THE
BOOK OF
RESOLUTIONS
OF THE UNITED METHODIST CHURCH
2004

THE
BOOK OF
RESOLUTIONS
OF THE UNITED METHODIST CHURCH
2004

The United Methodist Publishing House
Nashville, Tennessee

THE BOOK OF RESOLUTIONS OF THE UNITED METHODIST CHURCH 2004

This book is printed on elemental chlorine-free, acid-free paper.

ISBN 0-687-02414-5

Software Edition (Book of Resolutions with Book of Discipline)
Windows Version on CD-ROM, ISBN 0-687-06162-8

04 05 06 07 08 09 10 11 12 13 —10 9 8 7 6 5 4 3 2 1

MANUFACTURED IN THE UNITED STATES OF AMERICA

PREFACE

The Book of Resolutions has been published after each General Conference since 1968. This edition includes all resolutions that are currently valid. Resolutions that have been rescinded or superseded have been removed from this 2004 edition.

When approved by the General Conference, resolutions state the policy of The United Methodist Church on many current social issues and concerns. Only the General Conference speaks for The United Methodist Church (*Book of Discipline*, ¶ 509).

The 2000 General Conference approved a rule stating: "Resolutions shall be considered official expressions of The United Methodist Church for eight years following their adoption, after which time they shall be deemed to have expired unless readopted. Those that have expired shall not be printed in subsequent editions of the *Book of Resolutions*" (*Book of Discipline*, ¶ 510.2a). This edition has been prepared in accordance with that rule.

This 2004 edition presents the resolutions in seven sections: (1) The Natural World, (2) The Nurturing Community, (3) The Social Community, (4) The Economic Community, (5) The Political Community, (6) The World Community, and (7) Other Resolutions. The first six section titles match the sections of the Social Principles, United Methodism's foundational statement on social issues (printed after the User's Guide). The date of General Conference adoption appears at the end of each resolution.

To assist readers in study and use of the resolutions, this edition includes:

—User's Guide
—Grouping of related resolutions
—Index

The 2004 *Book of Resolutions* is published by The United Methodist Publishing House—Neil M. Alexander, president and publisher, and Harriett Jane Olson, book editor of The United Methodist Church. Marvin W. Cropsey, a staff member of The United Methodist Publishing House, served as the principal editor. The late Carolyn D. Minus, former General Board of Church and Society staff member, wrote the User's Guide.

CONTENTS

THE NATURAL WORLD
Environment/Energy

Nuclear Issues

THE NURTURING COMMUNITY

Ecumenical Issues

Church Structure

Family

Hispanic Concerns

Asian Concerns

Intolerance/Tolerance

Human Sexuality

Spirituality

Violence

THE SOCIAL COMMUNITY

Accessibility/Equal Access

Administrative Guidelines

African Americans

Children

Cultural Issues

Alcohol and Other Drugs

CONTENTS

Housing and Homelessness

Immigration

Mental Health

Missions

Native Americans

CONTENTS

Organ and Tissue Donation

Persons Living with HIV and AIDS

Rights of the Aging

Suicide

Population

Poverty

Racism

Rural Issues

CONTENTS

CONTENTS

Native Americans

Stewardship Issues in the Church

United States Economic Issues

Work/Leisure

THE POLITICAL COMMUNITY

Basic Freedoms

Church and State

Criminal Justice

Education

CONTENTS

Immigration

Military Service

Political Responsibility

United States Legislative Issues

THE WORLD COMMUNITY

Justice and Law

19

War and Peace

OTHER RESOLUTIONS

United Methodist Guidelines

Request for Study

USER'S GUIDE

What's the purpose of the *Book of Resolutions?*

The Book of Resolutions, 2004, published by The United Methodist Publishing House, collects in one volume all current and official social policies and other resolutions adopted by the General Conference of The United Methodist Church. These resolutions are:

• *Official policy statements* for guiding all the work and ministry of The United Methodist Church on approximately 200 subjects;
• *Educational resources* for The United Methodist Church on many of the important issues affecting the lives of people and all God's creation;
• *Guides and models* for helping United Methodist members and groups relate a lively biblical faith to action in daily life;
• *Resource materials* for persons preparing public statements about United Methodist concerns on current social issues.

The Book of Resolutions, 2004 is primarily a reference tool for church members and leaders. It is not a book that you will sit down to read from cover to cover.

You might not get acquainted with these resolutions until you are in the midst of some controversy in your congregation, or something happens regarding a particular subject in your community (or state, or nation). You may find that your denomination's policies give you more "food for thought." Maybe you will agree with the denomination's position. On the other hand, you may disagree. Either is all right. At the least, you know your church cares and wants you to be a knowledgeable and caring Christian about the issues of the day.

Furthermore, you may look to some of the statements in this book for spiritual guidance as you make an important decision in your life about work, home, family life, or use of money and other resources.

Can you answer some of my questions?

Why do we have all these social policies and resolutions?

The resolutions say, "We care!" Delegates to the General Conference of The United Methodist Church believe that we each need and deserve the guidance of the whole denomination as we face daily hopes, struggles, joy, or pain. The resolutions and Social Principles express our Church community's beliefs and give us evidence that the Church means for God's love to reach into situations faced each day, not just on Sunday mornings. Not all of us are intimately involved with each issue, but someone, somewhere, is.

Isn't *The Book of Discipline* enough?

The Book of Discipline establishes a framework for each part of United Methodism. The General Conference decided in 1968 that for reasons of length, these resolutions should be published in a volume separate from the Discipline. While *The Book of Resolutions* is not legally binding, it is an official guide from our denomination to be used responsibly for reference, encouragement, study, and support.

Why do the Social Principles appear in both the *Discipline* and in *The Book of Resolutions*?

The United Methodist Church puts the Social Principles in the *Discipline* (¶¶ 160–165) as one of our denominational foundation statements suggesting how faith is translated into action. Its broad principles (guides, not rules) are declarations to help us be in dialogue with one another about how faith motivates us to "get off the fence" and act.

The United Methodist Church puts the Social Principles in the front of *The Book of Resolutions* to help us relate the broad strokes of the Social Principles to more specific exploration and applications in resolutions.

Where do these policies and resolutions come from? How do they get adopted by General Conference?

They are sent in as petitions to General Conference every four years by general agencies, annual conferences, local churches, individual members, and groups. Once submitted as petitions, most of them are worked on by delegates in a legislative committee. The legislative committees accept, reject, or amend the petitions, then report their recommendations to the General Conference plenary; all delegates then vote on their recommendations.

Can I trust the statistics and data in these resolutions?

General source references are usually given when statistics are used in a resolution. Because such data may change during the years the resolution is valid, sometimes the resolution will provide more general descriptions of social conditions that make it urgent for the church to speak on a particular topic. Resolutions will take on more meaning when you secure local statistics and data on relevant topics.

Why do church social policies and U.S. government policies or positions seem so far apart on some of these issues?

The United Methodist Church membership extends beyond the U.S. boundaries; it is global. So, in many cases we are speaking to, from, or with more than one national government. Further, the Christian church must never be a mirror image of any government, whether Democrat or Republican, totalitarian or democratic. We know that Christians are obligated to be responsible and participating citizens under any governmental system, but that response and participation is to be interpreted in light of our faith.

As the Social Principles state, "Our allegiance to God takes precedence over our allegiance to any state" (¶ 164). And our church's public witness is first and foremost to be judged by God by whether it supports justice, love, and mercy, particularly for the poor and powerless.

Why can't the church just let us make up our own minds on these matters after it presents us neutral information on both sides of an issue?

Most importantly, The United Methodist Church believes God's love for the world is an active and engaged love, a love seeking justice and liberty. We cannot just be observers. So we care enough about people's lives to risk interpreting God's love, to take a stand, to call each of us into a response, no matter how controversial or complex. The church helps us think and act out of a faith perspective, not just respond to all the other "mind-makers-up" that exist in our society.

No information is truly neutral. This is true even of the most "hard scientific" data secured from the most advanced technology. These resolutions do strive for objectivity, not neutrality. There are usually more than "two sides" in important social controversies. Dialogue between different sides is critical in taking a stand. Faithfulness requires favoring what best demonstrates God's love and being willing to change when new perspectives or data emerge.

Is this something new in United Methodism?

Taking an active stance in society is nothing new for followers of John Wesley. He set the example for us to combine personal and social piety. Ever since predecessor churches to United Methodism flourished in the United States, we have been known as a denomination involved with people's lives, with political and social struggles, having local to international mission implications. Such involvement is an expression of the personal change we experience in our baptism and conversion.

Is there a difference between a social policy and a resolution?

The terms are used almost interchangeably in The United Methodist Church. Most social issue resolutions refer to public policy matters, such as local, state, and federal government programs and legislation. Other statements focus on conditions affecting the church and the church's programs or funding.

How do people use this *Book of Resolutions?*

• An ordained minister went to console neighbor parents after their son committed suicide. At home later that evening, the pastor and his own family struggled in their grief to apply their faith to this troubling situation. What did the church say about suicide? How should a Christian act? The pastor found the 1980 *Book of Resolutions* absolutely silent on this topic. During the six years after that first personal encounter with ministry after a suicide, the pastor wrote letters and articles and talked with seminary faculty and national church staff. As a result, the 1988 General Conference adopted its first resolution on suicide. Instead of merely wishing for guidance from our church on this most difficult subject, this pastor gave constructive leadership in the church, and we now can find helpful perspectives in *The 2004 Book of Resolutions.*

• A bishop and an annual conference board of church and society wanted to share a United Methodist position against the death penalty with their governor, who had to consider clemency for a death row inmate. They visited the governor and delivered a letter stating their own views of this particular situation and describing why The United Methodist Church opposes the death penalty. They used the resolution on capital punishment in *The Book of Resolutions* as the official policy of The United Methodist Church to support their plea for clemency.

• An adult church school group studied the foreign policy discussion topics called "Great Decisions," issued annually by the Foreign Policy Association. They compared its resources with positions in the relevant United Methodist policies from *The Book of Resolutions* for several evenings of lively study.

• Another adult class meeting on Sunday morning always studied faith and contemporary issues. For nearly six months, the members used *The Book of Resolutions* to guide their study and discussion. Different members made presentations on some aspect of the resolutions; then they used the study questions provided to stimulate some challenging discussion. Occasionally, they had guest speakers or used an audiovisual resource from their conference media center to amplify the subject.

• A nurse who is an active church member found the resolutions on "Universal Access to Health Care" and "Ministries in Mental Illness" to be helpful as she reflected on the strains in her job. She found it more possible to connect her faith to her discussions with coworkers about some of the major issues facing her profession in a big city hospital.

• A local church's outreach work area asked its administrative council to approve a congregational statement to the county zoning board favoring the construction of several low-income housing units. As part of their homework, the work area members reviewed the "Housing in the U.S.A." resolution in *The Book of Resolutions.* That resolution then served as a basis for their initiative; they even quoted from it when they testified at the zoning board.

How do I use *The Book of Resolutions?*

Read the preface. ————————————➤ It provides an orientation to the whole book.

Skim through the ————————————➤ Note: Resolutions are
table of contents.   listed under the section
of the Social Principles
to which they most
closely relate.

Check index for ————————————➤ Key words will help you
for specific references   locate resolutions

Example: If you want to know whether our denomination has
spoken about AIDS or HIV, you look for those entries
in the index. These subjects are referred to in a number of resolutions.

Example: What is there on "racism"? The index includes a num-
ber of references. You may also choose to look under
"African-American," "Native American," or "White
Privilege."

Find the text of the   • Note that the Social Principles include
Social Principles.   broad, fundamental statements grouped in
six sections between a preamble and a
creedal summary, "Our Social Creed."
• Review the "How can I understand the
Social Principles?" section in this User's
Guide. Use the diagrams in this section to
help interpret and look for meaning in the
Social Principles.

How can I understand the Social Principles?

The Book of Resolutions organizes almost all resolutions into the six areas of concern which form the major sections of the Social Principles. You may find it helpful to consider these six areas of concern as you explore specific resolutions.

One way of understanding the Social Principles is to consider the six sections as areas of concern: (1) the natural world, (2) the nurturing community, (3) the social community, (4) the economic community, (5) the political community, and (6) the world community.

The Natural World, the starting point for the areas of concern, provides the essential resources of life for all humankind.

Then add to the natural world the people of the world—of the World Community. All of us live in community, oftentimes becoming part of several communities. Together we make up the world community.

All of us also become a part of the Nurturing Community. Through the people with whom we interact most often—family, friends, local church, etc.—we shape our lives and the way we relate to other communities.

Three other communities impact both the nurturing community and the world community.

The Social Community (or cultural community) provides the arena where we live out our responsibilities and rights in our treatment of others.

The Economic Community, in which each of us functions, establishes production, distribution and employment systems; it creates both wealth and poverty.

The Political Community determines whether our rights are guaranteed and our basic freedoms are upheld. Directions and goals of our social and economic communities are debated and decided in this arena.

Decisions in all these communities have an impact on the natural world and vice versa.

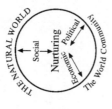

Our Social Creed

"Our Social Creed" (Section VII of the Social Principles) is a summary of the foregoing sections of the Social Principles in the form of a creed. While it is recommended by the general church for separate use in worship services, "Our Social Creed" is an integral part of the Social Principles.

Another way of considering the six sections of the Social Principles (the six areas of concern) is to look at: (1) the role of each section, (2) the predominant faith statement in each section, (3) our responsibility defined in each section, and (4) the issues discussed in each section. The chart on the next two pages summarizes the Social Principles in this way.

The Social Principles

CATEGORY	I The Natural World	II The Nurturing Community	III The Social Community	IV The Economic Community	V The Political Community	VI The World Community
ROLE	Provides for sustenance of all creation to be used with integrity	Provides the potential to nurture human beings into the fullness of their humanity.	Provides for means for determining the rights and responsibilities of the members toward one another	Provides directions for influencing economic policies.	Provides for the ordering of society.	Provides the setting for the interaction of nations.
FAITH STATEMENT	All creation is God's.	All persons are important and loved by God.	All persons are equally valuable in the sight of God.	All economic systems are under God's judgment.	All political systems are under God's judgment.	All of God's world is one world.

OUR RESPONSIBILITY	To value and conserve all natural resources.	To innovate, sponsor, and evaluate new forms of community.	To work toward societies in which social groups and individual values are recognized, maintained and strengthened.	To ensure that sound policies are developed that provide for full employment, adequate income, and so forth.	To take active responsibility for our government.	To work to develop the moral and spiritual capacity to achieve a stable world of love.
ISSUES	Water, air, soil, plants, energy utilization, animal life, space.	Family, Christian community, marriage, human sexuality, abortion, death.	Rights of minorities, children, youth and young adults, the aging, women, people with disabilities; alcohol/drugs, rural life.	Property, collective bargaining, work/leisure, consumption, poverty, migrant workers, gambling.	Basic liberties, political responsibility, freedom of information, civil obedience and civil disobedience, crime and rehabilitation, military service.	Nations and cultures, national power and responsibility, war and peace, justice and law.

How can I better understand the resolutions?

Each resolution shows:

- the rationale, or reasons for the resolution;
- the Social Principles paragraph to which that resolution relates (found at the conclusion of any resolution);
- the biblical references and/or theological concerns identified in this resolution;
- the major actions called for in that resolution for churches; individuals; church agencies; local, state, or national governments;
- the date the resolution was passed or amended and readopted by General Conference.

The Natural World

Resolution	Social Principles Paragraph	Biblical References Theological Concerns	Actions called for	Hymns to use
A Dioxin-Free Future	¶ 160A	Jesus' abundant life embraced physical well-being as well as emotional and spiritual health. Wesley and his followers have a long record of health/welfare ministries.	• Urge local churches, all church agencies and institutions to learn of suffering due to background levels of Dioxin • Urge general United Methodist agencies to work with companies and governments to support a gradual phase out of the production of Dioxin • Ask all United Methodists to take action to stop harm being done by the nonessential incineration of medical waste and encourage healthcare workers to adopt policies that will reduce or eliminate use of PVC plastic	"Open my eyes, that I may see" (*Hymnal*, 454) "God who shaped creation" (*Hymnal*, 443)

The Natural World

Resolution	Social Principles Paragraph	Biblical References Theological Concerns	Actions called for	Hymns to use
Nuclear Safety in the United States	¶ 160E	The God-given charge to humans to "guard and keep the earth" (Genesis 2:15). To ensure that God's creation is protected for present and future generations.	• Urge general United Methodist agencies to assist annual conferences in all aspects of information and action strategies on this issue. • Advocate for public policy, particularly regarding nuclear power, reviewing safety of operating plants, researching designs for plant safety, phasing out nuclear weapons production, establishing uniform safety standards for civilian and military nuclear operations, reevaluating U.S. nuclear waste policy, and conserving energy and enhancing alternative energy sources.	"A charge to keep I have" (*Hymnal*, 413) "Creating God, your fingers trace" (*Hymnal*, 109)

The Social Community

Resolution	Social Principles Paragraph	Biblical References Theological Concerns	Actions called for	Hymns to use
Rural Communities in Crisis	¶ 162N	God's gift of the land is a common gift to all humanity, requiring just patterns of land use (Lev. 25). Jesus commands us to love neighbor as self. The gospel challenges an ethic based on "bigness is better."	Issues over 72 comprehensive calls for change by the church at all levels, by local communities, and by state and federal governments. For example: • Churches to develop intentionally ministry to meet major needs in today's rural U.S.A.; to become public policy advocates; to model and support team and cooperative ministries; to emphasize ecology as part of Christian stewardship. • Federal legislation and programs to enable farm families to receive just return for their labor and investments; to develop just water and energy policies to recognize and protect rights of farm workers. • State and governments, private lending agencies, local governments, and community groups to be involved, together and separately overall, to develop a vision for agricultural life where programs and relations are just, participatory, and sustainable.	"Great is thy faithfulness" (Hymnal, 140) "Faith, while trees are still in blossom" (Hymnal, 508)

What do I do next?

Consider these questions for study and response to any of the resolutions:

• How familiar am I with the situation(s) described in this resolution?

• What are my reactions to this call for action by our church?

• How might reactions be different if we lived in another part of this country? lived in another country? were of a different economic class? attended a different church? if members of my family were present (or not present)?

• How could our local congregation creatively respond to the calls for action in the resolution?

• Are there groups in my area or state at work on this issue where I could join in action or learn more?

• What have I communicated to our congressional members or state legislators about our church's position on an issue of great importance?

• Who could we contact for more information or resources? Write to or call: Communications, General Board of Church and Society, 100 Maryland Avenue, N.E., Washington, DC 20002; (202) 488-5600 (www.umc-gbcs.org).

SOCIAL PRINCIPLES

PREFACE

The United Methodist Church has a long history of concern for social justice. Its members have often taken forthright positions on controversial issues involving Christian principles. Early Methodists expressed their opposition to the slave trade, to smuggling, and to the cruel treatment of prisoners.

A social creed was adopted by The Methodist Episcopal Church (North) in 1908. Within the next decade similar statements were adopted by The Methodist Episcopal Church, South, and by The Methodist Protestant Church. The Evangelical United Brethren Church adopted a statement of social principles in 1946 at the time of the uniting of the United Brethren and The Evangelical Church. In 1972, four years after the uniting in 1968 of The Methodist Church and The Evangelical United Brethren Church, the General Conference of The United Methodist Church adopted a new statement of Social Principles, which was revised in 1976 (and by each successive General Conference).

The Social Principles are a prayerful and thoughtful effort on the part of the General Conference to speak to the human issues in the contemporary world from a sound biblical and theological foundation as historically demonstrated in United Methodist traditions. They are a call to faithfulness and are intended to be instructive and persuasive in the best of the prophetic spirit; however, they are not church law. The Social Principles are a call to all members of The United Methodist Church to a prayerful, studied dialogue of faith and practice. (*See* ¶ 509.)

PREAMBLE

We, the people called United Methodists, affirm our faith in God our Creator and Father, in Jesus Christ our Savior, and in the Holy Spirit, our Guide and Guard.

We acknowledge our complete dependence upon God in birth, in life, in death, and in life eternal. Secure in God's love, we affirm the goodness of life and confess our many sins against God's will for us as we find it in Jesus Christ. We have not always been faithful stewards of all that has been committed to us by God the Creator. We have been reluctant followers of Jesus Christ in his mission to bring all persons into a community of love. Though called by the Holy Spirit to become new creatures in Christ, we have resisted the further call to become the people of God in our dealings with each other and the earth on which we live.

Grateful for God's forgiving love, in which we live and by which we are judged, and affirming our belief in the inestimable worth of each individual, we renew our commitment to become faithful witnesses to the gospel, not alone to the ends of earth, but also to the depths of our common life and work.

¶ 160.   I. THE NATURAL WORLD

All creation is the Lord's, and we are responsible for the ways in which we use and abuse it. Water, air, soil, minerals, energy resources, plants, animal life, and space are to be valued and conserved because they are God's creation and not solely because they are useful to human beings. God has granted us stewardship of creation. We should meet these stewardship duties through acts of loving care and respect. Economic, political, social, and technological developments have increased our human numbers, lengthened and enriched our lives. However, these developments have led to regional defoliation, dramatic extinction of species, massive human suffering, overpopulation, misuse and over-consumption of natural and nonrenewable resources, particularly by industrialized societies. This continued course of action jeopardizes the natural heritage that God has entrusted to all generations. Therefore, let us recognize the responsibility of the church and its members to place a high priority on changes in economic, political, social, and technological lifestyle to support a more ecologically equitable and sustainable world leading to a higher quality of life for all of God's creation.

A) Water, Air, Soil, Minerals, Plants—We support and encourage social policies that serve to reduce and control the creation of industrial byproducts and waste; facilitate the safe processing and disposal of toxic and nuclear waste and move toward the elimination of both;

encourage reduction of municipal waste; provide for appropriate recycling and disposal of municipal waste; and assist the cleanup of polluted air, water, and soil. We call for the preservation of old-growth forests and other irreplaceable natural treasures, as well as preservation of endangered plant species. We support measures designed to maintain and restore natural ecosystems. We support policies that develop alternatives to chemicals used for growing, processing, and preserving food, and we strongly urge adequate research into their effects upon God's creation prior to utilization. We urge development of international agreements concerning equitable utilization of the world's resources for human benefit so long as the integrity of the earth is maintained.

B) Energy Resources Utilization—Affirming the inherent value of nonhuman creation, we support and encourage social policies that are directed toward rational and restrained transformation of parts of the nonhuman world into energy for human usage and that de-emphasize or eliminate energy-producing technologies that endanger the health, the safety, and even the existence of the present and future human and nonhuman creation. Further, we urge wholehearted support of the conservation of energy and responsible development of all energy resources, with special concern for the development of renewable energy sources, that the goodness of the earth may be affirmed.

C) Animal Life—We support regulations that protect the life and health of animals, including those ensuring the humane treatment of pets and other domestic animals, animals used in research, and the painless slaughtering of meat animals, fish, and fowl. We encourage the preservation of all animal species including those threatened with extinction.

D) Space—The universe, known and unknown, is the creation of God and is due the respect we are called to give the earth.

E) Science and Technology—We recognize science as a legitimate interpretation of God's natural world. We affirm the validity of the claims of science in describing the natural world, although we preclude science from making authoritative claims about theological issues. We recognize technology as a legitimate use of God's natural world when such use enhances human life and enables all of God's children to develop their God-given creative potential without violating our ethical convictions about the relationship of humanity to the natural world.

In acknowledging the important roles of science and technology, however, we also believe that theological understandings of human experience are crucial to a full understanding of the place of humanity in the universe. Science and theology are complementary rather than mutually incompatible. We therefore encourage dialogue between the scientific and theological communities and seek the kind of participation that will enable humanity to sustain life on earth and, by God's grace, increase the quality of our common lives together.

F) Food Safety—We support policies that protect the food supply and that ensure the public's right to know the content of the foods they are eating. We call for rigorous inspections and controls on the biological safety of all foodstuffs intended for human consumption. We urge independent testing for chemical residues in food, and the removal from the market of foods contaminated with potentially hazardous levels of pesticides, herbicides, or fungicides; drug residues from animal antibiotics, steroids, or hormones; contaminants due to pollution that are carried by air, soil, or water from incinerator plants or other industrial operations. We call for clear labeling of all processed or altered foods, with pre-market safety testing required. We oppose weakening the standards for organic foods. We call for policies that encourage and support a gradual transition to sustainable and organic agriculture.

¶ 161. II. THE NURTURING COMMUNITY

The community provides the potential for nurturing human beings into the fullness of their humanity. We believe we have a responsibility to innovate, sponsor, and evaluate new forms of community that will encourage development of the fullest potential in individuals. Primary for us is the gospel understanding that all persons are important—because they are human beings created by God and loved through and by Jesus Christ and not because they have merited significance. We therefore support social climates in which human communities are maintained and strengthened for the sake of all persons and their growth. We also encourage all individuals to be sensitive to others by using appropriate language when referring to all persons. Language of a derogatory nature (with regard to race, nationality, ethnic background, gender, sexuality, and physical differences) does not reflect value for one another and contradicts the gospel of Jesus Christ.

A) The Family—We believe the family to be the basic human community through which persons are nurtured and sustained in mutual love, responsibility, respect, and fidelity. We affirm the importance of both fathers and mothers for all children. We also understand the family as encompassing a wider range of options than that of the two-generational unit of parents and children (the nuclear family), including the extended family, families with adopted children, single parents, stepfamilies, and couples without children. We affirm shared responsibility for parenting by men and women and encourage social, economic, and religious efforts to maintain and strengthen relationships within families in order that every member may be assisted toward complete personhood.

B) Other Christian Communities—We further recognize the movement to find new patterns of Christian nurturing communities such as Koinonia Farms, certain monastic and other religious orders, and some types of corporate church life. We urge the Church to seek ways of understanding the needs and concerns of such Christian groups and to find ways of ministering to them and through them.

C) Marriage—We affirm the sanctity of the marriage covenant that is expressed in love, mutual support, personal commitment, and shared fidelity between a man and a woman. We believe that God's blessing rests upon such marriage, whether or not there are children of the union. We reject social norms that assume different standards for women than for men in marriage. We support laws in civil society that define marriage as the union of one man and one woman.

D) Divorce—God's plan is for lifelong, faithful marriage. The church must be on the forefront of premarital and postmarital counseling in order to create and preserve strong marriages. However, when a married couple is estranged beyond reconciliation, even after thoughtful consideration and counsel, divorce is a regrettable alternative in the midst of brokenness. We grieve over the devastating emotional, spiritual, and economic consequences of divorce for all involved and are concerned about high divorce rates.

E) Single Persons—We affirm the integrity of single persons, and we reject all social practices that discriminate or social attitudes that are prejudicial against persons because they are single.

F) Women and Men—We affirm with Scripture the common humanity of male and female, both having equal worth in the eyes of God. We reject the erroneous notion that one gender is superior to another, that one gender must strive against another, and that members of one gender may receive love, power, and esteem only at the expense of another. We especially reject the idea that God made individuals as incomplete fragments, made whole only in union with another. We call upon women and men alike to share power and control, to learn to give freely and to receive freely, to be complete and to respect the wholeness of others. We seek for every individual opportunities and freedom to love and be loved, to seek and receive justice, and to practice ethical self-determination. We understand our gender diversity to be a gift from God, intended to add to the rich variety of human experience and perspective; and we guard against attitudes and traditions that would use this good gift to leave members of one sex more vulnerable in relationships than members of another.

G) Human Sexuality—We recognize that sexuality is God's good gift to all persons. We believe persons may be fully human only when that gift is acknowledged and affirmed by themselves, the church, and society. We call all persons to the disciplined, responsible fulfillment of themselves, others, and society in the stewardship of this gift. We also recognize our limited understanding of this complex gift and encourage the medical, theological, and social science disciplines to combine in a determined effort to understand human sexuality more completely. We call the Church to take the leadership role in bringing together these disciplines to address this most complex issue. Further, within the context of our understanding of this gift of God, we recognize that God challenges us to find responsible, committed, and loving forms of expression.

Although all persons are sexual beings whether or not they are married, sexual relations are only clearly affirmed in the marriage bond. Sex may become exploitative within as well as outside marriage. We reject all sexual expressions that damage or destroy the humanity God has given us as birthright, and we affirm only that sexual expression that enhances that same humanity. We believe that sexual relations where one or both partners are exploitative, abusive, or promiscuous are beyond the parameters of acceptable Christian behavior and are ultimately destructive to individuals, families, and the social order.

We deplore all forms of the commercialization and exploitation of sex, with their consequent cheapening and degradation of human personality. We call for strict global enforcement of laws prohibiting the sexual exploitation or use of children by adults and encourage efforts to hold perpetrators legally and financially responsible. We call for the establishment of adequate protective services, guidance, and counseling opportunities for children thus abused. We insist that all persons, regardless of age, gender, marital status, or sexual orientation, are entitled to have their human and civil rights ensured.

We recognize the continuing need for full, positive, age-appropriate and factual sex education opportunities for children, young people, and adults. The Church offers a unique opportunity to give quality guidance and education in this area.

Homosexual persons no less than heterosexual persons are individuals of sacred worth. All persons need the ministry and guidance of the church in their struggles for human fulfillment, as well as the spiritual and emotional care of a fellowship that enables reconciling relationships with God, with others, and with self. The United Methodist Church does not condone the practice of homosexuality and considers this practice incompatible with Christian teaching. We affirm that God's grace is available to all, and we will seek to live together in Christian community. We implore families and churches not to reject or condemn lesbian and gay members and friends. We commit ourselves to be in ministry for and with all persons.[1]

H) Family Violence and Abuse—We recognize that family violence and abuse in all its forms—verbal, psychological, physical, sexual—is detrimental to the covenant of the human community. We encourage the Church to provide a safe environment, counsel, and support for the victim. While we deplore the actions of the abuser, we affirm that person to be in need of God's redeeming love.

I) Sexual Harassment—We believe human sexuality is God's good gift. One abuse of this good gift is sexual harassment. We define sexual harassment as any unwanted sexual comment, advance or demand, either verbal or physical, that is reasonably perceived by the recipient as demeaning, intimidating, or coercive. Sexual harassment must be understood as an exploitation of a power relationship rather than as an exclusively sexual issue. Sexual harassment includes, but is not limited to, the creation of a hostile or abusive working environment resulting from discrimination on the basis of gender.

Contrary to the nurturing community, sexual harassment creates improper, coercive, and abusive conditions wherever it occurs in society. Sexual harassment undermines the social goal of equal opportunity and the climate of mutual respect between men and women. Unwanted sexual attention is wrong and discriminatory. Sexual harassment interferes with the moral mission of the Church.

1. See Judicial Council Decision 702.

J) Abortion—The beginning of life and the ending of life are the God-given boundaries of human existence. While individuals have always had some degree of control over when they would die, they now have the awesome power to determine when and even whether new individuals will be born. Our belief in the sanctity of unborn human life makes us reluctant to approve abortion. But we are equally bound to respect the sacredness of the life and well-being of the mother, for whom devastating damage may result from an unacceptable pregnancy. In continuity with past Christian teaching, we recognize tragic conflicts of life with life that may justify abortion, and in such cases we support the legal option of abortion under proper medical procedures. We cannot affirm abortion as an acceptable means of birth control, and we unconditionally reject it as a means of gender selection. We oppose the use of late-term abortion known as dilation and extraction (partial-birth abortion) and call for the end of this practice except when the physical life of the mother is in danger and no other medical procedure is available, or in the case of severe fetal anomalies incompatible with life. We call all Christians to a searching and prayerful inquiry into the sorts of conditions that may warrant abortion. We commit our Church to continue to provide nurturing ministries to those who terminate a pregnancy, to those in the midst of a crisis pregnancy, and to those who give birth. We particularly encourage the Church, the government, and social service agencies to support and facilitate the option of adoption. (See ¶ 161.K.) Governmental laws and regulations do not provide all the guidance required by the informed Christian conscience. Therefore, a decision concerning abortion should be made only after thoughtful and prayerful consideration by the parties involved, with medical, pastoral, and other appropriate counsel.

K) Ministry to those who have experienced an abortion—We urge local pastors to become informed about the symptons and behaviors associated with post-abortion stress. We further encourage local churches to make available contact information for counseling agencies that offer programs to address post-abortion stress for all seeking help.

L) Adoption—Children are a gift from God to be welcomed and received. We recognize that some circumstances of birth make the rearing of a child difficult. We affirm and support the birth parent(s) whose choice it is to allow the child to be adopted. We recognize the agony, strength, and courage of the birth parent(s) who choose(s) in hope, love, and prayer to offer the child for adoption. In addition, we also recognize the anxiety, strength, and courage of those who choose in hope, love, and prayer to be able to care for a child. We affirm and support the adoptive parent(s)' desire to rear an adopted child as they would a biological child. When circumstances warrant adoption, we support the use of proper legal procedures. When appropriate and possible, we encourage open adoption so that a child may know all information and people related to them, both medically and relationally. We support and encourage greater awareness and education to promote adoption of a wide variety of children through foster care, international adoption, and domestic adoption. We commend the birth parent(s), the receiving parent(s), and the child to the care of the Church, that grief might be shared, joy might be celebrated, and the child might be nurtured in a community of Christian love.

M) Faithful Care for Dying Persons—While we applaud medical science for efforts to prevent disease and illness and for advances in treatment that extend the meaningful life of human beings, we recognize that every mortal life will ultimately end in death. Death is never a sign that God has adandoned us, no matter what the circumstances of the death might be. As Christians we must always be prepared to surrender the gift of mortal life and claim the gift of eternal life through the death and resurrection of Jesus Christ. Care for dying persons is part of our stewardship of the divine gift of life when cure is no longer possible. We encourage the use of medical technologies to provide palliative care at the end of life when life-sustaining treatments no longer support the goals of life, and when they have reached their limits. There is no moral or religious obligation to use these when they impose undue burdens or only extend the process of dying. Dying persons and their families are free to discontinue treatments when they cease to be of benefit to the patient.

We recognize the agonizing personal and moral decisions faced by the dying, their physicians, their families, their friends, and their faith community. We urge that decisions faced by the dying be made with thoughtful and prayerful consideration by the parties involved, with medical, pastoral, and other appropriate counsel. We further urge that all persons discuss with their families, their physicians, and their pastoral counselors, their wishes for care at the end of life and provide advance directives for such care when they are not able to make these decisions for themselves. Even when one accepts the inevitability of death, the church and society must continue to provide faithful care, including pain relief, companionship, support, and spiritual nurture for the dying person in the hard work of preparing for death. We encourage and support the concept of hospice care whenever possible at the end of life. Faithful care does not end at death but continues during bereavement as we care for grieving families.

N) Suicide—We believe that suicide is not the way a human life should end. Often suicide is the result of untreated depression, or untreated pain and suffering. The church has an obligation to see that all persons have access to needed pastoral and medical care and therapy in those circumstances that lead to loss of self-worth, suicidal despair, and/or the desire to seek physician-assisted suicide. We encourage the church to provide education to address the biblical, theological, social, and ethical issues related to death and dying, including suicide. United Methodist theological seminary courses should also focus on issues of death and dying, including suicide.

A Christian perspective on suicide begins with an affirmation of faith that nothing, including suicide, separates us from the love of God (Romans 8:38-39). Therefore, we deplore the condemnation of people who complete suicide, and we consider unjust the stigma that so often falls on surviving family and friends.

We encourage pastors and faith communities to address this issue through preaching and teaching. We urge pastors and faith communities to provide pastoral care to those at risk, survivors, and their families, and to those families who have lost loved ones to suicide, seeking always to remove the oppressive stigma around suicide. The Church opposes assisted suicide and euthanasia.

¶ 162. III. THE SOCIAL COMMUNITY

The rights and privileges a society bestows upon or withholds from those who constitute it indicate the relative esteem in which that society holds particular persons and groups of persons. We affirm all persons as equally valuable in the sight of God. We therefore work toward societies in which each person's value is recognized, maintained, and strengthened. We support the basic rights of all persons to equal access to housing, education, communication, employment, medical care, legal redress for grievances, and physical protection. We deplore acts of hate or violence against groups or persons based on race, ethnicity, gender, sexual orientation, religious affiliation, or economic status.

A) Rights of Racial and Ethnic Persons—Racism is the combination of the power to dominate by one race over other races and a value system that assumes that the dominant race is innately superior to the others. Racism includes both personal and institutional racism. Personal racism is manifested through the individual expressions, attitudes, and/or behaviors that accept the assumptions of a racist value system and that maintain the benefits of this system. Institutional racism is the established social pattern that supports implicitly or explicitly the racist value system. Racism plagues and cripples our growth in Christ, inasmuch as it is antithetical to the gospel itself. White people are unfairly granted privileges and benefits that are denied to persons of color. Racism breeds racial discrimination. We define racial discrimination as the disparate treatment and lack of full access to resources and opportunities in the church and in society based on race or ethnicity. Therefore, we recognize racism as sin and affirm the ultimate and temporal worth of all persons. We rejoice in the gifts that particular ethnic histories and cultures bring to our total life. We commend and encourage the self-awareness of all racial and ethnic groups and oppressed people that leads them to demand their just and equal rights as members of society. We assert the obligation of society and groups within the society to implement compensatory programs that redress long-standing, systemic social deprivation of racial and ethnic people. We further assert the right of members of racial and ethnic groups to equal opportunities in employment and promotion; to education and training of the highest quality; to nondiscrimination in voting, in access to public accommodations, and in housing purchase or rental; credit, financial loans, venture capital, and insurance policies; and to positions of leadership and power in all elements of our life together. We support affirmative action as one method of addressing the inequalities and discriminatory practices within our Church and society.

B) Rights of Religious Minorities—Religious persecution has been common in the history of civilization. We urge policies and practices that ensure the right of every religious group to exercise its faith free from legal, political, or economic restrictions. We condemn all overt and covert forms of religious intolerance, being especially sensitive to their expression in media stereotyping. We assert the right of all religions and their adherents to freedom from legal, economic, and social discrimination.

C) Rights of Children—Once considered the property of their parents, children are now acknowledged to be full human beings in their own right, but beings to whom adults and society in general have special obligations. Thus, we support the development of school systems and innovative methods of education designed to assist every child toward complete fulfillment as an individual person of worth. All children have the right to quality education, including full sex education appropriate to their stage of development that utilizes the best educational techniques and insights. Christian parents and guardians and the Church have the responsibility to ensure that children receive sex education consistent with Christian morality, including faithfulness in marriage and abstinence in singleness. Moreover, children have the rights to food, shelter, clothing, health care, and emotional well-being as do adults, and these rights we affirm as theirs regardless of actions or inactions of their parents or guardians. In particular, children must be protected from economic, physical, emotional, and sexual exploitation and abuse.

D) Rights of Young People—Our society is characterized by a large population of young people who frequently find full participation in society difficult. Therefore, we urge development of policies that encourage inclusion of young people in decision-making processes and that eliminate discrimination and exploitation. Creative and appropriate employment opportunities should be legally and socially available for young people.

E) Rights of the Aging—In a society that places primary emphasis upon youth, those growing old in years are frequently isolated from the mainstream of social existence. We support social policies that integrate the aging into the life of the total community, including sufficient incomes, increased and nondiscriminatory employment opportunities, educational and service opportunities, and adequate medical care and housing within existing communities. We urge social policies and programs, with emphasis on the unique concerns of older women and ethnic persons, that ensure to the aging the respect and dignity that is their right as senior members of the human community. Further, we urge increased consideration for adequate pension systems by employers, with provisions for the surviving spouse.

F) Rights of Women—We affirm women and men to be equal in every aspect of their common life. We therefore urge that every effort be made to eliminate sex-role stereotypes in activity and portrayal of family life and in all aspects of voluntary and compensatory participation in the Church and society. We affirm the right of women to equal treatment in employment, responsibility, promotion, and compensation. We affirm the importance of women in decision-making positions at all levels of Church and society and urge such bodies to guarantee their presence through policies of employment and recruitment. We support affirmative action as one method of addressing the inequalities and discriminatory practices within our Church and society. We urge employers of persons in dual career families, both in the Church and society, to apply proper consideration of both parties when relocation is considered. We affirm the right of women to live free from violence and abuse and urge governments to enact policies that protect women against all forms of violence and discrimination in any sector of soceity.

G) Rights of Persons with Disabilities—We recognize and affirm the full humanity and personhood of all individuals with mental, physical, developmental, neurological, and psychological conditions or disabilities as full members of the family of God. We also affirm their rightful place in both the church and society. We affirm the responsibility of the Church and society to be in ministry with children, youth, and adults with mental, physical, developmental, and/or psychological and neurological conditions or disabilities whose particular needs in the areas of mobility, communication, intellectual comprehension, or personal relationships might make more challenging their participation or that of their families in the life of the Church and the community. We urge the Church and society to recognize and receive the gifts of persons with disabilities to enable them to be full participants in the community of faith. We call the Church and society to be sensitive to, and advocate for, programs of rehabilitation, services, employment, education, appropriate housing, and transportation. We call on the Church and society to protect the civil rights of persons with disabilities.

H) Equal Rights Regardless of Sexual Orientation—Certain basic human rights and civil liberties are due all persons. We are committed to supporting those rights and liberties for homosexual persons. We see a clear issue of simple justice in protecting their rightful claims where they have shared material resources, pensions, guardian relationships, mutual powers of attorney, and other such lawful claims typically attendant to contractual relationships that involve shared contributions, responsibilities, and liabilities, and equal protection before the law. Moreover, we support efforts to stop violence and other forms of coercion against gays and lesbians. We also commit ourselves to social witness against the coercion and marginalization of former homosexuals.

I) Population—Since the growing worldwide population is increasingly straining the world's supply of food, minerals, and water and sharpening international tensions, the reduction of the rate of consumption of resources by the affluent and the reduction of current world population growth rates have become imperative. People have the duty to consider the impact on the total world community of their decisions regarding childbearing and should have access to information and appropriate means to limit their fertility, including voluntary sterilization. We affirm that programs to achieve a stabilized population should be placed in a context of total economic and social development, including an equitable use and control of resources; improvement in the status of women in all cultures; a human level of economic security, health care, and literacy for all. We oppose any policy of forced abortion or forced sterilization.

J) Alcohol and Other Drugs—We affirm our long-standing support of abstinence from alcohol as a faithful witness to God's liberating and redeeming love for persons. We support abstinence from the use of any illegal drugs. Since the use of illegal drugs, as well as illegal and problematic use of alcohol, is a major factor in crime, disease, death, and family dysfunction, we support educational programs, as well as other prevention strategies, encouraging abstinence from illegal drug use and, with regard to those who choose to consume alcoholic beverages, judicious use with deliberate and intentional restraint, with Scripture as a guide.

Millions of living human beings are testimony to the beneficial consequences of therapeutic drug use, and millions of others are testimony to the detrimental consequences of drug misuse. We encourage wise policies relating to the availability of potentially beneficial or potentially damaging prescription and over-the-counter drugs; we urge that complete information about their use and misuse be readily available to both doctor and patient. We support the strict administration of laws regulating the sale and distribution of alcohol and controlled substances. We support regulations that protect society from users of drugs of any kind, including alcohol, where it can be shown that a clear and present social danger exists. Drug-dependent persons and their family members, including those who are assessed or diagnosed as dependent on alcohol, are individuals of infinite human worth deserving of treatment, rehabilitation, and ongoing life-changing recovery. Misuse or abuse may also require intervention, in order to prevent progression into dependence. Because of the frequent interrelationship between alcohol abuse and mental illness, we call upon legislators and health care providers to make available appropriate mental illness treatment and rehabilitation for drug-dependent persons. We commit ourselves to assisting those who have become dependent, and their families, in finding freedom through Jesus Christ and in finding good opportunities for treatment, for ongoing counseling, and for reintegration into society.

K) Tobacco—We affirm our historic tradition of high standards of personal discipline and social responsibility. In light of the overwhelming evidence that tobacco smoking and the use of smokeless tobacco are hazardous to the health of persons of all ages, we recommend total abstinence from the use of tobacco. We urge that our educational and communication resources be utilized to support and encourage such abstinence. Further, we recognize the harmful effects of passive smoke and support the restriction of smoking in public areas and workplaces.

L) Medical Experimentation—Physical and mental health has been greatly enhanced through discoveries by medical science. It is imperative, however, that governments and the medical profession carefully enforce the requirements of the prevailing medical research standard, maintaining rigid controls in testing new technologies and drugs utilizing human beings. The standard requires that those engaged in research shall use human beings as research subjects only after obtaining full, rational, and uncoerced consent.

M) Genetic Technology—The responsibility of humankind to God's creation challenges us to deal carefully with the possibilities of genetic research and technology. We welcome the use of genetic technology for meeting fundamental human needs for health, a safe environment, and an adequate food supply. We oppose the cloning of humans and the genetic manipulation of the gender of an unborn child.

Because of the effects of genetic technologies on all life, we call for effective guidelines and public accountability to safeguard against any action that might lead to abuse of these technologies, including political or military ends. We recognize that cautious, well-intended use of genetic technologies may sometimes lead to unanticipated harmful consequences.

Human gene therapies that produce changes that cannot be passed to offspring (somatic therapy) should be limited to the alleviation of suffering caused by disease. Genetic therapies for eugenic choices or that produce waste embryos are deplored. Genetic data of individuals and their families should be kept secret and held in strict confidence unless confidentiality is waived by the individual or by his or her family, or unless the collection and use of genetic identification data is supported by an appropriate court order. Because its long-term effects are uncertain, we oppose genetic therapy that results in changes that can be passed to offspring (germ-line therapy).

N) Rural Life—We support the right of persons and families to live and prosper as farmers, farm workers, merchants, professionals, and others outside of the cities and metropolitan centers. We believe our culture is impoverished and our people deprived of a meaningful way of life when rural and small-town living becomes difficult or impossible. We recognize that the improvement of this way of life may sometimes necessitate the use of some lands for nonagricultural purposes. We oppose the indiscriminate diversion of agricultural land for nonagricultural uses when nonagricultural land is available. Further, we encourage the preservation of appropriate lands for agriculture and open space uses through thoughtful land use programs. We support governmental and private programs designed to benefit the resident farmer rather than the factory farm and programs that encourage industry to locate in nonurban areas.

We further recognize that increased mobility and technology have brought a mixture of people, religions, and philosophies to rural communities that were once homogeneous. While often this is seen as a threat to or loss of community life, we understand it as an opportunity to uphold the biblical call to community for all persons. Therefore, we encourage rural communities and individuals to maintain a strong connection to the earth and to be open to: offering mutual belonging, caring, healing, and growth; sharing and celebrating cooperative leadership and diverse gifts; supporting mutual trust; and affirming individuals as unique persons of worth, and thus to practice shalom.

O) Sustainable Agriculture—A prerequisite for meeting the nutritional needs of the world's population is an agricultural system which uses sustainable methods, respects ecosystems, and promotes a livelihood for people that work the land.

We support a sustainable agricultural system that will maintain and support the natural fertility of agricultural soil, promote the diversity of flora and fauna, and adapt to regional conditions and structures—

a system where agricultural animals are treated humanely and where their living conditions are as close to natural systems as possible. We aspire to an effective agricultural system where plant, livestock, and poultry production maintains the natural ecological cycles, conserves energy, and reduces chemical inputs to a minimum.

Sustainable agriculture requires a global evaluation of the impacts of agriculture on food and raw material production, the preservation of animal breeds and plant varieties, and the preservation and development of the cultivated landscape.

World trade of agricultural products needs to be based on fair trade and prices, based on the costs of sustainable production methods, and must consider the real costs of ecological damage. The needed technological and biological developments are those that support sustainability and consider ecological consequences.

P) *Urban–Suburban Life*—Urban–suburban living has become a dominant style of life for more and more persons. For many it furnishes economic, educational, social, and cultural opportunities. For others, it has brought alienation, poverty, and depersonalization. We in the Church have an opportunity and responsibility to help shape the future of urban–suburban life. Massive programs of renewal and social planning are needed to bring a greater degree of humanization into urban–suburban lifestyles. Christians must judge all programs, including economic and community development, new towns, and urban renewal, by the extent to which they protect and enhance human values, permit personal and political involvement, and make possible neighborhoods open to persons of all races, ages, and income levels. We affirm the efforts of all developers who place human values at the heart of their planning. We must help shape urban–suburban development so that it provides for the human need to identify with and find meaning in smaller social communities. At the same time, such smaller communities must be encouraged to assume responsibilities for the total urban–suburban community instead of isolating themselves from it.

Q) *Media Violence and Christian Values*—The unprecedented impact the media (principally television and movies) are having on Christian and human values within our society becomes more apparent each day. We express disdain at current media preoccupation with dehumanizing portrayals, sensationalized through mass media "entertainment" and "news." These practices degrade humankind and violate the teachings of Christ and the Bible.

United Methodists, along with those of other faith groups, must be made aware that the mass media often undermine the truths of Christianity by promoting permissive lifestyles and detailing acts of graphic violence. Instead of encouraging, motivating, and inspiring its audiences to adopt lifestyles based on the sanctity of life, the entertainment industry often advocates the opposite, painting a cynical picture of violence, abuse, greed, profanity, and a constant denigration of the family. The media must be held accountable for the part they play in the decline of values we observe in society today. Many in the media remain aloof to the issue, claiming to reflect rather than to influence society. For the sake of our human family, Christians must work together to halt this erosion of moral and ethical values in the world community by:

1) encouraging local congregations to support and encourage parental responsibility to monitor their children's viewing and listening habits on TV, movies, radio and the Internet,

2) encouraging local congregations, parents and individuals to express their opposition to the gratuitous portrayal of violent and sexually indecent shows by writing to the stations that air them and the companies that sponsor them,

3) encouraging individuals to express their opposition to the corporate sponsors of these shows by the selection and purchase of alternate products.

R) Information Communication Technology—Because effective personal communication is key to being a responsible and empowered member of society, and because of the power afforded by information communication technologies to shape society and enable individuals to participate more fully, we believe that access to these technologies is a basic right.

Information communication technologies provide us with information, entertainment, and a voice in society. They can be used to enhance our quality of life and provide us with a means to interact with each other, our government, and people and cultures all over the world. Most information about world events comes to us by the broadcast, cable, print media, and the Internet. Concentrating the control of media to large commerical interests limits our choices and often provides a distorted view of human values. Therefore, we support the regulation of media communication technologies to ensure a variety of independent information sources and provides for the public good.

Personal communication technologies such as the Internet allow persons to communicate with each other and access vast information resources that can have commercial, cultural, political, and personal value. While the Internet can be used to nurture minds and spirits of children and adults, it is in danger of being overrun with commercial interests and is used by some to distribute inappropriate and illegal material. Therefore, the Internet must be managed responsibly in order to maximize its benefits while minimizing its risks, especially for children. Denying access in today's world to basic information communication technologies like the Internet due to their cost or availability, limits people's participation in their government and society. We support the goal of universal access to telephone and Internet services at an affodable price.

S) Persons Living with HIV and AIDS—Persons diagnosed as positive for Human Immune Virus (HIV) and with Acquired Immune Deficiency Syndrome (AIDS) often face rejection from their families and friends and various communities in which they work and interact. In addition, they are often faced with a lack of adequate health care, especially toward the end of life.

All individuals living with HIV and AIDS should be treated with dignity and respect.

We affirm the responsibility of the Church to minister to and with these individuals and their families regardless of how the disease was contracted. We support their rights to employment, appropriate medical care, full participation in public education, and full participation in the Church.

We urge the Church to be actively involved in the prevention of the spread of AIDS by providing educational opportunities to the congregation and the community. The Church should be available to provide counseling to the affected individuals and their families.

T) Right to Health Care—Health is a condition of physical, mental, social, and spiritual well-being, and we view it as a responsibility— public and private. Health care is a basic human right. Psalm 146 speaks of the God "who executes justice for the oppressed;/ who gives food to the hungry./ The Lord sets the prisoners free;/ the Lord opens the eyes of the blind." The right to health care includes care for persons with brain diseases, neurological conditions or physical disabilities, who must be afforded the same access to health care as all other persons in our communities. It is unjust to construct or perpetuate barriers to physical or mental wholeness or full participation in community.

We encourage individuals to pursue a healthy lifestyle and affirm the importance of preventive health care, health education, environmental and occupational safety, good nutrition, and secure housing in achieving health. We also recognize the role of governments in ensuring that each individual has access to those elements necessary to good health. Countries facing a public health crisis such as HIV/AIDS must have access to generic medicines and to patented medicines without infringing on a pharmaceutical company's patent/licensing rights. We affirm the right of men and women to have access to comprehensive reproductive health/family planning information and services which will serve as a means to prevent unplanned pregnancies, reduce abortions, and prevent the spread of HIV/AIDS.

U) Organ Transplantation and Donation—We believe that organ transplantation and organ donation are acts of charity, agape love, and self-sacrifice. We recognize the life-giving benefits of organ and other tissue donation and encourage all people of faith to become organ and tissue donors as a part of their love and ministry to others in need. We urge that it be done in an environment of respect for deceased and living donors and for the benefit of the recipients, and following protocols that carefully prevent abuse to donors and their families.

¶ 163. IV. THE ECONOMIC COMMUNITY

We claim all economic systems to be under the judgment of God no less than other facets of the created order. Therefore, we recognize the responsibility of governments to develop and implement sound fiscal and monetary policies that provide for the economic life of individuals and corporate entities and that ensure full employment and adequate incomes with a minimum of inflation. We believe private and public economic enterprises are responsible for the social costs of doing business, such as employment and environmental pollution, and that they should be held accountable for these costs. We support measures that would reduce the concentration of wealth in the hands of a few. We further support efforts to revise tax structures and to eliminate governmental support programs that now benefit the wealthy at the expense of other persons.

A) Property—We believe private ownership of property is a trusteeship under God, both in those societies where it is encouraged and where it is discouraged, but is limited by the overriding needs of society. We believe that Christian faith denies to any person or group of persons exclusive and arbitrary control of any other part of the created universe. Socially and culturally conditioned ownership of property is, therefore, to be considered a responsibility to God. We believe, therefore, governments have the responsibility, in the pursuit of justice and order under law, to provide procedures that protect the rights of the whole society as well as those of private ownership.

B) Collective Bargaining—We support the right of public and private (including farm, government, institutional, and domestic) employees and employers to organize for collective bargaining into unions and other groups of their own choosing. Further, we support the right of both parties to protection in so doing and their responsibility to bargain in good faith within the framework of the public interest. In order that the rights of all members of the society may be maintained and promoted, we support innovative bargaining procedures that include representatives of the public interest in negotiation and settlement of labor-management contracts, including some that may lead to forms of judicial resolution of issues. We reject the use of violence by either party during collective bargaining or any labor/management disagreement. We likewise reject the permanent replacement of a worker who engages in a lawful strike.

C) Work and Leisure—Every person has the right to a job at a living wage. Where the private sector cannot or does not provide jobs for all who seek and need them, it is the responsibility of government to provide for the creation of such jobs. We support social measures that ensure the physical and mental safety of workers, that provide for the equitable division of products and services, and that encourage an increasing freedom in the way individuals may use their leisure time. We recognize the opportunity leisure provides for creative contributions to society and encourage methods that allow workers additional blocks of discretionary time. We support educational, cultural, and recreational outlets that enhance the use of such time. We believe that persons come before profits. We deplore the selfish spirit that often pervades our economic life. We support policies that encourage the sharing of ideas in the workplace, cooperative and collective work arrangements. We support rights of workers to refuse to work in situations that endanger health and/or life without jeopardy to their jobs. We support policies that would reverse the increasing concentration of business and industry into monopolies.

D) Consumption—Consumers should exercise their economic power to encourage the manufacture of goods that are necessary and beneficial to humanity while avoiding the desecration of the environment in either production or consumption, and to avoid purchasing products made in conditions where workers are being exploited because of their age, gender, or economic status.

And while the limited options available to consumers make this extremely difficult to accomplish, buying "Fair Trade Certified" products is one sure way consumers can use their purchasing power to make a contribution to the common good. The International Standards of Fair Trade are based on ensuring livable wages for small farmers and their families, working with democratically run farming cooperatives, buying direct so that the benefits and profits from trade actually reach the farmers and their communities, providing vitally important advance credit, and encouraging ecologically sustainable farming practices. Consumers should not only seek out companies whose product lines reflect a strong commitment to these standards, but should also encourage expanded corporate participation in the Fair Trade market.

Consumers should evaluate their consumption of goods and services in the light of the need for enhanced quality of life rather than unlimited production of material goods. We call upon consumers, including local congregations and Church-related institutions, to organize to achieve these goals and to express dissatisfaction with harmful economic, social, or ecological practices through such appropriate methods as boycott, letter writing, corporate resolution, and advertisement. For example, these methods can be used to influence better television and radio programming.

E) Poverty—In spite of general affluence in the industrialized nations, the majority of persons in the world live in poverty. In order to provide basic needs such as food, clothing, shelter, education, health care, and other necessities, ways must be found to share more equitably the resources of the world. Increasing technology, when accompanied by exploitative economic practices, impoverishes many persons and makes poverty self-perpetuating. Therefore, we do not hold poor people morally responsible for their economic state. To begin to alleviate poverty, we support such policies as: adequate income maintenance, quality education, decent housing, job training, meaningful employment opportunities, adequate medical and hospital care, and humanization and radical revisions of welfare programs. Since low wages are often a cause of poverty, employers should pay their employees a wage that does not require them to depend upon government subsidies such as food stamps or welfare for their livelihood.

F) Migrant Workers—Migratory and other farm workers, who have long been a special concern of the Church's ministry, are by the nature of their way of life excluded from many of the economic and social benefits enjoyed by other workers. Many of the migrant laborers' situations are aggravated because they are racial and ethnic minority persons who have been oppressed with numerous other inequities within the society. We advocate for the rights of all migrants and applaud their efforts toward responsible self-organization and self-determination. We call upon governments and all employers to ensure for migratory workers the same economic, educational, and social benefits enjoyed by other citizens. We call upon our churches to seek to develop programs of service to such migrant people who come within their parish and support their efforts to organize for collective bargaining.

G) Gambling—Gambling is a menace to society, deadly to the best interests of moral, social, economic, and spiritual life, and destructive of good government. As an act of faith and concern, Christians should abstain from gambling and should strive to minister to those victimized by the practice. Where gambling has become addictive, the Church will encourage such individuals to receive therapeutic assistance so that the individual's energies may be redirected into positive and constructive ends. The Church should promote standards and personal lifestyles that would make unnecessary and undesirable the resort to commercial gambling—including public lotteries—as a recreation, as an escape, or as a means of producing public revenue or funds for support of charities or government.

H) Family Farms—The value of family farms has long been affirmed as a significant foundation for free and democratic societies. In recent years, the survival of independent farmers worldwide has been threatened by various factors, including the increasing concentration of all phases of agriculture into the hands of a limited number of transnational corporations. The concentration of the food supply for the many into the hands of the few, raises global questions of justice that cry out for vigilance and action. We call upon the agri-business sector to conduct itself with respect for human rights primarily in the responsible stewardship of daily bread for the world, and secondarily in responsible corporate citizenship that respects the rights of all farmers, small and large, to receive a fair return for honest labor.

We advocate for the rights of people to possess property and to earn a living by tilling the soil.

We call upon our churches to do all in their power to speak prophetically to the matters of food supply and the people who grow the food for the world.

I) Corporate Responsibility—Corporations are responsible not only to their stockholders, but also to other stakeholders: their workers, suppliers, vendors, customers, the communities in which they do business, and for the earth, which supports them. We support the public's right to know what impacts corporations have in these various arenas, so that people can make informed choices about which corporations to support.

We applaud corporations that voluntarily comply with standards that promote human well-being and protect the environment.

J) Trade and Investment—We affirm the importance of international trade and investment in an interdependent world. Trade and investment should be based on rules that support the dignity of the human person, a clean environment and our common humanity. Trade agreements must include mechanisms to enforce labor rights and human rights as well as environmental standards. Broad-based citizen advocacy and participation in trade negotiations must be ensured through democratic mechanisms of consultation and participation.

¶ 164.   V. THE POLITICAL COMMUNITY

While our allegiance to God takes precedence over our allegiance to any state, we acknowledge the vital function of government as a principal vehicle for the ordering of society. Because we know ourselves to be responsible to God for social and political life, we declare the following relative to governments:

A) Basic Freedoms and Human Rights—We hold governments responsible for the protection of the rights of the people to free and fair elections and to the freedoms of speech, religion, assembly, communications media, and petition for redress of grievances without fear of reprisal; to the right to privacy; and to the guarantee of the rights to adequate food, clothing, shelter, education, and health care. The form and the leaders of all governments should be determined by exercise of the right to vote guaranteed to all adult citizens. We also strongly reject domestic surveillance and intimidation of political opponents by governments in power and all other misuses of elective or appointive offices. The use of detention and imprisonment for the harassment and elimination of political opponents or other dissidents violates fundamental human rights. Furthermore, the mistreatment or torture of persons by governments for any purpose violates Christian teaching and must be condemned and/or opposed by Christians and churches wherever and whenever it occurs.

The Church regards the institution of slavery as an infamous evil. All forms of enslavement are totally prohibited and shall in no way be tolerated by the Church.

B) Political Responsibility—The strength of a political system depends upon the full and willing participation of its citizens. The church should continually exert a strong ethical influence upon the state, supporting policies and programs deemed to be just and opposing policies and programs that are unjust.

C) Church and State Relations—The United Methodist Church has for many years supported the separation of church and state. In some parts of the world this separation has guaranteed the diversity of religious expressions and the freedom to worship God according to each person's conscience. Separation of church and state means no organic union of the two, but it does permit interaction. The state should not use its authority to promote particular religious beliefs (including atheism), nor should it require prayer or worship in the public schools, but it should leave students free to practice their own religious convictions. We believe that the state should not attempt to control the church, nor should the church seek to dominate the state. The rightful and vital separation of churc and state, which has served the cause of religious liberty, should not be misconstrued as the abolition of all religious expression from public life.

D) Freedom of Information—Citizens of all countries should have access to all essential information regarding their government and its policies. Illegal and unconscionable activities directed against persons or groups by their own governments must not be justified or kept secret, even under the guise of national security.

E) Education—We believe that every person has the right to education. We also believe that the responsibility for education of the young rests with the family, faith communities, and the government. In our society, this function can best be fulfilled through public policies that ensure access for all persons to free public elementary and secondary schools and to post-secondary schools of their choice. Persons in our society should not be precluded by financial barriers from access to church-related and other independent institutions of higher education. We affirm the right of public and independent colleges and universities to exist, and we endorse public policies that ensure access and choice and that do not create unconstitutional entanglements between church and state.

F) Civil Obedience and Civil Disobedience—Governments and laws should be servants of God and of human beings. Citizens have a duty to abide by laws duly adopted by orderly and just process of government. But governments, no less than individuals, are subject to the judgment of God. Therefore, we recognize the right of individuals to dissent when acting under the constraint of conscience and, after having exhausted all legal recourse, to resist or disobey laws that they deem to be unjust or that are discriminately enforced. Even then, respect for law should be shown by refraining from violence and by being willing to accept the costs of disobedience. We do not encourage or condone, under any circumstances, any form of violent protest or action against anyone involved in the abortion dilemma. We offer our prayers for those in rightful authority who serve the public, and we support their efforts to afford justice and equal opportunity for all people. We assert the duty of churches to support those who suffer because of their stands of conscience represented by nonviolent beliefs or acts. We urge governments to ensure civil rights, as defined by the International Covenant on Civil and Political Rights, to persons in legal jeopardy because of those nonviolent acts.

G) The Dealth Penalty—We believe the death penalty denies the power of Christ to redeem, restore, and transform all human beings. The United Methodist Church is deeply concerned about crime throughout the world and the value of any life taken by a murder or homicide. We believe all human life is sacred and created by God and therefore, we must see all human life as significant and valuable. When governments implement the death penalty (capital punishment), then the life of the convicted person is devalued and all possibility of change in that person's life ends. We believe in the resurrection of Jesus Christ and that the possibility of reconciliation with Christ comes through repentance. This gift of reconciliation is offered to all individuals without exception and gives all life new dignity and sacredness. For this reason, we oppose the death penalty (capital punishment) and urge its elimination from all criminal codes.

H) Criminal and Restorative Justice—To protect all persons from encroachment upon their personal and property rights, governments have established mechanisms of law enforcement and courts. A wide array of sentencing options serves to express community outrage, incapacitate dangerous offenders, deter crime, and offer opportunities for rehabilitation. We support governmental measures designed to reduce and eliminate crime that are consistent with respect for the basic freedom of persons.

We reject all misuse of these mechanisms, including their use for the purpose of revenge or for persecuting or intimidating those whose race, appearance, lifestyle, economic condition, or beliefs differ from those in authority. We reject all careless, callous or discriminatory enforcement of law that withholds justice from all non-English speaking persons and persons with disabilities. We further support measures designed to remove the social conditions that lead to crime, and we encourage continued positive interaction between law enforcement officials and members of the community at large.

In the love of Christ, who came to save those who are lost and vulnerable, we urge the creation of a genuinely new system for the care and restoration of victims, offenders, criminal justice officials, and the community as a whole. Restorative justice grows out of biblical authority, which emphasizes a right relationship with God, self, and community. When such relationships are violated or broken through crime, opportunities are created to make things right.

Most criminal justice systems around the world are retributive. These retributive justice systems profess to hold the offender accountable to the state and use punishment as the equalizing tool for accountability. In contrast, restorative justice seeks to hold the offender accountable to the victimized person, and to the disrupted community. Through God's transforming power, restorative justice seeks to repair the damage, right the wrong, and bring healing to all involved, including the victim, the offender, the families, and the community. The Church is transformed when it responds to the claims of discipleship by becoming an agent of healing and systemic change.

I) Military Service—We deplore war and urge the peaceful settlement of all disputes among nations. From the beginning, the Christian conscience has struggled with the harsh realities of violence and war, for these evils clearly frustrate God's loving purposes for humankind. We yearn for the day when there will be no more war and people will live together in peace and justice. Some of us believe that war, and other acts of violence, are never acceptable to Christians. We also acknowledge that many Christians believe that, when peaceful alternatives have failed, the force of arms may regretfully be preferable to unchecked aggression, tyranny, and genocide. We honor the witness of pacifists who will not allow us to become complacent about war and violence. We also respect those who support the use of force, but only in extreme situations and only when the need is clear beyond reasonable doubt, and through appropriate international organizations. We urge the establishment of the rule of law in international affairs as a means of elimination of war, violence, and coercion in these affairs.

We reject national policies of enforced military service as incompatible with the gospel. We acknowledge the agonizing tension created by the demand for military service by national governments. We urge all young adults to seek the counsel of the Church as they reach a conscientious decision concerning the nature of their responsibility as citizens. Pastors are called upon to be available for counseling with all young adults who face conscription, including those who conscientiously refuse to cooperate with a system of conscription.

We support and extend the ministry of the Church to those persons who conscientiously oppose all war, or any particular war, and who therefore refuse to serve in the armed forces or to cooperate with systems of military conscription. We also support and extend the Church's ministry to those persons who conscientiously choose to serve in the armed forces or to accept alternative service. As Christians we are aware that neither the way of military action, nor the way of inaction is always righteous before God.

¶ 165.   VI. THE WORLD COMMUNITY

God's world is one world. The unity now being thrust upon us by technological revolution has far outrun our moral and spiritual capacity to achieve a stable world. The enforced unity of humanity, increasingly evident on all levels of life, presents the Church as well as all people with problems that will not wait for answer: injustice, war, exploitation, privilege, population, international ecological crisis, proliferation of arsenals of nuclear weapons, development of transnational business organizations that operate beyond the effective control of any governmental structure, and the increase of tyranny in all its forms. This generation must find viable answers to these and related questions if humanity is to continue on this earth. We commit ourselves as a Church to the achievement of a world community that is a fellowship of persons who honestly love one another. We pledge ourselves to seek the meaning of the gospel in all issues that divide people and threaten the growth of world community.

A) Nations and Cultures—As individuals are affirmed by God in their diversity, so are nations and cultures. We recognize that no nation or culture is absolutely just and right in its treatment of its own people, nor is any nation totally without regard for the welfare of its citizens. The Church must regard nations as accountable for unjust treatment of their citizens and others living within their borders. While recognizing valid differences in culture and political philosophy, we stand for justice and peace in every nation.

B) National Power and Responsibility—Some nations possess more military and economic power than do others. Upon the powerful rests responsibility to exercise their wealth and influence with restraint. We affirm the right and duty of people of all nations to determine their own destiny. We urge the major political powers to use their nonviolent power to maximize the political, social, and economic self-determination of other nations rather than to further their own special interests. We applaud international efforts to develop a more just international economic order in which the limited resources of the earth will be used to the maximum benefit of all nations and peoples. We urge Christians in every society to encourage the governments under which they live and the economic entities within their societies to aid and work for the development of more just economic orders.

C) War and Peace—We believe war is incompatible with the teachings and example of Christ. We therefore reject war as an instrument of national foreign policy, to be employed only as a last resort in the prevention of such evils as genocide, brutal suppression of human rights, and unprovoked international aggression and insist that the first moral duty of all nations is to resolve by peaceful means every dispute that arises between or among them; that human values must outweigh military claims as governments determine their priorities; that the militarization of society must be challenged and stopped; that the manufacture, sale, and deployment of armaments must be reduced and controlled; and that the production, possession, or use of nuclear weapons be condemned. Consequently, we endorse general and complete disarmament under strict and effective international control.

D) Justice and Law—Persons and groups must feel secure in their life and right to live within a society if order is to be achieved and maintained by law. We denounce as immoral an ordering of life that perpetuates injustice. Nations, too, must feel secure in the world if world community is to become a fact.

Believing that international justice requires the participation of all peoples, we endorse the United Nations and its related bodies and the International Court of Justice as the best instruments now in existence to achieve a world of justice and law. We commend the efforts of all people in all countries who pursue world peace through law. We endorse international aid and cooperation on all matters of need and conflict. We urge acceptance for membership in the United Nations of all nations who wish such membership and who accept United Nations responsibility. We urge the United Nations to take a more aggressive role in the development of international arbitration of disputes and actual conflicts among nations by developing binding third-party arbitration. Bilateral or multilateral efforts outside of the United Nations should work in concert with, and not contrary to, its purposes. We reaffirm our historic concern for the world as our parish and seek for all persons and peoples full and equal membership in a truly world community.

¶ 166.   VII. OUR SOCIAL CREED

We believe in God, Creator of the world; and in Jesus Christ, the Redeemer of creation. We believe in the Holy Spirit, through whom we acknowledge God's gifts, and we repent of our sin in misusing these gifts to idolatrous ends.

We affirm the natural world as God's handiwork and dedicate ourselves to its preservation, enhancement, and faithful use by humankind.

We joyfully receive for ourselves and others the blessings of community, sexuality, marriage, and the family.

We commit ourselves to the rights of men, women, children, youth, young adults, the aging, and people with disabilities; to improvement of the quality of life; and to the rights and dignity of all persons.

We believe in the right and duty of persons to work for the glory of God and the good of themselves and others and in the protection of their welfare in so doing; in the rights to property as a trust from God, collective bargaining, and responsible consumption; and in the elimination of economic and social distress.

We dedicate ourselves to peace throughout the world, to the rule of justice and law among nations, and to individual freedom for all people of the world.

We believe in the present and final triumph of God's Word in human affairs and gladly accept our commission to manifest the life of the gospel in the world. Amen.

(It is recommended that this statement of Social Principles be continually available to United Methodist Christians and that it be emphasized regularly in every congregation. It is further recommended that "Our Social Creed" be frequently used in Sunday worship.)

THE NATURAL WORLD

ENVIRONMENT/ENERGY

1. Caring for Creation—
A Study from a Native American Perspective

WHEREAS, we worship and honor a God who is Creator and Sustainer of all we have and are, and seek to cherish and care for God's creation, but have failed in our stewardship, and,

WHEREAS, in Christ God has healed our alienation from God and extended to use the first fruits of the reconciliation of all things, and

WHEREAS, God calls us to commit ourselves to extend Christ's healing to a suffering creation and await the time when even the groaning of creation will be restored to wholeness, and

WHEREAS, we are called to commit ourselves to work vigorously to protect and heal that creation for the honor and glory of God, whom we become fully aware of through Christ;

WHEREAS, we and our children face a growing crisis in the health of that creation in which we live, through which, by God's grace, we are sustained;

WHEREAS, we continue to degrade this creation through land degradation, deforestation, species extinction, water degradation, global toxification, the alteration of the atmosphere, and human and cultural degradation;

WHEREAS, many of the degradations are signs that we are pressing against the finite limits God has set for creation;

WHEREAS, with continued population growth, these degradations will become more severe and our responsibility is not only to bear and nurture children, but to nurture their home on earth and we recognize that human poverty is both a cause and a consequence of environment degradation;

WHEREAS, Native Americans whose religious cultures for centuries have taught them how to care for creation; and

WHEREAS, Native Americans through this unique perspective on caring for creation are convinced that environmental problems are more spiritual than technological;

Therefore, be it resolved, that the 2000 General Conference mandate the following:

1. That there be developed a four-year study on "Caring for Creation from a Native American Perspective."

2. The General Conference directs the Native American Comprehensive Plan working with program agencies of The United Methodist Church and other Native American entities, to develop the study.

3. That up to $80,000 be allocated to complete the study with resources, and provide a report with recommendations to the 2004 General Conference.

ADOPTED 2000

See Social Principles, ¶ 160A.

2. Cease Mountaintop Removal Coal Mining

WHEREAS, mountaintop removal coal mining is extremely profitable to the coal companies who practice it; and

WHEREAS, a large part of its profitability is that fewer miners are required than in the usual traditional methods of coal mining, and

WHEREAS, the entire tops of West Virginia mountains have been removed at Kayford, Kanawha County, at Blair, Boone County, at Sharpless, Logan County, and at Spruce River, Boone County, and at Wise County, Virginia, and mountaintop removal projects are proposed in Kentucky and Tennessee, and

WHEREAS, this removal of mountaintops has resulted in severe damage to homes of persons living in the nearby communities, along with damage to wells, the bombarding of their homes with " blast rock," and massive amounts of dust, and

WHEREAS, the millions and millions of tons of earth and rock removed from the tops of mountains are dumped into the valleys next to these mountains, totally destroying the springs and headwaters of streams in these valleys, along with all plant and animal life in them, and

WHEREAS, mountaintop removal mining, by destroying home places, is also destroying ancestral ground, sacred ground where generations after generations have lived, gone to church, married, made and birthed babies, taken family meals, slept in peace, died and been buried, and

WHEREAS, staff employees of the West Virginia Department of Environmental Protection and Department of Natural Resources testified before the West Virginia Legislature in its 1998 session that the long-term effect of mountaintop removal is unstudied and unknown, and that it should by stopped until its long-term effects are known, and

WHEREAS, Psalm 24:1 firmly reminds us that "The earth is the Lord's and the fullness thereof; and the world and they that dwell therein," and

WHEREAS, the sanctity and sacredness of human life and the natural environment should not be destroyed in the name of corporate profit,

Therefore, be it resolved, that the General Conference of The United Methodist Church, meeting in Cleveland, Ohio in May of the year 2000, implore those state and national governmental and regulatory agencies involved in mountaintop removal mining to halt this practice until scientific study of its long-term effect on human life and the natural environment has been accomplished.

ADOPTED 2000

See Social Principles, ¶ 160A.

3. A Dioxin-Free Future

Theological Foundation:

According to the Social Principles, "All Creation is the Lord's and we are responsible for the ways in which we use and abuse it" (¶ 160).

Background:

For nearly three decades, the scientific and health communities, including government agencies such as the U.S. Environmental

Protection Agency (EPA) and the World Health Organization (WHO) have been assessing the human health risks of dioxin—a class of chlorine-based persistent organic pollutants. The catalyst for this assessment was a finding through animal testing in the 1970s that dioxin was the most potent cancer-causing chemical ever studied.

Since the first EPA study, issued in 1985, major advances have been made in the scientific and health communities' analytical abilities to detect—and determine the impact of—trace amounts of dioxin. A major milestone in exposing the health risks associated with dioxin was the EPA's 1994 report entitled *The Scientific Reassessment of Dioxin.* This report affirmed health warnings made twenty years ago—that the "background" levels of *dioxin* pose a serious threat to the health of the general U.S. population.

Since 1994, the EPA report has been reviewed and revised based on comments from scientific peer review panels. An updated reassessment report was due in 2002. Despite recommendations from the Science Advisory Board that the report be finalized, EPA had not released the final report to the public at the time of this writing. However, based on the October, 2001 draft released and reviewed by panels, the conclusion remained the same: dioxin should be classified as a known human carcinogen—a view shared by the international community as expressed by WHO and within the United States through the U.S. Department of Health and Human Services and the National Institute of Health's National Toxicology Program. Exposure to toxic chemicals such as dioxin is widely suspected to be related to the continued high rates of cancer in the United States. The rate of testicular cancer has doubled in the past thirty years, the rate of prostate cancer has doubled in the past ten years, and the rate of breast cancer in the United States has risen from one in every twenty women in the 1960s to one in every eight women today. More women have died of breast cancer in the last two decades than the number of U.S. soldiers killed in World War I, World War II, and the Korean and Vietnam wars.

The EPA report stated that there is reason to believe that dioxins at extremely low levels cause a wide range of other serious health effects, including reproductive impairment, learning disabilities, developmental injuries, and the increased risk of diabetes and endometriosis. Furthermore, even low levels of dioxin impair the ability of the immune system to right infectious disease. The EPA report says that there is no level of dioxin below which the immune system is not affected.

The EPA concluded that the levels of dioxins already lodged in human bodies are already close to levels known to cause serious health problems. According to the EPA, the average person is exposed to dioxin levels 50 to 100 times greater than the maximum allowable amounts designated by the federal government in 1985.

Some persons have what the EPA calls "special" exposures, including certain occupational groups, people living near dioxin emitters, and people who consume higher than average levels of meat, fish, and dairy products. Human exposure to dioxins begins early in life, since dioxin crosses the placenta. Nursing infants take in four to twelve percent of their lifetime dose of dioxin within the first year of their lives, a period during which they are most susceptible to the effects of such toxins.

Ending toxic pollution, maintaining a clean environment, and using efficient, nonpolluting technologies are essential to a sound economy and a sustainable lifestyle. With a single program—dioxin phaseout— much of the world's most severe toxic pollution could be stopped.

The three largest sources of dioxin are incineration of chorine containing wastes, bleaching of pulp and paper with chlorine and the life-cycle of polyvinyl chloride (PVC). Of continued concern is the use of PVC products by the health care industry, especially the single use or short term use applications (i.e. "disposables"). These account for most of the organically bound chlorine in medical waste.

The American Public Health Association (APHA) has issued warnings, recognizing that "virtually all chlorinated organic compounds that have been studied exhibit at least one of a wide range of serious toxic effects such as endocrine dysfunction, developmental impairment, birth defects, reproductive dysfunction and infertility, immunosuppression and cancer, often at very low doses."

Remembering that "First Do No Harm" is a binding principle in medical ethics, the health care industry should pursue alternatives to PVC products. Appropriate alternative products composed of nonchlorinated material are currently available for many, though not all, health care uses of chlorinated plastics. Highly effective programs for the reduction of hospital waste have been initiated in the US and programs for the substitution of other materials for PVC are in place in some hospitals in Europe.

Acknowledging the ongoing risks associated with dioxin, The United Methodist Church:

- Calls on cancer research organizations to move to a prevention-based approach to cancer research and funding, including more studies on the relationship between cancer and chlorine-based toxins in the environment.
- Supports a phase out of the production of dioxin.
- Supports worker production programs for people working in industries that make toxic chemicals or result in toxic by-product and related chemicals, who may lose their jobs with a phaseout of these chemicals. Such programs could include a "Workers' Superfund" program.
- Challenges all United Methodist-related health care institutions, United Methodist health care professionals and workers, and United Methodist individuals and congregations to begin immediately to take action to change health care policies and practices in order to stop the harm being caused by nonessential incineration of medical waste and by generating a waste stream that is more toxic than necessary.
- Urges all health care facilities to explore ways to reduce or eliminate their use of PVC plastics.
- Calls upon all health care professionals and workers to encourage health care institutions with which they are associated to adopt policies that will lead to the reduction and elimination of the use of PVC plastics.
- Suggests that health care facilities hire or assign professional staff to evaluate the potential for persistent toxic pollution associated with the life-cycle of products the facility purchases.
- Strongly urges medical suppliers to develop, produce, and bring to market appropriate, cost-competitive products that can replace those that contain PVC or other chlorinated plastics. Any substitution for a chlorinated plastic product must provide a less toxic alternative with concern for the full public health implications of the replacement, including infections considerations.
- Encourages government oversight agencies and private accrediting bodies to incorporate requirements for education about the reduction of toxic pollution in their certification standards.

- Encourages study and evaluation of alternative products and practices that will lead to the reduction and elimination of the use of PVC products; also encourages programs to provide technical assistance and training to health care facilities that seek help in the reduction of their reliance on chlorinated plastics.
- Directs the General Board of Church and Society to cooperate with the General Board of Global Ministries to work with companies, governments, and medical institutions to implement the above recommendations.

ADOPTED 1996
AMENDED AND READOPTED 2004

See Social Principles, ¶ 160.

4. Steps Toward a Dioxin-Free Future

Theological Foundation

According to the Social Principles, "All Creation is the Lord's and we are responsible for the ways in which we use and abuse it" (¶ 160).

Background

1996 General Conference Resolution—"A Dioxin-Free Future": The 1996 General Conference of The United Methodist Church passed a resolution called "A Dioxin-Free Future," based on facts from the U.S. Environmental Protection Agency's 1994 Draft Dioxin Reassessment, which affirmed health warnings made 20 years ago—that the background levels of dioxin, a deadly chlorine-based chemical not found in nature, pose a serious threat to the health of the general U.S. population. (For specific health threats, please refer to the text of the resolution.)

The resolution supports a phase-out of the production of dioxin, beginning with immediate action on the three largest sources of dioxin: incineration of chlorine-containing wastes, bleaching of pulp and paper with chlorine, and the entire life cycle of polyvinyl chloride (PVC) plastic.

It also directs the General Board of Church and Society to cooperate with the Health and Welfare Ministries unit of the General Board of Global Ministries to work with companies, governments, and medical institutions to implement the above recommendations.

Medical waste incineration is a major source of dioxin contamination; this conclusion was raised by the same 1994 EPA Dioxin Reassessment report mentioned above.

Dioxins are created by the disposal of synthetic chlorinated organic compounds. Though the factors which determine dioxin formation during incineration are not fully understood, they are released into the environment during combustion of chlorinated plastic products, predominantly polyvinyl chloride (PVC).

The use of PVC products by the health care industry began after World War II and has grown rapidly, especially the single use or short term use applications (i.e. "disposables"). These account for most of the organically bound chlorine in medical waste.

The American Public Health Association's (APHA) warnings: The APHA in Resolution #9304 recognizes that "virtually all chlorinated organic compounds that have been studied exhibit at least one of a wide range of serious toxic effects such as endocrine dysfunction, developmental impairment, birth defects, reproductive dysfunction and infertility, immunosuppression and cancer, often at very low doses."

"First Do No Harm" is a binding principle in medical ethics.

Some alternatives are available or in development: Appropriate alternative products composed of nonchlorinated material are currently available for many, though not all, health care uses of chlorinated plastics. Highly effective programs for the reduction of hospital waste have been initiated in the U.S. and programs for the substitution of other materials for PVC are in place in some hospitals in Europe.

Be it resolved that the General Conference of
The United Methodist Church:

1. Challenges all United Methodist-related health care institutions, United Methodist health care professionals and workers, and United Methodist individuals and congregations to begin immediately to take action to change health care policies and practices in order to stop the harm being caused by the nonessential incineration of

medical waste and by generating a waste stream that is more toxic than necessary.

2. Urges all health care facilities to explore ways to reduce or eliminate their use of PVC plastics.

3. Calls upon all health care professionals and workers to encourage health care institutions with which they are associated to adopt policies that will lead to the reduction and elimination of the use of PVC plastics.

4. Suggests that health care facilities hire or assign professional staff to evaluate the potential for persistent toxic pollution associated with the life-cycle of products the facility purchases.

5. Strongly urges medical suppliers to develop, produce and bring to market appropriate, cost-competitive products that can replace those that contain PVC or other chlorinated plastics. Any substitution for a chlorinated plastic product must provide a less toxic alternative with concern for the full public health implications of the replacement, including infectious considerations.

6. Encourages government oversight agencies and private accrediting bodies to incorporate requirements for education about the reduction of toxic pollution in their certification standards.

7. Encourages study and evaluation of alternative products and practices that will lead to the reduction and elimination of the use of PVC products; also encourages programs to provide technical assistance and training to health care facilities that seek help in the reduction of their reliance on chlorinated plastics.

ADOPTED 1996
AMENDED AND READOPTED 2000

See Social Principles, ¶ 160A.

5. Energy Policy Statement

Humankind enjoys a unique place in God's universe. On the one hand, we are simply one of God's many finite creatures, made from the "dust of the earth," bounded in time and space, fallible in judgment, limited in control, dependent upon our Creator, and interdependent with all other creatures. On the other hand, we are created in the very image of God, with the divine Spirit breathed into us, and entrusted with "dominion" over God's creation (Genesis 1:26, 28; 2:7;

Psalm 8:6). We are simultaneously caretakers with all creation and, because of the divine summons, caretakers with God of the world in which we live. This hybrid human condition produces both the opportunity and the twin dangers for humans on this planet.

The first danger is *arrogance:* that we may overestimate the extent of human control over our environment and the soundness of human judgments concerning it; that we may underestimate the limits of the planet where we live; and that we may misunderstand "dominion" to mean exploitation instead of stewardship.

The second danger is *irresponsibility:* that we may fail to be the responsible stewards of the earth. As stewards entrusted with domin-ion, then, we will demonstrate our faith in God by shaping the new human society that will emerge in the twenty-first century. We cannot, therefore, neglect the task of seeking to embody in the world the val-ues that we hold in covenant with God. Nor can we forget the forgiv-ing grace in Jesus Christ, which alone makes us bold enough, or the hope in Christ, which alone keeps us from despair.

The Values Involved in Energy Policy

The decisions that humans are now making will either enhance or degrade the quality of life on the planet. We have entered an era of greater energy interdependence. As the world confronts global issues such as climate change, energy inequity, and pollution, energy-related problems will require international solutions based upon the values of justice and sustainability.

The Scripture that provides the motive for our action in the present energy crisis also lays the foundation for the values that we seek to realize. These values underlying the policies we advocate are justice and sustainability.

1. *Justice.* Ever since the first covenant between God and Israel, and especially since the eighth-century prophets, the people of God have understood that they bear a special concern for justice.

"Let justice roll down like waters,
and righteousness like an everflowing stream" (Amos 5:24)

is a cry echoed in hundreds of contexts throughout the Old and New Testaments. Biblical righteousness includes a special concern for the least and the last: the poor, the captive, the oppressed (Luke 4:18;

Isaiah 61:1-2). Energy policies that Christians can support, then, will seek to actualize the multifaceted biblical vision of justice. They will be policies that close rather than widen the gap dividing wealth and poverty, rich nations and poor. They will be measures that liberate rather than oppress. They will be programs that distribute fairly the benefits, burdens, and hazards of energy production and consumption, taking into consideration those not yet born as well as the living. They will thus be strategies that give priority to meeting basic human needs such as air, water, food, clothing, and shelter.

2. *Sustainability.* Only recently have we humans come to recognize that creation entails limits to the resources entrusted to us as stewards of the earth. In particular, we have come up against limits to the nonrenewable fuels available for our consumption and limits to our environment's capacity to absorb poisonous wastes. These double limits mean that humans can betray their stewardship either by using up resources faster than they can be replaced or by releasing wastes in excess of the planet's capacity to absorb them. We now know that humans have the capacity to destroy human life and perhaps even life itself on this planet, and to do so in a very short period of time. Energy policy decisions, therefore, must be measured by sustainability as a criterion in addition to justice. In tgerms of energy policy, sustainability means energy use that will not: (a) deplete the earth's resources in such a way that our descendants will not be able to continue human society at the level that is adequate for a good quality of life, and (b) pollute the environment to such an extent that human life cannot be sustained in the future. These guidelines for sustainability must include considerations of quality of life as well as mere biological continuance.

We enjoy a highly sophisticated, industrialized world. It is not a realistic option for us to return to a world where people read by candlelight and heat with wood. Also, we should be aware of the tragic effects that steadily increasing energy costs will have, especially upon the aged and poor members of our society. All options available to the rich nations are not open to peoples in other parts of the world; hence, we should endeavor to develop just and equitable energy policies.

We must creatively explore all sustainable energy options available to us. There are environmental problems connected with certain energy options. We believe that the environmental problems of each energy source should be fully assessed. For example, the large-scale use of our coal resources poses many problems. Underground mining, in addition to operational accidents, causes disabling illness or death from black lung. Strip-mining can despoil an area and ruin it for further use if restoration measures are not practiced. The burning of coal causes large-scale pollution and seriously alters the environment by increasing the carbon dioxide content of the atmosphere, contributing to global warming.

Hydroelectric power also has its problems. In addition to deaths from industrial accidents, many dam sites are (or were) attractive scenic areas. Destroying (or diminishing) such natural beauty areas is objectionable to most of us. Possible dam failure with the resultant flood damage must also be considered in evaluation of this source of power.

The use of petroleum products creates severe environmental problems. Tankers and offshore wells have created spills that have devastated seacoast areas; the damage is long-lasting or permanent. Air pollution, far from being under control, is a serious health problem, especially in centers of dense population.

The nuclear energy option also has many problems to be faced. The hazards in storing radioactive wastes for thousands of years and the destructive potential of a catastrophic accident involve a great risk of irreversible damage to the environment or to the human genetic pool.

1. We support strenuous efforts to conserve energy and increase energy efficiency. A transition to energy efficiency and renewable energy sources will combat global warming, protect human health, create new jobs, and ensure a secure, affordable energy future. Economists have concluded that a greater increase in end-use energy can be gained through conservation and energy efficiency than through any single new source of fuel. Furthermore, conservation is nonpolluting and job producing. We include under conservation: insulation, co-generation, recycling, public transportation, more efficient motors in appliances and automobiles, as well as the elimination of waste, and a more simplified lifestyle. The technology for such steps is already known and commercially available; it requires only dissemination of information and stronger public support, including larger tax incentives than are presently available.

2. All United Methodist churches, annual conferences, general boards and agencies are to be models for energy conservation by doing such things as: installing dampers in furnaces, insulating adequately all church properties, heating and lighting only rooms that

are in use, using air circulation, purchasing energy efficient appliances, and exploring alternative energy sources such as solar energy. Local churches, camps, and agencies are urged to become involved in programs such as the Energy Stewardship Congregation program, thereby witnessing our shared values of justice and sustainability.

3. All United Methodist Church programs and mission projects must model our sustainable and just energy values. We particularly urge the United Methodist Committee on Relief (UMCOR) and the General Board of Global Ministries (GBGM) to support and fund renewable and energy efficient mission projects; and we urge the Church Architecture Office of the General Board of Global Ministries to make energy conservation and the use of renewables a prime design feature in new building design and renovations.

4. We support increased government funding for research and development of renewable energy sources, especially solar energy, and government incentives to speed the application of the resulting technologies to our energy needs, wherever appropriate. The greatest national and international effort should be made in the areas of conservation and renewable energy sources.

5. We encourage international lending institutions and aid agencies to promote sustainable and just energy policies.

6. We oppose any energy policy that will result in continuing exploitation of indigenous peoples' lands. The despoiling of indigenous peoples' lands and the increased health and social-economic problems that have resulted because of oil exploration, hydroelectric projects, and the mining of coal and the milling of uranium must cease.

7. We support national energy programs that will not increase the financial burden on the poor, the elderly, and those with fixed incomes. If a rapid rise in the price of fuel is necessary to smooth out distortions in the energy economy, as many economists believe, then means should be found to cushion the impact of such price increases on the poor. Furthermore, energy policies must guarantee universal service to all consumers, protecting low-income and rural residents.

8. We support full cooperation of all nations in efforts to ensure equitable distribution of necessary energy supplies, the control of global warming, and rapid development and deployment of appropriate technologies based on renewable energy resources such as solar, wind, and water energy generation.

9. We strongly encourage The United Methodist Church at all levels to engage in a serious study of these energy issues in the context of Christian faith, especially the values of justice and sustainability.

ADOPTED 1980
AMENDED AND READOPTED 2000

See Social Principles, ¶ 160B.

6. U.S. Energy Policy and United Methodist Responsibility

Resolved:
1. Energy policy in the US must be based on sound scientific and ethical principles of respect for and justice within the World Community, focusing not on expanding supply through large scale projects but on managing the demand and developing renewable, alternative sources of energy. Specifically, the US must:
- move beyond its dependence on high carbon fossil fuels that produce emissions leading to climate change,
- ratify the Kyoto Protocol under the UN Framework Convention on Climate Change,
- concentrate on reducing carbon dioxide emissions within the US and not rely on mechanisms such as emission trading with other countries to meet our targets for emission reductions under international agreements,
- reduce our reliance on nuclear power, a technology for which there are still unresolved problems such as the safe disposal or safe storage of high level waste of nuclear reactors,
- manage demand through a high priority on conservation and energy efficiency,
- increase significantly research and development into such renewable energy sources as solar, wind, biomass, etc.,
- support development and utilization of appropriate technologies for small-scale, decentralized energy systems,
- support expansion of the infrastructure needed for public transportation and carpooling, and
- provide necessary support for individuals, families, and communities adversely affected by a transition away from fossil fuels, nuclear power, and large-scale hydro in order to

allow for alternative economic development, retraining, relocation, etc.

2. Members of local United Methodist churches are urged to show
leadership as stewards of God's creation and take concrete actions to:

- educate our congregants on energy production and usage in
  relation to global warming,
- conduct an energy audit of our homes, church facilities, and
  camp structures to identify sources of energy waste and the
  potential financial savings of energy-related improvements,
- make energy improvements to our homes, church facilities,
  and camp structures,
- replace light bulbs with compact fluorescent bulbs,
- expand our use of public transportation, carpooling, and tele-
  conferencing to reduce fossil fuel consumption,
- choose a cleaner vehicle that is the least polluting and most
  efficient,
- keep our vehicle's engine tuned and tires properly inflated,
- study the consequences of our consumer choices and take
  action to lessen our impact on the environment, and use our
  votes by telling our elected officials that we need laws that
  support the most important solutions to climate change:
  cleaner cars and cleaner power plants.

ADOPTED 2004

See Social Principles, ¶ 160B.

7. Environmental Justice for a Sustainable Future

Humankind is destroying the global ecological balance that provides the life-support systems for the planet. Signs of the crisis are evident all around us. The global ecological imbalance produces
environmental destruction.

Polluted air pervades the atmosphere. Garbage abounds, with little
space for disposal. Polluting gases destroy the ozone layer and cause
global warming. Deforestation leads to soil erosion, a lack of carbon
storage, inadequate water quantity and poor quality, and the loss of
species, resulting in a reduction in biological diversity. The misuse of

pesticides and fertilizers contributes to the poisoning of our soils and creates products harmful to all life.

Present social, political, and economic development structures fail to provide the basic necessities of food, clothing, and shelter for all our brothers and sisters around the world with more than 1.2 billion people currently living in absolute poverty. And the world population is projected to grow by another 3 billion people in the next fifty years. This growth, combined with higher standards of living, will pose severe strains on land, water, energy, and other natural resources.

Historical and Theological Concerns

Through the ages, a theological base for the domination of creation was found in Genesis 1:28: "Be fruitful and multiply, and fill the earth and subdue it; and have dominion over . . . every living thing that moves upon the earth." Misinterpretation of "subdue" and "dominion" has been used to justify much of the nature-destroying aspects of modern civilization.

The scale of human activity has grown so large that it now threatens the planet itself. Global environmental problems have become so vast that they are hard to comprehend. Between 1955 and 2000, the human population has more than doubled to 6.1 billion. During the same time, the consumption of fossil fuels has quadrupled with North Americans using fossil fuels at a per capita rate ten times greater than citizens of developing nations. The vast majority of scientific evidence suggests that the carbon dioxide from fossil fuels has already caused a measurable warming of the globe. Destruction of habitat, especially tropical rain forests, is causing the loss of species at an ever-increasing rate. Valuable topsoil is being depleted. There is a recurring hole in the ozone layer. More ultraviolet radiation now reaches the earth, which may cause more cancers, poorer crop growth, and damage to the immune systems of humans and other animals.

Confronted with the massive crisis of the deterioration of God's creation and faced with the question of the ultimate survival of life, we ask God's forgiveness for our participation in this destruction of God's creation. We have misused God's good creation. We have confused God's call for us to be faithful stewards of creation with a license to use all of creation as we see it. The first humans had to leave the garden of Eden when they decided they had permission to use all of creation despite warnings to the contrary. We have denied that

God's covenant is with all living creatures (Genesis 9:9). We have even denied that all of the human family should enjoy the covenant. We forget that the good news that we are called to proclaim includes the promise that Jesus Christ came to redeem all creation (Colossians 1:15-20).

We believe that at the center of the vision of shalom is the integration of environmental, economic, and social justice.

We are called to eliminate overconsumption as a lifestyle, thus using lower levels of finite natural resources.

We are called to seek a new lifestyle rooted in justice and peace.

We are called to establish new priorities in a world where 40,000 children die of hunger each day.

Therefore, we are called to a global sense of community and solidarity leading to a new world system of international relationships and economic/environmental order. In this way, the misery of 1.2 billion poor now living in absolute poverty can be alleviated and the living ecosystem be saved.

Principles for a Sustainable Future

The Social Principles of The United Methodist Church remind us that "all creation is the Lord's, and we are responsible for the ways in which we use and abuse it" (¶ 160). Development must be centered in the concept of *sustainability* as defined by the World Commission of Environment and Development: "to meet the needs of the present without compromising the ability of future generations to meet their own needs." The Christian understanding of sustainability encompasses this concept. Fundamental to our call as faithful witnesses is the meeting of human needs within the capacity of ecosystems. This ensures the security of creation and a just relationship between all people. Sustainable development, therefore, looks toward a healthy future in three vital areas: the social community, the economy, and the environment.

Conclusion

The United Methodist Church will strive for a global sense of community to help achieve social, economic, and ecological justice for all of creation.

We will focus on the conversion to sustainable practices in the following areas:

Atmosphere

- Support measures calling for the reduction of carbon dioxide, methane, nitrogen oxides, and sulfur dioxide, which contribute to acid rain and global climate change.
- Enforce agreements banning the use of chlorofluorocarbons (CFCs) to stop the depletion of the ozone layer.
- Support ratification and enforcement of international frameworks, such as Kyoto Protocol, that seek to reduce global greenhouse gas emissions.
- Support the cleanup of environmental problems through economic incentive, appropriate enforcement measures, and sanctions against those causing pollution.

Earth

- Support integrated and sustainable natural resource management.
- Commit to the "Greening of the World" through the limiting of all emissions of pollutants that damage forests and reforestation.
- Work for ecologically sound agricultural practices that produce healthy food and a clean environment.
- Protect biodiversity among both animals and plants.

Water

- Maintain that water is a basic human right not a commodity to be traded for profit.
- Support integrated, sustainable management to reduce or eliminate factors contributing to limited water quantity and poorer quality.

Energy

- Support improved energy conservation and greater reliance on new and renewable sources of energy.
- Support the development of eco-efficient mass transportation.
- Support a call for a sustainable national energy policy.

Actions/Recommendations

We call upon the agencies and local congregations of The United Methodist Church to take the following actions:

Council of Bishops

- Communicate to the church the urgency of responding to the ecological crisis.
- Model for the church a "ministry of presence" by going to places where humans and ecosystems are endangered by environmental destruction.

Connectional Table

- Initiate basic research on the changing attitudes on environmental issues among United Methodist members.
- Request each United Methodist agency to include an evaluation of their corporate action taken toward sustainable environmental practices as a part of their 2004-2008 Quadrennial Report.

General Board of Church and Society (GBCS)

- Develop programs that help annual conferences and local churches become more involved in sustainable practices in public policy and personal aspects of the ecological crisis. These programs would emphasize conversion to a sustainable society.

General Board of Discipleship (GBOD)

- Develop curriculum and programs (for all ages), in consultation with GBCS, that emphasize ecological responsibility as a key element of discipleship.

General Board of Global Ministries (GBGM)

- Join with the GBCS in working with mission partners to prepare for and participate in the implementation of Agenda 21

and the ongoing global dialogue on sustainability through the United Nation's Commission on Sustainable Development.
- Conduct a survey, with the assistance of all mission partners, to identify environmental concerns and develop projects geared to the solution of common concerns.
- Initiate an audit of all sponsored projects and meetings as to their environmental effect on the global ecological balance.
- Establish an eco-mission intern group to work on ecology issues.
- Include global environmental issues in the training of all GBGM missionaries.
- Facilitate dialogue between religious groups, other non-government organizations, and government agencies on the formation and methods of popular participation.

General Board of Higher Education and Ministry (GBHEM)

- Include a greater awareness in clergy education and training of the global ecological crises.

United Methodist Communications (UMCom)

- Produce programs that stress Christian responsibility for the future of creation and include models of The United Methodist Church's involvement in environmental justice.

General Council on Finance and Administration (GCFA)

- Assist the church in its effort to be ecologically responsible in its own use of resources by collecting statistics on local churches' and general agencies' use of energy, water, paper, and recycling to monitor the progress of the church in these aspects of stewardship.

General Board of Pension and Health Benefits (GBPHB)

- Develop investment guidelines, in consultation with agencies, to evaluate its securities on adherence to high standards of environmental accountability as evidenced by the adoption of an environmental code of conduct and a practice of transparency in public environmental reporting.

Local Congregations

• Develop programs to incorporate the concerns of ecological justice into their work in evangelism, social concerns, mission activities, stewardship, trustees, and worship.

ADOPTED 1992
AMENDED AND READOPTED 2004

See Social Principles, ¶ 160.

8. Environmental Law—The Precautionary Principle

As God's people we are called to stewardship of the earth and all that dwells therein.

At this point in human history, the human race is experiencing warning signs that our bodies and the natural environment have limits to their abilities to absorb and overcome the harm from some of our actions, technologies, and substances. These warning signs include the dying off of plant and animal species, the depletion of stratospheric ozone, global climate instability and increased rates of some learning disabilities, reproductive disorders, cancers, respiratory diseases including asthma, and other environmentally related illnesses.

In addition to the issue of pollution, the earth is experiencing environmental problems such as global climate instability, the loss of biodiversity, and the destruction of marine fisheries, which may threaten food supplies and lead to disastrous human health consequences.

There is continuing controversy in the promotion of world trade regarding the appropriate level of caution and protection of the environment. Where the preponderance of evidence would indicate that an activity will be harmful to the earth's environment, producers of pollution have insisted that there be "scientific certainty" on each point in question before caution is exercised. This policy results in very substantial harm occurring to the earth and its' creatures in order to prove that an activity is dangerous.

Current environmental regulations are aimed primarily at controlling pollution rather than taking the preventative approach of limiting the use, production or release of toxic materials in the first place. Under the current system, enterprises, projects, technologies and substances are in effect "innocent until proved guilty", and the vast majority of chemicals in production have not been adequately tested for their effects on humans and ecosystems.

Producers of pollution have repeatedly used their influence to delay preventative action, arguing that the immediate expense of redesign to achieve pollution prevention is unwarranted in the face of any uncertainty about eventual harmful health effects.

The Precautionary Principle is considered to be an emerging general principle of international environmental law. The United States signed and ratified the Rio Declaration on Environment and Development which states: "In order to protect the environment, the precautionary approach shall be widely applied by states according to their capabilities. Where there are threats of serious or irreversible damage, lack of full scientific certainty shall not be used as a reason for postponing cost-effective measures to prevent environmental degradation." (Rio Declaration on Environment and Development, June 14, 1992, 31 ILM 874)

Likewise the International Joint Commission in 1994 stated that "the burden of proof concerning the safety of chemicals should lie with the proponent for the manufacture, import or use of at least substances new to commerce in Canada and the United States, rather than with society as a whole to provide absolute proof of adverse impacts . . . The onus should be on the producers and users of any suspected toxic substance to prove that it is, in fact, both 'safe' and necessary, even if it is already in commerce." (International Joint Commission, Seventh Biennial Report Under the Great Lakes Water Quality Agreement of 1978 to the Governments of the United States and Canada, 1994)

Likewise the *Wingspread Statement* of January 1998, formulated by prominent members of the environmental community, states: "When an activity raises threats of harm to human health or the environment, precautionary measures should be taken even if some cause and effect relationships are not fully established. In this context the proponent of an activity rather than the public should bear the burden of proof. The process of applying the Precautionary Principle must be open, informed, and democratic and must involve potentially affected parties. The process must include a comprehensive, systematic examination of the full range of alternatives, including no action."

We urge all United Methodists in their daily lives and official capacities to hold society to this higher standard of care for God's creation; that where the preponderance of evidence indicates the probability of harm from some action, even in the absence of full scientific certainty, that an alternative path must be found.

In this context we advocate for significant increases in efforts toward pollution prevention, for identifying goals for reducing exposure to toxic chemicals, for incentives to replace known toxic chemicals with the least toxic alternatives, and we support the practice of organic farming methods in order to reduce the use of toxic chemicals in agriculture.

We encourage government at all levels to promote and abide by the Precautionary Principle in order to protect human health and the environment.

We urge the United States to honor the Precautionary Principle during the negotiations of international agreements and to work toward the establishment of the Precautionary Principle as a guiding principle of international law.

ADOPTED 2000

See Social Principles, ¶ 160*A, B, E,* and *F.*

9. Environmental Racism

Theological Background

In Isaiah we are given divine insight into our relations with one another "If you do away with the yoke of oppression, with the pointing finger and malicious talk and if you spend yourselves in behalf of the hungry and satisfy the needs of the oppressed then your light will rise in the darkness and your night will become like the noonday" Isaiah 58:9. We are further called both in Leviticus and by our Lord Jesus Christ to love our neighbors as ourselves. When we turn from this divine will, we as a broken people promote systems that are unjust and inequitable. One manifestation of these injustices is the persistent problem of racism.

Background:

The United Methodist Church is committed to understanding and eliminating racism. One generally ignored aspect is environmental

racism. People of color are disproportionately affected by toxic contamination due to the production, storage, treatment, and disposal
process of hazardous materials and wastes. African American,
Hispanic North American, Asian American, Native American, and
citizens of developing nations are usually the least able, politically
and economically, to oppose the sitings of these facilities.

As a result, their communities have become the dumping grounds
for waste with devastating economic and health consequences.

The pervasive problem of environmental racism within the United
States first came to light in the early 1980's. The birth of the environmental justice movement can be traced to the historic protest in 1983
in Warren County, North Carolina where over 500 people were
arrested for blocking the shipment of toxic waste (PCBs) to a landfill
in a predominantly black county. That same year, a General
Accounting Office (GAO, now Government Accountability Office)
study concluded "blacks make up the majority of the population in
three out of four communities where landfills are located."

In 1987, the United Church of Christ Commission for Racial Justice
issued the landmark report *Toxic Wastes and Race*. This report, expanding on the GAO findings, established that race—rather than poverty,
land value, or home ownership—is the most reliable predictor of
proximity to hazardous waste sites in the United States. And in 1992,
the National Law Journal study, *Unequal Protection*, uncovered racial
disparities in the enforcement of environmental protection laws. The
report highlighted a "racial divide in the way the US government
cleans up toxic waste sites and punishes polluters." According to the
report, "white communities see faster action, better results and stiffer
penalties than communities where blacks, Hispanics and other
minorities live. This unequal protection often occurs whether the
community is wealthy or poor."

These and other reports provided strong empirical evidence of
environmental racism.

Among the findings:

1. Race is consistently the most statistically significant variable in
the location of commercial hazardous waste facilities. Three of the
five largest commercial hazardous waste landfills in the United
States are located in communities of color; communities with commercial hazardous waste facilities have two to three times the aver-

age minority population of communities without such facilities; and three out of every five African Americans and Hispanic North Americans live in communities with toxic waste sites.[1] The African American community of Mossville in rural Louisiana is home to over thirty petrochemical and industrial plants located within a two-mile area. A US government report in 1999 highlighted alarming levels of dioxin in the blood of the residents and linked those levels to local exposures.

2. Communities where hazardous waste incinerators are sited tend to have large minority populations, low incomes, and low property values. The minority portion of the population in communities with existing incinerators is 98 percent higher than the national average. In Houston, Texas, six of eight municipal incinerators are located in predominantly African American neighborhoods.[2]

3. The asthma rate among African American children is 26 higher than that among white children. (US CDC) In 2002, 71% of African Americans live in counties that violate federal clean air standards compared with 58% of whites.

4. Fifty percent of the children in the United States suffering from lead poisoning are African American. At every income level, black children are contaminated with lead at twice the rate of white children.

5. Farm workers' children (mainly Hispanics) in the United States suffer a higher rate of birth defects due to their mothers' exposure to pesticides during the early stages of pregnancy. In farm worker communities, children with cancer are common. Pesticide exposure among farm workers can result in death, birth defects, cancer, nerve disorders, skin diseases, and other health complications.

6. Navajo teenagers have cancer rates seventeen times the national average, due to countless uranium spills on Navajo lands that contaminated their water, air, and soil.[3]

7. The growing trend during the 1980s and 1990s has been to dump toxic wastes in developing countries. Countries such as Liberia have been offered much-needed foreign capital if they accepted several shipments of toxic wastes in the past few years. Globalization has enabled environmental racism around the world, with developed

1. "Toxic Wastes and Race," Commission for Racial Justice, United Church of Christ, 1987.
2. Playing with Fire: Hazardous Waste Incineration, Greenpeace, 1991.
3. Center for Third World Organizing.

countries increasingly looking to developing countries as new dump ing grounds for unwanted and often toxic wastes. Unfortunately, these countries often lack the appropriate infrastructure to adequately handle the environmental and health problems that accompany these wastes.

As the evidence of environmental racism has grown, so has the number of grassroots activists committed to environmental justice. In 1991, the First National People of Color Environmental Leadership Summit gathered activists from across the country and around the world to share stories, strategies, struggles, and victories. The summit produced principles of environmental justice and a challenge to the mainstream, mostly white, environmental groups who were found to be exclusionary in both their composition and policies. A decade later, hundreds of activists gathered for a second summit to evaluate progress and develop strategies for continued work to combat persistent environmental racism.

In response to the demands of the environmental justice community, the Environmental Protection Agency established the Office of Environmental Equity (later changed to Office of Environmental Justice) to address inequities in environmental protection. In 1994, President Clinton issued Executive Order 12898 requiring federal agencies to develop strategies for ensuring compliance with principles of environmental justice and with a commitment that all communities have the right to safe and healthy environments.

Despite the clear evidence and growing awareness our society's attitude toward the production and disposal of hazardous products remains one of "out of sight, out of mind." But "out of sight, out of mind" is most often where the poor and powerless live and work. These communities have thus become toxic "sacrifice zones." Hazardous waste is still exposed in many communities such as Aniston, Alabama even in the year 2003. The work must continue. We must be persistent and consistent in exposing these atrocities with a commitment that all communities have a right to safe and healthy environments.

Other evidence suggests that the problem is worsening. The findings of the Interdenominational Hearings on Toxics and Minorities, held in September 1990, in Albuquerque, New Mexico, and the General Board of Church and Society-sponsored consultation on Responding to Communities Facing Toxic Hazards held in Baton Rouge, Louisiana, in October 1990, poignantly demonstrated that communities are still having problems related to toxic contamination more than ten years after the media exposed the problems. Our society's attitude toward the production and disposal of hazardous products is one of "out of sight, out of mind." But "out of sight, out of mind" is most often where the poor and powerless live and work. These communities have thus become toxic "sacrifice zones." The continued pattern of environmental racism represents a serious challenge to the conscience of all Christians. We therefore ask our local churches, conferences, and general agencies to join with other religious bodies and groups in actions to end this form of racism:

1. We request the Council of Bishops to address environmental racism in any formal communication to the denomination concerning racism or the environment.

2. We urge annual conferences, districts, local churches, and general agencies to become more involved with community groups working end environmental racism.

3. We urge all general program agencies and the General Commission on Religion and Race to:
   a. disseminate the "stories" of people and communities affected by environmental racism;
   b. find expertise, build leadership, and develop networks that can help empower people within communities in crisis; and
   c. develop programs that help annual conferences, districts, and local churches respond to these concerns.

4. We call upon the General Board of Church and Society to:
   a. advocate a moratorium on the siting of hazardous waste treatment, storage, and disposal facilities in low-income/people-of-color communities;
   b. advocate comprehensive legislation that remedies these injustices and adequately protects all citizens and the environment;
   c. advocate compliance with international agreements including the Basel Convention and Stockholm Convention to prevent the dumping of toxic wastes in developing countries; and
   d. develop programs that help annual conferences, districts, and local churches respond to these concerns.

5. We request the General Council on Ministries to assist the General Board of Church and Society in conducting research in this area.

6. We call upon the General Board of Pension and Health Benefits and other church investors to advocate in dialogue and shareholder resolutions with corporations on environmental racism issues and to urge companies to adopt environmental codes of conduct (such as the CERES Principles and to engage in greater transparency and public reporting modeled after the Global Reporting Initiative).

7. We urge individual United Methodists to:
   a. become aware of how and where their community's wastes are disposed and who in their community is adversely affected by the production and disposal of industrial chemicals; and
   b. make a personal commitment to reduce their use of hazardous chemicals by one each day;

8. We call upon the U.S. federal government to:
   a. institute comprehensive risk-assessment and health tracking studies of communities at risk and their affected populations;
   b. enable these communities to participate in clean-up decisions that affect them directly;
   c. fully fund the Office of Environmental Justice in the Environmental Protection Agency and pursue vigorous enforcement of environmental protection, civil rights and equal protection laws to end racial disparities in environmental protection;
   d. give these communities priority in receiving Superfund funding to clean up existing sites; and
   e. prohibit hazardous waste exports and imports.

9. We urge industry to:
   a. assess the adverse impacts of their production and disposal processes on workers and surrounding communities;
   b. implement comprehensive Toxics Use Reduction (TUR) programs;
   c. develop nontoxic alternatives to commonly used hazardous materials;
   d. comply with local, state, and federal environmental and safety laws;
   e. respond to community concerns and grievances;
   f. sign comprehensive environmental guidelines developed with public input, such as the CERES (Coalition for Environmentally Responsible Economies) Principles; and

g. develop industrywide standards for environmental accounting and auditing procedures similar to those required for financial accounting.

ADOPTED 1992
AMENDED AND READOPTED 2004

See Social Principles, ¶ 160; Resolution 7, "Environmental Justice for a Sustainable Future"; and Resolution 161, "A Charter for Racial Justice Policies in an Interdependent Global Community."

10. Environmental Stewardship

I. A Theology of Stewardship and the Environment

All creation is under the authority of God and all creation is interdependent. Our covenant with God requires us to be stewards, protectors, and defenders of all creation. The use of natural resources is a universal concern and responsibility of all as reflected in Psalm 24:1: "The earth is the Lord's and the fullness thereof."

In the Bible, a steward is one given responsibility for what belongs to another. The Greek word we translate as steward is *oikonomos*, one who cares for the household or acts as its trustee. The word *oikos*, meaning household, is used to describe the world as God's household. Christians, then, are to be stewards of the whole household (creation) of God. *Oikonomia*, "stewardship," is also the root of our word "economics." *Oikos*, moreover, is the root of our modern word, "ecology." Thus in a broad sense, stewardship, economics, and ecology are, and should be, related.

The Old Testament relates these concepts in the vision of *shalom*. Often translated "peace," the broader meaning of *shalom* is wholeness. In the Old Testament, *shalom* is used to characterize the wholeness of a faithful life lived in relationship to God. *Shalom* is best understood when we experience wholeness and harmony as human beings with God, with others, and with creation itself. The task of the steward is to seek *shalom*.

Stewards of God's Creation. The concept of stewardship is first introduced in the creation story. In Genesis 1:26, the Bible affirms that every person is created in God's image. But this gift brings with it a unique responsibility. Being created in God's image brings with it the responsibility to care for God's creation. God chose to give human beings a divine image not so we would exploit creation to our own ends, but so we would be recognized as stewards of God. To have dominion over the earth is a trusteeship, a sign that God cares for creation and has entrusted it to our stewardship. Our stewardship of all the world's resources is always accountable to God who loves the whole of creation and who desires that it exist in *shalom*. The intention of creation was that all should experience *shalom*, to know the goodness of creation. In the Old Testament, "fullness of life" means having enough, sufficient, to experience the goodness of creation. By contrast, our age has come to define "fullness of life" as more than enough. The desire of many for excess begins to deny enough for others, and *shalom* is broken. That all should participate in creation's goodness is a fundamental of stewardship.

Another theme of *shalom* is that in creation we are all related. Humans are not self-sufficient. We need God, others, nature. The story of the garden (Genesis 2) attempts to picture the complete and harmonious interrelatedness of all creation. There is *shalom* only when we recognize that interrelatedness and care for the whole. When we violate the rules of the garden, we are dismissed. In ecological terms, when we violate the principles of ecology, we suffer environmental damage.

As the story of the garden shows, God's intention of *shalom* was not carried out. Sin intervened, and the *shalom* was broken. But God offered a way to restore *shalom*—redemption. And as God's stewards we have a role in that redemption. Stewardship, then, is to become involved wherever wholeness is lacking and to work in harmony with God's saving activity to reconcile, to reunite, to heal, to make whole.

Stewardship has to do with how we bring all of the resources at our disposal into efficient use in our participation in the saving activity of God. Environmental stewardship is one part of our work as God's stewards. As stewards of the natural environment we are called to preserve and restore the air, water, and land on which life depends. Moreover, we are called to see that all life has a sufficient share of the resources of nature. With new hope rooted in Christ and with more obedient living as stewards of the earth, we can participate in God's healing of creation.

II. United Methodist Historical Concerns

Since the beginnings of the Methodist movement, there has been a concern with what we today call "environmental concerns." Wesley's emphasis on "cleanliness" came as he observed a land of open sewers, impure water, unplanned cities, and smoke-filled air. In the mines and mills, squalor and filth were everywhere, as was disease. The substantial decline in the death rate in England from 1700 to 1801 can be traced to improvements in environment, sanitation, and a wider knowledge of concepts of basic health such as those advocated by Wesley.

III. Principles for Christian Stewardship of the Environment

A. Responsible and Equitable Use of Natural Resources.

We support measures which will lead to a more careful and efficient use of the resources of the natural world. We urge United Methodists to analyze their consumption patterns and to seek to live a simple and less resource-dependent life.

We encourage programs which will recycle solid materials of all sorts—paper, glass, wood, building materials, metals, plastics, etc.

We urge United Methodists to participate actively in community recycling programs and urge the establishment of such programs in communities without these programs.

We believe that natural resources, outside the control of different nations, from the genes that form life to the air and outer space, are the common heritage of all humanity, and therefore must be developed and preserved for the benefit of all, not just for the few, both today and for generations to come.

We support the concept of common heritage where people have the right to enough of the resources of the universe to provide for their health and well-being; and we believe that God's creation is intended to be used for the good of all as a precious gift, not for warfare or economic oppression of others.

B. Right to Live in a Community Free of Toxic and Hazardous Substances.

We advocate that governments:

1. aggressively assess the extent of possible toxic and hazardous waste disposal problems within their jurisdictions;

2. require that the entity or entities responsible for the problem pay for hazardous waste cleanup and for any health damages caused by the improper or inadequate disposal of such substances; and

3. severely penalize those convicted of illegal disposal of hazardous and toxic materials.

We encourage measures to minimize the use of toxic and hazardous substances.

We oppose the practice of exporting materials banned in one nation for use in another nation.

We advocate that all parties with information on the health effects of a potentially toxic or hazardous substance make these data available to users of the substance.

We support measures to strengthen the public's right-to-know about chemical substances in their communities. Communities have a right to know whether their water, air, soil, or food is clean and free of toxic pollution.

We support applying the "Precautionary Principle," shifting the burden of proof to polluters to show that their air and water emissions are safe, rather than making citizens prove that emissions pose a health threat.

We support the right of those groups that would be affected by a nuclear, toxic, or hazardous material waste repository or incinerator to be involved actively in all decisions to locate such repositories or incinerators in their neighborhoods or jurisdictions.

We urge a halt to nuclear and toxic waste disposal at sea and stringent controls on toxic waste disposal in the soil.

C. Right to Clean Air.

We believe clean air is a basic right and necessity for all life. We must clean up and prevent air pollution, which threatens the health of our families and the survival of all life on the planet.

To ensure that we protect future generations and our natural environment from the harmful effects of air pollution and leave a legacy of clean air:

We advocate the adoption and strict enforcement of adequate standards (health-based air quality standards to protect vulnerable populations such as children, the elderly, and people with asthma) to control outdoor air pollutants such as vehicle and industrial smokestack emissions.

We urge all United Methodists to car pool, use mass transit, drive fuel efficient cars, and find other ways of reducing vehicle and industrial emissions.

We must give special attention to the long-term effects of air pollution, such as the depletion of the ozone layer, global warming, and acid rain; we support international and bilateral efforts to eliminate the cause of these problems.

We advocate that all large polluters, specifically power plants, refineries and chemical manufacturers, irrespective of age or fuel use, meet standards based on the least polluting process in each industrial sector.

We advocate the adoption and strict enforcement of adequate standards to control indoor air pollutants, such as chemical fumes from gas stoves and furnaces, pesticides, cleaning materials, formaldehyde, candles, paint, photocopy machines, radon and carpets, as well as particulates such as dust, mold, and asbestos fibers.

We advocate prohibiting smoking and providing adequate fresh air ventilation in all indoor facilities.

D. Minimization of Chemical Use.

We recommend the concept of integrated pest management (IPM), natural control systems, and crop rotation.

We urge that greater restrictions be placed on the export of restricted agricultural chemicals and that development and aid agencies encourage the use of agricultural techniques which rely less heavily on agricultural chemical use.

We recommend that industry, consumer groups, and governmental agencies aggressively investigate and study the long-range effects of chemicals used for the processing and preservation of food products, since many of these chemicals are harmful to animals and humans.

E. Responsible Land Use.

We encourage economic and farming practices which conserve and promote the improvement of topsoil.

We urge that governments provide farmers with incentives for more careful management of this precious resource.

We urge that the careful maintenance of the productivity of farm land be the central goal of all management of agricultural lands.

We urge governments to preserve the most productive soils for agricultural purposes.

We advocate for the preservation of forests (including reforestation), wetlands and wild areas for ecological balance, wildlife production, water quality, air quality, and the human spirit.

F. Preservation of the Diversity of Life.

We believe that the wondrous diversity of nature is a key part of God's plan for creation. Therefore, we oppose measures which would eliminate diversity in plant and animal varieties, eliminate species, or destroy habitats critical to the survival of endangered species or varieties.

We support national and international efforts to protect endangered species and imperiled habitats.

G. Right to Abundant and Clean Water.

The water on this planet is a sacred gift from God. To ensure that water remains pure and available to all:

We urge that steps be taken by all people to ensure more careful management and preservation of ground water sources.

We support the right of native peoples to the first use of waters on their lands.

We urge that industrial, municipal, agricultural and individual consumers of water develop and use water-conserving technology and practices.

We believe that water is a gift from God that needs to be kept clean. We advocate measures that will address polluted runoff that is threatening to public health; protection of waters for future generations; wetlands preservation to clean water and sustain wildlife; the public's right to know that their water is safe for drinking, swimming, and fishing; and effective enforcement against illegal pollution.

H. Responsible and Ethical Use of Technology.

We urge that the ethical and environmental effects of new technologies be fully examined before these technologies are used on a widespread basis. We acknowledge the constantly imperfect state of our knowledge of the effects of new technology and urge the development of those technologies most in accord with God's plan of wholeness for all creation.

I. Minimization of the Military's Impact on the Environment.

We oppose the production and testing of weapons designed to destroy or harm God's creation, such as all chemical, biological, and nuclear weapons.

We urge the abolishment of chemical, biological, and nuclear weapons and urge the cleanup of sites contaminated by chemical, biological, and nuclear weapons waste.

IV. Involvement

We urge all United Methodists, their local churches, boards and agencies to examine their roles as stewards of God's earth and to study, discuss, and work to implement this resolution.

All general agencies shall develop appropriate resources to implement this resolution.

ADOPTED 1984
REVISED AND READOPTED 2000

See Social Principles, ¶ 160B.

11. God's Creation and the Church

As disciples of Christ, we are called to be good stewards of God's creation. Accordingly, we call upon The United Methodist Church to adopt fresh ways to respond to the perils that now threaten the integrity of God's creation and the future of God's children.

Specifically, The United Methodist Church:

- designates one Sunday each year, preferably the Sunday closest to Earth Day, as a Festival of God's Creation, celebrating God's gracious work in creating the earth and all living things, incorporating it into the church's liturgical calendar, and developing appropriate ways for congregations to celebrate it;
- endorses the work of the National Religious Partnership for the Environment, and the World Council of Churches Climate

Change Program and urges conferences and congregations to support their activities and programs;

- supports the annual observance of the United Nations' World Environment Day and encourages conferences and churches to participate in programs such as Environmental Sabbath;
- recommends that annual conferences establish annual awards to honor prophetic defenders of God's creation from within their own constituencies;
- affirms the importance of nurturing, community-building approaches such as the Global Action Plan's Household Eco-Team Program designed to foster resource efficient lifestyle practices;
- encourages a simplified and environmentally sound lifestyle throughout the church and requests that Church agencies, conferences, and congregations be stewards of God's creation by reducing levels of consumption and participating in programs that reuse and recycle goods; and
- encourages United Methodist institutions to perform energy audits, improve energy efficiency, and pursue use of alternative clean energy sources such as wind and solar power where available.

ADOPTED 1996
AMENDED AND READOPTED 2004

See Social Principles, ¶ 160*B*.

12. Law of the Sea

We recognize that "All creation is the Lord's, and we are responsible for the ways in which we use and abuse it" (¶ 160).

We are called to repent of our devastation of the physical and non-human world, because this world is God's creation and is therefore to be valued and conserved.

Nowhere is this need greater than in relation to the sea. In 1970 the United Nations agreed that those areas of the seabed beyond national boundaries were the "common heritage" of humankind. This means that the resources belong to everyone.

The best hope for global cooperation is through the United Nations, where representatives of the nations of the world developed the Law of the Sea.

The Law of the Sea conference worked to produce a fair and just law for the ocean, in which all nations will benefit. No one nation will have all of its interests satisfied, but mechanisms will be set up to maintain order and peace, and both developed and developing countries will have worked on the regulations.

The Law of the Sea Treaty is concerned with protecting this "common heritage" of humanity. It would:

- guarantee unimpeded access to over 100 straits, facilitating commercial transportation;
- prevent conflicts over fishing waters;
- enforce environmental regulations forbidding countries to dump harmful wastes that spoil the ocean waters;
- share equitably the ocean resources, oil, fish, minerals, and prohibit unjust exploitation of these resources by the powerful;
- regulate access to the waters of coastal countries to permit research of the marine environment;
- limit the continuing extension of national sovereignty over international waters and settle legal disputes arising therefrom;
- prevent the division of the world into competing camps depending on powerful navies; and
- create an international agency to manage cooperatively the international seabed resources.

We also affirm our support for the evolution of effective "commons" law, such as the treaties for the Antarctic, climate, biodiversity, and outer space, which support our obligations of stewardship, justice, and peace.

Further, we urge all United Methodists to become informed about the Law of the Sea and to call upon their governments to commit themselves to just and equitable implementation of the Law of the Sea and to the ratification of the treaty.

ADOPTED 1980
AMENDED AND READOPTED 1996
READOPTED 2004

See Social Principles, ¶ 160A.

13. Protection of Water

In the Bible water, in both its physical and spiritual dimensions, is a gift. God covenants with Gods people and extends invitations to them to experience fullness of life. A measure of this abundant life is Gods offer of water as a free gift without cost or price (Isaiah 55:1). Both water as an element and water of life as a healing agent (Revelation 22:17) are a gift of God to everyone who thirsts. Further, the Bible offers examples of God and humans intervening in people's water crises, and providing water (Genesis 21:19; Genesis 24:15-21; Numbers 20:9-11). Water is an integral part of God's radical expression of God's love to all humanity. Water cannot be monopolized or privatized. It is to be shared like air, light, and earth. It is God's elemental provision for survival for all God's children together on this planet.

The problem is:

- Water use is increasing everywhere. The world's six billion inhabitants appropriate 54 percent of all accessible water.
- Globally, 69 percent of all water used on a yearly basis is used by agriculture; industry accounts for 23 percent, and domestic households account for 8 percent.
- Excess withdrawals, withdrawal at a rate greater than can be charged naturally is occurring in parts of the Arabian Peninsula, China, India, Mexico, the former Soviet Union, and the United States.
- One toilet flush uses as much water as an average person in a developing country uses in a whole day, to drink, cook, wash, and clean.
- Many of the 840 million people in the world who go hungry live in water scarce regions.
- 2.3 billion people suffer from diseases linked to dirty water.
- Around the world there is a cumulative pollution of aquifers and water sources by agriculture, industry, and mining waste.
- "If water usage continues in its present form the results will be devastating to the earth and its inhabitants. Each generation must ensure that the abundance and quality of water is not diminished as a result of its activities . . . water must be protected at any cost" (Maude Barlow: *Blue Gold: The Global Water Crisis and the Commodification of the World's Water Supply*) .

Therefore be it resolved the people called United Methodists
- shall affirm and educate that water is a basic human right to be shared and enjoyed by all God's people;
- shall encourage and develop strategies for guiding principles protecting our water supply;
- shall support the United Nations World Summit on Sustainable Developments commitment to reduce by half the number of people without sustainable access to safe drinking water by 2015;
- shall affirm and teach methods to support the International Year of Freshwaters commitment to protect and respect our water resources as individuals, communities, countries, a global family of concerned citizens;
- shall encourage and commit to good water management by all entities, corporations and communities;
- shall push companies that pollute to provide funds and services to clean waters that they pollute; and
- shall urge that all countries take responsibility for the way they use water.

Other resolutions:
Book of Resolutions, 1996, page 90, "Reduction of Water Usage"
Book of Resolutions, 1996, page 78, "Environmental Stewardship": Water
Resolution #10, "Environmental Stewardship": Right to Abundant and Clean Water
Resolution #7, "Environmental Justice for a Sustainable Future": Water

ADOPTED 2004

See Social Principles, ¶ 160A.

14. Recycling and the Use of Recycled Products

In Genesis 1:26-28, 2:7 and Psalm 8:6, God created all people in God's image, and gave them responsibility for creation. The Social Principles of The United Methodist Church state: "all creation is the Lord's and we are responsible for the ways in which we use and abuse it." The deterioration of the environment is a global problem. As Christians we are called to "place a higher priority on changes in economic, political, social, and technological lifestyle to support a more ecologically equitable and sustainable world leading to a higher quality of life for all of

God's creation" (Social Principles ¶ 160). As members of God's human community, we are called to be stewards of the land.

Since 1972 the General Conference has requested boards and agencies to use recycled paper. In 1996, the General Conference called for a phase-out of dioxin.

Therefore, be it resolved that the General Conference recommends that:

- general boards, agencies and publishers use recycled and "processed chlorine free" paper where economically feasible;
- United Methodist publishers collaborate in a study of ways to facilitate progress toward the goal of "processed chlorine free" paper, and report on progress to the 2004 General Conference;
- United Methodist agencies and churches educate the public and promote awareness of the benefits of recycling on the environment; and
- United Methodist agencies and churches participate in recycling programs for paper, plastic, glass and metal.

ADOPTED 2000

See Social Principles, ¶ 160.

NUCLEAR ISSUES

15. Nuclear Safety in the United States

Theology

God has given humans a special charge to "guard and keep" the earth (Genesis 2:15). Nuclear technology presents a special challenge to our call to be stewards of God's creation (Psalm 8:6-8) because of the risks involved in the production, handling, and disposal of long-lived nuclear byproducts (such as plutonium) in the energy and weapons-production cycles. Until society discontinues the use of nuclear power to produce energy and weapons, we have a special responsibility to ensure that God's creation be protected for present and future generations by insisting that the entire production cycle be as safe as possible.

The problem of nuclear safety is of worldwide concern. It is the responsibility of the church to use its influence internationally to prevent the devastation that could result from nuclear disasters.

United Methodist Policy

Through its Energy Policy Statement, The United Methodist Church affirmed the need to explore all sustainable energy options while highlighting the environmental risks posed by certain options including nuclear power. "The hazards in storing radioactive wastes for thousands of years and the destructive potential of a catastrophic accident involve a great risk of irreversible damage to the environment or to the human genetic pool."[1] Furthermore, the Church has reiterated its opposition to "the production and testing of weapons designed to destroy or harm God's creation, such as . . . nuclear weapons. We urge the abolishment of chemical, biological, and nuclear weapons and urge the cleanup of sites contaminated by chemical biological and nuclear weapons waste."

Background

Nuclear Power

Although there has been a pause in construction of new nuclear capacity in the United States—no nuclear plants have been ordered since 1978 and none has come on-line since the Tennessee Valley Authority's Watts Bar 1 reactor ordered in 1970 and licensed to operate in 1996—the waste generated by current nuclear operations continues to pile up and policy-makers are debating the merits of encouraging construction of new nuclear reactors. In the United States there are currently 103 licensed reactors operating at 65 plants in 31 states. Worldwide, nearly 433 reactors generate roughly 17% of global electricity.

The accident at Chernobyl on April 28, 1986—and its legacy of radiation, contamination, and cancer—demonstrated the dangers involved in the production of nuclear energy. This accident was much larger than the one at Three Mile Island in 1979. However, the Nuclear Regulatory Commission's Reactor Safety Study points out that accidents even larger than Chernobyl are possible for U.S. reactors. Despite the difference between the design of the Chernobyl plants and the designs of most U.S. plants, there are, according to the Reactor

1. Joshua Gordon, as cited by Christopher Flavin, Worldwatch Paper 75: "Reassessing Nuclear Power: The Fallout from Chernobyl"; March 1987.

Safety Study, many accident scenarios possible in U.S. plants that could lead to substantial releases of radiation. In March 2002, at the Davis-Besse nuclear plant near Toledo, Ohio, authorities discovered that leaking boric acid had corroded a six-inch hole in the reactor vessel head leaving only a quarter-inch-thick stainless steel liner to prevent a potentially catastrophic release of reactor cooling water. This most recent example of safety-related shortcomings at nuclear plants further increases concerns raised after the September 11, 2001 terrorist attacks that the Nuclear Regulatory Commission's oversight is insufficient and additional security and safety measures are needed.

Department of Energy Reactors

The Department of Energy (DOE) operates more than 200 nuclear facilities. Among its main responsibilities are the production and testing of this country's nuclear weapons program. The DOE facilities are generally more antiquated than civilian plants and are not subject to review by outside agencies. Five of these facilities are the main nuclear weapons production reactors. Four are located on the Savannah River in South Carolina; the fifth is the "N-Reactor" at Hanford, Washington (a complex where poor disposal of wastes in the past has created a radioactive landfill known as "one of our largest contaminated areas"). The containment systems in these plants have been criticized as being inadequate and not capable of meeting minimum civilian standards. In 1986, the DOE agreed to submit its five weapons reactors to state and federal waste disposal rules and shut down the Hanford "N-Reactor" for safety improvements. The cleanup of the Hanford site alone could cost over $100 billion. Yet most DOE plants continue to be exempt from the far more rigorous examination of commercial reactors by the Nuclear Regulatory Commission.

Emergency Planning and State Rights

After the Three Mile Island accident, rules were instituted to improve public safety in case of a nuclear accident. The new rules required the participation, in emergency planning exercise, of local and state officials. In 1986, the Nuclear Regulatory Commission, in response to two state governors' challenge to the viability of utility-produced emergency plans, requested that it be allowed to approve utility emergency evacuation plans in the event that state and local officials refuse to participate in the emergency-planning process. This rule change would ease the licensing of future nuclear reactors and seriously diminish public participation and review of safety measures, as well as increase the dangers of a serious accident.

Nuclear Wastes

One of the most controversial and costly components of the nuclear fission process is the creation of radioactive byproducts. The Nuclear Regulatory Commission divides wastes into two different categories according to the level and duration of radioactivity: high-level and low-level wastes. Each reactor produces an annual average of 20 tons of highly radioactive spent nuclear fuel and 50-200 cubic meters of low-level radioactive waste. Since the 1950s, the Department of Energy has been searching for a viable way to dispose of the wastes created by commercial nuclear reactors (irradiated fuels) and high-level wastes from weapons production. These wastes are highly radioactive and will remain radioactive. Presently, these wastes are stored within nuclear facility sites, creating what one member of Congress called hundreds of "de facto nuclear waste dumps." Over the past six decades, these by-products have been accumulating at storage sites throughout the country, including an estimated 45,000 tons of spent nuclear fuel at civilian nuclear power plants with another 2,000 tons generated annually.

The Nuclear Waste Policy Act of 1982 (NWPA) set a schedule for the location, construction, and operation of two high-level waste geologic repositories, one in the east, and one in the west. Amendments to NWPA in 1987 restricted the repository site studies to one location: Yucca Mountain. This site is located in Nevada, a state which itself has no nuclear reactors, and on land considered sacred to the Western Shoshone and Paiute. To a large extent, political considerations have taken precedence over safety and scientific considerations, and there has been improper and inadequate consultation and cooperation with state governments and Native American tribes. In 2002, Yucca Mountain was designated as the nuclear fuel repository over the objections of Nevada's elected officials, tribal representatives, and environmental advocates. Proponents of the site highlighted the area's geological stability despite the occurrence of an earthquake registering 4.3 on the Richter scale the month of the Congressional vote.

Construction of the Yucca Mountain repository will not be completed for years and shipments of the radioactive waste—raising deep safety concerns for the millions of residents living along shipment routes—will take decades. While billed as creating a "central repository" for waste, spent nuclear fuel must remain for years on site before it is "cool" enough to transport, so this process would merely create a new, larger storage site in addition to the 100-plus on-site storage facilities that would continue to store nuclear waste.

Recommendations

The United Methodist Church expresses its deep concern over the use of a technology with severe environmental and health impacts without appropriate and extensive safety measures in the production, handling, and disposal processes. We also reiterate our opposition to the use of nuclear technology for the production of weapons.

We recommend:

1. *Reviewing the safety of operating plants.* Each of the 107 operating commercial plants in the U.S. should be reviewed by the Nuclear Regulatory Commission and the Office of Technology Assessment of the U.S. Congress to identify design deficiencies and weaknesses that could contribute to or cause an accident.

2. *Instituting improvement programs.* Improvement programs should be instituted in areas of demonstrated weak performance such as management, personnel performance, equipment reliability, and contractor accountability.

3. *Researching new designs for plant safety.* New designs for existing and future nuclear plants should be researched and developed so as to eliminate the potential of a core meltdown accident.

4. *Phasing out nuclear weapons production.* We urge the closing down of the five weapons-producing reactors and the Rocky Flats Plutonium Processing Plant, a thorough cleanup of any remaining nuclear wastes at these sites, and no more nuclear arms testing.

5. *Establishing uniform safety standards for civilian and military nuclear operations.* We support having all nuclear operations in the U.S. subject to uniform basic safety provision. All Department of Energy nuclear operations should be licensed and reviewed by an independent agency such as the Nuclear Regulatory Commission or the Environmental Protection Agency. Department of Energy contractors should be held accountable to the same standards as civilian facility contractors and operators.

6. *Protecting neighboring populations.* We urge that due attention be given to the protection of populations living near nuclear power plants or along routes used to transport nuclear materials by ensuring the communities' participation in emergency evacuation plans. We support maintaining evacuation planning zones for all areas within ten miles from a nuclear facility, and engaging the full participation of state and local officials in the planning process. We believe that the safety of all potentially exposed populations should be the guide in safety improvements to nuclear power plants, not narrow cost-benefit analysis.

7. *Instituting full liability and compensation.* We hold that those corporations and governments responsible for nuclear accidents should be liable for cleanup and restitution to all victims of an accident.

8. *Reevaluating the U.S. nuclear waste policy:*
   a. We urge a moratorium on DOE's proposed nuclear waste repository program;
   b. We urge Congress to establish an independent commission to review DOE's nuclear waste repository and Monitored Retrievable Storage Programs and to provide increased funding for the development of waste management technologies that will allow prolonged storage at the reactor site;-
   c. We urge that full public participation and consultation in any future nuclear waste repository siting and transportation routing be guaranteed through provision of grants to affected localities, states, and Native American tribes; and
   d. We urge a moratorium of the building of nuclear power facilities until an adequate national plan is developed and implemented for the permanent disposal of nuclear waste products.

9. *Decommissioning.* We urge that the full cost of decommissioning (the dismantling and disposing of obsolete or closed power plants) be paid by the entities responsible for the construction and operation of nuclear facilities, not ratepayers or taxpayers.

10. *Conserving energy and finding alternative energy sources.* The greatest national effort should be made in the areas of conservation and renewable energy sources. We support increased government funding for research and development of technologies that would decrease dependence upon nuclear energy as an electricity source and urge the development of incentives, including tax and appliance standards, to speed the adoption of these technologies.

11. *Cooperating with annual conferences.* We urge the general church agencies of The United Methodist Church to assist central and annual conferences in their efforts to learn more about nuclear safety. Specifically, we urge general agencies of The United Methodist Church to assist annual conferences who have identified nuclear safety problems related to nuclear facilities, waste sites, and transportation routes within the bounds of those annual conferences.

We particularly urge the General Board of Church and Society to identify qualified nuclear safety experts who could assist annual conferences to understand and respond to nuclear waste and nuclear safety concerns in their areas.

ADOPTED 1988
AMENDED AND READOPTED 1992
AMENDED AND READOPTED 2004

See Social Principles, ¶ 160E.

THE NURTURING COMMUNITY

ECUMENICAL ISSUES

16. Support of Joint Declaration on the Doctrine of Justification

WHEREAS, in 1999 a Joint Declaration on the Doctrine of Justification was confirmed and signed by the Lutheran World Federation and the Roman Catholic Church, and

WHEREAS, the document is the product of many years of dialogue around this substantive and historically divisive issue, and

WHEREAS, the Joint Declaration "has this intention, namely, to show that on the basis of their dialogue...[They] are now able to articulate a common understanding of our justification by God's grace through Jesus Christ. It does not cover all that either church teaches about justification; it does encompass a consensus on basic truths of the doctrine of justification and shows that the remaining differences in its explication are no longer the occasion for doctrinal condemnations" (JDDJ, pg. 5), and

WHEREAS, the Resolution of the Officers of the World Methodist Council at their meeting in Abuja, Nigeria, September 15-19, 2003 supports and affirms this declaration expressing "our deep hope that in the near future we shall also be able to enter into a closer relationship with Lutherans . . . and with the Roman Catholic Church in accordance with this declaration of our common understanding of the doctrine of justification" (WMC, pg. 5).

Therefore, be it resolved, that The United Methodist Church expresses its gratitude and appreciation for the Joint Declaration between the Lutheran World Federation and the Roman Catholic Church and the response of the Officers of the World Methodist

Council, as well as its encouragement to the Council in its efforts to seek continued dialogue on this, and other matters.

ADOPTED 2004

See Social Principles, ¶ 161*B*.

CHURCH STRUCTURE

17. Living Into the Future

We commend to The United Methodist Church at all levels the following transformational directions. These central ideas are at the heart of the needed change in The United Methodist Church.
1. Center on Christian formation.
2. Call forth covenant leadership.
3. Empower the connection for ministry.
4. Strengthen our global connection and ecumenical relationships.
5. Encourage doctrinal and theological discourse.

These valuable principles and ideas need to be brought to life at every level of the UMC over the next quadrennium. Each organizational level of the church from the local congregation through all levels of the general church should begin to live out these transformational directions.

To guide us this way the General Conference charges the General Council on Ministries:

1. To work with the church in discerning God's will for its work and living as biblical people in the Wesleyan tradition through a style of leadership that is collegial, cooperative, inclusive, and actively practices hospitality.

2. To model the articulation of a clear and compelling ministry vision through a holistic process that focuses the work of all the parts.

3. To determine the most effective design for the work of the general agencies.
- Developing specific ways for agencies to integrate their work for greater collaboration and elimination of duplication;
- Determining how general agencies can better provide resources for annual conferences and local churches;

- Recommending to the 2004 General Conference the best way to staff the work beyond annual conferences and determining where the responsibility for personnel should be vested;
- Developing ways of evaluating the results of the work of the agencies.

4. To assist local congregations and annual conferences in their efforts to organize in such ways that enable them to live out the transformational directions in the context of their ministry while maintaining the connectional nature of the church.

5. To relate to annual conferences and build mutual relationships with annual conference leadership to assist them in living out the transformational directions.

6. To continue the dialogue about the global nature of The United Methodist Church.

In order to be good stewards of the time and money invested in the Connectional Process Team Report, it and all its related research are forwarded to the GCOM, with deep appreciation, as resource material for its ongoing work.

The results of this work shall be contained in the General Council on Ministries report to the 2004 General Conference.

ADOPTED 2000

See Social Principles, ¶ 161B.

18. Support Present Orders of Ministry

WHEREAS, diaconal ministers, local pastors, deacons, and elders have been living into the new United Methodist ordering of ministry as framed by the 1996 General Conference; and

WHEREAS, during the past quadrennium we have engaged in prayer, conversation, action, and planning for the future which have inspired our ministries and opened new paths for mission,

Therefore, be it resolved, that the General Board of Higher Education and Ministry:

1. Declare the 2001-2004 quadrennium as a time for discerning the ministry of the church as laity, diaconal ministers, local pastors, deacons, and elders continue to live into and embody faithful ministry in The United Methodist Church;

2. Hold consultations throughout the quadrennium with the groups named above to explore the ways we are able to support one another and enhance our common and distinctive ministries, all for the purpose of building and equipping the Body of Christ and sharing God's good news with the world. The consultations would be hosted by the General Board of Higher Education and Ministry;

3. Support the present orders of ministry so they can emerge with increasing fullness, focusing on supportive and clarifying legislation rather than restructuring or restrictive legislation.

ADOPTED 2000

See Social Principles, ¶ 161.

19. Affirmation for the Women's Division

WHEREAS, the Women's Division of the General Board of Global Ministries is charged by the Discipline to "be an advocate for the oppressed and dispossessed with special attention to the needs of women and children; (to) work to build a supportive community among women; and (to) engage in activities that foster growth in the Christian faith, mission education, and Christian social involvement" (paragraph 1317); and

WHEREAS, the Women's Division continues its educational ministries, its outreach in the name of Christ, its work for justice, peace, human community, and its compassionate service with women, children and youth; and

WHEREAS, for over 135 years, the Women's Division has never wavered from its total commitment to the Gospel of Jesus Christ and serving women, youth and children with mission education, opportunities for spiritual growth, opportunities for Christian social involvement and financial support for mission at home and around the world; and

WHEREAS, the Women's Division continues to stand in solidarity with women, youth and children by addressing issues such as violence, rape, incest, terrorism, exploitation and all levels of discrimination and work with other Christian groups to address and eliminate poverty and hunger as the Gospel of Jesus Christ requires; and

WHEREAS, the Women's Division continues to be at the heart of the denomination's missionary movement by working with Bible women, missionaries and deaconesses and to function as an integral structure and administrative entity with the General Board of Global Ministries;

Therefore, be it resolved, that the General Conference affirms the powerful witness of the Women's Division in our church and our world; 135 years of faithful service to Christ and the church, its current commitment to mission and its dedication to work within the General board of Global Ministries;

Be it further resolved, that the General Conference affirm the powerful witness of the Women's Division in our church and our world;

Be it further resolved, that the General Conference upholds the current structure of the Women's Division and the organization of United Methodist Women.

ADOPTED 2004

See Social Principles, ¶161.

FAMILY

20. Adoption in a Global Context

Every child is a child of God and deserves to grow up in a safe, healthy, and loving family environment. For a variety of reasons, including unwanted pregnancy, family violence, addictions, or poverty, children are placed for adoption with hopes for a better future.

Those seeking to adopt a child are faced with many challenges and concerns about the high costs of adoption, international laws and restrictions, interracial or intercultural differences, the availability of licensed agencies, and the long waiting times for processing adoptions.

International adoptions have increased dramatically in recent years. In some cases, this has created a lucrative multi-million dollar a year market in the business of "baby selling." High costs of international adoption call into question issues of stewardship while making it cost-prohibitive for families with moderate or low incomes. An international adoption may give a child a new opportunity to live a more abundant life with greater opportunities. However, removing children from their native land can have dire consequences, either because of unresolved prejudices held by the adoptive parents or because the children are unable to adjust emotionally or socially to their new homes. Neither is intercountry adoption a solution to the problems of high birth rates or poverty in the countries of origin. Countries where babies are being considered for adoption are concerned whether they may suffer a "brain drain" since typically only healthy babies, without disabilities or birth defects, are chosen by adoptive parents.

While some may pursue the adoption of children from other countries, many thousands of children in the foster care system wait in vain for families to adopt them. Adoption advocates point out that children who are under care in the foster care system are viewed as "less desirable" by potential adoptive parents, because these children may come from difficult or painful families of origin or may have been harmed by years in successive and less-than-ideal placements. A form of "ageism" prevails in the adoption process, both in the selection of parents and the placement of children.

Cross-racial adoption also presents many challenges. There are divisions over the "correctness" of interracial or cross-cultural adoption. Too often interracial adoption is based on economic class differences, or ability to provide for the child's needs. A family becomes a biracial or multicultural family when they adopt a child of a different race or culture than their own and, therefore, should be sensitive to the societal impact of racism or xenophobia upon the child. Adoptive parents should not neglect the history and heritage of the child's family of origin (if known) and should affirm racial ancestry and culture. Studies have shown that children from ethnic backgrounds different from their parents grow up with a stronger sense of identity and self-esteem if their birth ethnicity has been positively communicated within the family. Great sensitivity also needs to be expressed with regard to the intricacies of the social welfare system and the impact that adoption may have on Native Americans and other ethnic minorities.

Complex social problems which severely impact children, including racism, poverty, alcoholism, and family violence, need other approaches in addition to foster care and adoption.

In a time when many parents are seeking to adopt children, and when many children are needing a loving, caring family, The United Methodist Church affirms adoption as a means to create and strengthen families. Given the multiple challenges posed by adoption, we call upon all United Methodists, local churches, annual conferences, and general agencies to:

- encourage adoptive parents to respect and affirm the cultural and racial background of the adopted child;
- make adoption more affordable by supporting increased financial assistance to middle- and low-income families considering adoption;
- support regulations and policies that enable more qualified foster care families and qualified extended family members to more easily adopt children in their care;
- promote conditions which would make adoption unnecessary by supporting programs which will improve the living conditions of children in their families, their communities and their countries of origin; and provide access to counseling services for adoptive parents;
- in cases where information and contact is desirable for the well-being of the child, work through recognized organizations to make contact between adoptive and birth families; and
- encourage those entering into the adoption process to work only with licensed adoption agencies.

ADOPTED 2000

See Social Principles, ¶ 161*K*.

21. Support for Adoption

The Social Principles of The United Methodist Church, in the section on "The Nurturing Community," paragraph A) "The Family," state: "We believe the family to be the basic human community through which persons are nurtured and sustained in mutual love, responsibility, respect, and fidelity." They further acknowledge that the family encompasses a wide range of options. One of those options is the family that includes adopted children.

Clinical and social service agencies that relate professionally to adoption issues look for and encourage the same attitudes and behaviors that should apply for birth children. These attitudes and behaviors include: parental love; parental responsibility; encouragement of identity development of the child; physical, emotional, and economic security of the child; educational growth of the child; and socialization of the child.

Studies done by a variety of clinical and educational agencies and institutions concur that the six factors mentioned above, expressed in various forms, are vital for a sense of stability and dependability experienced by children in a family system.

Some of the most recent studies of families and children have been done by the Search Institute of Minneapolis, Minnesota, which has identified forty developmental assets that help children grow in a healthy, caring, and responsible environment.

External assets include: support (e.g., the family provides a high level of love and support; the child experiences caring neighbors); empowerment (e.g., children are valued by being placed at the center of family life; the parent(s) serve(s) others in the community); boundaries and expectations (e.g., the parent(s) and other adults model positive, responsible behavior; the parent or parents have realistic expectations for children's growth and development); and constructive use of time (e.g., the parent(s) expose(s) children to a variety of creative activities; the parent(s) provide(s) positive, supervised time at home).

Internal assets include: commitment to learning (e.g., family members are motivated to do well in school, work, and community; the parent(s) enjoy(s) learning and demonstrate(s) this through personal learning activities); positive values (e.g., the family values caring, helping behaviors; the family values honesty); social competencies (e.g., parental planning and decision-making behaviors are modeled and observed; peaceful conflict resolution is modeled and observed); and positive identity (e.g., the family models high self-esteem; the family has a positive view of the future).

It has been observed that as the above-mentioned assets are experienced, children and families demonstrate stability and growth regardless of whether children are of birth origin or adopted. *Therefore*, The United Methodist Church supports and encourages adoption by all persons who demonstrate these attitudes, behaviors, and assets.

ADOPTED 2004

See Social Principles, ¶ 161L.

22. Support for Clergy Families

Over the last many years, clergy and their families have continued to express serious concerns for the stresses they bear in their congregations and districts. This phrase, "life in the fishbowl," describes how pastor and staff therapist Frank J. Stalfa sees the lives of clergy and their spouses and family members in our local congregations. The image is painfully accurate about the situation filled with unrealistic expectations, virtually nonexistent boundaries for privacy and personal time, disrupted lives, crisis in careers and educational programs, unending demands of congregational needs, and pressure for spouses and "PKs" (preacher's kids) to be perfect, "model" Christians.

PK syndrome is documented in research on children and youth in clergy families, and it names the pressure on clergy children to set a high standard for other children to follow (the perfect student, the model son/daughter, the high-achieving youth)—potentially limiting their individuality and development.

In a 1992 survey by *Leadership*, on the causes for marriage problems in clergy families, these were the most frequently named: insufficient time together (81%); use of money (71%); income level (70%); communication difficulties (64%); congregational differences (63%); differences over leisure activities (57%) followed by difficulties raising children, pastor's anger toward spouse, differences over ministry career and spouse's career. A significant and troubling 80% of clergy reported that they believed their pastoral ministry negatively affected their families.

In a study of spouses of district superintendents, *Giving Voice: A Survey and Study of District Superintendents' Spouses in the United Methodist Church,** the detailed list of concerns and problems included the following: gossip and criticism, lack of family time, raising children alone, constant stress, unrealistic work loads, emotional and energy drains, sense of isolation in times of conflict, and the struggle to find spiritual nurture in that setting. This survey and study found these key issues:

- Family lifestyle;
- Careers of spouses;
- Self-care or lack of it;
- Sense of isolation, anger, and frustration.

*Giving Voice: A Survey and Study of District Superintendents' Spouses in The United Methodist Church, by Sylvia B. Corson, published by the General Board of Higher Education and Ministry, Nashville, 1999.

It is important to note that while the majority of clergy spouses are female, a growing number of these spouses are male. Noteworthy is the difference in how these men are treated: rather than being called the clergy spouse, they are the "men married to ministers," and the expectations placed on female clergy spouses are not placed on these male clergy spouses. Their development of a separate personal and professional identity may not be the struggle it is for many female spouses who fight to keep a career or family time or educational opportunities. This survey suggests that expectations of clergy spouses may be not only traditional but gender-related.

With the changing nature of our clergypersons in the Church, roles of their spouses and families have changed, blurred, shifted. Dual career clergy families can see career-ending moves and increased pressure on spouses to leave careers and educational programs. Anger, frustration, hostility, and isolation are all mentioned by clergy spouses in surveys of their feelings about this developing crisis in congregational relationships.

The increasing concerns heard from these "model" or "invisible" or "fishbowl" families are similar across the denomination in U.S. and global congregations. And it is unthinkable to believe that congregations intentionally wish this stress and pain. Certainly, many parishioners would find it unacceptable that their expectations and demands (spoken and unspoken) would cause such stress on their clergy family.

Christian Community for All Our Families

As United Methodists we envision churches and congregations in which all of God's children are welcome at the Table, all are nurtured and respected for their own gifts and talents, and all are transformed to be Christ to others in the world. We are a Church of Open Hearts, Open Minds, and Open Doors, regardless of gender, regardless of family status.

Our Church places high value on our families, yet the needs and crises of our clergy family, "the invisible family," may go unnoticed, unidentified, unaddressed. Clergy families are like every other family with strengths and stresses similar to our own. They need privacy and boundaries that protect personal life just as our families do.

What Can Be Done?

The roles of clergy spouse and family are unique and frequently taken for granted. These roles are, nonetheless, critical to the success of the clergy's ministry. Sustaining the emotional, spiritual, physical, and economic health of our clergy families is a ministry to be recommended to every congregation and district.

We can support our clergy families by doing the following:

- First, examining our own attitudes, perceptions, and expectations and identifying where we are unrealistic;
- Asking ourselves the questions that will identify any sexism or racism in our expectations and assumptions: *If this clergy spouse/family member were another gender or another race, would I have the same expectations? Would I make the same assumptions?*
- Remembering they are human and have their own personal and professional lives;
- Providing safe and honest sharing for clergy families when stress mounts;
- Encouraging clergy families to seek help, even taking the initiative to provide resources and support;
- Regularly clarifying and keeping our expectations realistic, recognizing that pedestals are for statues;
- Reserving family time and protecting family life boundaries;
- Avoiding stereotypic demands of a clergy spouse as an extension of the clergy or as another professional at the service of the congregation.

We can share the effective and renewing models working in Episcopal areas and conferences around the Church, including but not limited to these:

- The Arkansas Episcopal Area's Partners in Ministry Surveys and Renewal Retreats.
- Iowa Conference's *"What Do I Do If...?"*—*Basic Information Handbook for Clergy Spouses,* similar to those used in Northern Illinois, Memphis, and Southern Indiana conferences.
- Clergy Transitions Programs in several conferences.
- Florida Conference's program of nurture, healing, and preventative care to clergy and their families, *Shade and Fresh Water.* (The three-part approach includes a therapeutic presence for families in crisis or need, including professional counseling and safe space; a preventative program for clergy

families in transition in appointments; and a sustaining program encouraging healthy modeling of well-balanced lives.)
- Varied programs, guidance, and initiatives of organizations like The Center for Ministry, the Center for Pastoral Effectiveness and Spiritual Direction, and websites like "Desperate Preacher's Site."
- Ongoing collaboration between the General Commission on the Status and Role of Women, the General Board of Higher Education and Ministry, and the General Commission on Religion and Race.

Therefore, be it resolved that, the General Conference of The United Methodist Church calls on each of the following to address this growing crisis among our clergy families:

1. The General Commission on the Status and Role of Women will work collaboratively with the General Board of Higher Education and Ministry and other general boards and agencies to convene a denominational forum focusing on clergy spouse and families issues as experienced globally, the programs and resources available to clergy families, cabinets and bishops, conferences, and local congregations. The commission will report the feedback from the forum to the 2008 General Conference with recommendations for further study or action.

2. Bishops, cabinets, and boards of ordained ministry will promote specific conference resources, training and orientation models, and counseling assistance programs to all clergy and families.

3. The General Board of Higher Education and Ministry will enhance the training for staff-parish relations committees to provide useful strategies and resources.

4. Staff-parish relations committees will use strategies and training resources for their members in these specific concerns of clergy and families.

5. The General Commission on the Status and Role of Women and the General Board of Higher Education and Ministry will convene a summit of staff and members of related general agencies including the Board of Pension and Health Benefits, the Commission on Religion and Race, the Board of Church and Society, and the General Board of Global Ministries, to research issues affecting clergy spouses and families in the global United Methodist Church, to identify and promote existing relevant resources, plan the development of needed additional resources to address these concerns, and make any legislative recommendations to the 2008 General Conference.

6. District superintendents and their spouses may be called on to provide modeling and leadership for their clergy families in successful strategies. Superintendents will prioritize this issue as they work with local congregations in transitions and ongoing appointments.

7. Annual conference commissions on the status and role of women will survey spouses and families of clergy to assist annual conferences, bishops and cabinets, and general agencies in gathering data and developing resources and strategies in response to the challenges of life in the clergy family.

8. The research findings of GCSRW, GBHEM, and other general boards and agencies, will be published in a summary document and made available for use by United Methodist annual and central conferences, and other denominations and religious bodies.

ADOPTED 2004

See Social Principles, ¶ 161A.

23. Caring for Clergy Spouses, Children, and Youth During Divorce

WHEREAS, clergy families may experience severe tensions that sometimes lead to marital separation and/or divorce; and

WHEREAS, clergy and their spouses in such situations may need mediation and counseling and may not seek it voluntarily; and

WHEREAS, children of clergy families that are going through divorce often find that their normal pattern of spiritual formation and their congregational lives are interrupted during those times of painful transitions; and

WHEREAS, clergy spouses are often vulnerable in such situations, being unaware of provisions in *The United Methodist Book of Discipline* and the General Board of Pension and Health Benefits of The United Methodist Church; and

WHEREAS, spouses may need assistance in obtaining guidance, support and temporary housing; and

WHEREAS, members of the Board of Ordained Ministries and the cabinet encounter situations in which assistance is needed,

Therefore, be it resolved, that each annual conference be encouraged to make available through the Board of Ordained Ministries a trained team of children and youth advocates. The role of advocates will be to represent the concerns of children and youth throughout the divorce review process to include providing parents with resource information on those persons or agencies that provide mediation and counseling for children and youth who are experiencing the divorce of their parents; and

Be it further resolved, that each annual conference be encouraged to study and make available to families of clergy an explanation of the requirements for clergy and the rights of spouses during a marital separation or divorce, in accordance with the *Book of Discipline* and the General Board of Pension and Health Benefits.

ADOPTED 2000
AMENDED AND READOPTED 2004

See Social Principles, ¶ 161D.

24. May as Christian Home Month

WHEREAS, we believe that families in our world, at this hour, stand at a critical juncture, in the midst of destructive pressures that are daily taking their toll; and that The United Methodist Church has the opportunity, potential, and responsibility to respond to the urgent needs of families,

Therefore, be it resolved, that General Conference declare the month of May Christian Home Month, with emphasis upon family worship in the home, worship and program planning in the congregation, and prayer on behalf of families. We call upon the Office of Family Ministries of the General Board of Discipleship to produce resources for the support of Christian Home Month for use in the congregation and in the home.

ADOPTED 1992
AMENDED AND READOPTED 2004

See Social Principles, ¶ 161A.

25. Responsible Parenthood

We affirm the principle of responsible parenthood. The family, in its varying forms, constitutes the primary focus of love, acceptance, and nurture, bringing fulfillment to parents and child. Healthful and whole personhood develops as one is loved, responds to love, and in that relationship comes to wholeness as a child of God.

Each couple has the right and the duty prayerfully and responsibly to control conception according to their circumstances. They are, in our view, free to use those means of birth control considered medically safe. As developing technologies have moved conception and reproduction more and more out of the category of a chance happening and more closely to the realm of responsible choice, the decision whether or not to give birth to children must include acceptance of the responsibility to provide for their mental, physical, and spiritual growth, as well as consideration of the possible effect on quality of life for family and society.

To support the sacred dimensions of personhood, all possible efforts should be made by parents and the community to ensure that each child enters the world with a healthy body and is born into an environment conducive to the realization of his or her full potential.

When through contraceptive or human failure an unacceptable pregnancy occurs, we believe that a profound regard for unborn human life must be weighed alongside an equally profound regard for fully developed personhood, particularly when the physical, mental, and emotional health of the pregnant woman and her family show reason to be seriously threatened by the new life just forming. We reject the simplistic answers to the problem of abortion that, on the one hand, regard all abortions as murders, or, on the other hand, regard abortions as medical procedures without moral significance.

When an unacceptable pregnancy occurs, a family—and most of all, the pregnant woman—is confronted with the need to make a difficult decision. We believe that continuance of a pregnancy that endangers the life or health of the mother, or poses other serious problems concerning the life, health, or mental capability of the child to be, is not a moral necessity. In such cases, we believe the path of mature Christian judgment may indicate the advisability of abortion. We support the legal right to abortion as established by the 1973 Supreme Court decision. We encourage women in counsel with husbands, doctors, and pastors to make their own responsible decisions concerning the personal and moral questions surrounding the issue of abortion (*see* ¶ 161*J*).

We therefore encourage our churches and common society to:

1. provide to all education on human sexuality and family life in its varying forms, including means of marriage enrichment, rights of children, responsible and joyful expression of sexuality, and changing attitudes toward male and female roles in the home and the marketplace;

2. provide counseling opportunities for married couples and those approaching marriage on the principles of responsible parenthood;

3. build understanding of the problems posed to society by the rapidly growing population of the world, and of the need to place personal decisions concerning childbearing in a context of the well-being of the community;

4. provide to each pregnant woman accessibility to comprehensive health care and nutrition adequate to ensure healthy children;

5. make information and materials available so all can exercise responsible choice in the area of conception controls. We support the free flow of information about reputable, efficient, and safe nonprescription contraceptive techniques through educational programs and through periodicals, radio, television, and other advertising media. We support adequate public funding and increased participation in family planning services by public and private agencies, including church-related institutions, with the goal of making such services accessible to all, regardless of economic status or geographic location;

6. make provision in law and in practice for voluntary sterilization as an appropriate means, for some, for conception control and family planning;

7. safeguard the legal option of abortion under standards of sound medical practice;

8. make abortions available to women without regard to economic standards of sound medical practice, and make abortions available to women without regard to economic status;

9. monitor carefully the growing genetic and biomedical research, and be prepared to offer sound ethical counsel to those facing birth-planning decisions affected by such research;

10. assist the states to make provisions in law and in practice for treating as adults minors who have, or think they have, venereal diseases, or female minors who are, or think they are, pregnant, thereby eliminating the legal necessity for notifying parents or guardians prior to care and treatment. Parental support is crucially important and most desirable on such occasions, but needed treatment ought not be contingent on such support;

11. understand the family as encompassing a wider range of options than that of the two-generational unit of parents and children (the nuclear family); and promote the development of all socially responsible and life-enhancing expressions of the extended family, including families with adopted children, single parents, those with no children, and those who choose to be single;

12. view parenthood in the widest possible framework, recognizing that many children of the world today desperately need functioning parental figures, and also understanding that adults can realize the choice and fulfillment of parenthood through adoption or foster care;

13. encourage men and women to actively demonstrate their responsibility by creating a family context of nurture and growth in which the children will have the opportunity to share in the mutual love and concern of their parents; and

14. be aware of the fears of many in poor and minority groups and in developing nations about imposed birth-planning, oppose any coercive use of such policies and services, and strive to see that family-planning programs respect the dignity of each individual person as well as the cultural diversities of groups.

ADOPTED 1976
AMENDED AND READOPTED 1996
READOPTED 2004

See Social Principles, ¶ 161A, G, H, J.

26. Putting Children and Their Families First

"We believe the family to be the basic human community through which persons are nurtured and sustained in mutual love, responsibility, respect and fidelity." Children are "acknowledged to be full human beings in their own right, but beings to whom adults and society in general have special obligations. All children have the right to quality education. Moreover, children have the rights to food, shelter, clothing, health care, and emotional well-being as do adults, and these rights we affirm as theirs regardless of actions or inactions of their parents or guardians. In particular, children must be protected from economic, physical, emotional, and sexual exploitation and abuse." (From Social Principles of The United Methodist Church in *The Book of Discipline*.)

The Problem

Growing up whole and healthy is increasingly difficult for children. They face weakening support systems throughout society, from home to school to church, at the very time they are struggling with unprecedented stresses. They are forced to grow up too quickly, to make significant life choices at a younger and younger age.

The percentage of children in poverty is the most widely used indicator of child well-being. Growth in the ranks of poor children in the United States over the past few decades has not been due to an increase in the number of welfare-dependent families; rather, it is because the ranks of the working poor have been growing. For example, between 1976 and 2000, the number of children living in economically poor families who were totally dependent on welfare fell from 2.8 million to 1.1 million. At the same time, the number of children living in economically poor families who had income from jobs, but no financial public assistance, increased from 4.4 million to 6.9 million. A major reason for these discrepancies was a significant change in the way the U.S. government provides public assistance to low- and no-income families. Despite the enormous wealth in the United States, the child poverty rate is among the highest in the developed world.

(from "KIDS COUNT DATA BOOK 2002")

Globally, children are increasingly at risk from the effects of poverty. UNICEF reported, in its 2002 Annual Report, that "a child born today has a one-in-four chance of being born into poverty—a life of poor health, missed education and increased violence, insecurity and discrimination." Poverty inflicts irreparable damage on young bodies and minds. Nearly 11 million children under the age of five die each year from common illnesses and malnutrition associated with poverty. Poverty undermines the health, abilities and potential of millions more children.

Public Policy Implications

In light of the critical nature of the problems described above, The United Methodist Church should press for public polices that:

1. guarantee basic income for all families regardless of structure;

2. provide basic support services for families in economic crisis, including food and nutrition programs, crisis respite care, and home care services;

3. mandate full and complete access to health and medical care, including health maintenance, prenatal and well-baby services, and mental health services for all family members, including a highly under-served group: young children and teens;

4. assure safe and affordable housing for families without regard to number and ages of children; and

5. safeguard protective services for children at risk of abuse.

Too often we engage in public policy debate, make new laws and cut budgets and programs without putting the highest priority on how any change or policy will affect children and their families.

We call upon United Methodists to ask the following questions of any pending legislation, any budget cut, any new policy:

1. Are children's needs and well-being considered first and foremost in evaluating health and welfare, or any other national, state, or local policy?

2. Will this program or policy make fewer children poor or increase the likelihood of children growing up healthy, educated, and prepared to work and contribute to the future productivity of the economy?

3. Will this program or policy make families more self-sufficient, enabling parents to work by providing them with jobs and the tools of work (education and training, child care, health care, child support enforcement, before and after-school care)?

4. Will this program or policy support families in providing care, nurture, safety, and stability to children?

5. Will this program or policy help the many who have little rather than the few who have much?

6. Will this program or policy help families stay together and care for children?

7. Does this program or policy refrain from punishing children for the actions or inactions of their parents or guardians?

8. Will this program or policy actually save money in the long run, rather than gain a short-sighted savings that leaves the next generation to pay the price?

9. Is this program or policy as fair to children as to adults, to women as to men, and to poor as to affluent families?

10. Will this program or policy provide young people with opportunities for a meaningful future, while celebrating the contributions they make in the present?

11. Will this program develop in children a sense of responsibility for themselves and their communities?

Legislators and other public leaders should be held accountable to citizens and voters for their answers to these questions and for the results of their actions.

Church Program and Policy Implications

Churches must strengthen and expand their ministry and advocacy efforts on behalf of children and their families. A coordinated ministry that serves families with children in the congregations and in the larger community, that works hand-in-hand with human service providers and ecumenical colleagues, and that addresses the public policy concerns listed above is needed in every church and community.

The church has traditionally emphasized the integrity of the institutions of marriage and family and the responsibilities of parenthood. While these emphases should be maintained, a holistic ministry with families must, of necessity, be based on the broadest possible definition of family so that the great variety of structures and configurations will be included. Grandparents often function as parents, and many families are headed by single parents or "blended" through divorce and re-marriage. Adoption, fostering, and extended family structures are among those that need the church's ministry.

Churches need to understand that all the problems described here happen to individuals and families inside the congregation as well as in the community. It is critically important that each congregation deal openly with the needs of its members and its community and begin developing appropriate ministry responses for children and their families. Support groups, hotlines, shelters, parenting classes, treatment programs. home care services, nutrition and feeding programs, and after-school tutoring and mentoring programs are especially needed in many communities; they are programs that churches are often well-suited to sponsor or support.

A network of child-serving institution and agencies, from community centers to residences for at-risk children and youth, exists across the church. Many are local expressions of national or international mission, and others are related to annual conferences. These agencies meet critical needs and urgently require the financial, volunteer, and prayer support of congregations.

The Council of Bishops, in its 2001 document on the Initiative on Children and Poverty, said that: "In a world constituted by division and competition, in which the gap between the rich and the poor widens like a yawning chasm and human life is reduced to a marketable commodity, while the impoverished majority of the earth becomes invisible to the prosperous few, it is the church that is called to be the visible and tangible presence of a community built upon grace."

We Call upon The United Methodist Church to:

1. generate a plan in every local church for assessing ministry with children (in the congregation and in the community) and implementing a vision for ministry with children and their families that takes seriously the facts and perspectives presented above. This plan is to be overseen by the official decision-making body of every local church. The manual *Putting Children and Their Families First: A Planning Handbook for Congregations** can guide the process.

2. use the Bishops' Initiative on Children and Poverty manual Community with Children and the Poor: A Guide for Congregational Study* in every local church.

3. celebrate the Children's Sabbath in every local church each October. Utilize the resource manual* developed annually by the Children's Defense Fund.

4. increase awareness of the needs of children and their families by challenging the church's leaders (including bishops, general agency staff, director of connectional ministries, superintendents as well as local church clergy and lay leaders) to spend the equivalent of one full day each year as a volunteer at a local outreach ministry that serves children, such as a community center, child care center, tutoring or parenting program, or shelter for homeless families.

5. continue and strengthen a task force formed of persons from general church agencies who work on issues of child and family advocacy, in order to coordinate work. The task force will be convened annually by the Office of Children's Ministries of the General Board of Discipleship.

ADOPTED 2004

See Social Principles, ¶ 161A.

*Order from Service Center (1-800-305-9857).

27. Nurturing Marriage and Family

WHEREAS, according to the Social Principles of The United Methodist Church, "We believe the family to be the basic human community through which persons are nurtured and sustained in mutual love, responsibility, respect, and fidelity"; and

WHEREAS, we recognize that support from a faith community can help every family, no matter what its configuration, to more effectively provide safety, nurture growth, and sustain healthy relationships; and

WHEREAS, many families throughout our world today suffer because of poverty, inadequate health care, violence in the home, violence in their communities, lack of knowledge for developing healthy relationships, and inadequate resources for times of transition or crisis; and

WHEREAS, we recognize that healthy marriages have a positive impact on all members of a family; and

WHEREAS, we believe that United Methodist general agencies, annual conferences, and congregations can join together to strengthen and support marriages and families;

Therefore, be it resolved, that the 2004 General Conference of The United Methodist Church support efforts to nurture families and marriages.

1. We call upon pastors to take seriously the importance of premarital counseling for those seeking marriage.

2. We call upon congregations to offer classes and programs related to parenting, relationships, faith formation in the family, communication skills, conflict management, marriage preparation, marriage enrichment, and coping with crisis.

3. We call upon pastors and congregations to offer support and resources for families in all their various configurations.

4. We call upon annual conferences to assist congregations through the development, identification, and promotion of programs and resources for family ministries.

5. We call upon the General Board of Higher Education and Ministry to offer resources for clergy in marriage preparation and marriage enrichment and in developing healthy relationships within their own families.

6. We call upon seminaries to train clergy in marriage preparation, marriage counseling, and marriage enrichment.

7. We call upon the General Board of Church and Society to study state and federal legislation (both proposed and already in effect) related to strengthening marriages and families and to make recommendations to Boards of Church and Society in annual conferences regarding the possible impact of such legislation.

8. We call upon The United Methodist Publishing House to continue publication of materials in support of marriage, parenting, and family life.

9. We call upon the General Board of Discipleship to continue to develop, identify, and promote resources and materials for marriage and family ministries, including but not limited to the yearly development of resources for Christian Home Month.

ADOPTED 2004

See Social Principles, ¶161A.

HISPANIC CONCERNS

28. Rio Grande Conference

WHEREAS, the Hispanic population continues to grow in the Southwest, especially in the states of Texas and New Mexico; and

WHEREAS, the Hispanic people continues to struggle as a marginalized people in a process of cultural, political, economic, social and educational transition; and

WHEREAS, the Hispanic people are in need of spiritual support in this transitional process to facilitate the development of its spiritual life so it will be a means to a complete and total transformation; and

WHEREAS, the Rio Grande Conference, the only Hispanic Annual Conference of The United Methodist Church, historically and traditionally exists to minister with and to the Hispanic people of Texas and New Mexico; and

WHEREAS, the Rio Grande Conference has provided leadership and resources as part of its connectional responsibilities to all levels of The United Methodist Church,

Therefore, General Conference is committed to a real spirit of accompaniment with the Rio Grande Conference as an extension of its mission and ministry with the Hispanic people, and this commitment is expressed in the following ways:

1. acknowledging the historic tradition of the Rio Grande Annual Conference as the only Hispanic conference of The United Methodist Church ministering to the Hispanic people;

2. affirming the ministry of the Rio Grande Conference as collaborators with The United Methodist Church in mission with and to the Hispanic people;

3. supporting the ministry of the Rio Grande Conference in its commitment to the Hispanic people in Texas and New Mexico with resources from general agencies of The United Methodist Church for a continued development of the leadership and resources appropriate to minister to Hispanics in those states.

ADOPTED 2000

See Social Principles, ¶ 161.

29. Annual Conference Strategic, Comprehensive Plans for Hispanic/Latino-Latina Ministries

WHEREAS, God calls us to proclaim God's mighty acts (1 Peter 2:9) and to be good stewards of God's manifold grace, serving one another with whatever gift each has received (1 Peter 4:10), and to organize ourselves for the work of ministry (Ephesians 4:7-13); and

WHEREAS, our United Methodist heritage integrates missional action with organizational support; and

WHEREAS, *The Book of Discipline 2000* declares that "the mission of the Church is to make disciples of Jesus Christ by proclaiming the good news of God's grace and thus seeking the fulfillment of God's reign and realm in the world" (¶ 121), and that "each annual conference is responsible to focus and guide the mission and ministry of The United Methodist Church within its boundaries by envisioning the ministries necessary to live out the mission of the church in and through the annual conference; providing encouragement, coordination, and support for the ministries of nurture, outreach, and witness in districts and congregations for the transformation of the world; ...developing and strengthening ethnic ministries, including ethnic local churches and concerns...." (¶ 607); and

WHEREAS, according to the 2000 United States census analysis, the people group in the United States called Hispanic/Latino-Latina has increased 58 percent from 1990 to 2000 and is projected to be 25 percent of the United States population by 2040; and

WHEREAS, these figures represent an undercount and do not reflect information about undocumented persons; and

WHEREAS, according to the General Board of Global Ministries Office of Research's analysis of the census data, every annual conference of The United Methodist Church in the United States has within its boundaries a growing Hispanic/Latino-Latina population; and

WHEREAS, for three quadrennia the General Conference has approved the National Plan for Hispanic/Latino-Latina Ministry as a mission initiative of the whole church, and it is a comprehensive plan of evangelization with Hispanic/Latino-Latina communities by the whole church; and

WHEREAS, in direct relationship to the implementation of the National Plan for Hispanic/Latino-Latina Ministry, 600 faith communities have been established in 52 conferences, 900 lay missioners have been equipped and deployed, 75 new Hispanic/Latino-Latina congregations have been started in 35 conferences, 70 existing Hispanic/Latino-Latina churches in 35 conferences have been strengthened, and 900 outreach ministries have been established in 52 conferences; and

WHEREAS, according to the Office of the National Plan for Hispanic/Latino-Latina Ministry's estimates, the Hispanic/Latino-Latina membership in The United Methodist Church has increased by 40 percent from 1996 to 2002; and

WHEREAS, according to the Office of the National Plan for Hispanic/Latino-Latina Ministry's estimates, Hispanic/Latino-Latina persons represent less than 1 percent of the total membership of The United Methodist Church and Hispanic/Latino-Latina congregations represent approximately 1 percent of all United Methodist chartered churches; and

WHEREAS, these figures represent an undercount due to difficulties in reporting the number of Hispanic/Latino-Latina members in multicultural churches and non-Hispanic/Latino-Latina congregations, and the number of Hispanic/Latino-Latina congregations sharing facilities with other ethnic and cultural churches; and due to difficulties in the lack of reports from some Hispanic/Latino Latina congregations; and

WHEREAS, in spite of the National Plan for Hispanic/Latino-Latina Ministry and other missional efforts, advances and success in reaching the people group called Hispanic/Latino-Latina and the increased presence of Hispanic/Latino-Latina persons in the United Methodist connectional system, the people group in the United States called Hispanic/Latino-Latina represents a huge mission field,

Therefore, be it resolved, that by December 31, 2006, every annual conference in the United States shall develop a strategic, comprehensive plan for Hispanic/Latino-Latina ministries within its boundaries, and this plan will include, but not be limited to, socio-economic, cultural, and religious analysis of the Hispanic/Latino-Latina communities that will be served; and strategies to strengthen existing Hispanic/Latino-Latina ministries and congregations, to start new ministries and congregations, to identify, equip, and deploy clergy and laity leaders, and to identify and deploy material and financial resources.

Be it further resolved, that the Council of Bishops, the National Plan for Hispanic/Latino-Latina Ministry, the General Board of Discipleship and the General Board of Global Ministries ensure that the conference comprehensive plans are in place by the indicated date and provide support and consultation in the development of the plans.

ADOPTED 2004

See Social Principles, ¶161.

ASIAN CONCERNS

30. Indochina Ministries

WHEREAS, there are 450,000 Cambodian, 350,000 Hmong and Laotian, and over 13 million Vietnamese Americans in the United States and there are twelve Cambodian fellowships and congregations, eleven Hmong fellowships and congregations, three Laotian fellowships and nineteen Vietnamese fellowships and congregations; and

WHEREAS, the political situation has changed rapidly in Indochina at the present time,

Therefore, be it resolved, that the General Conference celebrates God's grace in many recent events in Indochina, that the General Board of Global Ministries has established the Methodist Center in Phnom Penh and appointed two missionary couples in Cambodia since 1998;

Be it further resolved, that the General Conference highly recommend annual conferences, general boards, and agencies: (1) to assess new mission opportunities among Cambodians, Hmong, Laotians, and Vietnamese in Indochina and set appropriate goals, especially in Laos and Vietnam; (2) to commission more Indochinese Americans who hear a call to minister in their ancestral homes; (3) to establish networking and sponsorship from annual conferences, general boards, and agencies regarding mission plans and General Advance Specials that concern Indochinese, especially in Laos and Vietnam.

ADOPTED 2000

See Social Principles, ¶ 161.

31. Indochinese-American Ministries

WHEREAS, since the end of the Vietnam War in 1975, the US has joined many countries around the world in opening their homes and their lands to the refugees from Indochina. There are 450,000 Cambodian, 350,000 Hmong and Laotian, and over 13 million Vietnamese-Americans in the US at the present time; and

WHEREAS, there was no official Methodist ministry in the three countries of Cambodia, Laos and Vietnam in Indochina before 1975 Through the resettlement process, the UM local churches and their members have opened their hearts and their homes to welcome refugees from Indochina. As of September 1999, there are twelve Cambodian fellowships and congregations, eleven Hmong fellowships and congregations, three Laotian fellowships, and nineteen Vietnamese fellowships and congregations. This was made possible through the loving care, support, and witness in words and deeds of the UM local churches, their members, and with the seeds from Vietnamese Christians of other denominations in Vietnam and strong support of the annual conferences, general boards, and agencies; and

WHEREAS, there are six ordained Hmong, two ordained Laotian, one ordained Cambodian, and thirteen ordained Vietnamese UM clergy; and

WHEREAS, more ordained clergy are needed as in: one Cambodian, ten Hmong, three Laotian and twenty Vietnamese to meet the urgent needs of new congregational growth; and

WHEREAS, there are more opportunities for newcomers to open their hearts and minds to the gospel than when they are well settled and especially more chance for the first generation to listen to the good news of our Lord than the second or third generations,

Therefore, be it resolved, that the General Conference of the UMC celebrate God's wonderful grace, blessings, and providence through these new emerging Indochinese-American ministries in the last twenty-five years;

Be it further resolved, that the 2000 General Conference commends local churches, annual conferences, general boards, and agencies in their effort to reach out to these new groups;

Be it further resolved, that the 2000 General Conference highly recommend annual conferences, general boards, and agencies to make further efforts in congregational development, training in church and society outreach, preparing Sunday School materials, worship materials, and literature as well as conducting leadership training and recruitment for both Indochinese-American lay and clergy in order to meet the urgent needs of the forty-five fellowships and congregations at the present time and the goal for thirty more in the next ten years.

ADOPTED 2000

See Social Principles, ¶ 161.

INTOLERANCE/TOLERANCE

32. Being the Church Amid Disagreement

To the people called United Methodists, with the hope that through prayer and holy conferencing, we will engage each other in love and grace as we deal with issues upon which we disagree:

As a church facing a new millennium we continue to disagree, sometimes bitterly. Important biblical, theological and scientific questions remain in dispute among persons of good will. This has been true on many issues throughout the history of our denomination. Called as United Methodists to be vigilant on issues of inclusiveness, we urge the church to pause in reflection on the process of disagreement. What hopes would we lift up for our own denomination? When we engage in deeply felt struggle for the truth, emotions run high. Our human nature moves us to yearn for "victory"—for winning the debate, making judgment in hopes it will settle the controversy that causes us discomfort and pain as a community. The "meaning" of any communication has two parts: the content, ideas, or position on the issue, and the feelings we have about those ideas. In prolonged disagreement, we may find ourselves stepping on the feelings of others in our urgency to find the true, winning position. We remind ourselves as a community of faith to remember who we are, what both civil and religious communities perceive about us in our discord, and what we have called ourselves to be as a church.

Biblical and Theological Reflections and a Parable for Our Time

In "The Ministry of all Christians," (¶ 138), we hold ourselves accountable to this call:

"We recognize that God made all creation and saw that it was good. As a diverse people of God who bring special gifts and evidences of God's grace to the unity of the church and to society, we are called to be faithful to the example of Jesus' ministry to all persons."

We can heed this call to value all of God's creation as good, and all of God's children as capable of bringing special gifts to our church and to society. These special gifts can be gifts of engaged listening, careful feedback during disagreement, and suspension of judgment and retribution. The diverse people of God are indeed that—*diverse*. We do not always agree. But if we heed this call to value all of God's creation, we show our world how to disagree in remarkable and loving ways.

Jesus shared a parable that speaks powerfully to our time. In the parable of the wheat and the weeds (Matthew 13:24-30), he shares a story about difference, discord, and judgment that becomes a parable of grace. When asked if the weeds should not be culled from the wheat field, the householder claimed the responsibility to judge what would happen to the weeds when the harvest came. The householder did not dispute that there were weeds in the fields, but the judgment of which were weeds and what would happen to them was the householder's to make. The householder refuses to judge at the beginning. This is a story about rushing to judgment, and Jesus shares a caution based on our human nature to take action on assumptions that may or may not be true. When separation is graciously postponed, what is perceived as weed may be found to be wheat indeed! The reign of God as we know it now, as we experience it, as we try to be faithful within it, is not precise and neat and orderly. This imprecision comes as a grace to us. First of all, it frees us from the building of walls that exclude and efforts to have a "pure" community. Surely careful thought must be given to the articulation of Christian doctrine and the exposition of Christian behavior. But the grace of imprecision allows us to keep those who differ with us within the concern and the care of God. Secondly, strengthened and guided by the grace of God, we must make our own prayerful decisions about good and evil, about right and wrong as clearly as possible. But the ultimate judgment upon others and upon ourselves is not ours to make. Only God can make such judgments, and in due course this will be done. In the meantime, we must be more patient with one another. Because we do not have to sort out now who is and who is not within the reign of God, we can live with openness and freedom toward others. We must not separate ourselves from those who see things differently. This is a parable about grace and about being faithful in living it.

How Shall We Disagree?

In every community, there will be conflict and differences of opinion, some quite strongly held. How we disagree, more so than which position prevails, has a powerful impact on many audiences. As caring Christians, we carry responsibility for this impact whether or not we are aware of it. These are some of those audiences watching how we Christians disagree, argue, and debate together:

- young people, our youth and children who watch us as role models for their lives,
- our local congregations looking for wisdom and guidance in their ministry,
- leaders of our nations and local communities worldwide,

- those about whom we debate, for most discord is rooted in experiences of human lives, even the extreme example of less scrupulous, even reckless persons who may use our protestations and the invisible atmosphere our discord creates to justify their acts of violence.

Power of a Discerning Question

In the midst of engaged debate, our ability to listen to one another can weaken. True listening, hearing feelings as well as ideas, can be enhanced when we can focus for a time on questions that help us discern one another's positions on matters of importance. Questions that might help us do this are:

1. How shall we agree to treat one another while we disagree?

2. How can we show hospitality to one another while we disagree?

3. What hopes for The United Methodist Church do we have in common?

4. When confronting divisive issues along which hard lines have been drawn, can we temporarily suspend decision-making in order, through prayer, silence and study, to discern the appropriate response for these times?

5. How can we use this period of discernment to deepen our understanding of all positions on the issue?

6. Until we can agree on a resolution, can we agree to suspend motions, decisions, policy development that will assert one position over the other?

7. How could we use this time of suspended judgment to deepen our understanding of all positions on the issue?

8. What are the positive and negative effects of our disagreement on our congregations, our members, our clergy and laity, and on the communities where we serve?

9. What action as a community of faith should we take in light of these effects?

10. What would we like the nature of our community in The United Methodist Church to be when this issue that divides us is finally resolved?

Ministry of Mindfulness

Local congregations, study groups, cabinets, clusters and districts, annual, central and General Conferences can be holy and hopeful places of discord. Regardless of our positions on controversial issues, we can practice a ministry of mindfulness of the impact of our discord. Some strategies may be helpful in these settings:

1. Begin by sharing and studying relevant scripture, as scripture is our primary authority, and also consulting additional aspects of the Wesleyan quadrilateral-tradition, reason, and experience.

2. Begin sharing where we agree.

3. Remember to honor our relationships to each other as children of God.

4. Practice the art of "feedback"—true feedback in which many positions are shared and heard, and repeated back.

5. Place emphasis on the "spiritual discipline of true listening"—attending and listening for the feelings of the others as well as their ideas.

6. Use facilitators to maintain safe spaces for difficult feelings and ideas to be shared.

7. Address the issues. In the absence of consensus, share clearly and candidly what we are willing to risk for the sake of justice and compassion.

8. Be mindful not to attack the messenger when discussing the message.

9. Use principles of mediation, focusing on interests (what we would like to happen, how we would envision things to be) rather than the positions or stands we take to get there.

10. Speak faithful hope for the possibility of future reconciliation and resolution. What will it be like when we are through this discord?

11. Practice "holy conferencing"—infusing debate and dialogue with prayer, silence, and more prayer. Pray for each other, for our church, for future possibilities, for hope, and for guidance of the Holy Spirit as we move through discord.

12. Utilize resources available to our groups, congregations, conferences and agencies to strengthen our sense of community, especially in disagreement.

13. Pray for and practice the discipline of patience. Forging new understandings and agreements will take intentional effort.

ADOPTED 2000

See Social Principles, ¶ 161.

HUMAN SEXUALITY

33. Church to Be in Ministry to Persons of All Sexual Orientations

WHEREAS, we affirm our belief in the inestimable worth of each individual because we are human beings created by God and loved through and by Jesus Christ, and we affirm all persons as equally valuable in the sight of God (Preamble to Social Principles and ¶ 65G and 66, *1996 Book of Discipline*); and

WHEREAS, baptism is God's gift of unmerited grace through the Holy Spirit and marks the entrance of persons into the church and its ministries of love, justice, and service (¶ 310, *1996 Book of Discipline*); and

WHEREAS, we affirm that through baptism God has made us members of one body of Christ so that all who follow Jesus have spiritual gifts to share for the common good (1 Corinthians 12:4-27); and

WHEREAS, in addressing the nurturing function of Christian fellowship, our United Methodist Social Principles assert that human sexuality is a complex gift of which we have limited understanding (¶ 161G); and

WHEREAS, we believe that homosexual persons no less than heterosexual persons are individuals of sacred worth and that all persons need the ministry and guidance of the church in their struggles for human fulfillment, as well as the spiritual and emotional care of a fellowship that enables reconciling relationships with God, with others, and with self (¶ 161G); and

WHEREAS, an individual confronting his or her own minority sexual orientation and/or that of a close family member, friend, or associate often experiences isolation, confusion, and fear when he or she needs information, guidance, and support ("Teens at Risk," *2000 Book of Resolutions*); and

WHEREAS, we recognize that teens dealing with questions about sexual orientation are at a greater risk for suicide ("Teens at Risk," *2000 Book of Resolutions*); and

WHEREAS, the teachings and actions of Jesus demonstrated radical inclusion of those rejected by mainstream society; and

WHEREAS, a resolution was adopted at General Conference, 1996, which issued a call to our churches to reach out in love and compassion to all persons, regardless of sexual orientation, becoming beacons of love in a stormy sea of hatred, discrimination, and violence ("Call for a Rebirth of Compassion," *2000 Book of Resolutions*); and

WHEREAS, we are called to renew our commitment to become faithful witnesses to the gospel, not alone to the ends of the earth, but also the depths of our common life and work (Preamble to the Social Principles),

Therefore, be it resolved, that The United Methodist Church dedicate itself to a ministry of Christ-like hospitality and compassion to persons of all sexual orientations, and to a vision of unity through openness to the spiritual gifts of all those who have been baptized into the Body of Jesus Christ. Such ministry and openness may include: welcoming sexual minorities, their friends, and families into our churches and demonstrating our faith in a loving God; a willingness to listen and open our hearts to their stories and struggles in our churches, districts, annual conferences, and General Conference; encouraging study and dialogue around issues of sexuality; and praying for all those who are in pain and discord over our Christian response to this controversial issue.

ADOPTED 2000

See Social Principles, ¶ 161G.

34. Dialogue on Homosexuality

WHEREAS, in consultation with the Council of Bishops, the General Commission on Christian Unity and Interreligious Concerns (GCCUIC) would develop conversation around homosexuality in the spirit of understanding and care for all persons within the United Methodist family; and

WHEREAS, building on the model of the GCCUIC's 1999 Conference, "In Disagreement, Charity: Conversation on Homosexuality," these dialogues would seek to engage the church in discerning God's guidance on these matters; and

WHEREAS, in accepting leadership for developing this series of dialogues, the GCCUIC would forego any role in developing or supporting any legislative changes to the *Book of Discipline*. This moratorium would ensure an open and fair context for thoughtful and prayerful discussion of issues that impact the unity of the church; and

WHEREAS, funding for these dialogues would come from special grants that the GCCUIC would submit to the General Council on Finance and Administration,

Therefore, be it resolved, that the 2000 General Conference request the GCCUIC to sponsor a series of dialogues during the 2001-2004 quadrennium on issues related to homosexuality and the unity of the church.

ADOPTED 2000

See Social Principles, ¶ 161G.

35. Report of the Task Force on Homosexuality and the Unity of the Church

WHEREAS, The United Methodist Church has struggled for many years over the issue of homosexuality, and

WHEREAS, the General Commission on Christian Unity and Interreligious Concerns (GCCUIC) remains committed to pursuing unity within the church as a gift and calling of God, and

WHEREAS, the 2000 General Conference directed the GCCUIC to lead the church in dialogue on issues related to homosexuality and the unity of the church (Resolution Number 29, *Book of Resolutions 2000*, page 134), and

WHEREAS, the 2000 General Conference directed the GCCUIC to report on this work within The United Methodist Church; and

WHEREAS, the GCCUIC has been privileged to listen to the hopes, fears, concerns, and suggestions of hundreds of persons across The United Methodist Church, and

WHEREAS, the GCCUIC has worked to create open, grace-filled spaces for persons with contending viewpoints to learn to know each other authentically, to explore divergent understandings through prayerful and civil dialogue, and whenever possible, to experience healing and reconciliation, and has developed models that promote this kind of grace-filled and civil dialogue, and

WHEREAS, the GCCUIC has employed these models to engage the Council of Bishops, the General Council on Ministries, representatives of the five national racial/ethnic caucuses of The United Methodist Church, as well as youth and young adults in productive conversations; and has developed resources for dialogue in local churches, districts, and annual conferences, and

WHEREAS, the GCCUIC was directed by the 2000 General Conference to forgo any advocacy on this issue at the 2004 General Conference related to the position or language of *The Book of Discipline,*

Therefore, be it resolved, that the 2004 General Conference of The United Methodist Church receives the report of the Task Force on Homosexuality and the Unity of the Church of the GCCUIC and commends the report to the whole Church, and

Be it further resolved, that the 2004 General Conference encourages further dialogue throughout The United Methodist Church designed with worship at the center to lead to greater understanding, love, and care for each other, and with the hope that our struggles with these concerns will take a more civil character to the benefit of us all.

ADOPTED 2004

See Social Principles, ¶ 161G.

36. Sexual Abuse Within Ministerial Relationships

There is little doubt that sexual misconduct in church and society is a significant and troubling topic for our communities and congregations worldwide. We are aware that this unwanted behavior damages the moral environment where people worship, work, and learn. In 1996, the General Conference made a commitment to focus on sexual misconduct within the church and take action to address this brokenness and pain within The United Methodist Church. (Book of Resolutions 1996, p. 128; 2000, p. 135)

Power and Responsibility

These words of Ann Smith capture the essence of this critical issue: "The abuse of power occurs when we use power to gratify our own needs rather than to carry out God's sacred trust. It happens when we refuse to own the responsibility of guardianship that comes with the privilege of power... until we understand that power is the responsibility to give, instead of the opportunity to take, we will continue to abuse it." (*Alive Now,* Sept./Oct. 1996)

In accordance with *The Book of Discipline,* ¶ 161F, all human beings have equal worth in the eyes of God. As the promise of Galatians 3:26-29 states, " all are one in Christ"; therefore, we as United Methodists support equity among all persons without regard to ethnicity, situation or gender. In our congregations and settings for ministry, we seek to create an environment of hospitality for all persons, male or female, which is free from misconduct of a sexual nature and encourages respect, equality and kinship in Christ.

Those in positions of authority in the church, both clergy and lay, have been given much responsibility, vested with a sacred trust to maintain an environment that is safe for people to live and grow in God's love. Misconduct of a sexual nature inhibits the full and joyful participation of all in the community of God. Sexual misconduct in church and ministry settings impedes the mission of Jesus Christ. Ministerial leaders have the responsibility not only to avoid actions and words which hurt others, but also to protect the vulnerable against actions or words which cause harm.

As our children, youth and adults come to worship, study, camps, retreats, and schools of mission, they bring a heightened awareness of the issues of sexual abuse, sexual harassment, incest, rape, and sexual assault. In the safety and sanctity of the church's settings, we as church leaders and volunteers can be confronted with questions and disclosures of sexual violence and abuse from persons in our churches. We as clergy or lay ministers are asked for guidance and support from vulnerable and sometimes broken individuals. As we enter these pastoral and ministerial relationships, we do so facing the complexity of risk, vulnerability, and moral/ethical dilemmas. It is not only our pastors who find themselves searching for good information and wise advice to share; it is also our lay and clergy, volunteer and paid persons who fill ministerial roles with children, youth, young adults, and adults. These leaders may find themselves needing information and sufficient training or preparation for their ministry. All will need an appropriate and affirming ethic to guide their own behavior within a ministerial relationship with a group or individual parishioner. Clarity about the nature and scope of sexual misconduct is essential.

Sexual misconduct by either a lay person or clergy person within a ministerial relationship can be defined as a betrayal of sacred trust, a violation of the ministerial role, and the exploitation of those who are vulnerable in that relationship. Sexual abuse within the ministerial relationship occurs when a person within a ministerial role of leadership (lay or clergy, pastor, educator, counselor, youth leader, or other position of leadership) engages in sexual contact or sexualized behavior with a congregant, client, employee, student, staff member, coworker, or volunteer. (*1996 Book of Resolutions,* p. 130)

"Sexualized behavior" is behavior that communicates sexual interest and/or content. Examples include, but are not limited to displaying sexually suggestive visual materials; making sexual comments or innuendo about one's own or another person's body; touching another person's body; hair; or clothing; touching or rubbing oneself in the presence of another person; kissing; and sexual intercourse.

"Sexual harassment and sexual abuse within the ministerial relationship" represent an exploitation of power and not just "inappropriate sexual or gender-directed conduct." Sexual harassment is a continuum of behaviors that intimidate, demean, humiliate, or coerce. These behaviors range from the subtle forms that can accumulate into a hostile working, learning, or worshipping environment to the most severe forms of stalking, assault, or rape. It is important to see both sexual harassment and sexual abuse within relationships at work, school, or church as part of this continuum of brokenness. (*1996 Book of Resolutions,* p. 130)

Those in Ministerial Roles

Both laity and clergy fill ministerial roles in our church programs. In addition to clergy or professional staff, any United Methodist may fill a ministerial role by participating in such ministries as:
- leading and participating in lay speaking ministries;
- counseling or leading events for children, youth, and adults;
- teaching and leading in church schools for children, youth, and adults;
- counseling victims of violence, domestic violence, or sexual abuse;
- counseling couples about marriage, divorce, or separation;
- filling the pulpit temporarily;
- volunteering to chaperone trips, work camps, or special events;
- working in Walks to Emmaus and Chrysalis retreats;
- mentoring;
- supervising church staff members; and
- serving as missionaries.

SEXUAL ABUSE WITHIN MINISTERIAL RELATIONSHIPS

Survey Results on Our Progress

In 1996, the General Conference confronted the topic of sexual abuse and sexual harassment within the ministerial relationship. It called for the development of policies in our churches, conferences, agencies, and schools. It further called for training and advocacy practices. The General Conference also called for a survey of progress as a denomination conducted by the General Commission on the Status and Role of Women in cooperation with other general agencies.

Surveys of annual conferences and local congregations reveal that our progress in four areas is not enough: prevention, education, intervention, and healing. The General Conference continues to call for additional technical assistance in several areas:

1. resources for various constituencies within the church addressing prevention, education, intervention, and healing after lay or clergy sexual misconduct;

2. more training (entry level, follow-up, and advanced) for the various constituencies within the church addressing prevention, education, intervention, and healing;

3. discovery, development and implementation of models for intervention and healing in order to provide a consistent and thorough response when complaints of lay or clergy sexual misconduct are initiated;

4. development of a model for ongoing assessment of policies, practices, and responses of conferences in addressing clergy and lay sexual misconduct;

5. appropriate handling of the presence and involvement of legally convicted sexual offenders in local congregational activities and ministry;

6. opportunities for annual conferences to share their resources and experiences in responding to complaints of clergy and lay misconduct of a sexual nature.

Therefore be it resolved, that The United Methodist Church renews its stand in opposition to the sin of sexual misconduct and abuse within the church. It further recommits all United Methodists to the eradication of sexual misconduct in all ministerial relationships, and calls for:

1. The General Commission on the Status and Role of Women to continue to convene and coordinate a cooperative work team to address the areas of prevention, education, intervention, and healing with regard to lay and clergy misconduct of a sexual nature. The team

will include persons from the General Board of Global Ministries, the General Board of Higher Education and Ministry, the General Council on Finance and Administration, the General Commission on the Status and Role of Women, the General Board of Discipleship, the General Board of Church and Society, and up to four additional persons from throughout the connection with expertise in these areas.

    a. The work team's expenses, including but not limited to costs of travel, will be paid from the existing budgets of the participating agencies.

    b. The work team will report its findings, actions, conclusions, and recommendations to the 2008 General Conference, including proposals for legislation if necessary.

2. The General Commission on the Status and Role of Women, in cooperation with the various sponsoring bodies, to provide resources for leaders of lay events and programs within the church in order to help train and equip them to raise this important issue with laity (including lay speakers, lay leaders, Christian educators, persons in mission, leaders in Schools of Christian Mission, Walks to Emmaus, Chrysalis, and National Youth Ministry Organization events and training, and projects for young people through the Shared Mission Focus on Young People).

3. The General Commission on the Status and Role of Women, through the cooperative work team, to ensure that resources for laity and clergy in ministerial roles are identified and promoted by the participating agencies for use in conferences, districts or clusters, and local congregations.

4. The Council of Bishops to reaffirm its commitment to preventing and eradicating sexual harassment, abuse and misconduct in the church through education, training, and sharing of resources. Each Episcopal area will develop ongoing plans to coordinate persons involved in prevention and intervention, including but not limited to: district superintendents, boards of ordained ministry, boards of laity, advocates, intervention and healing teams, trained mediators, and staff-parish relations committees.

5. United Methodist-related schools of theology to provide training on the prevention and eradication of sexual harassment, abuse, and misconduct within the ministerial relationship.

6. Annual conference boards of ordained ministry to provide education (entry level, follow-up, advanced) for all appointed clergy and for all newly appointed clergy and commissioned members. Annual

conferences are also encouraged to provide similar education and training for those employed in ministerial leadership.

7. The General Board of Church and Society to continue to advocate for just laws that will help eradicate sexual harassment and abuse.

ADOPTED 1996
REVISED AND READOPTED 2000
REVISED AND READOPTED 2004

See Social Principles, ¶ 161I.

37. Eradication of Sexual Harassment in The United Methodist Church and Society

Since the mid 1970's when the term "sexual harassment" was first named by Lin Farley, the world has seen an extraordinary evolution in awareness, laws and litigation, policies, advocacy, and international collaboration to eradicate sexual harassment in the workplace. In our own communities we have moved from debating whether or not sexual harassment is even a problem to witnessing women and men join together across national boundaries to address it in multinational workplaces. Sexual harassment is regularly named as an element of sexual violence in the U.S. and around the world. It is named as a priority problem in the Ecumenical Decade of Churches in Solidarity with Women in 1998, the UN Conference on Women in Beijing in 1995, the reports of the International Labor Organization, in courts martial in the US military, and position statements of the European Women's Lobby (EWL) to the European Union. It is the subject of major media attention when a coalition of women from the USA and Japan join to protest a multinational corporation's handling of it.

Legal and Policy Development in the U.S.

1970's: The earliest studies of U.S. workers showed that 40-60 percent of women and about 15 percent of men had experienced sexual harassment at work. In that same era, courts in the U.S. found that gender-based behavior that inhibited people from doing their job, and thus earning a living, violated laws prohibiting sex discrimination.

1980: The U.S. Equal Employment Opportunity Commission issued guidelines on the identification and elimination of sexual harassment as an illegal form of sex discrimination in workplaces. Sexual harassment was defined as "unwelcome sexual advances, requests for sexual favors, and other verbal or physical conduct of a sexual nature when: 1) submission to the conduct is made either explicitly or implicitly a term or condition of an individual's employment, or 2) submission to or rejection of the conduct by an individual is used as a basis for employment decisions affecting such individual, or 3) the conduct has the purpose or effect of unreasonably interfering with an individual's work performance or creating an intimidating, hostile, or offensive working environment."

1986: In a landmark decision, the U.S. Supreme Court in Meritor v. Vinson substantially clarified and strengthened the concept of "unwanted conduct," named sexual harassment as a form of illegal sex discrimination, and found that companies may be held liable for the misbehavior of an employee against another.

1992: The U.S. Supreme Court in a significant decision added another venue where sexual harassment is illegal—in the school classroom and playground, the college or university, and in the vocational training programs. The courts agreed that students, like workers, should not be demeaned, humiliated, or intimidated on the basis of their gender to the point it interferes with their education. Thus began extraordinary efforts to raise the awareness of teachers, students, parents, and communities that patterns of harassing behaviors can be started early.

1998-99: In another landmark ruling, the Supreme Court ruled that schools may be held liable for students' harassment of other students if officials knew about it and did nothing to stop it. This ruling in Davis v. Monroe came one year after the Court's five major rulings in 1998 increasing employers' potential liability for harassment on the job.

In U.S. studies at the end of the 90's, 50-60 percent of women and 15-20 percent of men reported experiencing sexual harassment at work. While women are the predominant targets of harassment, men are targets as well with increasing numbers of reports coming from working men. At the close of the century, the Equal Employment Opportunity Commission reported that the number of complaints of sexual harassment at work from women and men had increased eight times over this decade.

ERADICATION OF SEXUAL HARASSMENT

The United Methodist Church's Efforts

1908: The original Social Creed of The Methodist Episcopal Church contains the prophetic call to stand "for such regulation of conditions of labor for women as shall safeguard the physical and moral health of the community."

1981: The General Commission on the Status and Role of Women called for all United Methodist general agencies to have clear policies on sexual harassment for employees. All of the agencies responded and adopted policies.

1988: Just two years after the first major ruling of the U.S. Supreme Court prohibiting sexual harassment in the workplace, the General Conference defined sexual harassment, named it as sin, and recognized it as a problem within our churches, agencies, and institutions. In early recognition of the importance of policies and procedures, the General Conference called for clear policies and procedures establishing grievance procedures for victims and penalties for offenders (*1996 Book of Resolutions*, p. 481).

1990: The General Council on Ministries issued its report on a survey of United Methodist clergy, laity, college and seminary students, and nonclergy church employees ("Sexual Harassment in The United Methodist Church"). It concluded, "The presence of sexual harassment in the environments associated with The United Methodist Church interferes with the moral mission of the church and disrupts the religious activity, career development, and academic progress of its participants. This study shows that unwanted sexual behavior takes place in a variety of circumstances in the church and has a range of negative consequences for its victims."

1992: The General Conference called for every annual conference, agency, and United Methodist-related institution to have policies and procedures in place. While the General Board of Church and Society would continue to monitor and advocate for just laws eradicating harassment in society, the General Commission on the Status and Role of Women was called on to assess the effectiveness of the church's efforts to eradicate it in our programs and structures. The General Conference added "sexual harassment" as a "chargeable offense" for clergy and laity in ¶ 2702, *Book of Discipline*.

1995: The General Commission on the Status and Role of Women conducted a survey of annual conferences in the U.S. and Puerto Rico. Policies were in place in schools of theology and UM-related colleges and universities, general agencies, and in a majority of annual conferences.

1996: Adopting the resolution, "Sexual Abuse Within the Ministerial Relationship and Sexual Harassment Within The United Methodist Church" (*1996 Book of Resolutions*, p. 128), the General Conference affirmed the progress made in training, education, and policy development over the previous quadrennium. In addition to this ongoing work, it called for all local churches to adopt policies and procedures, and it added ¶ 161*I* "Sexual Harassment" to the *Book of Discipline*.

1998: A coordinated agency effort resulted in the "Sexual Ethics in Ministry Survey" of annual conferences in the U.S. Annual conferences identified what they needed in tools and resources to continue their own progress in healing, education, intervention and prevention of sexual harassment.

Evolving International Research and Policy

1980's: Research studies in Canada, Europe, and the former Soviet Union showed sexual harassment was widespread across international borders. While research methods varied from country to country, all the studies revealed the same thing: sexual harassment was a problem in the world's workplaces, with serious implications for its victims, the perpetrators, companies and organizations, and nations as a whole. It was a serious problem related to the abuse of power using gender to intimidate, coerce, demean, and humiliate. Whether the harassers were office workers, police officers, attorneys, or waiters, whether in Europe, North or South America, Asia, Africa or the Pacific region, the patterns of harassment and the impact on victims and witnesses looked the same from country to country.[1]

Internationally, sexual harassment is seen as a barrier to the full participation of women in the workplace, and destructive to working environments for men and women.[2]

1992: International studies (International Labor Organization 1992[3]) showed there are no typical victims of sexual harassment, but those most likely to be harassed are those perceived as vulnerable and

1. Susan L. Webb, Shock Waves: The Global Impact of Sexual Harassment, 1994.

2. Jane Aeberhard-Hodges, "Sexual harassment in employment: recent judicial and arbitral trends," *International Labour Review*, V. 135 N. 5, 1996.

3. "Violence at Work," *International Labor Organization Report*, survey of job violence and psychological harassment in 32 countries, 1999.

financially dependent . . . divorced, separated and widowed women,single parents, lesbians, racial/ethnic women, women working in traditionally male-dominated jobs, younger women, and temporary workers. The study found that women at particular risk for job violence are health care workers, teachers, social workers, taxi drivers, and retail workers. The ILO also found that while women are more likely to be harassed, men who are subjected to harassment have the same kind of vulnerabilities: young men new to the workforce, men working in jobs traditionally dominated by women, racial/ethnic men, and gay men.

1998: At the closing event of the Ecumenical Decade of Churches in Solidarity with Women, "sexual harassment" appeared regularly in the testimonies of women and young women from many nations. In international gatherings, sexual harassment is regularly listed as one dimension of violence against women. Whether it was the UN Conference on Women in Beijing, the Conference on Development in Cairo, or the Decade Festival in Harare, these gatherings continue to identify the elimination of violence against women (physical, spiritual, psychological, sexual, structural, or economic) as a top priority for the world community.

1999: In collaborative action, the United Nations Development Fund for Women (UNIFEM) established its Trust Fund in Support of Actions to Eliminate Violence Against Women,[4] disbursing more than $600,000 in grants for local, regional, and global initiatives. This indicates a growing recognition by governments and local groups that violence against women is a fundamental violation of women's rights with devastating consequences for women's health and well-being and for society as a whole.

As the century closed, women's organizations in Europe, the USA, South America, Africa, and Asia advocated for the eradication of sexual harassment in the multinational workplace. One startling example of women and men coalescing to demand an end to this form of violence was the work of women's organizations in the U.S. with over 50 organizations in Japan to protest the actions of Mitsubishi following the allegations of sexual harassment in a U.S.-based plant. This high profile example of hostile work environment reminds us that "Seku hara" sexual harassment in any language, is harmful for workers, businesses, communities, and nations.

4. UNIFEM Global Campaign to Eliminate Violence Against Women, 1999.

Why We Must Be Concerned?

Generally, anyone can be a target in the workplace—women, men, youth, interns, volunteers, all racial/ethnic groups, any level of employee. In the learning place, any student of either gender, any grade, any teacher or professional, or any volunteer in a school program can be a target. In the church it can happen to a variety of persons, for example a staff person, pastor, committee or council chairperson, church school teacher or helper, student, camper, counselor, youth worker, or chaperone. The verb "to harass" is roughly translated "to set a dog on someone." This is what harassment feels like to a victim; it is demeaning, humiliating, frightening, isolating, and intimidating. The experience can be devastating to the individual, damaging self-esteem, productivity, and ability to earn wages; and, it can result in illness, absenteeism, poor performance, loss of promotions and opportunities. For students it can result in failure, absenteeism, isolation from peers, loss of self-esteem and therefore learning potential, withdrawal from teams and groups, and illness. Families of targets and others in the work and learning place are also victims of the hostile, intimidating environment harassment creates.

There is good reason why Fortune 500 companies declared sexual harassment as the "business issue of the 90's." There is sound moral reasoning behind The United Methodist Church's declaration that sexual harassment is a sin against individuals and communities, and is a chargeable offense for our clergy and laity. Even more profound are the devastating effects on persons when it happens in a faith community. Spiritual life, theological language and meaning, and relationships are jeopardized. For some, the loss of a sense of safety and sanctuary can be permanent.

What Now Must We Do?

Worldwide, advocates of employed women have this concern: equal access for women to resources, employment, markets, and training in order to participate fully in their own economic development. To this end they call for the elimination of sexual harassment and other forms of discrimination in the workplace. Other issues include the need for comparable international data on the incidences of harassment against women at work across international boundaries; the implementation and enforcement of policies and laws that prohibit sexual harassment and gender-based violence in the work-place, and the urgency for governments and agencies worldwide to make contributions to initiatives seeking to raise awareness of young women and eradicate all forms of sexual violence.

In The United Methodist Church, we are aware that ongoing vigilance is needed to keep effective, updated policies and procedures in all places in the church. Regular, up-to-date training of our lay and clergy leaders is an ongoing ministry of our church. Advocacy and intervention teams have been working in many conferences, and every episcopal area needs to maintain working, effective channels and procedures. Since the children and youth in our church school and youth groups are experiencing this behavior at school, how much more could we as local churches do to resource and support them in recognizing, stopping, and dealing with sexual harassment in their own lives?

God's Call to Live in Hospitable Community

Sexual harassment is a barrier to hospitality. This alienating, sinful behavior causes brokenness in relationships—the opposite of God's intention for us in human community.

From the first biblical stories of human community in the garden to the letters of Paul to the first Christian communities, we learn that all of us, both female and male, are created in the image of God, and thus have been made equal in Christ. From the beginning God intended us to live out our equality in relationship with one another and in community. Yet in our brokenness, we have given greater value and power to some over others based on gender, race, culture, age, status, or ability.

Jesus' ministry reminds us amid this brokenness that we can experience whole relationships with one another and with God. And thus we are called to be stewards of God's community of hospitality where there is not only an absence of harassment, but also the presence of welcome, respect, and equality.

Therefore, the General Conference calls for increased efforts worldwide to eradicate sexual harassment in the denomination and its institutions including these strategies:

1. the General Commission on the Status and Role of Women and the General Board of Global Ministries continue to work together with international women's organizations on efforts to eradicate violence against women in our communities worldwide;

2. the General Commission on the Status and Role of Women in collaboration with appropriate agencies continue to develop educational resources to assist United Methodists throughout the connection in understanding the issues of sexual harassment in church and society;

3. the General Commission on the Status and Role of Women in cooperation with the General Board of Higher Education and Ministry identify and develop resources on sexual harassment specific to those in ordained ministry and to lay leaders, students, faculty ,and administrators of United Methodist-related educational institutions;

4. episcopal leaders implement plans to address and eradicate sexual harassment in each episcopal area with attention to prevention, education, intervention, and healing measures;

5. the General Commission on the Status and Role of Women will continue to monitor and assess the church's progress in eradicating sexual harassment and will report to the 2004 General Conference the specific areas to be strengthened within the life of the church including policy development, education, and training;

6. annual conferences throughout the connection will encourage their local and national governments to collect accurate data on the incidence and nature of sexual harassment in their workplaces. They will also encourage their national governments to adopt laws, policies, and procedures for eradicating sexual harassment. Annual conferences are encouraged to utilize this data and experiences to plan initiatives to raise awareness throughout the conferences;

7. the General Board of Church and Society and the General Board of Global Ministries will advocate for laws that prohibit sexual harassment in U.S. workplaces, and continue to provide resources to the denomination on international initiatives to eradicate harassment and other forms of violence against women;

8. the General Commission on the Status and Role of Women and the General Board of Global Ministries in collaboration with the General Commission on Christian Unity and Interreligious Concerns will work cooperatively with the World Council of Churches "Decade to Overcome Violence" (2001-2010); and

9. the General Commission on the Status and Role of Women shall continue to conduct ongoing self-assessment of The United Methodist Church's progress to eradicate this behavior from the church, and to

strengthen initiatives to eradicate it from our diverse societies around the world.

ADOPTED 1992
REVISED AND ADOPTED 2000

See Social Principles, ¶ 161*I*.

SPIRITUALITY

38. Support Chrysalis at All Levels of the Church

WHEREAS, this is a ministry given to us from the Upper Room; and

WHEREAS, this brings a spiritual awareness of Jesus Christ to our youth in a unique, loving, patient, and kind way; and

WHEREAS, we rejoice in the truth which is revealed in this effort to involve our youth in a very important ministry in the Chrysalis movement; and

WHEREAS, youth may return to their local churches and be present and future leaders of the church,

Therefore, be it resolved, that:

1. The General Conference urge all Annual Conferences to increase their efforts and resources in the Chrysalis movement so that the youth of our churches know and are in touch with Christ; and

2. The General Conference urge each conference to work in connection with the General Conference Council on Ministries, and that adequate funding be provided within each annual conference budget for Chrysalis ministries as outlined in the menu from the Upper Room for this extremely important ministry; and

3. The General Conference encourages churches to enlist and involve their youth, girls and boys, in the life and work of Chrysalis so that they may return and be leaders within their own congregations.

Furthermore, General Conference encourages the General Board of Discipleship and Upper Room ministries to continue their emphasis on Chrysalis.

ADOPTED 2000

See Social Principles, ¶ 161*A*.

39. Support the Walk to Emmaus at All Levels of the Church

WHEREAS, the Walk to Emmaus is given to us from the Upper Room; and

WHEREAS, this ministry brings a spiritual awareness of Jesus Christ to all adults in a unique, loving, patient, and kind way; and

WHEREAS, we rejoice in the truth which is revealed in this effort; and

WHEREAS, this ministry involves our members in a very important ministry; and

WHEREAS, this ministry enables members to return to their local churches and be present and future leaders of the church,

Therefore, be it resolved, that General Conference:

1. urges all annual conferences to increase their efforts and resources in the Walk to Emmaus so that the adults of our churches know and are in touch with Christ;

2. encourages churches to enlist and involve their adult members, men and women, in the life and work of the Walk to Emmaus so that they may return and be leaders within their own congregations; and

3. encourages the General Board of Discipleship and Upper Room ministries to continue their emphasis on Walk to Emmaus.

ADOPTED 2000

See Social Principles, ¶ 161.

40. Affirmation for the Historic Doctrines of the Christian Faith

WHEREAS, The Constitution of The United Methodist Church, in its Restrictive Rules (*see* ¶ 17-22), protects both the Articles of Religion and the Confession of Faith as doctrinal standards that shall not be revoked, altered, or changed (*Book of Discipline*, p. 58).

Therefore, be it resolved, that the 2004 General Conference affirms its commitment to the historic doctrines of the Christian faith as taught in the Scripture and affirmed in the historic creeds of the Church, in the United Methodist Articles of Religion, and in the sermons of John Wesley.

ADOPTED 2004

See Social Principles, ¶161.

41. Recover Doctrinal Heritage and Encourage Biblical and Theological Dialogue

WHEREAS, the sharing of theological differences should be a common reality within our church; and

WHEREAS, biblical and theological dialogue needs to be part of the fabric of our life together in all aspects of the church's life; and

WHEREAS, the church needs ways to strengthen our ability for dialogue and doctrinal discernment; and

WHEREAS, the issues of faith and order could be developed, struggled with, and result in new perspectives being shared; and

WHEREAS, using discernment in various levels of the church would truly be a celebration if resources were shared as a gift with one another; and

WHEREAS, all bodies of the church should be encouraged to engage in biblical and theological dialogue.

Therefore, be it resolved , that we affirm the disciplinary role of the bishops and the General Commission on Christian Unity and Interreligious Concerns in fostering biblical and theological dialogue at all levels of the church and do not support the establishment of a separate Commission on Faith and Order.

Be it further resolved, that we affirm the Church in its desire to recover and develop our distinctive doctrinal heritage, catholic, and reformed and thereby support enabling doctrinal re-invigoration for the sake of authentic renewal, faithful evangelism, and ecumenical dialogue and social witness.

Be it further resolved, that we encourage the Church at all levels to offer models and training for leaders (i.e. local church pastors, district superintendents, directors of connectional ministries, laity, etc.) on how to facilitate biblical and theological dialogue. In addition, we urge every general agency to incorporate within its training of church leaders, models of biblical and theological discourse using diverse training modules that reflect upon the diversity of The United Methodist Church.

Be it further resolved, that the 2004 General Conference and all entities of the Church be urged to model biblical and theological dialogue for The United Methodist Church.

ADOPTED 2004

See Social Principles, ¶ 161.

VIOLENCE

42. Pornography and Sexual Violence

The issue of pornography has undergone a dramatic change over the past two decades, one that shifts the definition, increases the complexity, and requires a new level of discussion. The use of violent, aggressive themes accompanying sexually explicit material has continued to increase. Cable television, the Internet, and other new technology have made sexually aggressive media widely available, particularly to children and youth. Pornography is frequently relied upon as a source of information about sexuality. The church needs to lead society in articulating an ethic that affirms God's good gift of human sexuality and that protects the vulnerable from sexual violence and coercion. For this task, we stand on solid ground, from Scripture and from our Social Principles:

"So God created humankind in God's own image, in the image of God was the human created; male and female God created them. . . . And God saw everything that was made, and behold, it was very good" (Genesis 1:27, 31, RSV-An Inclusive Language Lectionary, NCCC, 1983).

> *"We recognize that sexuality is God's good gift to all persons. We believe persons may be fully human only when that gift is acknowledged and affirmed by themselves, the church, and society. . . . we recognize that God challenges us to find responsible, committed and loving forms of expression. . . . We reject all sexual expressions that damage or destroy the humanity God has given us as birthright. . . . We deplore all forms of the commercialization and exploitation of sex, with their consequent cheapening and degradation of human personality. . . . We recognize the continuing need for full, positive, and factual sex education opportunities for children, youth and adults. . . ."* (from The Social Principles of The United Methodist Church, ¶ 161G).

Common understandings of pornography no longer serve us well. Some of us may believe pornography is a social evil because it is sexual, while others may defend pornography as a universal right to freedom of expression because it is sexual. Yet the truth is that pornography is not about sexuality; it is about violence, degradation, exploitation, and coercion.

While there is not widespread agreement on definitions, the following are suggested as the basis for dialogue:

Pornography is sexually explicit material that portrays violence, abuse, coercion, domination, humiliation, or degradation for the purpose of arousal. In addition, any sexually explicit material that depicts children is pornographic.

The impact of pornography on behavior is difficult to measure. While there is little evidence that consuming pornography causes an individual to commit a specific act of sexual aggression, several studies suggest that such consumption may predispose an individual to sexual offenses, and that it supports and encourages sexual offenders to continue and escalate their violent and abusive behavior. Few dispute the fact that a society that supports multibillion dollar industries promoting sexual violence as entertainment and portraying the abuse and torture of women and children in a sexual context is a society in trouble.

Pornography is inextricably linked to the oppression of women. Its appeal will continue as long as sexual arousal is stimulated by images of power and domination of one person over another, most often male over female. Pornography is also fundamentally linked to racism; women of color are invariably portrayed in the most violent and degrading ways. The destructive power of pornography lies in its ability to ensure that attitudes toward sexuality will continue to be influenced by images that negate human dignity, equality, and mutuality. Pornography contributes to alienation in human relationships and distorts the sexual integrity of both women and men.

The explosion of the Internet in recent years has made access easier for providers and consumers of pornography, and especially for adults who sexually abuse children. There is mounting evidence that pedophiles routinely use the Internet to lure children into their hands. A staggering number of chat rooms promote rape, incest, sex with children, child prostitution, and other criminal and violent behaviors.

Pornographic materials are being transmitted in cyberspace on a global scale, permitting access by both adults and children. Disclaimers warning of graphic materials on these sites have not prevented children from viewing them. Most sites offer free "previews" of graphic, obscene, and violent images and are linked to other sites. According to the United States Commission on Pornography, 12- to 17-year-old adolescents are among the largest consumers of pornography.

Those portrayed in Internet pornographic images are typically women, especially women of color. Female bodies are treated as objects and commodities, and female body parts are dismembered and magnified for pornographic effect and cyber-sexual consumption. The global nature of the Internet and its lack of regulation enables such materials that may be legal in one country to be accessed in a country where they may be illegal. National boundaries are easily crossed, and there is no international code of conduct to monitor pornographic material.

Care should be taken that children and youth are protected from pornographic materials. The supervision and love of Christian parents and other caring adults, supported by the extended church family, are the primary source of sex education. A comprehensive approach to sex education offers an additional basis for countering pornography. Children, youth, and adults need opportunities to discuss sexuality and learn from quality sex education materials in families, churches and schools. An alternative message to pornography, contained in carefully prepared age-appropriate sex education materials that are both factual and explicit and portray caring, mutually consenting relationships between married adults, is needed. Materials should be measured by the intentions expressed and the goals served, not by the degree of explicitness of sexual imagery. If we fail to provide such materials, accompanied by parental and adult supervision, we risk reliance of children and youth on pornography as the primary source of information about sexuality.

The temptation to embrace easy answers must be resisted. Government censorship is not an effective tool to deal with pornography. To acknowledge pornography as harmful is not to sanction every possible legal remedy. Censorship carries an inherent risk that it will be used to limit sex education materials and erotica simply because they are sexually explicit. Yet to honor the right to freedom of speech is not to authorize expression of all ideas by any means possible. We know that the exercise of freedom must take place within a framework of social responsibility, with particular regard for the vulnerability of children and youth. A corporate decision not to allow pornography, such as by an online provider, is not censorship; it is corporate responsibility.

The United Methodist Church is already on record naming sexual violence and abuse as sins and pledging to work for their eradication ("Domestic Violence and Sexual Abuse," *2000 Book of Resolutions*) and stating that "children must be protected from economic, physical and sexual exploitation and abuse" (The Social Principles, ¶ 162C).

Understanding pornography to portray violence, abuse and humiliation in a sexual setting, and understanding any sexually explicit depiction of children to be pornographic, we affirm that The United Methodist Church is opposed to pornography. We further affirm our commitment to quality sex education and our resistance to censorship. We call upon The United Methodist Church, its general agencies, annual conferences and local churches, to:

1. educate congregations about the issue of pornography;

2. seek strategies, other than government censorship, to reduce the proliferation of pornography;

3. work to break the link between sex and violence;

4. monitor and limit access by children and youth to pornography and sexually explicit material;

5. participate in efforts to ban child pornography and protect child victims;

6. promote the use of United Methodist and other quality sex education materials that help children and youth gain an understanding of and respect for mutually affirming sexuality;

7. provide educational sessions for parents on minimizing the risk to children from Internet usage. Encourage parents to establish rules for teenagers and children; encourage parents to utilize screening technology;

8. call for social responsibility in all media, including the Internet and in all public libraries, and work with local, national, and international groups that advocate for global media monitoring of images of women, men and children; and

9. participate in ecumenical and/or community efforts that study and address the issue of pornography.

ADOPTED 1988
REVISED AND ADOPTED 2000

See Social Principles, ¶ 161H.

THE SOCIAL COMMUNITY

ACCESSIBILITY/EQUAL ACCESS

43. Annual Accessibility Audit

WHEREAS, our Social Principles state, "We affirm the responsibility of the Church and society to be in ministry with children, youth, and adults with mental, physical, developmental, and/or psychological and neurological conditions or disabilities" (¶ 162G); and

WHEREAS, the Americans with Disabilities Act calls for all public buildings to be made accessible to people with disabilities,

Therefore, be it resolved, that all United Methodist churches shall conduct an annual audit of their facilities to discover what barriers impede full participation of people with disabilities. Plans shall be made and priorities determined for the elimination of all barriers, including architectural, communication, and attitudinal barriers. The Accessibility Audit for Churches, available from the Service Center, General Board of Global Ministries, 7820 Reading Road, Cincinnati, OH 45222, (800) 305-9857, shall be used in filling out the annual church/charge conference reports.

ADOPTED 1992
AMENDED AND READOPTED 2004

See Social Principles, ¶ 162G.

44. Accessibility Grants for Churches

WHEREAS, it is essential that The United Methodist Church as a denomination find a way to assist individual churches in the annual conferences to find grant money to assist them in becoming more accessible by removing architectural barriers; and

WHEREAS, our denomination establishes many programs around specific groups of people, whether they be ethnic groups or age-targeted groups; and

WHEREAS, each of the groups that the church claims an interest in and sets priorities for includes persons with disabilities. There are more than 54 million in the United States alone. The United Nations recently focused on the issue of disability by calling for institutions to become more accessible; and

WHEREAS, several years ago, $500 grants were awarded to churches that were qualified, to help them increase their accessibility;

Therefore be it resolved, that it would be appropriate to set aside monies to again provide accessibility grants or loans to churches in each of the annual conferences. The program could be administered from within the General Board of Global Ministries.

ADOPTED 2000

See Social Principles, ¶ 162G.

45. Compliance with the Americans with Disabilities Act for Employers

WHEREAS, the General Board of Global Ministries, on October 16, 1979, called "United Methodists to a new birth of awareness of the need to include, assimilate, receive the gifts, and respond to the needs, of those persons with mental, physical, and/or psychologically handicapping conditions, including their families"; and

WHEREAS, the General Conference resolved in 1980 to take major steps in adapting facilities, new and existing, such as "church sanctuaries, educational buildings, parsonages, camps, colleges, or other church-related agencies or facilities" so that they meet minimum guidelines for "barrier-free construction" (*see* "Barrier-Free Construction for People with Disabilities"); and

WHEREAS, President Bush signed into law the Americans with Disabilities Act (ADA); and

WHEREAS, love without justice is empty and meaningless, and it is unjust to deny anyone employment based solely on human-created obstacles; and

WHEREAS, it is fitting that Christians be a "cloud of witnesses" for the secular world;

Therefore, be it resolved, that all United Methodist churches investigate and attempt to comply with Title I of the ADA, which states that employers "may not discriminate against qualified individuals with disabilities" and will "reasonably accommodate the disabilities of qualified applicants or employees unless undue hardship would result."

ADOPTED 1992
AMENDED AND READOPTED 1996
READOPTED 2004

See Social Principles, ¶ 162G.

46. United Methodist Implementation of Americans with Disabilities Act

WHEREAS, our human rights as stated by the United States of America Constitution are God given, and we can set priorities unto ourselves apart from the rest of His creation, and

WHEREAS, these priorities are applied to our life and what it means to us, how we live it, who we are and to become, and *anyone* can have an attainable priority to direct their life, and

WHEREAS, by applying the use of our love with all our heart, soul, mind, and strength in our time, money, and attitudes we can perceive our priorities within ourselves and others, and

WHEREAS, God's grace is with us throughout our lives: birth, disease, accident, crime, and aging, yet, not realizing it till it's been revealed, and

WHEREAS, we *all* are instruments of God's grace in other people's lives when we are open to His grace, and

WHEREAS, we are all priests—the whole church is the holy priesthood, those called to be a mediator between God and a needful world representing Jesus Christ—where *all* are to share God's love and salvation with other people, and

WHEREAS, God's love for us is unconditional; God loves us for who we are—not what we are or how we look; Christ died for us while we were yet sinners, and this great love moves us to accept this gift in our hearts of a living relationship with God as a priority for *all* our lives, and

WHEREAS, we are consciously living our lives in relationship with God that can be nurtured through the spiritual discipline of living in God's presence, and these lives are courageous and joyful—not tragic or brave, and

WHEREAS, study brings our minds to Christ like lives, equips us to fulfill the highest calling of *all* of us, and

WHEREAS, Christian study brings *all* to a knowledge of God and knowledge of the world to serve God, and

WHEREAS, sacred moments and practices (through services and discipline) bring us to know, experience, and live in the presence of Christ through the church *(meaning everyone)*, including the serving and receiving of the sacraments, and

WHEREAS, baptism and Holy Communion are upheld by all Christian traditions and have been given to us so we may live on growing as disciples in every part of our life, and

WHEREAS, showing Christ as being real and important for others, we *all* must live authentically as our serving Christ gives our hands to Christ by making a friend, being a friend, and introducing our new friend to the friend of all friends—Jesus Christ, and

WHEREAS, through the Resolution of the "Annual Accessibility Audit" (#43, adopted in 1992), Social Principles, ¶ 162G "Rights of Persons with Disabilities," and the section in the *Book of Discipline* on inclusiveness (¶ 138) gives the opportunity for *each person*, and congregation to make a plan for serving Christ, and

WHEREAS, even with God's gift of grace and a new life in Christ, we can still sin in many forms, yet there is still forgiveness, realizing and admitting our sin (physically and spiritually) in our lives as the first step to overcome them, and

WHEREAS, through prayer, repentance, surrendering anew, counseling, and creating a new plan to reevaluate and prioritize to God's direction in *all* our lives, and

WHEREAS, by becoming disciples, we can reply to the call of Christ with *all* our hearts, minds, souls, strengths, hands, and feet as we are able to walk with Jesus and grow into His likeness as our highest priority; to share Christ and to learn to love as Jesus loved, and

WHEREAS, people all around us, including the church, are in need of God's transforming love for living in this world and can be changed whenever we bring Christ's love and truth working within our church, family, work, social environments, and our private times, and

WHEREAS, we are edified by God's grace for growth in our relationships as we live in obedience to His call, the Holy Spirit teaches and empowers us to love as Jesus loved and to mature in the likeness of Christ as children imitate their parents, to be focused upon our call in humble service, and

WHEREAS, the body of Christ is the gathering of *all* disciples who offer their lives to proclaim Christ in the world, and *every member* of the body of Christ has been given special gifts for ministry that need to be sought and exercised to build up the church, to form healthy, living communities, and to show Christ's life of love in concrete ways "that the world may believe," and

WHEREAS, we are called to persevere in grace for the rest of our lives by weekly attendance, commitment to share support, accountability, and guidance, and

WHEREAS, *all* are sent out by Christ's Great Commission, to be Christ's apostles in today's world in the midst of obstacles that can be overcome through Christ and other Christians, and

WHEREAS, there are 56 million disabled citizens at any one time in the United States, and

WHEREAS, disabled persons are real people, with real voices and real choices whose lives have been stolen within ALL cultures within America comprised of young, middle-aged, seniors, veterans, parents, husbands, wives, children from all races and all ethnic backgrounds, and

WHEREAS, people with disabilities constitute a discrete and insular minority, subjected to a history of purposeful unequal treatment and placed in a position of political powerlessness in American society and within the church, and

WHEREAS, prejudice and discrimination against people with disabilities based on unjustified stereotypes continues, with disparate treatment and disenfranchisement, and

WHEREAS, such discrimination and prejudice denies people with disabilities the opportunity to pursue opportunities in society and within the Church on an equal basis, to live in their own homes so as to be close to family, friends, work, school, church, recreation, social stimulation, libraries, theaters, community centers, museums, and medical facilities, and

WHEREAS, accommodation for our disabled people (parishioners and visitors alike) are part of our reaching out through the provisions of *The Book of Discipline* through Church and Society empowers and frees us to advocate for personal assistants, accessibility in public and private areas, housing, transportation, and technology to do so, and

WHEREAS, through Church and Society we have a duty to bring justice and fairness in our civil responsibilities (like voting or serving in civil government) for our people with disabilities for Medicaid, Medicare, vocational rehabilitation, housing, education, job training, in-home services, and transportation—all of which are *everyone's* civil right, and

WHEREAS, this inability to participate fully in American society and within the church robs people with disabilities of the opportunity to claim any degree of independence and costs the United States (including the church) billions of dollars annually in unnecessary expenses from enforced dependency and non-productivity, and

WHEREAS, the body of Christ, the church, need to be vigilant as consumers, advocates, and legislators to reserve funding and accountability to promote choice for persons with disabilities, and

WHEREAS, the Americans with Disabilities Act (ADA) was signed into law by George Bush in 1990 to, in his words, "in the unjustified segregation and exclusion of persons with disabilities from the mainstream of American life," and

WHEREAS, the United States Supreme Court promoted community living through its OLMSTEAD decision, which urges all 50 states to *plan* for people living in the community over institutional placement, and

WHEREAS, the ADA's primary goal is to promote access to *all* aspects of social interaction including education, employment, commerce, recreation, government, and transportation, and

WHEREAS, the ADA provides the means for full implementation of the Act and legal recourse to redress discrimination on the basis of physical disability, and

WHEREAS, The United Methodist Church has brought closely within itself to help people as taught by our Lord Jesus Christ those who are hungry, thirsty, sick or in prison,

Therefore, be it resolved, that the assembled delegates to this General Conference of The United Methodist Church 2004 affirm our support of the full implementation of the provisions of the Americans with Disabilities Act of 1990, and

Be it further resolved, the General Conference of The United Methodist Church urge all our congregations to implement and enforce the provisions of the ADA and all disability-related programs within every area that members of The United Methodist Church reside with the same vigor and interest as they would any other law affecting their able-bodied constituency.

ADOPTED 2004

See Social Principles, ¶ 162G.

47. Assisting Personal Mobility

WHEREAS, the International Organization of Mobility Providers estimates that some 22,000,000 persons worldwide lack personal mobility because of land mines, polio, wartime injuries, and a host of other causes, and

WHEREAS, these persons usually live in dire poverty, are marginalized from society, hidden away in back rooms, and are often seen as embarrassments, and

WHEREAS, these persons of God's creation often live lives of misery and discomfort, "scuttling around on the ground like crabs" (the description of a missionary in Congo), eating the dust and mud of streets and trails, looking at people's feet, and

WHEREAS, such persons seldom have an adequate social life, being unable to attend school, go to church, visit relatives, or attend community events, and

WHEREAS, they long to be productive members of society, but must depend on others for mobility, and

WHEREAS, mobility devices are available that can provide for these persons a degree of mobility giving to them the fullness of human dignity, comfort, hope and productivity they deserve, and

WHEREAS, personal mobility should be a human right for all of God's people,

Therefore, be it resolved, that the next quadrennium shall be declared a time to focus on the need for providing personal mobility as an act of justice and compassion; and

Be it further resolved, that every entity of The United Methodist Church respond generously with time and resources: to analyze the mobility needs in their community and other parts of the world; to collaborate with people in need of enhanced mobility and with organizations involved with them; and to seek appropriate ways to address needs that have been identified.

ADOPTED 2004

See Social Principles, ¶ 162G.

48. Eradication of Sexism in the Church

WHEREAS, sexism continues to be a pervasive and systematic force within our church and our society; and

WHEREAS, sexism deprives the church and society of the opportunity to use the skills and talents that women have; and

WHEREAS, a General Commission on the Status and Role of Women 2003 survey of local churches in the United States found that only 57% have policies against sexual harassment; inclusive language studies are rare in local congregations; and urban congregations more frequently have inclusive language studies, harassment policies, and diverse use of female lay persons (as Board of Trustees members and ushers, for example); and

WHEREAS, this survey also found that bishops who are female appointed more district superintendents who were female, and their conferences had more local congregations with sexual harassment policies in place than conferences with Bishops who were male; and

WHEREAS, the Church remains committed to the eradication of sexual harassment against children, employees, volunteers, clergy and their families, and congregants. Yet sexual misconduct remains a serious problem in our conferences, and an alarming number of local congregations do not have policies, procedures, or training in place for laity and clergy in stopping and preventing sexual harassment and misconduct; and

WHEREAS, the Church continues to lose clergywomen (particularly clergywomen of color) from local church ministry into more welcoming forms of ministry. A persistent, subtle, and often unchallenged sexism denies women in The United Methodist Church the opportunity to participate fully and equally in all areas of the Church;

Therefore, be it resolved, that the General Conference affirm the work and the necessity for the continuance of the General Commission on the Status and Role of Women and of the annual conference related commissions and counterparts; and

Be it further resolved, that each annual conference commission or counterpart be given the financial backing to pursue projects that are aimed at educating the members of the local churches about the issues of sexism and at sponsoring the leadership events that enable the annual conference commission members to be better advocates for all who seek equity and inclusiveness; and

Be it further resolved, that each annual conference, United Methodist seminary, and all United Methodist-related institutions are called to have policies on sexual harassment and equal opportunity; and

Be it further resolved, that each annual conference and local congregation is called have policy, procedures, and training opportunities in place for lay and clergy in stopping and preventing sexual harassment and misconduct; and that progress to full compliance will be reported through the Episcopal Office to the General Commission on the Status and Role of Women at the Commission's request. The Commission will be responsible to report to General Conference 2008; and

Be it further resolved, that the General Conference support the General Commission on the Status and Role of Women as the advocacy and monitoring agency of women's issues for increasing opportunities for females in leadership, promoting equality in filling decision-making posts, and fostering inclusiveness in all facets of The United Methodist Church.

ADOPTED 1996
AMENDED AND READOPTED 2004

See Social Principles, ¶ 162F.

49. Homosexuals in the Military

Basis: The United States of America, a nation built on equal rights, has denied the right of homosexuals to actively serve their country while being honest about who they are. Meanwhile, The United Methodist Church is moving toward accepting all people for who they are. The United Methodist Church needs to be an advocate for equal civil rights for all marginalized groups, including homosexuals.

Conclusion: The U.S. military should not exclude persons from service solely on the basis of sexual orientation.

ADOPTED 1996

See Social Principles, ¶ 162H.

50. Rights of All Persons

A portion of the world's population is gay, lesbian. bisexual, and transgender (GLBT). Around the world, political and religious institutions have targeted GLBT persons for discrimination in housing, employment, health care, and access to redress for such discrimination. Some falsely portray the basic human rights laws that protect GLBT persons from hate crimes as unfair "legal preference."

It is particularly disturbing when religious values are used to justify persecution of select groups. Christians proclaim that all people are God's children deserving the protection of their human and civil rights. Our Social Principles gives us clear direction in this matter:

We insist that all persons, regardless of age, gender, marital status, or sexual orientation, are entitled to have their human and civil rights ensured (¶ 161G).

The rights and privileges a society bestows upon or withholds from those who comprise it indicate the relative esteem in which that society holds particular persons and groups of persons. We affirm all persons as equally valuable in the sight of God. We therefore work toward societies in which each person's value is recognized, maintained, and strengthened (¶ 162).

Therefore, all United Methodists are called upon:

1. to refrain from signing petitions and to vote against measures that advocate the denial of basic human and civil rights to anyone;

2. to educate congregation and community alike about the position of the United Methodist *Discipline* on civil rights and its broad applications; and

3. to stand against any political or physical acts that deny human and civil rights and the sacred worth of all persons.

4. to advocate for initiatives which would prohibit job and housing discrimination based on sexual orientation and gender identity throughout the world; and

5. to advocate for initiatives which provide for extra penalties for crimes which are expressly committed for the purpose of harming someone based solely on their race, color, national origin, religion, sexual orientation, gender identity, gender, or disability.

Therefore, be it resolved, that the General Board of Church and Society develop education tools designed to provide for open and healthy dialogue and understanding of sexuality in the world with the specific goal of protecting the human and civil rights of gay, lesbian, bisexual and transgender persons.

We do this as part of our Christian witness and ministry. Never let it be said that United Methodists were silent during this attack on the rights of all.

ADOPTED 1996
AMENDED AND READOPTED 2004

See Social Principles, ¶ 161G and ¶ 162A and H.

ADMINISTRATIVE GUIDELINES

51. National Cooperative Parish Ministry Leadership Team

WHEREAS, the Sixth National Cooperative Parish Ministry Consultation convened in St. Louis, Missouri, on November 13-16, 2003, with 376 persons in attendance; and,

WHEREAS, the National Cooperative Parish Ministry Leadership Team, composed of persons from both town/rural and urban settings coordinated the event along with representatives from the General Board of Global Ministries, the General Board of Discipleship, and the General Commission on Christian Unity and Interreligious Concerns; and,

WHEREAS, the Sixth Consultation included United Methodists as well as ecumenical partners who serve rural and urban cooperative parish ministries in a variety of multiracial settings;

WHEREAS, the Consultation included help—shops, briefings, panels, plenary addresses, power-point presentations, networking, and witnessing, all of which were highly affirmed as serving of great value to the ministry of United Methodist charges, single churches, circuits, and cooperative projects, ministries, and parishes; and,

WHEREAS, the effectiveness of cooperative projects, ministries, and parishes for the purposes of congregational nurturing, outreach to communities of the poor and marginalized, and witnessing to Christian commitments in rural, urban and suburban communities was affirmed; and

WHEREAS, The United Methodist Church is experiencing a decline in the number of ordained clergy persons and will need to find ways to enlist and train persons for new models of ministry, among such models being those that will seek to work in cooperative projects, ministries, and parishes;

Therefore, be it resolved that the National Cooperative Parish Ministry Leadership Team be commended for its planning and leading of the Sixth Consultation on Cooperative Projects, Ministries, and Parishes: Pathways With Promise and for the cooperative ministry resources it has developed throughout the 2001-2004 quadrennium; and,

Be it further resolved, that the general boards and agencies, the annual conferences, districts, and local churches of The United Methodist Church be called on to implement processes that will eventuate in understandings of how to initiate needed cooperative projects, ministries, and parishes and to facilitate their movement toward local and global mission and ministry; and,

Be it further resolved, that appreciation be conveyed to the General Board of Global Ministries, the General Board of Discipleship, and the General Commission on Christian Unity and Interreligious Concerns for their financial support and active participation; and

Be it further resolved, that these boards and agencies of The United Methodist Church be called on to continue providing encouragement and financial support for the ongoing work of the National Cooperative Parish Ministry Leadership Team; and,

Be it further resolved, that the General Board of Higher Education and Ministry be requested also to collaborate with the National Cooperative Parish Ministry Leadership Team in its work; and

Be it further resolved, that the General Board of Global Ministries, the General Board of Discipleship, the General Commission on Christian Unity and Interreligious Concerns, and the General Board of Higher Education and Ministry be called upon to undergird the National Cooperative Parish Ministry Leadership Team as it prepares a Seventh Consultation on Cooperative Projects, Ministries and Projects for the 2005-2008 quadrennium.

ADOPTED 2004

See Social Principles, ¶ 162N.

52. Plan to Support Cooperative Parish Ministry

WHEREAS, the 376 participants in the Sixth Consultation on Cooperative Projects, Ministries, and Parishes: Pathways with

Promise, coordinated by the National Cooperative Parish Ministry Leadership Team, held in St. Louis, MO, on November 13-16, 2003, affirmed the benefits of congregations working together to make disciples of Jesus Christ and shape communities that reflect the reign of God; and

WHEREAS, cooperative ministry is an intentional style of team ministry that enables groups of congregations and their pastors and laity in a defined geographic area, as United Methodists and ecumenically, to work together in ministries of nurture, outreach, and witness; and

WHEREAS, cooperative forms of ministry are proven to enhance lay leadership development, to provide greater support and peer accountability among clergy, and to further connectional awareness and increased resourcing from the connectional church; and

WHEREAS, the Cooperative Ministry Common Table, under the leadership of the General Council on Ministries and involving the National Leadership Team on Cooperative Parish Ministry, meeting at the site of the Sixth Consultation on Cooperative Projects, Ministries, and Parishes explicitly recognized and affirmed the need for support of cooperative ministry from bishops and cabinets, annual conferences, districts, local churches, and general boards and agencies, and seminaries;

Therefore, be it resolved, that the cooperative ministry movement be supported by:

1. all boards and agencies of The United Methodist Church collaborating and working together around issues concerning cooperative ministries, i.e., training, resources, financial assistance, technical assistance, etc.;

2. bishops and cabinets fulfilling the requirements that are in *The Book of Discipline* of The United Methodist Church, concerning cooperative ministries, i.e., training, consultation, deployment of personnel, etc.;

3. bishops and cabinets giving priority to cooperative ministries in the appointment making process;

4. seminaries including training and field experiences for students to learn skills for working in team settings such as cooperative projects, ministries, and parishes;

5. courses of study for local pastors including training and field experience to learn skills for working in team settings that include cooperative projects, ministries, and parishes;

6. cabinets encouraging United Methodist congregations to work together in cooperative ecumenical parishes;

7. cabinets and conference administrative leaders giving special attention to cooperative projects, ministries, and parishes as effective strategies for developing and maintaining ministry in a wide variety of congregations and communities, i.e., rural, urban, declining, stable, growing, racial/ethnic and multicultural, large and small membership churches, etc.;

8. cabinets and other annual conference leaders giving attention to encouraging cooperative projects, ministries, and parishes, as means by which to reach out and start new congregations in areas such as apartment complexes, mobile home parks, recreational areas, prisons, retirement homes, unincorporated sections of communities, etc.

ADOPTED 2004

See Social Principles, ¶162N.

53. Church and Community Workers

WHEREAS, current social and economic needs across the U.S.A. call upon the church for attention and action in accordance with Christ's teachings; and

WHEREAS, financial undergirding of human service programs by the public sector on all levels has failed to meet the needs of people; and

WHEREAS, developing contacts and linkages between local church/cooperative ministries and community groups is key to the understanding of and response to human hurt and need, and is a primary strength of the church and community ministry program; and

WHEREAS, for many decades church and community workers have worked effectively in mission outreach with The United Methodist Church in town and rural, urban, and specialized settings; and

WHEREAS, church and community workers are the only cadre of missionaries serving within the bounds of the U.S.A. who are employed and assigned by the General Board of Global Ministries;

Therefore, be it resolved, that the General Board of Global Ministries continue to recruit, enlist, train, adequately fund, and deploy church and community workers, and

Be it further resolved, that the funding partnership continue between the local area, annual conference, and the General Board of Global Ministries in order to place church and community workers in economically depressed areas where they are desperately needed.

ADOPTED 1992
REVISED AND READOPTED 2000

See Social Principles, ¶ 162P.

54. Use of Church Facilities by Community Groups

Encouragement shall be given for the use of local church facilities by community groups and agencies that serve social and service needs of the total community that are in keeping with the mission of The United Methodist Church.

ADOPTED 1970
AMENDED AND READOPTED 2000

See Social Principles, ¶ 162.

55. Volunteers in Mission

WHEREAS, the United Methodist Volunteers in Mission (UMVIM) movement is one of the most dynamic mission outreach programs of the denomination today; every conference has a UMVIM Coordinator in place. Some jurisdictions have paid full-time UMVIM coordinator who, because of the time commitment, able to assist their respective conferences more effectively than those coordinators in a part-time or volunteer position; and

WHEREAS, although United Methodist Volunteers in Mission is a major mission outreach now, with thousands of United Methodists participating annually, the potential is much greater; and

WHEREAS, the church needs to invest in ways which will enhance the program, involve even more United Methodists, and bring Christ's love to people and churches in need around the world. Full-time jurisdictional coordinators will be a great help in the expansion of this effective, hands-on mission and service outreach of The United Methodist Church,

Therefore, we recommend that every jurisdiction include in its budget a line item to cover the salary, professional expenses, and office expenses for a jurisdictional United Methodist Volunteers in Mission coordinator. In addition, we request the General Board of Global Ministries to enter into discussion with the central conferences relative to discovering the possibility of Volunteers in Mission programs in those conferences.

ADOPTED 2000

See Social Principles, ¶ 162.

56. Young Adult Ministries Organization

WHEREAS, the only established ministry for young adults is the Student Movement whose target audience is limited to college students and no forum or structure exists that allows for self-determination for young adults; and

WHEREAS, young adults are vital members of The United Methodist Church; and

WHEREAS, not all ministries are applicable to all age groups; and

WHEREAS, The United Methodist Church has ministries specifically designed for persons with common interests,

Therefore, be it resolved, that there be a study team formed to dialogue, research, and plan to evaluate the continually changing needs of young adult ministry. Additionally the team will make recommendations for:

1. assisting local churches and annual conferences in developing effective ministries for 18-30-year-old young adults;

2. assessing the need and funding pattern for organizations that focuses on church-wide effort on young adult ministry at the general church, annual conference and central conference level where they do not currently exist;

3. finding and learning from vital local ministries for young adults;

4. designing strategies for reaching out to young adults in relevant ways; and

5. creating a long-term plan which will allow The United Methodist Church to be on the "cutting edge" of ministry with young adults.

The effort shall be a collaborative partnership between the National Youth Ministry Organization, the United Methodist Student Movement, the General Board of Discipleship, and the General Board of Global Ministries. Selected staff persons shall serve as resource persons for the team. Each of these boards shall choose a non-board member to serve on the study team. All other general agencies (¶ 702.2) shall designate one young adult board member or staff person from their agency to participate on the study team.

The study team shall seek to be inclusive giving special attention to age, geographic representation, and educational and marital status. Expenses for each of the participants shall be covered by their respective agency. The General Board of Discipleship shall have the responsibility to convene the study team and provide adequate administrative resources. Upon completion of the report, the study team shall report back to the General Board of Discipleship.

ADOPTED 2000

See Social Principles, ¶ 162D.

AFRICAN AMERICANS

57. African American Family Life

Our Social Principles state that "we believe the family to be the basic human community through which persons are nurtured and sustained in mutual love, responsibility, respect, and fidelity" (¶ 161A).

Families of all types in the United States are vulnerable to social and economic change.

African American families today face problems of epidemic proportions from violence within the geographical community, new and virulent health problems, a high rate of cardiovascular illness, and economic stress.

We call upon the General Board of Discipleship to identify or create resources and materials to assist local churches in developing a program of mentoring, counseling, and referral that includes strategies to strengthen African American family life and to produce a listing of these resources to be distributed to and promoted in each annual conference.

ADOPTED 1992
AMENDED AND READOPTED 2000 AND 2004

See Social Principles, ¶ 162A.

58. A History of Blacks

An examination and assessment of the Methodist legacy in America reveals that Black persons and their contributions continue to receive inadequate credits, and there are more written resources available about Blacks in the history of Methodism.

Literature about Black persons in the Methodist history and/or literature written from the perspective of the Black ethos is perceived as resources primarily for Black persons, while an important element in the interrelationship of the different groups within the church family is to respect thoroughly and understand the uniqueness and contributions of Black persons in the evolving history of Methodism and the U.S.A.

We call upon the General Commission on Archives and History and The United Methodist Publishing House, in joint consultation with the General Commission on Religion and Race, to determine the most effective means to identify additional Black literary and historical records that have not been acknowledged and/or published; promote the use of these and other such resources among whites and other racial and ethnic minorities; and encourage training sessions led by Blacks using these resources that acknowledge the contributions of Black persons to the legacy and heritage of Methodism in the United States of America and the world and that a listing of these resources be distributed to each conference.

ADOPTED 1992
AMENDED AND READOPTED 2004

See Social Principles, ¶ 162A.

59. Resourcing Black Churches in Urban Communities

WHEREAS, the struggle for social, economic, and political survival of Black people in the United States is manifested in their historical migration to urban centers; and

WHEREAS, the problems that have evolved through the decade now face this population of people, isolated from access to the material resources needed to unleash its power and creativity in a manner that will build rather than destroy communities; and

WHEREAS, the Black United Methodist churches in urban communities have historically been centers of spiritual nurture and social and political action that have cared for the youth and offered viable alternatives to the negative aspects of decaying urban centers; and

WHEREAS, there is a demonstrated need in all urban communities in this country for strong, vital Black congregations to reach into the hurts and pains of the community and provide the spiritual revival that is needed in order to reclaim individuals and communities and manifest the healing power of God to combat drugs, violence, and a growing sense of hopelessness; and

WHEREAS, the gospel mandates that we "seek the welfare of the city where I have sent you into exile, and pray to the LORD on its behalf, for in its welfare you will find your welfare" (Jeremiah 29:7); and

WHEREAS, Black United Methodist congregations in urban communities are called, as are all churches, to minister to the needs of persons in the communities where the church is located; and

WHEREAS, the conditions in urban communities for Black persons continue to worsen, and the need for grounding in a faith and reliance on the power of God for the strength and vision to reclaim and rebuild strong, proud, faith-centered communities grows daily while the resources and persons in Black urban congregations decrease;

Therefore, be it resolved, that the General Conference direct the General Board of Discipleship to develop programs and strategies that will enable the development of Black leadership, and specific programs and strategies that will foster financial self-sufficiency, such as launching a stewardship education program.

Be it further resolved, that the General Board of Global Ministries work with existing Black churches in urban communities to develop and maintain vital congregations providing practical ministries that address the spiritual, social, and economic decline in these communities.

Be it further resolved, that the General Board of Global Ministries coordinate its work in strengthening Black urban congregations with the General Board of Discipleship, the annual conferences and urban ministry units of annual conferences, the Strengthening the Black Church for the Twenty-First Century initiative.

ADOPTED 1992
AMENDED AND READOPTED 2004

See Social Principles, ¶ 162A.

60. Black Leadership

Be it resolved, that The United Methodist Church in all of its annual conferences will actively seek to identify Black clergy and laity for leadership positions at the local, district, annual conference, jurisdictional, and general church levels. Such active identification may be accomplished through:

- the conducting of district leadership training seminars, to which at least three members of each predominantly Black church have been invited;
- the establishment of a "mentor system" in which an effective Black leader would become a mentor to a potential Black leader and would encourage and assist that person in the full development of his or her leadership skills;
- the frequent fellowshipping of racial and ethnic congregations, leading to an understanding and knowledge of racial differences; and
- bishops' and district superintendents' actively choosing Black United Methodists to fill appointive positions in the district, annual conference, jurisdictional, and general church levels.

Be it further resolved, that each conference shall include a report of its progress in its annual conference journal.

ADOPTED 1992
AMENDED AND READOPTED 2004

See Social Principles, ¶ 162A.

61. Observance of Martin Luther King Jr. Day

The prophetic witness of Dr. Martin Luther King, Jr. for justice and peace embodies the spirit of the Social Creed, the Social Principles of The United Methodist Church and the inclusiveness of our denomination. His words continue to inspire and guide our commitment to the whole Gospel:

"We cannot be truly Christian people so long as we flaunt the central teachings of Jesus: brotherly love and the Golden Rule."—Martin Luther King, Jr.

"Was not Jesus an extremist for love—'Love your enemies, bless them that curse you, pray for them that despitefully use you." Was not Amos an extremist for justice—'Let justice roll down like waters and righteousness like a mighty stream.' Was not Paul an extremist for the gospel of Jesus Christ—'I bear in my body the marks of the Lord Jesus.' Was not Martin Luther an extremist—'Here I stand; I can do none other so help me God.' Was not John Bunyan an extremist—'I will stay in jail to the end of my days before I make a butchery of my conscience.' Was not Abraham Lincoln an extremist—'This nation cannot survive half slave and half free.' Was not Thomas Jefferson an extremist—'We hold these truths to be self-evident, that all men are created equal.' So the question is not whether we will be extremist but what kind of extremist will we be. Will we be extremists for hate or will we be extremists for love? Will we be extremists for the preservation of injustice—or will we be extremists for the cause of justice? In that dramatic scene on Calvary's hill, three men were crucified. We must not forget that all three were crucified for the same crime—the crime of extremism. Two were extremists for immorality, and thusly fell below their environment. The other, Jesus Christ, was an extremist for love, truth and goodness, and thereby rose above his environment.—Martin Luther King, Jr.

The observance of Martin Luther King Jr. Day enriches and strengthens our social witness today.

Therefore, be it resolved, that each annual conference observe Martin Luther King Jr. Day with appropriate services of commemoration in recognition of Dr. King; and on that day we recommend that we close the bishops' office, all conference offices, all district offices, all local church offices, and, where feasible, business offices of church-related institutions; and that we support local activities surrounding the celebration of Dr. King's life and ministry; that we encourage local school districts not to hold classes on Martin Luther King Jr. Day; and that if local school districts hold classes, we encourage them to use Martin Luther King Jr. Day to celebrate Dr. King's work and address the need for the continuing struggle for justice.

ADOPTED 1992
AMENDED AND READOPTED 2004

See Social Principles, ¶ 162A.

62. Support Reparations for African Americans

WHEREAS, the General Conference acknowledges and profoundly regrets the massive human suffering and the tragic plight of millions of men, women, and children caused by slavery and the transatlantic slave trade; and

WHEREAS, at the conclusion of the Civil War, the plan for the economic redistribution of land and resources on behalf of the former slaves of the Confederacy was never enacted; and

WHEREAS, the failure to distribute land prevented newly freed Blacks from achieving true autonomy and made their civil and political rights all but meaningless; and

WHEREAS, conditions comparable to "economic depression" continue for millions of African Americans in communities where unemployment often exceeds 50 percent; and

WHEREAS, justice requires that African American descendants of the transatlantic slave trade be assured of having access to effective and appropriate protection and remedies, including the right to seek just and adequate reparation or satisfaction for the legacy of damages, consequent structures of racism and racial discrimination suffered as a result of the slave trade; and

WHEREAS, Isaiah 61:1-3 provides a model for reparations: "He has sent me to bind up the brokenhearted, to proclaim freedom for the captives, . . . to proclaim the year of the Lord's favor,... and provide for those who grieve in Zion—to bestow on them a crown of beauty instead of ashes, the oil of gladness instead of mourning, and a garment of praise instead of a spirit of despair."; and,

WHEREAS, January 5, 1993, Congressman John Conyers Jr. (D-Mich.) introduced H.R. 40 to the House of Representatives, calling for the establishment of the Commission to Study Reparation Proposals for African Americans, "acknowledging the fundamental injustice, cruelty, brutality and inhumanity of slavery in the United States from 1619 to the present day," for the purpose of submitting a report to Congress for further action and consideration with respect to slavery's effects on African American lives, economics, and politics;

Therefore, be it resolved:

1. that we support the discussion and study of reparation for African Americans;

2. that we petition the President, the Vice President, and the United States House of Representatives to support the passage and signing of H.R. 40;

3. that a written copy of this petition be delivered to the President and Vice President of the United States, the United States Senate

Majority Leader, the House Speaker, and House Member John Conyers Jr.

4. that the General Commission on Religion and Race and the General Board of Church and Society develop a strategy for interpretation and support of passage of H.R. 40;

5. That the appropriate general boards and agencies of The United Methodist Church develop and make available to its members data on the history of slavery and the role of theology in validating and supporting both the institution and the abolition of the slave trade; and

6. That we call upon The United Methodist Church to acknowledge the memory of the victims of past tragedies and affirm that, wherever and whenever these tragedies occur, they must be condemned and their recurrence prevented

ADOPTED 1996
AMENDED AND ADOPTED 2004

See Social Principles, ¶ 162A.

CHILDREN

63. Childcare and the Church

Today's Families

Families today need the church to provide quality, loving care in a safe, stimulating learning environment. More parents of both genders and all socioeconomic classes are entering the labor force, returning to school, and returning to job training programs. More parents are choosing to remain single. Although the number of divorces in the United States shows recent indications of decreasing, the number of children living in a single-parent-headed household continues to increase. With men and women waiting until later in life to become parents, their work patterns are already established and they often continue in those patterns after having children. With increasing awareness of the benefits of early childhood education, parents are seeking programs that enhance their children's physical, mental, emotional, social, and spiritual growth. The strain of parenting is recognized in cases of child neglect and abuse, as we see through daily reports of the media. There is a need for respite care outside the home to allow parents to resolve issues of neglect and abuse. Parents of a single child or of children with a wide age range recognize the need for their child or children to participate in regular socialization opportunities. Children with special needs, long-term health care needs, and minor illnesses also need childcare while parents must work.

Our Call

Our service of infant baptism in The United Methodist Church recognizes the sacredness of each person from birth and our responsibility to nurture each child in the faith. In proclaiming that sacredness and recognizing each child as a child of God, we in the church carry a commitment to help enable people to live life in the fullness that Jesus proclaimed.

We promise ". . . We will surround these persons with a community of love and forgiveness, that they may grow in their service to others . . ." (*The United Methodist Hymnal,* page 40). In recognition of this promise and in response to the sacredness of all children, our vision for childcare must include a vision of services available to all families on an equitable basis. "The Christian faith mandates us to recognize and respond to the value of each human person. Our task as the church is to minister to the needs of all persons and to ensure for them a caring community where all may be nurtured in a dignified and loving manner. This mandate is to be seen not as a burden, but rather as an opportunity." (Adopted 1984. From *The Book of Resolutions of The United Methodist Church,* 1996. Copyright © 1996 by The United Methodist Publishing House. Used by permission; page 224.) Through the particular ministry of childcare, we extend the nurturing ministry of the church and proclaim justice to children, families, and communities.

Childcare is not only a nurturing concern but also a pastoral and prophetic concern for the church. The church has important responsibilities in initiating, encouraging, and participating in the highest quality of childcare for children and families, not only in the local community but also nationwide.

Therefore, we recommend the following:

1. *See childcare as planned ministry.* Each congregation of The United Methodist Church that houses or supports any childcare program

must intentionally assess its understanding of discipleship as it relates to this program. Childcare is a valid expression of the Christian faith. However, programs in local churches too often exist without much thought to intentional ministry. Concerns often focus on budgeting and facility use instead of the ministry of the programs. When this happens, misunderstandings arise between the childcare program and the congregation, and missed opportunities occur for witnessing and mirroring the Christian faith. Each childcare program may encompass one or all of the following expressions of ministry. A particular congregation may choose any avenue of ministry, but it is important that each congregation be intentional, involving thought and prayer. What are the congregation's gifts for ministry with children? What is the mission of childcare? How is the intentional ministry a part of the daily operation of the program?

Congregations must determine how the childcare program embraces the church's mission.

a. Nurture includes Christian education, stewardship, and worship. In a program that focuses on nurture, spiritual development through Christian education is central. An intentional part of the curriculum should be the selection of stories (biblical and secular) and methods, and the integration of "God talk" and Christian values into daily conversations and interactions. When celebrations follow the church year, and when themes are based on Christian concepts, our faith traditions are an intentional part of the curriculum. Also included in nurture is stewardship. In our childcare programs, we reflect our commitment to being God's stewards in the ways we use and allocate our physical resources. We also reflect an understanding of the precarious balance of the world in an ecological sense. When children are cared for, they learn to care for others and for their world.

b. Outreach includes the areas of advocacy, safety, health, welfare, and equity, and how well they are addressed in our communities. Embracing outreach as a part of a weekday ministry program follows our traditional roots of caring for the needs of the community. As a congregation responds to the needs of people in the community through weekday ministry, the community and the congregation discover many blessings. Such a program addresses safety issues, social justice issues, equity issues, and health issues. Specialty childcare that addresses community issues might include care for infants, ill children, children of families at risk, children with special needs, children who are survivors of abuse, children with language barriers, migrant or refugee children, school-age children, and young adolescents. Each congregation should determine the unmet needs of their surrounding community. When possible, congregations should work collaboratively with other community agencies and groups to assure that needs are being met without duplication of efforts and in support of each other. When unable to meet the needs of a community, congregations must be outspoken advocates for needs of children in their community.

c. Witness includes the areas of evangelism, membership care, and spiritual formation. In embracing witness as our particular expression of ministry, we proclaim God active in our lives. As Jesus told us to proclaim the good news, so we must through our childcare ministries. Through these ministries, we can minister to the spiritual needs of children and their families. Not to do so is to turn our backs on our call to go into the world proclaiming the message of Jesus Christ.

A witness to our faith speaks clearly through the actions of weekday ministry boards, through the caring love of the staff, through the use of developmentally appropriate practices, through gentle and caring words, through the curriculum, through the environment of the facilities, and through the attitude of the congregation.

Every congregation of The United Methodist Church needs to define its ministry through childcare and include a statement of this ministry through weekday programs as part of employee handbooks, parent handbooks, community statements, and church reports.

2. *Uphold the quality of childcare in the church.* Any time a child enters a childcare program housed in a church, expectations are raised regarding quality of the program, behavior of the childcare staff and church staff, and adherence to the Christian doctrines of love and justice. Whether a congregation sees itself as actually sponsoring the program or as merely a landlord, since the program is in the church, families have different expectations than if they were taking their child to a commercial childcare facility. A church cannot divorce itself, either morally or legally, from what takes place in its building through childcare programs.

a. Program Reviews: For this reason, annual review of the child-care program should take place. Concern should be given to the curriculum, the involvement of the congregation with the program, pastoral availability to families and staff involved in childcare, safe and clean buildings and equipment, and the highest quality in staff and staff support. The process for the program review must be jointly determined by the childcare staff, church personnel, and informed, interested laity. A plan must be in place.

b. Licensing: The purpose of licensing standards is to protect children. Safety, health, space, and staff requirements provide a foundation for establishing and maintaining good programs for children. The regulations of basic health and safety conditions in a building/program that serves children are the appropriate responsibility of the state and do not interfere with the free exercise of religion. United Methodists have been meeting such standards for years in other areas of the life of the church, such as camping. A congregation is responsible to provide the best care for children when they gather in a church building. Regarding licensing procedures, congregations should seek to at least meet, if not surpass, the standards set in their community. Even if a program is license-exempt by the state, an effort should be made to meet licensing requirements for safety and for integrity. Congregations should also seek to be actively informed about such licensing procedures and requirements and should work to reform such regulations when they do not mandate standards that serve the best interests of children.

c. Self-Study: Through a self-study process, every childcare facility can look for ways to evaluate the care provided. Churches should follow some process of self-study for their childcare programs on a regular basis. Such studies involve both the childcare providers and the congregation and allow them to continuously assess the effectiveness of the ministry they are providing. These self-studies are available through some annual conferences, the Ecumenical Child Care Network, and the National Association of Early Childhood Programs (a division of the National Association for the Education of Young Children).

d. Personnel: As congregations seek to support childcare programs, salary, benefits, and support of the staff of these programs should be of concern and subject to review and discussion to insure the best for the children and families involved. Congregations must assure that children are served through the best caregivers. Congregations have a responsibility to advocate for higher pay and benefits for childcare workers. These professional caregivers should maintain excellence and integrity in the important job they do, and they should be appropriately compensated for it.

With increased concern around issues of child abuse, congregations need to assure that all childcare providers have been adequately screened for child abuse and neglect in accordance with laws of local jurisdiction, especially in the area of sexual misconduct. Appropriate screening protects the children, the childcare providers, and the congregation. The personnel issue also includes a concern for the education and training of childcare workers. A yearly plan for continuing education should be part of the congregation's support for childcare providers. Many childcare providers have extensive training and education in the field. They are good sources for training of those who work with children in other areas of the church, including childcare workers for Sunday services, Sunday school teachers, and vacation Bible school teachers. For those who are hired without proper training and education, the congregations should sponsor and encourage attendance at continuing education events.

3. *Be advocates for quality childcare.* Going beyond the congregation, United Methodists should be diligent advocates for childcare nationwide. The following suggestions are for individuals and groups within congregations who seek to better the place of children in American society:

   a. Become informed about childcare conditions existing today and the issues involved in the design of an adequate public policy for childcare. Address the issues through eliciting a response of commitment from the policy makers.
   b. Use the appropriate councils and agencies of the church to monitor public policy at federal, state, and local levels of government.
   c. Become involved not only in church conferences and meetings but in the larger arena of childcare through such organizations as the Children's Defense Fund, the National Association for the Education of Young Children, and the Ecumenical Child Care Network.

d. Call upon staff at the General Board of Church and Society in Washington, DC, and within each annual conference. They are charged with particular responsibility for the church's involvement in public policy processes in order to monitor, serve as an advocate for, raise issues concerning, and bring the voice of the church to bear on childcare policy development.

e. Call upon the staff of the General Board of Discipleship and the United Methodist Publishing House to express arising needs as they relate to program support, needed curriculum, and policies regarding church and childcare center relationships.

f. Call upon the General Board of Global Ministries to assist churches in responding to childcare needs in their communities with appropriate programs and resources.

g. Call upon the General Board of Discipleship in consultation with the General Council on Finance and Administration to make available to local congregations resources that address legal aspects and procedures to follow in establishing childcare facilities and/or programs.

ADOPTED 2000

See Social Principles, ¶ 162C.

64. Eradicating Abusive Child Labor

In the Gospels, the disciples' attitude toward God was measured by their attitude toward children and their ability to "become as a little child." The protection of childhood and the nurture of children are, therefore, among our most sacred human responsibilities. Reflecting this, the Social Principles of The United Methodist Church uphold the rights of children to growth and development, adequate nutrition, health services, housing, education, recreation, protection against all forms of racial discrimination, cruelty, neglect, and exploitation.

However, throughout the world, childhood itself is under assault by new as well as historic forces. Today's child, in too many parts of the world, must not only cope with warfare, famine, and pestilence at an early age, but is too often denied childhood itself by being forced into labor under abusive and destructive conditions. Many millions of children around the world labor in work that is coerced, forced, bonded, enslaved or otherwise unfair in wages, injurious to health and safety, and/or obstructive of educational or moral development.[1]

WHEREAS, the majority of child labor is found in informal sectors of the world's poorest economies, a growing element in global competition is the employment of children in developing-country export industries making products such as vegetables, fruit, tea, coffee, glass, garments, brassware, leather goods, and hand-knotted carpets for sale on the international market. The oriental carpet industry employs one of the most abusive forms of bonded child labor, involving perhaps as many as one million children in South Asia.[2]

In the United States, as many as 200,000 children work in agriculture as paid or unpaid labor, often under dangerous conditions without adequate protection, and at significant risk to their education.

The United Nations and the International Labor Organization (ILO) have established universal principles to protect children from such abuse, including the International Covenant on the Rights of the Child and the ILO Convention No. 138 for Minimum Age for Admission to Work. These international conventions have been ratified by many countries, not including the United States.

There is growing awareness in international-development agencies that child labor is not a byproduct of generalized poverty, but is rooted in specific policies that disproportionately neglect or disadvantage certain populations—ethnic, caste, or gender groups—and that unbalanced development policies have contributed to the exacerbation of child labor.[3]

We therefore call on The United Methodist Church:

1. to support public policies that include the ratification and enforcement of international labor conventions regarding child labor, affirmed by The United Methodist Church in the resolution on the "Rights of Workers" (adopted 1988), and the Convention on the Rights of the Child, affirmed by The United Methodist Church in the resolution on the "Ratification of Human Rights Covenants and Conventions";

2. to work to eradicate the evils of child labor through encouraging the appropriate agencies and units to join the Child Labor Coalition,

1. A. Bequele and W.E. Myers, First Things First in Child Labor: Eliminating Work Detrimental to Children, ILO and UNICEF, 1995; pages 1-27.

2. U.S. Department of Labor, *By the Sweat and Toil of Children*, 1994.

3. Pharis J. Harvey, "Where Children Work: Child Servitude in the Global Economy," *The Christian Century*, April 5, 1995; pages 362-65.

a broad-based coalition of medical, welfare, religious, consumer, labor, and human-rights organizations in the United States, and to support such consumer initiatives as the RUGMARK campaign, initiated in India by UNICEF, the South-Asian Coalition on Child Servitude, and others to label and market oriental carpets made without exploited child labor;

3. to support legislative and administrative measures to enforce bans against the international trafficking in goods made by child labor;

4. to support unilateral and multilateral aid and development policies that attack the root causes of child labor, such as lack of basic education, gender and caste prejudice, and unbalanced development schemes that disadvantage certain populations; and

5. to work toward the reform of United States labor laws to provide better protection of farm workers' rights and to bring child labor restrictions into conformity with international standards.

ADOPTED 1996
REVISED AND ADOPTED 2000

See Social Principles, ¶ 162C.

65. Reducing the Risk of Child Sexual Abuse in the Church

Jesus said, "Whoever welcomes [a] child . . . welcomes me" (Matthew 18:5). Children are our present and our future, our hope, our teachers, our inspiration. They are full participants in the life of the church and in the realm of God.

Jesus also said, "If any of you put a stumbling block before one of these little ones . . . it would be better for you if a great millstone were fastened around your neck and you were drowned in the depth of the sea" (Matthew 18:6). Our Christian faith calls us to offer both hospitality and protection to the little ones, the children. The Social Principles of The United Methodist Church state that "children must be protected from economic, physical, emotional and sexual exploitation and abuse" (¶ 162C).

Tragically, churches have not always been safe places for children. Child sexual abuse, exploitation, and ritual abuse1 occur in churches, both large and small, urban and rural. The problem cuts across all economic, cultural, and racial lines. It is real, and it appears to be increasing. Most annual conferences can cite specific incidents of child sexual abuse and exploitation within churches. Virtually every congregation has among its members adult survivors of early sexual trauma.

Such incidents are devastating to all who are involved: the child, the family, the local church, and its leaders. Increasingly, churches are torn apart by the legal, emotional, and monetary consequences of litigation following allegations of abuse.

1. "Ritual abuse" refers to abusive acts committed as part of ceremonies or rites; ritual abusers are often related to cults, or pretend to be.

2. God calls us to make our churches safe places, protecting children and other vulnerable persons from sexual and ritual abuse. God calls us to create communities of faith where children and adults grow safe and strong. In response to this churchwide challenge, the following steps should be taken to reduce the risk of child sexual abuse:

A. Local churches should:

1. develop and implement an ongoing education plan for the congregation and its leaders on the reality of child abuse, risk factors leading to child abuse, and strategies for prevention;

2. adopt screening procedures (use of application forms, interviews, reference checks, background clearance, and so forth) for workers (paid and unpaid) directly or indirectly involved in the care of children and youth;

3. develop and implement safety procedures for church activities such as having two or more nonrelated adults present in classroom or activity; leaving doors open and installing half-doors or windows in doors or halls; providing hall monitors; instituting sign-in and sign-out procedures for children ages ten or younger; and so forth;

4. advise children and young persons of an agency or a person outside as well as within the local church whom they can contact for advice and help if they have suffered abuse;

5. carry liability insurance that includes sexual abuse coverage;

6. assist the development of awareness and self-protection skills for children and youth through special curriculum and activities; and

7. be familiar with annual conference and other church policies regarding clergy sexual misconduct.

B. Annual conferences should:

1. develop safety and risk-reducing policies and procedures for conference-sponsored events such as camps, retreats, youth gatherings, childcare at conference events, mission trips, and so forth; and

2. develop guidelines and training processes for use by church leaders who carry responsibility for prevention of child abuse in local churches. Both sets of policies shall be developed by a task force appointed by the cabinet in cooperation with appropriate conference agencies. These policies shall be approved by the annual conference and assigned to a conference agency for implementation. It is suggested that the policies be circulated in conference publications and shared with lay professionals and clergy at district or conference seminars.

C. *The General Board of Discipleship and the General Board of Global Ministries should:*

1. cooperatively develop and/or identify and promote the following resources;

2. sample policies, procedures, forms, and so forth for reducing the risk of sexual abuse and exploitation of children and youth in local churches, both in relation to their own sponsored programs and to any outreach ministries or other programs for children or youth that use church space;

3. child abuse prevention curriculum for use in local churches;

4. training opportunities and other educational resources on child sexual abuse and exploitation and on ritual abuse; and

5. resources on healing for those who have experienced childhood sexual trauma.

ADOPTED 1996
READOPTED 2004

See Social Principles, ¶ 162C.

66. Child Soldiers

Background[1]

Children represent the future of human civilization and the future of every society. To permit them to be used as pawns of warfare, whether

1. Background information provided verbatim from the Report of the United Nations Secretary General's Special Representative for Children and Armed Conflict to the General Assembly, 12 October 1998, "Protection of children affected by armed conflict."

as targets or perpetrators, is to cast a shadow on the future. From generation to generation, violence begets violence, as the abused grow up to become abusers. Children who are thus violated carry the scars of fear and hatred in their hearts and minds. Forced to learn to kill instead of pursuing education, the children of conflict lack the knowledge and skills needed to build their own futures and futures of their communities. For society, the lives destroyed and the opportunities lost can have devastating effects on its long-term stability and development.

As the Preamble to the Charter of the United Nations emphasizes, our first duty is "to save succeeding generations from the scourge of war." In this we have failed profoundly. Not only are millions of children still the victims of war, far too often they are its principal targets and even its instruments. Presently, in approximately 50 countries around the world, children are suffering from the effects of conflict and its aftermath.

For all the children deliberately massacred or caught in crossfire or maimed by antipersonnel land mines, many more have been deprived of their physical, mental, and emotional needs in societies at war. Millions have lost their homes and their parents, not to mention years of education and their youth. Some have been permanently traumatized by the events they have witnessed and experienced. In today's internecine conflicts, children are specifically targeted in strategies to eliminate the next generation of potential adversaries. To the same end, children, especially girls, have been made the targets of sexual abuse and gender-based violence on a large scale. Most cynically, children have been compelled to become instruments of war, recruited or kidnaped to become child soldiers, thus forced to give violent expression to the hatred of adults. In all, an estimated 2 million children have been killed in situations of armed conflict since 1987, while three times that number have been seriously injured or permanently disabled.

The international community has an obligation to be concerned about the protection of all noncombatants caught in the midst of violent conflicts. Yet there is an urgent need to focus special attention on the plight of children. They are the ones least responsible for conflict, yet most vulnerable to its excesses. Children, as the most innocent and powerless victims of armed conflict, require special protection. In zones of conflict, international advocacy and intercession are essential to ensure that parties to conflict commit themselves to the protection of children from exploitation, abuse, and brutalization. The international community must ensure that those who target children do not continue to do so with impunity.

The United Methodist Church urges:

1. The General Boards of Global Ministries and Church and Society, and the Bishops' Initiative on Children and Poverty to work with local churches to implement the recommendations of the World Council of Churches (Eighth Assembly, Harare, Zimbabwe) to:

- call for an immediate moratorium on the recruitment and participation of children as soldiers and the demobilization of existing child soldiers;
- work to prevent the compulsory or voluntary recruitment or re-recruitment of former soldiers, taking particular account of the needs of former girl soldiers;
- promote the establishment of international standards to this effect, in particular the adoption of an optional protocol to the Convention on the Rights of the Child raising the minimum age from 15 to 18 years for all forms of recruitment and participation in hostilities; and
- urge their national governments to adopt and apply such standards in their own national legislation.

2. The General Boards of Global Ministries and Church and Society, and Bishops' Initiative on Children and Poverty to:

- offer humanitarian assistance, where possible, to children traumatized by the experience of having been a child soldier; and
- urge United Methodists in the United States to demand that the United States government ratify the United Nations Convention on the Rights of the Child which only the United States and Somalia have not ratified.

ADOPTED 2000

See Social Principles, ¶¶ 162C and 164G.

67. Children's Sabbath

WHEREAS, "The program calendar of the denomination shall include only the Special Sundays approved by General Conference, Special Sundays approved by ecumenical agencies to which The

United Methodist Church is officially related, and the days and seasons of the Christian Year" (*1996 Book of Discipline*, ¶ 266); and

WHEREAS, the General Board of Global Ministries, Women's Division and the General Board of Church and Society have officially endorsed the 1999 Children's Sabbath of the ecumenically endorsed Children's Defense Fund; and

WHEREAS, the National Council of the Churches of Christ in the U.S.A., an ecumenical agency of which The United Methodist Church is a member, also endorses the National Observance of the Children's Defense Fund Children's Sabbath; and

WHEREAS, the United Methodist Bishops Initiative on Children and Poverty has been extended into the next quadrennium (2001-2004), without identifying a specific date of churchwide celebration and prayer for children and those living in poverty throughout the world;

Therefore, be it resolved, that the second weekend of October be identified as the Children's Sabbath on the program calendar of The United Methodist Church throughout the next quadrennium,

Be it further resolved, that this weekend is not to be classified as a churchwide special Sunday with offerings, or a special Sunday without churchwide offerings. The inclusion of said weekend is the inclusion of a special date approved by an ecumenical agency to which The United Methodist Church is officially related, with said observance requiring no financial support on the part of The United Methodist Church.

ADOPTED 1996
REVISED AND READOPTED 2000

See Social Principles, ¶ 162C.

68. Don't Allow Parents to Withhold Children's Medical Care

WHEREAS, the Federal Child Abuse Prevention and Treatment Act requires states participating in the grant program to include the failure to provide needed medical care in their definitions of child neglect; and

WHEREAS, the U.S. Congress enacted the above religious exemption to the requirement in 1996; and

WHEREAS, the religious exemption discriminates against a class of children, depriving them of protections to which other children are entitled; and

WHEREAS, many children have died or suffered permanent injury because their parents believed that the law allowed them to withhold medical care on religious grounds;

Therefore, be it resolved, that The United Methodist Church calls upon the U.S. Congress to repeal Section 5106i of Title 42 of the U.S. Code, which states, "Nothing in this subchapter and subchapter III, of this chapter, shall be construed as establishing a federal requirement that a parent or legal guardian provide a child any medical service or treatment against the religious beliefs of the parent or legal guardian . . . "

ADOPTED 2000

See Social Principles, ¶ 162C.

69. Prohibit Corporal Punishment in Schools and Child-Care Facilities

WHEREAS, schools and child-care facilities are the only institutions in America in which striking another person for the purpose of causing physical pain is legal,

WHEREAS, corporal punishment is humiliating and degrading to children and sometimes causes physical injury,

WHEREAS, it is difficult to imagine Jesus of Nazareth condoning any action that is intended to hurt children physically or psychologically,

WHEREAS, corporal punishment sends a message that hitting smaller and weaker people is acceptable,

WHEREAS, corporal punishment is used most often on poor children, minorities, children with disabilities, and boys,

WHEREAS, there are effective alternatives to corporal punishment that teach children to be self-disciplined rather than to submit out of fear,

WHEREAS, schools and child-care centers should inspire children to enjoy learning and school and child-care personnel should be able to encourage positive behavior without hitting children,

Therefore, be it resolved, that The United Methodist Church calls upon all states to enact laws prohibiting corporal punishment in schools and day and residential child-care facilities.

ADOPTED 2004

See Social Principles, ¶ 162C.

70. Discipline Children Without Corporal Punishment

WHEREAS, corporal punishment models aggressive behavior as a solution to conflict,

WHEREAS, some research has associated corporal punishment with increased aggression in children and adults, increased substance abuse, increased risk of crime and violence, low self-esteem, and chronic depression,

WHEREAS it is difficult to imagine Jesus of Nazareth condoning any action that is intended to hurt children physically or psychologically,

WHEREAS, time-outs and deprivation of privileges are as effective as corporal punishment in stopping undesirable behavior,

WHEREAS, the effectiveness of corporal punishment decreases with subsequent use and therefore leads caretakers to hit children more severely,

WHEREAS, children must eventually develop their own conscience and self-discipline, which are fostered by a home environment of love, respect, and trust,

Therefore, be it resolved, that The United Methodist Church encourages its members to adopt discipline methods that do not include corporal punishment of their children.

And be it further resolved, that The United Methodist Church encourages congregations to offer opportunities for dialogue and education on effective discipline of children.

ADOPTED 2004

See Social Principles, ¶ 162C.

CULTURAL ISSUES

71. African American Methodist Heritage Center

WHEREAS, Black Methodists for Church Renewal, Inc. (BMCR), a caucus of The United Methodist Church, has engaged in a process to establish and provide for the maintenance of an African American Methodist Heritage Center, connected with a historically Black institution, that will preserve and protect artifacts and be accessible for research about African American people in Methodism; and

WHEREAS, in spite of the best efforts of many, there is no single repository for the history, memories, and stories of those of African descent, who have been a part of Methodism since its inception in the mid 18th century and those of African descent who have stayed throughout Methodism's history; and

WHEREAS, the depositing of these artifacts will be symbolic of the stones that Joshua directed to be taken from the River Jordan and placed as a monument so that generations to come will always remember the trials and triumphs of our journey (Joshua 4:19-24); and

WHEREAS, BMCR has been in consultation with the General Commission on Archives and History, and both entities have entered into an agreement wherein the General Commission on Archives and History will be the temporary repository until a permanent location can be found in a historic African American United Methodist institution; and

WHEREAS, the General Commission on Religion and Race strongly supports the work of the Heritage Center as a partner in the collection of historical documents related to the Central Jurisdiction and views the Heritage Center as, possibly, the future home of materials related to the General Commission on Religion and Race Central Jurisdiction Recovery Project.

Therefore, be it resolved, that the General Conference of The United Methodist Church meeting in 2004 commend BMCR and the General Commission on Archives and History for their cooperation in the development of such a project and applaud all those who will work to assure this great legacy of our common history.

Be it further resolved, that all United Methodists find ways and means to be supportive of this project with their prayers, their memorabilia, and their gifts to ensure the successful completion of this project.

Be it further resolved, that the General Commission on Religion and Race be supportive of this initiative through its advocacy and consultative responsibilities.

Be it further resolved, that the African American Methodist Heritage Center, Inc., initiated by BMCR, in consultation with the General Commission on Archives and History, establish an endowment fund through The United Methodist Church Foundation and seek authorization, if appropriate, to solicit gifts in this fund for the purpose of financial support of the African American Methodist Heritage Center and its growth.

ADOPTED 2004

See Social Principles, ¶ 162A.

72. Affirming the Use of Diverse Languages in the United States and Opposing a Constitutional Amendment Making English the Official Language

The United States is a land whose inhabitants are enriched by diverse traditions, languages, and cultures. While English is the most commonly used or "primary" language of the country, there have always been other languages present throughout the history of the nation. Native American languages and Spanish were already spoken when the first English colonists arrived. Throughout that same history, there have been various efforts to prescribe the use of English and to proscribe the use of other languages. These efforts sometimes resulted in legislation that had the effect of legalizing discrimination against various language minority groups, as was the case for German, Swedish, French, Greek, and Italian immigrants who came to this country in great numbers during the nineteenth century. However, such legislative attempts were eventually overcome by the constitutional principles of equal rights for all. The acknowledgment of English as the primary language of the United States does not deny the right and contribution of other languages or the inherent right of people to retain and speak their mother tongues.

In recent years, there have been renewed efforts in different parts of the country to make English the official language of the nation. Notwithstanding their unsuccessful attempts to pass a constitutional amendment, we are now seeing concerted efforts to bring the same policy to state and local levels. We are concerned that the movement to declare constitutionally English as the official language of the nation is not based upon any real need but, in fact, may be motivated by an effort to deny the pluralistic foundation of the country and to deny the dignity and wholeness of persons from different racial and ethnic groups who rightly considered their languages an integral part of their cultures. We fear the real purpose of some may be not so much to make English the *official* language of the U.S. as to make English the *exclusive* language of the nation.

For example, there is an English-only "movement" that has gained more national recognition. Organizations such as "U.S. English" and "English First" continue gaining support through active national activities and local English-only campaigns. In addition to promotion of their principles through the media, they are also involved in various legislative and lobbying activities. These include efforts to pass a constitutional amendment making English the official language of the United States, opposition to federal legislation for bilingual education, voting-rights bills, and the FCC licensing applications for Spanish-language broadcasts.

These efforts and their implications are another manifestation of the systemic racism that has infected this country for generations. The English-only movement blames the deterioration of the American fabric on immigration and the use of languages other than English. It contends that the nation's unity rests upon the use of an official language. It defines multiculturalism and multilingualism as "anti-unity." Consequently, the movement, if successful, could further discriminate against and segregate the racial and ethnic population of the United States. Essential information such as the 911 emergency telephone number, hospital emergency rooms, police, firefighters, language services, bilingual education, and interpreters in the judicial system might be denied.

As Christians, we believe that we are children of God, created in God's image, and members of the family of God.

We believe that diversity is a gift of the creative genius of God and that languages are an expression of the wisdom of God.

We believe that competence in the English language is important to participate fully in the life of the United States, but we also acknowledge the fact that we live in a global context, the global family of God, where people and nations experience interdependency at all levels and where the acquisition of a second language represents a better understanding of other people's cultures, hopes, and dreams.

We believe that our nation needs to take advantage of the rich contributions that the ethnic/language groups bring to this country by preserving those languages and encouraging North Americans to learn other languages.

We believe that it is the will of God that each human being is affirmed as a whole person and that it is in the acceptance and interchange of our uniqueness that we find oneness—total wholeness—*shalom*.

We oppose the attempt to rob a person of his or her language as dehumanizing and as a denial of that person's wholeness.

We oppose the English-only movement as a manifestation of the sin of racism.

Therefore, be it resolved, that the General Conference shall:

1. express in writing to the President of the United States its support for practices and policies that permit provision of information in

languages appropriate to the residents of communities and its opposition to the movement that seeks to make English the only language of the United States, which movement is discriminatory and racist;

2. forward this resolution to members of Congress, governors, and the legislatures of the fifty states and territories;

3. commend this resolution to all United States annual conferences for promotion and interpretation within the annual conferences; and

4. ask the General Board of Church and Society to make this resolution an urgent item in their agenda for lobbying, constituency education, and advocacy.

ADOPTED 1988
AMENDED AND ADOPTED 2000

See Social Principles, ¶ 162.

73. Biracial/Multiracial Inclusive Language

WHEREAS, in 1967 the US Supreme Court ruled in Loving vs. Virginia that interracial marriages could not be banned, and a rise in interracial marriages has since occurred producing what can be identified as biracial children and a generation following, multiracial children; and

WHEREAS, the US Census Bureau has identified a significant biracial/multiracial population by reporting in 2001 that biracial/multiracial population is 2.4 percent of the total US population, 6,826,228; specifically, stating that the percentage of children being raised by one parent of a different race is 2.3 percent white, 6.3 percent black, 54 percent Native American, 18 percent Asian, and 13 percent other; and

WHEREAS, it has been reported that out of 35 percent of the current population (those born between 1982 and 2002) one in five have one immigrant parent, and when polled, 82 percent stated that they would date or marry outside their race[1]; and

WHEREAS, we are told that in Christ there is no Jew or Greek, there is no longer slave or free, there is no longer male and female (Galatians 3:28), we as a church should not be exclusive toward race, but actively inclusive; and

1. Howe, Neil and William Strauss. *Millennials Rising*. New York : Vintage Books, 2000. pp. 14-15, 218.

WHEREAS, in spite of our faith, many of our own forms within our church are exclusive requiring the growing population of biracial/multiracial people to choose between one parent or another, by requiring churchgoers to identify themselves by selecting only one of the six classical racial options: Asian, Black, Euro-American, Hispanic, Native American, and Pacific Islander;

Therefore, be it resolved, that The United Methodist Church expand its inclusive language in all aspects of the church to include biracial/multiracial persons by offering racial identification options that are not limiting but embracing of persons with more than one racial or ethnic background.

ADOPTED 2004

See Social Principles, ¶ 162A.

74. Replace Term "Ethnic Minority" with "Ethnic Person"

Be it resolved, that given the global nature of The United Methodist Church, that General Conference 2004 take action to remove the term *ethnic minority* from all future United Methodist *Disciplines* as a nomenclature for ethnic people or groups. Given the racial history of the United States of America, the term *minority*, for many people, is not only a means for describing the number of persons of a particular ethnic group but is often heard and experienced by ethnic persons to mean less than and not equal to in worth to the whole. Therefore, the term *minority* diminishes our capacity as United Methodists to see ourselves as part of the body of Christ where all persons are considered to be gifted, whole and equal but yet different.

Be it further resolved, that the term *racial/ethnic persons* replace the term *ethnic minority* where it is not feasible to name a particular ethnic group.

ADOPTED 2004

See Social Principles, ¶ 162A.

75. Holocaust Memorial Day (Yom HaShoah)

In recent years, Jewish communities have developed the custom of remembering the Holocaust (Shoah) on the Jewish calendar at a designated time each year. This observance has become a powerful means of educating people about this historical atrocity and sensitizing them to present and potential violence rooted in racial hatred.

WHEREAS, "In the twentieth century there is particular shame in the failure of most of the church to challenge the policies of governments that were responsible for the unspeakable atrocities of the Holocaust" (*Building New Bridges in Hope, Book of Resolutions* 1996);

WHEREAS, as the same document observes, "[t]he Christian Church has a profound obligation to correct historical and theological teachings that have led to false and pejorative perceptions of Judaism and contributed to persecution and hatred of Jews"; and

WHEREAS, we are currently (May 2000) remembering the 55th anniversary of the end of World War II;

Therefore, be it resolved, that the 2000 General Conference calls The United Methodist Church to contrition and repentance of its complicity in "the long history of persecution of the Jewish people" and asks the General Commission on Christian Unity and Interreligious Concerns to give special programmatic emphasis to Holocaust awareness and to prepare resources for use in local congregations, annual conferences and their Conference Commissions on Christian Unity and Interreligious Concerns or equivalent structures to enable them to become more aware of the Holocaust and its impact, and

Be it further resolved, as a sign of our contrition and our solidarity with the Jewish community, the General Conference urges the promotion of observance of Yom HaShoah, Holocaust Memorial Day, each spring in United Methodist local congregations and urges the General Commission on Christian Unity and Interreligious Concerns, in cooperation with other agencies of The United Methodist Church, in a time of increasing anti-Semitism, to work with our own denominations' history with regard to this tragedy and find ways to support the work against anti-Semitism in the world today and to prepare resources for local congregations to observe Yom HaShoah.

We continue to pray for God's grace to speak in Jesus' name against bigotry, hatred, genocide, or other crimes against humanity whenever we encounter them.

ADOPTED 2000

See Social Principles, ¶ 162.

76. Support for Multicultural and Ethnic-Specific Ministries

"The World is my parish" said John Wesley, the founder of Methodism. These words have been the motto of United Methodists throughout many generations. Today, when we seem to be living in the midst of an explosion of diversity, once again these words come alive and become more relevant. Even when racial/ethnic/cultural diversity has been a reality in the United States from its very beginnings, this diversity has reached a momentum in our common history both in church and in society. Mobility, advanced technology, war, political instability, and socioeconomic realities have brought the diversity of the world into our very own neighborhoods and churches, creating a challenge to old principles of church growth such as the homogenous theory.

In response to this reality, many churches have begun by developing multicultural ministries. However, the concern has been raised that the current trend for multicultural ministries has been placed in opposition to the continued development and strengthening of the racial/ethnic local church. Frequently the choice of a multicultural ministry has been done at the expense of what has been called ethnic specific ministries, e.g. Asian, Black, Hispanic, Pacific Islander, and Native American ministries. In other instances, multicultural ministries are being used to dismiss the uniqueness of the different groups; and/or simply as a superficial face make-up (a few different faces in the congregation) that does not impact the life, leadership style, and decision-making of the congregation. In these cases, multiculturalism can be a disguised form of racism.

WHEREAS, the General Commission on Religion and Race is mandated by the Church to ensure the equal participation of all believers as members of the same body that is the body of Christ; and

WHEREAS, the question of multicultural congregations or ethnic specific congregations is not an either/or proposition for inclusiveness but rather two distinct paths needed to achieve the inclusive spirit revealed to us at Pentecost, when people understood each other, not through a common language, but through the power of the Spirit who affirmed and embraced everyone (each one spoke in his/her own tongue), making of many, One; and

WHEREAS, a truly multicultural congregation is more than "token" participation of racial/ethnic persons, but is one that incorporates into the worship style, leadership, and entire ministry cultural elements of the different racial/ethnic groups present in the congregation thus ensuring that everyone has a place at the table where power is shared (resources and decision-making) and where conflict is managed collaboratively, and where everyone brings gifts to the mutually "owned table," and where the entire congregation is shaped by all and not by one dominant group; and

WHEREAS, ethnic specific ministries have historically been a source of strength, encouragement, and empowerment for people of color, and have enabled people to move outside of their local congregations to participate in the larger church and have contributed greatly to the inclusiveness of the church; and

WHEREAS, it is important that the church is sensitive to the context of all people and reaches people where they are, including culture and language; and

WHEREAS, one of the principles of inclusiveness is self-determination, and people of color in their continued quest for empowerment in the midst of a racist church and society should have the power to determine if their cultural and spiritual needs are best met in an ethnic specific congregation or in a multicultural one; and

WHEREAS, on many occasions an "ethnic specific" congregation can be the beginning of becoming a multicultural church; and

WHEREAS, multicultural ministries should be look upon as one of the models of the inclusive and multicultural church, and that there are many ways in which the church can be multicultural and inclusive without being together in the same worship service always, such as community work, mission, children and youth, church governance, etc.

Be it Resolved that:

The United Methodist Church's commitment to inclusiveness affirms the continued development and strengthening of the racial/ethnic congregations as well as the development and strengthening of congregations that respect, understand, and embrace diversity becoming truly multicultural congregations as defined above;

The Council of Bishops give direction to their annual conferences on this issue so that local churches are provided with resources and guidance in their efforts to respond to their diverse communities;

The General Board of Global Ministries and the General Board of Discipleship continue providing leadership and resources in the development of racial/ethnic congregations and multicultural congregations where everyone has a place at the table and power is shared;

The General Commission on Religion and Race continues collaborating with the General Board of Global Ministries, the General Board of Higher Education and Ministry, the General Board of Church and Society, and the General Board of Discipleship in the development of resources that undergird the creation and the strengthening of multicultural and ethnic specific ministries;

The United Methodist seminaries incorporate into their curriculums the subjects needed to prepare students who will be able to minister in different and diverse settings.

ADOPTED 2004

See Social Principles, ¶ 162A.

77. Inclusiveness in All Dimensions of the Church

A door of opportunity has been opened to The United Methodist Church—the opportunity to consolidate endeavors to discern the barriers to racial and cultural inclusiveness. Many annual conferences responded to the action of the 1992 and 1996 General Conferences calling upon annual conferences to develop "programs to emphasize inclusiveness in all dimensions of the church." However, many annual conferences have not yet responded to that call.

In recognition of the need to plan in order to implement intentions to be inclusive, the 2004 General Conference reaffirms the commitment that each annual conference, led by the bishop and cabinet, develop comprehensive programs that place fresh emphasis upon inclusiveness—cultural, racial, lingual, gender—throughout the life and ministry of The United Methodist Church.

These plans should provide that strategies similar to those outlined in the resolution adopted in 1992 continue:

1. that this program include a conference-wide enlistment and recruitment program that seeks clergy and laity who will give themselves to cross-racial and cross-cultural appointments, to begin new Sunday schools and congregations among poor people and people of color;

2. that the program include a determined effort to enlist and recruit some of the most competent, experienced pastors for such cross-racial and cross-cultural appointments rather than simply enlisting the newest clergy;

3. that local churches are trained and enabled to reach out to their surrounding communities;

4. that this "inclusive" emphasis include asking and actively encouraging all multistaff congregations to deliberately make their staffs inclusive in terms of gender, race, and ethnicity;

5. that goals and strategies be established in each conference so that cross-racial and cross-cultural appointments become normative for the conference and one of the essential ways in which the conference engages in the mission of Christ;

6. that the program include experiences for the conference lay and clergy leadership that increase their knowledge and understanding of all the people and cultures who reside within the borders of the conference;

7. that this conference program include programs for children and youth, such as multicultural camps, human-relations conferences/ seminars, and various kinds of work camps;

8. that the conference program include the enlisting and recruitment of young adults to become "people in mission" who work on a subsistence basis or pay their own way;

9. that this program enable the establishment of new congregations—rural, suburban, and urban—in town and country;

10. that this program will encourage diversity in styles and kinds of ministries, in worship styles, and in language and thought forms in order to enable the gospel and The United Methodist Church to again have impact on working-class people, the poor, people of color, and other target groups of people;

11. that this program make appointments of clergy to ministries of justice and peace, to ministries of prevention and rehabilitation in drug abuse, and to children and young people caught in the spiraling crisis of drugs, violence, racism, and poverty;

12. that each conference program will include assisting local congregations and pastors in sharing-facilities situations to develop an "inclusive" model for the congregation, even though worship services occur in several languages, and in eliminating the "landlord-tenant" model of relationships;

13. that the program include a provision that we will no longer sell church buildings in the urban areas to churches of other denominations but will instead place clergy and laity in those situations, assisting them in finding the way to create a new people in that place for mission to the people in that community;

14. that the conference program will include a major training and additional skills strategy, using pastors' schools, annual conference sessions, and United Methodist theological schools (where a United Methodist seminary is not within the bounds of the conference or area, the conference should enlist schools of other denominations) to create resources for the inclusive ministry and to empower conference clergy and laity; and

15. that this conference program also include innovative ministries in urban, suburban, and rural areas, so that an unfettered gospel can do the work of the Crucified and Risen One.

Further, that as annual conferences continue to revise and perfect their inclusiveness programs, that special attention be given to the following points of concentration:

1. that Comprehensive Plans for Racial Ethnic Ministries be reviewed, revised, and implemented. Further, that the Comprehensive Plans incorporate the recommendations of the national plans adopted by General Conference, the National Plan for Hispanic/Latino-Latina Ministries, the Native American Comprehensive Plan, Strengthening the Black Church for the 21st Century, Advancing United Methodist Ministries Among Korean Americans, the Asian Ameerican Language Ministry Plan, and other plans for racial and ethnic ministries that may be approved by General Conference;

2. that bishops and cabinets design specific strategies with timelines to make cross-racial and cross-cultural appointments the norm rather than the exception. That these strategies include preparation of pastors, congregations, and pastor-parish relations committees before an appointment is made, and provisions for support for pastors and congregations in cross-racial and cross-cultural appointments;

3. that annual conference leaders at all levels—local church, district, conference, bishops, and cabinets—seek ways to enhance their skills in the areas of interpersonal communication, cross-cultural communication, and conflict management and resolution. The General Commission on Religion and Race may be consulted for resources;

4. that councils on ministries (or their equivalent) provide opportunities for ongoing dialogueamong people of different races, cultures, ethnicities, gender, ages, abilities, disabilities, and theological perspectives at all levels of the conference about what it means to be the inclusive church.

And further, that the delegates at the various jurisdictional conferences and their nominating committees be urged to be intentional in their nominations to the various general boards and agencies to ensure that racial/ethnic persons are elected to these boards and agencies in representative numbers; and that the nominating committees of each annual conference include in their nomination and election process an equitable number of racial/ethnic persons on every board and agency.

We call upon the General Commission on Religion and Race to monitor the progress of each annual conference's plans for inclusiveness and the content of jurisdictional and conference nominations reports.

ADOPTED 1996
AMENDED AND READOPTED 2004

See Social Principles, ¶ 162A and H.

78. Prejudice Against Muslims and Arabs in the U.S.A.

Today in the United States of America there are approximately 3 million persons who are adherents of Islam. Arab Americans, both Christian and Muslim, constitute a growing number of persons in the American population. These persons are suffering the effects of a particularly virulent prejudice too often aided and abetted by statements and images in the media and by rhetoric from some of the highest political leadership. The suffering of this community has increased dramatically since the tragic events of September 11, 2001.As part of the fabric of racism in the U.S.A., in which both subtle and violent acts continue against ethnic groups and persons, such acts are also being perpetrated against the Arab and Muslim communities in the U.S.A. These expressions of racism manifested in violent acts have also increased since September 11, 2001.

Arab American organization offices, mosques, and Islamic centers have been bombed and torched. Leaders of these communities have been murdered and questionable uses of law have been utilized to stifle the rights of association and freedom of expression. Arab persons and/or persons looking like Arabs are being detained in airports and other places without justification. They are continually subjected to harassment and discrimination. Though discriminatory acts against Arabs and Muslims do not stand in isolation from similar acts perpetrated against other racial and ethnic persons in the

U.S.A., their existence and effects upon Arabs and Muslims have been little acknowledged in U.S. society, with concomitant deleterious effect on U.S. perceptions, internationally, as they touch upon relations with predominantly Arab and Muslim nations and organizations.

Therefore, The United Methodist Church, in the knowledge that Jesus calls us to the blessings of peacemaking and reminds us that the highest law is to love God and neighbor, calls its members and its leaders:

1. To oppose demagoguery, manipulation, and image making that seeks to label Arabs and Muslims in a negative way;

2. To counter stereotypical and bigoted statements made against Muslims and Islam, Arabs and Arabic culture;

3. To increase knowledge of neighbor by study and personal contact that yield a greater appreciation of the Muslim and Arabic contributions to society;

4. To act decisively to include Arabs and Muslims in interfaith and community organizations;

5. To pray for the perfection of community among us and to participate fully in the process of bringing it into being; and

6. To publicly denounce through statements from the Council of Bishops and the General Board of Church and Society current practices that discriminate against this community.

In order to aid United Methodists to respond to this call, all boards, agencies, and institutions of The United Methodist Church are requested to provide resources and program and, where appropriate, to act in advocacy.

ADOPTED 1988
AMENDED AND READOPTED 2000
AMENDED AND READOPTED 2004

See Social Principles, ¶ 162B.

79. Spiritual Unity in Human Diversity

WHEREAS, The United Methodist Church is experiencing conflicting expressions of faith and biblical theology; and

WHEREAS, The United Methodist Church incorporates confessional traditions (i.e., the Articles of Religion and the Confession of Faith from *The Book of Discipline, 1992)* and inclusive tradition ("The Catholic Spirit" sermon by John Wesley); and

WHEREAS, *The Book of Discipline, 1992* (Part II: "Doctrinal Standards and Our Theological Task") "preserves the inherent tension between doctrinal standards and theological exploration . . . [and] involves dialogue, debate, and some conflict" ("Biblical Wisdom and Current Theological Ferment," Council of Bishops, October 31-November 4, 1994); and

WHEREAS, maintaining an inclusive spirit about doctrinal, theological, and language issues serves the greater purpose of helping people to affirm faith in Jesus Christ and to appropriate the historic confessions of the Church; and

WHEREAS, confessing faith in scriptural truth honors rich diversity in the biblical witness and informs a deeper understanding of diversity among people of faith; and

WHEREAS, "indeed, the body does not consist of one member but of many. . . . [and] God arranged the members in the body, each one of them, as he chose. . . . The eye cannot say to the hand, 'I have no need of you,' nor again the head to the feet, 'I have no need of you.' On the contrary, the members of the body that seem to be weaker are indispensable, and those members of the body that we think less honorable we clothe with greater honor, and our less respectable members are treated with greater respect; whereas, our more respectable members do not need this. But God has so arranged the body, giving the greater honor to the inferior member, that there may be no dissension within the body, but the members may have the same care for one another" (1 Corinthians 12:14-25);

Therefore, be it resolved, that The United Methodist Church reject any spirit that seeks to divide the body of Christ (and especially The United Methodist Church) and that cuts off the confessing and inclusive heritages by which United Methodists know themselves to be people of God; and

Be it further resolved, that we affirm our biblical faith in Jesus Christ and the spiritual gift of unity in human diversity.

ADOPTED 1996
READOPTED 2004

See Social Principles, ¶ 162.

80. Support for Five Ethnic National Plans

WHEREAS, ¶ 138 of *The Book of Discipline, 2000* states "As a diverse people of God who bring special gifts and evidences of God's grace to the unity of the Church and to society, we are called to be faithful to the example of Jesus' ministry to all persons"; and

WHEREAS, ¶162.A of The Social Principles affirms the ministry to all persons and states "We rejoice in the gifts that particular ethnic histories and cultures bring to our total life"; and

WHEREAS, five ethnic national plans (Asian Language Ministry, Hispanic, Korean, Native American, and Strengthening the Black Church) have affirmed and have made significant contributions to the growth and strengthening of major ethnic ministries; and

WHEREAS, continuing needs for the five ethnic national plans (Asian Language Ministry, Hispanic, Korean, Native American, and Strengthening the Black Church) are clearly demonstrated by their successes in making disciples of Christ; and

WHEREAS, funding for these ethnic national plans are essential and critical in order to continue ministry to ethnic people;

Therefore, be it resolved that, this General Conference of The United Methodist Church expresses its support for continuing existence and funding of the ethnic national plans.

ADOPTED 2004

See Social Principles, ¶ 162A.

81. The Church's Response to Ethnic and Religious Conflict

Would that you knew the things that make for peace.
—Jesus of Nazareth (Luke 19:42)

The tragic conflicts in such places as Bosnia, India, Indonesia, the Middle East, Nigeria, Rwanda, Northern Ireland, and Sri Lanka, as well as interethnic conflict in the United States, reveal the deep potential for hatred, fear, and religious belief to stir up violence in humankind. These conflicts pose a great challenge to the Christian church as the mediator of Jesus' gospel of love and reconciliation in the world, as well as to the wider religious community. The church's pain is only made greater by the fact that so many of these violent conflicts pit one religious group against another.

When his disciples James and John saw it, they said, "Lord, do you want us to command fire to come down from heaven and consume them [a Samaritan village]?" But he turned and rebuked them. (Luke 9:54-55)

We confess that as Christians we too have responded to religious and ethnic differences out of fear, ignorance and even hatred. We have too quickly resorted to violence as a means of resolving conflicts.

The rising tide of violence in the world threatens to engulf communities, nations, and world civilizations. It is time for the church to become proactive in resolving conflict nonviolently and developing alternatives to violence. Specifically:

- we call upon the General Board of Global Ministries to continue discussions with Christian Peacemakers, Witness for Peace, International Solidarity Movement, and other nonviolent movements that provide a Christian presence in situations of international, interreligious, and interethnic conflict, to explore the possibility of including United Methodists on the teams that are sent to areas of conflict;
- we call upon the General Board of Global Ministries to incorporate the principles of nonviolent conflict resolution and interethnic and interreligious dialogue in the Shalom Zone Program;
- we call upon the General Board of Church and Society, together with the General Commission on Religion and Race and the General Commission on Christian Unity and Interreligious Concerns to hold a series of interreligious dialogues to develop new approaches to mutual understanding, respect, and cooperation, and to develop, for use in local church and community settings, guidelines on how to set up local dialogues and how to develop and implement alternatives to violence;
- we call upon our seminaries and United Methodist-related colleges and universities to offer courses on alternatives to violence and to sponsor local community initiatives to diffuse ethnic and religious conflict. We also call on our seminaries to encourage the study of the theological roots of violence and of Jesus' teachings on nonresistance and resisting evil; and
- we call upon the U.S. government, working with the United Nations, to give leadership **by** redirecting funds from its for-

eign military exercise training programs to the UN High Commission for Human Rights and other international human rights organizations for the tasks of peacemaking, peacekeeping, reconstruction, and rehabilitation. This means reallocating funds from building weapons to building communities, from teaching to kill to teaching to protect life. Modest beginnings in such an effort can be seen in community policing initiatives in many of our cities, in the peacekeeping force in Bosnia, and in the nonviolent transition to democracy in South Africa;

• we call upon the General Board of Discipleship, together with the General Board of Global Ministries, to address our growing multi-faith contexts in developing church school curriculum by utilizing resources from ecumenical and interfaith organizations;

• we call upon local churches to be engaged in "Creating Interfaith Community"—a Women's Division-initiated mission study—throughout the coming quadrennium;

• we call upon annual conferences to organize high school and adult trips through United Methodist Seminars (a program offered by Women's Division and the General Board of Church and Society) or United Methodist Volunteers in Mission to study Ethnic and Religious Conflicts and alternatives to violence.

ADOPTED 1996
AMENDED AND READOPTED 2004

See Social Principles, ¶ 162*A* and *B*.

ALCOHOL AND OTHER DRUGS

82. Alcoholic Beverage Advertising at the Olympics

WHEREAS, the Bible tells us that our bodies are "temples of the living God" (1 Corinthians 6:13-20) and since we are created in God's own image, we should strive to perfect our bodies in God's image;

WHEREAS, the founders United Methodism provide historical undergirdings for our strong witness on abstinence from alcohol;

Susanna Wesley in a letter to John Wesley influenced and urged piety with these words: *"Take this rule: whatever weakens your reason, impairs the tenderness of your conscience, obscures your sense of God, or takes off the relish of spiritual things; in short, whatever increases the strength and authority of your body over your mind, that thing is sin to you, however innocent it may be in itself"; and*

WHEREAS, John Wesley in his sermon on the use of money urges, *'Neither may we gain by hurting our neighbor in his body. Therefore we may not sell anything which tends to impair health. Such is, eminently, all that liquid fire commonly call 'drams' or spirituous liquor"; and*

WHEREAS, sports events display athletic ability, and the Olympics are an exhibition of the highest achievement in athletic ability; and

WHEREAS, the consumption of alcoholic beverages inhibits athletic ability rather than increases it; and

WHEREAS, the consumption of alcoholic beverages contributes to many problems in society such as automobile accidents, assaults on women and children, suicide, and drowning, to mention a few; and

WHEREAS, advertising of alcoholic beverages will associate them in the mind of the public with the highest achievement in athletic ability, which is a false message;

Therefore, be it resolved, that The United Methodist Church strongly protests beer or any alcoholic beverage being advertised at or near all Olympics games or any other sporting event,

And be it further resolved, that we consider it scandalous for any alcoholic beverage to be listed as a sponsor of the Olympics event, or any other national or international sports organization,

And be it further resolved, that the secretary of the General Conference is instructed to send a copy of this resolution to the Olympic Organizing Committees.

ADOPTED 2000
AMENDED AND READOPTED 2004

See Social Principles, ¶ 162J.

83. Drug and Alcohol Concerns

As God's children and participants in the gift of abundant life, we recognize the need to respond to those who know brokenness from the widespread abuse of alcohol and other drugs in our world. The experience of God's saving grace offers wholeness to each individual. In light of the reality of alcohol and other drug abuse, the church has a responsibility to recognize brokenness and to be an instrument of education, healing, and restoration. First, we must be committed to confronting the denial within ourselves that keeps individuals and nations from overcoming their struggle with alcohol and other drug abuse. Second, the alcohol and other drug problem must be understood as a social, economic, spiritual, and health problem. Third, the church has a fundamental role in reorienting the public debate on alcohol and other drugs by shifting the focus from punishment to prevention and treatment. This is rooted in the Christian belief in the ongoing possibilities for transformation in the life of each individual and in our world.

The alcohol and other drug crisis has reached global proportions. More alcohol and other drugs are produced and consumed than ever before. In consuming countries, with their attendant problems of poverty, racism, domestic violence, hopelessness, and material despair, alcohol and other drug abuse is a part of a continuing cycle of economic and spiritual turmoil.

Abuse of legal drugs (alcohol, tobacco, and pharmaceuticals) remains a leading cause of disease and death around the world. While recreational use of illegal drugs in the United States has declined, the use of drugs remains socially acceptable as levels of addiction and abuse continue to rise.

Growing numbers of cities, small towns, and rural areas around the world are caught in a web of escalating alcohol and other drug-related violence. As the findings of the regional hearings in the United States stressed: "Drug addiction crosses all ethnic, cultural, and economic backgrounds." Social systems are dangerously strained under the heavy weight of alcohol and other drug-related health and social problems. Meanwhile, the supply of drugs from developing countries continues to grow in response to high demand from the developed countries.

The United States policy response to the drug crisis has focused almost exclusively on law enforcement and military solutions. This policy, in some cases, has led to the erosion of precious civil liberties and human rights, especially for poor and minority communities.

International strategies should reflect the need for balanced, equitable economic growth and stable democratic governments in drug-producing developing countries. Most importantly, any alternative strategy must be rooted in local communities. The most creative and effective approaches to the present crisis begin at the local level.

The United Methodist Church has long opposed abuse of alcohol and other drugs. In 1916, the General Conference authorized the formation of a Board of Temperance, Prohibition, and Public Morals "to make more effectual the efforts of the church to create public sentiment and crystallize the same into successful opposition to the organized traffic in intoxicating liquors."

During the 1988-92 quadrennium, The United Methodist Church launched a comprehensive Bishops' Initiative on Drugs and Drug Violence, which, through regional hearings across the United States, deepened the denomination's awareness of alcohol and other drug problems. The report of these hearings concluded: "Therefore, The United Methodist Church must play a key role in confronting drug and alcohol addiction. . . ." Today, The United Methodist Church remains committed to curbing drug traffic and the abuse of alcohol and other drugs.

In response to the alcohol and other drug crisis, The United Methodist Church commits itself to a holistic approach, which emphasizes prevention, intervention, treatment, community organization, public advocacy, and abstinence. Out of love for God and our neighbors, the church must have a positive role by offering a renewed spiritual perspective on this crisis. We commend local congregations, annual conferences, and general agencies and seminaries to take action in the areas of alcohol, tobacco, and other drugs.

I. Alcohol

Alcohol is a *drug*, which presents special problems because of its widespread social acceptance. We affirm our long-standing conviction and recommendation that abstinence from alcoholic beverages is a faithful witness to God's liberating and redeeming love.

This witness is especially relevant because excessive, harmful, and dangerous drinking patterns are uncritically accepted and practiced. Society glamorizes drinking, and youthful immaturity can be exploited for personal gain. The costs associated with alcohol use/abuse are more than the costs associated with all illegal drugs combined. Worldwide, millions of individuals and their families suffer as a result of alcoholism. The medical consequences of alcohol abuse include fetal alcohol syndrome—which is a preventable cause of mental retardation—cardiac defects, and pre- and postnatal growth retardation. Chronic alcohol consumption can have a damaging effect on every body organ, including brain, liver, heart, stomach, intestines, and mouth. Alcohol is a factor in many other social problems such as crime, poverty, and family disorder. The societal costs of alcohol abuse include lost productivity, increased health-care costs, loss of lives in vehicular accidents, and criminal activity.

Thus, The United Methodist Church bases its recommendation of abstinence on critical appraisal of the personal and societal costs in the use of alcohol. The church recognizes the freedom of the Christian to make responsible decisions and calls upon each member to consider seriously and prayerfully the witness of abstinence as part of his or her Christian commitment. Persons who practice abstinence should avoid attitudes of self-righteousness that express moral superiority and condemnatory attitudes toward those who do not choose to abstain. Because Christian love in human relationships is primary, abstinence is an instrument of love and sacrifice and always subject to the requirements of love.

Our love for our neighbor obligates us to seek healing, justice, and the alleviation of the social conditions that create and perpetuate alcohol abuse.

Therefore:

1. We urge individuals and local congregations to demonstrate active concern for alcohol abusers and their families. We encourage churches to support the care, treatment, and rehabilitation of problem drinkers.

2. We urge churches to include the problems of alcohol and the value of abstinence as a part of Christian education.

3. We encourage individuals and local congregations to develop prevention education for family, church, and community. We encourage sound empirical research on the social effects of alcohol.

4. We oppose the sale and consumption of alcoholic beverages within the confines of United Methodist Church facilities and recommend that it be prohibited.

5. We ask individuals and local congregations to study and discuss the problem of driving while intoxicated and impaired by alcohol or other drugs, and we support legislation to reduce such activity.

6. We direct the General Board of Discipleship and The United Methodist Publishing House to incorporate educational material on alcohol and other drug problems, including the material on preven-

tion, intervention, treatment, and the value of abstinence throughout its graded literature.

7. We expect United Methodist-related hospitals to treat the alcoholic person with the attention and consideration all patients deserve. We urge the worldwide health-care delivery system to follow this example.

8. We urge all legislative bodies and health-care systems and processes to focus on and implement measures to help meet the special needs of those disproportionately affected by alcohol use.

9. We favor laws to eliminate all advertising and promoting of alcoholic beverages. We urge the General Board of Church and Society and local churches to increase efforts to remove all advertising of alcoholic beverages from the media. We urge special attention to curbing promotions of alcoholic beverages on college campuses as well as racial minority communities.

10. We urge the Federal Trade Commission to continue developing better health hazard warning statements concerning the use of alcohol.

11. We ask the United States government to improve interagency coordination of drug and alcohol abuse efforts so that there are uniform policies and regulations, and we look forward to the cooperation of all governments in these areas.

II. Tobacco

The use of tobacco is another form of drug abuse, even though it is legal. Overwhelming evidence links cigarette-smoking with lung cancer, cardiovascular diseases, emphysema, and chronic bronchitis. In addition, cigarette-smoking can negatively affect a developing fetus, and secondary smoke is a known carcinogen. The United Methodist Church discourages all persons, particularly children, youths and young adults, from using any form of tobacco.

We commend the suspension of cigarette advertising on radio and television. We are concerned about other advertisements that associate smoking with physical and social maturity, attractiveness, and success, especially those targeted at youth, racial minorities, and women. We support the Federal Trade Commission's rules requiring health warning statements in cigarette packaging. We are also concerned that the tobacco industry is marketing tobacco in developing countries. *Therefore:*

1. We recommend that tobacco use be banned in all church facilities.

2. We recommend a tobacco-free environment in all public areas.

3. We recommend the prohibition of all commercial advertising of tobacco products.

4. We support expanded research to discover the specific mechanisms of addiction to nicotine. We urge the development of educational methods that effectively discourage the use of tobacco and methods to assist those who wish to stop using tobacco.

5. We urge the Department of Agriculture and other government agencies to plan for and assist the orderly economic transition of the tobacco industry—tobacco growers, processors, and distributors—into industries more compatible with the general welfare of the people.

6. We support National Comprehensive Tobacco Control Legislation that includes provisions to: a) reduce the rate of youth smoking by increasing the price of cigarettes; b) protect tobacco farmers by helping them shift from tobacco to other crops; c) give the FDA full authority to regulate nicotine as a drug; d) fund anti-tobacco research and advertising, as well as education and prevention campaigns.

III. Drugs

The United Methodist Church recognizes the widespread use and misuse of drugs that alter mood, perception, consciousness, and behavior of persons among all ages, classes, and segments of our society. Pharmacologically, a drug is any substance that by its chemical nature alters the structure or function of any living organism. This broad definition encompasses a wide range of substances, many of which are psychoactive and have the potential for abuse. These include marijuana, narcotics, sedatives and stimulants, psychedelics, and hallucinogens. Additionally, commonly used products such as glue, paint thinners, and gasoline have the potential to be abused as inhalants.

A. Marijuana

Like alcohol and tobacco, marijuana is frequently a precursor to the use of other drugs. The active ingredient is THC, which affects the user by temporarily producing feelings of euphoria or relaxation. An altered sense of body image and bouts of exaggerated laughter are commonly reported. However, studies reveal that marijuana impairs short-term memory, altering sense of time and reducing the ability to perform tasks requiring concentration, swift reactions, and coordination. Some countries permit the use of marijuana in medicines. Recently, some states in the United States have passed legislation permitting the medical use of marijuana. The medical use of any drug should not be seen as encouraging recreational use of the drug. We urge all persons to abstain from all use of marijuana, unless it has been legally prescribed in a form appropriate for treating a particular medical condition.[1]

B. Sedatives and Stimulants

Sedatives, which include barbiturates and tranquilizers, are prescribed appropriately for treatment of anxiety. These legally prescribed drugs need to be taken only under appropriate medical supervision. The use of this class of drugs can result in dependence.

Severe physical dependence on barbiturates can develop at doses higher than therapeutic doses, and withdrawal is severe and dangerous. The combination of alcohol and barbiturates is potentially lethal.

Stimulants range from amphetamines to mild stimulants such as caffeine and nicotine. Prescribed for obesity, sleep disorders, hyperactivity, fatigue, and depression, stimulants produce a temporary sense of vitality, alertness, and energy.

Unlike other stimulants, cocaine has limited medical uses. When the powder form is inhaled, cocaine is a highly addictive central nervous system stimulant that heightens the body's natural response to pleasure and creates a euphoric high, and has the potential to be extremely lethal. "Crack," a crystallized form of cocaine, is readily available because of its lesser cost. Addiction often comes from one use of the substance.

C. Psychedelics or Hallucinogens

Psychedelics or hallucinogens, which include LSD, psilocybin, mescaline, PCP, and DMT, produce changes in perception and altered states of consciousness. Not only is there limited medical use, the use of these drugs may result in permanent psychiatric problems.

1. Performance Resource Press, Inc., Troy, Michigan.

D. Narcotics

Narcotics are prescribed for the relief of pain, but the risk of physical and psychological dependencies is well documented. Derived from the opium plant, natural narcotics include heroin, morphine, codeine, and percodan, while synthetic narcotics include methadone and meperidine.

Therefore, as The United Methodist Church:

1. We oppose the use of all drugs, except in cases of appropriate medical supervision.

2. We encourage the church to develop honest, objective, and factual drug education for children, youths, and adults as part of a comprehensive prevention education program.

3. We urge the church to coordinate its efforts with ecumenical, interfaith, and community groups in prevention, rehabilitation, and policy statements.

4. We encourage the annual conferences to recognize the unique impact of drugs and its related violence upon urban and rural areas and provide appropriate ministries and resources.

5. We strongly encourage annual conferences to develop leadership training opportunities and resources for local church pastors and laity to help them with counseling individuals and families who have alcohol and other drug-related problems; counseling those bereaved by alcohol and other drug-related deaths and violence; and teaching stress management to church workers in communities with high alcohol and other drug activity.

6. We support National Comprehensive Tobacco Control Legislation that includes provisions to: a) reduce the rate of youth smoking by increasing the price of cigarettes; b) protect tobacco farmers by helping them shift from tobacco to other crops; c) give the FDA full authority to regulate nicotine as a drug; d) fund anti-tobacco research and advertising, as well as education and prevention campaigns.

7. We urge redevelopment of more effective methods of treatment of drug abuse and addiction.

8. We support government policies concerning drugs that are compatible with our Christian beliefs about the potential transformation of all individuals.

9. We urge all United Methodist churches to work for a minimum legal drinking age of twenty-one years in their respective states/nations.

10. We support strong, humane law-enforcement efforts against the illegal sale of all drugs, and we urge that those arrested for possession and use of illegally procured drugs be subject to education and rehabilitation.

ADOPTED 1996
AMENDED AND ADOPTED 2000
AMENDED AND READOPTED 2004

See Social Principles, ¶ 162J.

84. Keep Children Free of Drugs and Alcohol

WHEREAS, our Christian faith calls us to teach and lead children in the right way; and

WHEREAS, over a third of children begin using alcohol before they are teens; and

WHEREAS, one in ten young teens is a regular user of marijuana and other drugs; and

WHEREAS, alcohol and drugs bring harm to growing bodies and minds; and

WHEREAS, it is illegal in most states to sell or give alcoholic beverages to those under 21 and illicit use and selling of "controlled" drugs is a crime at any age; and

WHEREAS, the Justice Department reports that many school programs aimed to help young people have not deterred their use of alcohol and other drugs; and

WHEREAS, young people with inner stamina, self-esteem, and faith more readily can say, "no" to drugs and alcohol;

Therefore, be it resolved, that we, the 2000 General Conference of The United Methodist Church, support efforts to keep children drug free and safe that young people can have full lives, avoiding use of beverage alcohol and illicit drugs and say "no" to them.

1. We call upon individual families to pray for their children and to teach their children by precept and example the preference of avoiding beverage alcohol and illicit drugs and resisting peer pressures for their use.

2. We call upon all people to pray and give moral and financial support to community, church and other efforts to discourage children and teens from use of alcohol and drugs.

3. We call upon our local congregations to pray for the children and to include in their Christian education programs for young people and their families studies emphasizing the ill effects of drugs and alcohol and the importance of avoidance of them.

4. We further call upon local congregations to have annual observances of a Drug and Alcohol Awareness Sunday and to challenge young people and their elders to say "no" as an aspect of their commitment to Jesus Christ.

5. We call upon our fellow citizens to support legislation that will help to curtail availability of alcoholic beverages to youth and to support public programs that help to instill values in young people that will help them to have drug-and-alcohol-free lives.

6. We call upon other religious bodies to join us in adopting resolutions and supporting efforts to curtail alcohol and drug abuse in our communities, states, and nation.

7. We direct the General Board of Church and Society and the General Board of Discipleship to develop and promote resource materials to implement this concern within the connection.

ADOPTED 2000

See Social Principles, ¶ 162J.

85. Drinking on Campus

WHEREAS, according to a new survey by the Centers for Disease Control and Prevention, binge drinking is on the rise in the United States and is climbing fastest among 18- to 20-year-olds who are too young to drink legally; and

WHEREAS, this survey also revealed that episodes of binge drinking, defined as having five or more drinks in one sitting, increased 17% among all adults between 1993 and 2001, and shot up 56 percent among 18 to 20 year olds; and

WHEREAS, United Methodist colleges do provide an environment suitable for pursuing a higher education in a Christian atmosphere; and

WHEREAS, the United Methodist-related colleges and universities do have policies related to alcohol use and abuse on the campuses; and

WHEREAS, the United Methodist-related colleges and universities spent over $1.5 million to address issues related to alcohol abuse on their campuses; and

WHEREAS, many students nationwide continue to engage in binge drinking and drinking to get drunk, with an alarming percentage of students reporting alcohol-related incidents, such as missing classes, personal injuries, sexual assault, or other forms of violence and vandalism;

Therefore, be it resolved, that The United Methodist Church continue to address this issue through:

1. collaborating with the Special Program on Substance Abuse and Related Violence (SPSARV) staff and Interagency Task Force and the General Board of Higher Education and Ministry, and partnering with the college presidents and/or staff of United Methodist-related institutions, as well as other agencies and programs that are working on the issue of reducing college drinking;

2. promoting an alternative lifestyle that encourages "wellness" without drugs and alcohol, seeking authentic advocates for this alternative lifestyle, and having these advocates promote this image on United Methodist campuses around the world;

3. carrying out the five components of SPSARV on college campuses: Leadership Development, Community Demonstration Programs, Advocacy, Grants, and Educational and Promotional Resources;

4. strongly recommending that United Methodist-related colleges and universities uphold abstinence from drinking alcohol as a viable and faith-based option, and that these institutions provide/continue to provide programming and social events that foster such an environment;

5. strongly urging campus leadership to remove alcohol-promoting advertisements from the campuses and sports events.

ADOPTED 2004

See Social Principles, ¶ 162J.

86. Reduction of Alcohol-Related Problems

WHEREAS, the Scriptures, when viewed in their entirety, are clear on the intoxicating and harmful effects of alcoholic beverages, but do in fact approach the use of alcohol with a stance of cautious moderation, within certain limits; and

WHEREAS, the Scriptures provide warrant for alcohol consumption with careful attention to use, as distinguished from high-risk use, abuse, and addiction, while applying the principles of discernment which we are called to exercise on other life issues; and

WHEREAS, The United Methodist Church is challenged to apply the ethical guidelines of Scripture to a contemporary culture in which alcoholic beverages play a prominent role, for which we pay a heavy price in both human and economic terms; and

WHEREAS, there is substantial evidence that patterns of casual alcohol use, problematic use, dependence and addiction are prevalent within our fellowship, and may be as prevalent among members of The United Methodist Church as they are in society at large; and

WHEREAS, the Social Principles place emphasis solely on abstinence as "a faithful witness," while at the same time encouraging us to "assist those who have become dependent, and their families," thereby leaving an attention gap between abstinence and dependence; and

WHEREAS, the Social Principles encourage us to assist dependent people "in finding freedom through Jesus Christ and in finding good opportunities for treatment, for ongoing counseling, and for reintegration into society," but we find that the few resources dedicated to prevention, treatment and rehabilitation stand in stark contrast to the great needs that exist; and,

WHEREAS, John Wesley, the founder of the Methodist Movement, was extremely aware of the effects of drunkenness on individuals and families, including members of his own extended family, but was charitable to those individuals affected by alcohol in his culture; and

WHEREAS, John Wesley reserved his strongest language for the economic aspects of business enterprises that promoted indiscriminate alcohol consumption in a famous sermon, in which he urged his listeners to "gain all you can," but not at the expense of another person's property, health, and spiritual well-being; and

WHEREAS, our Doctrinal Standards and General Rules states that "We believe it is the duty of Christian citizens to give moral strength and purpose to their respective governments...;" and the Social Principles exhort us to "continually exert a strong ethical influence upon the state, supporting policies and programs deemed to be just and opposing policies and programs that are unjust;" and

WHEREAS, concepts of Christian discipleship, stewardship and justice demand that we attend to the human and economic damage caused by high-risk consumption, while recognizing the needs of our addicted brothers and sisters, whether they are within our fellowship or outside of it; and

WHEREAS, *The Book of Resolutions* (2000) presents several other sources of alcohol-related concerns, including industry promotion and advertising (72, now 82); a comprehensive view of the problem as "a social, economic, spiritual and health problem," and commitment to "a holistic approach which emphasizes prevention, intervention, treatment, community organization, and abstinence," and improvement of interagency coordination in this area (73, now 83); keeping children free of alcohol, including legislation and public programs (74, now 84); and concerns about drinking on campus (75, now 85); and

WHEREAS, reason and experience inform us that sole concentration on abstinence all too often breeds judgmental attitudes, drives troubled people even deeper into despair and secretive behavior, discriminates against people who need healing, invites hypocrisy and closes off opportunities to witness to God's love and grace; and

WHEREAS, the legacy of the Temperance Movement of an earlier century has been transformed by new social forces and scientific findings into a vigorous public health movement, with emphasis on pro-health alcohol policies that place individual responsibility in the context of social norms and practices; and

WHEREAS, more than three decades of research have shown that alcohol abuse, dependence and addiction have widespread effects on persons, families, communities, and institutions, and have documented not only the extent of the physical and social consequences but also the economic effects on health care, medical services, workforce productivity, crime and violence, child welfare, corrections, public safety, social services, education, and mental health; and

WHEREAS, recent research has shown that underage drinkers account for almost 20 percent of all alcohol consumed and adults who drink excessively are responsible for more than 30 percent of the alcohol consumed in the U.S., and industry profits are derived from those consumers; and

WHEREAS, marketing research has shown that youth were 60 times more likely to see alcoholic beverage commercials than "responsibility ads" created by the industry, and that for every drinking and driving prevention ad, alcohol companies aired 172 product promotion ads; and

WHEREAS levels of low-risk, acceptable consumption and guidelines for responsible use have been issued by the U.S. Department of Agriculture and the U. S. Department of Health and Human Services, limiting consumption to one standard drink per day for women and two standard drinks per day for men, but abstinence for (a) persons under the age of 21, (b) persons who are in recovery from alcohol dependence or alcoholism, (c) persons whose parents or other family members have experienced alcohol-related problems, (d) women who are trying to conceive or are pregnant, (e) persons who plan to drive or engage in activities that require attention or skill, and persons using prescription or over-the-counter medications; (f) persons who may put self or others at risk in other ways as a result of consumption; and

WHEREAS, we understand that "moderation" is in itself a problematic concept, given the psychoactive properties of ethyl alcohol, which challenges our judgment and awareness, so that slogans such as "know when to say when" or "just say no" make little sense to a person who is in the grip of addiction; and

WHEREAS, the alcohol industry has shown in many ways that it is far more interested in profits than in the health, safety and welfare of the people, more interested in expanding its customer base to insure its economic viability, blaming its customers for alcohol-related problems, and refusing steadfastly to define what it means by "responsible drinking," to the point that even their "responsibility" messages serve its own interests, attempting thereby to absolve itself of corporate responsibility; and

WHEREAS, those who profit from the production, distribution, promotion and sale of alcoholic beverages have been allowed to assume a privileged position in the formation of public policy and legislation at local, state and national levels, a degree of power and influence which has succeeded in dissuading the public, including the faith community, from taking appropriate action as citizens; and

WHEREAS, funding for prevention and for treatment of addicted people continues to be woefully inadequate, considering the magnitude of the problem, leaving millions of Americans without needed services, and the social costs of alcohol-related problems continue to rob our economy of resources needed to deal with poverty and disease, while the industry opposes every effort to offset these costs by increases in alcohol excise taxes; and

WHEREAS, prevention research strongly recommends a comprehensive community-wide approach, which acknowledges that individual behavior is powerfully shaped by one's environment, the rules and regulations of social institutions, community norms, mass media messages, and accessibility of alcohol; and

WHEREAS, a community, state, and nation which allows a product with high potential for misuse and abuse to be produced, promoted, distributed and valued for routine consumption is ethically obligated to care about those who succumb to the risks and adverse consequences, especially when those risks and consequences are incompletely understood by the consumer; and

WHEREAS, the concerned citizens of our nation call for faith community leadership on this issue, leadership that transcends special economic interests and considers the public interest, leadership that pursues action rather than continued pronouncements; able and willing to challenge industry practices, when others have a defeatist attitude and consider the industry invincible in matters of social policy;

Therefore, be it resolved, that the members of The United Methodist Church take a firm stand to reduce alcohol-related problems, not only as a personal matter, but as a concern for congregation, community, state and nation, and communicate that stand effectively, rather than passively, through action to change the social norms; and

Be it further resolved that, the gap between abstinence and addiction be closed, using the entire Bible as our ethical guide, and that The United Methodist Church promote an ethic that is consistent with personal, spiritual and societal concern for health, safety and well-being; that such ethic be one that (a) accepts abstinence in all situations; (b) accepts judicious consumption, with deliberate and intentional restraint, in low-risk situations; (c) actively discourages consumption in high-risk situations; and (d) actively discourages heavy consumption in all situations; and

Be it further resolved that, guidelines for moderate consumption, as issued by the U.S. Department of Agriculture (U.S. Dietary Guidelines) and the U. S. Department of Health and Human Services, as stated above, be encouraged in educational efforts; and

Be it further resolved that, The United Methodist Church pursue a course of action that reflects the ethical imperative, that prevention of alcohol-related problems and treatment and rehabilitation of those who become addicted should be available and accessible to all those in need, as well as their families, neighbors, fellow church members, employers, and others whose lives are directly affected; and

Be it further resolved that, the members of The United Methodist Church take action to reduce the domination of industry agenda on state and local levels and encourage our legislators to place the health and safety concerns ahead of profitability; and

Be it further resolved that, The United Methodist Church support public policy proposals that would increase the rates of fees and excise taxes paid by the industry to the various states for the privilege of selling beer, wine and spirits, with proceeds earmarked for the development of prevention, treatment and other measures to reduce alcohol-related problems; and

Be it further resolved that the General Board of Church and Society during the 2005-2008 quadrennial study this issue and make recommendations to the 2008 General Conference with a comprehensive statement that addresses the critical global emphasis,; and

Be it finally resolved that, The United Methodist Church increase its efforts to provide guidance to its annual conferences, to work toward wholeness, compassion, reconciliation and healing, community, alternatives to incarceration and restorative justice, to give help and hope to those who feel helpless and hopeless, and to advise congregations on ways in which members can advocate for pro-health alcohol policies at local, state, and national levels.

ADOPTED 2004

See Social Principles, ¶ 162J.

87. Drugs and AIDS

According to the United Nations' AIDS estimates, approximately 40 million people worldwide are living with HIV/AIDS. Of these, two to three million are injecting drug users. Many more have used, and continue to use, alcohol and other drugs.

The international drug trade knows no boundaries or frontiers and has no specific national identity. It is now worth an estimated $400 billion per year and is organized and managed like a multinational corporation. Drugs of all kinds are now produced in all regions of the world. Despite its illegality, drug production and distribution has become a major source of revenue for many countries. The most lucrative markets remain in the United States and western Europe, but consumption is spreading fast in eastern Europe, Southeast Asia, and throughout Africa.

In the United States, an estimated one-third of HIV/AIDS cases are related to injecting drug use. Substance abuse is directly tied to the increase in HIV/AIDS among women. Women are primarily infected with HIV through injecting drugs (48 percent) or heterosexual transmission from an infected partner, who is often himself a drug user (54 percent).

Research has shown over and over again that drug use, injected or otherwise, can affect decision-making, especially about engaging in unsafe sex, which in turn can endanger one's health as well as the health of others. A research study conducted by The National Center on Addiction and Substance Abuse revealed that of the 15 to 24-year-olds surveyed:

- 50 percent say "people their age" mix alcohol or drugs and sex "a lot."
- 73 percent believe that their peers often don't use condoms when alcohol and drugs are in the picture.
- 37 percent want more information about how alcohol or drugs might affect their decisions about having sex.

In response to the alcohol, drug and HIV/AIDS crisis in the world, The United Methodist Church commits itself to a holistic approach of awareness, education, prevention, treatment, community organizing, public advocacy and abstinence. Out of our love and concern for our brothers, sisters and children in our local and global communities, we therefore:

1. urge the Office of the Special Program on Substance Abuse and Related Violence (SPSARV) of the General Board of Global Ministries and all boards and agencies of the Church to work cooperatively on issues related to drugs and AIDS;

2. encourage local churches to include problems of alcohol, drug abuse and unsafe sex and the value of abstinence as part of Christian education;

3. encourage United Methodist churches and institutions to provide support, comfort and care to those afflicted with alcohol-related problems, drug addiction and HIV/AIDS within their given mandate;

4. urge the Federal Government to improve interagency cooperation and coordination to fight the double scourge of drugs and AIDS;

5. make available creative programs and activities for school children, youth and young adults that keep them away from alcohol and
drug abuse; and

6. promote and make available peer education models based on
empowerment and self-determination.

ADOPTED 2004

See Social Principles, ¶ 162J.

ECUMENICAL ISSUES

88. Building New Bridges in Hope

"God whom Christians have come to know in Jesus Christ, has created all human beings in the divine image and . . . God desires that all
people live in love and righteousness. . . .

"While we are committed to the promotion of mutual respect and
understanding among people of all living faiths, we as Christians recognize a special relationship between Christians and Jews because of
our shared roots in biblical revelation."[1]

A Quest for New Understanding

What is the relationship that God intends between Christianity and
Judaism, between Christians and Jews? In The United Methodist
Church, a search for understanding and appropriate response to this
important theological and relational question has been under way for
some time. A significant step in the development of United Methodist
understanding of and intention for Christian-Jewish relations was
taken in 1972, when the General Conference adopted a position statement under the title *Bridge in Hope*. This denominational statement
urged church members and congregations to undertake "serious
new conversations" with Jews in order to promote "growth in mutual

1. "The Churches and the Jewish People, Towards a New Understanding," adopted at
Sigtuna, Sweden, by the Consultation on the Church and the Jewish People, sponsored by
the World Council of Churches, 1988.

understanding."[2] As it has been studied and used, *Bridge in Hope* has served as a strong foundation for United Methodist-Jewish dialogue in many settings.

Since 1972, other Christian denominations, as well as ecumenical bodies in which The United Methodist Church participates, such as the World Council of Churches, have also made statements on Christian-Jewish relations. Those voices have contributed to our further knowledge, reflection, and understanding. At the same time, we have learned much from the many relationships and dialogues that have flourished between Jews and Christians locally, nationally, and internationally.

Especially crucial for Christians in our quest for understanding has been the struggle to recognize the horror of the Holocaust as the catastrophic culmination of a long history of anti-Jewish attitudes and actions in which Christians, and sometimes the church itself, have been deeply implicated. Dialogues with Jewish partners have been central for Christians in our process of learning of the scope of the Holocaust atrocities, acknowledgment of complicity, and responsibility, repentance, and commitment to work against anti-Semitism in all its forms in the future.

We are aware, however, that the Christian-Jewish bridge of understanding has only begun to be constructed. The United Methodist Church is committed to continuing clarification and expansion of our knowledge of Judaism and to strengthening our relationships with Jewish people. We seek mutual exploration of the common ground underlying Christianity and Judaism as well as that which makes each faith unique. This statement is an expression of the principles of that commitment.

Foundation for United Methodist Understandings of Christian-Jewish Relations

As expressed in its Constitution, The United Methodist Church has long been strongly committed to the unity of the church: "As part of the church universal, The United Methodist Church believes that the Lord of the church is calling Christians everywhere to strive toward unity. . . ."[3] For many years, The United Methodist Church has devoted

2. *Bridge in Hope, Jewish-Christian Dialogue,* adopted by the General Conference of The United Methodist Church, 1972.
3. *The Book of Discipline of The United Methodist Church, 1992,* Constitution, Division One, Article 5; page 22.

itself at all levels of church life to building partnerships with other Christian denominations in striving to reveal the reality of the one Body, the whole church of Jesus Christ. "We see the Holy Spirit at work in making the unity among us more visible."[4]

By its *Book of Discipline,* The United Methodist Church is also dedicated to "serious interfaith encounters and explorations between Christians and adherents of other living faiths in the world." We believe that "Scripture calls us to be both neighbors and witnesses to all peoples. . . . In these encounters, our aim is not to reduce doctrinal differences to some lowest common denominator of religious agreement, but to raise all such relationships to the highest possible level of human fellowship and understanding."[5] In an interdependent world of increasing awareness of the vitality and challenges of religious pluralism, we are called to "labor together with the help of God toward the salvation, health, and peace of all people."[6]

As with all theological questions, United Methodists approach the issues of interfaith relationships, including Christian-Jewish dialogue, by seeking understanding of God's will in Scripture in the context of tradition, reason, and experience. In that spirit and with that intention, we affirm the following principles for continued study, discussion, and action within The United Methodist Church, with other Christians, and especially with Jews.

United Methodist Guiding Principles for Christian-Jewish Relations

In order to increase our understanding of and with peoples of other living faith traditions, of ourselves as followers of Jesus Christ, and of God and God's truth, The United Methodist Church encourages dialogue and experiences with those of other faiths. For important and unique reasons, including a treasury of shared Scripture and an ancient heritage that belong to us in common but which also contain our dividedness, we look particularly for such opportunities with Jews. United Methodist participation in Christian-Jewish dialogue and relationships is based on the following understandings:

4. *The Book of Discipline of The United Methodist Church, 1992,* Doctrinal Standards, Our Theological Task; page 84.
5. Ibid.
6. Ibid.

1. There is one living God, in whom both Jews and Christians believe.

While the Jewish and Christian traditions understand and express their faith in the same God in significantly different ways, we believe with Paul that God, who was in Christ reconciling the world to God's own self (2 Corinthians 5:18-19), is none other than the God of Israel, maker of heaven and earth. Above all else, Christians and Jews are bonded in our joyful and faithful response to the one God, living our faith as each understands God's call.

2. Jesus was a devout Jew, as were many of his first followers.

We know that understanding our Christian faith begins by recognizing and appreciating this seminal fact. Neither the ministry of Jesus and his apostles nor the worship and thought of the early church can be understood apart from the Jewish tradition, culture, and worship of the first century. Further, we believe that God's revelation in Jesus Christ is unintelligible apart from the story of what God did in the life of the people of Israel.

Because Christianity is firmly rooted in biblical Judaism, we understand that knowledge of these roots is essential to our faith. As expressed in a statement from the Consultation on the Church and Jewish People of the World Council of Churches: "We give thanks to God for the spiritual treasure we share with the Jewish people: faith in the living God of Abraham, Isaac, and Jacob; knowledge of the name of God and of the commandments; the prophetic proclamation of judgment and grace; the Hebrew Scriptures; and the hope of the coming Kingdom. In all these, we find common roots in biblical revelation and see spiritual ties that bind us to the Jewish people."[7]

3. Judaism and Christianity are living and dynamic religious movements that have continued to evolve since the time of Jesus, often in interaction with each other and with God's continual self-disclosure in the world.

Christians often have little understanding of the history of Judaism as it has developed since the lifetime of Jesus. As a World Council of Churches publication points out: "Bible-reading and worshiping Christians often believe that they 'know Judaism' since they have the Old Testament, the records of Jesus' debates with Jewish teachers and the early Christian reflections on the Judaism of their times. . . . This attitude is often reinforced by lack of knowledge about the history of

7. "The Churches and the Jewish People. . . . "

246

Jewish life and thought through the 1,900 years since the parting of the ways of Judaism and Christianity."[8]

As Christians, it is important for us to recognize that Judaism went on to develop vital new traditions of its own after the time of Jesus, including the Rabbinic Judaism that is still vibrant today in shaping Jewish religious life. This evolving tradition has given the Jewish people profound spiritual resources for creative life through the centuries. We increase our understanding when we learn about the rich variety of contemporary Jewish faith practice, theological interpretation, and worship, and discover directly through dialogue how Jews understand their own history, tradition, and faithful living.

4. *Christians and Jews are bound to God though biblical covenants that are eternally valid.*

As Christians, we stand firm in our belief that Jesus was sent by God as the Christ to redeem all people, and that in Christ the biblical covenant has been made radically new. While church tradition has taught that Judaism has been superseded by Christianity as the "new Israel," we do not believe that earlier covenantal relationships have been invalidated or that God has abandoned Jewish partners in covenant.

We believe that just as God is steadfastly faithful to the biblical covenant in Jesus Christ, likewise God is steadfastly faithful to the biblical covenant with the Jewish people. The covenant God established with the Jewish people through Abraham, Moses, and others continues because it is an eternal covenant. Paul proclaims that the gift and call of God to the Jews is irrevocable (Romans 11:29). Thus, we believe that the Jewish people continue in covenantal relationship with God.

Both Jews and Christians are bound to God in covenant, with no covenantal relationship invalidated by any other. Though Christians and Jews have different understandings of the covenant of faith, we are mysteriously bound to one another through our covenantal relationships with the one God and Creator of us all.

5. *As Christians, we are clearly called to witness to the gospel of Jesus Christ in every age and place. At the same time, we believe that God has continued, and continues today, to work through Judaism and the Jewish people.*

Essential to the Christian faith is the call to proclaim the good news of Jesus Christ to all people. Through the announcement of the gospel

---

8. "Ecumenical Considerations on Jewish-Christian Dialogue, 1993," World Council of Churches, paragraph 1.6.

in word and work comes the opportunity for others to glimpse the glory of God, which we have found through Jesus Christ. Yet we also understand that the issues of the evangelization of persons of other faiths, and of Jews in particular, are often sensitive and difficult. These issues call for continuing serious and respectful reflection and dialogue among Christians and with Jews.

While we as Christians respond faithfully to the call to proclaim the gospel in all places, we can never presume to know the full extent of God's work in the world, and we recognize the reality of God's activity outside the Christian church. It is central to our faith that salvation is accomplished not by human beings, but by God. We know that judgment as to the ultimate salvation of persons from any faith community, including Christianity and Judaism, belongs to God alone.

It is our belief that Jews and Christians are coworkers and companion pilgrims who have made the God of Israel known throughout the world. Through common service and action, we jointly proclaim the God we know. Together through study and prayer, we can learn how the God we believe to be the same God speaks and calls us continually into closer relationship with one another, as well as with God.

6. *As Christians, we are called into dialogue with our Jewish neighbors.*

Christians and Jews hold a great deal of Scripture, history, and culture in common. And yet, we also share 2,000 painful years of anti-Semitism and the persecution of Jews by Christians. These two apparently discordant facts move Christians to seek common experiences with Jews, and especially to invite them into dialogue to explore the meaning of our kinship and our differences. Our intention is to learn about the faith of one another and to build bridges of understanding.

While for Christians, dialogue will always include testimony to God's saving acts in Jesus Christ, it will include in equal measure listening to and respecting the understanding of Jews as they strive to live in obedience and faithfulness to God and as they understand the conditions of their faith.

Productive interfaith dialogue requires focused, sustained conversation based on willingness to recognize and probe genuine differences while also seeking that which is held in common. We are called to openness so that we may learn how God is speaking through our dialogue partners. As stated in the World Council of Churches' "Guidelines on Dialogue": "One of the functions of dialogue is to allow participants to describe and witness to their faith on their own

terms. . . . Participants seek to hear each other in order to better understand each other's faith, hopes, insights, and concerns."[9] Fruitful and
respectful dialogue is centered in a mutual spirit of humility, trust,
openness to new understanding, and commitment to reconciliation
and the healing of the painful wounds of our history.

7. *As followers of Jesus Christ, we deeply repent of the complicity of the
church and the participation of many Christians in the long history of persecution of the Jewish people.*

The Christian church has a profound obligation to correct historical
and theological teachings that have led to false and pejorative perceptions of Judaism and contributed to persecution and hatred of
Jews. It is our responsibility as Christians to oppose anti-Semitism
whenever and wherever it occurs.

We recognize with profound sorrow that repeatedly and often in
the last 2,000 years, the worship, preaching, and teaching of the
Christian church has allowed and sometimes even incited and
directed persecution against Jews.

The church today carries grave responsibility to counter the evil done
by Christians to Jews in the Crusades, the Inquisition, and the pogroms
of Eastern Europe and elsewhere, carried out in the name of Jesus
Christ. In the twentieth century there is the particular shame in the
failure of most of the church to challenge the policies of governments
that were responsible for the unspeakable atrocities of the Holocaust.

Historically and today, both the selective use and the misuse of
Scripture have fostered negative attitudes toward and actions against
Jews. Use of New Testament passages that blame "the Jews" for the
crucifixion of Jesus have throughout history been the basis of many
acts of discrimination against Jews, frequently involving physical violence. There is no doubt that traditional and often officially sanctioned
and promulgated Christian teachings, including the uncritical use of
anti-Jewish New Testament writings, have caused untold misery and
form the basis of modern anti-Semitism.

Misinterpretations and misunderstanding of historical and contemporary Judaism continue, including the mistaken belief that Judaism
is a religion solely of law and judgment while Christianity is a religion
of love and grace. The characterizations of God in the Hebrew Bible
(called the Old Testament by Christians) are rich and diverse; strong

9. "Guidelines on Dialogue," adopted at London Colney, England, by the Consultation
on the Church and the Jewish People of the Unit on Dialogue and People of Living Faiths
and Ideologies, World Council of Churches, 1981, paragraph 3.4.

images of a caring, compassionate, and loving deity are dominant for Jews as well as for Christians. Further, there are parallels between New Testament Christian understandings of the "spirit of the law" and contemporaneous theological developments in first-century Jewish theology.

The church has an obligation to correct erroneous and harmful past teachings and to ensure that the use of Scripture, as well as the preparation, selection, and use of liturgical and educational resources, does not perpetuate misleading interpretations and misunderstanding of Judaism.

It is also essential for Christians to oppose forcefully anti-Jewish acts and rhetoric that persist in the present time in many places. We must be zealous in challenging overt and subtle anti-Semitic stereotypes and bigoted attitudes that ultimately made the Holocaust possible, and which stubbornly and insidiously continue today. These lingering patterns are a call to Christians for ever-new educational efforts and continued vigilance, so that we, remembering and honoring the cries of the tortured and the dead, can claim with Jews around the world to be faithful to the post-Holocaust cry of "Never Again."

8. As Christians, we share a call with Jews to work for justice, compassion, and peace in the world in anticipation of the fulfillment of God's reign.

Together, Jews and Christians honor the commandment to love God with all our heart, soul, and might. It is our task to join in common opposition to those forces—nation, race, power, money—that clamor for ultimate allegiance. Together, we honor the commandment to love neighbor as self. It is our task to work in common for those things that are part of God's work of reconciliation. Together, we affirm the sacredness of all persons and the obligation of stewardship for all God has created.

Jews still await the messianic reign of God foretold by the prophets. Christians proclaim the good news that in Jesus Christ, "the kingdom of God is at hand"; yet we, as Christians, also wait in hope for the consummation of God's redemptive work. Together, Jews and Christians long for and anticipate the fulfillment of God's reign. Together, we are "partners in waiting." In our waiting, we are called to witness and to work for God's reign together.

9. As United Methodist Christians, we are deeply affected by the anguish and suffering that continue for many people who live in the Middle East region that includes modern Israel.

We commit ourselves through prayer and advocacy to bring about justice and peace for those of every faith.

Within The United Methodist Church, we struggle with our understanding of the complexity and the painfulness of the controversies in which Christians, Jews, and Muslims are involved in the Middle East. The issues include disputed political questions of sovereignty and control, and concerns over human rights and justice. We recognize the theological significance of the Holy Land as central to the worship, historical traditions, hope, and identity of the Jewish people. We are mindful of this land's historic and contemporary importance for Christians and Muslims. We are committed to the security, safety, and well-being of Jews and Palestinians in the Middle East, to respect for the legitimacy of the state of Israel, to justice and sovereignty for the Palestinian people, and to peace for all who live in the region.

As we join with others of many religious communities in wrestling with these issues and searching for solutions, we seek to work together with other Christians, Jews, and Muslims to honor the religious significance of this land and to bring about healthy, sustainable life, justice, and peace for all.

New Bridges to Christian-Jewish Understanding

The above statements of principle and affirmation offer a foundation for theological reflection within The United Methodist Church and with other Christians on our understanding of our relationships with the Jewish people. They are meant to be the basis of study, discussion, and action as we strive for greater discernment within the church.

Further, we hope that the statements of guiding principle will be important as bases of cooperative efforts, and especially for dialogue between United Methodists (sometimes in the company of other Christians) and Jewish communities, as we mutually explore the meaning of our kinship and our differences.

Using the foregoing foundation and principles, The United Methodist Church encourages dialogue with Jews at all levels of the church, including and especially local congregations. It is also hoped that there will be many other concrete expressions of Jewish-Christian relationships, such as participating in special occasions of interfaith observance, and joint acts of common service and programs of social transformation. These offer great opportunity to Christians and Jews to build relationships and together work for justice and peace (*shalom*) in our communities and in the world, serving humanity as God intends.

We dare to believe that such conversations and acts will build new bridges in hope between Christians and Jews, and that they will be among the signs and first fruits of our sibling relationship under our parent God. Together, we await and strive for the fulfillment of God's reign.

ADOPTED 1996
READOPTED 2004

See Social Principles, ¶ 162B

89. Called to Be Neighbors and Witnesses— Guidelines for Interreligious Relationships

Nations of the world are growing increasingly interdependent politically and economically. The various world religious communities are also encountering each other in new ways. Religions of Asia and Africa are showing new life and power within their homelands and are spreading to other continents, creating new multireligious societies, especially in western nations. New sects, cults, and ideologies are emerging and ancient traditions are receiving renewed attention. To an unprecedented degree, the wonders of the information age bring the world's rich religious diversity into our homes and communities.

The emergence of religiously diverse societies and the new dynamics in old religious communities have prompted many faith communities to reconsider how they relate to one another and to prevailing secular ideologies. This represents a great opportunity for learning and an enhanced understanding of our common concerns. Yet, there is also danger that religious tensions will lead to oppression of religious minorities and curtailment of religious freedom with real potential for armed conflict. At a time when worldwide problems of human suffering due to poverty, wars, and political oppression are so vast and pervasive that no one faith group can solve them, tensions between religious groups often prevent the level of cooperation needed to respond more adequately. As ancient religions demonstrate new life and power to speak to the deepest human concerns,

Christians are pressed toward a deeper understanding of other faith traditions and a reexamination of their own claims to a global mission to all people.

What are the implications of this religiously diverse situation for Christian theology and ministry? What does it mean to be a faithful follower of and witness to Jesus Christ? What does it mean to affirm the Lordship of Jesus Christ in a religiously pluralistic world? Can we, of different faith traditions, live together as neighbors, or will diverse religious loyalties result in mutual antagonism and destruction? What are the resources United Methodist Christians bring for building constructive relationships between persons of different religions?

The United Methodist Church provides this statement as guidance to its members and congregations in facing these questions in their relations with persons who hold other faith perspectives.

Called to Be Neighbors

For some Christians, it may seem strange even to refer to "persons who hold other faith perspectives." Some are accustomed to calling them "non-Christians" or "nonbelievers." These attitudes may have developed out of confidence in the ultimate truth of our own faith perspective or from limited experience of and insensitivity to other traditions, to the truth they may contain, and to the profound meaning and purpose they give to the lives of people. How, then, are we to relate to those who seem different from us religiously?

Scripture gives us many images of neighborliness which extends across conventional boundaries. In the Old Testament (Genesis 12), we find God challenging Abraham and Sarah to go live among strangers. In the New Testament, Jesus breaks convention by speaking with the Samaritan woman at the well (John 4:6-30) and shows how she can be reached through dialogue. Speaking with a lawyer (Luke 10:25), Jesus reminds him that his neighbor, the one to whom he should show love and compassion, and from whom he may receive grace, may be a stranger. Today, our Lord's call to neighborliness (Luke 10:27) includes the "strangers" of other faith traditions who live in our towns and cities. It is not just that historical events have forced us together. Christianity itself impels us to love our neighbors and to seek to live in contact and mutually beneficial relationships, in community, with them.

What does it mean to be a neighbor? It means to meet other persons, to know them, to relate to them, to respect them, and to learn about their ways which may be quite different from our own. It means to create a sense of community in our neighborhoods, towns and cities and to make them places in which the unique customs of each group can be expressed and their values protected. It means to create social structures in which there is justice for all and that everyone can participate in shaping their life together "in community." Each race or group of people is not only allowed to be who they are, but their way of life is also valued and given full expression.

Christians distinguish several meanings of "community." One definition expresses their relationships as members of one another in the body of Christ, the church, a people called together by Christ, a "communion of saints" who work toward the reign of God. A broader definition points to the relationship that is shared with others in the wider human community, where Christians are concerned for peace, justice, and reconciliation for all people. Other faiths also have their understanding of "community." The vision of a "worldwide community of communities" commends itself to many Christians as a way of being together with persons of different religious convictions in a pluralistic world.

Ultimately, this is to shift the question from, "To which church do we belong?" to "Have we participated in promoting the work of the Holy Spirit?" That suggests that we United Methodist Christians, not just individually, but corporately, are called to be neighbors with other faith communities (such as Buddhist, Jewish, Muslim, Hindu, and Native American), and to work with them to create a human community, a set of relationships between people at once interdependent and free, in which there is love, mutual respect, and justice.

Called to Be Witnesses

Within this religiously diverse community, Christians, trusting in Jesus Christ for their salvation, are called to witness to him as Lord to all people (Acts 1:8). We witness to our Lord through words which tell of his grace, through deeds of service and social change that demonstrate his love, and through our life together in the Christian community, exhibiting God's power to heal, reconcile, and unite.

When Jesus issued his famous missionary mandate, "Go therefore and make disciples of all nations" (Matthew 28:20), the Greek word is *poreuthentes*. This literally means "to depart, to leave, to cross boundaries." Thus, a witness to Jesus Christ is one who can bridge boundaries, be they geographic, sociological, racial, or cultural. The gospels tell story after story of Jesus crossing boundaries and reaching to outsiders, drawing them into his circle. As disciples of Jesus, our outreach draws upon the gospel call to be even more than neighbors. We are to proclaim and witness to the God who has bound humanity together in care for one another, regardless of the differences between us.

As relationships with persons of other faith communities deepen, Christians discover how often our witness has been unneighborly, how much we have talked and how little we have listened, and how our insensitive and unappreciative approaches have alienated sincere truth seekers and persons who already have strong faith commitments. We become aware that we frequently communicate attitudes of superiority regarding our own faith, thereby perpetuating walls and hostilities between us as human beings. These can only restrict Christian witness.

As United Methodist Christians reflect anew on our faith and seek guidance in our witness to and encounter with our new neighbors, we rediscover that God who has acted in Jesus Christ for the salvation of the whole world, is also Creator of all humankind, the "one God and Father of all, who is Lord of all, works through all, and is in all" (Eph. 4:6 TEV). Here Christians confront a profound mystery—the awareness of God who is related to all creation and at work in the whole of it, and the experience of God who has acted redemptively for the whole creation in Jesus Christ. Christians witness to God in Jesus Christ in the confidence that here all people can find salvation and in the trust that because of what we know of God in Jesus, God deals graciously and lovingly with all people everywhere.

Dialogue—A Way to Be Neighbors

"Dialogue" is the word which has come to signify an approach to persons of other faith communities which takes seriously both the call to witness and the command to love and be neighbors. To be engaged in dialogue is to see witnessing and neighborliness as interrelated activities. Rather than a one-sided address, dialogue combines witnessing with listening. It is the intentional engagement with persons who hold other faith perspectives for purposes of mutual under-standing, cooperation, and transformation.

"Dialogue" may be as informal as a conversation in the marketplace or as formal as the leader of one religious group explaining to others its belief or worship life. Dialogue is more than an individual or aca-demic enterprise. It also involves groups or communities of people holding different convictions who reach out to one another. This com-munity orientation gives a practical bent to interreligious dialogue.

In dialogue, one individual or group may seek relationship with another in order to expose misunderstandings and stereotypes and to break down barriers that separate and create hostility and conflict. Ethnic or religious communities may approach each other in dialogue in order to resolve particular problems or to foster cooperation in deal-ing with a local, national, or even global situation of human suffering. At its deepest level, dialogue is both learning about and sharing our faith through its stories and images. Each partner learns from the rich store of wisdom of the other, and each expresses his or her own deep-est conviction in the faith that it has truth worth sharing with the other.

Through dialogue with persons of other faith communities, new insights are received regarding God's activity in the world today, the divine purpose for humankind as a whole, and the place of the Christian community within these purposes. It is also a common experience for Christians to feel the need to express their own faith with greater clarity. We trust in the Holy Spirit to make known new and different insights through such encounters.

Even though Jews, Christians and Muslims share the same covenant, in many of our cities and towns we continue to live as strangers to each other. A positive foundation from which to connect with persons in other faith communities is recognition of some of the gifts they bring to the human community. For instance, through Judaism, Christians can connect to the covenantal faithfulness of God; Islam illustrates the joy of life lived in obedience to God's will; the spiritualities of indigenous peoples encourage a deep reverence for God's natural creation; Buddhism offers contemplative ways to con-nect to the divine; and Hinduism in its varieties brings the gift of tol-erance. Engaging in dialogue with positive expectation offers the possibility of sharing mutually beneficial spiritual gifts as well as overcoming past hostilities.

Dialogue frequently has been misunderstood. Some see it as limited to the commonalities that exist between different religious traditions.

It is important to discern and explore those commonalities and to utilize them to strengthen relationships. But there is more! Dialogue offers to both partners the opportunity of enriching their own faith through the wisdom of the other. In the process it helps overcome the deep mistrust, hatred, hostility, and conflict that characterize so many intercultural and interreligious relations. Each religious community asserts that its faith offers a way to resolve conflict in positive ways and has resources for building community among diverse peoples. Dialogue seeks to provide an environment which allows space for differences, builds on the positive affirmations of each faith, and brings them into relationship with each other.

Dialogue—A Way to Witness

The only precondition for dialogue—sometimes a challenging one—is a true willingness to enter a relationship of mutual acceptance, openness, and respect. Effective dialogue requires that both partners have deep convictions about life, faith, and salvation. True dialogue requires that Christians not suspend their fundamental convictions concerning the truth of the gospel, but enter into dialogue with personal commitment to Jesus Christ and with the desire to witness to that faith. Effective dialogue also requires that Christians be truly open to persons of other faith communities, to their convictions about life, truth, and salvation and to their witness, as others also feel called to witness to their faith and teachings about the meaning of life. Engagement in dialogue is a form of Christian ministry.

Is not this urge to witness an obstacle to interreligious dialogue? It often has been, but it need not be. Where there is listening as well as speaking, openness and respect as well as concern to influence, there is dialogue and witness. Indeed, dialogue at its most profound level is an exchange of witness. Participants share with each other their perceptions of the meaning of life, of ultimate reality, salvation and hope, and the resources of their faith for enabling community. In genuine "dialogue," we "witness and are witnessed to." The most effective dialogue takes place when both sides really do care that the other hear, understand, and receive the other's wisdom. Part of our witness is our openness to hearing the witness of the other.

Dialogue at these depths holds great promise. Long-cherished convictions may be modified by the encounter with others. Misunderstanding may be clarified, potential hostilities reconciled, and new insights regarding one's own faith may emerge in contrast to that of another. The depths of another's faith may be so disclosed that its power and attractiveness are experienced. Dialogue is a demanding process, requiring thorough understanding of one's own faith and clear articulation of it to the other person. It asks that we "translate" our perspectives to one another with integrity, that we have the patience and attentiveness to discern what meaning words and images have for the other persons as well as ourselves.

Dialogue is not a betrayal of witness. Dialogue and witness are wrongly placed in opposition to each other. They need each other. Dialogue creates relationships of mutual understanding, openness ,and respect. Witness presses dialogue to the deepest convictions about life, death, and hope.

Many persons of other faiths are suspicious that dialogue is a new and more subtle tool for conversion. In some ways this is inevitable since Christians do want others to learn of and receive the truth and grace we know in Jesus Christ. The difference between dialogue and other forms of witness is that it is a context for learning from the other the truth and wisdom of the other faith as well as sharing with the other the truth and wisdom of our own. We leave to the Holy Spirit the outcome of our mutual openness. Our concern is to be obedient to our own call to witness and to follow the imperative to be loving and neighborly to persons of other faith communities. In dialogue, these deeply held truths encounter each other in witness and love, so that greater wisdom and greater understanding of truth may emerge which benefit all parties in the dialogue. As we exhibit courtesy, reverence, and respect and become neighbors, fears of each other are allayed, and the Holy Spirit works within these relationships.

Neighbors and Witnesses—Into the New Millennium

The command to love one's neighbors and the call to witness to Jesus Christ to all people are inseparably linked. The profound challenge which this represents for United Methodist Christians can be seen most sharply in the new religious movements which have arisen in recent years. These movements have become a source of concern for many Christians. Some groups seem to utilize methods that are manipulative and coercive.

However, many people have found new vision, meaning, and hope in some of these new faith perspectives. These new religious movements are very diverse and they should not be lumped together indiscriminately, condemned, and dismissed. Neither should they automatically be embraced as valid expressions of human dignity and freedom. Careful study and contact will enable Christians to distinguish those which are manipulative and coercive and which are to be challenged for reasons of faith.

As we take seriously this calling to be witnesses and neighbors to people of all faith communities, old and new, we become aware of the biblical caution not to bear false witness (Matthew19:18) and the admonition to live at peace with all people (Hebrews 12:14). How are we to avoid bearing false witness unless we know our neighbors and understand their faith commitments? How can one truly love a neighbor and hold back what to Christians is the greatest of all gifts—God becoming present to people in Jesus Christ? How can we live peacefully together, unless we are willing to be neighborly? How can we say we love our neighbor if we are unwilling to be attentive to the message and the gifts which God has given him or her? Love of neighbor and witness to Christ are the two primary attitudes United Methodist Christians must affirm in their relationship with persons of other faith traditions. When we affirm our love for the neighbor, we discover that God has given us another gift—people in other faith communities. We join hands with them to fight against the evil powers and principalities of this earth.

God is calling United Methodists into a new millennium full of its own challenges and opportunities. We seek to learn how the Holy Spirit works among all peoples of the world, especially among those in other religious traditions. We desire to read the holy texts that others believe to be inspired by God and to open ourselves to the power and spiritual insights held in the stories, images, and rituals of other traditions. And we pray for guidance as we yearn to proclaim the Savior whom we know among people who believe in other saviors and lords. May all our mission and witness to the peoples of this world be inspired by the Holy Spirit and centered in the love taught us by Jesus Christ.

Guidelines for Interreligious Relationships

The following guidelines will assist United Methodists to be faithful to their call to witness and the call to be neighbors with persons of other faith communities.

1. Identify the various faith communities in your area and begin to familiarize your congregation with them. This may involve planned experiences which bring faith communities into contact with one another or the formation of study groups which provide an introduction to other faith traditions.

2. Initiate dialogues with other faith communities, remaining sensitive to areas of historic tension yet open to the possibilities for deepened understanding and new insight. Each partner must forthrightly face the issues that cause separation as well as those that create unity.

3. Work in practical ways with persons of other faith communities to resolve economic, social, cultural and political problems in the community. Soup kitchens, food pantries, Habitat for Humanity projects and other such efforts can be an effective focus for shared concerns for the common good.

4. Together with persons of other faith traditions, plan community celebrations with an interreligious perspective. Prepare carefully. Sensitivity to the integrity of each tradition is essential. Care should be taken not to relativize all religious symbols and practices nor minimize religious differences.

5. Develop new models of community building which strengthen relationships and allow people to dwell together in harmony while honoring the integrity of their differences.

Intent

The intent in developing interreligious relationships is not to amalgamate all faiths into one religion. We Christians have no interest in such syncretism. To engage in interreligious dialogue is neither to endorse nor to deny the faith of other people. In dialogue we seek insight into the wisdom of other traditions and we hope to overcome our fears and misapprehensions about them. Far from requiring a lessening of commitment to Christ, effective dialogue is only possible when one's own faith is strong, and may ultimately serve to deepen or extend it.

We Christians are seeking to be neighbors with persons whose religious commitments are different from our own and to engage each other about the deepest convictions of our lives. In our assurance of and trust in God's grace in Jesus Christ, we open ourselves to dialogue and engagement with persons of other faith communities and to other Christians whose understandings may be different from our own.

This interreligious engagement challenges United Methodist Christians to think in new ways about our lives in the broader human community, about our mission, evangelism, service, and our life together within the Christian church. We seek to promote peace and harmony with persons of other religious traditions in our various towns, cities, and neighborhoods. Yet we do not hide our differences, nor avoid conflicts, but seek to make them constructive. In each place, we share our lives with each other, we witness and are witnessed to, we invite others into the Christian community and we are invited into theirs. Our prayer is that the lives of all in each place will be enriched by the differences of others, that a new sense of community may emerge, and that others may receive the gift of God in Christ, while we receive the gifts which have been given them.

ADOPTED 1980
REVISED AND ADOPTED 2000

See Social Principles, ¶ 162B.

90. Continue Membership in Churches Uniting in Christ

WHEREAS, the Constitution of The United Methodist Church states that the dividedness in the church of Jesus Christ "is a hindrance to its mission in the world" and has committed us to ecumenical involvement; and,

WHEREAS, the predecessor churches of The United Methodist Church were founding members of Churches Uniting in Christ (formerly Consultation on Church Union), and The United Methodist Church has been an active supporter of COCU/CUIC for more than 30 years; and,

WHEREAS, the 1988 General Conference of The United Methodist Church affirmed the COCU Consensus as an authentic expression of the apostolic faith and a sufficient theological foundation for covenanting; and,

WHEREAS, the 1996 General Conference adopted *Churches in Covenant Communion: Churches of Christ Uniting* as the definitive agreement for joining with other churches in covenant communion; and,

WHEREAS, the 1999 plenary of the Consultation on Church Union approved a *Call to Christian Commitment and Action to Combat Racism* and recommends a process using the materials and implementing action within the member communions; and,

WHEREAS, the 2000 General Conference of The United Methodist Church:

- affirmed the progress of the Consultation on Church Union in its journey toward greater visible unity among the member churches under the name of Churches Uniting in Christ; and
- affirmed the following *Marks of Unity* as goals on the journey to be lived out when in accord with *The Book of Discipline*:

1. Mutual recognition of each other as authentic expressions of the one church of Jesus Christ,

2. Mutual recognition of members in one baptism,

3. Mutual recognition that each affirms the apostolic faith of Scripture and tradition which is expressed in the Apostles' and Nicene Creeds and that each seeks to give witness to the apostolic faith in its life and mission,

4. Provision for celebration of the Eucharist together with intentional regularity,

5. Engagement together in Christ's mission on a regular and intentional basis, especially a shared mission to combat racism,

6. Intentional commitment to promote unity with wholeness and to oppose all marginalization

and exclusion in church and society based on such things as race, age, gender, forms of disability, sexual orientation, and class,

7. Appropriate structures of accountability and appropriate means for consultation and decision making,

8. An ongoing process of theological dialogue; and

WHEREAS, the 2000 General Conference of The United Methodist Church directed: (1) the Council of Bishops and the General Commission on Christian Unity and Interreligious Concerns (GCCUIC) to lead The United Methodist Church in its membership in the Consultation on Church Union and to continue dialogue with covenanting partners, clarifying questions and developing a covenanting process; and (2) the Council of Bishops and the GCCUIC to promote the *Call to Christian Commitment and Action to Combat Racism* throughout The United Methodist Church and to advocate for its study and implementation; and

WHEREAS, on January 19, 2002, "A Service of Dissolution" was conducted to mark the dissolution of the Consultation on Church Union; and

WHEREAS, on January 20, 2002, the covenanting partners witnessed the inauguration of a new relationship as Churches Uniting In Christ (CUIC) growing in faith together, worshiping God together, combating racism together, proclaiming the Gospel together, pursuing wholeness together, and being church together;

Therefore, be it resolved, that the 2004 General Conference of The United Methodist

Church reaffirm its membership in and support of Churches Uniting in Christ in accordance with *The Book of Discipline* 2000, and

Be it further resolved, that the 2004 General Conference direct the Council of Bishops and the General Commission on Christian Unity and Interreligious Concerns to lead The United Methodist Church in its membership in Churches Uniting in Christ and in being a good neighbor.

ADOPTED 2004

See Social Principles, ¶ 162.

91. Continue Membership in the National Council of Churches

WHEREAS, the Constitution of The United Methodist Church states that the dividedness in the church of Jesus Christ "is a hindrance to its mission in the world" and has committed us to ecumenical involvement; and,

WHEREAS, The United Methodist Church and its predecessor churches have been charter members of the National Council of the Churches of Christ in the U.S.A.; and,

WHEREAS, The NCCCUSA is a "community through which the churches are seeking to make visible their unity given in Christ"; and,

WHEREAS, the NCCCUSA is "an instrument of the churches' ecumenical witness to live responsibly in mutual accountability and service"; and,

WHEREAS, the NCCCUSA provides a unique opportunity for denominational representatives to share divergent traditions in matters of faith and practice; and,

WHEREAS, the NCCCUSA provides a channel for denominational cooperation in Christian education, mission and justice issues, communications, interfaith matters, evangelism, and relationships with local ecumenical expressions; and,

WHEREAS, United Methodist delegates from each of the jurisdictions have offered distinguished leadership to the NCCCUSA, and successive General Conferences have supported the continuing membership in the NCCCUSA since its founding in 1950; and,

WHEREAS, we rejoiced in the celebration of the fiftieth anniversary of the founding of the NCCCUSA in 2000,

Therefore, be it resolved, that the 2004 General Conference of The United Methodist Church reaffirm its membership in and support of the National Council of the Churches of Christ in the U.S.A., in accordance with the 2004 *Book of Discipline,* ¶2404.2.a.

ADOPTED 1992
AMENDED AND ADOPTED 2000, 2004

See Social Principles, ¶ 162.

92. Continue Membership in the World Council of Churches

WHEREAS, the Constitution of The United Methodist Church states that the dividedness in the church of Jesus Christ "is a hindrance to its mission in the world" and has committed us to ecumenical involvement; and,

WHEREAS, The United Methodist Church and its predecessor churches were founding members of the World Council of Churches (WCC); and,

WHEREAS, United Methodist delegates in leadership positions among the over 330 member churches continue to make significant contributions to this world wide body, and the General Conference and the Council of Bishops have continued to offer strong commitment for the WCC; and,

WHEREAS, we rejoice in the continuing leadership of Kathryn Bannister (Kansas West Annual Conference) as a president of the WCC; and,

WHEREAS, the United Methodist delegates from each of the jurisdictions and central conferences have offered distinguished leadership in the WCC, and successive General Conferences have supported the continuing membership in the WCC since its founding in 1948;

Therefore, be it resolved, that the 2004 General Conference of The United Methodist Church reaffirm its membership in and support of the World Council of Churches, in accordance with the 2004 *Book of Discipline* (¶ 2404.3).

ADOPTED 2004

See Social Principles, ¶ 162.

93. Continue Membership in the World Methodist Council

WHEREAS, the Constitution of The United Methodist Church states that the dividedness in the church of Jesus Christ "is a hindrance to its mission in the world" and has committed us to ecumenical involvement; and,

WHEREAS, The United Methodist Church and its predecessor churches have been members of the World Methodist Council since its first session in 1881 (under the name of the Ecumenical Methodist Conference); and,

WHEREAS, the World Methodist Council is an appropriate forum for Wesleyans; and

WHEREAS, the United Methodist delegates have offered distinguished leadership to the WMC, and successive General Conferences have supported the continuing membership in the WMC since its founding in 1950;

Therefore, be it resolved, that General Conference of 2004 reaffirm its membership in and support of the World Methodist Council, in accordance with the 2004 *Book of Discipline* (¶ 2403.1); and,

Be it further resolved, that the General Conference encourage The United Methodist Church to support "Achieving the Vision," the current endowment initiative of the World Methodist Council to ensure the future mission and ministry of the Council.

ADOPTED 2004

See Social Principles, ¶ 162.

94. Guidelines for Cooperation in Mission

WHEREAS, the World Methodist Council has recommended the following be adopted by its member churches:

People of the Wesleyan heritage look upon the whole world as their parish. They feel committed to preach the gospel of Jesus Christ to all people.

Many of the churches in that Methodist tradition are responding anew to the call for mission in the whole world. There are changing patterns of migration and increasing movements of peoples, both geographically and spiritually. As a result new Methodist missions are started in areas where there are already communities and churches of the Wesleyan tradition working. In places, this has created confusion and unhealthy competition and has been an offense to the gospel. Sometimes, both clergy and laity seek to move from one church to another.

It is natural to those who are in the tradition of John Wesley to seek out and respond to new opportunities and to respond to requests for help. We want to stretch out our hand to all whose heart is as our heart and to work closely together. Our instinct is to share as fully as possible with all who share with us in the same mission. We are therefore committed to support each other in our work and to do nothing that would undermine each other.

In this fluid situation the World Methodist Council finds it necessary for the sake of its common mission to ask its member churches to agree on some principles and guidelines on this matter.

Three basic principles should apply especially to all such Methodist work being done by different member churches in the same area.
- Respect
- Courtesy
- Communication and consultation

Two consequences follow:

1. When any member churches of the WMC are intending to support and endorse new work in an area of the world, before agreeing officially:
- Other member churches should be notified.
- Advice should be sought in order to minimize, or prevent, any duplication of resources.

We are aware that the needs of people of particular languages or cultures may make new mission work necessary. But the principles of respect, courtesy, and communication should ensure that all our traditions can delight in new manifestations of the work of God's Spirit. The Holy Spirit often works beyond our own boundaries and limitations. At the same time, whenever possible, we would encourage those involved in "new" Methodist movements to link with an existing church. We believe it is possible to order our relationships in a cooperative way and to help new fellowships to seek the most appropriate church to join.

2. The same principle should apply where member churches presently find themselves working alongside each other in various countries:

- Different Methodist traditions should be encouraged to join together, or at least to work in a spirit of consultation and cooperation.
- Different Methodist traditions should communicate fully with each other, and thereby share resources and experience for the furtherance of God's Kingdom.

No member churches should be working in competition with each other, because this implies the breakdown of respect, courtesy, and communication. Good practice would be to develop regular meetings and clear protocols governing the relationship of churches together in particular areas.

The World Methodist Council, through its officers, offers its good services to provide a platform and the channels necessary for information and consultation between its member churches on these matters.

Therefore, be it resolved, that The United Methodist Church adopts these guidelines in its commitment to the pursuit of Christ's call to Christian unity and in a spirit of solidarity with other member churches of the World Methodist Council.

ADOPTED 2004

See Social Principles, ¶162.

95. Continuation of Commission on Pan-Methodist Cooperation and Union

WHEREAS, the Constitution of The United Methodist Church states that the dividedness in the church of Jesus Christ "is a hindrance to its mission in the world" and has committed us to ecumenical involvement; and

WHEREAS, the Constitution of The United Methodist Church calls for our church to "seek, and work, for unity at all levels of church life" (¶ 6); and

WHEREAS, The United Methodist Church has a historical relationship and shared tradition with the African Methodist Episcopal Church, The African Methodist Episcopal Zion Church, and the Christian Methodist Episcopal Church; and

WHEREAS, the Third Consultation of Methodist Bishops in 1983 approved a request calling for the creation of a Commission on Pan-Methodist Cooperation as a successor to the Pan-Methodist Bicentennial Committee and the Missional Thrust Convocation; and

WHEREAS, the General Conference of 1984 authorized involvement in a Commission on Pan-Methodist Cooperation "to define, determine, plan, and, in cooperation with established agencies of the several denominations, execute activities to foster meaningful cooperation" (¶ 2403.2); and

WHEREAS, the Commission on Pan-Methodist Cooperation was duly convened and inaugurated on May 27, 1985; and

WHEREAS, the Sixth Consultation of Methodist Bishops in April 1995 approved a resolution to the respective General Conferences calling for the creation of a Commission on Union whose purpose was to build on the work of the earlier Study Commission established in 1994; and

WHEREAS, the Commission on Union was duly convened and inaugurated on December 2, 1997; and

WHEREAS, representatives from the African Methodist Episcopal, African Methodist Episcopal Zion, Christian Methodist Episcopal, and The United Methodist churches labored in the Commission on Pan-Methodist Cooperation on models of cooperation while the representatives of the four denominations labored in the Commission on Union on various models of union; and

WHEREAS, the 2000 and 2004 General Conferences of the four denominations took action to consolidate the Commission on Pan-Methodist Cooperation and the Commission on Union into the Commission on Pan-Methodist Cooperation and Union, which was convened and inaugurated on November 29, 2000; and

WHEREAS, we affirm the consolidation of the two former Commissions to form the Commission on Pan-Methodist Cooperation and Union to better oversee the continuing cooperative work toward union; and

WHEREAS, the first and most difficult lesson that the Commission on Pan-Methodist Cooperation and Union has learned during the past quadrennium is that, as with any worthwhile efforts that are of God, progress is slow and only comes with constant discernment of the will of the Holy Spirit; and

WHEREAS, the work of the Commission on Pan-Methodist Cooperation and Union has produced encouraging opportunities for cooperation in program ministries as noted in the Commission's report to the General Conferences; and

WHEREAS, the Commission on Pan-Methodist Cooperation and Union continues to struggle with the difficult issues of reconciliation, cooperation, and union, in the midst of repentance and forgiveness; and

WHEREAS, we celebrate the changes enacted by the [United Methodist] General Conference of 2000 to include Pan-Methodist representatives as full members of all United Methodist general agencies; and

WHEREAS, events and activities planned and held across the Pan-Methodist connection can work for the unit we seek,

Therefore, be it resolved, that the 2004 General Conference of The United Methodist Church continue the work of the Commission on Pan-Methodist Cooperation and Union and authorize the provision of its membership and budget; and

Be it further resolved, that the 2004 General Conference further endorse and promote the implementation of the Pan-Methodist Initiative on Children in Poverty; and

Be it further resolved, that the Commission on Pan-Methodist Cooperation and Union be composed of nine (9) persons from each Pan-Methodist denomination: three bishops, three clergy, and three lay persons, one of whom should be a young adult (either clergy or lay), with sensitivity given to continuity of participation.

Models of union shall continue to be instituted and tested by the Commission on Pan-Methodist Cooperation and Union throughout the next quadrennium.

Progress reports shall continue to be made regularly to each body of bishops and to each of the General Conferences no later than 2010.

The quadrennial budget of the Commission on Pan-Methodist Cooperation and Union shall be $140,000 to be allocated proportionately to each Pan-Methodist denomination based on membership.

Be it further resolved, that a Pan-Methodist approach be given to any major event planned by a general agency of The United Methodist

Church, by the agency's notifying early in the planning stage: (1) the corresponding agency or responsible staff in the other Pan-Methodist denominations, and (2) the members of the United Methodist delegation on the Commission on Pan-Methodist Cooperation and Union; and

Be it further resolved, that the General Council on Ministries or its successor agency as defined by *The Book of Discipline* establish a Pan-Methodist approach to its coordinating responsibilities.

ADOPTED 2004

See Social Principles, ¶162A.

96. Encounter with Christ in Latin America and the Caribbean

WHEREAS, the missional initiative Encounter with Christ in Latin America and the Caribbean of the General Board of Global Ministries has achieved the initial goal of one million dollars on behalf of our United Methodist partnership in mission with the Methodist churches of Latin America and the Caribbean; and

WHEREAS, the stated goal of twenty-five million dollars to constitute the Encounter permanent fund in order to provide earned income for comprehensive mission partnership provides one means of securing resources to undergird a holistic strategy on Latin America and the Caribbean; and

WHEREAS, the initial success in securing funding for Encounter, and the experience in mission education in sharing the need and opportunities for partnership in witnessing to Christ through the Methodist churches of the region might be utilized in the development of a special program for the region; and

WHEREAS, the Encounter with Christ initiative seeks to strengthen the unity and shared mission outreach of Methodist churches bound together through the Council of Evangelical Churches of Latin America and the Caribbean (CIEMAL) and the Methodist Church of the Caribbean and the Americas (MCCA); and

WHEREAS, the VIII General Assembly of CIEMAL, meeting in Piracicaba, Brazil, in May, 2003, affirmed the importance of Encounter for the churches of the region, and unanimously agreed to make a special contribution to Encounter and include support for Encounter in the yearly CIEMAL budget;

Therefore, be it resolved, that General Conference celebrate the achievement of reaching the initial goal of one million dollars for this missional initiative that was endorsed as a priority for United Methodists by previous General Conference action, express gratitude to a host of supporters, and call upon annual conferences, local churches, and individuals to renew and increase their commitment in order to reach the twenty-five million dollar goal.

ADOPTED 2004

See Social Principles, ¶162.

97. Resolution of Intent—With a View to Unity

In 1750, John Wesley wrote the sermon "Catholic Spirit," in which he presented his views on mutual tolerance among those seeking to unite in love:

". . . And 'tis certain, so long as 'we know' but 'in part', that all men [sic] will not see all things alike. It is an unavoidable consequence of the present weakness and shortness of human understanding that several men will be of several minds, in religion as well as in common life. So it has been from the beginning of the world, and so it will be 'till the restitution of all things'.

"Nay farther: although every man necessarily believes that every particular opinion which he holds is true (for to believe any opinion is not true is the same thing as not to hold it) yet can no man be assured that all his own opinions taken together are true. Nay, every thinking man is assured they are not, seeing *humanum est errare et necire*—to be ignorant of many things, and to mistake in some—is the necessary condition of humanity. This therefore, he is sensible, is his own case. He knows in the general that he himself is not mistaken; although in what particulars he mistakes he does not, perhaps cannot, know.

"I say, perhaps he cannot know. For who can tell how far invincible ignorance may extend? Or (what comes to the same thing) invincible prejudice; which is often so fixed in tender minds that it is afterwards impossible to tear up what has taken so deep a root. And who can say, unless he knew every circumstance attending it, how far any mistake is culpable? Seeing all guilt must suppose some concurrence of the will—of which he only can judge who searcheth the heart.

"Every wise man therefore will allow others the same liberty of thinking which he desires they should allow him; and will no more insist on their embracing his opinions than he would have them to insist on his embracing theirs. He bears with those who differ from him, and only asks him with whom he desires to unite in love that single question. 'Is thine heart, as my heart is with thy heart?' " (*The Works of John Wesley*, Volume 2, Sermons II, "Catholic Spirit," 83-85).

Unfortunately, in Wesley's 1784 abridgment of the Thirty-Nine Articles of the Church of England, and not in keeping with the tone of "Catholic Spirit," a number of strong statements against the Roman Catholic Church were included.

In 1970 the General Conference adopted a resolution of intent. It was offered to the conference by Albert Outler on behalf of the Theological Study Commission on Doctrine and Doctrinal Standards. Engaged in the debate, among others, were Harold A. Bosley, Robert E. Cushman, and Georgia Harkness. The resolution was adopted as presented (*Journal of the 1970 General Conference, The United Methodist Church*, 255). However, the resolution was not included in, or was mistakenly deleted from, *The Book of Resolutions of The United Methodist Church*, 1970.

At the General Conference of 1992, a new resolution, "Ecumenical Interpretations of Doctrinal Standards," offered by the General Commission on Christian Unity and Interreligious Concerns, was received, adopted, and subsequently printed in *The Book of Resolutions of The United Methodist Church*, 1992 (245-46). Although grounded in the Study Commisssion's resolution of intent, this document is not as comprehensive in its scope as was the original, with specific reference to our current understanding of the composition of our Doctrinal Standards.

The original resolution of intent is resubmitted as a substitute for "Ecumenical Interpretations of Doctrinal Standards":

WHEREAS, it is common knowledge that the context of the original Thirty-Nine Articles (1563—and specifically Articles XIV, XIX, XXI, XXII, XXIV, XXV, XXVIII, XXX) was bitterly polemical, it is of prime importance in an ecumenical age that they should be reconsidered and reassessed. They were aimed, deliberately, at the Roman Catholic Church in a time of reckless strife, and were a mix of the theological and nontheological convictions of embattled schismatics fighting, as they believed, for national survival and evangelical truth. John Wesley's hasty abridgement (1784) of the original Thirty-Nine Articles (down to twenty-four) retained seven out of the ten of these anti-Roman references (XIV, XV, XVI, XVIII, XIX, XX, XXI) in his enumeration. This reflects his conviction as to their applicability to the Roman Catholic Church as he perceived it at the time. This much must be recognized and acknowledged as belonging to our inheritance from our Anglican-Wesleyan past.

It is, however, one of the virtues of historical insight that it enables persons, in a later age, to recognize the circumstances of earlier events and documents without being slavishly bound to their historical evaluation, especially in a subsequent epoch when relationships have been radically altered. Such a transvaluation will enable us freely to relegate the polemics in these articles (and the anathemas of Trent, as well) to our memories "Of old, unhappy, far-off tales/And battles long ago" and to rejoice in the positive contemporary relationships that are being developed between The United Methodist Church and the Roman Catholic Church, at levels both official and unofficial.

Therefore, be it resolved, that we declare it our official intent henceforth to interpret all our Articles, Confession, and other "standards of doctrine" in consonance with our best ecumenical insights and judgment, as these develop in the light of the Resolution of the 1968 General Conference on "The Methodist Church and the Cause of Christian Unity" (*Book of Resolutions 1968,* 65-72). This implies, at the very least, our heartiest offer of goodwill and Christian community to all our Roman Catholic brothers and sisters, in the avowed hope of the day when all bitter memories (ours and theirs) will have been redeemed by the gift of the fullness of Christian unity, from the God and [Creator] Father of our common Lord, Jesus Christ (*Journal of the 1970 General Conference, The United Methodist Church,* 255).

ADOPTED 2000

See Social Principles, ¶ 162.

EDUCATION

98. Education, The Gift of Hope

WHEREAS, John Wesley was a "unique and remarkable educator (who) gave to the whole Methodist movement . . . a permanent passion for education"[1], and

1. *The Story of Methodism,* Halford E. Luccock, Paul Hutchinson, Robert W. Goodloe (Abingdon Press, 1926; page 361).

WHEREAS, Wesley believed that persons develop their full God-given potential when they educate their mind as well as nurture their spirit; and

WHEREAS, the historic United Methodist concern for education is witnessed through commitment to educational opportunity for all persons regardless of gender or ethnic origin, or economic or social background; and

WHEREAS, this commitment continues as United Methodist individuals, congregations, colleges, campus ministries, and other groups become involved in local education in their communities; and

WHEREAS, these efforts make a significant contribution to furthering access, advancing and enhancing student learning, and advocating for the continued improvement of educational opportunity; and

WHEREAS, educators, families, and communities are concerned about substance abuse and violence in our schools and communities, along with other social problems which undermine the safety of children and the quality of their lives in school and in society at large; and

WHEREAS, United Methodists have a moral concern to take initiatives to support and create alliances involving educators, community leaders, and students to address the challenges of contemporary education and to work to resolve the threats to quality education; and

WHEREAS, the 1996 General Conference of The United Methodist Church received *Education: The Gift of Hope,* a study of the historic and current United Methodist concern for education, and urged every local church to use the study to understand our historic educational concern and to become enlivened in educational partnerships in the local community; and

WHEREAS, the General Board of Higher Education and Ministry has revised *Education: The Gift of Hope,* to address concerns about drugs and violence in our schools and to further remind United Methodists of the Wesleyan challenge to become involved in local efforts in education;

Therefore, be it resolved, that every local United Methodist congregation is encouraged to study *Education: The Gift of Hope* to learn of our heritage and concern; and

Be it further resolved, that each local congregation develop a strategy for being in partnership with local educators, community leaders, and students in providing a positive, safe, helpful, and hopeful environment in which students can live and learn and grow.

ADOPTED 1996
AMENDED AND READOPTED 2000

See Social Principles, ¶ 162D.

99. Revitalizing The United Methodist Church and Theological Education

The United Methodist Church has a long, rich tradition in American higher education. American Methodism has been committed to education since its inception. At the Christmas Conference of 1784, the first action was the election of a bishop and the establishment of Cokesbury College in Abingdon, Maryland. This action was symbolically and substantively important because the conference unquestionably spoke and acted on two high priority items. One was leadership (electing the bishop), and the other was program (establishing Cokesbury College).

Soon thereafter, newly elected Bishop Francis Asbury wrote to all Methodists, reminding them of their obligation to erect a school in the vicinity of every church, "to give the key of knowledge in a general way to your children, and those of the poor in the vicinity of your small towns and villages."[1] Bishop Asbury set the church-wide vision "to give the key of knowledge" as a program priority, and securing local church resources "to erect a school in the vicinity of every church." Thus, "millions of working-class Methodists gave their nickels, dimes, and crumpled dollar bills . . . to the apportionments and special appeals that built our hospitals, orphanages and colleges. Motivated by their commitment to Christ, ordinary people made extraordinary sacrifices to accomplish visionary goals."[2]

The United Methodist education pipeline became an integral part of the connectional system. The pipeline is leadership development, and it must start in the local church, continue in the schools, colleges, universities, theological schools and campus ministry units, and then produce leaders for the church and world. Local churches, together with scholarship support, sent their youth to our colleges and universities. World-class graduates, equipped with general and professional education, were gushing out of the United Methodist education pipeline and became leaders in the church and the world. In the early 1960s, however, The United Methodist Church's program priorities shifted away from education, and today, the historic partnership between church and campus has been weakened therefore contributing to the erosion and rusting of the pipeline.

1. Elliott, T. Michael, et al., eds. *To Give the Key of Knowledge: United Methodists and Education, 1784-1976,* (Nashville: National Commission on United Methodist Higher Education, 1976), 13.
2. Snyder, Dean, "Too few stars in our crown," *UMConnection,* February 20, 2002.

The pipeline has eroded and rusted as there are fewer young people in the church and the leadership pool is dwindling. We struggle to get the best and brightest for clergy as research shows there are declining numbers of clergy with MDIVs; there is a small percentage of students entering college who plan to attend seminary; and there are fewer young people who see ordination as elder as a significant vocation.

It is very alarming to review the membership composition of The United Methodist Church in the United States, for these data further explain how the pipeline is rusted. Membership below the age of 18 consists of only 4.6% (or 383,000), while membership above the age of 40 consists of 80.1%. The average age of church members is 57 years old. Only 9.9% of clergy members are below the age of 39. Of 8,292,809 members of The United Methodist Church, Asian Americans comprise only 0.8%, African Americans 5.1%, Hispanic Americans 0.6%, Native Americans 0.2%, Pacific Islanders 0.1%, and white Americans 93.2%. Among the clergy members, Asian Americans comprise 2.2%, African Americans 5.6%, Hispanic Americans 1.2%, Native Americans 0.4%, Pacific Islanders 0.3%, and white Americans 90.4%. Female clergy members comprise only 18.5% of 44,539 clergy members, while 63% of the members of the church are females.

In facing this reality, we must ask, "What is the future of The United Methodist Church?" In order to resolve this most urgent issue, The United Methodist Church must have a clear vision, dynamic leadership, purposeful and focused programs, and faithful stewardship, such as the early Methodists had at the 1784 Christmas Conference.

The General Board of Higher Education and Ministry (GBHEM) proposes that the 2004 General Conference adopt the following strategic vision and goals as a denominational priority:

Vision

A new generation of Christian leaders will commit boldly to Jesus Christ and be characterized by intellectual excellence, moral and spiritual courage, and holiness of heart and life.

Goal 1

The United Methodist Church, throughout its connection, will identify, recruit, educate, and prepare young people for Christian vocations with a special focus on first generation United Methodists.

Goal 2

The United Methodist Church, throughout its connection, will collaborate with United Methodist-related schools, colleges, universities, theological schools, and campus ministry units to build a new education pipeline that will generate dynamic leaders for the church and world.

Goal 3

The United Methodist Church, throughout its connection, will embrace its tradition of excellent, educated leadership by sharing success stories from its ministries in higher education, theological education, and campus ministry in ways that create a desire to be a part of its vibrant ministries.

We urge the 2004 General Conference to approve this resolution for the purpose of revitalizing The United Methodist Church and to mandate that the General Board of Higher Education and Ministry be fully responsible for implementing the resolution.

ADOPTED 2004

See Social Principles, ¶ 162.

100. The Right of All to Quality Education

The Social Principles acknowledge that children are full human beings in their own right (Social Principles, ¶ 162C). Children have a right to education, and parents and governments have an obligation to provide them with the access to an adequate education. "Thus, we support the development of school systems and innovative methods of education designed to assist every child toward complete fulfillment as an individual person of worth. All children have the right to quality education" (¶ 162C).

The United Methodist Church is committed to the "achievement of a world community that is a fellowship of persons who honestly love one another. We pledge ourselves to seek the meaning of the gospel in all issues that divide people and threaten the growth of world community" (¶ 165).

In our tradition, education is not just about learning to read and write, or about mathematics and geography, or about history and science. Education is about acquiring the necessary skills and knowledge we need for the survival of a democratic society. Education is the vehicle through which the community secures its continued existence and development through the transmission of its accumulated knowledge and ideological aims to other generations.

This is also true for the Israelites as for any of the peoples of the ancient world. Walter A. Elwell points out that in the Hebrew Scripture we find "repeatedly that the success of the community and the continuity of its culture were conditioned by the knowledge of and obedience to God's revealed law (Joshua 1:6-8). Thus, to ensure their prosperity, growth, and longevity as the people of Yahweh, Israel's mandate was one of education—diligently teaching their children to love God, and to know and obey his statutes and ordinances (Deuteronomy 6:1-9). Likewise, the New Testament record links the success of the church of Jesus Christ, as a worshiping community of 'salt and light' reaching out to a dark world, to the teaching of sound doctrine" [1] (see also John 13:34-35; Romans 12:1-2; Ephesians 4:14; Titus 2:1).

Clearly, the above example highlights the importance of teaching children about the faith, however; it also illustrates the importance of educating children in general. The above illustrates the need to instill in our children values that could benefit the entire human family. Thus, we can echo the international community in asserting that education is a human right. We can also affirm that education is a social and spiritual benefit from which no one should be barred or impeded.

Unfortunately, the right to education remains one of the most widely and systematically violated of all human rights. Today, 115 million children are not enrolled in school; the majority of them girls. Forty percent (40%) of children in Africa receive no education. Another 150 million children start primary school but drop out before they have completed four years of education, the vast majority before they have acquired basic literacy skills. Unless urgent action is taken, they will join the ranks of nearly 1 billion illiterate adults in the world.

The benefits of an education are enormous. A good education helps people gain access to better paying jobs, thus, helping reduce the number of people who live in poverty. By the same token, a good education is essential for a sustained economic growth. Education provides people with skills and empowers them to take advantage of new opportunities. Completing just five years of education can increase agricultural efficiency significantly. In addition, studies have shown that educating girls not only raises their future wages, but dramatically reduces infant and maternal mortality rates.

1. Elwell, Walter A. "Entry for 'Education in Bible Times'" *Evangelical Dictionary of Theology*.<http://www.biblestudytools.net/Dictionaries/BakerEvangelicalDictionary/bed.cgi?number=1218. 1997

People across the world are increasingly demanding that the right to education for all children be upheld. Governments, local communities and community-based organizations in poor countries are striving, often in spite of the most appalling adversity, to educate their children. In April 2003, two million people took part in the Global Campaign for Education's week of action and called for an end to the global crisis in education.

In 2000 many communities around the world responded to The United Nations' call to "Education for All." In addition, the United Nations' "Millennium Development Goals" document includes a goal to achieve universal primary education by 2015. Rich countries have repeatedly promised that poor countries with credible national education plans would not be allowed to fail due to a lack of resources, but this promise has not yet been translated into action. The World Bank estimates that $10 billion to $15 billion will be needed each year to achieve this goal. If current trends continue, 88 countries will not deliver primary education for all their children by 2015. Rich countries and the World Bank must increase and improve aid for basic education.

Therefore, the General Conference of The United Methodist Church calls on the United States, the European Union, Japan and other rich nations as well as the International Monetary Fund and the World Bank to deliver on their promises to the world's children by providing substantial and sustained increases in aid for basic education in poor countries. The International Monetary Fund must not press governments to cut education spending as a means to "balance" their budgets, or to stimulate the economy.

In addition, we urge United Methodists in countries around the world to advocate their governments to provide such support for their children's education.

ADOPTED 2004

See Social Principles, ¶ 162D.

GENETICS

101. Bioethics Task Force

In light of the rapid development of biotechnology and related research, including, but not limited to, research dealing with human cloning and the mixing of human stem cells with animal or human embryos, we recommend that the General Board of Church and Society form a bioethics task force to advise the church on relevant ethical issues.

ADOPTED 2000

See Social Principles, ¶ 162M.

102. New Developments in Genetic Science

I. Foreword

The 1988 General Conference approved a statement affirming the positive prospects and warning of the potential dangers of genetic technologies. The General Conference authorized the establishment of a representative task force to:

1. review and assess scientific developments in genetics and their implications for all life;

2. take initiatives with industrial, governmental, and educational institutions involved in genetic engineering to discuss further projections and possible impact;

3. convey to industry and government the sense of urgency to protect the environment as well as animal and human life;

4. support a moratorium on animal patenting until the task force has explored the ethical issues involved;

5. cooperate with other churches, faith groups, and ecumenical bodies sharing similar concerns;

6. explore the effects of the concentration of genetic engineering research tasks and applications in a few crops; and

7. recommend to the 1992 General Conference such further responses and actions as may be deemed appropriate. The term *genetic science* was adopted to identify collectively the aforementioned issues, and the task force was thus named the Genetic Science Task Force.

The task force was appointed in March 1989. Task force members include scientists, educators, health professionals, ethicists, theologians, a social worker, a lawyer, and a farmer. Informational hearings in the following areas provided basic data on the issues: Houston and College Station, Texas; Boston, Massachusetts; Washington, D.C.; San

Leandro, California; Ames, Iowa; Durham, North Carolina; and Oak Ridge, Tennessee.

Testimony was received from geneticists, physicians, theologians, ethicists, social workers, attorneys, officers of biotechnology companies, journalists, insurance executives, governmental regulatory agency representatives, educators, and persons with genetic disorders and the family members of such persons. The hearing process formed the basis of the recommendations contained in this resolution. A more complete discussion of issues can be found in the complete report of the task force to General Conference.

II. Our Theological Grounding

The United Methodist doctrinal/theological statement affirms that "new issues continually arise that summon us to fresh theological inquiry. Daily we are presented with an array of concerns that challenge our proclamation of God's reign over all of human existence" (1988 *Book of Discipline*, ¶ 69).

One of the concerns that merits critique in light of theological understandings is genetic science. The urgent task of interpreting the faith in light of the biotechnology revolution and evaluating the rapidly emerging genetic science and technology has only begun. The issues demand continuing dialogue at all levels of the church as persons from diverse perspectives seek to discern and live out God's vision for creation.

The following affirmations provide the theological/doctrinal foundation of the task force's work and recommendations. These historic affirmations represent criteria by which developments and potential developments in biotechnology are evaluated by the community of faith, the church. The task force urges the whole church to join in the urgent task of theological inquiry in what has been called the genetic age.

A. All creation belongs to God the creator

Creation has its origin, existence, value, and destiny in God. Creation belongs to God, whose power and grace brings the cosmos out of nothingness, order out of chaos, and life out of death. Creation is a realm of divine activity as God continually seeks to bring healing, wholeness, and peace. All creation is accountable to God; therefore, all existence is contingent, finite, and limited. Creation has been declared "good" by the Creator, and its goodness inheres in its fulfillment of the divine purpose. The goodness of our genetic diversity is grounded in our creation by God.

B. Human beings are stewards of creation

While human beings share with other species the limitations of finite creatures who owe their existence to God, their special creation "in the image of God" gives them the freedom and authority to exercise stewardship responsibly. This includes the knowledge of human life and behavior as it is being expanded by genetic science. The biblical imperative is that human beings are to nurture, cultivate, and serve God's creation so that it might be sustained. Humans are to participate in, manage, nurture, justly distribute, employ, develop, and enhance creation's resources in accordance with their finite discernment of God's purposes. Their divinely conferred dominion over nature does not sanction exploitation and waste; neither does responsible stewardship imply refusal to act creatively with intelligence, skill, and foresight.

The image of God, in which humanity is created, confers both power and responsibility to use power as God does: neither by coercion nor tyranny, but by love. Failure to accept limits by rejecting or ignoring accountability to God and interdependency with the whole of creation is the essence of sin. Therefore, the question is not, Can we perform all prodigious work of research and technology? but, Should we? The notion that the ability to do something is permission to do it ignores the fundamental biblical understanding of human beings as stewards accountable to the Creator and as contingent, interdependent creatures. Although the pursuit of knowledge is a divine gift, it must be used appropriately with the principle of accountability to God and to the human community and the sustainability of all creation.

C. Technology in service to humanity and God

God has given human beings the capacity for research and technological invention, but the worship of science is idolatry. Genetic techniques have enormous potential for enhancing creation and human life when they are applied to environmental, agricultural, and medical problems. When wisely used, they often provide positive—

though limited and imperfect—solutions to such perplexing social problems as insufficient food supply, spread of disease, ecological deterioration, overpopulation, and human suffering. When used recklessly, for greedy profit, or for calculated improvement of the human race (eugenics), genetic technology becomes corrupted by sin. Moreover, we recognize that even the careful use of genetic technologies for good ends may lead to unintended consequences. We confess that even our intended consequences may not be in the best interest of all.

D. From creation to redemption and salvation

Redemption and salvation become realities by divine grace as we respond in faith to God's action in Jesus Christ to defeat the powers of sin that enslave the human spirit and thwart the realization of God's purposes for creation. Jesus Christ is the incarnation of God's eternal Word and wisdom. His redemptive life, ministry, death, resurrection, and sending of the Spirit reveal God's vision for humanity. Having distorted God's good intention for us in creation, we now are called to be conformed to God's true image in Jesus Christ.

Through the affirmation of the goodness of creation and the saving work of Christ, God has claimed all persons as beloved sons and daughters with inherent worth and dignity. Therefore, we understand that our worth as children of God is irrespective of genetic qualities, personal attributes, or achievements. Barriers and prejudices based on biological characteristics fracture the human family and distort God's goal for humanity. The community of Christ bears witness to the truth that all persons have unity by virtue of having been redeemed by Christ. Such unity respects and embraces genetic diversity, which accounts for many differences among people. Love and justice, which the Scriptures uplift and which Jesus Christ supremely expresses, require that the worth and dignity of the defenseless be preserved and protected. As the community of Christ, the church seeks to embody love and justice and to give of itself on behalf of the powerless and voiceless.

E. God's reign is for all creation

The coming of God's reign is the guiding hope for all creation. Hebrew Scripture and the life, teaching, death, and resurrection of Jesus Christ affirm that God's reign is characterized by liberation from all forms of oppression, justice in all relationships, peace and good will among all peoples, and the healing of all creation. It is both the vision of God's new heaven and new earth and the recognition of our limits that must inform and shape our role as stewards of earth and life in the emerging age of genetics. It is in the context of God's sovereignty over all existence, our hope for the coming of God's reign, our awareness of our own finitude, and our responsibility as stewards that we consider these issues and the following recommendations.

III. Issues in the Development of Genetic Research and Technology

A. Why the Church is addressing these issues

God's sovereignty over all creation, our status as stewards of creation's resources, and the church's nature as a nurturing and prophetic community living toward God's reign over all existence propel us to consider the theological/ethical implications of genetic science. As genetic science probes the very structure of biological life and develops means to alter the nature of life itself, the potential for relief of suffering and the healing of creation is enormous. But the potential for added physical and emotional suffering and social and economic injustice also exists. Developments in genetic science compel our reevaluation of accepted theological/ethical issues, including determinism versus free will, the nature of sin, just distribution of resources, the status of human beings in relation to other forms of life, and the meaning of personhood.

B. Genetic science affects every area of our lives

The food we eat, the health care we receive, our biological traits, and the environment in which we live are all affected by research and developments in genetic science. As stewards of and participants in life and its resources, we seek to understand, to evaluate, and to utilize responsibly the emerging genetic technologies in accordance with our finite understanding of God's purposes for creation. The divine purpose includes justice, health, and peace for all persons, and the integrity and ecological balance of creation. The uses of genetic science have the potential for promoting as well as thwarting these aspects of the divine purpose.

Genetic issues are much more pressing than is generally recognized. Every community contains individuals and families who daily face genetic concerns in the workplace or as result of their own genetic makeup. The rapid growth of genetic science has increased our awareness of these concerns, has created new concerns, and has accelerated the theological, ethical, and pastoral challenges that genetics poses to persons of faith.

C. Scientific change now leads societal change

The rise in importance of science and technology has been one of the most significant developments in the last 400 years. Beginning with the industrial revolution, we have witnessed a succession of revolutions: the technological, the atomic, and the biological. Each of these revolutions has presented society with a host of religious challenges and threats that have taken enormous and ongoing efforts to resolve constructively. The very nature of work, perceptions of the world, international relations, and family life has changed in part because of these revolutions.

A major dimension of the biological revolution is genetic science. Less than fifty years ago, the actual genetic substance of living cells, DNA, was firmly identified. Now, altering DNA in plants and animals, even humans, in order to correct disorders or to introduce more desirable characteristics is being done. Genetic developments in medicine and agriculture promise to alter the very nature of society, the natural environment, and even human nature. Christians must evaluate these developments in light of our basic understanding of God as creator and of humans as stewards of creation, including technology.

D. Genetic science challenges society

Biotechnology based on genetic research is already upon us. Thousands of people and millions of dollars are devoted to genetic science. Gene therapy has already been introduced as an experimental medical treatment. Extensive research is being conducted in plant and animal genetics, with significant implications for the food supply, farm policy, agricultural economics, and ecological balance. The efforts to identify the estimated one hundred thousand human genes (the Human Genome Project) are well underway with funding from both the National Institutes of Health and the U.S. Department of Energy.

In spite of the rapid growth in genetic research, many people tend to see genetics merely as an extension of the changes in medical, agricultural, and other technologies. In fact, genetic science crosses new frontiers as it explores the essence of life. The implications of genetic research and development are so far-reaching that society must consider the effect of these developments on persons, animal and plant life, the environment, agriculture, the food supply, patent policies, and medicine. Delays in commercializing some of the technologies may afford society and the church additional time to address the implications, but the time available for serious reflection on the consequences of these technologies prior to their implementation is brief.

IV. Questions About Biotechnology

New developments in technology always challenge society's imagination and understanding. Technology is often viewed either with awe or with fear. The popular view of the geneticist alternates between a saint who cures all disease and a mad scientist who creates monsters or perverts life. The extreme image must be avoided as society raises questions about the technologies themselves and questions how they should be properly developed and controlled. Although genetic technologies are similar to other technologies, genetic science and technology force us to examine, as never before, the meaning of life, our understanding of ourselves as humans, and our proper role in God's creation.

Several basic questions can provide a framework within which to evaluate the effect of genetics (or any other new technology) on any segment of society. The questions revolve around issues of appropriateness, availability, efficacy, and accessibility.

V. The Patenting of Life Forms

The patenting of life forms is a crucial issue in the debate over access to genetic technologies. Some claim that patenting of life will give complete control to the owner and so limit access. Others insist that the scientists and funding agencies or institutions must have some return on their investment. A compromise that many societies have worked out in order to provide economic returns for those who have developed a technology while providing access, eventually, to the entire society is the patent, or exclusive control of a technological invention for a period of years. But should exclusive ownership rights apply to the gene pool? In 1984, the General Conference of The United Methodist Church declared genes to be a part of the common heritage of all peoples. The position taken by the church in 1984 is consistent with our understanding of the sanctity of God's creation and God's ownership of life. Therefore, exclusive ownership rights of genes as a means of making genetic technologies accessible raises serious theological concerns. While patents on organisms themselves are opposed, process patents—wherein the method for engineering a new organism is patented—provide a means of economic return on investment while avoiding exclusive ownership of the organism and can be supported.

VI. Affirmations/Recommendations/Conclusions

A. General

1. We affirm that knowledge of genetics is a resource over which we are to exercise stewardship responsibly in accordance with God's reign over creation. The use of genetic knowledge in ways that destabilize and fragment creation is resisted as a violation of God's vision of justice, peace, and wholeness.

2. We caution that the prevalent principle in research that what *can* be done *should* be done is insufficient rationale for genetic science. This principle should be subject to legal and ethical oversight in research design and should not be the prevalent principle guiding the development of new technologies. Applications of research to technologies need moral and ethical guidance.

3. We urge adequate public funding of genetic research so that projects not likely to be funded by private grants will receive adequate support and so that there will be greater accountability to the public by those involved in setting the direction of genetic research.

4. We urge that genes and genetically modified organisms (human, plant, animal) be held as common resources and not be exclusively controlled, or patented. We support improvements in the procedures for granting patents on processes and techniques as a way to reward new developments in this area.

B. Medical recommendations

1. Testing and Treatment
   a. We support the right of all persons to health care and health-care resources regardless of their genetic or medical conditions.

b. We support equal access to medical resources, including genetic testing and genetic counseling by appropriately educated and trained health-care professionals. We affirm that responsible stewardship of God's gift of human life implies access of all persons to genetic counseling throughout their reproductive life.

c. We support human somatic gene therapies (recombinant DNA therapies that produce genetic changes in an individual which cannot be passed to offspring) that prevent or minimize disease and its effects. But we believe these therapies should be limited to the alleviation of suffering caused by disease. We urge that guidelines and government regulations be developed for the use of all gene therapies. We oppose human germ-line therapies (those that result in changes that can be passed to offspring) because of the possibility of unintended consequences and of abuse. With current technology it is not possible to know if artificially introduced genes will have unexpected or delayed long-term effects not identifiable until the genes have been dispersed in the population.

We oppose both somatic and germ-line therapies when they are used for eugenic purposes or enhancements, that is, to provide only cosmetic change or to provide social advantage.

Furthermore, we urge that government regulations and professional organization guidelines be developed and effectively implemented for all gene therapies.

d. We call on all nations to ban human cloning (the intentional production of genetically identical or essentially identical human beings and human embryos), whether such cloning is funded privately or through government research.

e. We call for a ban on medical and research procedures which intentionally generate "waste embryos" which will knowingly be destroyed when the medical procedure or the research is completed.

2. Privacy and confidentiality of genetic information

a. We support the privacy of genetic information. Genetic data of individuals and their families shall be kept secret and held in strict confidence unless confidentiality is waived by the individual or his or her family, or unless the collection and use of genetic identification data are supported by an appropriate court order.

b. We support increased study of the social, moral, and ethical implications of the Human Genome Project. We support wide public access to genetic data that do not identify particular individuals.

c. We oppose the discriminatory or manipulative use of genetic information, such as the limitation, termination, or denial of insurance or employment.

C. Agriculture

1. We support public involvement in initiating, evaluating, regulating, and funding of agricultural genetic research.

a. We believe the public has an important policy and financial role in ensuring the continuation of research that furthers the goal of a safe, nutritious, and affordable food supply.

b. We believe that the public should have input into whether a research effort, or its products, will serve an unmet need in food and fiber production and processing. We urge United Methodists to be active participants in achieving this accountability in all areas of the world.

c. We believe that the benefits of research applications should accrue to the broadest possible public, including farmers and consumers.

2. We support the sustainability of family farms, natural resources, and rural communities and urge that genetic research in agriculture and food products promote these goals.

D. Environment

1. As stewards of the planet Earth, we should strive to perpetuate all of God's living creations as long as possible. We should be concerned not only with the well-being of humans, but also with the wholeness of the rest of creation. We should try to maintain ecological balance as God intended. Technologies such as genetic engineering can affect ecological balance. Genetic technologies must be used carefully to help sustain the planet.

2. We caution that genetically engineered organisms be released into the environment only after careful testing in a controlled setting that simulates each environment in which the organisms are to be used.

3. We urge the development of criteria and methodologies to anticipate and assess possible adverse environmental responses to the release of genetically engineered organisms.

4. We urge that prior to the release of each organism, plans and procedures be developed to destroy genetically engineered organisms that may cause adverse environmental responses.

E. What the church can do

1. Expand education and dialogue around ethical issues in the development of genetic science and technology.

   a. We request that The United Methodist Church and its appropriate boards and agencies educate laity and clergy on the issues of genetic science, theology, and ethics by conducting workshops and seminars, producing resource materials, and training pastors and laypersons to deal constructively with these issues. Sessions on the ethical implications of genetics technology should be included as part of seminary training, continuing education requirements for clergy, Christian educators' training events, adult and youth Sunday school curriculum, schools of mission and schools of church and society, and campus ministry programs.

   b. We request that clergy be trained to provide pastoral counseling for persons with genetic disorders and their families as well as those facing difficult choices as a result of genetic testing. These choices might include decisions such as those related to reproduction, employment, and living wills. Churches are encouraged to provide support groups for individuals and families affected by genetic disorders.

   c. We call on the church to support persons who, because of the likelihood of severe genetic disorders, must make difficult decisions regarding reproduction. We reaffirm the 1988 General Conference (*1988 Book of Discipline,* ¶ 71G) position opposing the termination of pregnancy solely for the purpose of gender selection.

   d. We urge theological seminaries to offer courses and continuing education events that equip clergy to address theological and ethical issues raised by scientific research and technology.

   e. We urge the church to establish and maintain dialogue with those persons working to develop or promote genetics-based technologies.

The complexity and multifaceted implications of genetic science require continuing interaction among scientists, technologists, theologians, ethicists, industrial and corporate leaders, government officials, and the general public. The church can facilitate dialogue on the emerging issues. The Genetic Science Task Force hearings revealed a strong interest on the part of persons from various perspectives, experiences, and interests in exploring the ethical, theological, and societal implications of developments in genetics. Providing a forum for informed discussion will enable the church to inform the public, raise relevant theological/ethical concerns, expand and deepen theological exploration in light of contemporary developments, and more adequately support scientists and technologists who seek to live out their faith in their vocations.

The ethical concerns of the church need to be interjected into the laboratory, the factory, and the halls of government in an ongoing manner. Local churches, districts, annual conferences, and appropriate general agencies should participate in dialogues with university, industry, and government bodies.

2. Produce resources to educate on genetics issues. General agencies of the church should develop additional interpretive resources on genetics issues.

    a. United Methodist Communications is urged to cooperate with the General Board of Church and Society to develop an episode of "Catch the Spirit" highlighting persons who testified to the Genetics Science Task Force.

    b. The Board of Discipleship is urged to develop curriculum materials stressing the ethical dimensions of the widespread use of genetic technologies in health, agriculture, and other industries.

    c. The Division of Health and Welfare Ministries of the General Board of Global Ministries is urged to develop materials in cooperation with United Methodist-affiliated hospitals on the ethical issues families may face regarding the use of new diagnostic tests and other procedures.

    d. The General Board of Higher Education and Ministry is urged to survey seminaries and United Methodist-affiliated schools for academic courses related to genetic science and to make this listing available through its publications.

    e. The General Council on Ministries Research Section is urged to survey United Methodist general agencies and annual conferences requesting the names of informed speakers in the following categories:

1) families affected by genetic disorders;
2) clergy with experience in the fields of genetics research or genetics counseling;
3) genetic counselors, social workers, psychologists, and other counseling professionals who work with individuals and families with genetic disorders;
4) social and physical scientists researching the effect of genetic technologies on society;
5) environmental, agricultural, and biomedical scientists;
6) theologians and ethicists;
7) farmers and others concerned about agricultural and environmental effects of these technologies;
8) technologists and representatives of industry;
9) physicians knowledgeable in genetic issues, especially obstetrician-gynecologists and pediatricians; and
10) educators.

3. Continue and increase The United Methodist Church's work in the area of genetics.

a. The General Council on Ministries is urged to convene a meeting of general agency staff in early 1993 to review the work each agency plans in the 1993-1996 quadrennium relative to the ethics of genetic science technologies.

b. The General Board of Church and Society is urged to continue its work in these areas, to publish a summary of the hearings it conducted on genetic science, and to monitor legislative and governmental actions related to genetic technologies.

c. All general agencies are urged to cooperate with ecumenical groups as they seek to coordinate actions regarding the use of knowledge gained from genetic science. Concern for justice for persons and the integrity of all life should form the basis of our ecumenical witness.

d. Local churches are urged to study the issues raised in this statement and to act on the recommendations.

ADOPTED 1992
AMENDED AND READOPTED 2000

See Social Principles, ¶ 162M.

103. Human Cloning

Cloning has sparked enormous and sustained concern in the general public, including the church. For the purposes of this document, human cloning means the intentional production of genetically identical or essentially identical human beings and human embryos. Cloning touches on many crucial questions about human nature, raises hopes and expectations, and brings to the fore uncertainties and fears. While we do not see obvious benefits of human cloning and while we recognize potential dangers of cloning, we also acknowledge the excitement that this new research generates for advances in medicine, agriculture, and other scientific endeavors.

As United Methodists, our reflections on these issues emerge from our faith. We remember that creation has its origin, value, and destiny in God, that human beings are stewards of creation, that technology has brought forth both great benefit and great harm to creation. As people of faith, we believe that our identity as human beings is more than our genetic inheritance, our social environment, or the sum of the two. We are created by God and have been redeemed by Jesus Christ. We recognize that our present human knowledge on this issue is incomplete and finite. We do not know all of the consequences of cloning (psychological, social, or genetic). It is important that the limits of human knowledge be considered as policy is made.

Therefore, we submit the following policy positions:

1. We call for a ban on all human cloning, including the cloning of human embryos. This would include all projects, privately or governmentally funded, that are intended to advance human cloning. Transcending our concerns with embryo wastage are a number of other unresolved and barely explored concerns with substantial social and theological ramifications: use or abuse of people, exploitation of women, tearing of the fabric of the family, the compromising of human distinctiveness, the lessening of genetic diversity, the direction of research and development being controlled by corporate profit and/or personal gain, and the invasion of privacy. These unresolved concerns generate significant distrust and fear in the general public.

2. We call for a ban on therapeutic, medical, research, and commercial procedures which generate waste embryos. The methods of concurrent research protocols in cloning necessitate the production of excess or "waste embryos," which are ultimately destroyed.

3. We commit to the widespread discussion of issues related to cloning in public forums, including United Methodist schools, seminaries, hospitals, and churches. Given the profound theological and moral implications, the imperfection of human knowledge, and the tremendous risks and social benefits, we urge that there be a moratorium on cloning-related research until these issues can be discussed fully by both the general public including significant participation from communities of faith, as well as by experts in agricultural and biological science, public policy, ethics, theology, law, and medicine, including genetics and genetic counseling. The psychological and social effects of cloning on individuals, families, parental relationships, and the larger society should be fully discussed. Those presently affected by in vitro fertilization, surrogacy, artificial insemination, and other reproduction technologies should be consulted to provide insight into some related psychological and social issues.

4. We call on all nations to ban human cloning and to identify appropriate government agencies to enforce the ban. Appropriate social and governmental bodies must monitor and guide research and developments in the field. Concern for profit and commercial advantage should be balanced by consideration for individual rights, the interest of wide constituencies, and the common good of future generations.

ADOPTED 2000

See Social Principles, ¶ 162*M*.

104. Guidelines for Developing Genetically Modified Organisms

"In the beginning when God created the heavens and the earth, the earth was a formless void and darkness covered the face of the deep, while a wind from God swept over the face of the waters. . . . And God said, "Let the waters bring forth swarms of living creatures, and let birds fly above the earth across the dome of the sky. . . . So God created the great sea monsters and every living creature that moves, of every kind, with which the waters swarm, and every winged bird of every kind. And God saw that it was good" (Genesis 1:1-2, 20-21) .

All of creation is a good gift of God, brought into glorious being out of nothingness and shaped out of chaos. All life, including human life, is created. It is finite, contingent, and limited and is sustained through God's loving care and attention, calling forth of new creation, moment-to-moment, in uncountable abundance in God's world. The tapestry of God's creation is woven with the beauty of extravagant diversity. From bacteria to begonias to our own lives, the diverse interconnected fabric of life calls forth our awe and wonder.

Human communities, in our incredibly diverse web of relationships, carry with them complex and widely differing traditions, (his/her) stories, and relationships with the rest of creation. In addition to nurturing the spirit, God's creatures provide nourishment and sustenance for each other in abundant and diverse ways. In human culture, hunting and gathering, plowing and planting, breeding and feeding, have grown in ways that reflect God's penchant for difference. The climates, soils and lands of different geographical regions differ dramatically in their ecologies. Farming, hunting, and other patterns for sustaining human life vary widely within countries and across the world. These differences also are a reflection God's gloriously expressed diversity.

Reflecting on this diversity and the continuing presence of God's grace in our lives, United Methodists must address the threats to bio- and agricultural diversity posed by current activities in genetic engineering of plants and animals. These technologies are emerging within the context of a history of the overuse of land, the homogenization of agriculture, and the brutal exploitation of non-human animal life in search of ever higher profits.

We have exploited God's soils, landscapes, plants, and animal life merely for their commercial value, forgetting our proper roles as limited, graced stewards of God's creation. Our relationship with creation is one of "entrustment." And we have not fulfilled that trust.

Humans, and particularly North American agricultural practices have lost or obliterated strains of corn and apples, reduced the varieties of cattle and sheep to a virtual handful, bred chickens that do not ever get to walk, and turkeys so large they cannot even stand, much less fly. Multinational agri-business has sought to expand profits and control of agricultural practices by exporting such exploitative practices to peoples in the developing world. These practices have also threatened the diversity of the human community. The voices of farmers in such developing contexts urge North American Christians to seek repentance and wisdom as we embark on the next wave of bio-engineering: genetic modification.

Given this context, we urge extreme caution. The General Conference of The United Methodist Church in 2000 stated, "At this point in human history, the human race is experiencing warning signs that our bodies and the natural environment have limits to their abilities to absorb and overcome the harm from some of our actions, technologies, and substances." (See "Environmental Law—The Precautionary Principle.") Medical and scientific research is only beginning to identify the long-term synergistic effects of what we have done to our ecosystems and what we are doing to our food.

Genetic modifications of plants, animals, and microbes must not speed the destruction of God's creation. With genomic technology, we are involved in the manipulation of life at a basic level. There may be possibilities for significant benefits for humanity. There are also, perhaps even greater, possibilities for unforeseen catastrophe. As finite recipients of God's grace and God's call to stewardship, we can only proceed with repentance for past transgression and a willingness to cultivate the crucial virtue of patience. We must proceed on the basis of faithful precaution, seeking God's help in discerning temptations to do apparent "goods" from faithful loving action as Jesus did in his sojourn in the desert (Luke 4:1-44).

Among the specific concerns that warrant our study and action are:

- The distribution of genetically engineered grains to starving, impoverished, and war-ravaged peoples where the grain cannot be used later for crops to be sold in developed world markets. Many African countries that might receive genetically modified grain from the US would not be able to later export that grain to Europe or Japan where genetically modified grain imports are restricted. They also may not be able to export the grain if the strains have been patented.
- The refusal by food donor nations to mill genetically modified grains before distribution so the grains' seeds would not contaminate genetically engineered, organism-free ecosystems is an additional problem.
- The failure of grain exporters to disclosure of the genetically modified nature of the grain being distributed
- Engineering plants and animals to produce pharmaceuticals
  - Including the moral aspects of these procedures particularly on animals
  - Including the dangers of such animals and plants ending up in the food supply

- Release of genetically engineered (GE) seeds and growing GE crops without adequate safety and ecological impact testing
    - Including the role of profit-oriented corporate interests in the process
    - Including the lack of scientific evidence supporting a declaration of "substantial equivalence between GE and non-GE foods"
    - Including the dearth of knowledge of the long-term health effects of genetically modified organisms.
    - Including genetic contamination of non-genetically modified species and varieties and the impact on organic farmers
    - Including issues of legal liability and intellectual property
    - Including the problem of contaminating exports to preclude organic farming standards
- The effects of genetically modified traits in the overall food system of a region
    - Increasing trend toward monoculture of crops
    - Increasing elimination of farm animal diversity
- The engineering of genetically modified organisms to allow greater use of specific pesticides
    - Including the need to use more rather than less pesticides as advertised
- The adverse economic impacts on farmers of using genetically modified crops
- The engineering of toxins into food crops as insecticides and the concomitant expansion of insect resistance to those toxins.
    - Including the adverse impact on organic farmers whose only pesticide has been naturally occurring insect toxins
    - Including the impact of pesticide-resistant insects on the spread of disease
- The lack of labeling of fields containing GE crops
    - Including the impact on surrounding farmers seeking to use non-GE crops
- The lack of regulation and universal labeling of genetically modified foods

- Including clear labeling to distinguish true organic foods and organically grown products that involved genetically modified organisms
- The production and marketing of agricultural products that have been engineered to produce no seed or sterile seed so that farmers cannot plant seed from the crops they have raised
- Multinational financial and trade institutions' promotion of GE as a solution to global problems of hunger
  - Including interpretation of World Trade rules to prevent local governments from determining their own rules regarding genetically modified organisms
  - Including the imposition of the use of GE crops as a condition of receiving international assistance
- The loss of genetic diversity, including the consequences of the loss of native seed and animal varieties, is a concern.
  - Including the impact of "industrial agriculture" on the impetus to create monocultures
- The genetic engineering of plants and animals and the patenting of genes, plants, and animals raise major theological and ethical concerns.
  - the moral and ethical questions surrounding the proscription of "use" of any for of life to a single party or entity in the face of creation as a gift
  - Including the moral and ethical issues surrounding the proscription of access to knowledge that might help diagnose or treat diseases

Three Ethical Guidelines

It is possible to change the technology-driven direction of agriculture and rural development to one that is respectful and appreciative of creation as a gift of God that reflects our responsibilities as stewards and establishes right relationships of sustainability with creation. But we need guidelines. A sustainable agriculture must have three attributes:

1. It must be just. A just society and a just agriculture provide the means whereby people can share in the inheritance of the earth so that all life can fully be maintained in freedom and community. The purpose of a just agriculture should be the maintenance and renewal of

the necessary resources for food, clothing, and shelter, for now and for the future, recognizing the needs for space and sustenance of all of God's creatures.

2. It must be participatory. For an agriculture to be just, everyone has the right to be consulted and the needs of all species to thrive be considered. Participation in human society and in the ongoing process of creation is the necessary condition for justice. Ethical human participation requires recognition of everyone's right to be consulted and understood, regardless of that person's economic, political, or social status. Participation is not possible without power. In such decision-making, everyone has the right to be consulted about such issues as expenditures for armaments, nuclear power, and forms of employment, social services, and so forth. However, the power of participation in decision making should be weighted to local participation due to local community relationships and local risks rather than to economic or political centers of power.

3. It must be appropriate. Appropriate agriculture is appropriate to the region, context, and conditions of the area. It is one where the idea of permanent carrying capacity is maintained, where success (agriculture, energy production, forestry, water use, industrial activity) is measured by whether or not it sustains the soil and the ecosystems necessary to assure continuing supplies of healthful food. Rather than by the criteria of yields per acre or profits, appropriate agriculture ensures that waste products can be absorbed back into the ecosystem without damage.

Sustainable agriculture—just, participatory, and appropriate— would meet basic human needs for food and fiber, regenerate and protect ecosystems, be economically viable, enhance the quality of life for farm families, be supportive of rural communities, be socially just, and be compatible with spiritual teachings that recognize the earth as a common heritage and responsibility. For Christians, the idea of sustainability flows directly from the biblical call to human beings to be stewards of God's creation.

Be it resolved that:

The General Board of Church and Society continue to monitor developments in this area, but especially advocate for the following:

1. The right of nations to set their own standards related to genetically modified organisms and their importation.

2. Labeling of genetically modified organisms.

3. Testing of genetically modified organisms to assure their safety to human health and the environment.

That other agencies of the church work to educate about the concerns raised in this resolution.

ADOPTED 2004

See Social Principles, ¶ 162M.

HEALTH CARE

105. Care for People Who Are Hard-of-Hearing

WHEREAS, an inclusive church seeks to be accessible to people who are deaf/hard-of-hearing,

Therefore, be it resolved, that the Commission on General Conference, beginning in 2004, budget for the full funding of Professional American Sign Language Interpretation for delegates and nondelegates to General Conference. This is to be coordinated by the General Board of Global Ministries.

ADOPTED 2000

See Social Principles, ¶ 162G.

106. Closed Captioning

WHEREAS, United Methodists and other engaged in ministry and mission with The United Methodist Church include those who have reduced or no ability to hear sounds; and

WHEREAS, these persons are thereby denied access to the rich resources of videotaped messages, stories and programs; and

WHEREAS, technology exists to provide such productions with "closed captioning,"

Therefore, be it resolved, that The United Methodist Church encourages all videos produced by the general church, its agencies, committees, or authorized task forces to include closed captioning.

ADOPTED 2000

See Social Principles, ¶ 162G.

107. Communications Access for People Who Have Hearing and Sight Impairment

Because The United Methodist Church believes that all United Methodists are full members of the church and is committed to ministry by and with people with disabilities; and

Public accommodations such as restaurants, hotels, theaters, doctors' offices, pharmacies, retail stores, museums, libraries, parks, private schools, and daycare centers may not discriminate on the basis of disability, effective January 26, 1992.

Auxiliary aids and services must be provided to individuals with vision or hearing impairments or other individuals with disabilities so that they can have an equal opportunity to benefit, unless an undue burden would result. (from a synopsis prepared by the Civil Rights Division, U.S. Department of Justice)

And because, despite sincere efforts on the part of the church, people with disabilities are still confronted by barriers to communications within the church;

We call upon the church to:

1. increase its awareness; and

2. use appropriate technologies to make essential communications accessible to people who are deaf and hearing impaired, including:

   a. considering production of alternative versions of church-produced video, films, or other audiovisuals at meetings for people who are deaf or hearing impaired, and people who are blind or partially sighted; and

   b. considering the use of assistive technologies in telephone communications for persons who are deaf or hearing impaired.

ADOPTED 1992
AMENDED AND READOPTED 1996
READOPTED 2004

See Social Principles, ¶ 162G.

108. Correcting Injustices in Health Care

Introduction

We all recognize the need for adequate health care for ourselves and our families. In the last two decades there have been many options brought before the people of this nation and some have been serious attempts to provide for all. However, most proposals have continued to exclude some portion of society from access to adequate health care. The debates seem to have subsided, but problems of providing adequate care to individuals are actually increasing with time.

Tremendous Medicaid budget cuts are pending. These cuts would surely further limit health care access for the poor and the physically or mentally challenged. Health Maintenance Organizations (HMOs), and the like, interfere with physicians' treatment plans. In effect, HMOs deny legitimate claims by developing regulations on getting approvals for treatment that both patients and doctors have difficulty understanding or satisfying. It has been estimated that today's physician spends about one-third of his or her time satisfying these regulations and seeking approvals for treatment, time the physician could be spending with patients. Because there are so many public and private health care insurance organizations the result is an insurmountable bureaucratic complex; a system which tends to confuse virtually every aspect of insurance coverage for the patients and the practitioners.

Now is the time for a comprehensive single-payer health care program that will provide adequate health care to all without placing further barricades to access.

Failed Solutions

Private health insurance, in all its forms, continues to increase its premium cost while limiting care and/or increasing deductibles and co-payments for care. However, these increases do not necessarily reflect rises in the actual costs of treatments. Premiums must rise in order to keep adequate profit margins for owners and investors. It has been estimated that the cost of administration of Medicare is 4 percent to 5 percent of its budget, while the typical private company's budget for administration and profit is about 25 percent.

Furthermore, when there is no institutional or employer provider of health insurance, personal policies are offered by companies at extraordinary rates. The average family, much less the working poor, simply cannot afford personal policies. They can cost $ 2,000 or more in premiums with deductibles ranging from $1,500 to $5,000 per year for each individual.

Private insurance companies usually impose annual or lifetime limits on the amount of benefits payable, whether the policy is individual, group, or institutional. These harsh policies leave the lingering worry that with a catastrophic illness or injury such limits may be reached, abruptly stopping all insurance benefits and leaving the policy beneficiary completely uninsured. Then to get care, the individual must sell and/or spend all assets, including homes, financial holdings, lifetime savings accounts, etc., in order to qualify for Medicaid and restore any medical coverage at all.

Recently two bills were offered in Congress and defeated. There can be little doubt that active lobbying of Congress by health insurance companies and their associations was a factor in the defeats. These bills would have required some additional expenses for health care insurance companies, perhaps eating into current profits. We can be fairly certain, however, that those expenses would eventually have been passed along to the premium payer, preserving high profits.

[The Patients' Bill of Rights Act of 1998 (S. 2529) (or its subsequent version) seeks to provide certain guarantees to patients in HMOs and other private systems. These guarantees included portable policies, rights to information, grievance procedures and other important accommodations for the patient. However, it offers to do this while preserving the current health care system. This bill may have been helpful to some but necessitated compromise with profit motivation and would have added another bureau.]

[The Healthy Americans Act (S. 2074) was "to guarantee for all Americans, affordable, and comprehensive health care coverage." This sounded good on the surface, but it still relied on private insurers in most cases. It did provide a way to eliminate cost to the very poor, and a sliding scale of premiums up to 400 percent of the poverty line income. It was to be administered by the individual states, creating fifty new bureaus responsible to a new national agency and eliminating none of the existing bureaus.]

Many states are developing programs to provide health care to all minors, regardless of family income. These programs stop at age 18, regardless of income. They are insufficient to the nation as a whole and, though significantly relieving distress on families and individuals, they are only temporary.

President Clinton's health care initiatives were an attempt to seek compromise between the private insurers and the needs of the nation. They were an attempt to place responsibilities and limits on insurers while providing a somewhat comprehensive package of benefits to the nation. He was accused of creating a massive bureaucracy and limiting the autonomy of private corporations. He was accused of creating a system that was too expensive.

However, then and now there exists a massive bureaucratic complex which manages health care: fifty state Medicaid systems, the Veteran's Administration, the Railroad Employees insurance program, federal and state employee systems, health care for retired military personnel (formerly know as CHAMPUS), Medicare and countless private insurance companies including, HMOs, PPOs, Medicare Supplemental Plans, etc. What makes this massive bureaucratic complex worse is that none of the bureaus communicate in similar terms: not to patients, not to physicians, not to hospitals, which barricades providers and patients from filing and receiving payments on legitimate claims. Furthermore, this system increases administrative costs for everyone: doctors, hospitals, patients, other health care providers, and the private insurance companies entrusted to provide our care. The bureaucratic complex has become an incredible burden to society.

Myriad Injustices in the Current System

It has become clear that Managed Care Companies, HMOs, PPOs, and the like, interfere with the physician's ability to develop comprehensive treatment plans for his or her patients. They require that a decision be made by the corporation about treatment cost and efficacy and, in most cases, decisions are made by individuals much less qualified than the patient's physician or the specialist a physician may recommend. In fact, persons with little or no medical training often make those decisions. Many insurance companies hire nurses to review the physicians' diagnoses and treatment plans. While it is unusual for nurses to oversee doctors, it is also evident that these nurses have had no contact with the patient under review. Furthermore, those decisions are made with primary consideration for the costs to the corporation, not for the optimum health of the patient. In the current climate physicians who prescribe treatments or tests not pre-approved by the insurance corporation face severe financial penalties or other disincentives to optimum patient care.

Managed Care was supposed to be a way of providing care to increasing numbers of patients; however, there are actually increasing numbers of uninsured. The very poor, the affluent, the employees of government and large corporations, and many receiving adequate pensions plus Medicare are insured. The self-employed, recently unemployed, middle income, and working poor simply cannot afford personal policies. And even though some states are developing programs to provide health care to all minors regardless of family income, they are only temporary, leaving the child uninsured when reaching the age of majority.

The government tries to fill the gap with the Medicaid systems. While Medicaid (some states have different names for similar programs) provides some care to the poor, it does not encourage primary nor comprehensive care and disqualifies applicants with borderline incomes. Also, the Medicaid systems remain under constant attack as one of the first places to cut state budgets. Our civil leadership may claim health care as a priority but this tendency belies their credibility on this issue. When Medicaid budgets are cut, the poor suffer. After cuts, those in the greatest need and at highest risk have fewer benefits. In an already crippled system further cuts to Medicaid spending result in leaving more people with inadequate health care.

Private insurance companies, also, impose insurmountable limits to health care, even in the best of plans. Annual or lifetime limits on the amount of benefits payable leave the lingering worry that, with a catastrophic illness or injury, such a limit may be reached, abruptly stopping all insurance benefits and leaving the premium payer uninsured. The current private health insurance system, with its high profit margins, further contributes to an unhealthy society by forcing people to choose between health insurance and sustenance, housing, or the other needs of a family; thus basic health insurance becomes too expensive for the average individual or family.

An increasing number of middle income families, the working poor, the elderly, and many in minority communities do not receive health insurance benefits from their employers, cannot pay for any health care insurance, and do not qualify for Medicaid. If a health catastrophe should strike, they must deplete all assets in order to qualify for Medicaid, including selling of a home or surrendering a lifetime of savings. While not only placing these families in financial jeopardy, these circumstances contribute to poverty, constant worry, and despair among many. The devastating expense of a long-term or terminal illness, inadequate care in general, and the extraordinary cost of insurance all contribute to keeping many minorities in the poverty cycle, dependent on welfare and other forms of assistance, and imprisoned in struggling and dangerous communities.

Even in our United Methodist connection more and more annual conferences and more and more parishes are feeling the burden of providing health care to their clergy and their lay staff. Small churches, even multiple point parishes, have difficulty paying for private health insurance. If conferences institute "ability to pay" programs, the wealthier churches become benefactors for the smaller ones, possibly eroding their own financial security over time or depleting funds for other important ministries.

Virtually no one can pay cash for health care and the profit motivated private health insurance companies depend on this, making the system usurious. Moreover, the insurance corporations and associations, with money to spend, lobby and cajole our representatives to keep the current system in place, in spite of its inadequacies and its injustices. Even now, these same companies want to limit a patient's right to sue in civil court when the company breaches its own contract to provide benefits, regardless of the suffering or death a benefit denial may cause. In these types of cases a benefit denial is tantamount to medical malpractice. Competition for premium dollars and concern for high profits have taken priority over necessary care at actual cost. It is evident that private insurance companies are prone to deny claims while continuing to receive premiums, favoring higher profit over the "health and wholeness" of the weakened, the worried, and the sick.

Resolution

Therefore, as it is unconscionable that any human being should ever be denied access to adequate health care due to economic, racial, or class barriers; and The United Methodist Social Principles state in the introduction to paragraph 162, "The rights and privileges a society bestows upon or withholds from those who comprise it indicate the relative esteem in which that society holds particular persons and groups of persons . . . .", and in ¶ 162C, ". . .Children have the rights to food, shelter, clothing, health care. . . .", and in ¶ 162T, "Health care is a basic human right. . . . It is unjust to construct or perpetuate barriers to physical wholeness. . . . We also recognize the role of government in ensuring that each individual has access to those elements necessary to good health."; and the Council of Bishops has endorsed the Universal Declaration for Human Rights which clearly claims health care as right due to every world citizen;

Therefore, be it resolved, that The United Methodist Church expressly adopt the claim of health care as a "basic human right" and that this claim be the hallmark of our United Methodist efforts in this area of advocacy; and

Be it further resolved, that The United Methodist Church now demands health care as a basic human right and as an entitlement for all Americans, including Native Americans, and legal resident aliens; and

Be it further resolved, that The United Methodist Church will exert its influence in any arena and wherever possible to bring about substantive change in the health care system, respecting the hallmark of health care as a "basic human right"; and

Be it further resolved, that compassion and healing be the primary motivation in developing a health care system that is just and inclusive and recognizing this, The United Methodist Church now calls for implementation of a totally nonprofit health care insurance system, a single-payer system administered by the federal government; and

Be it further resolved, that The United Methodist Church endorses the health care system described in the American Health Security Act of 1995 (H.R. 1200, The McDermott Bill), or a very similar system, one which guarantees complete freedom for patients to choose their physicians and health care providers and for physicians to provide and prescribe needed and appropriate care; and

H.R. 1200 combines all government health care programs (e.g. Medicare, CHAMPUS, Federal Employees, Railroad Employees, etc.) into one, eliminates Medicaid by providing care to the poor, and eliminates all the layers and permutations of health care insurance administration and service bureaus, both public and private. This bill provides a comprehensive package of health care including: primary care, emergency and hospital care, long-term care, drugs and prescriptions, drug and alcohol recovery treatment, dental care, etc. This care is paid for by an across-the-board employers excise tax of about 8 percent of gross wages for each employee and about a 2 percent personal income tax and reasonable "co-pays" with no lifetime or annual limits on coverage. No health tax would be collected from anyone whose income is 100 percent of or below the poverty line. A sliding scale is used for those whose income is between 100 percent and 200 percent of the poverty line.

Be it finally resolved, that The United Methodist Church publicly advocate and fervently lobby the federal government to protect and provide for rights to health care and to take up measures such as the American Health Security Act.

ADOPTED 1992
REVISED AND ADOPTED 2000

See Social Principles, ¶ 162T.

109. Health and Wholeness

Introduction

All human beings have been created in the image of God and are called to abundant life. In the biblical story of the woman with the hemorrhage, Jesus provides an example of his healing ministry that includes the spiritual as well as the physical status of the person.

And behold, a woman who had suffered from a hemorrhage for twelve years came up behind him and touched the fringe of his garment; for she said to herself, "If I only touch his garment, I shall be made well." Jesus turned, and seeing her he said, "Take heart, daughter; your faith has made you well." And instantly the woman was made well (Matthew 9:20-22, Revised Standard Version).

The United Methodist Church believes that its mission is to continue the redemptive ministry of Christ, including teaching, preaching, and healing. Christ's healing was not peripheral but central in his ministry. The church, therefore, understands itself as called by the Lord to the holistic ministry of healing: spiritual, mental emotional, and physical.

Health in this sense is something beyond, but not exclusive of, biological well-being. In this view, health care is inadequate when it fixes its attention solely on the body and its physiological functions, as is any religion that focuses its interest entirely on the spirit. Taking the Gospel mandates seriously, United Methodists are called to work toward a healthy society of whole persons. Part of our task is to enable people to care for themselves and to take responsibility for their own health. Another part of our task is to ensure that people who are ill, whether from illness of spirit, mind, or body, are not turned aside or ignored but are given care that allows them to live a full life. A related obligation is to help society welcome the sick and the well as full members, entitled to all the participation of which they are capable. People who are well, but different from the majority, are not to be treated as sick in order to control them. Being old, developmentally disabled, or physically disabled is not the same as being sick. Persons in these circumstances are not to be diminished in social relationships by being presumed to be ill. We see this task as demanding concern for spiritual, political, ethical, economic, social, and medical decisions that maintain the highest concern for the condition of society, the environment, and the total life of each person.

Human suffering is caused by a variety of factors—the environmental, social, and personal factors mentioned, as well as others that remain unknown to us.

Environmental Factors. Clean air, pure water, effective sanitary systems for the disposal of wastes, nutritious foods, adequate housing, and hazard-free workplaces are essential to health. The best medical system cannot preserve or maintain health when the environment is disease-producing.

Social Factors. Inadequate education, poverty, unemployment, lack of access to food, stress-producing conditions, and social pressures reinforced by marketing and advertising strategies that encourage the use of guns, tobacco, alcohol, and other drugs are detrimental to good health.

Personal Habits. Overeating or eating non-nutritious foods, substance abuse (including alcohol, tobacco, barbiturates, sedatives, and so forth) are clearly destructive to health. Failure to exercise or to rest and relax adequately are also injurious to health. Overeating and undereating, due to food security emergencies or eating disorders, are opposite but not unrelated health crises.

Although medical care represents a very important part of health care, it does not include the whole. More medical care does not always equal better health.

Medical care in much of the world has evolved too much as disease care rather than health care. Disease prevention, public health programs, and health education appropriate to every age level and social setting are needed globally. Services should be provided in a compassionate and skillful manner on the basis of need, without discrimination as to economic status, mental or physical disability, race, color, religion, sex, age, national origin, language, or multiple diagnosis.

A Just Health System

Within a just society, every person has a right to:

1. basic health services that are accessible and affordable in each geographic and cultural setting;

2. an environment that promotes health;

3. active involvement in the formulation of health-care activities that meet local needs and priorities;

4. information about his or her illness, and to be an active participant in treatment and rehabilitation;

5. receive compassionate and skilled care;

6. a health-care system sensitive to cultural needs and medical/ethical critique; and

7. access to funding sources where necessary for basic health services.

Health Insurance

For all persons to have adequate access to needed health-care services, public financing must be a significant part of an overall health insurance plan. Public funding is necessary to pay for insuring those who cannot pay part or all of the necessary premiums required.

Health Maintenance

Many health problems and illnesses are preventable if we accept the fact that health maintenance requires understanding of the unity of the human body, mind, and spirit. The whole person needs proper nutrition, exercise, the challenge to learn and grow, and an acknowledgement that this is a lifelong process. We recognize that these needs are difficult to meet when environmental factors contribute to ill health. But we must acknowledge the fact that we have separated spiritual health from physical health. In Western Protestant interpretation of health and healing, the union of the body and spirit is often dismissed. Cultures that respect and revere that union are often disregarded or looked upon in a condescending manner. The early church did not make these distinctions, nor did Jesus in his healing ministry. We must, if we are to obtain good health, unite the body and spirit in our thinking and actions.

Therefore, as Christians we accept responsibility for modeling this holistic, preventive style of health maintenance. We commit ourselves to examining the value systems at work in our society as they impact the health of people and to working for programs and policies that enable people to breathe clean air, drink clean water, eat wholesome food, and have access to adequate education and freedom that enable mind and spirit to develop.

Medical Services

We support the following principles of access to health services:

1. In a just society, all people are entitled to basic maintenance and health-care services. We reject as contrary to our understanding of the gospel the notion of differing standards of health care for various segments of the population.

2. Health care should be comprehensive, including preventive, therapeutic, and rehabilitative services.

3. Religious and other appropriate forms of counseling should be available to all patients and families when they are called upon to make difficult medical choices, so that responsible decisions, within the context of the Christian faith, may be made concerning organ transplants, use of extreme measures to prolong life, abortion, sterilization, genetic counseling, institutionalization, and death with dignity.

4. We encourage development of community support systems that permit alternatives to institutional care for such groups as the aging, the terminally ill and mentally ill, and other persons with special needs.

5. Professional health-care personnel should be recruited and appropriately educated to meet the health-care needs of all persons. Especially urgent is the need for physicians trained in geriatric medicine. Special priorities should be established to secure among the professional group at least proportional representation of women and minorities who are now seriously under-represented.

6. In areas where medical services are not available or are under-supplied, we urge private or public funding to provide the full range of needed services. To meet these goals, we recommend the reallocation of funds from armaments to human services, both nationally and internationally (Social Principles, ¶ 165C).

7. Regional planning processes should coordinate the services rendered by all health-care institutions, including those funded by governments, to create a more effective system of health services in every area. Priorities should be established for the provision of health services, such as preventive care, mental-health services, home care, and health education.

8. Corrective measures should be taken where there is maldistribution or unavailability of hospital beds, intermediate care and nursing home care, home-delivered care, neighborhood health centers, community mental-health centers, and emergency care networks.

9. We encourage medical education for laypersons that will enable them to effectively evaluate medical care they need and are receiving.

10. We support the medical community in its effort to uphold ethical standards and to promote quality assurance.

11. We support and encourage medical volunteers.

Health and Wholeness Ministry

As United Methodists, we are called to a ministry of health and wholeness. Therefore, we challenge our membership to:

1. make health concerns a priority in the church, with special emphases that include but are not limited to women's health concerns; appropriate, unbiased, informed diagnosis and treatment of older adults; preventive care (including health education); special health concerns and needs of children and youth; and establishment of networks for information sharing and action suggestions;

2. support the provision of direct-health services where needed and to provide, as we are able, such services in hospitals and homes, clinics, and health centers;

3. accept responsibility for educating and motivating members to follow a healthy lifestyle reflecting our affirmation of life as God's gift;

4. become actively involved at all levels in the development of support systems for health care in the community, including: dependent care (respite and twenty-four-hour care, in-home and short-term out-of-home care), meals, programs for women in crisis, halfway houses, support systems for independent living, and family support systems;

5. become advocates for a healthful environment; accessible, affordable health care; continued public support for health care of persons unable to provide for themselves; continued support for

health-related research; and provision of church facilities to enable health-related ministries;

6. become involved in a search for Christian understanding of health, healing, and wholeness and the dimensions of spiritual healing in our congregations and seminaries;

7. encourage colleges, universities, hospitals, and seminaries related to The United Methodist Church connectional units to gain an added awareness of health issues and the need for recruitment and education of persons for health-related ministries who would approach such ministries out of a Christian understanding and commitment; and

8. support public policies and programs that will ensure comprehensive health-care services of high quality to all persons on the principle of equal access.

While public and private health initiatives are attempting to create manageable and sustainable health care services in the United States, we urge all parties to recall an early observation in the health care debate. As long ago as 1983, a presidential Committee on Medical Ethics wrote: "Measures designed to contain health care costs that exacerbate existing inadequacies or impede the achievement of equity are unacceptable from a moral standpoint."

All six billion members of God's global family live along a spectrum from sick to well. Lessons learned in every society—from the United States to every other one—are valuable to the health of all. Our goal will be the greatest health for all people in all respects.

ADOPTED 1984
AMENDED AND READOPTED 2000

See Social Principles, ¶ 162T and ¶ 165C.

110. Observance of Health Care Justice Sabbaths

Health Care Justice Sabbaths have been observed by the United Methodist and other congregations since their inauguration in 1994 by the Interreligious Health Care Access Campaign.

Health Care Justice Sabbath observances permit persons of faith to demonstrate their faithfulness to the goal of health care for all in keeping with the healing ministry of Jesus Christ and in recognition of the restoration of health as a sign of the presence of God's kingdom.

Rather than specifying a particular date for this observance, the campaign encouraged communions and congregations to select a Sabbath date that reflected their individual commitment to issues of health and wholeness. In support of this interfaith effort and in faithful witness to the beliefs articulated in the United Methodist Social Principles on Heath Care. The United Methodist Church calls congregations to designate one Sunday during the calendar year for the observance of a Health Care Justice Sabbath.

The Health Care Justice Sabbath is a day of rejoicing and reflection. It is a time for thanksgiving for the health and well-being enjoyed by many in our world community and thanksgiving for the diverse caregivers who minister to our needs. It is a time to reflect on those who are sick, who struggle with chronic illnesses, who lack access to the health-care services they need, and who are denied those basic elements essential to achieving health. It is a time to reflect on acts of health care mercy and acts of health care justice and how each supports the other. It is a time to focus on our belief that health care is a right and a responsibility, public and private. It is a time to challenge our communities of faith to seek their role in making "Health Care for All" a reality.

To assist congregations in their observance of a Health Care Justice Sabbath, resources will be made available by the General Board of Church and Society.

ADOPTED 1996
AMENDED AND READOPTED 2004

See Social Principles, ¶ 162T.

111. The Church and Deaf Ministries

A Time for Action

Strategy and Structure for Strengthening the Connection with the Greater Deaf Community for the New Century.

A new era demands a new approach. As the greater deaf community desires to serve the church and become a resource for the whole connection, it is recommended that the General Conference of 2000 adopt the proposed plan for "Strengthening the Connection with the Greater Deaf Community for the New Century."

Structure

1. A Steering Committee shall be established by an assigned staff member of the General Board of Global Ministries.

2. There shall be ten (10) members recruited for the steering committee as follows: two deaf, two deafened, two hard of hearing, one deaf-blind, one deaf institutional ministry professional, and two clergy with experience in ministry with the greater deaf community.

3. It is strongly urged that the committee be inclusive with regard to gender, ethnicity, jurisdictions, and different sign language and hearing abilities.

4. The initial meeting will be called by the staff member of the General Board of Global Ministries during the first year of the quadrennium and the Steering Committee members shall elect their own officers.

Tasks and Objectives of the Steering Committee

1. The initial meeting of the Steering Committee shall be to establish and organize an overall agenda for the quadrennium. This agenda will include two training events where the Steering Committee and other invited members of the greater deaf community and hearing advocates will be trained in various areas of outreach to include but not be restricted to:
- presentation and advocacy skills for strengthening the connection with the greater deaf community;
- becoming resources for the general church, annual conferences, faith communities, and local churches;
- working with general boards and agencies for strengthening the connection with the greater deaf community;
- creating action plans and legislation for annual conferences and General Conference.

2. The Steering Committee shall also identify general boards and agencies as well as target annual conferences and seminaries for strengthening the connection with the greater deaf community.

3. All trained persons will be expected to serve in teams of two or more to provide resources, leadership, and a presence for the greater deaf community at annual meetings of the targeted general boards and agencies, annual conferences, and seminaries.

4. Targeted general boards and agencies will provide adequate agenda time at their annual meetings for the 2000-2004 quadrennium for these trained teams to educate, inform, and lead them to strengthen their connection with the greater deaf community.

5. Targeted annual conferences will agree to provide adequate time and access to conference staff and cabinet to educate, inform, and lead them to strengthen their connection with the greater deaf community.

6. Targeted seminaries will agree to provide adequate time and access to administration, faculty, and staff to educate, inform, and lead them to strengthen their connection with the greater deaf community.

7. Teams shall report back to the Steering Committee for direction and development as the process of strengthening the connection with the greater deaf community continues through the quadrennium.

Accountability

The Steering Committee of "Strengthening the Connection with the Greater Deaf Community for the Next Century" will be accountable to an assigned section of the General Board of Global Ministries sharing yearly progress reports and evaluation. The steering committee shall also report to The United Methodist Congress of the Deaf for discussion, sharing information, and plans for implementation.

Summary

As The United Methodist Church prepares to enter into a new century, one of our most pressing concerns is to strengthen our connection with one another and with our world. Methodism has a long history from its origins with John Wesley of commitment to its connection with the forgotten communities of our world. The United Methodist Church's connection with the greater deaf community is a history of forgotten stories and forgotten people. Never has there been a more important time to act as God's people and strengthen our connection with the greater deaf community for the next century.

ADOPTED 2000

See Social Principles, ¶ 162G.

112. United Methodist Response to Hospital Mergers

WHEREAS, a crisis in health care is occurring in communities across the United States because of the ever-increasing number of hospital mergers, and

WHEREAS, such mergers often put the availability of AIDS prevention information, fertility services, artificial insemination, tubal ligations, vasectomies, condom distribution, contraceptive medication and devices, "morning after" pills, and abortion services at risk; and

WHEREAS, such mergers can result in the denial of certain types of end-of-life health care; and

WHEREAS, the effect of these mergers is most severe in poorer communities that have limited health care options to begin with; and

WHEREAS, these mergers are usually completed, often with the assistance of public money, before the public is even aware they are happening or what the consequences will be;

Therefore, be it resolved, that the General Board of Church and Society and the Women's Division work to alert their constituencies concerning this crisis in reproductive and end-of-life health care, and

Be it further resolved, that the General Board of Church and Society and the Women's Division expand their health and wholeness public policy advocacy to include this critical issue of reproductive and end-of-life health care; and

Be it further resolved, that the General Board of Church and Society and the Women's Division work in cooperation with appropriate community groups to make resource materials available to local churches; such materials to include briefing papers, articles, action alerts, sample sermons, and information on gaining legal intervention when necessary to deal with the crisis of increasingly limited reproductive and end-of-life health care in their communities.

ADOPTED 2000

See Social Principles, ¶ 162T.

113. Universal Access to Health Care

The health care system in the United States is in need of serious systemic change. We call for legislation that will provide universal access to quality health care with effective cost controls.

John Wesley was always deeply concerned about health care, providing medical services at no cost to the poor in London and emphasizing preventive care. The first Methodist Social Creed (adopted in 1908) urged working conditions to safeguard the health of workers and community.

Through its many hospitals and health-care facilities around the world, as well as public-policy advocacy for health, The United Methodist Church continues to declare its commitment to quality and affordable health care as a right of all people.

The concern of The United Methodist Church for health is rooted in our biblical understanding that salvation embraces wholeness of mind, body, and spirit. Jesus revealed the meaning of divine love in his acts of healing for all and the meaning of justice in his inclusion of all persons in the healing and saving power of God. The redemptive ministry of Christ, which focused on healing and wholeness—spiritual, mental, physical, and emotional—is our model for health ministry.

Persons in the United States have been conditioned to expect quality health care. The United States has one of the lowest overall mortality rates compared with other countries. Its medical technology expertise is evident in the many success stories of curing severe illness and prolonging life. The quality of medical training in the United States has also been very high, benefiting those who have access to the services of doctors and other health professionals.

Unfortunately, the excesses of the present system are beginning to erode many of these achievements. Millions of Americans are denied appropriate health care simply because of their economic status and/or disability. Within this group are some of the most vulnerable members of society, particularly children. Even those adults who are working are not spared: a substantial number of those without insurance belong to families with steadily employed workers. Many working people also belong to another large group in danger—those who are inadequately or underinsured.

Not surprisingly, the poor, the aging, women, children, people with disabilities, and persons of color are most at risk in this system. The infant mortality rate in the United States is the worst among the "developed" countries. Black women die from cervical cancer at three times the rate of white women. Black Americans have a significantly lower life-span than white Americans and Hispanics have the least access to the health care system of any group. Native Americans, besides suffering greatly from alcoholism, have a substantially higher tuberculosis rate than average U.S. rates. Recent immigrants who experience health problems find the health care system poorly equipped to meet their needs.

Even persons with middle income have difficulty finding affordable, quality care. Families in which a member suffers from catastrophic illness find their health insurance premiums priced so high they can no longer afford them, or in some cases, insurance is canceled. Businesses are overwhelmed with the cost of health insurance, a problem The United Methodist Church is also facing. The dissatisfaction with the U.S. health system ranks highest among the middle class in many surveys.

The health care system is extremely costly in the United States, consuming more of the gross national product than Canadian health-care costs.

Finally, the providers of health care and corporate America both are unhappy with the present system. Doctors object to excessive paperwork, malpractice suits, and inadequate government programs. Hospitals can no longer stay financially sound under existing policies. Corporate America has called for radical change because our economic position in the world is being eroded by rising health costs. Unions, as well, are unhappy, and a large number of strikes in recent years have stemmed from disputes over health care.

We therefore seek legislation that incorporates the following principles:

Principle 1

We seek a national health-care plan that serves and is sensitive to the diversity of all people in the United States and its territories.

Principle 2

We seek a national health-care plan that will provide comprehensive benefits to everyone, including preventive services, health promotion, primary and acute care, mental-health care, and extended care.

Principle 3

We seek a national health-care plan with an equitable and efficient financing system drawn from the broadest possible resource base.

Principle 4

We seek a national health-care plan that provides services based on equity, efficiency, and quality, with payments to providers that are equitable, cost-efficient, and easy to administer and understand.

Principle 5

We seek a national health-care plan that reduces the current rapid inflation in costs through cost-containment measures.

Principle 6

We seek a national health-care plan that is sensitive to the needs of persons working in the various components of the health care system and gives special attention to providing not only for affirmative action in the recruitment, training, and employment of workers, but also for just compensation for all workers at all levels and for retraining and placement of those displaced by changes in the health care system.

Principle 7

We seek a national health-care plan that promotes effective and safe innovation and research for women and men in medical techniques, the delivery of health services, and health practices.

Principle 8

We seek a national health-care plan that assesses the health impacts of environmental and occupational safety, environmental pollution, sanitation, physical fitness, and standard-of-living issues such as housing and nutrition.

We, in The United Methodist Church, are called to a ministry of healing. *Therefore,* we challenge our church to:

1. Support the Interreligious Healthcare Access Campaign and its public-policy advocacy to provide access to universal health care for all;

2. Educate and motivate persons to pursue a healthy lifestyle, thus avoiding health problems by practicing preventive medicine;

3. Affirm the role of Christlike care in institutions that provide direct health services by units of The United Methodist Church;

4. Develop a curriculum model on universal health-care advocacy suitable for United Methodist Church seminaries; and

5. Ensure that persons representative of the groups most directly affected by inaccessibility to quality health care participate in all levels of efforts by The United Methodist Church directed toward the implementation of a national health-care policy.

ADOPTED 1992
AMENDED AND READOPTED 2000

See Social Principles, ¶ 162T.

114. Support for the Religious Coalition for Reproductive Choice

WHEREAS, The United Methodist Church was a founding member of the Religious Coalition for Reproductive Choice in 1973, and

WHEREAS, the General Board of Church and Society and the Women's Division of the General Board of Global Ministries are currently members of the Religious Coalition, along with national organizations from 14 denominations, including the Episcopal Church, Presbyterian Church (USA), United Church of Christ, Unitarian Universalism, Reform and Conservative Judaism, and

WHEREAS, these Coalition member organizations hold a wide variety of views regarding policies relating to specific issues of reproductive choice such as when life and personhood begins but, nevertheless, share common religious values, have official pro-choice policies, and are committed to working together to ensure reproductive choice for all persons through the moral power of religious communities, and

WHEREAS, the Religious Coalition supports the right of all persons to have access to a wide range of reproductive health services including sexuality education, family planning services, contraception, abortion services, affordable and quality health and child care, and

WHEREAS, the Religious Coalition's All Options Clergy Counseling program trains clergy of many faiths to assist women in discerning the course of action that they believe is best in a case of unintended pregnancy, and

WHEREAS, internationally, the Religious Coalition is an accredited non-governmental organization with the United Nations Department of Public Information which supports international family planning services in such areas as South Africa where the Coalition works with churches on HIV/AIDS education and prevention, and

WHEREAS, the Coalition's efforts help counter attempts to enact restrictive legislation that would impose specific religious views about abortion and reproductive health on persons of all faiths, and

WHEREAS, factions within the United Methodist Church whose stated goal is to have the General Conference go on record in opposition to all abortions regardless of the reason are working towards the goal of severing all United Methodist ties with the Religious Coalition for Reproductive Choice;

Therefore, be it resolved, that the United Methodist 2004 General Conference go on record in support of the work of the Religious Coalition for Reproductive Choice, and

Be it further resolved, that the 2004 General Conference affirm the continued membership of the General Board of Church and Society and the Women's Division of the General Board of Global Ministries in the Religious Coalition for Reproductive Choice.

ADOPTED 2004

See Social Principles, ¶ 162T.

115. Faithful Care for Persons Suffering and Dying

Christians affirm that human beings are creatures of God. As such, we are not the authors of our own existence, but receive our lives as gifts from God, who has made us as embodied spirits, capable of transcendence but also vulnerable to illness, accident, and death. God has endowed human beings with capacities for freedom, knowledge, and love, so that we might freely enter into the communion with God and each other for which we were made. The Creator's gift of liberty has been abused and distorted by sin. In Jesus Christ and the Holy Spirit we meet God as Savior, Redeemer, and present Advocate, who has acted in love to free us and all creation from captivity to the power of sin and death. To know God in these ways enables us to receive God's sovereignty over life and death not just as a limit or a neutral fact. It is a source of comfort and peace, as we wait for the final victory over death which is the hallmark of the finished work of redemption.

Therefore, Christians gather as forgiven sinners, redeemed by Christ and empowered by the Holy Spirit to discern and to choose the path of faithfulness to God and one another, as a community seeking to know and to do the truth. It is within the framework of these affirmations, and within the context of these relationships, that we grapple with the questions of faithful care for the sick and the dying.

Through the examples and command of Jesus Christ, the church receives the task of ministering to the sick, relieving what suffering can be relieved and undertaking to share and to lighten that which cannot be eliminated. This mandate calls upon us to address all the needs of the sick. These needs include relief from pain and other distressing symptoms of severe illness, but they also embrace the need for comfort and encouragement and companionship. These needs are expressed particularly by the very ill and the dying who confront fear and grief and loneliness. They are in critical need for emotional and spiritual care and support. The duty to care for the sick also calls upon us to work to reform the structures and institutions by which health care is delivered when they fail to provide the comprehensive physical, social, emotional, and spiritual care needed by those facing grave illness and death.

Care for the dying is an aspect of our stewardship of the divine gift of life. As human interventions, medical technologies are only justified by the help that they can give. Their use requires responsible judgment about when life-sustaining treatments truly support the goals of life, and when they have reached their limits. There is no moral or religious obligation to use them when the burdens they impose outweigh the benefits they offer, or when the use of medical technology only extends the process of dying. Therefore, families should have the liberty to discontinue treatments when they cease to be of benefit to the dying person. However, the withholding or withdrawing of life sustaining interventions should not be confused with abandoning the dying or ceasing to provide care. Even when staving off death seems futile or unreasonably burdensome to continue, we must continue to offer comfort care—effective pain relief, companionship and support for the patient in the hard and sacred work of preparing for death.

Historically, the Christian tradition has drawn a distinction between the cessation of treatment and the use of active measures by the patient or care-giver which aim to bring about death. If death is deliberately sought as the means to relieve suffering, that must be understood as direct and intentional taking of life, whether as suicide or homicide. This United Methodist tradition opposes the taking of life as an offense against God's sole dominion over life, and an abandonment of hope and humility before God. The absence of affordable, available comfort care can increase the pressure on families to consider unacceptable means to end the suffering of the dying.

Health Insurance in the United States

(While this section explores this topic in the United States context, we encourage further understanding and knowledge of practices and traditions around the globe.)

In the United States today, many millions of people have either no health insurance or grossly inadequate coverage which gives them no reliable access to medical treatment. Even for those who do have basic access, good quality comfort care—including effective pain relief, social and emotional support and spiritual counsel—is often not available from a medical system geared toward cure and rehabilitation rather than care for the dying. Such circumstances leave people with a distorted choice between enduring unrelieved suffering and isolation, and choosing death. This choice undermines rather than enhancing our humanity. When cost control measures and for-profit health care institutions bring economic pressures directly to bear on treatment decisions such as the cessation of care, the United States system of health care financing and administration has distorted and corrupted the practice of medicine. We as a society must assure patients situations where their desire not to be a financial burden does not tempt them to choose death rather than receiving the care and support that could enable them to live out their remaining time in comfort and peace.

Pastoral Care

The church's unique role for persons facing suffering and death is to advocate for and provide care in all of its dimensions to the very sick in the form of pastoral care. Such pastoral care is the calling of the whole community of faith, not only pastors and chaplains. Because Christian faith is relevant to every aspect of life, no one can cope successfully with life's pain and suffering and ultimate death without the help of God through other people. In Pastoral care God's help and presence are revealed. Persons offering and receiving pastoral care include the patient, the community of faith, family, friends, neighbors, other patients, and health-care teams.

Those offering pastoral care empathize with suffering patients and share in the wounds of their lives. They listen as patients express their feelings of guilt, fear, doubt, loneliness, hurt, and anger. They can provide resources for reconciliation and wholeness and assist persons in reactivating broken or idle relationships with God and with others. They can provide comfort by pointing to sources of strength, hope, and wholeness, especially reading Scriptures and prayer.

This same pastoral care must be provided to the family and friends of those who are suffering and dying. They too, must have an opportunity to share their feelings of guilt, hurt, anger, fear, and grief. Grieving persons need to be reminded that their feelings are normal human responses that need not cause embarrassment or guilt. Families have long-established patterns of relationships and attention to the entire family unit must be incorporated into pastoral care. Religious, cultural, and personal differences among family and friends must be considered with special sensitivity.

Health care workers also need pastoral care. Doctors and, especially, support staff have intimate contact with dying persons in ways experienced by few others. They live in the tension of giving compassionate care to patients while maintaining professional detachment. Pastoral care for health-care workers means helping them take loving care of themselves as well as their patients.

Pastors and chaplains are called especially to sustain the spiritual growth of patients, families, and health-care personnel. They bear witness to God's grace with words of comfort and salvation. They provide nurture by reading the Scriptures with patients and loved ones; by Holy Communion; by the laying on of hands; and by prayers of repentance, reconciliation, and intercession. They provide comfort and grace with rituals of prayer or anointing with oil after miscarriage, or after a death in a hospital, nursing home, or hospice. They develop rituals in connection with a diagnosis of terminal illness, of welcome to a hospice or nursing home, or of return to a local congregation by persons who have been absent for treatment or who have been in the care of a loved one.

In all these ways, pastoral-care givers and the community of faith are open to God's presence in the midst of pain and suffering, in order to engender hope, and to enable the people of God to live and die in faith and in holiness. They assist persons in coming to peace with themselves and others as they accept the realization that death is not always an enemy. They affirm that there is only one possible ending to the Christian story. Regardless of the tragedies and triumphs, the youthfulness or the age, the valleys of doubt and despair, the suffering and loss, and the soaring as things turn out all right—we come to the only one certain end: "I am the resurrection and the life. Those who believe in me, though they die, will live, and every one who lives and believes in me shall never die" (John 11:25-26, NRSV).

In addition to offering comfort and hope, pastoral-care givers are trained to help patients understand their illness and can assist families in understanding and coming to grips with information provided by medical personnel. Pastoral-care givers are especially needed when illness is terminal and neither patients nor family members are able to discuss this reality freely.

The complexity of treatment options and requests by physicians for patient and family involvement in life-prolonging decisions require good communication. Pastoral-care givers can bring insights rooted in Christian convictions and Christian hope into the decision-making process. If advance directives for treatment, often called "living wills," or "durable powers of attorney" are contemplated or are being interpreted, the pastoral-care givers can offer support and guidance to those involved in decision-making. They can facilitate discussion of treatment options, including home and hospice care.

Decisions concerning faithful care for the suffering and the dying are always made in a social context that includes laws, policies, and practices of legislative bodies, public agencies and institutions, and the social consensus that supports them. The social context of dying affects individual decisions concerning treatment and care and even the acceptance of death. Therefore, pastoral-care givers must be attentive to the social situations and policies that affect the care of the suffering and dying and must interpret these to patients and family members in the context of Christian affirmations of faithful care.

United Methodist Response

To insure faithful care for the suffering and dying it is recommended that United Methodists:

1. Acknowledge dying as part of human existence, without romanticizing it. In dying, as in living, mercy and justice must shape our corporate response to human need and vulnerability.

2. Accept relief of suffering as a goal for care of dying persons rather than focusing primarily on prolonging life. Pain control and comfort-giving measures are essentials in our care of those who are suffering.

3. Educate and equip Christians to consider treatments for the suffering and the dying in the context of Christian affirmations of God's providence and hope. This should be done especially through preaching and adult Christian education programs addressing these issues.

4. Train pastors and pastoral care-givers in the issues of bio-ethics as well as in the techniques of compassionate companionship with those who are suffering and dying.

5. Acknowledge, in our Christian witness and pastoral care, the diverse social, economic, political, cultural, religious and ethnic contexts around the world where United Methodists care for the dying.

ADOPTED 2004

See Social Principles, ¶ 161*M* and ¶ 162*T*.

HOUSING AND HOMELESSNESS

116. Homelessness in the United States

The biblical mandate to care for the poor is clear as put forth in Isaiah 58:6-7 where God says "Is not this the fast that I choose . . . to share your bread with the hungry, and bring the homeless poor into your house; [and] when you see the naked, to cover them?" The homeless are most assuredly the people of God—the people of God who call the church to both repentance and action. They are the hungry we are asked to feed, the strangers we are to welcome, and the naked that we are to clothe. They are the sick and imprisoned we are commanded to visit (Matthew 25:31-36). Theologian Walter Brueggemann says, "The Bible itself is primarily concerned with the issue of being displaced and yearning for a place." What we must seek for all people is safe, sanitary, and affordable housing. The church is called to not only seek to provide shelter but we must do more than house the homeless, we must build community. Home as a promise to the homeless must be the ongoing commitment of the church.

In the most materially rich nation in the world, the homeless are all around us. They are the lonely who pass their time talking to themselves in every big city and small town in the nation. They are rural families without the economic means to travel long distances to shelters and other public services. The homeless are people who have been displaced and discarded. Their numbers alone make them a nation of strangers, highly mobile and rootless, surrounded by wealth, glamour, and excess of all of that which they so desperately lack. Even in a strong economy, no less than 2.3 million adults and children, nearly one percent of the population is likely to experience a spell of homelessness at least once during a year; the numbers grow larger as the economy recedes.

Homelessness is a crisis that strikes at the soul of the nation and at the heart of the church. A study by the U.S. Conference of Mayors revealed a sharp rise of homelessness in major cities in 2000. The study estimates that on average, single men comprise 40 percent of the homeless population, families with children 40 percent, single women 14 percent, and unaccompanied minors four percent. The homeless population is estimated to be 50 percent African-American, 35 percent white, 12 percent Hispanic, two percent Native American, and one percent Asian. An average of 22 percent of homeless people in the cities are considered mentally ill; 34 percent are substance abusers; 20 percent are employed; and 11 percent are veterans.

Homelessness has many faces and many causes, but its root is in the failure of the nation to commit itself through public policies and programs to eradicate poverty. Homelessness and poverty cannot be separated. A comprehensive, all-out attack on poverty must be waged. In order to wage this attach the following factors must be addressed:

- Lack of community support for de-institutionalized people with chronic mental illness
- Discontinuance or reduction of public benefits to significant numbers of elderly and disabled people
- A minimum-wage structure that locks the working poor into poverty
- Loss of family farms
- Closure of plants and businesses
- An economy increasingly built on low-paying temporary and seasonal jobs with few or no benefits
- The increasing number of single-parent households with associated low incomes

- The lack of housing for people with AIDS
- Displacement of inner-city residents by urban renewal.

In addition to the above, the shortage of affordable housing also contributes greatly to this plight of homelessness. In its 2002 report, the Millennial Housing Commission, a bipartisan commission created by Congress, found that housing affordability is the single greatest challenge facing the nation.

Homelessness is both a rural and an urban problem. The rural homeless tend to be young, white, and female. Rural shelters are scarce, so homeless people often double up with friends and relatives. The Housing Assistance Council has found that rural homeless people are migrant workers, displaced renters, bankrupt farmers, and laid-off workers. Native Americans and other residents on Indian reservations are increasingly found among the rural homeless. Extremely high unemployment, coupled with the increased numbers of Native American people returning to live on reservations, has placed undue burdens on an already overtaxed and inadequate social service system. Rural homeless people often migrate to cities, thus contributing to urban homelessness.

The United Methodist Church must continue to affirm the right of all persons to live without deprivation in safe, sanitary, and affordable housing. The United Methodist Church must clearly assert that inequitable public policies, unfair and discriminatory private-sector practices have deprived many of that right. The church must teach its constituents that homelessness is a violation of human dignity and an affront to the biblical mandate to do justice. We must use all our power to eliminate the causes of homelessness and to work along with others to eradicate it. The Bible calls us to commit ourselves to welcoming the stranger into our midst and to seeing all people as belonging to the family of God. The church must recognize in deed as well as word that homeless people are our neighbors, seek to learn who are the homeless in our communities and speak out on their behalf in our congregations and in the larger community.

The following actions are recommended to general agencies, annual conferences, and local churches:

1. General Agency Recommendations:
   a. Provide to clergy and laity educational, training resources and opportunities that address the root causes of homelessness and provide models for addressing the problem.

b. Urge seminaries to include courses in their curriculum that help prepare clergy for effective leadership around systemic contradictions in our society that create poverty and homelessness.

c. Encourage annual conferences to include courses in their plans for continuing education for clergy at least once a quadrennium.

d. Continue to support and work with national, regional, and local housing advocacy groups to implement this resolution.

e. Join with other communions to promote affordable housing for low-income persons through the National Low-Income Housing Coalition, the National Coalition for the Homeless, the National Alliance to End Homelessness, and other appropriate networks.

f. Document and affirm the work of local churches and service providers who provide needed ministries of compassion to homeless persons through church-based soup kitchens, transitional housing programs, shelters, food pantries, clothes closets, and rent and utility assistance programs. Promote their efforts throughout the local church by soliciting financial contributions and volunteer support, and by encouraging members to contribute specialized skills and technical assistance.

g. Identify effective existing models and provide new models for local congregations and clergy who wish to undertake Bible study and theological reflection around the root causes of homelessness.

2. Annual Conference Recommendations:

a. Participate in "End Homelessness in Ten Years" grassroots efforts led by the National Alliance to End Homelessness

b. Inform clergy and laity of the avenues available to churches to become involved in housing development by exposing them to different models used to address the lack of affordable housing.

c. Adopt a resolution on homelessness encouraging actions at the congregational level to address the homeless crisis in local communities.

d. Encourage local churches to conduct a survey on homelessness in their areas to determine what services are currently being provided and to discover gaps in services toward which the church should direct its efforts.

e. Support cooperative parishes as a major strategy for responding to the problem of homelessness.

3. Local Church Recommendations:
   a. Involve clergy and laity in local church volunteers networks, direct-service programs, ecumenical coalitions for the homeless, directories of local service providers, speaking opportunities for groups such as Habitat for Humanity, and workshops led by local homeless advocates and the homeless themselves.
   b. Promote local church-based community organizing efforts to empower neighborhoods and influence government at every level.

4. All Levels of the Church: Call upon Congress to pass comprehensive national housing legislation, as outlined in the General Conference resolution on housing.

ADOPTED 2004

See Social Principles, ¶ 162A.

117. Housing in the U.S.A.

The Scriptures look ahead to that ideal day when all persons will enjoy pleasant, peaceful, and secure shelter under their own vines and fig trees and "no one shall make them afraid" (Micah 4:4 NRSV).

In many portions of the Gospel, we find Jesus seeking out homes for retreat and renewal, for fellowship and hospitality. Similarly, all persons are entitled to dwelling places that provide for safety, privacy and recreation.

The Social Principles statement of The United Methodist Church declares: "We hold governments responsible for . . . guarantee of the rights to adequate . . . shelter" (¶ 164A). We reaffirm this right as well as the assertion of the 1972 General Conference that "housing for low income persons should be given top priority" (*1972 Book of Resolutions*).

The need for adequate housing at affordable costs is critical today.

Love for neighbor demands that Christians care about how adequately their neighbors are sheltered. Christians should identify with those who suffer daily from a shortage of available, decent, safe, and sanitary housing. There are many levels and forms of deprivation. Nearly every American town and city has its "homeless," those who exist literally without any form of shelter, living under bridges, in cars and abandoned buses, carrying their entire possessions with them in a few shopping bags.

Millions of families huddle together in densely overcrowded apartments, rural shacks, ancient house trailers, converted warehouses, and condemned or abandoned buildings. Many of our fellow citizens live in housing that lack such necessities as running water or plumbing, and others have no permanent housing (the homeless) because the remainder of us fail to recognize their plight or simply do not care enough.

Since December of 1986, families with children have become the fastest growing homeless group. While The United Methodist Church affirms the pervasive powers of families as "creators of persons, proclaimers of faith perspectives and shapers of both present and future society," it must continue its condemnation of policies that ignore the causal relationship between shortages of low-income housing and the lack of initiative or political will to ensure that safe and affordable housing is available to all citizens.

The deinstitutionalization of persons diagnosed as mentally ill or recovering, or who could live full lives with minimal supervision, is a concept of worth. However, a lack of regional and community planning has allowed many people to be released from a variety of institutions with no place to go, no affordable housing on the budgets allotted to persons through federal or state funds, and no supervised environment for those who need it. Few services exist to maintain supervised, semi-independent, safe, affordable housing. The National Institute of Mental Health estimates that one third of the homeless have mental health problems. Some are persons who were deinstitutionalized with no support; others became ill because of the environment of homelessness.

"Am I my brother's keeper?" (Genesis 4:9, NRSV) becomes a challenging alternative when concerned United Methodists begin to address the phenomenon of increased homeless families in our country. We must grapple with ways to meet the needs of the homeless. We must be more open to using church buildings that are outmoded and excess land in urban and rural areas. We must examine needs and services in our communities and develop a better understanding of our role in local, state, and federal policy development. We commend United Methodists who are engaged in the effort to change such intolerable housing conditions. We commend every such individual, local church, interfaith group, nonprofit, for-profit, and government effort. We endorse with gratitude and appreciation the thousands of dollars and untold hours of voluntary service that United Methodists dedicate to this battle to improve human shelter in our country. We urge local churches, districts, and annual conferences to strengthen every housing ministry taking place within their communities by providing additional financial, technical, counseling, and spiritual resources.

Many specific activities deserve greater United Methodist support.

A. At the local level

Local churches, individually or in cooperation with other churches, can identify specific housing needs existing in their communities. Often, bringing to public consciousness the plight of people in need of shelter is the first step toward alleviating such need. Sometimes the use of existing church buildings can graphically demonstrate both the need and a solution that then can be developed more fully through the use of other facilities and financial resources.

Formation of nonprofit and limited-divided housing corporations or housing cooperatives is a viable approach in many situations. There are excellent opportunities for establishing housing construction, management, and advocacy programs. However, expert consultative and technical services generally are needed from the earliest conception. We urge the use of the services provided by the General Board of Global Ministries. We urge landowners, apartment and housing managers, and policy boards to allow federally subsidized tenants to inhabit their dwellings. This is a serious problem at this time, because U.S. government policy recommends selling up to 30 percent of public housing units for private development. The net result is displacement of the poor. Availability of housing for them is limited because of discrimination and a reluctance on the part of the government to maintain federally subsidized housing monies for privately owned housing.

B. At the regional level

The atmosphere of conflict infects the relationship between cities, towns, suburban areas, counties, and states throughout our nation. Too often, competition for use of land cloaks subtle racism. Economic profit, likewise, often is used to justify a lack of concern for the impact of taxation measures. Uncoordinated planning and development results in jobs being located beyond the reach of those most in need of work. The "trickle-down theory" of housing occupancy masks a selfish motivation and results in the maintenance and expansion of existing ghettos, causes the formation of new ghettos, and enforces negative attitudes that support class and racial segregation. We urge United Methodists to challenge all such practices and to engage in every activity to eliminate such vestiges of discrimination from our nation.

Every urbanized area in our country is required to have some form of a regional planning agency. Most rural areas have some similar agency, such as an area development district. Generally these political structures have considerable influence upon housing patterns, planning, production, and usage. Most can have citizens' advisory groups that develop strategy proposals and monitor private and governmental housing activities. We urge United Methodists to become knowledgeable of and involved in such planning agencies.

C. At the national level

Since the enactment of the National Housing Act of 1949, the United States has set a goal that every citizen be housed in "decent, safe and sanitary housing." Yet the reality is that we are farther from that goal today than ever before. In part, this is due to growth of population and the ever-increasing gap between those who are economically well-off and those who are not. But in large measure, the disparity is due to an unwillingness of our elected representatives to use general tax revenues to achieve the goals more fully. Generally, legislators feel they represent the views of their electorate and receive very little support for using tax dollars to build more housing for low- and moderate-income families. The moral commitment first stated in 1949 and restated in every subsequent Housing Act by Congress (1959, 1968, 1974, 1978) has gone greatly unheeded. If "decent, safe and sanitary housing" is to be a citizen's right, a much greater moral outcry must be raised.

Therefore, we call upon United Methodists to undertake a concerted effort to impress upon their elected representatives a profound concern over the continuing housing deficiencies existing in our cities, towns, and rural areas. Much more effort needs to be made to influence the legislative processes that affect housing, including improving existing laws, developing more imaginative approaches where possible, and providing adequate funding for housing designated to meet the needs of the ill-sheltered.

(1) Subsidized Rental Housing (Section 8) and Public Housing

Under the Section 8 Housing Assistance Payments Program, renters normally pay a percentage of their income for rent, and the federal government makes up the difference between that and the HUD-(Department of Housing and Urban Development) established Fair Market Rent. We support this program for subsidizing rents as one way of opening up more housing units to low-income families and yet expecting such families, when possible, to provide their fair share of costs. However, the reality is that there are just not enough units of housing available at a cost that can be afforded by the poor, even with payment assistance. There is a great need for developing more housing units. In 1985, more than 8 million low-income renters were in the market for the available 4.2 million units at an affordable (minimum of 25 percent of income) price.

The Temporary Aid to Needy Families (TANF) is the primary source of income for many people who now find themselves homeless. The amount of money that many families with children receive is lower than the average cost of housing in many states. This situation will exacerbate when TANF recipients are terminated due to the term limits now imposed by federal and state governments.

We are greatly concerned over the rapidly increasing trend toward converting rental housing to condominiums for sale. Too often in practice this means pushing people out of housing they can afford to rent but can't afford to buy. We therefore recommend that the rate of condominium conversion of rental units be slowed, or that percentages of the units be set aside with affordable rental rates. Further, we urge local housing authorities to offset this trend by encouraging increased housing stock of subsidized rental units.

We support use of a wide variety of subsidized housing approaches in order to meet a greater demand to house needy people. However, the development of a "voucher" program with no ceiling on the actual rent that can be charged and no local community guarantee of housing set aside for the poor will not alleviate the present situation.

Public housing continues to be a vital necessity in both urban and rural areas. Every incorporated city, town, and county can and should provide public, well-constructed, and well-managed rental housing for those who cannot obtain it on the open market. Nearly 50 percent of all housing is now occupied by the elderly. Since the church has traditionally expressed concern and provided care of the aging, it is especially crucial that this program is continued, expanded, and adequately funded.

We must at all times critically examine the setting at the local, state, and federal levels, because governmental policies affect the funding, improvement, and provision of housing resources for any given community. The Federal Administration between 1981 and 1988 tried to eliminate or reduce the main federal programs used by states and local governments to help the poor and the homeless. The Community Development Block Grant Program, General Revenue Sharing, and the Temporary Emergency Food Assistance Program (TEFAP) have all been affected. The Community Development Block Grant Program budget has been cut almost yearly. General Revenue Sharing was eliminated. The Administration has targeted for elimination the Temporary Emergency Food Assistance Program. Congress has repeatedly come to the rescue of these programs and in 1986 passed a law allowing the homeless to receive Aid to Families with Dependent Children (Now Temporary Aid to Needy Families), social security, and Medicaid.

(2) Fair Housing

Fair housing in our nation has regressed dramatically. Because housing remains segregated in most places in the United States, schools tend to be segregated and jobs tend to be located at inconvenient distances from ethnic neighborhoods.

We therefore call upon the U.S. Congress to provide the Department of Housing and Urban development with "cease and desist" enforcement powers, and we encourage HUD to apply these powers evenly and with relentless determination to ensure equal access to affordable housing in all markets. We support state and local legislation that would strengthen fair housing enforcement across the country. We also support HUD funding for states with laws that are substantially equivalent to federal law. We also call for the expansion of coverage in the Fair Housing Act to provide protection for people with disabilities.

Equal access to housing not available represents an unrealizable right. Therefore, to fulfill equal opportunity objectives we urge that more housing be built and offered at prices most persons can afford to pay.

A. Redlining

We deplore the practice of "redlining" as it occurs in many urban areas. This generally means that financial institutions, insurance companies, and mortgage brokers collectively make it difficult for homeowners to secure adequate financing and insurance at reasonable rates in a certain neighborhood of a given urban community. We ask that all necessary steps be taken, through negotiation and legislation, to eliminate this immoral practice, and that churches take the lead in encouraging financial support arrangements that rejuvenate instead of destroy our neighborhoods. Vigilant monitoring by the religious community can forestall such unhealthy practices.

We support existing laws such as the Home Mortgage Disclosure Act, which provides information to the public on where banks and savings and loans make their loans, and the enlarged Community Reinvestment Act, which mandates that banks and savings and loans have the responsibility to serve the credit needs of moderate and lower-income communities.

We urge compliance of the institutions in which the church deposits funds with the Home Mortgage Act; and we support such additional regulations and laws that will ensure reinvestment in currently red-lined communities, in a way that will not result in unjust displacement of elderly, poor, ethnic, and other persons.

B. *Housing for older adults and people with disabilities*

The Section 202 federal program is a bright spot in an otherwise dismal picture of housing for older adults and people with disabilities of any age. Restricted to sponsorship by nonprofit groups (the majority of which are related to religious groups), the 202 continues to offer a direct ministry opportunity. Since it is a loan guarantee program with lower-than-market interest rates, it needs to be funded at much more realistic levels than in the past. There is also a need for expanding the congregate housing services project for semi-independent older adults or people with disabilities. The steady increase in age of our population is evidence for the need to expand the 202 program until the need for this type of rental housing for the elderly has been met. This program provides support services for persons using 202 housing and is cost effective because it allows people who might have to be institutionalized to live in much lower-cost housing.

(3) *Housing for Native Americans*

Housing policy, as in other aspects of national policy and practices toward Native American tribes, is grossly inadequate. We call for a substantial increase in programs at the federal level and for the implementation of state and local housing programs in every possible way, so that the shocking condition of substandard reservation housing can be quickly improved. Special efforts through programs of United Methodist general agencies, in partnership with ethnic conferences and funds for ethnic ministry, should be supportive of actions to improve housing for Native Americans.

(4) Financing of Housing

Traditionally, the vast majority of housing in our country has been financed through the private money-lending industry. There is little likelihood that this would need to change if the traditional principles against usury are followed. But more attention needs to be given to developing ways mortgage money can be made available to low-income persons for home ownership, and to provide rental housing for low-income people. Federal and state programs aid the moderate- and upper-income segments of our population quite well, but similarly helpful programs for the lower-income sector of the population do not exist. The 1980s saw the greatest benefit go not to the neediest families, but to those who are sufficiently well off to purchase homes.

The higher the family income, the more these tax immunities breaks help. Three fourths of these tax immunities breaks go to homeowners in the top 15 percent of the income bracket. Poor or lower-middle class homeowners get only 3 percent of the tax immunities breaks. Government-subsidized mortgage programs need to be developed that can also aid the lower-middle class and poor individuals and families.

In contrast to the rapid growth in federal aid to move well-to-do homeowners through the Internal Revenue Code, Congress has continued to cut the federal budget in areas that greatly affect poor working families.

New methods of private financing need to be developed so that traditional money sources are not withdrawn from the housing industry in favor of other, more profitable forms of investment.

Recommendations

A number of federal programs as well as some state programs exist today to make possible the meaningful participation of church groups in providing adequate housing in a wholesome environment. We encourage United Methodist churches to join in such programs that require minimal capital investment but substantial commitment of time and energy. Churches should be aware that these programs are available in both urban and rural areas. More church groups ought to:

1. Be concerned about the conditions of housing in their communities;

2. Use the tools available (e.g., General Board of Global Ministries Housing Consultant Services) to provide better housing;

3. Dedicate a special day or Sunday as a Day of Prayer and Action for Shelter, as has been developed by Habitat for Humanity (contact the General Board of Global Ministries for special resources); and

4. Develop a sense of mission and assume responsibility as stewards to meet these needs without expectation of monetary reward.

5. Encourage the establishment and full funding of a Community and State Fair Housing Trust Fund.

In implementing any housing ministry, church people must maintain great sensitivity to community needs and work to achieve community participation and control. Tenants' need for adequate, reasonably priced and energy-efficient housing should be recognized. Care must always be exercised to ensure our Christian involvement as "enablers" rather than "controllers." Our goal must always be to enable those we help to be in control of their own lives, futures, and destinies. Whatever the form of community organization, housing production, management, or ownership of a housing project, every effort should be made at each developmental step to ensure that those who are being aided are afforded the opportunity, and indeed, are required, to take every action necessary to direct the undertaking. Wherever possible, we must train rather than service, transfer power rather than decide, empower rather than control. In this as in all other aspects of housing ministries, United Methodists should seek the best technical guidance and ensure the greatest professional competence for such a ministry. Let us equip ourselves and provide the widest possible range of supportive assistance to individuals, congregations, districts, conferences, and all forms of cooperative groups sharing similar goals and policies so that our fellow citizens may achieve, as their right, "decent, safe and sanitary housing" as soon as possible.

ADOPTED 1988
AMENDED AND READOPTED 2000

See Social Principles, ¶ 162A.

IMMIGRATION

118. Opposition to the Illegal Immigration
Reform and Immigrant Resolution Act

WHEREAS, the Holy Scriptures call us as the community of God to give shelter, protection and help to sojourners living amongst us, reminding us that we, too, were foreigners in other times; and

WHEREAS, the Council of Bishops of The United Methodist Church through its document *To Love the Sojourner* has given the various boards, commissions, and agencies of The United Methodist Church direction as we relate to undocumented persons that live in our communities; and

WHEREAS, undocumented persons possess certain inalienable rights named and lifted in the International Declaration on Human Rights, the United Nations charter, as well as the documents concerning immigration of the Geneva Convention, and the Constitution of the United States Bill of Rights; and

WHEREAS, one of the most critical issues facing the Hispanic community today is the need for amnesty for the undocumented immigrants living within the United States; and

WHEREAS, being an undocumented person is NOT a crime;

Therefore, be it resolved, that we, The United Methodist Church, declare that the *Illegal Immigration Reform and Immigrant Resolution Act* is evil and unjust, and that the enforcement thereof results in immediate and insufferable human rights violations, discrimination, and oppression.

We call the United States government to accountability and insist upon:

1. changes in, and possible abolition of, the 1996 immigration law;

2. the continued existence of a unified Immigration and Naturalization Service, rather than a division into administrative and enforcement prosecutorial branches, and

3. the development of an amnesty program for undocumented persons to be implemented immediately.

Be it further resolved, that the General Conference move to create a task force to be responsible for agencies working on behalf of The United Methodist Church that is composed of staff from the following church boards and agencies: General Board of Global Ministries, General Commission on Religion and Race, General Board of Church and Society, with a minimum of two bishops, legal advisers, and

Methodists Associated to Represent the Cause of Hispanic Americans (MARCHA) representation.

ADOPTED 2000

See Social Principles, ¶ 162.

119. Refugees, Immigrants, and Visitors to the United States of America

United Methodists are called to be faithful to God and to God's actions in the world. As United Methodists we believe that God is the parent of all—that all people are created in God's image and that it is the right of all people to have a full and abundant life. We believe that the resources of creation are God's gift for all people. We believe that as people of God we need to be open to others and welcome especially the sojourners in our midst.

The United States of America prides itself as being open to ethnic diversity. However, United States citizens have not always held to that ideal. While some people have been welcomed, others have remained in the outskirts of U.S. cultural core and fabric. Furthermore, the reality is that with time U.S. borders have been getting narrower and often a spirit of hostility and racism toward the sojourners in the U.S.—refugees, immigrants, and visitors—has grown to the point of rejection and discrimination.

A glaring example of discrimination and injustice is the denial of entry visas to legitimate invitees from around the world, in particular the delegates to the 2004 General Conference coming from the Central Conferences in Africa and the Philippines. These are delegates of color whose denial of entry by the U.S government to a legitimate event such as the General Conference—which is well announced and scheduled—is unacceptable and unconscionable.

The tragic events of September 11, 2001, rather than helping U.S. citizens become more open and welcoming to the people who seek relief from economic and political pressures as well as from hunger and war in their countries, have blurred their vision and have created a distorted concept of national identity. Refugees, immigrants, and visitors from Africa, Asia, Latin America, and very specially the Middle East are being unjustly harassed and persecuted. In the name of the law, refugees and immigrant families are being separated, and many persons are being sent back to their countries disregarding the political, emotional, physical, and spiritual consequences of such action. There is fear and anguish in the sojourners in our midst. There is mistrust and hostility toward the sojourners in our midst. Visitors' visas to enter the United State have become increasingly difficult and expensive to obtain.

The United Methodist Church's position has been clear on the issue of immigration, including those who while working in the U.S. and making their contribution do not have the needed documents for residence. The 2000 General Conference adopted a resolution that specifically charged The United Methodist Church to declare the "Illegal Immigration Reform and Immigrant Resolution Act" evil and unjust and to call the United States government to accountability and insist upon changes and possible abolition of the 1996 Immigration law, the continued existence of a unified Immigration and Naturalization Service, rather than a division into administrative and enforcement prosecutorial branches, and the development of an amnesty program for undocumented persons (Resolution #118, "Opposition to the Illegal Immigration, Reform and Immigrant Resolution Act").

WHEREAS, the immigrant and refugee community, as well as, from Africa, Asia, Latin America, and the Pacific are currently suffering the effects of discriminatory immigration policies. We therefore call The United Methodist Church;

1. to affirm and remind the church through the Council of Bishops, United Methodist Communications and the General Board of Church and Society, the position of The United Methodist Church regarding the rights of refugees, immigrants, and undocumented persons to seek a better life in the United States;

2. to affirm and remind the President of the United States of America, the U.S. Congress, and other government officials of The United Methodist Church's position on immigration as described in the Resolution on Immigration (Resolution #118) adopted by the 2000 General Conference and on this resolution;

3. to promote and distribute both resolutions through the Council of Bishops, United Methodist Communications, and the General Board of Church and Society;

4. to call local churches to seek ways to welcome, assist, and empower the refugee, immigrant, visitors, and undocumented persons in their neighborhood, and to denounce the persecution of the sojourner in the U.S. as prejudicial and racist;

5. to request the General Board of Church and Society to work for public policy that is hospitable to visitors to the United States in every step of entry and visit to the U.S. from visa application to the time while they are enroute to and are accepted entry into the United States;

6. to request that immediately upon adoption by the General Conference, the Secretary of the General Conference will send a copy of this resolution to the President of the United States, the Speaker of the U.S. House of Representatives, the President of the U.S. Senate, and the U.S. Secretary of State.

ADOPTED 2004

See Social Principles, ¶ 162.

MENTAL HEALTH

120. Abusive Treatment Methods for Persons with Mental Disabilities

A large part of the ministry of our Lord focused on persons with mental disabilities. Such persons are children of God and, therefore, our brothers and sisters within God's family. The full and equal rights of persons with mental disabilities are enshrined in the Social Principles of The United Methodist Church.

Yet the use of abusive treatment methods as "therapy" for persons with mental disabilities still occurs. Such abusive treatment methods are used both on adults and children, and programs that rely on such abusive treatment methods are often funded by tax revenues. A number of organizations that advocate for persons with mental disabilities have already taken a stand against abusive treatment methods.

The United Methodist Church joins in affirming the right of persons with disabilities to freedom from abusive treatment methods. We oppose the use of any form of punishment for children or adults with mental disabilities in any case where such punishment would be considered illegal, abusive, or unconscionable if applied to a child or adult who is not disabled. In particular, we condemn as unacceptable the following practices:

1. treatment methods that result in physical injury or tissue damage to the person;

2. verbal abuse or insult, humiliation, or degradation;

3. prolonged isolation from others;

4. denial of food, warmth, hygiene, contact with other human beings, or other necessities of life;

5. the use of electric shock or noxious substances as a form of punishment;

6. the use of any punishment on a child with a mental disability that would be considered child abuse if used on a child with no disabilities;

7. neglect;

8. the misuse of physical or chemical restraint; and

9. the threat of any of the above treatments.

Any therapy used in the treatment of persons with mental disabilities must be potentially beneficial to the person. As an alternative to abusive treatment methods, we support the use of positive approaches in the treatment of persons with mental disabilities. Positive approaches affirm the humanity of these persons and recognize that the needs and desires of such persons are not significantly different from those of other persons. Our obligation to persons with mental disabilities is to support and assist them in their efforts to live lives as rich and rewarding as possible.

We call upon all public and private agencies and service providers involved in treating persons with mental disabilities to adopt and uphold the standards set forth in this resolution.

We call upon United Methodist Church-related institutions and agencies, including hospitals, homes, schools, and universities, to adopt and uphold the standards set forth in this resolution and to support research on positive treatment methods.

We call upon governments at all levels to end immediately the expenditure of public revenues on any agency or program that fails to adopt and uphold the standards set forth in this resolution.

The United Methodist Church declares itself to be open to persons with mental disabilities and their families, and the church commits itself to support such persons and families and to accommodate their needs within our community. We further pledge our support to help persons with mental disabilities and their families find appropriate services, programs, and supports, and to protect them from abusive treatment methods.

ADOPTED 1996
READOPTED 2004

See Social Principles, ¶ 162G.

121. Caring Communities—The United Methodist Mental Illness Network

The mission to bring all persons into a community of love is central to the teachings of Christ. We gather as congregations in witness to that mission, welcoming and nurturing those who assemble with us.

Yet we confess that in our humanity we have sometimes failed to minister in love to persons and families with mental illness. We have allowed barriers of ignorance, fear, and pride to separate us from those who most need our love and the nurturing support of community.

To support United Methodist congregations in their goal to reach out to persons and families with mental illness, the General Board of Church and Society established the United Methodist Mental Illness Network of "Caring Communities," congregations and communities in covenant relationship with persons and families with mental illness.

United Methodist congregations are called to join the Caring Communities Program:

- to educate their members about mental illness;
- to enter into a covenant relationship of understanding and love with persons and families with mental illness, in order to nurture them; and
- to reach out to the larger community.

ADOPTED 1996
AMENDED AND READOPTED 2004

See Social Principles, ¶ 162G and T.

122. The Church and People with Mental, Physical, and/or Psychological Disabilities

We call United Methodists to a new birth of awareness of the need to accept, include, receive the gifts of, and respond to the concerns of those persons with mental, physical, and/or psychological disabilities, including their families.

Because the experience of disabilities is included in all racial, social, sexual, and age groupings, and this experience is common to every family and at some time in every life;

And because a large part of the ministry of our Lord focused on persons with conditions such as mental, physical, psychological, and/or neurological disabilities;

And because the body of Christ is not complete without people of all areas of life;

And because we cannot afford to deny ourselves fellowship with these persons and must intentionally develop more healthy attitudes and behavioral responses to people with disabilities;

And because there exist inadequacies in the church and in society with regard to concerns for the rights of people with disabilities, utilization of talents, and their full participation within the life of the church and society;

And because of more suffering and exclusion from the fellowship of the church of persons with mental, physical, and/or psychological conditions;

And believing that the church is most faithful to the teachings and example of Jesus when it expresses love in concrete ways in a mutual ministry with those who are outcasts, neglected, avoided, or persecuted by society;

And believing in the legacy of John Wesley, Phillip Otterbein, and Jacob Albright, who held that vital piety flows into compassionate ministry;

And knowing that prevailing societal norms unduly glorify the conditions of youthful beauty, mental alertness, and material affluence to the exclusion and avoidance of those whose disabilities put them outside these norms,

Therefore, we pledge ourselves to:

Accessibility:

1. Renew and increase our commitments as a church to the development of a barrier-free society, especially in the many facilities of the church and parsonages. To indicate the seriousness of our intent, we must set time limits to ensure the greatest physical accessibility in the shortest feasible periods and extend our policy of not providing funding through or approval by United Methodist agencies unless minimum guidelines are met, which include but are not limited to:

    a. providing adequate access to sanctuary pews, altars, chancel areas and pulpit, classrooms, and restrooms;

    b. providing curb cuts, ramps with at least a 1:12 inclination or platform lifts; and

    c. providing facilities with equipment and supplies to meet the needs of persons with seen and unseen disabilities, including persons with vision and/or hearing impairments.

2. All meetings of The United Methodist Church, beyond the local church, be accessible to people with disabilities. As general church agencies, jurisdictions, annual conferences, and districts nominate people with disabilities to their boards and committees, it is necessary for these boards and committees to accommodate these persons.

3. All United Methodist churches are asked to conduct an audit of their facilities to discover what barriers impede the full participation of people with disabilities. Steps should then be taken to remove those barriers. The accessibility audit for churches is a recommended resource available from the General Board of Global Ministries.

Awareness:

1. Sensitize and train local church pastors to the needs and opportunities for those who have a disability and their families to better minister to and with them.

2. Lead the local churches in attitudinal change studies, to the end that the people called United Methodists are sensitized to the gifts, needs, and interests of people with disabilities, including their families.

3. Take advantage of the great opportunities for our church to work cooperatively with other denominations who also are addressing these issues and extend an active invitation to work jointly where possible.

4. Suggest one Sunday each year as Access Sunday to sensitize people to our accessibility concerns.

Adequate Resources:

1. Provide resources through the church at all levels, including curricula, for persons with various disabilities, such as those who are blind, deaf, para—or quadriplegic, mentally retarded, psychologically or neurologically disabled, and so forth, so that each individual has full opportunity for growth and self-realization with the community of faith and the society at large.

2. Strongly recommend that all curriculum material be so designed that it can be adapted to meet the needs of people with disabilities; that curriculum material portray people with disabilities in leadership roles within church and society; that curriculum material reflect the Guidelines for the Elimination of Handicappist Language as produced by the General Council on Ministries.

Affirmative Action:

1. Include in all our efforts of affirmative action the concerns and interests of people with disabilities, particularly in the active recruitment and encouragement of these persons for leadership roles, both clergy and lay, within the church and its agencies, in hiring practices, job security, housing, and transportation.

2. Urge the General Board of Higher Education and Ministry to monitor annual conference boards of ordained ministry so that people with disabilities are given equal treatment in the steps to ordained ministry.

3. Strongly urge that our schools of higher education and theological training provide specialized courses for faculty and students in the awareness and appreciation of gifts, needs, and interests of people with disabilities. This must include the emphasis of accessibility and equal employment in these institutions, as well as those in the larger society. Accreditation by the University Senate should be withdrawn where persons who are disabled are excluded, either from attendance, services, or employment.

4. Strongly urge local churches to conduct needs-assessment surveys. Such a survey would suggest to a local church what particular actions must be taken to fully include people with disabilities within the life of the church.

Advocacy Within the Church:

Implement within each annual conference methods of recruiting, sensitizing, and training persons as advocates to work with and on behalf of people with disabilities on a one-to-one basis and to enable them to achieve their human and civil rights as well as to assume their rightful place in the life of the church and community. Each annual conference should also develop the larger concern of advocacy for people with disabilities to enable them to achieve appropriate housing, employment, transportation, education, and leisure-time development.

THE CHURCH AND PEOPLE WITH DISABILITIES

Advocacy Within the Society:

While there is much to be done within the church to make real the gospel of inclusiveness with regard to people with disabilities, there is a world society that also must be made aware of the concerns and needs of these persons. We admonish the church and its people to stand alongside people with disabilities and to speak out on their rights in society. These rights include access to jobs, public transportation and other reliable forms of transportation, adequate housing, and education. We are people under orders to minister to and with all God's children. We are all a people in pilgrimage! We have too often overlooked those of God's children who experience life in different ways from ourselves. We pledge ourselves to an inclusive, compassionate, and creative response to the needs and gifts of people with mental, physical, and/or psychological disabilities.

Barrier-Free Construction for People with Disabilities:

Be it resolved, that church monies from agencies of The United Methodist Church beyond the local church be granted, loaned, or otherwise provided only for the construction of church sanctuaries, educational buildings, parsonages, camps, colleges, or other church-related agencies or facilities that meet minimum guidelines in their plans for barrier-free construction;

That local churches utilizing their own funds or funds secured through lending agencies and institutions beyond The United Methodist Church be urged to make adequate provision in their plans to ensure that all new church buildings shall be of barrier-free construction;

That local churches be urged to adapt existing facilities through such programs as widening doorways, installing ramps and elevators, eliminating stairs where possible, providing handrails, adequate parking facilities, and rest rooms so that people with disabilities may take their appropriate place in the fellowship of the church; and

That the appropriate national agencies provide technical information for local churches to assist in providing barrier-free facilities.

ADOPTED 1984
AMENDED AND READOPTED 1996, 2004

See Social Principles, ¶ 162G.

349

123. Ministries in Mental Illness

Mental illness is a group of brain disorders that cause disturbances of thinking, feeling, and acting. Treatment should recognize the importance of a nonstressful environment, good nutrition, and an accepting community. Treatment should also recognize the importance of medical, psychiatric, emotional and spiritual care, psychotherapy or professional pastoral psychotherapy—in regaining and maintaining health. Churches in every community are called to participate actively in expanding care for the mentally ill and their families and communities.

John Wesley's ministry was grounded in the redemptive ministry of Christ with its focus on healing that involved spiritual, mental, emotional, and physical aspects. His concern for the health of those to whom he ministered led him to create medical services at no cost to those who were poor and in deep need, refusing no one for any reason. He saw health as going beyond a simple biological well-being to wellness of the whole person. His witness of love to those in need of healing is our model for ministry to those who are suffering from mental illness.

All aspects of health—physical, mental, and spiritual—were of equal concern to Jesus Christ, whose healing touch reached out to mend broken bodies, minds, and spirits with one common purpose: the restoration of well-being and renewed communion with God and neighbor. But those whose illness brought social stigma and isolation, such as the man of Gadara, whose troubled spirit caused fearsome and self-destructive behavior, were embraced and healed with special compassion (Mark 5:1-34). When the man of Gadara said his name was "Legion; for we are many" (verse 9), his comment was suggestive of the countless individuals, in our time as well as his, whose mental dysfunction—whether genetically, environmentally, chemically, socially, or psychologically induced—causes fear, rejection, or shame, and to which we tend to respond with the same few measures no more adequate for our time than for his: stigmatization, isolation, incarceration, and restraint.

We confess that our Christian concepts of sin and forgiveness, at the root of our understanding of the human condition and of divine grace, are sometimes inappropriately applied in ways that heighten paranoia or clinical depression. Great care must be exercised in ministering to those whose brain disorders result in exaggerated self-negation, for while all persons stand in need of forgiveness and reconciliation, God's love cannot be communicated through the medium of forgiveness for uncommitted or delusional sins.

We reaffirm our confidence that God's unqualified love for all persons beckons us to reach out with fully accepting love to all, but particularly to those with disabling inability to relate to themselves or others due to mental illness.

Research published since 1987 has underscored the physical and genetic basis for the more serious mental illnesses, such as schizophrenia, manic-depression, and other affective disorders.

Public discussion and education about mental illness are needed so that persons who suffer from brain disorders, and their families, can be free to ask for help. This includes freedom from the stigma attached to mental illness that derives from a false understanding that it is primarily an adjustment problem caused by psychologically dysfunctional families. Communities need to develop more adequate programs to meet the needs of their mentally ill members. This includes the need to implement state and local programs that monitor and prevent abuses of mentally ill persons, as well as those programs that are intended to replace long-term hospitalization with community-based services.

The process followed in recent years of deinstitutionalizing mental patients has corrected a long-standing problem of "warehousing" mentally ill persons. However, without adequate community-based mental-health programs to care for the dehospitalized, the streets, for too many, have become a substitute for a hospital ward. Consequently, often the responsibility, including the costs of mental-health care, have simply been transferred to individuals and families or to shelters for the homeless that are already overloaded and ill-equipped to provide more than the most basic care. Furthermore, the pressure to deinstitutionalize patients rapidly has caused some mental-health systems to rely unduly upon short-term chemical therapy to control patients rather than upon more complex programs that require longer-term hospitalization or other forms of treatments where research provides successful outcomes achieved. Such stopgap treatment leads to repeated short-term hospitalizations, with little or no long-term improvement in a person's ability to function.

The church, as the body of Christ, is called to the ministry of reconciliation, of healing, and of salvation, which means to be made whole. We call upon the church to affirm ministries related to mental illness that embrace the role of community, family, and the healing professions in healing the physical, social, environmental, and spiritual impediments to wholeness for those afflicted with brain disorders and for their families.

1. We call upon all local churches, districts, and annual conferences to support the following community and congressional programs:
   a. adequate public funding to enable mental-health systems to provide appropriate therapy;
   b. expanded counseling and crisis intervention services;
   c. workshops and public awareness campaigns to combat stigmas;
   d. housing and employment for deinstitutionalized persons;
   e. improved training for judges, police, and other community officials in dealing with mentally ill persons;
   f. community and congregational involvement with patients in psychiatric hospitals and other mental-health-care facilities;
   g. community, pastoral, and congregational support for individuals and families caring for mentally ill family members;
   h. more effective interaction among different systems involved in the care of mentally ill persons, including courts, police, employment, housing, welfare, religious, and family systems;
   i. education of their members in a responsible and comprehensive manner about the nature of the problems of mental illness facing society today, and the public-policy advocacy needed to change policies and keep funding levels high;
   j. active participation in helping their communities meet both preventive and therapeutic needs related to mental illness; and
   k. the work of the National Alliance for the Mentally Ill (NAMI), Washington, D.C., a self-help organization of mentally ill persons, their families, and friends, providing mutual support, education, and advocacy for those persons with severe mental illness and urging the churches to connect with NAMI's religious outreach network. We also commend to the churches Pathways to Promise: Interfaith Ministries and Prolonged Mental Illnesses, St. Louis, Missouri, as a necessary link in our ministry on this critical issue.
2. We call upon seminaries to provide:
   a. technical training, including experience in mental-health units, as a regular part of the preparation for the ministry, in order to

help congregations become more knowledgeable about and involved in mental-health needs of their communities.

3. We call upon the general agencies to:

   a. advocate systemic reform of the health-care system to provide more adequately for persons and families confronting the catastrophic expense and pain of caring for mentally ill family members;

   b. support universal access to health care, insisting that public and private funding mechanisms be developed to ensure the availability of services to all in need, including adequate coverage for mental-health services in all health programs;

   c. advocate community mental-health systems, including public clinics, hospitals, and other tax-supported facilities, being especially sensitive to the mental-health needs of culturally or racially diverse groups in the population;

   d. support adequate research by public and private institutions into the causes of mental illness, including, as high priority, further development of therapeutic applications of newly discovered information on the genetic causation for several types of severe brain disorders;

   e. support adequate public funding to enable mental-health-care systems to provide appropriate therapy; and

   f. build a United Methodist Church mental illness network at the General Board of Church and Society to coordinate mental-illness ministries in The United Methodist Church.

ADOPTED 1992
AMENDED AND READOPTED IN 2004

See Social Principles, ¶ 162T.

124. Healing of Post-Abortion Stress

WHEREAS, we recognize that there is a legal right to an abortion, we also recognize that some regret that event later in life,

WHEREAS, the church should be about offering healing ministries for all types of brokenness,

Therefore, be it resolved that the 2004 General Conference of The United Methodist Church urge pastors to become informed about the symptoms and behaviors associated with post-abortion stress; and

Be it further resolved that the 2004 General Conference of The United Methodist Church encourage local churches to make available contact information for counseling agencies that offer programs to address post-abortion stress for all seeking help.

ADOPTED 2004

See Social Principles, ¶ 162T.

125. Mental Illness, Mental Health Courts, and the Christian Community

We believe all persons with a mental illness diagnosis should have access to the same basic freedoms and human rights as other persons living in a free society. We understand that there is a fine line of distinction between criminal violation of the law and behavior that is criminalized because law enforcement agencies have had no other recourse for handling persons whose behavior and actions have been the result of mental illness symptoms which affect thinking, perceptions, and behavior. We oppose the use of jails and prisons for the incarceration of persons who have serious, persistent mental illnesses for whom treatment in a secure hospital setting is far more appropriate. Moreover, many incarcerated persons with mental illness need psychiatric medications. Citing economic reasons as the cause for failure to provide medications to a person who needs them is unacceptable as is imposing medication compliance as a condition of release or access to treatment and other services. We believe that all states should understand and embrace an ethical understanding of the compassionate intent of the law in the establishment of mental health courts when mental illness is a factor in law enforcement. We believe all persons confined for the purpose of mental illness treatment in an accredited psychiatric facility, either public or private, shall have all their human rights respected, including their [legal] right to have input into their treatment plan, medications, and access to religious support as State laws allow. We also hold all treatment facilities, public and private, responsible for the protection of these rights.

We further believe all mental health treatment facilities; public and private, including outpatient treatment programs, should take seriously the religious and nonreligious spiritual needs of persons with a mental illness who find help and hope for their life through their faith in God or in a power higher than themselves.

We acknowledge that persons with a mental illness diagnosis who exhibit difficult or disruptive behaviors often do so because they have

354

experienced traumatic events such as abuse or domestic violence, have lived a life of physical or emotional poverty, or have been deprived of social experiences and have limited social skills and etiquette. We believe that some persons with a mental illness who exhibit acting-out or difficult behaviors do so because they have often been lonely, misunderstood, powerless, or are without joy in their lives.

We believe mental illness courts, properly established, regulated and administered could be maintained in every jurisdiction to handle cases involving persons with serious mental illnesses; insure compassionate and ethical treatment, and avoid whenever possible criminalizing the behaviors that result from symptoms which affect thinking, perceptions, and behavior.

We believe The Church and local congregations have a responsibility for the role they play in advocating for the lives of adults as well as children and teens who have mental illnesses; whose experiences have included pastoral care and other spiritual opportunities they have had prior to diagnosis and may be denied now because of stigma and their difficult behaviors. We believe these responsibilities include educational opportunities and the right to literacy. We believe in the perpetuation of Christian and spiritual values in our society relating to the development of pastoral leadership skills to understand mental illness and be able to mediate with persons in their congregations and their communities concerning the issues and needs of persons who have a mental illness. We further believe congregations and private foundation boards on which Christians sit and have authority or influence have a significant role to play in advocating for the support of ministries that address these issues.

ADOPTED 2004

See Social Principles, ¶ 162T.

MISSIONS

126. Communities of Shalom

WHEREAS, the General Conference responded to the Los Angeles crisis of 1992 by creating a new strategy called Communities of Shalom, which incorporates evangelism and community action;

WHEREAS, Communities of Shalom focus on spiritual renewal, congregational development, community economic development, health, and strengthening race and class relationships;

WHEREAS, Communities of Shalom strategy has spread throughout the United States and Africa, in rural and urban settings; and

WHEREAS, the need for Communities of Shalom continues to grow; *Therefore, be it resolved,* that The United Methodist Church:

1. strongly urge the continual expansion of Shalom ministries throughout the United States and the world for communities in crisis and transition;

2. through the General Board of Global Ministries, resource Communities of Shalom through training and technical assistance;

3. affirm the Shalom Committee and its continued work with the General Board of Global Ministries and other general church agencies. The committee shall be composed of twelve (12) members and two ex-officio members. There shall be six members selected by the Council of Bishops, three by the General Board of Global Ministries and three selected by the Shalom Committee for expertise. A staff person of the General Board of Global Ministries and a staff person of the General Board of Pensions shall serve as ex-officio members with vote;

4. charge all general church agencies to explore and develop opportunities to work collaboratively to assist local churches with the Communities of Shalom strategy; and

5. endorse the solicitation of Shalom resources from foundations, corporations, government sources, individuals, and churches utilizing the Advance, a foundation structure, and other necessary strategies.

ADOPTED 2004

See Social Principles, ¶ 162P.

127. Mission Personnel in the United States

WHEREAS, mission personnel in the United States, which includes church and community workers, US-2s, mission interns, summer interns, community developers, rural chaplains, lay missioners, and others, have faithfully and effectively enabled The United Methodist

Church to facilitate mission and ministry across the United States in settings often neglected and overlooked by others; and

WHEREAS, for many people in the United States, life is becoming increasingly difficult, with the basic necessities of food, shelter, health care, job and educational opportunities, childcare, and transportation required for daily survival often being beyond reach; and

WHEREAS, God continues to hear the cries of the oppressed, impoverished, and neglected people; and

WHEREAS, God continues to call persons to offer themselves for service with the poor to provide both compassionate care and personal empowerment; and

WHEREAS, The United Methodist Church, with its unique Wesleyan traditions of identity and advocacy with the poor and its historical focus on social issues and human development, is challenged by God to be radically attentive and responsive to marginalized and dispossessed people and to bear responsibility for keeping their plight before the total church and world community; and

WHEREAS, mission personnel in the United States provide leadership vital to initiate and maintain cooperative ministries, including communities of shalom and missionary programs, and other efforts that focus attention on the needs of women, children, youth, racial and ethnic populations, the aging, and people with disabilities in both rural and urban areas;

Therefore, be it resolved, that The United Methodist Church reaffirm its commitment to impoverished people and oppressed communities in the United States by creating and maintaining among its highest levels of priority the recruitment, training, and placement of mission personnel in the United States who can enable people, churches, and communities to move beyond their present circumstances to participate in healthy, whole communities;

Be it further resolved, that new and innovative means of providing financial support for mission personnel in the United States be developed as The United Methodist Church at all levels confronts the challenge to deal with limited available resources.

ADOPTED 1996
AMENDED AND READOPTED 2004

See Social Principles, ¶ 162.

NATIVE AMERICANS

128. A Study of Native American Land

WHEREAS, in 1988 the General Conference of The United Methodist Church passed a resolution directing various agencies of the church, and Native American church entities, to develop a comprehensive study and report on the use by The United Methodist Church of American Indian Lands for mission purposes since 1784, in consultation with the Native American International Caucus and the Oklahoma Indian Missionary Conference, and

WHEREAS, this land use study has been completed, and

WHEREAS, The United Methodist Church is eliminating all resolutions passed in 1988 and prior, and

WHEREAS, the Native People of this land are STILL experiencing blatant disregard for their treaty rights in the loss of tribal land bases, and,

WHEREAS, The United Methodist Church owns property throughout this country on ancestral Indian land;

Therefore, be it resolved, that General Conference direct the General Board of Global Ministries (GBGM) to report on the use by The United Methodist Church of American Indian lands for mission purposes since 1784, in consultation with the Native American International Caucus and the Oklahoma Indian Missionary Conference; and

Be it further resolved, that the GBGM board report include the disposition of any unused land; and

Be it further resolved, that the GBGM report these findings to the 2004 General Conference.

ADOPTED 2000

See Social Principles, ¶ 162A.

129. Comity Agreements Affecting Development of Native American Ministries

WHEREAS, certain annual conferences of The United Methodist Church have used the alleged Comity Agreement as the basis for their functional relationship among Native Americans, limiting their capability to develop Native American ministries in certain geographical areas; and

WHEREAS, the effects of practicing the concept of a Comity Agreement by The United Methodist Church have resulted in the failure of the Church to follow through with the biblical mandate of propagating the gospel to all nations and, further, have caused the failure of the church to create the climate for leadership development of Native Americans; and

WHEREAS, such a Comity Agreement would be discriminatory in that it would violate the right of Native Americans to associate with the denomination of their choice;

Therefore, be it resolved, that The United Methodist Church states, as a matter of policy, that it is not a party to any interdenominational agreement that limits the ability of any annual conference in any jurisdiction to develop and resource programs of ministry of any kind among Native Americans, including the organization of local churches where necessary.

ADOPTED 1980
READOPTED 2000

See Social Principles, ¶ 162A.

130. Concerning Demeaning Names to Native Americans

In our society today, there is a growing debate and discussion about the appropriateness of using Native American names as nicknames for professional sports teams and university mascots. As the publication *Words That Hurt, Words That Heal,* produced by The United Methodist Church, highlights, the use of names and language is a powerful instrument for good and destructive purposes. It is demeaning to Native Americans and other members of our society to depict Native Americans as violent and aggressive people by calling a sports team the "Braves" or the "Warriors." The implication is that all Native Americans are aggressive and violent people. This use of nicknames is not conducive to the development of a society committed to the common good of its citizenry.

In "The United Methodist Church and America's Native People" (*The Book of Resolutions, 1992;* page 178), The United Methodist Church has issued a call for repentance for the church's role in the dehumanization and colonization of our Native American sisters and brothers. In light of this stand and the fact that we strongly believe the continued use of Native American names as nicknames is demeaning and racist, we urge all United Methodist-related universities, colleges, and schools to set an example by replacing any nicknames that demean and offend our Native American sisters and brothers; and we support efforts throughout our society to replace such nicknames, mascots, and symbols.

ADOPTED 1996
READOPTED 2004

See Social Principles, ¶ 162A.

131. Respecting the Native American Legacy and Tradition

The United Methodist Church has denounced the continued use of Native American names as nicknames for sport teams as racist and dehumanizing. Respecting the Native American legacy and tradition has been a critical issue for the General Commission on Religion and Race and the General Commission on Christian Unity and Interreligious Concerns.

United Methodists have not been the sole voice on this issue. Many other communions, religious groups, and secular organizations have addressed this concern in the form of statements, articles, protests, and resolutions. However, in spite of these efforts, Native American names and symbols are still being used by sport teams.

WHEREAS, The United Methodist Church is committed to the elimination of racism within the church and within society, and

WHEREAS, The United Methodist Church is equally committed to participate actively in the continued struggle of building the true community of God where reconciliation comes together with justice and peace, and

WHEREAS, The United Methodist Church rejects the use of Native American names and symbols for sport teams, and considers the practice a blatant expression of racism:

Therefore, be it resolved, that the General Conference calls upon all the general agencies, annual conferences, and United Methodist Church-related organizations and institutions, upon selecting locations for their meetings and events in cities that sponsor sport teams using Native American names and symbols, to hold meetings and events in cities that do not sponsor sport teams using Native American names and symbols, and make public the position of The United Methodist Church regarding sport teams using Native American names and symbols.

ADO PTED 2004

See Social Principles, ¶162A.

132. Confession to Native Americans

WHEREAS, the gospel calls us to celebrate and protect the worth and dignity of all peoples; and

WHEREAS, the Christian churches, including The United Methodist Church and its predecessors, have participated in the destruction of Native American people, culture, and religious practices; and

WHEREAS, the churches of this country have not sufficiently confessed their complicity in this evil; and

WHEREAS, the churches have been blessed by having members who are Native Americans as well as by engaging in dialogue with Native Americans who practice their traditional religions; and

WHEREAS, confession of our guilt is a first step toward the wholeness that the churches seek through the ecumenical movement;

Therefore, be it resolved, that the United Methodist General Conference confesses that The United Methodist Church (and its predecessor bodies) has sinned and continues to sin against its Native American brothers and sisters and offers this formal apology for its participation, intended and unintended, in the violent colonization of their land; and

Be it further resolved, that The United Methodist Church pledges its support and assistance in upholding the American Indian Religious Freedom Acts (P.L. 95-134, 1978) and within that legal precedent affirms the following:

1. the rights of the native peoples to practice and participate in traditional ceremonies and rituals with the same protection offered all religions under the Constitution of the United States of America;

2. access to and protection of sacred sites and public lands for ceremonial purposes; and

3. the use of religious symbols (feathers, tobacco, sweet grass, bones, and so forth) for use in traditional ceremonies and rituals.

Be it further resolved, that the General Conference recommends that local churches develop similar statements of confession as a way of fostering a deep sense of community with Native Americans and encourages the members of our Church to stand in solidarity on these important religious issues and to provide mediation when appropriate for ongoing negotiations with state and federal agencies regarding these matters.

ADOPTED 1992
READOPTED 2004

See Social Principles, ¶ 162A.

133. Ecumenical Dialogues on the Native Community

WHEREAS, in Methodism there has been a strong attraction toward native cultures, yet, at the same time, there has been an inherent desire to change, control, or destroy the traditional lifeways. As Christianity enters the third millennium since the birth of Jesus Christ, the church continues to be torn by the double legacy of both attraction and repulsion which was modeled by John Wesley over two-and-a-half centuries ago.

WHEREAS, historically, the churches have not known or understood the native people within and outside the church. However, native people had a sacred relationship with the Creator thousands of generations before the colonial imposition of Christianity. The church has had a long pattern of following the prevailing attitudes of U.S.A. society, rather than promoting attitudes of proper respect and support. This has resulted in a lack of understanding, harmony, balance, and healing among native communities.

WHEREAS, ecumenical dialogues bringing together native Christians including members of the native American church, traditional practitioners, and other spiritual and ceremonial leaders have been conducted by the General Commission on Christian Unity and Interreligious Concerns in order to build bridges of understanding, respect, and healing of native communities; and

WHEREAS, in accordance with Scripture and a desire to bring Methodism into the modern-day life of native people, and to forge a means of protecting what remains of traditional lifeways, the General Commission on Christian Unity and Interreligious Concerns has initiated a dialogue process; and

WHEREAS, in order to ensure a path toward the unity of generations, the General Commission on Christian Unity and Interreligious Concerns has worked with other ecumenical entities and communions to address the issues of power, prestige and privilege in relation to Native American communities and Native American leadership,

Therefore, be it resolved, that the 2000 General Conference:

1. Urge local congregations of The United Methodist Church to engage in dialogue with a native community to begin a journey of understanding the native perspective of unresolved issues of identity, community, hostility, and empowerment. This dialogue will assist the church in its own understanding of responsibility to empower native families and communities by affirming native culture and tradition; and

2. Call upon these partnerships to incorporate in these discussions the misappropriation and selling of native heritage and cultural ways. The consequences of these actions can be detrimental and lead to unacceptable practices within and outside the native community.

ADOPTED 2000

See Social Principles, ¶ 162A.

134. Health Care for Native Americans

WHEREAS, Native Americans are the most socio-economically deprived minority group in the United States; and

WHEREAS, the United States government is bound by treaty to provide health care for all Native Americans; and

WHEREAS, the United States government now provides these medical services through Indian Health Services, United States Public Health Service, Department of Health and Human Services; and

WHEREAS, medical services currently provided by the Indian Health Services for health education and prenatal care have contributed to a rapid decline in infant mortality among Native Americans; and

WHEREAS, similar successes of these health programs are likely to have occurred for all Native Americans living in the United States; and

WHEREAS, despite these successes, the federal government is constantly threatening to cut the Indian Health Services Program; and

WHEREAS, any funding cuts could severely curtail or cancel health care for a large number of eligible Native Americans; and

WHEREAS, a small number of Native Americans can afford to buy private health insurance,

Therefore, be it resolved, that all Native Americans have access to adequate medical services to ensure a balance of physical, mental, and spiritual well-being for the "Journey Toward Wholeness"; and that the United States Congress allows no decrease in federal funds to operate Indian health facilities.

Be it further resolved, that the General Board of Church and Society submit this resolution, on behalf of the General Conference, to all United States senators and legislators who have Indian Health Services within their respective state.

ADOPTED 1988
AMENDED AND READOPTED 2000

See Social Principles, ¶ 162A.

135. Human Rights of Native People of the Americas

WHEREAS, many of the indigenous Native people living in the Americas are held captive by government, social, and economic policies that violate their rights as human beings; and

WHEREAS, these policies deny the worth and God-given right of every human being to live free of injustice, discrimination, and fear; and

WHEREAS, the human rights of Native people of the Americas have been and continue to be grossly violated by various governments that suppress freedom; and

WHEREAS, indigenous Native people of the Western Hemisphere Americas are in countries experiencing civil war, and their lives are continually threatened and endangered; and

WHEREAS, our religious faith calls us to affirm the dignity and worth of every human being and to struggle with our oppressed brothers and sisters for justice; we are called to "proclaim release to the captives . . . to set at liberty those who are oppressed" (Luke 4:18, RSV),

Therefore, be it resolved, that we petition the 2000 General Conference to direct the General Board of Church and Society to design, coordinate, and facilitate, in consultation with the Native American International Caucus, and all other appropriate United Methodist Native American organizations, a strategy that will bring the power of moral and religious influence of The United Methodist Church and the government of the United States to bear upon the struggles of the oppressed Native people of the Americas.

ADOPTED 2000

See Social Principles, ¶ 164*A*.

136. Increased Support for Programs Impacting Native American Higher Education

WHEREAS, the National United Methodist Native American Center, Inc., supports and endorses the goal of optimum educational achievement for all United Methodist Church members; and

WHEREAS, the concept of illiteracy is unacceptable in a time when society projects a formal demeanor of progress and opportunity for all members; and

WHEREAS, past support for The United Methodist Church for the participation of Native Americans in higher education has been minimal, productive, and appreciated; and

WHEREAS, a trend of decreasing Native American participation in higher education is beginning to appear at the national and regional levels; and

WHEREAS, the consistently rising costs of higher education contribute considerably to the decrease of Native American participation in higher education; and

WHEREAS, recent statistics suggest an upward trend of academic success for Native Americans currently participating in higher education; and

WHEREAS, the National United Methodist Native American Center, Inc., supports the philosophy that every person has a right to an education and it is society's responsibility to enable every person to obtain this right; and

WHEREAS, the foundation to Native American growth and progress in society lies within the domain of formal education;

Therefore, be it resolved, that the General Conference endorse and support the funding, development, implementation, and assessment of a higher education recruitment/retention forum, sponsored by The United Methodist Church for Native Americans throughout the denomination's regions, to be organized and managed by the National United Methodist Native American Center, Inc., in cooperation with local churches reflecting a significant population of Native Americans.

Be it further resolved, that the General Conference encourage The United Methodist Church to utilize the information and materials generated as a result of the forum for sensitizing and familiarizing non-Indian membership about Native Americans in their respective communities.

ADOPTED 1992
READOPTED 2004

See Social Principles, ¶ 162A.

137. Native American Ministries Sunday

WHEREAS, the Native American population continues to shift in larger numbers from the rural areas to the urban population centers; and

WHEREAS, the human conditions of numerous Native Americans in the rural and urban environments reflect a legacy of poverty and socioeconomic denial; and

WHEREAS, there is a serious shortage of Native American pastors and trained professionals to respond to the human conditions in the Native American communities; and

WHEREAS, there is a National United Methodist Native American Center, which has been created to recruit, train, and deploy Native American leadership; and

WHEREAS, the financial support that is required to sustain the center is beyond the capability of the Native American communities; and

WHEREAS, the 1988 General Conference approved Native American Awareness Sunday (now known as N.A.M. Sunday) as a means for providing opportunities for the denomination to support Native American ministries;

Therefore, be it resolved, that all annual conferences promote the observance of the Native American Ministries Sunday and encourage local churches to support the Sunday with programming and offerings.

Be it further resolved, that the agencies that develop and provide resources for this special day report to the General Commission on Religion and Race their plans, strategies, and timelines for addressing the goals and objectives related to Native American Ministries Sunday.

ADOPTED 1992
READOPTED 2004

See Social Principles, ¶ 162A.

138. Native American Center

WHEREAS, the National United Methodist Native American Center, Inc. (NUMNAC) has functioned as one of four national centers focused on ethnic enlistment, training, and assistance in the deployment of ordained and diaconal ministry and other professional leaders in their respective communities; and

WHEREAS, NUMNAC has operated admirably with a limited staff of the executive director, associate director, and an administrative assistant; and

WHEREAS, NUMNAC's previous funding was authorized by the General Conference with linkage responsibilities resting with the General Board of Higher Education and Ministry (GBHEM); and

WHEREAS, NUMNAC's service record over the past 19 years has been extremely contributory to active Native American recruitment into the ordained ministry, higher education opportunities for United Methodist Native American students, Native American youth involvement in The United Methodist Church, pastoral care and training for current ministry, spiritual reinforcement in Native American congregations, communication between Native American and non-Indian churches, and research relating to the growing cultural diversity within The United Methodist Church; and

WHEREAS, there exists a continuous need for Native American understanding, sensitivity, input, and participation among and within the church administration and general community; and

WHEREAS, NUMNAC's past funding has limited the expansion of programs to benefit Native American clergy,

Therefore, be it resolved, that the 2000 General Conference endorse 2001-2004 funding of NUMNAC through subline of the World Service Fund titled "Other Ministries, National United Methodist Native American Center." NUMNAC board and staff will raise any additional funds needed to fulfill program goals and needs; and

Be it further resolved, that the 2000 General Conference endorse NUMNAC's current functions and roles as related to its initial goals and objectives, its proposed activities for 2001-2004 quadrennium, and that it be supported by related entities of The United Methodist Church as a center for Native American cultural, spiritual and contemporary training for United Methodist clergy and lay people.

ADOPTED 2000

See Social Principles, ¶ 162A.

139. Pastoral Care and the AIDS Epidemic in Native American Communities

WHEREAS, the AIDS disease is of epidemic proportions; and

WHEREAS, pastoral care training does not take into consideration the unique cultural and spiritual healing methods of the Native American community; and

WHEREAS, a national consultation on pastoral care and AIDS for Native Americans would provide sound cultural insights for The United Methodist Church in the area of pastoral care for Native American pastors; and

WHEREAS, a program of this nature would provide nurture for Native American pastors and their continuing education,

Therefore, be it resolved, that the General Board of Higher Education and Ministry and the National United Methodist Native American Center continue to develop culturally relevant curriculum materials regarding pastoral care and AIDS in the Native American community; and

Be it further resolved, that General Conference encourage the National United Methodist Native American Center and the General Board of Higher Education and Ministry to hold, as soon as possible, a National Consultation on Pastoral Care and AIDS in the Native American community using this curriculum, consistent with the availability of independent funding.

ADOPTED 1992
READOPTED 2004

See Social Principles, ¶ 162*A* and *S*.

140. Native American Social Witness Program

WHEREAS, Native American churches have historically been seen as being on the receiving end of mission and ministry; and

WHEREAS, yet many social concerns are presently being addressed by Native American communities; and

WHEREAS, the potential and need for social justice ministries among Native Americans is tremendous, and Native American congregations have been put into the role of recipient rather than being empowered,

Therefore, be it resolved, 2000 General Conference directs the General Board of Church and Society to make available to every Native American United Methodist Church, upon request, ministry training and consultation on social witness during the 2001-2004 quadrennium. Such a program will be designed and patterned after the gospel of Jesus Christ, which will empower congregations to engage in social witness to their respective Native American communities.

ADOPTED 2000

See Social Principles, ¶ 162*N*.

141. Native American Dialogue About "Chief Wahoo"

WHEREAS, any language, image, or depiction of material which diminishes or demeans persons on the basis of racial or ethnic characteristic as racial harassment is sin; and

WHEREAS, The United Methodist Church has gone on record in the 1996 General Conference as denouncing any organization or team that uses offensive racist logos[1]; and

1. *1996 Book of Resolutions*, p. 217, "Concerning Demeaning Names to Native Americans"

WHEREAS, the "Chief Wahoo" caricature, owned by the Cleveland Indian Professional Baseball Team, does demean and diminish Native Americans by denying them recognition as human beings in the baseball team's use and abuse for economic profits; and

WHEREAS, the use of negative and denigrating images, and the acceptance of such images by a large segment of media viewing persons, increases the struggles of young Native Americans to develop strong self-esteem needed to compete effectively within dominant culture; and

WHEREAS, the "Chief Wahoo" mascot increases the isolation, confusion, and hostility which is expressed so graphically by the statistical records of such social dysfunction as alcoholism, school drop-out rates, teen suicide and violence, and family disintegration among Native Americans; and

WHEREAS, the controversy over "Chief Wahoo" deflects attention from the ongoing struggle by all minority groups, including Native Americans, for equality coupled with respect for their traditional values and customs; and

WHEREAS, persons who fail to or refuse to recognize the human worth of their fellow human beings may diminish themselves and their ability to relate effectively with other people and the openness of mind and spirit which prepares them to relate more fully to the Divine.

Therefore, be it resolved, that the Native American International Caucus affirms the sacred value of all of God's creation, including those who participate in and are loyal to the use of "Chief Wahoo" as a logo.

Be it further resolved, that United Methodist Native Americans hope for reconciliation with such persons and that such reconciliation will require dialogue, mutual respect, and sensitivity by persons on all sides of this controversy. We invite such dialogue, and

Be it further resolved, that The United Methodist Church direct appropriate church agencies, in consultation with appropriate Native American entities, to engage the Cleveland community and the ownership of the Cleveland Indian Professional Baseball Team in a dialogue of understanding and sensitivity with demeaning ethnic caricatures and mascots.

ADOPTED 2000

See Social Principles, ¶ 162A.

142. Native American History and Contemporary Culture as Related to Effective Church Participation

WHEREAS, current literature and research suggest a substantial "communication gap" between Native Americans and non-Indian United Methodist Church entities, specifically as it relates to non-Indian entities comprehending the concept of Native American life, culture, language, spirit, values, and such; and

WHEREAS, this vague communication has been a consistent problem over history, with minimal effort from non-Indian entities to change their attitudes toward Native Americans until recent trends; and

WHEREAS, such attitude of society reflects a growing trend toward developing and implementing a system accommodating, to a high degree, cultural diversity; generally speaking, society is beginning to demonstrate comprehension of the term *multicultural* education as related to the year 2000 and is making efforts to become even more informed; services that once perpetuated Eurocentric society only are now examining the values of the ever-growing ethnic populations and attempting to integrate these values into their service activities (education, government, health, business, and such); and

WHEREAS, there are substantial numbers of ethnic professionals capable of providing effective instruction in cultural diversity as related to The United Methodist Church's current and future thrusts; and

WHEREAS, there still is a critical need for The United Methodist Church to become concretely familiar with its Native American membership in order to ensure their religious, denominational, spiritual, and emotional well-being; and

WHEREAS, there is an expressed concern from The United Methodist Church's Native American membership that racism and prejudice are significant contributors to the absence of Native American representation in the church's hierarchy; and

WHEREAS, the formal means of eliminating this condition is through the formal instruction in Native American history, culture, and contemporary affairs of non-Indian entities of The United Methodist Church;

Therefore, be it resolved, that General Conference advocate the development and implementation of a training policy whereby Native American history, culture, and contemporary affairs will be an integral part of ministry and administrative training for all aspects of The United Methodist Church;

Be it further resolved, that General Conference designate the National United Methodist Native American Center, Inc., as the center for the research, development, and training components of the requested curriculum;

Be it further resolved, that General Conference support a policy that the concept of "Indian preference" be utilized in the selection of instructors and speakers for the proposed training components.

ADOPTED 1992
READOPTED 2004

See Social Principles, ¶ 162A.

143. Native American Religious Freedom Act

WHEREAS, tribal people have gone into the high places, lakes, and isolated sanctuaries to pray, receive guidance from God, and train younger people in the ceremonies that constitute the spiritual life of Native American communities; and

WHEREAS, when tribes were forcibly removed from their homelands and forced to live on restricted reservations, many of the ceremonies were prohibited; and

WHEREAS, most Indians do not see any conflict between their old beliefs and the new religion of the Christian church; and

WHEREAS, during this century the expanding national population and the introduction of corporate farming and more extensive mining and timber industry activities reduced the isolation of rural America, making it difficult for small parties of Native Americans to go into the mountains or to remote lakes and buttes to conduct ceremonies without interference from non-Indians; and

WHEREAS, federal agencies began to restrict Indian access to sacred sites by establishing increasingly narrow rules and regulations for managing public lands; and

WHEREAS, in 1978, in an effort to clarify the status of traditional Native American religious practices and practitioners, Congress passed a Joint Resolution entitled "The American Indian Religious Freedom Act," which declared that it was the policy of Congress to protect and preserve the inherent right of Native Americans to believe, express, and practice their traditional religions; and

WHEREAS, today a major crisis exists in that there is no real protection for the practice of traditional Indian religions within the framework of American constitutional or statutory law, and courts usually automatically dismiss Indian petitions without evidentiary hearings; and

WHEREAS, while Congress has passed many laws that are designed to protect certain kinds of lands and resources for environmental and historic preservation, none of these laws is designed to protect the practice of Indian religion on sacred sites; and

WHEREAS, the only existing law directly addressing this issue, the American Indian Religious Freedom Act, is simply a policy that provides limited legal relief to aggrieved American Indian religious practitioners,

Therefore, be it resolved, that the General Board of Global Ministries and the General Board of Church and Society make available to the church information on the American Indian Religious Freedom Act; and

Be it further resolved, that the General Board of Church and Society support legislation that will provide for a legal cause of action when sacred sites may be affected by governmental action; proposed legislation should also provide for more extensive notice to and consultation with tribes and affected parties; and

Be it further resolved, that the General Board of Church and Society may enter and support court cases relating to the American Indian Religious Freedom Act; and

Be it further resolved, that the General Board of Church and Society communicate with the Senate Committee on Indian Affairs, declaring that the position of The United Methodist Church, expressed through the 1992 General Conference, is to strengthen the American Indian Religious Freedom Act of 1978 and preserve the God-given and constitutional rights of religious freedom for Native Americans.

ADOPTED 1992
AMENDED AND READOPTED 2004

See Social Principles, ¶ 162A.

144. Native American Representation in The United Methodist Church

WHEREAS, the population of Native Americans has grown dramatically during the past two decades; and

WHEREAS, this trend of population growth is accompanied by a substantial positive interest in Native American culture and history in regard to The United Methodist Church participation among traditionally noninterested individuals; and

WHEREAS, leadership of The United Methodist Church has recently demonstrated a sincere desire to "include" Native Americans in the decision-making activity of the church; and

WHEREAS, there is a significant need to recruit Native Americans into "role model" positions within the church as a means to enhance church membership, ministry numbers, and an overall understanding of contemporary Native American life as related to racial communication; and

WHEREAS, current attitudes among Native Americans reflect a critical desire to present and communicate accurate Native American perspectives to, and for, decision-making bodies of The United Methodist Church; and

WHEREAS, there is currently a minute number of Native Americans serving on the national United Methodist Church policy-making boards, management committees, education boards, finance committees, information areas, and such; and

WHEREAS, current trends suggest a decrease in church membership and attendance among Native American citizenry;

Therefore, be it resolved, that General Conference strongly support the following tasks as related to accurate Native American representation and participation on local, regional, and national policy-making, managerial, and implementation/evaluation boards/committees of The United Methodist Church:

1. Establish a policy of defining Native American identity as "any individual who can provide verification of membership in a tribe of the United States";

2. Develop a policy that will ensure that Native Americans will be identified, selected, and placed on pertinent boards and/or committees as previously stated; and

3. Urge national, regional, and annual conference activities to select Native American representation from Native American individuals who have a background of relevant Native American history, cultural sensitivity, and contemporary affairs.

Be it further resolved, that The United Methodist Church supports the integration of a policy on Native American definition within *The*

Book of Discipline, specific to the current and future regard of Native American representation on such national, regional, and local efforts.

ADOPTED 1992
READOPTED 2004

See Social Principles, ¶ 162A.

145. Native American Young Adults in Mission

WHEREAS, by treaty obligation many Native American tribes are recognized as "nations" within the territorial boundaries of the United States; and

WHEREAS, the General Board of Global Ministries of The United Methodist Church sponsor the Mission Intern Program, and the **Mission Personnel Program Area of the Board** assigns young adults overseas , and within the boundaries of the United States to develop leadership skills; and

WHEREAS, opportunities for mission and evangelism exist within Native American nations and tribes within the territorial boundaries of the United States;

Therefore, be it resolved, that the Mission Personnel Program Area be directed to assign Native American young adults in "Native American Nations and Tribes" within the boundaries of the United States and in overseas assignments.

ADOPTED 1992
AMENDED AND READOPTED 2004

See Social Principles, ¶ 162A.

146. Native People and The United Methodist Church

Most European Americans are isolated from the issues of justice for the United States' native people by the remoteness of reservations or native territories, the lapse of time, the comparative invisibility of natives in the urban setting, the distortions in historical accounts, and the accumulation of prejudices. Now is the time for a new beginning, and The United Methodist Church calls its members to pray and work for that new day in relationship between indigenous native peoples, other minorities, and European Americans.

The United Methodist Church has been forced to become more sharply aware and keenly conscious of the destructive impact of the unjust acts and injurious policies of the United States government upon the lives and culture of U.S. American Indians, Alaska natives, and Hawaiian natives. In the past, the white majority population was allowed to forget or excuse the wrongs that were done to the indigenous peoples of this land. Today, U.S. American Indian and Alaska natives and Hawaiian natives are speaking with a new and more unified voice, causing both the government and the American people to reexamine the actions of the past and to assume responsibility for the conditions of the present.

A clear appeal is being made for a fresh and reliable expression of justice.

The call is being made for a new recognition of the unique rights that were guaranteed in perpetuity of U.S. American Indians by the treaties and legal agreements that were solemnly signed by official representatives of the United States government. A plea is being raised regarding the disruption of Alaska and Hawaiian natives who were not granted the legal agreements protecting their culture and land base.

The time has come for the American people to be delivered from beliefs that gave support to the false promises and faulty policies that prevailed in the relations of the United States government with the United States of America's native peoples. These beliefs asserted that:

1. white Europeans who came to this continent were ordained by God to possess its land and utilize its resources;

2. natives were not good stewards of the environment, permitting nature to lie in waste as they roamed from place to place, living off the land;

3. the growing white population tamed nature and subdued the natives and thus gave truth to the assumption that the white race is superior;

4. the forceful displacement of the natives was a necessary and justifiable step in the development of a free land and a new country; and

5. the white explorers and pioneers brought civilization to the natives and generously bestowed upon them a higher and better way of life.

Rarely are these beliefs now so blatantly set forth, yet they are subtly assumed and furnish the continuing foundation upon which unjust and injurious policies of the government are based.

These beliefs, in former times, permitted the government, on the one hand, to seize lands, uproot families, break up tribal communities, and undermine the authority of traditional chiefs. On the other hand, the beliefs enabled the government to readily make and easily break treaties, give military protection to those who encroached on native lands, distribute as "free" land millions of acres of native holdings that the government designated as being "surplus", and systematically slay those natives who resisted such policies and practices.

In our own time, these beliefs have encouraged the government to:

1. generally assume the incompetence of natives in the management and investment of their own resources;

2. give highly favorable leasing arrangements to white mining companies, grain farmers, and cattle ranchers for the use of native lands held in trust by the federal government or historically used as supportive land base;

3. use job training and other government programs to encourage the relocation of natives from reservations or native territories to urban areas;

4. utilize government funds in projects that are divisive to the tribal or native membership and through procedures that co-opt native leadership;

5. extend the control of state government over native nations that are guaranteed federal protection;

6. terminate federal services and protection to selected native nations and further deny federal recognition to others;

7. engage in extensive and expensive litigation as a means of delaying and thus nullifying treaty rights and aboriginal land claims;

8. pay minimal monetary claims for past illegal confiscation of land and other native resources;

9. lump together United States natives with other racial minorities as a tactic for minimizing the unique rights of native peoples; and

10. punitively prosecute the native leaders who vigorously challenge the policies of the federal government.

The church is called to repentance, for it bears a heavy responsibility for spreading false beliefs and for unjust governmental policies and practices. The preaching of the gospel to America's native people was often a preparation for assimilation into white culture. The evangelizing of the native nations often affected the policies of the government.

The church has frequently benefited from the distribution of native lands and other resources. The church often saw the injustices inflicted upon native peoples but gave assent or remained silent, believing that its task was to "convert" the heathen.

The church is called through the mercy of almighty God to become a channel of the reconciling Spirit of Jesus Christ and an instrument of love and justice in the development of new relations between native nations, other minorities, and whites, in pursuit of the protection of their rights.

The United Methodist Church recognizes that a new national commitment is needed to respect and effect the rights of American Indians and Alaska and Hawaiian natives to claim their own identities, maintain their cultures, live their lives, and use their resources.

The United Methodist Church expresses its desire and declares its intention to participate in the renewal of the national responsibility to the United States of America's native people.

The United Methodist Church calls its congregations to study the issues concerning American Indian and Alaska and Hawaiian native relations with the government of the United States; to develop an understanding of the distinctive cultures and the unique rights of the native people of the United States; to establish close contacts wherever possible with native persons, tribes, and nations, and to furnish support for:

1. the right of native people to live as native people in this country;

2. the right of native people to be self-determining and to make their own decisions related to the use of their lands and the natural resources found on and under them;

3. the right of native people to plan for a future in this nation and to expect a fulfillment of the commitments that have been made previously by the government, as well as equitable treatment of those who were not afforded legal protection for their culture and lands;

4. the right of American Indian nations to exercise the sovereignty of nationhood, consistent with treaty provisions;

5. the right of Alaskan natives to maintain a subsistence land base and aboriginal rights to its natural resources; and

6. the right of native Hawaiians to a just and amicable settlement with the United States through federal legislation related to aboriginal title to Hawaiian lands and their natural resources.

The United Methodist Church especially calls its congregations to support the needs and aspirations of America's native peoples as they struggle for their survival and the maintenance of the integrity of their culture in a world intent upon their assimilation, Westernization, and absorption of their lands and the termination of their traditional ways of life.

Moreover, we call upon our nation, in recognition of the significant and cultural attainments of the native peoples in ecology, conversation, human relations, and other areas of human endeavor, to receive their cultural gifts as part of the emerging new life and culture of our nation.

ADOPTED 1980
REVISED AND ADOPTED 2000

See Social Principles, ¶ 162A.

147. Regarding Native American Culture and Traditions as Sacred

For hundreds of years Native Americans, Native Alaskans, and Native Hawaiians, compelled by the gospel have chosen to become disciples of Jesus Christ. In doing so, we have affirmed with the voices of the saints that all that is necessary for salvation, relationship with God and our brothers and sisters, is contained in the gospel of Jesus Christ. We bear witness to the mercy of God through our faith, continuing in discipleship and ministry.

Government and religious institutions intentionally destroyed many of our traditional cultures and belief systems. To assimilate our peoples into mainstream cultures, as children many of our ancestors were forcibly removed to boarding schools, often operated by religious institutions, including historical Methodism. Historically, Native peoples have been targets by those seeking land and other natural resources. Genocide became a tool of greed and a response to fear. While attempting to erase Native people from existence, traditional cultures also fell victim to acts of genocide.

As Native Christians, we affirm for the church and ourselves that many elements of our traditions and cultures are consistent with the gospel of Jesus Christ, and the teachings of the church. We affirm that the Holy Spirit is faithful in guiding us in holy living within our cultures and the broader culture. We recognize that just as in the broader culture, not all expressions of traditional cultures are appropriate for all believers; God is faithful in leading us to acceptable worship and continued growth in grace, as tribal people. We further affirm that our identity as Native, or tribal persons is pleasing to our Creator, and vital to the body of Christ. We affirm for each other that our languages, cultures, identities, and many traditions are pleasing to God and have the potential to refresh the church and offer hope to the world. To be less is to be other than what God is asking us to be in our time.

We further believe that many of our Native traditions affirm the presence of God, our need for right relationship with our Creator and the world around us, and a call for holy living. Both through corporate and personal conviction our people individually and tribally are led by the Spirit of God to a greater awareness of God. Traditional beliefs, consistent with the gospel and the historic witness of the church should not be understood as contrary to our beliefs as Native Christians. Furthermore, the testimony of historic and contemporary Native Christians should be counted in the historic witness of the church.

WHEREAS, we believe that God's creating presence speaks to us through our languages and cultures and that such testimony is vital to the ongoing work of the church among our people and;

WHEREAS, many Native traditions were erroneously feared, rather than understood as vehicles for the grace of God, and;

WHEREAS, such fears have resulted in persecution of traditional Native peoples and Native Christians, and;

WHEREAS, many traditions have been misinterpreted as sin, rather than varying cultural expressions leading to a deeper understanding of our creator;

Therefore, be it resolved, that the General Conference of The United Methodist Church affirms the sacredness of Native people, their languages, their cultures, and their gifts to the church and the world.

Be it further resolved, that we believe in the faithful leadership of the Holy Spirit in assisting us as individuals and communities in the preservation of those cultures and the continuation of their faith; that just as there are many parts of the body of Christ, there are many Native traditions, languages, customs, and expressions of faith; that in the best of Native traditions, the church, and the spirit of ecumenism, we allow for the work of the Spirit of God among our communities and tribes without prejudice.

Therefore, be it further resolved, that being justified by faith, we will honor as sacred those practices that: call us back to the sacredness of

Native people; affirm as beautiful their identity among the world's peoples; lead us into right relationship with our Creator, creation, and those around us; and call us into holy living. We call upon the world, the church, The United Methodist Church, and the people of The United Methodist Church to receive the gifts of Native people as people of God.

ADOPTED 2004

See Social Principles, ¶ 162A.

148. The Protection of Native American Sacred Sites

WHEREAS, in 1978, in an effort to clarify the status of traditional Native American religious practices and practitioners, Congress passed a Joint Resolution entitled "The American Indian Religious Freedom Act," which declared that it was the policy of Congress to protect and preserve the inherent right of American Indians to believe, express, and practice their traditional religions; and

WHEREAS, today a major crisis exists in that there is no real protection for the practice of traditional Indian religions within the framework of American constitutional or statutory law, and courts usually automatically dismiss Indian petitions without evidentiary hearings; and

WHEREAS, while Congress has passed many laws that are designed to protect certain kinds of lands and resources for environmental and historic preservation, none of these laws are designed to protect the traditional sacred sites of Native American tribes for the purpose of Native American traditional religious practice; and

WHEREAS, the only existing law directly addressing this issue, the American Indian Religious Freedom Act, is simply a policy that provides limited legal relief to aggrieved American Indian religious practitioners; and

WHEREAS, the 1992 General Conference of The United Methodist Church went on record as supporting the rights of all Native Americans, Christian and traditional alike,

Therefore, be it resolved, that the General Board of Church and Society continue to support legislation that will provide for a legal cause of action when sacred sites may be affected by governmental action; proposed legislation should also provide for more extensive notice to and consultation with tribes and affected parties; and

Be it further resolved, that, on behalf of the whole United Methodist Church, the General Board of Church and Society may enter and support court cases relating to the American Indian Religious Freedom Act; and

Be it further resolved, that the General Board of Church and Society communicate with the Senate Select Committee on Indian Affairs, declaring that the position of The United Methodist Church, expressed through the 2000 General Conference, is to strengthen the American Indian Religious Freedom Act of 1978 and preserve the God-given and constitutional rights of religious freedom for American Indians, including the preserving of traditional Native American sacred sites of worship.

ADOPTED 2000

See Social Principles, ¶ 164A.

149. Native American Tribal Sovereignty Protection Initiative

WHEREAS, prior to European contact the indigenous nations of this continent were sovereign, autonomous and self-regulating; and

WHEREAS, prior to the American Revolution, the sovereign status of indigenous nations was recognized through nation-to-nation relationships with the major European powers. These relationships were maintained with the newly formed American government, who formulated 371 treaties with Indian nations between 1778-1871; and

WHEREAS, these treaties were and are regarded as sacred and enduring texts by American Indians and Alaska Natives, as sacred and enduring as the U. S. Constitution and Bill of Rights are to all American citizens. Therefore, it was disturbing that the U.S government could ignore their trust responsibilities through the violation of treaties and other promises; and

WHEREAS, indigenous persons were once sole occupants of this continent and estimated to number 10 million or more north of Mexico, their land base has been decimated to 2.3 percent of the U.S., and, according to the 2000 census, their population to 2.4 million. This decimation was rationalized according to (a) the European belief in their "discovery" of the new world, (b) the arrogance of manifest destiny and (c) the egregious destruction of the Native concept of tribal communal land; and

WHEREAS, tribal sovereignty is understood as an inherent international right of Native nations, and it encompasses various matters, such as jurisdiction over Indians *and* non-Indians on tribal lands, education and language, child welfare and religious freedom. Land is both the physical and spiritual foundation of tribal identity, as stated by Kidwell, Noley and Tinker (2001) in *A Native American Theology:* "Land is today the basis upon which tribal sovereignty rests, the rights of Indian people to live upon, use and to govern in a political sense the members of the tribe who live on the land and those whose tribal membership gives them an association with it" (p. 15); and

WHEREAS, early U.S. Supreme Court decisions support and affirm tribal sovereignty, most notably the Marshall trilogy of cases in the 19th century, and Winter v. S. (1908). Most recent Court decisions have contradicted earlier rulings and undermine tribal sovereignty; and

WHEREAS, a recently conducted survey by an independent research firm demonstrates that 75 percent of the American public supports tribal government over Native lands, and 74 percent believe that federal and state officials should make tribal self-government a priority; and

WHEREAS, in *The Book of Resolutions*, Resolution 144 calls that support be furnished for the rights of Native people according to the following points (relative to self-determination and sovereignty):

- The right of Native people to be self-determining, and make their own decisions;
- The right of Native people to plan for a future in this nation, and to expect a fulfillment of commitments that have been made previously by the government, as well as equitable treatment of those who were not afforded legal protection for their culture and lands;
- The right of Native nations to exercise their sovereignty consistent with treaty provisions; and

WHEREAS, the National Congress of American Indians (NCAI) has appealed to religious institutions and their congregations to urge the moral responsibility of the U.S. government in upholding treaty obligations and trust responsibilities to Native peoples. NCAI has promulgated the Tribal Sovereignty Protection Initiative as a proactive effort in light of recent threats to tribal sovereignty from the federal government, including a conservative Supreme Court;

Therefore, be it resolved, that The United Methodist Church affirms all aspects of Resolution 144; and

Be it further resolved, that, in response to the NCAI appeal and the Tribal Sovereignty Protection Initiative, The United Methodist Church hereby urges the moral responsibility of the United States government and calls upon governmental agencies and entities within the United States to uphold and honor all treaty obligations and trust responsibilities to Native peoples; and

Be it further resolved, that the Council of Bishops and the General Board of Church and Society, in consultation with the United Methodist Native American International Caucus (NAIC) and the National United Methodist Native American Center (NUMNAC), present this resolution to the NCAI Executive Director, the NCAI President, the Senators and Representatives of the United States Congress, the President of the United States, the U.S. Secretary of the Interior, the U.S. Assistant Secretary of Indian Affairs, and the United Methodist Jurisdictional Task Forces on Native American Ministries; and

Be it further resolved, that The United Methodist Church hereby urges all clergy and laity to educate themselves and their congregations about historical and contemporary aspects of tribal sovereignty, including action steps that concerned individuals and congregations can take to support American Indians and Alaska and Hawaiian Natives. (For resources, contact the United Methodist Native American International Caucus.)

ADOPTED 2004

See Social Principles, ¶162A.

ORGAN AND TISSUE DONATION

150. National Donor Sabbath

In the interest of urging members and others to consider becoming future organ and tissue donors, The United Methodist Church encourages its congregations to join in the yearly ecumenical and interfaith celebration of National Donor Sabbath. Usually held two weekends before Thanksgiving, this national event is an expression of our Christian gratitude for the gift of life.

Congregations may choose a variety of ways to educate persons about organ and tissue donation. Examples of ways churches currently participate include developing special liturgies, bulletin inserts, sermons on the subject and church school discussions.

Waiting lists for organ and tissue transplants are long and the need is great. National Donor Sabbath provides yet another way United Methodists can help save lives.

ADOPTED 2000

See Social Principles, ¶ 162U.

151. Organ and Tissue Donation

WHEREAS, selfless consideration for the health and welfare of all persons is at the heart of the Christian ethic; and

WHEREAS, organ and tissue donation is a life-giving act, since transplantation of organs and tissues is scientifically proven to save the lives of persons with terminal diseases and improve the quality of life for the blind, the deaf, and persons with life-threatening illnesses; and

WHEREAS, organ donation may be perceived as a positive outcome of a seemingly senseless death and is thereby comforting to the family of the deceased and is conducted with respect, and with the highest consideration for maintaining the dignity of the deceased and his or her family; and

WHEREAS, moral leaders the world over recognize organ and tissue donation as an expression of humanitarian ideals in giving life to another; and

WHEREAS, thousands of persons who could benefit from organ and tissue donation continue to suffer and die due to lack of consent for donation, due primarily to poor awareness and lack of an official direction from the church,

Therefore, be it resolved, that The United Methodist Church recognizes the life-giving benefits of organ and tissue donation and thereby encourages all Christians to become organ and tissue donors by signing and carrying cards or driver's licenses, attesting to their commitment of such organs upon their death to those in need, as a part of their ministry to others in the name of Christ, who gave his life that we might have life in its fullness.

ADOPTED 1984
AMENDED AND READOPTED 2000

See Social Principles, ¶ 162U

PESONS LIVING WITH HIV AND AIDS

152. A Covenant to Care: Recognizing and Responding to the Many Faces of AIDS IN THE U.S.A.

United Methodists have been in ministry since the beginning of the of the HIV/AIDS pandemic. They have followed the way of healing, ministry, hospitality, and service shown by Jesus Christ. According to the Gospel of Luke (4:16-21), Jesus identified himself and his task with that of the servant Lord, the one who was sent to bring good tidings to the afflicted, hope to the brokenhearted, liberty to the captives, and comfort to all who mourn, giving them the oil of gladness and the mantle of praise instead of a faint spirit (Isaiah 61:1-3). God's Word calls us to a ministry of healing, a ministry that understands healing not only in physiological terms but also as wholeness of spiritual, mental, physical, and social being.

The Context of Caring Ministry in the United States

In recent years, AIDS in the United States has received less media attention, but that does not mean the disease has gone away. Though medical drugs can prolong the life of people who have been infected, there is no cure for AIDS. Not only must our commitment to ministry continue, but it must also expand, particularly in the area of prevention education.

HIV/AIDS affects and infects a broad cross-section of people in the United States and Puerto Rico: all ages, all races, both sexes, all sexual orientations. The cumulative number of AIDS cases reported to Centers for Disease Control (CDC) through December 2001 is 816,149. Adult and adolescent AIDS cases total 807,074 with 666,026 males and 141,048 females.[1]

1. Centers for Disease Control and Prevention (CDC). *HIV/Aids Surveillance Report 2001*, 13, no. 2:1-44. http://www.cdc.gov/hiv/stats/hasr1302.htm (31 January 2003).

In the early 1980s, most people with AIDS were gay white men. Overall incidences of new cases of AIDS increased rapidly through the 1980s, peaked in the early 1990s, and then declined. However, new cases of AIDS among African Americans increased. By 1996, more cases of AIDS were reported among African Americans than any other racial/ethnic population. The number of people diagnosed with AIDS has also increased among Hispanics, Asians/Pacific Islanders, and Native Americans/Alaska Natives.[2] In 2001, the rate of adult/adolescent AIDS cases per 100,000 population was 76.3 among African Americans, 28.0 among Hispanics, 11.7 among Native Americans/Alaska Natives, 7.9 among whites, and 4.8 among Asians/Pacific Islanders.[3] Though national surveillance data does not record the hearing status of people with HIV/AIDS, the Department of Health and Human Services believes that deaf and hard of hearing people have been disproportionately infected with HIV.[4]

As of December 2001, according to CDC estimates, 850,000 to 950,000 people in the United States were infected with HIV. One-quarter of these were unaware of their status! Approximately 40,000 new HIV infections occur each year: about 70 percent men and 30 percent women. Of these newly infected people, half are younger than 25. Almost half of the men are African American, 30 percent are white, 20 percent are Hispanic. Among newly infected women, approximately 64 percent are African American, 18 percent are white, and 18 percent are Hispanic. A small percentage of men and women are part of other racial/ethnic groups.[5] No longer is HIV a disease of white gay men or of the east and west coast; it has not been for more than a decade. In 2001, 39 percent of persons with AIDS were living in the South, 29 percent in the Northeast, 19 percent in the West, 10 percent in the Midwest, and 3 percent in the U.S. territories.[6]

2. A HIV and Aids—United States, 1981-2000," Morbity and Mortality Weekly Report, 50, no. 21 (June 01, 2001): 430-4. http://www.cdc.gov/mmwr/preview/mmwrhtml/mm5021a2.htm (31 January 2003).

3. National Institute of Allergy and Infectious Diseases (NIAID), Fact Sheet: HIV Statistics (December 2002). http://www.niaid.nih.gov/factsheets/aidsstat.htm (31 January 2003).

4. Department of Health and Human Services (HRSA) APrograms: Deaf and Hard of Hearing and IV/AIDS,@ http://hab.hrsa.gov/programs/factsheets/deaffact.htm (4 March 2003).

5. National Institute of Allergy and Infectious Diseases (NIAID), Fact Sheet: HIV Statistics (December 2002). http://www.niaid.nih.gov/factsheets/aidsstat.htm (31 January 2003).

6. Centers for Disease Control and Prevention, AU.S. HIV and AIDS Cases Reported Through December 2001 Year-End Report,@ Surveillance Report, 13, No. 2 http://www.cdc.gov/hiv/stats/hasr1302/commentary.htm (31 January 2003).

United Methodist churches, districts, and conferences can help to stop the spread of HIV/AIDS by providing sound, comprehensive, age-appropriate preventive education, including information that abstinence from sex and injection drug use is the safest way to prevent HIV/AIDS. In addition, the church can provide grounding in Christian values, something that cannot be done in public schools or in governmental publications on HIV/AIDS.

Youth and Young Adults: AIDS is increasingly affecting and infecting our next generation of leaders, particularly among racial and ethnic minorities. In the United States, HIV is the fifth leading cause of death for people between the ages of 25 and 44. Among African American men in this age group, HIV has been the leading cause of death since 1991. In 1999, among African American women, 25 to 44 years old, HIV was the third leading cause of death. Many of these young adults were infected in their teens and early twenties. At least half of all new HIV infections are estimated to be among people under 25 with the majority of infections occurring through sexual contact.[7]

Racial and Ethnic Minorities: African Americans, Hispanics and Native Americans have been disproportionately infected with HIV/AIDS. Representing only an estimated 12 percent of the total US population, African Americans make up almost 38 percent of all AIDS cases reported in the country. Almost 63 percent of all women reported with AIDS were African American.[8]

It is critical to prevent patterns of risky behaviors that may lead to HIV infection before they start. Clear communications between parents and their children about sex, drugs, and AIDS is an important step. Church, school, and community-based prevention education is another step. Youth and young adults must be actively involved in this process, including peer education.

The large and growing Hispanic population in the United States is also heavily affected by HIV/AIDS. In 2000, Hispanics represented 13 percent of the US population (including residents of Puerto Rico) but accounted for 19 percent of the total number of new cases of AIDS reported that year.[9]

7. Centers for Disease Control and Prevention, "Young People at Risk: HIV/AIDS Among America's Youth" http://www.cdc.gov/hiv/pubs/facts/youth.htm (31 January 2003).

8. Centers for Disease Control and Prevention, AHIV/AIDS among African Americans@ http://www.cdc.gov/hiv/pubs/facts/afam.htm (31 January 2003)

9. Centers for Disease Control and Prevention, AHIV/AIDS among Hispanics in the United States@ http://www.cdc.gov/hiv/pubs/facts/hispanics.htm (31 January 2003).

Women: AIDS among women has been mostly "an invisible epidemic" even though women have been affected and infected since the beginning. AIDS has increased most dramatically among women of color. African American and Hispanic women together represent less than 25 percent of all women in the United States, yet account for more than 75 percent of reported cases of AIDS. In 2000, African American and Hispanic women represented an even greater proportion (80 percent) of cases of AIDS reported in women.[10] Of newly infected women in 2001, approximately 64 percent were African American and 18 percent were Hispanic.[11] In 2000, 38 percent of women reported with AIDS were infected through sexual contact with HIV-positive men while injection drug use accounted for 25 percent of cases. In addition to the direct risks associated with drug injections (sharing needles), drug use is also fueling the heterosexual spread of the epidemic. A significant proportion of women infected sexually were infected by injection drug-using men. Reducing the toll of the epidemic among women will require efforts to combat substance abuse and reduce HIV risk behaviors. [12]

People who are Deaf, Late-Deafened, and Hard of Hearing: In the United States, as many as 40,000 deaf and hard-of-hearing individuals are believed to be living with HIV disease.[13] Health experts suspect that HIV prevalence in the deaf community may be higher than in the hearing community, but comprehensive data is lacking. An indicator is that one in seven deaf people has a history of substance abuse, compared with one in ten hearing people.[14] Research has also shown that deaf high school students have much less knowledge about HIV transmission than their hearing counterparts. Because 75 percent of the culturally deaf community uses American Sign Language (ASL) as their primary means of communication, ASL is the

10. Centers for Disease Control and Prevention, AHIV/AIDS among US Women,@ 2002 www.cdc.gov/hiv/pubs/facts/women.httm) (31 January 2003).

11. Centers for Disease Control and Prevention, HIV Prevention Strategic Plan Through 2005. January 2001. http://www.cdc.gov/nchstp/od/hiv_plan/default.htm (31 January 2003).

12. Centers for Disease Control and Prevention, AHIV/AIDS among Hispanics in the United States,@ 2002 http://www.cdc.gov/hiv/pubs/facts/hispanics.htm (31 January 2003).

13. Office of HIV/AIDS Policy. Conference proceedings: National Meeting on the Deaf and Hard of Hearing. Washington, DC: U.S. Department of Health and Human Services; 2000.

14. Peinkoffer JR. HIV education for the deaf, a vulnerable minority. Public Health Rep. 1994;109:390-6.

most effective means of communication of HIV/AIDS information for this group; but the message must be clear. At a United Methodist HIV/AIDS event in 2002, a speaker noted that deaf people have died and others have delayed medical treatment because they believed themselves healthy when they saw the sign for "HIV" and "positive" conveyed to them in ASL. They thought HIV positive meant "good result" and did not realize that they were being told they were infected.[15] It also should be noted that over 98 percent of those with hearing loss, including many elderly people, do not know sign language. In prevention education contexts, assistive listening systems and devices, such as "pocket talkers," should be used to aid those who are hard of hearing.

Older Adults: The number of those 50 and older infected with HIV is increasing at twice the rate of those under 50, according to experts on aging at Baylor College of Medicine in Houston who are targeting older Americans for safer sex education.[16] The myth that older people are sexually inactive has produced dreaded consequences. The most prevalent behavior risks for older adults are multiple sexual partners and having a partner with risk behavior. Since they are not worried about pregnancy, older couples are less likely to use condoms and, therefore, increase their risk of infection. Most older people mistakenly believe that if they are heterosexual and don't inject drugs, they cannot get AIDS. Reaching this group of people with HIV prevention messages means exploring avenues such as church, widows' support groups at senior centers, and Golden Age Clubs at community centers and churches.

Drug-Associated HIV Transmission: Since the epidemic began, injection drug use (IDU) has accounted for more than one-third (36 percent) of AIDS cases in the U.S. Racial and ethnic minorities in the U.S. are most heavily affected by IDU-associated AIDS. In 2000, IDU-associated AIDS accounted for 26 percent of all cases among African Americans and 31 percent among Hispanic adults and adolescents, compared with 19 percent of all cases among white adults/adolescents. Non-injection drugs such as cocaine also contribute to the spread of the epidemic when users trade sex for drugs or money, or

15. Melissa Lauber, ASilence on HIV/AIDS Spells Death, Church Leaders Warn,@ December 10, 2002 http://gbgm-umc.org/health/aids/dcconference.cfm (5 March 2003).

16. Centers for Disease Control and Prevention, *CDC HIV/STD/TB Prevention News Update* (November 11, 2002) citing Carolyn Poirot , "Risk of AIDS Rising for Older Adults" *Star-Telegram* (November 6, 2002) http://lists.cdcnpin.org/pipermail/prevention-news/2002-November/000353.html (31 January 2003).

when they engage in risky sexual behavior that they might not engage in when sober.

HIV prevention and treatment, substance abuse prevention, and sexually transmitted disease treatment and prevention services must be better integrated to take advantage of the multiple opportunities for intervention—first, to help uninfected people stay that way; second, to help infected people stay healthy; and third, to help infected individuals initiate and sustain behaviors that will keep themselves safe and prevent transmission to others.[17]

The Challenge for Ministry

Across the United States, in churches large and small, pastors and laity have asked, "What can my church do?" Churches can build on areas which are already doing well; they can covenant to care. Churches and other United Methodist organizations need to continue or begin compassionate ministry with persons living with HIV/AIDS and their loved ones. In terms of prevention education, United Methodists have an opportunity to teach not only the facts about HIV transmission and how to prevent infection but to relate these facts to Christian values. Congregations can do HIV/AIDS prevention education in broader contexts, such as human sexuality and holistic health, as well as addressing societal problems, such as racism, sexism, addiction, and poverty. We call on United Methodists to respond:

1. Churches should be places of openness and caring for persons with AIDS and their loved ones. We ask congregations to work to overcome attitudinal and behavioral barriers in church and community that create stigma and discrimination of persons with AIDS and their loved ones. Congregations can offer Christian hospitality and become arks of refuge to all. We must remember that:

- the face that AIDS wears is always the face of a person created and loved by God;
- the face that AIDS wears is always the face of a person who is someone's mother or father, husband or wife, son or daughter, brother or sister, loved one or best friend;
- the face that AIDS wears is always the face of a person who is the most important person in someone else's life.

17. Centers for Disease Control and Prevention, ADrug-Associated HIV Transmission Continues in the United States,@ 2002 http://www.cdc.gov/hiv/pubs/facts/idu.htm (31 January 2003).

2. Each congregation and annual conference, through their Church and Society committees, should mobilize persons for legislative advocacy at the local, state and national levels to support for HIV/AIDS initiatives in the United States. These advocacy efforts will be strengthened through partnerships with organizations/coalitions who are currently involved in this issue.

3. Educational efforts about AIDS should use reliable medical and scientific information about the disease, transmission, and prevention. Spiritual resources must also be included to enable people to address issues related to discipleship, ministry, human sexuality, heath and wholeness, and death and dying. Education helps to prepare congregations to respond appropriately when they learn that a member has been infected by the HIV virus or diagnosed with AIDS. It can lead to the development of sound policies, educational materials and procedures related to the church school, nurseries, and other issues of institutional participation. Prevention education can save lives.

4. Each congregation should discern the appropriate response for its context. Ministries should be developed, whenever possible, in consultation and collaboration with local departments of public health and with other United Methodist, ecumenical, interfaith, and community-based groups concerned about the HIV/AIDS pandemic. Congregations can organize to provide spiritual, emotional, physical and/or financial support to those in their community who are caring at home or elsewhere for a person who has AIDS. Projects might include observing events such as World AIDS Day (December 1) and the Black Church Week of Prayer for the Healing of AIDS (first week in March), sponsoring support groups for people with AIDS and their loved ones, developing strong general church programs for children and youth that also include AIDS education, pastoral counseling, recruiting volunteers, and offering meeting space for community-based organizations, including groups trying to overcome substance abuse and sexual addiction.

5. The United Methodist Church has a congregational HIV/AIDS ministry called the Covenant to Care Program, whose basic principle is "If you have HIV/AIDS or are the loved one of a person who has HIV/AIDS, you are welcome here." We commend those who have been in ministry through this program and recommend "Covenant to Care" to all United Methodist organizations. More information

is available on the General Board of Global Ministries' Web site at http://gbgm-umc.org/health/aids/.[18]

ADOPTED 2004

See Social Principles, ¶ 162S.

153. World AIDS Day Observance

Each year, World AIDS Day is observed on December 1. It is a time for special programs on HIV/AIDS education and religious worship services that focus on intercessory and healing prayer, hope in God, and love and compassion in the midst of the HIV/AIDS pandemic.

We recommend that United Methodists be encouraged to observe World AIDS Day on or around December 1. We further recommend that voluntary offerings be given to "Global HIV/AIDS Program Development" (UMCOR Advance #982345-7).

Materials for World AIDS Day are available each year from UNAIDS (*http://www.unaids.org*), the General Board of Church and Society(*http://www.umc-gbcs.org*), and the General Board of Global Ministries (*http://gbgm-umc.org/health/*) of The United Methodist Church.

ADOPTED 1996, AMENDED AND READOPTED 2004

See Social Principles, ¶ 162S.

154. United Methodist Global AIDS Fund Distribution

WHEREAS, for twenty years the General Conference of The United Methodist Church has spoken with prophetic compassion to the global issue of HIV/AIDS. Our resolutions, however, have not been matched by a resolve to commit significant financial and denominational resources in the struggle for education, prevention, treatment and care in the worldwide struggle against HIV/AIDS; and

18. For more information about the Covenant to Care program or the church and HIV/AIDS Ministries, contact: Health and Welfare Ministries, General Board of Global Ministries, Room 330, 475 Riverside Drive, New York, NY 10115; Voice Phone: 212-870-3871; FAX: 212-870-3624; TDD: 212-870-3709; E-Mail: aidsmin@gbgm-umc.org.

WHEREAS, the United Nations has now declared the pandemic a "global emergency," saying human life is threatened everywhere and world security is at risk as the planet faces the worst health crisis in 700 years; and

WHEREAS, with 42 million people infected, more than 20 million already deceased, and 16,000 new infections daily, the leaders of all the nations in the world unanimously asked faith-based organizations to join them in the battle to save human life; and

WHEREAS, to date the response of Christians, including United Methodists, has been minimal, particularly in comparison to our resources and other commitments;

Therefore, be it resolved, that the 2004 General Conference commits itself to establishing the United Methodist Global AIDS Fund (UMGAF). During the 2005-2008 quadrennium, United Methodists will raise $3 million through apportionments and match this with an additional $5 million through Advance gifts;

Be it further resolved, that of the total money raised in each annual conference for UMGAF, 25 percent shall be retained by the annual conference that raised it, to be used in programs combating HIV/AIDS in their region and in other global connectional projects. Each annual conference shall designate an appropriate agency for the promotion and distribution of these funds.

Be it further resolved, that of the total money raised in each annual conference for the United Methodist Global AIDS Fund, 75 percent shall be remitted by the conference treasurer to the treasurer of the General Council on Finance and Administration for distribution to a new Global AIDS Initiatives Committee (with no more than ten total representatives from the General Board of Global Ministries, Council of Bishops, General Board of Church and Society, Youth and Young Adults Ministries, and three persons not serving with any of these agencies).

Be it further resolved, that this Global AIDS Initiatives Committee will be responsible for the promotion, use, supervision and distribution of these funds. The United Methodist Global AIDS Fund will:

1. assist local congregations and conferences in identifying and creating global partnerships for mutual HIV/AIDS ministry;

2. provide support for projects sponsored by local congregations or organizations related to The United Methodist Church, partner autonomous Methodist churches and the ecumenical church;

3. encourage partnerships between congregations and conferences in the United States and Methodist congregations and ecumenical

organizations globally that are engaged in the struggle against HIV/AIDS;

4. advocate for social justice, particularly related to increasing governmental and non-governmental funding and issues regarding the role of pharmaceutical companies;

5. develop appropriate promotional materials and funding guidelines; and

6. Engage the leadership of a person with appropriate skills for a special global AIDS assignment (#4091c).

ADOPTED 2004

See Social Principles, ¶ 162S.

RIGHTS OF THE AGING

155. Abuse of Older Adults

WHEREAS, 1.5 to 2 million older adults are maltreated annually in the U.S.; and

WHEREAS, only one in every eight of these cases is reported; and

WHEREAS, the older adult population will double by the year 2030; and

WHEREAS, elder abuse and neglect take many forms, such as beatings, sexual abuse, improper use of restraints, improper use of medications, verbal abuse, isolation abuse, stealing possessions, misuse or waste of assets, and a failure to provide food/fluids, medication, medical care, shelter and clothing.

Therefore, be it resolved, that we call on The United Methodist Church to break the silence and to address this social ill through education and awareness, information, counseling and referral services, support systems, and reports to the proper authorities when abuse is suspected.

Therefore, be it further resolved, that the Older Adult Committee and the appropriate general agencies provide resources and materials to address the issue.

ADOPTED 2000

See Social Principles, ¶ 162E.

156. Aging in the United States—The Church's Response

I. The Situation

Older adult membership in The United Methodist Church is growing rapidly. In the past, the role of older people in congregations was limited, either by choice or circumstance. Congregations often viewed older adults as a liability rather than emphasizing the potential for a renewed or visionary ministry. Many of the myths and stereotypes of aging and older persons are changing.

During the past 100 years, life expectancy in the United States has increased by almost 28 years. The number of persons 65 years of age and older has grown from 3.1 million in 1900 (4.1 percent of the total population) to 33.5 million in 1995 (12.8 percent of the total population). This number is expected to increase from 34.7 million in the year 2000 (13 percent) to 70 million in the year 2030 (20.0 percent). In 1995, persons reaching age 65 had an average life expectancy of an additional 17.4 years (18.9 years for females and 15.6 years for males). By 2030, minority populations will represent 25 percent of the elderly population, up from 13 percent in 1990. The older population includes a disproportionate number of women (145 women to 100 men) and persons with a wide range of capacities, from active, healthy, and employed to fragile, frail, and chronically disabled.

As a result of better health care, nutrition, and job safety, many more Americans are living into older adulthood. By the year 2030, there will be proportionately more older adults than young people in the population. Every day in the United States 5,600 people celebrate their sixty-fifth birthday, and 4,550 persons, 65 years or older, die. The result is an increase of 1,050 older adults per day.

Most older persons have at least one chronic condition and many have more. Hospital expenses accounted for the largest share of health expenditures for older persons. Benefits from government programs, including Medicare, Medicaid, and others, covered about two-thirds of the health expenditures for older persons.

Lack of adequate health insurance is the most pressing health issue faced by older adults today. Private health insurance is so expensive that it is affordable or impossible to buy because of the exclusions for "existing conditions." This problem is made worse because persons that were not employed outside the home often have no claim on employer-based group policies in which the employed spouse participated if divorce or death occurs, and they have fewer job options with good insurance plans if they choose to work outside the home.

Medicare is a health insurance program primarily for persons over the age of 65. Medicaid provides a supplement to Medicare primarily for low-income persons. Medicare only covers about 40 percent of most older adults' individual medical expenses. Older adults who have need for specialized residences, or their families, often have no choice but to opt for a nursing home that is covered by Medicaid. This is more costly and usually not the choice of the parties involved.

Although most older persons live in urban places, they also comprise a large proportion of rural populations where facilities and resources for them are extremely limited. Health care availability, transportation, and job opportunities are often lacking in rural areas. This condition is complicated further by a disproportionately low allocation of federal funds to meet the needs of the rural elderly.

Race and ethnicity are important determinants of the residential patterns of elderly people. While about one third of all older persons live in central cities, one half of all African Americans and Hispanics over 65 is heavily concentrated in urban areas. The popular shifts in housing patterns brought about by urban renewal and gentrification (higher-income persons buying property in formerly poor neighborhoods) and the resultant increase in homeowner taxes have a major impact on the elderly, especially minorities. Houses that have been paid for are lost because of the tax increases, or low rents rise astronomically.

We need to dispel the common misunderstanding that aging is synonymous with senility and dementia, and that older persons are unable or unmotivated to learn, grow, and achieve. Opportunities for continuing education and growth have long been unmet by a system geared to the needs of the young. Hearing and vision loss and other physical or biological changes may impede or change the way an older adult learns; however, old age can be a time of continual learning.

Like society, faith communities are "graying," but at an even faster rate. It isn't unusual to find many local churches having an older adult membership that represents over 60 percent of their total membership, with some even higher! This is due in part to younger and middle-aged adults choosing not to participate in congregations.

Some problems that beset older persons are the result of the social and physical process of aging. These include changes in work, family, and community roles; the reduction of energy; and the increase in chronic illness and impairments. These conditions can lead to increased dependence on others for life's necessities. Other problems faced by the elderly are the result of subtle and overt discrimination by social and political institutions. Being old today is not easy, in either the church or society. If the situation of older persons is to be improved, the church must act.

II. A Theological Response

Aging is a process involving the whole life span from birth to death. The response of the church begins with a theological understanding of aging concerned with the whole life process rather than with only its final stages. The meaning of life, rather than death, is the central point from which to theologize about aging. In The United Methodist Church, there are many legitimate theological understandings of the meaning of life in its progression from birth to death. The position presented here is one attempt to express this meaning.

1. All of creation is God's work (Genesis 1). Human beings are only a small part of the totality of life forms. The aging process is universal in all life forms. Birth, aging, and death are all part of divine providence and are to be regarded and taught as positive values. This does not in any way mean that such things as birth defects, disease, or deaths at an early stage in life are the will of God.

2. As Christians, the mystery of God's involvement in the person of Jesus Christ provides us with a unique source of divine help (grace) in our passage through life's successive stages. This is especially significant in the later stages, when spiritual maturation and well-being can be experienced even in times of physical decline. The power of the cross is a special revelation of how suffering can be reconciling and redemptive. Faith in the Resurrection provides us with an assurance of the abiding presence of the Risen Lord (Matthew 28:20) and the Holy Spirit (John 14:16-19; 2 Corinthians 3:17-18; Romans 8:9-11), and the permanence of our relationship with God beyond the mystery of death. In this spiritual presence we also find the source of the potential of all persons for self-transcendence. God's act in Christ was for life abundant (John 10:10) in all stages of life. Christ also gives us our traditional Wesleyan vision of the goal of ultimate perfection

(Matthew 5:48). The grace of God in Christ is therefore important throughout life, including its last stages.

3. In response to this saving grace, we believe in the inevitable need to walk in the ways of obedience that God has enabled (Ephesians 2:8-10). These ways are defined by love for God and neighbor (Mark 12:28-31; Romans 13:8-9). It is therefore the privilege of Christians to serve all persons in love, including older persons with their special needs. Furthermore, since God's grace is not conditioned by any human standards of worthiness or usefulness (2 Corinthians 5:19), all persons are valuable to God (Matthew 6:25-30). In the larger pattern of human needs and rights, those of elderly persons must be consciously and intentionally included.

4. Older persons are not simply to be served but are also to serve; they are of special importance in the total mission of the church. Since the Christian vocation has no retirement age, the special contributions of elderly persons need conscious recognition and employment. The experience of all older persons, and the wisdom of many, are special resources for the whole church.

5. The church as the body of Christ in the world today (1 Corinthians 12:27) is God's method for realizing the reconciliation accomplished by Christ (Colossians 1:16-20). As such, it intentionally sponsors institutional forms that help reconcile persons of all ages to one another and to God. This especially includes those institutions designed to meet the needs of elderly persons and to keep them fully incorporated into the body of Christ. The church also is charged with an abiding concern for justice for all. It should work tirelessly for the freedom of all persons to meet their own fullest potential and to liberate those who are captive to discrimination, neglect, exploitation, abuse, or poverty.

III. Calls to Action

A. By society at all levels

United Methodists are called to advocate for the elimination of age discrimination in personal attitudes and institutional structures. We should pursue this advocacy vigorously and in cooperation with appropriate private and public groups, including all levels of government. Our efforts should be based on the following:

1. Religious institutions make a unique and significant contribution to human life. Living involves ethical issues and value decisions. *Therefore,* a religious presence is important to the quality of total community life.

2. Governments should play a critical role in ensuring that all benefits are available to all elderly persons to improve their quality of life. Christians should support governmental policies that promote sharing with those who are less fortunate. This does not absolve either the institutional church or individual Christians from responsibility for persons in need.

3. A standard of basic survival support systems should be accepted and established in our society and made available to all persons. These systems should include: health care, transportation, housing, and income maintenance at a minimum. Christians need to identify and promote those facilities and services that ensure opportunities for prolonged well-being. These services need to be provided within the financial means of the elderly, with appropriate public subsidy when necessary. They include the following:

   a. universal comprehensive health insurance program;
   b. health-resources systems special to the needs of the elderly that are comprehensive, accessible, and feasible within available resources (these include long-term care, hospice care, home health care, and health maintenance organizations);
   c. health-education systems that emphasize proper nutrition, proper drug use, preventive health care, and immunization as well as information about the availability of health resources within the community;
   d. training for medical and social service personnel concerning the special cultural, physical, psychosocial, and spiritual aspects and needs of the elderly;
   e. adequate housing that is both affordable and secure, with protections that massive tax and rental increases will not create displacement, and transportation systems that meet the special needs of the elderly;
   f. national legislation correcting the disparity in Medicare's failure to cover either assisted living residences or dementia-specific housing, or home nursing care;
   g. a basic governmental income-maintenance system adequate to sustain an adequate standard of living affording personal dignity;

    h. basic pension systems benefit levels adequate to meet economic needs at least equal to the defined poverty level, supplementation by benefits from public funds;

    i. continuing educational and counseling opportunities for the elderly in pre-retirement planning, in work-related training, in interpersonal retirement relationships, and in personal enrichment;

    j. formal and informal community associations such as public and private centers that foster social, recreational, artistic, intellectual, and spiritual activities to help persons overcome loneliness and social isolation;

    k. continuing employment opportunities for those who desire them in flexible, appropriate work settings related to varying lifestyles; and

    l. opportunities for volunteer work and paid employment that best utilize the skills and experiences of the elderly.

4. Finally, our society is called upon to respond to a basic human right of the elderly: the right to faithful care in dying and to have personal wishes respected concerning the number and type of life-sustaining measures that should be used to prolong life. Living wills, requests that no heroic measures be used, and other such efforts to die with faithful care should be supported.

B. By the church at all levels

    1. *All levels of the church are called to:*

        a. practice non-discrimination in the church on the basis of age in hiring, deployment, and promotion of older workers, including the appointment of clergy;

        b. include ministries by, with and for older adults as an essential and intentional component of the church and its mission;

        c. promote flexible retirement and eliminate mandatory retirement based solely on age;

        d. develop theological statements on death and dying that recognize the basic human right to faithful care of the dying;

        e. address the questions raised by the declining quality of life; stimulate research to connect the improvement of the quality of life with longevity of life, raised by increased longevity;

    f. develop ethical guidelines for dealing with difficult medical decisions that involve the use of limited resources for health and life insurance;

    g. authorize appropriate research, including a demographic study of members of The United Methodist Church, to provide greatly needed information on the psycho-social and spiritual aspects of aging; and

    h. establish a properly funded pension system with an adequate minimum standard for all clergy and church-employed lay persons and their spouses, including the divorced spouse.

2. *Each local church is called to:*

    a. become aware of the needs and interests of older people in the congregation and in the community, including the places in which they reside, and to express Christian love through person-to-person understanding and caring;

    b. intentionally sponsor ministries in institutions designed to meet the needs of older adults, such as nursing homes, assisted living residences, and dementia-specific housing as well as the homes of older adults living alone, as we keep these older persons fully incorporated in the body of Christ;

    c. affirm the cultural and historical contributions and gifts of ethnic elderly persons;

    d. acknowledge that ministry by, with, and for older adults is needed in congregations of all sizes;

    e. support, equip, and train lay volunteers with a dedication for this important ministry;

    f. develop a barrier-free environment in which the elderly can function in spite of impairments;

    g. develop an intentional ministry with older adults that:

    h. ensures life maintenance for each person related to adequate food, health service, mobility, personal security, income, and other personal services;

    i. offers opportunities for life enrichment including intellectual stimulation, social involvement, spiritual cultivation, and artistic pursuits;

    j. encourages life reconstruction when necessary, including motivation and guidance in making new friends, serving new roles in the community that help people cope with loss, and providing support systems for older adults experiencing losses; and

k. affirms life transcendence, including celebration of the meaning and purpose of life through worship, Bible study, personal reflection, and small-group life;

l. recognizes that older persons represent a creative resource bank available to the church and to involve them in service to the community as persons of insight and wisdom (this could include not only ministry to one another, but also to the larger mission of the church for redemption of the world, including reaching the unchurched);

m. relates to secular retirement communities within its boundaries;

n. fosters intergenerational experiences in the congregation and community including educating all age groups about how to grow old with dignity and satisfaction;

o. ensures that the frail are not separated from the life of the congregation but retain access to the sacraments and are given assistance as needed by the caring community;

p. provides support and information for adults caring for aging parents;

q. cooperates with other churches and community agencies for more comprehensive and effective ministries with older persons;

r. accepts responsibility for an advocacy role in behalf of the elderly; and

s. develops older-adult ministries responsible to the church council. A staff position or older adult council may be needed to facilitate this ministry with older adults.

3. *Each annual conference is called to:*

a. provide leadership and support through its council on ministries or alternative structure for an intentional ministry to older persons in its local churches, with special attention to the needs of women and minorities;

b. develop a program of job counseling and retirement planning for clergy and lay employees;

c. share creative models of ministry and a data bank of resources with the local churches and other agencies;

d. define the relationship between the annual conference and United Methodist-related residential and non-residential facilities for the elderly, so that the relationships can be clearly understood and mutually supportive;

e. recruit persons for professional leadership in working with the elderly;

f. serve as both a partner and critic to local church and public programs with the elderly, promoting ecumenical linkages where possible;

g. support financially, if needed, retired clergy and lay church workers and their spouses who reside in United Methodist long-term care settings;

h. promote Golden Cross Sunday and other special offerings for ministries by, for, and with the elderly; and

i. recognize that older persons within the conference, both lay and clergy, represent a significant and experienced resource that should be utilized in both the organization and mission of the conference.

4. *General boards and agencies are called to:*

a. examine the pension policies of the general church and their impact related to the needs of those who are single (retired, divorced, or surviving dependents of pensioners);

b. create specific guidance materials for ministry by, for, and with the elderly;

c. prepare intergenerational and age-specific materials for church school and for other special studies in the local church;

d. promote advocacy in behalf of all the elderly, but especially those who do not have access to needed services because of isolation, low income, or disability (this might include advocacy for health care, income maintenance, and other social legislation);

e. assist institutions for the elderly to maintain quality care and to develop resource centers for ministry with and by the elderly;

f. create a variety of nonresidential ministries for the elderly;

g. coordinate general church training in ministry with the elderly;

h. provide for formal coordination on aging issues;

i. advocate the special concerns and needs of older women and minorities; and

j. utilize older persons as a creative resource bank in the design and implementation of these objectives.

5. *Retirement and long-term care facilities related to the church are called to:*

a. develop a covenant relationship with the church to reinforce a sense of joint mission in services with the elderly;

b. encourage the provision of charitable support and provide a channel for the assistance of the whole church; and
c. encourage both residential and nonresidential institutional settings that emphasize the spiritual, personal, physical, and social needs of the elderly.

6. *Finally, seminaries and colleges are called to:*
   a. provide seminarians with instruction on aging and experiences with older persons in the curriculum;
   b. prepare persons for careers in the field of aging;
   c. develop special professorships to teach gerontology, and to provide continuing education for those who work with the elderly;
   d. engage in basic and applied research related to aging, and communicate the findings;
   e. develop a system for sharing research results with the church; and
   f. enable the elderly to enroll in courses and degree programs and to participate generally in the life of educational institutions.

IV. Summary

Concern for older persons in the church is theologically grounded in the doctrine of Creation, in the meaning of God's work in Christ, in the response to grace that leads us into service, in the continuing value of older persons in the larger mission, and in the nature of the church as an agent of redemption and defender of justice for all.

Older adults deserve respect, dignity, and equal opportunity. The United Methodist Church is called to be an advocate for the elderly, for their sense of personal identity and dignity, for utilization of experience, wisdom, and skills, for health maintenance, adequate income, educational opportunities, and vocational and avocational experiences in cooperation with the public and private sectors of society.

The aging process is part of God's plan for life, with the good news of Christ's redemption giving hope and purpose. United Methodists are called to live this message through words and deeds in the church and in society.

ADOPTED 1988
REVISED AND ADOPTED 2000

See Social Principles, ¶ 162E.

SUICIDE

157. Suicide: A Challenge to Ministry

The apostle Paul, rooted in his experience of the resurrected Christ, affirms the power of divine love to overcome the divisive realities of human life, including suicide:

> For I am convinced that neither death, nor life, nor angels, nor rulers, nor things present, nor things to come, nor powers nor height, nor depth, nor anything else in all creation will be able to separate us from the love of God in Christ Jesus our Lord.   (Romans 8:38-39)

Paul's words are indeed sources of hope and renewal for persons who contemplate suicide, as well as for those who grieve the death of friends and family members who have committed suicide. These words affirm that in those human moments when all seems lost, all may yet be found through full faith.

A Christian perspective on suicide thus begins with an affirmation of faith: Suicide does not separate us from the love of God.

Unfortunately, the church throughout much of its history has taught just the opposite, that suicide is an unforgivable sin. As a result, Christians, acting out of a sincere concern to prevent suicide, often have contradicted Christ's call to compassion.

For example, victims have been denounced and presumed to be in hell, and families have been stigmatized with guilt and inflicted with economic and social penalties.

The purpose of this statement is to challenge and guide our caring ministries to reduce the number of suicides and to share God's grace so that the lives of those touched by suicide may be enriched, dignified and enabled for ministry to others.

Demography of Suicide

Suicide is the eleventh leading cause of death claiming 30,000 lives each year or one every 18 minutes. More than 4,000 0f those who commit suicide annually are under age 25. Because suicide occurs at all ages, it is the fifth leading cause of lost potential life, according to the U.S. Centers for Disease Control and Prevention (CDC). Furthermore, it is estimated that between 500 and 1,500 people seek care in emergency rooms each day for suicide attempts. Research indicates that in any given year 20 percent of all high school students seriously consider suicide.

Suicide rates vary by age, gender and ethnicity but affects all peoples, regardless of education or socioeconomic status. The highest rate of suicide generally occurs among white males in later life. Among some Native American and Alaskan Native groups, however, rates among youth are several times higher that the U.S. population as a whole. About 80 percent of those who commit suicide are male, but females are much more likely to attempt suicide.

"It is generally agreed that not all deaths that are reported as suicides are reported as such. Deaths may be misclassified as homicides or accidents where individuals have intended suicide by putting themselves in harm's way and lack of evidence does not allow for classifying the death as suicide. Other suicides may be misclassified as accidental or undetermined deaths in deference to community or family." (National Strategy for Suicide Prevention, 2001; p.32)

Risk and Protective Factors of Suicide

Specific groups in society appear more vulnerable to suicide than others, especially if they experience certain precipitants (events in their lives such as disease, loss of family, friends, job, severe trama, or other stress factors) and have easy access to a method for ending their lives, that is, if they are in an enabling environment. Studies show that 90% of those who die by suicide suffer from a diagnosable mental illness, substance abuse, or both. These factors—vulnerability, precipitating events, enabling environment—must be recognized and addressed if there is to be any reduction to the suicide rate.

Youth experience alienation and rejection by society, family, and the church when dealing with sexual-identity issues, including homosexuality. For many youth, the only perceived way out is suicide.

Social interconnections, social support and life skills are shown to provide protection from suicide. These methods can be learned, and youth training, such as that taught annually by the Arkansas Youth Suicide Prevention Commission, is a major force for suicide intervention and prevention.

Societal Attitudes

The prevailing attitudes of society, both secular and religious, have been to condemn the victim and ignore the victim's family and friends

There are always two parties to a death; the person who dies and the survivors who are bereaved . . . the sting of death is less sharp for the person who dies than it is for the bereaved survivor. This, as I see it, is the capital fact about the relation between the living and the dying. There are two parties to the suffering that death inflicts; and in the apportionment of the suffering the survivor takes the brunt.

—Arnold Toynbee, from *Man's Concern with Death*

Churches have denied funerals and memorial services to bereaved families. Victims' remains have been banned from cemeteries. Medical examiners have falsified records for families so they can receive economic aid. Federal and state surveys of attitudes toward suicide confirm a broad spectrum of responses ranging from fear, denial and resistance to widespread support for suicide prevention. Social and religious stigma is widespread. One report told of a long-time teacher of church youth who lost her son to suicide. When she returned to her class a few weeks later, she was told that because her son had taken his life, she was no longer to teach. In contrast, several denominations have in recent years adopted informed and more compassionate statements on suicide for their members. Frequently mentioned are the needs to remove social stigmas that discourage youth and others from seeking the help they need and for providing mental health opportunities for those who suffer from depression and suicidal ideation. The understanding support of family and friends as a major factor in providing such effective support is now more widely appreciated.

The Church's Response

Recognizing that the church's historical response to suicide includes punitive measures intended to prevent suicide and that there is no clear biblical stance on suicide, the General Conference of The United Methodist Church strongly urges the employment of major initiatives to prevent suicide, following the guidelines of the National Strategy for Suicide Prevention issued by the U. S. Department of Health and Human Services. Additionally, the General Conference recommends to the boards, agencies, institutions, and local churches of The United Methodist Church that the ministry of suicide prevention should receive urgent attention. Survivors of loss through suicide and suicide attempts should also receive priority concern in the overall ministry of the Church. Harsh and punitive measures (such as denial of funeral or memorial services, or ministerial visits) imposed upon families of suicide victims should be denounced and abandoned. The church should participate in and urge others to participate in a full, community-based effort to address the needs of people at risk and their families. Each annual conference and local church should respond to issues of ministry related to suicide prevention and family-support services.

It must be emphasized that suicide increases in an environment or society that does not demonstrate a caring attitude toward all persons. The church has a special role in changing societal attitudes and harmful social environment of individuals and families. To promote this effort, the church should do the following:

1. the General Board of Discipleship shall continue to develop curriculum for biblical and theological study of suicide and related mental and environmental health problems and promote the programs recommended by the American Association of Pastoral Counseling and the use of scientific research of the Centers for Disease Control and Prevention, the National Institutes of Health, and other credible institutions in the private sector, such as organizations within the National Council of Suicide Prevention ;

2. the General Board of Higher Education and Ministry shall develop materials for United Methodist-related seminaries to train church professionals to recognize treatable mental illness associated with suicide (e.g., depression) and to realize when and how to refer persons for treatment; it shall ensure that all pastoral counseling programs include such training and strategies for ministry survivors of suicide loss and suicide attempts ; and seek attention to suicide in courses in Bible, Christian Ethics, Preaching and Religious Education as well as Pastoral Care;

3. the General Board of Church and Society shall continue to support public policies that: (a) promote access to mental-health services for all persons regardless of age, (b) remove the stigma associated with mental illness, and (c) encourage "help-seeking" behavior;

4. embrace all persons affected by suicide, including young children, in loving community through support groups and responsive social institutions, call upon society through the media to reinforce (following published guidelines for reporting suicide and related matters) the importance of human life and to advocate that public policies include all persons' welfare, and work against policies that

devalue human life and perpetuate cultural risk factors (i.e., nuclear armaments, war, racial and ethnic prejudice);

5. affirm that we can destroy our physical bodies but not our being in God, and affirm that a person stands in relationship to others, but in our efforts to be more compassionate and care giving, avoid glamorizing the deaths of those who take their lives, especially young people. The loss of every person is a loss in community;

6. support the United Methodist childcare institutions that provide treatment for emotionally disturbed children, youth, and their families and retirement communities that are home for those where suicide rates are highest; and

7. strengthen the youth ministries of the local church, helping the young people experience the saving grace of Jesus Christ and participate in the caring fellowship of the church.

Conclusion

"The church is called to proclaim the gospel of grace and, in its own life, to embody that gospel. It embodies that gospel when it is particularly solicitous of those within its number who are most troubled, and when it reaches beyond its own membership to such people who stand alone." (Dr. Philip Wogaman, professor of Christian Social Ethics, Wesley Theological Seminary).

ADOPTED 1988
AMENDED AND READOPTED 1996
AMENDED AND READOPTED 2004

See Social Principles, ¶ 161M.

158. Teen Sexual Identity and Suicide Risk

In the year 2003 at least 700,000 high school students will attempt suicide—one in every 13 high school students in the United States. According to the U.S. Centers for Disease Control and Prevention, suicide rates among adults have steadied or even declined over the past few decades but teenage suicide rates have tripled.

A 1989 U.S. Department of Health and Human Services study found that teens dealing with issues of sexual identity are two to three times more likely to attempt suicide than are other youth.

The United Methodist Church, in Social Principles ¶ 162.H, states: Certain basic human rights and civil liberties are due all persons. We are committed to supporting those rights and liberties for homosexual persons.

The General Conference will establish and fund a task group which will:

- Publish, in laypeople's terms, a summary of current research on homosexual youth at risk for suicide;
- Work with organizations currently doing research on these issues;
- Provide a directory of agencies working on issues of teen suicide among youth dealing with issues of sexual identity;
- Publish a resource for congregations and families which provides accurate information, recommendations for programs, and pastoral guidance.
- Make recommendations for legislative actions within The United Methodist Church;
- Make recommendations for programs for youth through congregations, districts, conferences, mission agencies, United Methodist Women, United Methodist Men and other organizational bodies of The United Methodist Church.
- Report to the 2008 General Conference on its findings and work.

ADOPTED 2004

See Social Principles, ¶¶ 161G and 161M.

POPULATION

159. World's Population and the Church's Response

The creation of the world out of chaos into order is the initial biblical witness. In this witness is the affirmation of the freedom and responsibility of humankind. We affirm God to be the Creator, the one who grants us freedom, and the one to whom we are responsible.

God's ongoing creative and re-creative concern for the universe was expressed through Jesus Christ, who has called us to find the meaning of our lives in dual love of God and neighbor. In this context, we live responsibly before God, writing history by the actions of our lives. The imperative for the individual Christian and the Christian community is to seek patterns of life, shape the structures of society, and foster those values that will dignify human life for all.

We are living in an age of possibility in which we are called under God to serve the future with hope and confidence. Christians have no alternative to involvement in seeking solutions for the great and complex set of problems facing the world today. These issues are closely interrelated: hunger, poverty, disease, lack of potable water, denial of human rights, economic and environmental exploitation, overconsumption, technologies that are inadequate or inappropriate, rapid depletion of resources, and continuing growth of population. None can be addressed in isolation.

Nor can hunger, poverty, disease, injustice, and violence in the world be simplistically blamed on population growth. The rapidly swelling numbers of people, however, makes addressing these issues more challenging. The world's population is estimated to reach 9.2 billion by 2050, with the least developed countries having the highest fertility and population growth. The populations of those nations are expected to triple in the next 50 years, from 600 million to 1.8 billion. With each passing day we are discovering more and more connections between population and with sustainable development. As the population grows, it has an obvious impact on land use, water consumption, and air quality. Communities are called to be responsible stewards of all these resources. How can we protect God's gift of the natural environment and at the same time provide a place of sustainability for humans?

The high rates of malaria and HIV/AIDS diminish life for many of God's children. According to UNAIDS, it is predicted that by 2010 more than 80 million persons will have contracted the AIDS virus. And today malaria is found throughout the tropical and sub-tropical regions of the world and causes more than 300 million acute illnesses and at least one million deaths annually. (World Health Organization, 2001-2010 UN Decade to Roll Back Malaria)

Gender inequality in parts of the world exacerbates these complex issues. We know that in many nations, women are considered property and lack basic human rights such as protection under the law and access to education, housing, and jobs. Women comprise 70 percent of the world's poor and many are captives (knowingly or unknowingly) within patriarchal structures, policies, and practices.

We also recognize the growing numbers of elderly in the world's population. Many of them are among the world's most poor.

According to the United Nations Population Fund, there are almost 400 million people over the age of 60 in the developing world, and the majority are women. While just 8 percent of persons in developing countries today are older than 60, the proportion will jump to 20 percent in the next 50 years. As communities engage in sustainable development, it will be important for the needs of the aging to be considered, such as economic sustenance, health care, housing, and nutrition. We must also insure the elimination of violence against older persons and provide support and care for the many elderly who are caring for their children and grandchildren, including those affected by the HIV/AIDS pandemic.

As people of faith, we are called to educate ourselves about the interconnectedness of life's critical concerns and live as responsible stewards. The church can address these complex population-related issues on several fronts. We call on all United Methodists to:

1. access educational opportunities that focus on the issue of population and its inter-relatedness to other critical issues such as poverty, disease, hunger, environment, injustice, and violence, and to promote these opportunities in the local church;

2. urge that the United Methodist medical and mission facilities and programs provide a full range of reproductive health and family planning information;

3. take the lead in upgrading the status of women in societies and include women in all development planning and processes. One such action would be advocating for the United States to ratify the United Nations Convention for the Elimination of Discrimination Against Women (CEDAW) and to adopt the Equal Rights Amendment;

4. implement programs within The United Methodist Church that provide and/or enhance educational opportunities for girls and women, making it possible for them to achieve levels of self-sufficiency and well-being;

5. call upon governments to give high priority to addressing the malaria crisis and HIV/AIDS pandemic and urge adequate funding to eradicate and prevent these diseases;

6. call on the U.S. Congress and legislative bodies of the developed nations to recognize the crucial nature of population growth and to give maximum feasible funding to programs of population, environment, health, agriculture, and other technological-assistance programs for developing nations. International assistance programs should be based on mutual cooperation, should recognize the diver-

sities of culture, should encourage self-development and not dependency, and should not require "effective population programs" as a prerequisite for other developmental assistance;

7. call on governments and private organizations to place a high priority on research aimed at developing a range of safe, inexpensive contraceptives that can be used in a variety of societies and medical situations. Promote greater understanding of attitudes, motivations, and social and economic factors affecting childbearing; and

8. call on governments to implement systems of social insurance and support for older persons to ensure adequate economic sustenance and housing, and quality health care and nutrition.

ADOPTED 2004

See Social Principles, ¶162*I*.

POVERTY

160. Principles of Welfare Reform

As people of faith and religious commitment, we are called to stand with and seek justice for people who are poor. Central to our religious traditions, sacred texts, and teachings is a divine mandate to side with and protect the poor. Thus the scripture says: However, there should be no poor among you, for in the land the LORD your God is giving you to possess as your inheritance, he will richly bless you, if only you fully obey the LORD your God and are careful to follow all these commands I am giving you today. If there is a poor man among your brothers in any of the towns of the land that the LORD your God is giving you, do not be hardhearted or tightfisted toward your poor brother. Rather be openhanded and freely lend him whatever he needs. If one refuses to help the needy, the scripture continues:

"He may then appeal to the LORD against you, and you will be found guilty of sin...Give generously to him [the poor] and do so without a grudging heart; then because of this the LORD your God will bless you in all your work and in everything you put your hand to. There will always be poor people in the land. Therefore I command you to be openhanded toward your brothers and toward the poor and needy in your land" (Deuteronomy 4—5 and 7—11, NIV).

We share a conviction, therefore, that welfare reforms must not focus on eliminating programs but on eliminating poverty and the damage it inflicts on children (who are two thirds of all welfare recipients), on their parents, and on the rest of society.

We recognize the benefit to the entire community of helping people move from welfare into the job market when possible and appropriate. We fear, however, that reform will fail if it ignores labor-market issues such as unemployment and an inadequate minimum wage, and important family issues such as the affordable housing affordable childcare, pay equity, access to health care, and the economic value of care-giving in the home. Successful welfare reform must address these concerns as well as other issues, such as pay equity, affordable housing, and the access to health care.

We believe that people are more important than the sum of their economic activities. Successful welfare reform demands more than economic incentives and disincentives; it depends on overcoming both biased assumptions about race, gender, and class that feed hostile social stereotypes about people living in poverty and suspicions that people with perspectives other than our own are either indifferent or insincere. Successful welfare reform will depend ultimately upon finding not only a common ground of policies but a common spirit about the need to pursue them for all.

The following principles neither exhaust our concerns nor resolve all issues raised, but these principles will serve as our guide in assessing proposed legislation. We hope they may also serve as a rallying point for a common effort with others throughout the nation.

The General Conference of The United Methodist Church adopts "Principles of Welfare Reform," and directs them to be sent to the President of the United States, the speaker of the United States House of Representatives, and the United States Senate majority leader. In addition, annual conferences are asked to send this statement to appropriate state officials.

A Statement of Shared Principles of Welfare Reform

The goal of Welfare Reform must be to lift people out of poverty, not merely to reduce welfare rolls. To be effective in reducing poverty, the Work Opportunity and Personal Responsibility Act of 1996, commonly known as Temporary Aid to Needy Families (TANF), and related welfare laws should be based on the following principles. It must:

1. *Insure that poverty reduction is a central goal.* All welfare policies must work together to enable recipients and their families to leave poverty and achieve self-sufficiency. For example, cash benefits combined with wages and supportive services must be sufficient to allow each family to meet its basic needs.

2. *Provide sufficient federal and state funding.* Funding for welfare should at a minimum be indexed to the rate of inflation. Continuation of state maintenance of effort should be required.

3. Acknowledge the dignity of work, eliminate barriers to employment and provide training and education necessary for unskilled workers to get and hold jobs. Participation in post-secondary education should count as work. Supportive services provided should include childcare, transportation, and ancillary services to make participation possible and reasonable.

4. Continue and encourage public/private partnerships to train workers and help them find jobs. If public jobs are created, they should lead to family-sustaining wages, comply with workplace protection laws, and not displace current workers. States should provide means by which employment programs can be evaluated at the local level for effectiveness and fairness. *Allow welfare recipients to retain a substantial portion of wage earnings and assets* before losing cash, housing, health, child-care, food assistance or other benefits. In no case should former welfare recipients receive less in combined benefits and income as a result of working than they received while they were on welfare.

5. *Be available to all people in need.* Immigrants should have access to the same benefits that are available to citizens. Those who receive benefits should receive them according to their needs and for as long as the need exists.

6. *Not impose time limits on people who are complying with the rules of the program.* It is the state's responsibility to assure access to counseling, legal assistance, and information on eligibility for child support, job training and placement, medical care, affordable housing, food programs, and education.

7. *Acknowledge the responsibility of both parents and government to provide for the well-being of children.* Welfare should insure that children benefit from the active and healthy participation of parents—whether custodial or not—in their lives. The barriers to participation by mar-

ried parents in federal programs should be removed. There should be no family caps and no full-family sanctions. Children should benefit from successful state efforts to collect child support assistance from non-custodial parents through increasing the amount of collected child support that children receive.

8. *Address the needs of individuals with special situations.* People who have been victims of domestic violence or stalking must be protected and have their privacy maintained. Some with disabling conditions may need extended periods of time to become employable; and it must be recognized that some people cannot or should not work under any circumstances.

9. *Uphold and affirm every person's value, whether employed or not.* In compassion, we recognize that a small proportion of people on welfare may never be in a position to work outside the home. Exemptions should be offered for people with serious physical or mental illness, disabling conditions, or responsibilities as caregivers who work at home. States should have the option to use federal funds to help families to cope with multiple barriers to employment.

ADOPTED 1996
AMENDED AND READOPTED 2004

See Social Principles, ¶ 162*A.*

RACISM

161. A Charter for Racial Justice Policies in an Interdependent Global Community

Racism is the belief that one race is innately superior to all other races. In the United States, this belief has justified the conquest, enslavement, and evangelizing of non-Europeans. During the early history of this country, Europeans assumed that their civilization and religion were innately superior to those of both the original inhabitants of the United States and the Africans who were forcibly brought to these shores to be slaves. The myth of European superiority persisted and persists. Other people who came and who are still coming to the United States, by choice or by force, encountered and encounter racism. Some of these people are the Chinese who built the railroads as indentured workers; the Mexicans whose lands were annexed; the

Puerto Ricans, the Cubans, the Hawaiians, and the Eskimos who were colonized; and the Filipinos, the Jamaicans, and the Haitians who lived on starvation wages as farm workers.

In principle, the United States has outlawed racial discrimination; but in practice, little has changed. Social, economic, and political institutions still discriminate, although some institutions have amended their behavior by eliminating obvious discriminatory practices and choosing their language carefully. The institutional church, despite sporadic attempts to the contrary, also still discriminates.

The damage of years of exploitation has not been erased. A system designed to meet the needs of one segment of the population cannot be the means to the development of a just society for all. The racist system in the United States today perpetuates the power and control of those of European ancestry. It is often called "white racism." The fruits of racism are prejudice, bigotry, discrimination, and dehumanization. Consistently, African Americans, Hispanics, Asians, Native Americans, and Pacific Islanders have been humiliated by being given inferior jobs, housing, education, medical services, transportation, and public accommodation. With hopes deferred and rights still denied, the deprived and oppressed fall prey to a colonial mentality that acquiesces to the inequities, occasionally with religious rationalization.

Racist presuppositions have been implicit in U.S. attitudes and policies toward Asia, Africa, the Middle East, and Latin America. While proclaiming democracy, freedom, and independence, the U.S. has been an ally and an accomplice to perpetuating inequality of the races and colonialism throughout the world. The history of The United Methodist Church and the history of the United States are intertwined. The "mission enterprise" of the churches in the United States and "Westernization" went hand in hand, sustaining a belief in their superiority.

We are conscious that "we have sinned as our ancestors did; we have been wicked and evil" (Psalm 106:6, *Today's English Version*). We call for a renewed commitment to the elimination of institutional racism. We affirm the 1976 General Conference Statement on The United Methodist Church and Race, which states unequivocally: "By biblical and theological precept, by the law of the church, by General Conference pronouncement, and by Episcopal expression, the matter is clear. With respect to race, the aim of The United Methodist Church is nothing less than an inclusive church in an inclusive society. The

United Methodist Church, therefore, calls upon all its people to perform those faithful deeds of love and justice in both the church and community that will bring this aim into reality."

Because we believe:

1. that God is the Creator of all people and all are God's children in one family;

2. that racism is a rejection of the teachings of Jesus Christ;

3. that racism denies the redemption and reconciliation of Jesus Christ;

4. that racism robs all human beings of their wholeness and is used as a justification for social, economic, and political exploitation;

5. that we must declare before God and before one another that we have sinned against our sisters and brothers of other races in thought, in word, and in deed;

6. that in our common humanity in creation all women and men are made in God's image and all persons are equally valuable in the sight of God;

7. that our strength lies in our racial and cultural diversity and that we must work toward a world in which each person's value is respected and nurtured; and

8. that our struggle for justice must be based on new attitudes, new understandings, and new relationships and must be reflected in the laws, policies, structures, and practices of both church and state.

We commit ourselves as individuals and as a community to follow Jesus Christ in word and in deed and to struggle for the rights and the self-determination of every person and group of persons. Therefore, as United Methodists in every place across the land, we will unite our efforts within The United Methodist Church:

1. to eliminate all forms of institutional racism in the total ministry of the church, giving special attention to those institutions that we support, beginning with their employment policies, purchasing practices, and availability of services and facilities;

2. to create opportunities in local churches to deal honestly with the existing racist attitudes and social distance between members, deepening the Christian commitment to be the church where all racial groups and economic classes come together;

3. to increase efforts to recruit people of all races into the membership of The United Methodist Church and provide leadership-development opportunities without discrimination;

4. to create workshops and seminars in local churches to study, understand, and appreciate the historical and cultural contributions of each race to the church and community;

5. to increase local churches' awareness of the continuing needs for equal education, housing, employment, and medical care for all members of the community and to create opportunities to work for these things across racial lines;

6. to work for the development and implementation of national and international policies to protect the civil, political, economic, social, and cultural rights of all people such as through support for the ratification of United Nations covenants on human rights;

7. to support and participate in the worldwide struggle for liberation in church and community; and

8. to support nomination and election processes that include all racial groups employing a quota system until the time that our voluntary performance makes such practice unnecessary.

ADOPTED 1980
READOPTED 2000

See Social Principles, ¶ 162A.

162. Act of Repentance for Racism

There is no longer Jew or Greek, there is no longer slave or free, there is no longer male or female; for all of you are one in Christ Jesus.

(Galatians 3:28)

WHEREAS, the Constitution of The United Methodist Church in Article IV mandates racial inclusiveness; and

WHEREAS, The United Methodist Church and its predecessor organizations in years past have participated, as institutions, in acts which have perpetuated the sin of racism, which continues to be a barrier to Christian unity; and

WHEREAS, at this time, The United Methodist Church is involved in conversations of the Commission on Pan-Methodist Cooperation and the Commission on Union, which has helped bring to the forefront of consciousness the particular acts of racism which led to the formation of the African Methodist Episcopal, African Methodist Episcopal Zion, and the Christian Methodist Episcopal denominations, and also the formation of the Central Jurisdiction within The United Methodist Church; and

WHEREAS, there is a need among United Methodists for education concerning the church's past history, especially in the areas of African-American race relations; and

WHEREAS, the Commission on Union and the Commission on Pan-Methodist Cooperation affirm United Methodist efforts toward repentance for past and present sins of racism; and

WHEREAS, the Council of Bishops has joined the General Commission on Christian Unity and Interreligious Concerns in preparation for a liturgical act of repentance for racism; and

WHEREAS, confession and repentance for racism is but a first step toward the changing of hearts leading to healing and wholeness;

Therefore, be it resolved, General Conference adopts *Steps Toward Wholeness: Learning and Repentance,* a study guide which addresses the church's role in racism, concluding with a call for repentance; and requests all local congregations in the United States to engage in study sessions using *Steps Toward Wholeness.* All annual conferences are also requested to engage in a liturgical act of repentance in 2001.

ADOPTED 2000

See Social Principles, ¶ 162*A.*

163. Affirmative Action

The United Methodist Church has long been committed to the principle of social inclusiveness. That is, in keeping with the spirit of the gospel, we affirm that all persons—whatever their racial or ethnic identity, whatever their gender or national origin, whatever their physical state or condition—are full-fledged members of the human community with every one of the rights and privileges that such membership entails. The implementation of "affirmative action" reflects a shared understanding that diversity is a positive outcome of social inclusion that yields benefits for the entire community.

In light of that commitment, the church has, in years past, adopted a strong stand supportive of the concept of "affirmative action." Recently, this concept has been subjected to intense opposition. While some of the particular policies adopted under that rubric may be in need of revision—given developments that have occurred over the course of time—we would, at this moment, reconfirm our support for the basic concept. Inclusionary efforts that lead to diversity yield enriched environments for our daily living and learning.

The Declaration of the United Nations World Conference against Racism, Racial Discrimination, Xenophobia and Related Intolerance (Durban, South Africa, 31 August to 8 September 2001) contains the following affirmations:

- recognition of the need for special measures or positive actions for the victims of racism, racial discrimination, xenophobia and related intolerance in order to promote their full integration into society;
- recognition that such measures should aim at correcting the conditions that impair the enjoyment of rights;
- recognition of the need to encourage equal participation of all racial and cultural, linguistic and religious groups in all sectors of society; and,
- recognition of the need for measures to achieve appropriate representation in educational institutions, housing, political parties, legislative bodies, employment, especially in the judiciary, police, army and other civil services.

The concept of affirmative action emerged in response to the civil rights movements of the 1960s as one of a set of public policies designed to overcome a tragic history of racist and sexist practices throughout this nation and to create a more equitable social system in keeping with the spirit of the gospel and in keeping with the proclaimed democratic ideals of the American people.

Affirmative action is not intended to enable class privilege for the wealthy, such as using family legacies or donor contributions to gain personal advantages. The specific intent of affirmative action, given its origins, was to bring the prestige and power of government to bear on economic and educational institutions, requiring them to put into effect carefully conceived plans to admit qualified persons who traditionally had been excluded from participating in them—women, ethnic and racial minorities, and, at a later time, persons with disabilities.

Over the past three decades, programs of affirmative action have had a significant effect in the employment patterns of corporations and public agencies and in the character of the professional staff and student bodies of educational institutions, private and public. Proportionately, more women, racial and ethnic minorities, and people with disabilities have found their talents and training recognized than before such programs were instituted.

At the same time, however, many women, racial and ethnic minorities, and persons with disabilities, though fully competent, have confronted obstacles in these settings, stifling their advancement in education and in employment. Unemployment of racial and ethnic minorities remains appreciably higher than the national average. Women workers continue to earn less than male workers in the same or similar positions, and they continue to confront limitations in promotion to a more prestigious and responsible level of jobs. Persons with disabilities are bypassed regardless of their motivations.

Despite these persistent inequities, the concept of affirmative action is currently under severe attack. In some locations, it has been abolished as a public policy on several (somewhat different and not altogether compatible) grounds:

- that it promotes the hiring (in business) or admission (to institutions of higher education) of unqualified persons;
- that it discriminates unduly against white males;
- that it has a negative impact on the self-esteem of affirmative action candidates; and
- that its goals have been at this time fully realized and therefore it is no longer necessary.

In light of the evidence, however, (except in those cases where policies of affirmative action have been badly or improperly administered) all of these alleged grounds seem specious. The implementation of affirmative action has resulted in concrete gains for people of color and women in higher education and the corporate world. However persuasive they seem on the surface, they tend to slough off or to ignore the persistence of significant and widespread inequalities of opportunity affecting women, ethnic and racial minorities, and persons with disabilities throughout our social system.

From the perspective represented by The United Methodist Church, the most fundamental premise underlying the concept of affirmative action is both moral and spiritual. Concern for the disadvantaged and the oppressed is a major feature of the message of the Hebraic prophets and of Jesus. According to biblical teaching, we are mandated, in the face of inhumane discrimination—whether that discrimination is intended or unintended—to do what we can to redress legitimate grievances and to create a society in which the lives of each and all will flourish.

For this fundamental reason, we reconfirm our commitment to the concept of affirmative action. The use of numerical goals and timetables is a legitimate and necessary tool of effective affirmative action programs. This concept retains its pertinence as a means of attaining a more inclusive society in our educational systems, in our businesses and industries, and in religious and other institutions. No persons—whatever their gender, their ethnic or racial heritage, their physical condition—should be deprived of pursuing their educational or employment aspirations to the full extent of their talents and abilities.

Fairness is the rule for affirmative action guaranteeing more opportunities for all to compete for jobs. Indeed, the purpose of affirmative action has always been to create an environment where merit can prevail.

Rather than curtail or abolish programs in affirmative action, we should instead move toward the reallocation of the resources of our society to ensure the fullest opportunities in the fulfillment of life.

At the same time, given the tenacity of many forms of racism, sexism, and ableism—both blatant and subtle—the concept of affirmative action retains its relevance as part of an overall effort to create a more just and equitable social system.

Therefore, be it resolved, that the 2004 General Conference of The United Methodist Church calls upon all its members to:

1. affirm our Judeo-Christian heritage of justice and inclusiveness as a foundation for the concept of affirmative action;

2. constitute a model for others in society by practicing and strengthening our own affirmative action policies, whatever our station in life;

3. declare our support of efforts throughout the society to sustain and, where needed, strengthen affirmative action legislation and programs;

4. collaborate with movements and initiatives seeking to ensure effective participation of ethnic and racial minorities, women, and persons with disabilities in all sectors of our society; and

5. interpret the genuine meaning of affirmative action, dispelling the myths and responding to the specious appeals that would undercut and vilify affirmative action policies and programs.

Be it further resolved, that the 2004 General Conference reaffirm its mandate to implement affirmative action programs in all general church boards and agencies, annual conferences, church-related institutions, districts, and local churches.

Be it further resolved, that the General Commissions on Religion and Race and the Status and Role of Women continue to monitor The United Methodist Church and related institutions and to provide assistance in helping them move toward greater conformity with the principle of inclusiveness.

ADOPTED 1996
AMENDED AND READOPTED 2004

See Social Principles, ¶ 162A.

164. Annual Conference Responsibility to Eradicate Racism

WHEREAS, conferences within the United States are becoming more diverse; and

WHEREAS, it is predicted that within the United States, the population of persons of European descent will be less than 50 percent before 2050; and

WHEREAS, racism has been a systemic and personal problem within the U.S. and The United Methodist Church (UMC) and its predecessor denominations since its inception; and

WHEREAS, the UMC is committed to the eradication of racism; and

WHEREAS, it takes significant change, learning, time and healing to eradicate racism; and

WHEREAS, it takes significant attitudinal and systemic change to learn and to incorporate the gifts and contributions of the different racial-ethnic persons within the church's ministry, structures, and mission,

Therefore, be it resolved, that every annual conference within the U.S. have a strategy and program which educates and supports systemic and personal changes to end racism and work multiculturally, and

Be it further resolved, that an educational program which will include understanding systemic racism, a strategy for its eradication, appreciation and valuation of diversity, and guidelines for working with different groups in communities towards becoming an inclusive church be offered at least yearly within the annual conference, and

Be it further resolved, that all clergy and lay leadership be encouraged to participate in such a program and that all newly ordained clergy be required to participate in the program, and

Be it further resolved, that the General Commission on Religion and Race include as part of its review process the adherence of annual conferences in equipping and supporting leadership to eradicate racism and work multiculturally, and that as annual conferences develop and implement programs, results will be forwarded by the Conference Commission on Religion and Race (or other conference structures dealing with those responsibilities) to the General Commission on Religion and Race.

ADOPTED 2000

See Social Principles, ¶ 162A.

165. Affirmation of Commission on Religion and Race

WHEREAS, United Methodists reject racism as sin and a violation of our human dignity as children of God, and

WHEREAS, racism is still alive in both church and society, and

WHEREAS, The United Methodist Church has been committed to the elimination of racism since 1968 when it established the GCORR, and

WHEREAS, it is still crucial that the task of eliminating racism within the church is given to an independent agency with the sole purpose of seeking racial justice and racial inclusiveness,

Therefore, be it resolved that the 2004 General Conference affirms the existence of The Commission of Religion and Race as an independent monitoring agency for the elimination of racism, and that the GCORR continues with its explicit mandate of helping the church to be free of racism and become racially inclusive.

ADOPTED 2004

See Social Principles, ¶ 162A.

166. Affirmation of the Joint Task Force on Racism

WHEREAS, the annual conferences ratified a constitutional amendment adopted by the 2000 General Conference, pledging to work toward the elimination of racism within the society, the Church, its policies, and organizations; and

WHEREAS, "The United Methodist Church acknowledges that all persons are of sacred worth. All persons without regard to race, color, national origin, status, or economic condition, shall be eligible to attend its worship services, participate in its programs, receive the sacraments, upon baptism be admitted as baptized members, and upon taking vows declaring the Christian faith, become professing members in any local church in the connection" (The Constitution, Division One, ¶ 4, Article IV); and

WHEREAS, "Racial Justice—The United Methodist Church proclaims the value of each person as a unique child of God and commits itself to the healing and wholeness of all persons. The United Methodist Church recognizes that the sin of racism has been destructive to its unity throughout its history. Racism continues to cause painful division and marginalization. The United Methodist Church shall confront and seek to eliminate racism, whether in organizations or in individuals, in every facet of its life and in society at large. The United Methodist Church shall work collaboratively with others to address concerns that threaten the cause of racial justice at all times and in all places" (The Constitution, Division One, ¶ 5, Article V); and

WHEREAS, racism is an evil that knows no borders, affects people of all socioeconomic backgrounds, spares no one person as its victim, creates resentment and rage among those affected and erases the circle of humanity replacing it with dividing lines between the races. While the potential for racism lies in all of us, through the power of Jesus Christ the potential to eliminate it is well within our reach; and

WHEREAS, Christians must work together to help eliminate the lines of division and establish that all of God's children are members of the human race, regardless of racial and ethnic origin or the color of one's skin; and

WHEREAS, The United Methodist Church must acknowledge that steps have been made toward the goal of eliminating racism, celebrate and salute the groups that have made proactive efforts to alleviate tension caused by racism; and

WHEREAS, in love, the Church must hold accountable the groups in our midst that have not made efforts to alleviate racism and to bring together the children of God to live and be treated as Jesus intended; and

WHEREAS, Christians have a duty to spread the good news of Jesus Christ who loved each of us, died for us and was resurrected to prove his ultimate victory over death to win our souls. This duty requires much of the household of faith, one of which is to show and live in love with one another and to eliminate the destructive and life-taking sin of racism;

Therefore, be it resolved, that the 2004 General Conference will affirm the work of the Joint Task Force on Racism by recommending continued efforts to eliminate racism in church organizations and practices through the following steps:

1. All agencies within districts, annual conferences, and the general church, will assign a person with the specific responsibility to work on the elimination of racism.

2. All districts, annual conferences, and general agencies will establish a covenant that reflects how its members will live out its life in the performance of assigned responsibilities with the goal of eliminating racism. Each member and staff will be asked to sign the covenant as an outward sign of making this commitment.

3. All local churches, districts, annual conferences, and general agencies will find ways to celebrate diversity through Jesus' prophetic, redemptive, and incarnational presence throughout the Church.

ADOPTED 2004

See Social Principles, ¶162.

167. Membership in Clubs or Organizations that Practice Exclusivity

WHEREAS, membership held in any club or organization that practices exclusivity based on gender, race, or socioeconomic condition is clearly in violation of the stance of the United Methodist Social Principles;

Therefore, it is recommended, that United Methodists who hold memberships in clubs or organizations that practice exclusivity based on gender, race, or socioeconomic condition prayerfully consider whether they should work for change within these groups or resign their membership. If one decides to resign, we urge that the decision and reasons be made public. This reflects the intent and purpose of the Social Principles of The United Methodist Church.

ADOPTED 1992
READOPTED 2004

See Social Principles, ¶ 162A.

168. Project Equality

In consideration of long-established support by The United Methodist Church for fair employment practices; and

In consideration of a national policy for fair employment practices in the United States, which embraces legislation against unemployment discrimination; and

In the conviction that Project Equality, a voluntary cooperative interdenominational enterprise of churches, synagogues, and related institutions, provides a responsible, consistent, ethical, practical, effective, and positive means whereby The United Methodist Church and other churches can support fair employment practices in the United States; and

In recognition of The United Methodist Church's responsibility to make ethical use of its own financial resources through effective use of equal employment opportunity as one of its purchasing criteria; and

In recognition that Project Equality provides a technical-assistance resource to agencies and institutions of The United Methodist Church in the development of equal employment and affirmative action programs,

Therefore, be it resolved, that The United Methodist Church endorses Project Equality and recommends cooperation through participation, financial support, and utilization of the Project Equality "Buyer's Guide" in all purchases by United Methodist annual conferences, local churches, local or national institutions, agencies, and organizations.

ADOPTED 1992
AMENDED AND ADOPTED 2000

See Social Principles, ¶ 162*A*.

169. Racial Profiling in the USA

According to a study prepared by the Institute on Race and Poverty of the University of Minnesota Law School, and entitled "Components of Racial Profiling Legislation," racial profiling is one of the most pressing civil rights of our time. Racial profiling negatively affects all persons of color of all generations and income levels. It undermines the legitimacy of the criminal justice system and hinders effective policing in the communities that need it the most.

"A Resource Guide on Racial Profiling Data Collection Systems," published by the U. S. Department of Justice defines racial profiling as "any police-initiated action that relies on the race, ethnicity or national origin rather than behavior of an individual or information that leads the police to a particular individual who has been identified as being, of having been, engaged in criminal activity."[1]

Racial profiling is present at traffic stops by police officers when the use of race or ethnicity is the decisive factor that makes the officer stop, question, search, or arrest someone.

Racial profiling has been monitored in a number of jurisdictions, and in nearly all of these jurisdictions, it was found to be a significant problem. For example, a 1996 study in Maryland found that while African Americans accounted for only 16.9 percent of the drivers on I-95, they constituted 72.9 percent of the drivers stopped and searched by the Maryland police. [2]

Racial profiling affects law-abiding citizens as well as offenders. Innocent persons of color are stopped, questioned, and searched for reasons that would not lead to stops of white drivers. People of color report stops based on minor equipment violations such as items hanging from rearview mirrors and even stops followed by inquiries such as, "whose car is this you're driving?" or "what are you doing in this neighborhood?"

Racial profiling not only subordinates the civil rights of entire communities to the goals of criminal justice, but it is an ineffective crime prevention tool that ultimately victimizes the very people that it is supposed to protect—the noncriminal public.

A 1999 Gallup poll found nationally 42 percent of African Americans believe that they have been stopped by police because of their race, 77 percent of African Americans believe racial profiling is widespread, and 87 percent disapprove of the practice. Similar answers have been received among persons from other races and ethnic background. The same poll showed that although only 6 percent of whites believed they had been stopped by police because of their race or ethnic background, 56 percent of whites believe racial profiling was widespread, and 80 percent disapproved of racial profiling.[3]

1. Deborah Ramrez, Jack McDevitt, and Amy Farrel. "A Resource on Racial Profiling Data Collection Systems: Promising Practices and Lessons Learned," 3 (2000).
2. David A. Harris. "Driving While Black." Racial Profiling on Our Nation's Highways, and American Civil Liberties Union Special Report 21-22 (1999).
3. The Gallup Poll, September 21-November 16, 1999.

The widespread perception among people of color that they are unfairly targeted by the police because of their race or ethnic background has led to a lack of trust in the police. This mistrust harms both the police and communities of color, by impeding effective police work precisely within the communities of color that are the ones who need it the most. It is well known that people of color are more likely than whites to be victims of crime. However, mistrust of police hinders the cooperation that is needed between the communities and the police officers.

WHEREAS, racial profiling is an abhorrent manifestation of racism, and it is a painful and tragic reality in our lives, we call The United Methodist Church to:

- denounce through an official communication of the Council of Bishop, to the President of the United States of America, Congress, and the Attorney General, racial profiling as an unjust and evil reality that needs to be corrected; and
- enable the church body: annual conferences, districts and local churches, and under the leadership of the General Board of Church and Society and the General Commission on Religion and Race, to be proactive in educating the constituency about this issue and in establishing networks of cooperation with the criminal justice and the law enforcement systems.

ADOPTED 2004

See Social Principles, 162*A*.

170. White Privilege in the United States

European Americans enjoy a broad range of privileges denied to persons of color in our society, privileges that often permit them to dominate others who do not enjoy such privileges. While there are many issues that reflect the racism in U.S. society, there are some cases where racism is the issue, such as affirmative action, housing, job discrimination, hate crimes, and criminal justice. In addition, there are many broader social issues where racism is one factor in the equation, albeit often the major one.

Poverty is a serious problem in the U.S., but a far greater percentage of Black and Hispanic persons are poor than white persons.

Police brutality is much more prevalent in ethnic minority communities, partly because police in minority communities are usually a nonresident, mostly white occupying force.

Schools in white communities receive a far higher proportion of education dollars than those in minority communities, leading to larger class size, fewer resources, and inferior facilities.

While welfare affects the entire society, it hits minorities hardest. Although both Democrats and Republicans support tax credits for families to enable middle-class mothers to stay home with their children, welfare "reform" forces poor, single mothers to take low-paying jobs and leave their children to inadequate or nonexistent day care. Because more and better job opportunities are open to white persons, they are leaving the welfare rolls faster than minority persons, making minority persons a disproportionate segment of the welfare population.

Criminal "justice" is meted out more aggressively in racial minority communities than white communities. Nearly half of inmates in the U.S. are African American; one out of every fourteen Black men is now in prison or jail; one out of every four is likely to be imprisoned at some point during his lifetime.

If only one of these areas impacted ethnic minorities disproportionately, an explanation might be found in some sociological factor other than race. But where race is a common thread running through virtually every inequality in our society, we are left with only one conclusion: White, European Americans enjoy a wide range of privileges that are denied to persons of color in our society. These privileges enable white persons to escape the injustices and inconveniences which are the daily experience of racial ethnic persons. Those who are White assume that they can purchase a home wherever they choose if they have the money; that they can expect courteous service in stores and restaurants; that if they are pulled over by a police car it will be for a valid reason unrelated to their skin color. Persons of color cannot make these assumptions.

We suggest that the church focus not only on the plight of people living in urban or rural ghettos, but also on white privilege and its impact on white persons. For example, churches in white or predominantly white communities need to ask why there are no persons of color in their community, why the prison population in their state is disproportionately Black and Hispanic persons, why there are so few

Black and Hispanic persons in high-paying jobs and prestigious universities, why schools in white communities receive more than their fair share of education dollars, and why white persons receive preferential treatment from white police officers.

We ask the General Conference to recognize white privilege as an underlying cause of injustice in our society including our church and to commit the church to its elimination in church and society.

The rights and privileges a society bestows upon or withholds from those who comprise it indicate the relative esteem in which that society holds particular person and groups of persons.

We direct the General Board of Discipleship (GBOD), in consultation with the General Commission on Religion and Race (GCORR), to prepare a study guide on white privilege and its consequences in church and society.

We ask the Board of Church and Society in every annual conference to sponsor workshops on White privilege.

We direct the GCORR and the GBOD to jointly review and develop UM curriculum materials, with particular attention to those for children and youth, for the purpose of affirming children of all racial and ethnic groups, and to communicate in our curriculum materials that in our society, privileges that are taken for granted by white persons are often denied to others because of their racial and ethnic identity.

We ask each local church with a predominantly white membership: 1) to reflect on its own willingness to welcome persons without regard to race and to assess the relative accessibility in housing, employment, education and recreation in its community to white persons and to persons of color; and 2) to welcome persons of color into membership and full participation in the church and community and to advocate for their access to the benefits which white persons take for granted.

We challenge individual white persons to confess their participation in the sin of racism and repent for past and current racist practices. And we challenge individual ethnic persons to appropriate acts of forgiveness.

Finally, we call all persons, whatever their racial or ethnic heritage, to work together to restore the broken body of Christ.

ADOPTED 2000

See Social Principles, ¶ 162A.

RURAL ISSUES

171. Ministries of Rural Chaplains

WHEREAS, the General Conference of 1996 clearly affirmed the ministries of rural chaplains and called on The United Methodist Church to pursue rural chaplaincy as a significant means of resourcing renewal in rural churches and communities throughout the world; and

WHEREAS, the Rural Chaplains Association now has 201 certified members (women, men, laity and clergy, United Methodist and ecumenical) including African Americans, Caucasians, Hispanics, Native Americans, and persons from the international community (England, Philippines, Russia) with several persons in process from Mexico, and has initiated relationships with representatives from Africa, Australia, and Canada; and

WHEREAS, the Report on the National Comprehensive Plan for Town and Country Ministry, mandated by the General Conference of 1996, states that "Rapid changes are occurring in town and country . . . including the looming loss of thousands of family farms, the changing face of agricultural production, the growth of ethnic/migrant and other new populations; the emerging challenges of forestry, mining, fisheries and other industries such as small manufacturing and prisons; the prevalence of `Appalachian-like' economies in many places changing patterns of use and control; and struggles over environmental issues, water quality and hazardous waste disposal"; and

WHEREAS, rural communities in the United States and worldwide continue to experience: losses of agricultural employment and processing, mining, timbering, textile industries and of small family-owned businesses; a shortage of needed leadership and opportunities for youth; losses of human service institutions; exploitation of their poor and powerless; the destruction of environment; and lack of a balance of political power; and

WHEREAS, special learning events have been provided to rural chaplains on: long-term rural-family crisis; ministry in the midst of hate and violence; and the administrative and ministering capabilities of cooperative parish ministries, *shalom* ministries and ecumenical ministries in rural settings; and

WHEREAS, the Rural Chaplains Association has given significant attention to the causes and effects of the escalating control of agricultural and food products by powerful multinational corporations upon rural communities within the United States and the world; and

WHEREAS, rural chaplains are recognized as a special type of mission personnel of the General Board of Global Ministries for town and rural settings,

Therefore, be it resolved, that The United Methodist Church commend and reaffirm its commitment to rural chaplains and request the Rural Chaplains Association to increase its work nationally, internationally, and ecumenically with lay and clergy rural chaplains, many of whom carry out their ministries under trying conditions and in difficult places; and,

Be it further resolved, that the General Board of Global Ministries be commended for its support of rural chaplaincy as a significant means of resourcing the renewal of rural churches and communities throughout the world, and that the board be encouraged to continue its support of the Rural Chaplains Association in the future.

ADOPTED 1996
AMENDED AND READOPTED 2000

See Social Principles, ¶ 162N.

172. Support for All Who Minister in Rural Settings

WHEREAS, rural churches and communities provide unique settings for ministry; and

WHEREAS, this uniqueness calls for specially gifted people, both laity and clergy, who desire to serve in rural communities;

Therefore, be it resolved, that The United Methodist Church is called upon to affirm the value and worth of all those who minister in rural settings, to celebrate their gifts and grace, and to recognize their witness within The United Methodist Church.

Resolved, that The United Methodist Church is called upon to give particular recognition to licensed local pastors, laypersons assigned, lay missioners, and church and community workers.

Further be it resolved, that The United Methodist Church is called upon to support these persons in ways that promote more effective ministry.

Further be it resolved, that annual conferences and districts are called upon to explore with these individuals their unique gifts as they relate to service in rural areas, to identify those with gifts particularly suited to rural ministry, and to encourage such uniquely gifted persons to pursue ministry in rural settings.

Finally be it resolved, that annual conferences are called upon to establish support structures that provide for:

- Enhancement of pastoral family life,
- Resources for maintaining pastoral well-being,
- Structures and technology that encourage connectedness and accountability to the larger church, and
- Creative ways to address geographic dynamics.

ADOPTED 2004

See Social Principles, ¶ 162N.

173. Affirmation of Rural Chaplains

WHEREAS, the General Conference since 1996 has affirmed the ministries of rural chaplains and the Rural Chaplains Association, and called on The United Methodist Church to pursue rural chaplaincy as a significant means of enabling renewal in towns/villages and rural churches and communities throughout the world; and,

WHEREAS, the Rural Chaplains Association now has 214 members (women, men, laity and clergy, United Methodist and ecumenical), including several persons from the international community; and,

WHEREAS, rural chaplains are lay and clergy persons who have sensed the call to live in, work with, and advocate for town and rural persons, families, congregations, and communities; and,

WHEREAS, special emphasis is placed on responses to hate and violence, and advocacy for justice issues among all people, regardless of ethnicity, gender, age, or economic status; and,

WHEREAS, rural chaplains meet annually for support, encouragement, resourcing, and enrichment by means of workshops/consultations which explore biblical understandings and focus on person-related chaplaincy-type skills as well as understanding issues of food production and multi-national economics that impact family farmers, farm workers, migrants, and rural businesses and communities; and,

WHEREAS, rural chaplains work with other prophetic persons/ groups on the local level who are committed to long-term involvement aimed at developing local and outside resources to enhance the lives of rural congregations and communities; and,

WHEREAS, the Rural Chaplains Association greatly empowers the development of lay leadership, serves as one way of recognizing the gifts and graces of rural peoples, and unleashes new possibilities for God's Spirit to move across the countryside; and,

WHEREAS, rural chaplains will be an asset in the implementation of the National Comprehensive Plan for Town and Country Ministry approved by General Conference of 2000; and,

WHEREAS, the Rural Chaplains Association continues to develop international/global linkages, especially with Russia, Tadjikistan, and Guatemala, by exposing participants to the cultural, economic, political, ecological and religious life of their people;

Therefore, be it resolved, that rural chaplains continue being recognized as a special type of mission personnel of the General Board of Global Ministries for town and rural settings; and,

Be it further resolved, The United Methodist Church commend and reaffirm its commitment to rural chaplains as the Rural Chaplains Association increases its work nationally, internationally, and ecumenically with lay and clergy persons, many of whom carry out their ministries under trying conditions and in difficult places; and,

Be it further resolved, that the General Board of Global Ministries be encouraged to continue support of the Rural Chaplains Association in the future.

ADOPTED 2004

See Social Principles, ¶ 162N.

174. Call to the Churches for the Renewal of Rural Ministries

For 70 years the religious community has joined together through Agricultural Missions, Inc. as one way of supporting and accompanying rural communities around the world in their efforts to end poverty and injustice. For many years now rural communities in the United States and across the world have faced daunting new challenges in the wake of increasing globalization of food systems and promotion of policies that favor corporations over family farms.

Using global and regional trade agreements, corporations are controlling decisions that profoundly affect the lives of rural people.

Trade regulations and treaties, both current and under negotiation, such as the Free Trade Area of the Americas (FTAA), have conferred on corporations the right to supersede national farm policies in any nation, to demand access to local markets, and to purchase and own local water distribution systems and other essential services.

The market-based model of economic development fostered by the World Trade Organization, the World Bank and the International Monetary Fund and imposed through international trade agreements, such as the North American Free Trade Agreement (NAFTA), has resulted in and/or hastened the:

1. displacement of people from the land and the decline in the culture of the family farm;

2. belief among rural residents, particularly the youth, that there is no future in agriculture, leading to the impoverishment and eventual death of many rural communities;

3. increasing rates of farmer suicides and farm worker exploitation, as well as violence in the family and the community, substance abuse and related problems; and

4. violation of the integrity of God's creation as typified by the pollution of the air, land, and water and disruption of the ecology and climate on a global scale.

It is essential that the churches stand with those who work the land in their struggles and witness to their work. As churches, we need to provide material and moral support and raise our voices, lest by our silence the structures of power assume our consent to the injustices being committed against rural peoples and communities. We bear witness that alternatives that are just and sustainable are being developed, despite enormous odds, by the shared efforts of rural communities in many countries and regions. The Church needs to renew and expand relationships with these communities and struggles and make common cause with them.

The Church possesses the lenses of the gospel and has the responsibility to bring moral and ethical scrutiny to social and economic policy. The Church must play a critical and essential role in evaluating economic policies for consistency with the Scripture and the Christian principles of justice.

Therefore, we call The United Methodist Church to respond as worshiping congregations and as institutions responsible for providing moral guidance and prophetic vision to society at large and to impoverished people, in particular:

1. At the congregational level, pastors must be better equipped to address the despair affecting rural people, by working closely with local organizers and grassroots organizations.
2. At the institutional level, The United Methodist Church should:
    a. work with universities in the United States in rural areas and reclaim land-grant colleges, including historically black and Indian tribal colleges, to promote the interests of small-scale farmers instead of agribusinesses;
    b. consider setting up an ecumenical fund to assist small farmers threatened with bankruptcy to keep their farms and assist them in engaging in sustainable farming practices;
    c. promote a culture and economy of sufficiency, conservation, and thrift for corporate and individual lifestyles as best models of stewardship of God's creation;
    d. advocate a process of public audits to call to accountability agribusinesses, banks and other financial institutions (including the international financial institutions), and trans-national corporations and call on them to remedy the negative impact of their policies and activities on rural communities;
    e. strengthen its partnership with farm and rural community-based organizations and networks to educate and engage members on critical policy issues, including agricultural subsidies, food and trade policies, economic justice, and the integrity of creation;
    f. accompany farm workers in their struggles to secure healthy living conditions, decent wages, and the right to organize, and to support rural grassroots organizations that work with them in these endeavors; and
    g. develop concrete programs to demonstrate its solidarity with and accompaniment of small-scale, minority, and indigenous producers to secure their rights to their land and the fullness of life promised by Jesus Christ.

ADOPTED 2004

See Social Principles, ¶ 162N.

175. Town and Country Ministry

WHEREAS, the 1996 General Conference mandated the development of a National Comprehensive Plan for Town and Country Ministry, under the direction of the General Board of Global Ministries; and,

WHEREAS, a task force was formed, which produced such a plan, titled *Born Again in Every Place: The National Comprehensive Plan for Town and Country Ministry of The United Methodist Church*, that has been presented to the General Conference of 2000 as part of the report of the General Board of Global Ministries; and,

WHEREAS, the National Comprehensive Plan as accepted and reported by the General Board of Global Ministries calls for the formation of an interagency implementation team to develop goals and strategies for the complete implementation of the plan by the whole church,

Therefore, be it resolved, that the 2000 General Conference direct the General Board of Global Ministries to allocate funds in sufficient amount to support the formation and work of the Implementation Team for the National Comprehensive Plan for Town and Country Ministry to its full completion, as intended by the original mandate; and,

Be it further resolved, that the General Conference strongly recommend to the General Board of Global Ministries that representation from the task force which developed the plan be included on the Implementation Team.

ADOPTED 2000

See Social Principles, ¶ 162.

176. Rural Life Sunday Theme

WHEREAS, the 1996 General Conference mandated and assigned the development of a National Comprehensive Plan for Town and Country Ministry for The United Methodist Church in the United States; and

WHEREAS, the 2000 General Conference adopted the "National Comprehensive Plan for Town and Country Ministry of The United Methodist Church: Report to the General Conference 2000"; and

WHEREAS, among the goals summarized in the National Comprehensive Plan for Town and Country Ministry was, "To strengthen the relations between town and country and urban worshiping congregations and their communities"; and

WHEREAS, an objective stated to meet the above goal in the National

Comprehensive Plan for Town and Country Ministry called for a celebration in a General Conference session using the Rural Life Sunday theme for that year;

Therefore be it resolved that, the 2008 General Conference celebrate in session the Rural Life Sunday theme for that year.

ADOPTED 2004

See Social Principles, ¶ 162N.

177. Rural Communities in Crisis

The United Methodist Church has long witnessed to rural peoples and their concerns. Each General Conference since 1940 has suggested responses for improving rural church and community life and the economic and environmental well-being of rural peoples. The 1988 General Conference accepted a study on U.S. Agriculture and Rural Communities in Crisis, yet the crisis continues. Today we reaffirm that historical study and call The United Methodist Church to continue its commitment to rural church ministry and advocacy for agricultural and rural community concerns.

Theological Statement: Land, People, and Justice

God is the owner of the land (Leviticus 25); thus it is a gift in covenant that involves the stewardship of keeping and tending the land for present and future generations. As God's creation, land must be regenerated that it may sustain life and be a place of joy. It is a common gift to all of life, requiring just patterns of its use.

Social, economic and ecological justice with regard to the use of land is central to biblical law. The land itself is to receive a rest every seven years (Leviticus 25:4). Voluntary charity or occasional care of the land is not enough. Israel's failure to follow the laws related to the land was counted a cause of their exile to Babylon (2 Chronicles 36:21). Care of the land and the rights of the poor and needy are at the center of the Law. Adequate food is considered an inherent right, such that the poor could eat grapes in a neighbor's vineyard or pluck grain when passing by a field (Deuteronomy 23:24-25). Land owners are urged not to be too efficient in their harvest (Leviticus 19:9-10), so that it is possible for the needy to glean the fields.

Indeed, the concept of equal access to community resources according to one's need formed the basis of the covenant the community was expected to embody. Caring for one's neighbor, especially a poor neighbor, is a religious obligation. Jesus both inherits and fulfills this tradition when he says the commandment to love one's neighbor as oneself is second only to the commandment to love God (Matthew 22:38-40).

The prophets viewed patterns of economic exploitation, social class consciousness, judicial corruption, political oppression, failing to care for the land, and exclusiveness as in opposition to God's desire for full life and wholeness for all (Amos 2-8; Isaiah 5:1-13; 58:3-7; Jeremiah 2:7-8; Hosea 4:1-3). Some would suggest that both the contemporary world and Israel under the monarchy came to worship "bigness" more than God.

Today, rural parts of our world suffer from many of the same maladies as ancient Israel. Land holdings are increasingly concentrated in the hands of fewer owners. People pursue material wealth as the solution to other spiritual and economic problems. Creation itself groans under a burden of eroding topsoil, toxic waste and polluted waters. Neither the land nor most of the people who work the land can celebrate the wholeness God intended.

The U.S. Farm Crisis

Agriculture is a major component in the U.S. economy. Through the production of goods and services, agriculture has added about $90 billion annually to the national economy from 1995 to 2000. About 18 percent of all civilian jobs are in agriculture and related input and marketing industries. In addition, the agricultural sector regularly has a positive balance of trade. Women and ethnic minorities, including African-Americans, Hispanics, Native Americans, and Asians, have contributed immensely to the country's food production.

The benefits of the agricultural economy are widely skewed. Agriculture is recognized as an inherently volatile industry, especially for family farmers.

The Crisis Affecting Agriculture Is:

1. The Loss of Family Farmers—Amid chronically difficult rural economics, the patterns of land ownership and control are ever less diverse. The U.S Department of Agriculture National Commission on

Small Farms reported in 1998 that there are 300,000 fewer farmers than in 1979, and farmers are receiving 13 percent less income for every consumer dollar spent. The loss of ethnic-owned and small-scale farms are even greater. Today there are 2.1 million farmers and ranchers. About 94 percent of U.S. farms are small, but they receive only 41 percent of all farm receipts. Most disappearing farms are family-sized units. A family farm is not defined by acreage but as an agricultural production unit and business in which the management, economic risk, and most of the labor (except in peak seasons) are provided by the family and from which the family receives a significant part, though not necessarily the majority, of its income. Family farms vary by region and commodity.

2. Increased Concentration and Corporate Agriculture—U.S. government policy choices have perpetuated the greater concentration of assets and wealth into fewer larger farms and agribusiness firms. Federal farm programs and tax policies have historically benefited large farms the most. Large farms that depend on hired farm workers receive exemptions from federal labor laws allowing them the advantage of low-wage costs. (See Resolution #236, "Rights of Farm Workers in the U. S.") The ownership and control over agricultural assets is increasingly concentrated in fewer and fewer hands. Factory farms have become the dominant method of raising meat in the United States. Four firms now control over 80 percent of the beef market. Farmers have little to no control over the prices set for their products. Many family farmers are caught in a web of contracts with large, vertically-integrated agribusiness conglomerates that dictate almost everything farmers do: erecting farm buildings, choosing feed, installing lighting. Emerging agricultural technologies use ever greater levels of capital to enable fewer people to produce food. As a result, income and opportunities have shifted from farms to the companies that produce and sell products to farmers. The dominant trend is a few, large, vertically-integrated firms controlling the majority of food and fiber products in an increasingly global processing and distribution system.

3. Farm Income—Net farm income and net farm operator household income are two measures of the relative ability of farmers to finance and sustain their farming operations and provide for their families. By either measure, it is apparent that the combination of plummeting commodity prices, high input expenses and production risks continue to threaten the economic sustainability of family farm-

ers. Without government farm programs and disaster assistance as a partial replacement for adequate commodity prices, even more producers would be forced off their farms.

4. Ecological Damage—Factory farms, especially those that produce livestock such as hogs, are poisoning their communities. These farms have taken root mainly where zoning laws were weak or nonexistent or in states that prohibited lawsuits against agricultural operations. The inevitable by-product of huge concentrations of animals is huge concentrations of manure that is stored in open lagoons. The water is eventually sprayed on farmland, although there is usually far more manure than local fields can absorb. In such quantities, manure becomes a toxic substance. Spills and groundwater contamination are always a risk as is airborne contamination of water from ammonia, which rises from the lagoons and falls into low-lying rivers and estuaries. More than five billion tons of topsoil is lost every year and the intensive use of pesticides results in more than 14 million Americans drinking water that routinely contains pesticides.

5. Pervasive Discrimination—African American and other racial ethnic farmers are even less likely than white farmers to benefit from any changes in the rural/farm economy. Surveys of Native American farmers suggest that their situation may be nearly as bleak. Farming is the leading occupation among Native Americans living on reservation lands. Asian and Hispanic Americans have historically been excluded from significant farm ownership. African Americans, Hispanics and Native Americans have not received fair and equitable service from the U.S. Department of Agriculture. The USDA has long tolerated discrimination in the distribution of program benefits and has misused its power to influence land ownership and farm profitability. Farm program regulations shut out racial ethnic farmers from the benefits that have helped larger white producers survive the changes in agriculture. The USDA remains insensitive to the needs of racial ethnic farmers and neglects its responsibility to reach out and serve all who need their services. (*See* Resolution #235, "Rights of African American Farmers.")

6. Trade—Trade agreements have brought few benefits to family farmers. Current trade negotiations fail to address the causes of and needs for the many types of practices that characterize agricultural trade: domestic food safety, security for all countries, agricultural commodity/supply demand imbalances that results in adequate

returns to producers, and the concentrated market power that exists among a limited number of agricultural market participants.

7. Biotechnology/Genetically Modified Organisms (GMOs)—The rapid introduction of commercial genetically engineered animals, seeds and crops with inadequate research, testing and regulation may cause unintended ecological, health, social, economic and cultural consequences. GMOs affect the entire food chain and pose an indirect threat to the future well-being of farmers and nations hoping to ensure food security. The majority of genetically engineered crops currently on the market are produced and marketed by large private companies seeking primarily to generate a return on shareholders' investments. Private control of genetically engineered agriculture, coupled with emerging global trade policies that protect the interests of patent rights holders, makes food systems more vulnerable to shifting global economic trends and threatens the sovereignty and very existence of local food systems. Non-segregated and unlabeled genetically engineered crops put farmers at risk of losing highly profitable markets, fail to protect the consumers from agricultural products whose safety is not yet proven, and deny consumers' the right to choose. Genetically engineered seeds and crops are promoted as a solution to world hunger and malnutrition. Moral, consumer and producer concerns, informed by independent scientific knowledge, need to be addressed.

Rural Community in Crisis

The rural United States today is a contrast between beauty and desecration, isolation and industrialization, wealth and poverty, power and oppression, freedom and exploitation, abundance and hunger, individualism and dependence. U.S. Census data and other sources count the overall rural poverty rate at 14.6 percent, while 33 percent of African Americans, 27 percent of Hispanics, and 30 percent of Native Americans in rural areas are poor. More children in rural areas live in poverty than children in urban areas. Of the 50 counties in the U.S. with the lowest per-capita income, only one is in a metropolitan area; of the other 49, many are very rural with income based on agriculture. For six years in a row (1996 to 2001), the people living in the great plains of the United States have had the lowest income regionally. Only 6.3 percent of rural Americans live on farms. Farming accounts for only 7.6 percent of rural employment, which is dominated by low wage industries. Rural incomes remain lower than the urban median. Among poor families, those in rural areas are more likely to be working poor.

Nearly 30 percent of non-metropolitan households—more than 6.2 million—have at least one major housing problem, most often the burden of cost (paying more than 30 percent of income for housing). A 2000 survey found eighth-graders in rural schools were 32 percent more likely than those in metropolitan areas to have used marijuana, 52 percent more likely to have used cocaine, 29 percent more likely to have used alcohol, and twice as likely to have smoked cigarettes. Rural residents tend to have poorer health care access, lower health insurance coverage, and little or no managed care availability. Rural communities have little or no public transportation.

Call for Change: What Needs to Be Done?

A. Local churches and annual conferences are called to:

1. Develop specific ministries to meet major needs that exist today in rural United States, including:
   a. taking responsibility for assisting with mending the brokenness of community life in rural society;
   b. strengthening their ministry and mission with rural churches and communities;
   c. lifting up the responsible stewardship of natural resources; and
   d. building bridges of understanding and partnership between rural, suburban and urban congregations and communities.
2. Place personnel strategically in order to respond to rural needs; insist that pastoral appointments be made with the needs of entire communities in mind, and not just the needs of the congregation.
3. Become public policy advocates, speaking out as a church, creating awareness and understanding, and bringing about positive change.
4. Be in partnership with seminaries to develop programs, including "teaching" parishes and internships, to equip ministers to serve in rural areas.
6. Develop programs to invest conference foundation funds in rural economic development needs.
7. Discover ways to enable the racial ethnic ownership of farmland.

B. The general church is called to:

1. Use its seminaries to prepare clergy to be more effective pastors in rural areas, using the "missionary training" model, knowing that many ministers not accustomed to rural life enter into areas where there is a new "language," a new lifestyle, a new culture.

2. Cooperate ecumenically and with other groups beyond the church to develop responses to the problems of rural areas.

3. Better learn the skills of personnel placement so that appointed ministers in rural areas will tenure long enough to build trusting, understanding relationships necessary for pastoring the community. Place more mission (and similar) personnel in rural ministries.

4. The General Board of Church and Society and the General Board of Global Ministries work with family farm organizations to address the crisis facing family farmers and rural communities and monitor agricultural genetically engineering developments and educate United Methodists of its impact on the food chain.

5. Recognize Rural Life Sunday as a special day in the church year, combining in the one day the emphases of Rural Life Sunday, Soil Stewardship Day, Earth Day, World Environment Day, and Rogation Sunday.

C. Federal legislators and administrators, as they develop farm and rural policies, are called to:

1. Develop national agricultural policies that enable farmers to significantly increase net farm income, improve the quality of rural life and increase the number of family farmers so that farmers may continue to provide a reliable supply of food and fiber and serve as stewards of the nation's resources. These new policies would:
    a. reverse the loss of family farms;
    b. ensure a fair price at the marketplace;
    c. provide credit to family farmers at affordable interest rates;
    d. develop a marketing and government support system that will guarantee the cost of production to farm families;
    e. initiate participatory democratic processes with farmers to determine if mandatory production goals, which would discourage overproduction of some commodities, are needed to move toward a balance between supply and demand;
    f. reform government payments to benefit family farmers, rather than large corporate and wealthy farming interests;

g. create programs that would enable new families to enter farming as a vocation;

h. create incentives for family farmers to shift from current production-oriented modes to a sustainable and regenerative agriculture;

i. ensure the participation of family farmers regardless of race and sex; and

j. implement the recommendations of the reports National Commission on Small Farms and the Civil Rights at the United States Department of Agriculture.

2. Discourage concentration in ownership and control of land and money and move toward land reforms that broaden ownership of land by stronger anti-trust laws and enforcement, a ban on corporate meatpacker ownership of livestock, and create safeguards and amend laws for growers involved in contract agriculture to give them the bargaining power they need to demand fair contracts.

3. Require soil and water conservation practices as well as increased funding for farm operations that participate in federal programs; include farmers in the planning of such requirements and the enforcement of national organic standards.

4. Reform federal tax laws to remove unfair competition and discourage tax shelter-motivated capital in agriculture.

5. Maintain an emphasis on direct loan activity, resist attempts to reduce the level of direct loans in favor of guarantees, and increase the Limited Resources Loan program for qualified farmers.

6. Provide for commodity reserves, isolated from the market, to be established at a level adequate to protect consumers from supply disruption and meet domestic agricultural disaster and global humanitarian food aid requirements.

7. Ensure that most federally-supported programs of research and education in agriculture focus on small and medium-sized family farm operations, with special attention paid to racial ethnic farmers, and that county committees, which administer these programs, be inclusive of women and racial ethnic farmers.

8. Fund major new research initiatives and programs through the federal land grant institutions, including black land grant colleges, to ensure the development of long-term, sustainable, and regenerative agriculture.

9. Develop farm policies that will encourage farm-owned and controlled businesses and cooperatives for processing, distributing, and marketing farm products.

10. Develop policies that will respect the guaranteed land and water rights of all racial ethnic peoples.

11. Develop and support programs in cooperation with community-based organizations and cooperatives to improve the quality of life in depressed rural areas, with attention given to health care, transportation, education, employment, value-added agriculture, law enforcement, housing, job training, and environmental protection.

12. Develop national and regional water and energy policies that assure that those who benefit from energy and water projects pay a substantial portion of those costs.

13. Recognize and protect the right of farm workers to organize into unions of their own choosing, to be covered by minimum wage laws, and to receive adequate benefits, including social security, health care, and unemployment.

14. Develop a fair trade policy that stabilizes domestic markets, ensures consumer access to an adequate, safe and affordable food supply, discourages dumping[1], allows all countries to develop farm programs that provide fair prices, reduces agricultural subsidies by rich countries, and respects each country's needs and traditions for food security, policies on the importation of genetically modified food, conservation of natural resources, and fair distribution of economic opportunity.

15. Prohibit the importation of produce containing residues of pesticides or other chemicals that are banned for U.S. producers, and revise permitted residue levels when the pesticide is banned.

16. Seek out international cooperation in developing an international food policy.

17. Address GMOs/genetically engineered agriculture by prohibiting patents and exclusive rights to products and processes by companies and individuals that are in the public domain; ensuring that protecting the reward system for innovations does not impede the distribution of the necessities of life; not requiring a country to import genetically engineered seeds and crops; and requiring truthful and accurate labeling so that dietary needs and nutritional considerations can be attended to and, if warranted, epidemiological studies can be done.

1. Dumping: The intentional export of goods priced below the cost of production leading to a disruption of global markets. However the power of participation in decision making should be weighted to local participation due to local community relationships and local risks rather than to economic or political centers of power.

Three Ethical Guidelines

Food is not merely another market commodity. Food is essential to life and is sacred culturally to all people. We can change the direction of U.S. agriculture and rural development, but we need guidelines. A preferred agriculture must have three attributes:

1. It must be just. A just society and a just agriculture provide the means whereby people can share in the inheritance of the earth so that all life can fully be maintained in freedom and community. The purpose of a just agriculture should be for the maintenance and renewal of the necessary resources for food, clothing, and shelter, for now and for the future.

2. It must be participatory. For agriculture to be just, everyone has the right to be consulted. Participation in society and in the ongoing process of creation is the necessary condition for justice. Participation requires recognition of everyone's right to be consulted and understood, regardless of that person's economic, political, or social status.

Participation is not possible without power. In such decision-making, everyone has the right to be consulted about such issues as expenditures for armaments, nuclear power, forms of employment, social services, and so forth.

3. It must be sustainable. A sustainable agriculture is one where the idea of permanent carrying capacity is maintained, where yields (agriculture, energy production, forestry, water use, industrial activity) are measured by whether or not they are sustainable rather than by the criteria of yields per acre or profits. In a sustainable agriculture, waste products can be absorbed back into the ecosystem without damage.

A just, participatory, and sustainable agriculture would meet basic human needs for food and fiber, regenerate and protect ecosystems, be economically viable, enhance the quality of life for farm families, be supportive of rural communities, be socially just, and be compatible with spiritual teachings that recognize the earth as a common heritage and responsibility. For Christians, the idea of sustainability flows directly from the biblical call to human beings to be stewards of God's creation.

ADOPTED 2004

See Social Principles, ¶ 162N.

178. Accessible and Affordable Leadership Training

WHEREAS, the 2000 General Conference adopted the "National Comprehensive Plan for Town and Country Ministry of The United Methodist Church: Born Again in Every Place"; and

WHEREAS, among the goals summarized in the National Comprehensive Plan for Town and Country Ministry was "To Recognize, train and utilize lay leadership in town and country ministries"; and

WHEREAS, also among the goals summarized in the National Comprehensive Plan for Town and Country Ministry was "To Provide effective pastoral leadership for all town and country churches"; and

WHEREAS, the foundational study that lead to the development of the National Comprehensive Plan for Town and Country Ministry found that "The laity made two overwhelming appeals to the connectional system: 1) 'provide us with training and resources appropriate to town and country situations,' and 2) 'listen to us about matters affecting church life and potential in our communities'"; and

WHEREAS, "one of the most critical issues facing the church is the quality of pastoral leadership"; and

WHEREAS, town and country churches are best served by pastors who are sensitive and understand the nature of town and country ministries and are adequately supervised; and

WHEREAS, the distances to educational facilities and training make it difficult for many clergy and laity to take advantage of and receive adequate training;

Therefore, be it resolved, that the General Board of Discipleship and conference agencies responsible for lay training and leadership develop distance learning, internet options, and other methods to recognize, train, and utilize lay leadership in ways that are accessible, affordable, and context appropriate to town and country settings, and

Be it further resolved, that United Methodist agencies, seminaries, Course of Study schools, licensing schools and other avenues of preparing pastoral leadership further develop accessible, affordable, and context appropriate methods that will prepare those appointed or assigned to understand the culture of town and country communities in order to serve more effectively in those settings.

ADOPTED 2004

See Social Principles, ¶ 162N.

179. Support and Protection of Rural People

WHEREAS, rural people, rural communities and rural congregations are of great value in God's creation and have many gifts and strengths to share with the world community; and

WHEREAS, farming, ranching, other agricultural endeavors, trucking, migrant work, timbering, recreation, fishing and river work, rural factories, and small businesses of numerous kinds, as elements of rural life, undergird the economy of the world; and

WHEREAS, rural people contribute to the abundance of our world economy, but often do not receive benefits commensurate with their efforts; and

WHEREAS, developments in communication technology and improved transportation systems have done much to eliminate problems of isolation and distance in some parts of the world, while further isolating people from each other in other parts of the world; and

WHEREAS, the health and well-being of God's creation rests upon the vitality of our worldwide rural people who are caretakers of the land, water, and air; and

WHEREAS, The United Methodist Church, recognizing the sacredness of creation care, has a long history of ministry within rural places throughout the world;

Therefore be it resolved, that The United Methodist Church, as it is in ministry in rural places, affirms that:

1. rural residents around the world deserve the option of living and prospering in the communities where they live, and the goals and policies of the governments that relate to rural places should provide this option;

2. rural people around the world deserve a sense of purpose and authentic hope, equitable and continuing spiritual care; satisfying economic opportunity to meet basic needs for food, clothing, and shelter; nurture and protection for children and youth; security for the elderly and those who abilities are challenged; equitable access to affordable health care and education; and opportunities for recreation and spiritual renewal;

3. as stewards of creation, rural people around the world have a right to determine how land, water, air, and other resources within their communities, especially in areas of limited population, are to be used, with particular attention given to land use and control being

exercised by all who live within an area and/or own land within a given area while respecting the legal rights of owners of real property.

ADOPTED 2004

See Social Principles, ¶ 162N.

URBAN ISSUES

180. Holy Boldness: Reaffirming a National Plan for Urban Ministry

As United Methodists, our biblical and Wesleyan heritage calls us to transform urban churches and communities with holy boldness. A comprehensive urban-ministry plan called Holy Boldness sets forth a vision, goal areas, and outcomes to organize and resource congregations and church-based community organizations for transforming urban and suburban congregations and communities through the gospel of Jesus Christ.

Holy Boldness is a grassroots movement that empowers congregations and church-based organizations to develop local strategies for urban ministry. Its objective is to work within present structures and existing resources to leverage new opportunities for urban ministry.

In support and acknowledgment of the valuable role of Holy Boldness in the life of the church, the General Conference of The United Methodist Church reaffirms the Holy Boldness plan and:

1. commends the ministry of urban churches and church-based organizations that share the gospel of Jesus Christ through prophetic vision and proclaiming God's Word;

2. urges more congregations and church-based organizations to become covenanting partners with the Holy Boldness Urban Ministry Plan and work toward developing and carrying out local strategies that address Holy Boldness goal areas: contextual urban theology, urban evangelism, leadership development, community economic development, eradication of racism, strengthening multicultural relationships, and health and healing;

3. urges the General Board of Church and Society and the General Board of Global Ministries to support public policy initiatives based on the goals of Holy Boldness;

4. mandates the general church agencies' staff having responsibility for urban concerns and/or the general secretary's designee(s) from Religion and Race, Discipleship, Global Ministries, Communications, Higher Education and Ministry, Council on Ministries, and Church and Society, and a representative from the Council of Bishops to work together to develop collaborative agency strategies for resourcing as well as to review existing resources that may be channeled for the Holy Boldness Urban Ministry Plan; and

5. charges the designated representative staff of the previously cited general church agencies to work with the Office of Urban Ministries of the General Board of Global Ministries to report to the 2004 General Conference on the effectiveness of the Holy Boldness Urban Ministry Plan's ability to:

    a. organize and mobilize congregations and church-based organizations to accomplish local church and community transformation, and

    b. evaluate the effectiveness of collaboration within the general church agencies to resource and enable the plan to be carried out in local urban contexts.

Holy Boldness: A National Urban Ministry Plan

Change is inevitable, but transformation is optional. As The United Methodist Church, we have the opportunity to transform urban churches and communities with holy boldness. The Holy Boldness plan is not an exact plan, but a dynamic tool for organizing and mobilizing people for urban transformation. It recognizes that there are regional and local differences and invites churches and church-based community organizations to develop local strategies to carry out the Holy Boldness goals.

Goal Areas

The goal areas identified for this plan were determined through a national survey of laity, pastors, church-related community-organization staff, conference staff, and bishops. The plan does not presume to address every urban church and community need, but it is a first step toward organizing and mobilizing United Methodists to work locally on goals for church and community transformation. The goal areas are:

1. Urban theology;
2. Urban evangelism and congregational development;
3. Eradicating racism and other forms of oppression;
4. Developing and strengthening multicultural relationships;
5. Community economic development;
6. Leadership development; and
7. Wholeness, healing, and health.

Asset-Based

While there are serious urban problems inside and outside the church, transformation is possible through the resources and strengths of the church and community. The Holy Boldness plan calls for churches and communities to identify their assets and build on these assets as people are mobilized for transformation. Some of the assets are:

1. God's transforming power through Jesus Christ;
2. The local church and church-based community organizations;
3. The people in churches and cities who represent a wide variety of racial and ethnic traditions and have the talents for transformation;
4. United Methodist general agencies and schools; and
5. Ecumenical and interfaith partners.

Congregation-Based

As a church, we are blessed with congregations, church-related community organizations, and institutions that seek to transform urban communities. All are important to the life of urban communities and will be challenged to work toward the goals of the Urban Plan. The plan calls for a significant focus on local urban congregations that are in need of development, are strategically located, and have the opportunity to share God's love in word and deed. If the church is to transform communities, the local church is critical.

Collaborative Effort

Urban transformation requires a collaborative effort by local churches working in cooperation with other denominations, community organizations, businesses, and governmental institutions. Collaboration will need to continue to occur beyond city limits by collaborating with suburban and central city churches that have committed volunteers, resources and relational roots in inner-city neighborhoods, and with exurbia churches that share similar problems, all of which strengthen ministry.

Collaboration will also need to continue to occur at the national level. General church agencies working together to identify common strategies can realize mutual accomplishments. The national strategies should link with local strategies and needs. National collaboration must also involve other ecumenical and interfaith bodies and national urban resources.

Covenant-Inspired

The Urban Plan invites people, churches, church-based community organizations, and church agencies to covenant to work toward the established goals. Churches and organizations will continue to review the plan and make a commitment to work toward the goals in their setting. Covenanting churches and groups will continue to become part of a nationwide network for support, idea development, and resourcing. Hundreds of churches and church-related organizations/agencies will be invited to covenant to work toward the plan's goals.

Holy Boldness

Churches and church-related community organizations will continue to be encouraged to take authority and responsibility in being bold and holy to accomplish the Urban Ministry Plan goals. This will continue to require local strategies and local ownership. With God's help, transformation of urban congregations and communities is possible.

United Methodist Urban Ministry Vision

The United Methodist Church must practice "holy boldness" in urban areas as evidenced by the church:

1. risking all we have to share God's transforming love as experienced through Jesus Christ in both word and deed;
2. ministering with and among the poor;
3. transforming and developing urban congregations;

4. celebrating and honoring diversity within the congregation, church-related organizations, agencies, and the community;

5. living and proclaiming God's justice and equality in every situation without fear of being isolated and ridiculed;

6. being an agent for healing in the midst of broken lives and communities; and

7. effectively developing the spiritual, social, and physical well-being of individuals and communities.

Goals

Urban Theology—Urban leaders must:

1. teach within churches and church-related organizations, and be examples in the community that urban ministry is based in the person, ministry, and stories of Jesus Christ, who provided an example of meeting the physical needs of others and proclaiming the saving power of God;

2. expand the urban academy with a strong urban theology component, as well as practical components for carrying out our theology in the world through community development, eliminating racism, strengthening multicultural relationships, urban evangelism, leadership development; and

3. encourage congregations to model a theology that serves all people and focuses on the poor and marginalized.

Urban Evangelism and Congregational Development:

The United Methodist Church must:

1. develop the necessary support and systems to enable longer pastoral appointments;

2. design resources and training to help congregations communicate the gospel of Jesus Christ effectively in a diverse and changing urban environment;

3. use existing resources and develop new resources for urban congregational Bible study to deepen people's faith and challenge them to live the gospel;

4. develop a prayer network that links churches in partnerships (this can include urban churches with suburban or exurbia churches); and

5. increase the number of worshipers in urban congregations through evangelism and outreach to the neighborhood in which the church is located and other community networks.

Eradicating Racism and Other Forms of Oppression:

The United Methodist Church must:

1. oganize local and national support systems for those willing to risk pursuing the vision and agenda of eliminating racism;

2. highlight model programs that challenge and work toward eradicating racism and other forms of oppression in the congregation and the community so that other congregations can develop similar efforts; and

3. be sensitive to racism in all urban training experiences.

Developing and Strengthening Multicultural Relationships:

1. develop the resources for, and encourage congregations to participate in, cultural immersion and cross-cultural experiences; and

2. design new and use existing church resources for the arts, music, worship, and Bible study that model, encourage, and strengthen multiculturalism.

Community Economic Development:

The United Methodist Church must:

1. continue and further expand the Communities of Shalom Initiative as a holistic strategy for developing communities and strengthening congregations;

2. provide training and technical assistance to help churches engage in systemic change and community economic development by working with an existing community-development corporation or by starting a community-development corporation where necessary;

3. assist churches in learning how they can raise additional dollars for community development from sources outside the church;

4. assist congregations in utilizing their buildings for community economic development and outreach; and

5. continue to support the national United Methodist community-development loan fund that helps United Methodist congregations and individuals invest money for community development through churches.

Leadership Development:

The United Methodist Church must:

1. expand the Hispanic Plan model of lay missioner for urban leadership;

2. empower laity and clergy for ministry and mission by educating them to work through the structure of The United Methodist Church;

3. continue training lay and clergy leadership for urban ministry, including advocacy and effective change in public and private life; and

4. intentionally recruit more clergy and laity for urban ministry and offer them opportunities to be involved in "hands-on" experiences.

Wholeness, Healing, and Health:

The United Methodist Church must:

1. increase the understanding of how people are marginalized and what can be done to develop wholeness, healing, and health;

2. assist congregations in developing a comprehensive understanding of how they can be healing agents in their neighborhoods and bring about a healthy community;

3. challenge congregations and agencies to develop ways to improve the spiritual, social, and physical well-being of individuals and communities;

4. communicate through the Holy Boldness network models of ministry with the homeless, the hungry, people who are HIV-positive, individuals who are physically and mentally ill, victims of violence, and people with addictions; and

5. publicize successful models where spiritual development by congregations and/or community organizations has brought about wholeness, healing, and health in urban settings.

ADOPTED 1996
AMENDED AND READOPTED 2000

See Social Principles, ¶ 162P.

181. Special Emphasis for Ministries Within Major Urban Centers

WHEREAS, the Christian church—and the Methodist movement—began in city communities; and

459

WHEREAS, a majority of the world's population now lives in cities for the first time in history; and

WHEREAS, the fastest-growing populations in the United States are among the Asian, Hispanic, and African American people; and

WHEREAS, The United Methodist Church has a deep commitment to build ministry among the poor and the marginalized; and

WHEREAS, there are high concentrations of human needs, and incidences of human injustice within the communities of our cities;

Therefore be it resolved, that the United Methodist Church continue a special emphasis on ministry within our major urban centers by:

1. incorporating intentional, multiracial ministry;
2. implementing outreach and inclusion within the local church congregational life;
3. evangelizing the poor and oppressed;
4. providing strong pastoral and lay leadership;
5. increasing the financial and human resources available for ministry in our cities;
6. uniting our Methodist families—the African Methodist Episcopal Church, the African Methodist Episcopal Zion Church, the Christian Methodist Episcopal Church, and The United Methodist Church—to make one powerful Methodist voice and presence in our cities; and
7. leading the way for ecumenical and interfaith initiatives to revitalize the communities.

Be it further resolved, that each general agency and each jurisdictional conference take appropriate steps to implement this ongoing initiative.

ADOPTED 2004

See Social Principles, ¶162P.

VIOLENCE

182. Acts of Hate

The world has been inundated with acts of hate in recent years. Persons from around the world have lashed out in anger and fear, persecuting those whom they see as different, such as:

- in the United States—Jasper, Texas, a Black man was dragged to his death behind a truck by white drivers; and
- in Wyoming—a gay student was viciously attacked and left to die; and
- in countries such as Kosovo, Rwanda and others—genocide and ethnic cleansing.

Thousands of stories appear around the world in the media where persons have acted out of fear and bigotry to harm others emotionally, physically, and/or spiritually. Jesus said: "Love your enemies, do good to those who hate you, bless those who curse you, pray for those who abuse you" (Luke 6:27 NRSV). Instead of taking lives, we are called as Christian people "to lay down our lives for one another" (1 John 3:16 NRSV). We must be willing to walk into the houses of sin and eradicate the sin that tears lives apart.

That is why we as United Methodists must stand in direct opposition to any person or group that would choose to harm another individual's life, liberty, property, or family. We must unite around the world to make a Christian witness that acts against persons because of their national origin, religion, gender, age, race, or sexual orientation will not be tolerated. We will then "Commit ourselves to be in ministry for and with all persons" (¶ 161G, Social Principles).

Therefore, be it resolved, that the General Conference of The United Methodist Church reaffirms its historical commitment not to tolerate acts of hate inside or outside the church. The church shall respond to the victims and the perpetrators of these acts with compassion as witnessed in Jesus Christ. We oppose any and all acts of hate, or attempts to make people feel of less worth, fear for their well-being, or lose spiritual presence in their lives.

Further, be it resolved, that The United Methodist Church, with assistance from the appropriate boards, agencies, and local churches continue to educate:

- Christians on faithful responses to acts of hate;
- children and youth on the sins of hate and bigotry through Sunday School materials, United Methodist Youth Fellowship resources, and special projects that are done in several languages;
- seminary students and clergy on the trends of hate in the world and how the church can faithfully prevent and respond to acts of hate; and

- all persons in The United Methodist Church about the sins of hatred and bigotry that have been committed in our United Methodist Church against our members and against those with whom we seek to minister.

Be it further resolved, that the members of The United Methodist Church:

- be active participants in civic or religious organizations that promote unity and diversity and work to eradicate acts of hate;
- take strong nonviolent action in opposition to hate groups;
- work to fulfill a ministry to those individuals who would choose to be a part of hate groups and show them the compassion and saving grace of Jesus Christ;
- promote diversity dialogue and programs in all churches, annual conferences, central conferences, general agencies, campus ministry units, and any other place where The United Methodist Church has a witness;
- enlist the various boards and agencies to work together to create a Mediation Team Resource Kit that focuses on hate mediation for distribution to local churches and annual conferences; and
- support a restorative-justice response to hate crimes, which aims at dialogue, accountability, and healing between victims and offenders rather than at adding more punishment of offenders if their crime was motivated by hate.

ADOPTED 2000

See Social Principles, ¶ 162A.

183. Expressing Grief for Acts of Violence

WHEREAS, violence permeates our society, perpetrated by those who hurt others because of the color of their skin, their sexual orientation, their religious identity, or no reason at all; and

WHEREAS, violence exists in many nations including but not limited to Northern Ireland, the former Yugoslavia, Israel, Palestinian-controlled territories, Iraq, Liberia, Myanmar, Pakistan, Afghanistan, Sudan, West Timor, and the Russian federation where "ethnic cleansing," deportations, tyrannical rulers, religious intolerance, war, and civil unrest scar the lives of millions and have resulted in despicable acts of murder and genocide; and

WHEREAS, The United Methodist Church grieves over this violence;

Therefore, be it resolved, that The United Methodist Church be in ministry to our grieving communities. Our congregations shall include avenues for young people to share joys, concerns, fears, and aspirations in a violence-free environment. Our Council of Bishops shall express a voice of hope for our nation, working with members of Congress, the President, and state governments to support funding for programming that gives youth alternatives to violence and criminal activity.

Be it further resolved, that United Methodist congregations, youth and campus ministries and church agencies promote opportunities where we may be a witness to a grieving nation, helping to heal wounds of violence in our communities, witnessing through work groups, Bible studies, community outreach, prayer and involvement in ecumenical and interfaith groups and coalitions.

Be it further resolved, that the United Methodist Council of Bishops and the leaders of our pan-Methodist family express a voice of hope for those who suffer from violence throughout the world community, and that the bishops act as beacons of light, working with the United Nations and leaders of national states to bring about more peace and justice in our global community.

Be it further resolved, that we as United Methodists and individuals within the global community seek to reconcile the violence found within our own hearts, seek forgiveness for the injustices we ourselves have committed to each other, our friends and family, and the larger community. Whether it be our actions or our thoughts, our words or our deeds, our voice or our silence, if we have done wrong, we seek forgiveness. We pray for mercy as we seek to walk more humbly with our God, with our families and friends, with our communities, and with ourselves.

Be it further resolved, that we United Methodists express our grief for the broken covenants of the church, both in The United Methodist Church and the church universal; we define a broken covenant as being actions that we may have committed in the name of faith that have locked persons out of relationships with Jesus Christ and the church, whether it be because of differences, prejudices, or through ignorance. We seek forgiveness for acts of violence committed in the name of faith.

We accept the call of our living God as presented in Scripture, in Micah 6:8, where God's requirements are presented: "He has shown you, O man, what is good. And what does the Lord require of you? To do justly, and to love mercy, and to walk humbly with your God." As we grieve we know that Jesus Christ calls us to rise up and to minister to a broken community that it may heal and that we may one day live in a community free from violence.

ADOPTED 2000

See Social Principles, ¶ 162A.

184. Hate Crimes

WHEREAS, hate crimes result from the intentional selection of victims or property as the object of violence because of the actual or perceived race, color, religion, national origin, ethnicity, gender, disability, or sexual orientation of the individual victim or owners of the property; and

WHEREAS, the national climate in the past decade has resulted in the increased public attention to hate crimes as evidenced by the Midwest killing spree by Benjamin Smith, the dragging death of James Byrd in Jasper, Texas, the killings and injuries at Columbine High School in Littleton, Colorado, the burning and defacing of churches and synagogues and countless other incidents throughout the United States which have not received widespread public attention; and

WHEREAS, hate crimes have increasingly involved children, youth and young adults as perpetrators and victims thereby causing intense stresses on family units, schools, and churches; and

WHEREAS, the eradication of hate crimes will intrinsically impact the challenge for the church and society to eliminate hatred and bigotry;

Therefore, be it resolved, that The United Methodist Church accept and move to implement the following recommendations:

General church:

- renew the church's stand and commitment against hate crimes in any form and in any place.

The United Methodist Church through its agencies:

- encourage law-enforcement personnel to maintain records on hate crimes and to bring to justice the perpetrators of such violence and intimidation;
- support hearings on hate crimes, particularly in those states where statistics reveal an increase in the activity of the Ku Klux Klan and other hate groups; and
- support congressional hearings when there are allegations of government involvement or negligence exacerbating such violence.

Annual conference/districts:

- call every annual conference to develop specific plans which will enable local churches to respond to hate group activities;
- develop support group(s) for persons active in antiracism strategies and for persons ministering to victims of hate crimes.

Local churches:

- recommend that a response team to deal with hate crime and violence in church and society be established by cabinets and bishops (compare with Eastern Pennsylvania model). Attention should be given to providing resources and assistance with children, youth, and young adults in churches, schools, and family units.

Individuals:

- should not be silent. If you are subject to an act of bigotry or racial violence, tell someone. Tell your family, your friends, neighbors, the church; seek support for yourself. Report the incident to police. Insist that the crime be reported as a "hate crime."

ADOPTED 2000

See Social Principles, ¶ 162A and G.

185. Hate Crimes in the United States

The United Methodist Church has a long history of addressing social issues related to race and gender. Today, addressing these issues requires that we deal with the increasing incidents of hate crimes.

Ku Klux Klan, Christian Identity groups, Neo-Nazis, and other hate groups initiate people into their groups by requiring them to do acts of hate, such as assaulting racial-ethnic people, beating or killing persons perceived to be homosexual, desecrating synagogues, and burning churches with racial-ethnic or multicultural membership. Hundreds of churches and synagogues have been burned or vandalized in recent years. Race-based hate crimes have targeted all racial, ethnic, and religious groups and immigrants. Assaults against people perceived to be gay or lesbian are increasing at alarming rates and are characterized by particular viciousness.

But it is not just hate groups who perpetrate such crimes. According to a recent study by the American Psychological Association,"most hate crimes are carried out by otherwise law-abiding young people who see little wrong with their actions. Alcohol and drugs sometimes help fuel these crimes, but the main determinant appears to be personal prejudice . . . such prejudice is most likely rooted in an environment that disdains someone who is 'different' or sees that difference as threatening." According to The White House Conference on Hate Crimes report, "teenagers and young adults account for a significant proportion of the country's hate crimes—both as perpetrators and victims." Children are not born with hatred; they are taught hatred. We, as part of society, have a responsibility to condemn hate and violence and to teach our children not to hate.

The United Methodist Church must be proactive in resisting hate and teaching young people and all members how to live in our diverse social world without passively accepting the rise of hate and bigotry. When church members do nothing about hate language or horrifying atrocities, such as the murders of James Bird and Matthew Shepherd, and have not actively taught tolerance, we participate in the social support of hate.

Resolutions that address such issues are not new to United Methodists. More than one hundred references in *The Book of Resolutions of The United Methodist Church* address various aspects of our commitment to the elimination of racism in all its forms. In particular, the 1996 resolution, "Global Racism: A Violation of Human

Rights," states that United Methodists will "work in coalition with secular groups to monitor and actively combat the activities of hate groups, extremist groups, and militia groups in the United States and other parts of the world" (*The Book of Resolutions of The United Methodist Church, 1996*, page 256).

Although The United Methodist Church is in conflict over the place of gay and lesbian people in the church, there is agreement that in the larger society, sexual orientation is not grounds for revoking human rights. In the "Social Principles" of *The Book of Discipline*, it states that "certain basic human rights and civil liberties are due all persons. We are committed to supporting those rights and liberties for homosexual persons. . . . Moreover, we support efforts to stop violence and other forms of coercion against gays and lesbians" (¶ 162H).

Violence, hate, and civil rights violations go against the long heritage of United Methodist commitment to justice for all persons. Today, it is increasingly apparent that such commitment must be translated into action in new ways.

Therefore, be it resolved, that The United Methodist Church, through its general boards, agencies, and other appropriate structures will:

1. provide biblically based resources that address hate crimes and intolerance for both young people and adults;

2. create resources to help United Methodists analyze the language of intolerance among groups that use religious language and emotionally charged images;

3. organize letter writing campaigns and denominational and ecumenical delegations to meet with government officials to advocate for passage, funding, and implementation of strong hate crimes laws and for holding congressional hearings on hate crimes;

4. fund local, community-based networks which educate for tolerance and provide support for the victims of hate crimes;

5. track hate crimes through news media and other sources to provide information to the Women's Division and General Board of Global Ministries who work in partnership with other organizations tracking hate crimes to expand a national data base of such incidents;

6. engage in a media campaign to promote tolerance and report hate crimes. Monitor, respond to, and support media that promote tolerance while challenging programs that teach hate, stereotypes, prejudice and/or bigotry;

7. educate members that silence equals complicity with hate. When jokes, disparagements, stereotypes, or references to violence based on

identity or status pass without response, we participate in the growing culture of intolerance, hate, and violence;

8. research, organize, and advocate for local, state, and national hate crime laws that include any crimes committed based upon race, ethnicity, culture, status, religion, sexual orientation, gender, age, disability, and/or class;

9. support legislation that protects the civil rights of all persons;

10. work with ecumenical and interfaith groups to create worship resources and to hold worship services for tolerance;

11. work with diverse grassroots and national organizations to create joint strategies and actions to address hate crimes;

12. work through local organizations and local schools to review policies and training programs related to various forms of discrimination and sexual harassment based on gender and perceived sexual identity;

13. contact all governors urging that they appoint a task force to investigate hate crimes at state levels; and

14. encourage The United Methodist Church all over the world to engage in efforts to address hate-based activities in ways appropriate to their particular context.

ADOPTED 2000

See Social Principles, ¶ 162A and G.

186. Violence Against Women and Children

The deafening and disabling silence that has surrounded the abuse of women and children is being broken. We now know that overwhelming numbers of women and children in our churches and communities are being battered, raped, emotionally and psychologically abused, and physically and sexually assaulted. The abuse occurs in communities of every racial composition and every economic status, in rural areas as well as cities, in families adhering to every religion and to no religion. Silence will no longer shield us from our complicity in the violence nor from our failure to overcome it.

The Social Principles of The United Methodist Church affirm the family as "the basic human community through which persons are nurtured and sustained in mutual love, responsibility, respect, and fidelity." Clearly violence and abuse cannot be tolerated within such an understanding. The Social Principles are explicit: "We recognize that family violence and abuse in all its forms—verbal, psychological, physical, sexual—is detrimental to the covenant of the human community. We encourage the Church to provide a safe environment, counsel and support for the victim. While we deplore the actions of the abuser, we affirm that person to be in need of God's redeeming love."

We acknowledge the ways in which misinterpretation and misuse of Christian Scriptures and traditions have contributed to violence against women and children, and to the guilt, self-blame, and suffering which victims experience, and to the rationalizations used by those who abuse. A reexamination of those misused passages can help us reclaim traditions in ways that support victims and challenge abuse in the family.

Stories of violence against women and children are so common that we scarcely notice them, even in the Bible. Yet, they are there. Women, only a few of them even named, are abused, rejected, and raped by brothers, husbands, and strangers. Daughters are traded and sacrificed. A concubine wife is sliced into pieces by the master who traded her body for his own safety. Yet even this last, most violent story, in Judges 19, cannot be used to justify abuse for it ends with this command: "Consider it, take counsel and speak" (vs. 30). It is the silence, the unwillingness to acknowledge the horror, which leaves victims isolated, protects perpetrators, and thwarts healing. We are commanded to break the silence, to give credence to the stories, to be agents of wholeness and justice.

Jesus' concern for the victim is seen in the story of the Good Samaritan (Luke 10:25-37). By concluding this parable with the words, "Go and do likewise," Jesus indicates that we are to receive all people who have been violated or abused, who are weak or vulnerable, with particular compassion and caring. Jesus made it clear that meeting a legalistic obligation is not enough; we must go beyond the letter of the law in reaching out to comfort and assist those who have been harmed.

The church must re-examine the theological messages it communicates in light of the experiences of victims of domestic violence and sexual abuse. We must treat with extreme care the important, but often-misused, concepts of suffering, forgiveness, and the nature of marriage and the family.

Situations of violence and abuse exist in families in virtually every congregation; tragically, no church or community is exempt. As part of a research project conducted by the Ministries with Women, Children and Families program of the General Board of Global Ministries, pastors who had asserted their conviction that there were no families experiencing violence or abuse in their congregations were asked to mention the issues from the pulpit, using words like battering, rape, incest and child abuse. All those who reported related that members subsequently came to them with current stories of abuse in their families. Clearly, church families are not immune, and many are waiting for a signal that these concerns are appropriate ones with which to share and struggle in the community of faith.

The church is challenged to listen to the stories of victims and survivors and to seek information and guidance that will lead to wiser and more effective ways to minister with persons who experience domestic violence and sexual abuse. The church must be a refuge for people who are hurting, and it is an entirely appropriate place for these issues to be addressed. Many congregations are finding ways to demonstrate that the church is a place where people can feel confident in turning to first, not last, for comfort and healing.

People of faith should take the lead in calling for a just response by the community in the face of domestic violence and sexual abuse. Justice-making involves several steps: righteous anger; compassion for the victim; advocacy for the victim; holding the offender legally and spiritually accountable for his or her sin against the victim and the community; treatment for the offender; and prevention of further abuse by addressing the societal roots and not merely the symptoms of violence and abuse.

Policy Statements and Actions

The United Methodist Church affirms the sacredness of all persons and their right to safety, nurture and care. It names domestic violence and sexual abuse as sins and pledges to work for their eradication. The church commits itself to listen to the stories of battered spouses, rape victims, abused children, adult survivors of child sexual abuse, and all others who are violated and victimized. The church further commits itself to provide leadership in responding with justice and compassion to the presence of domestic violence and sexual abuse among its membership and within the community at large.

The following actions are commended to local congregations:

1. Create a church climate of openness, acceptance, and safety that encourages victims to speak of their pain and seek relief and healing.

2. Encourage all clergy and lay leaders to work collaboratively with community agencies on prevention strategies and to provide for the physical, emotional, and spiritual needs of victims, offenders, and other family members.

3. Adopt policy and procedures for keeping children and vulnerable adults safe from abuse in church facilities and programs.

4. Assess currently available prevention and response resources in the community and, where indicated as appropriate, initiate new programs and services. Wherever possible, undertake new programs ecumenically or as part of a community coalition.

5. Set up peer support groups for battered spouses, for adults who were sexually abused as children, and for rape victims. A trained resource person or professional counselor should be consulted for assistance in setting up peer support groups.

6. Encourage church members to volunteer their services to existing shelters, crisis centers, and other community services. Insist upon training for volunteers.

7. Re-examine, and change if necessary, scriptural and theological messages, cultures, and traditions that validate violence or abuse or support a view of women as subordinate to men or children as property of adults. Pay particular attention to church teachings on repentance and forgiveness.

8. Maintain a library of printed and video resources on domestic violence, sexual assault, child abuse and the role of the church. Develop a utilization plan.

9. Participate in Domestic Violence Awareness Month each October and Child Abuse Prevention Month each April in the United States, or similar emphases in other countries.

10. Urge clergy to preach on domestic violence and sexual abuse topics; urge congregants to host or cooperate in community education events and to highlight opportunities for involvement in prevention and service activities.

The following actions are commended to annual conferences, general agencies, and seminaries:

1. Provide, for clergy and laity, education and training that address domestic violence, sexual assault and child sexual abuse. Seminaries are urged to include courses in their curriculum, and annual confer-

ences are urged to offer courses in their continuing education programs for clergy.

2. Support policies, programs, and services that protect victims, hold offenders accountable, and provide support for family members.

3. Provide training in abuse prevention, detection, and intervention to church school teachers, youth leaders and pastors, and encourage them to use abuse prevention curriculum. Include specific guidelines and training for abuse reporting procedures.

4. Develop and implement clear policies to deal with sexual abuse by clergy and others who provide leadership in the church.

5. Encourage governments to ratify the United Nations Conventions on "The Elimination of All Forms of Discrimination Against Women" and on "The Rights of the Child" as minimum global standards to protect women and children.

ADOPTED 2004

See Social Principles, ¶ 162C and F.

187. Violent Coin-Operated Video Game Machines

The United Methodist Church advocates at state and federal levels for the elimination of violent games that specifically target children and youth, specifically those games that glorify death, show killing, and depict all acts of violence.

General Conference requests the General Board of Church and Society, the General Board of Global Ministries, and the General Board of Discipleship to develop resources, curriculum, and advocacy strategies that will seek to provide creative avenues to address conflict and violence in our society.

The denomination will use legislative and nonlegislative means at federal and state levels to reduce violence in our society, especially among the young, and to teach our young people conflict resolution strategies as an alternative to violence.

ADOPTED 2000

See Social Principles, ¶ 162Q.

188. Prohibition of Bullying

Be it resolved, and it is hereby resolved, that The United Methodist Church at all levels will:

- categorically oppose the practices of adult, youth, and child bullying, mobbing (also known as scapegoating);
- diligently work to increase societal awareness of these destructive behaviors; and
- intentionally validate, enlighten, support, and empower persons being injured by such behaviors in workplaces, in schools and in all environments.

ADOPTED 2004

See Social Principles, ¶ 162.

WOMEN

189. Churches in Solidarity with Women: From Solidarity to Accountability

On Easter Sunday 1988, the World Council of Churches (WCC) launched "An Ecumenical Decade of Churches in Solidarity with Women" from 1988-1998 to give churches the opportunity to respond to God's call to inclusiveness, solidarity with the oppressed, and the sharing of power and resources within communities.

Our Biblical Calling

Now that this Ecumenical Decade has come to a close, we are reminded of the prophetic tradition that calls the people of God to live and work in solidarity with the oppressed to bring oppression to an end. Rooted in the stories of Genesis is the declaration that all persons, female and male, are created in the image of God, the giver of life. We are also reminded of the affirmation that through our baptism, we are incorporated into the body of Christ, the new community where there is neither slave nor free, Jew nor Greek, male nor female... but all are one in Christ Jesus (Galatians 3).

Historical Recollections

In 1985, the United Nations "End of the Decade Conference" reminded us that millions of women and girls live on the margins of our societies. They find themselves on the fringes because of the sins of discrimination and prejudice. The margins of society are dangerous places not only for women, but for their families and communities that depend on women's well-being for their own social, economic, physical, and spiritual well-being.

In 1988, the WCC launched a new decade to focus anew on the work ahead, "An Ecumenical Decade of Churches in Solidarity with Women" from 1988-98. It was designed to build on the momentum of the UN Decade for Women. This Decade called us to end physical and emotional abuse of women, their economic insecurity and political powerlessness, and their exclusion from decision-making processes. It called for churches to encourage and empower the full contribution and participation of women in every aspect of society and the church.

In 1988, the General Conference of The United Methodist Church committed to: participate fully in the Decade, supporting full participation of women in decision-making and development bodies; support women doing theology and sharing spirituality; produce educational resources and programs on the marginalization and oppression of women; encourage all levels of our church to study the root causes of sexism and find ways to increase the participation of women in all aspects of the church; and increase the involvement of racial, ethnic, national minority, indigenous, immigrant, and refugee women and to support the WCC Women Under Racism Programme; continue work on the Forward Looking Strategies; encourage governments of our nations to commit to appropriate action for development that included the needs and perspectives of women; and support the ratification and implementation of the UN Convention on the Elimination of All Forms of Discrimination Against Women.

During the years that followed, listening teams collected stories called "Living Letters" and testimony of the endurance and determination of women to overcome oppression in these four major areas of concern:

1. violence against women in all forms and dimensions, both past and present;

2. economic injustice and the effects of the global economic crisis on women;

3. racism and xenophobia (fear/hatred of the strange/stranger), and their impact on women; and

4. exclusion of women from the full and creative participation in the life of the church.

In 1995, the Fourth International Conference on Women in Beijing lifted up economic justice for women, access to health care and family planning, participation of women in social and policy planning, violence against women, rights of women in inheritance, and women's roles in creating and promoting peace as central issues.

In 1996, the United Methodist General Conference recommitted the church to working on the goals of the Decade, and to focusing attention on these four areas of concern surfacing in the "Living Letters." The General Conference further committed us to address the spiritual and social brokenness that condemns women to lives of poverty, powerlessness, and violence. It called us to study, reflection, and advocacy for the full voice and participation of women in church and society.

From Solidarity to Accountability

At the end of this Ecumenical Decade, we as United Methodists can celebrate its learning, hopes, and recommendations. But, in the new millennium, we know that solidarity must grow into commitment and action. Indeed more is required. Accountability must follow these years of solidarity. Accountability means taking responsibility for acting on all the expressions of solidarity. Evidence of the fruits of our churches' labors will be found in changes in theological perspectives, the collection and assessment of data, shared power, active encouragement, specific recruitment, and support for success after recruitment. The work ahead presents new and old challenges which we must be ready to face.

The work of the Decade identified some pressing challenges, depicting brokenness in our human community: the need for safe places where women can speak out about injustice, violence, and practices that minimize women; the need to persist with each other in care as we struggle on issues about which we do not agree; and the need to attend and truly hear the perspectives of young women in our churches. While there was broad diversity on certain issues, there is no doubting the clarion call to eliminate violence against women in all dimensions. In order to realize a vision of community where all are valued and none are excluded, it will be necessary for churches to do the difficult, detailed work of accountability: carefully monitor structures and practices so that all forms of exclusion are eradicated. We as United Methodists are called to embrace this vision and join to pray, lament, seek scriptural hope, and begin the intentional work needed to move forward from solidarity to accountability. These four issues are key components of the Decade's learning:

Eradication of Violence

A critical priority is the eradication of violence. We must announce to the world that violence against women in all its dimensions is a sin. We must hold ourselves accountable for the elimination of violence and the renewal of our commitment to justice and peace among women, men, and children in our homes and communities.

Economic Justice

Economic justice, where poverty is neither tolerated nor justified, is a vital element in the vision of the Decade. Economic justice means the peoples of the south and east flourish with the peoples of the north and west, where a balance of power and wealth is restored, and where women and children no longer endure enforced or debilitating labor. Appropriate and just economic development holds the needs, perspectives, and contributions of women central. Churches are called to declare poverty and its dehumanizing consequences as a scandal against God.

Racism, Xenophobia, and Violence

Further, this vision holds that the fullness of life in Christ requires that no race or ethnicity be valued over another, and that churches in the name of Christ challenge all acts of ethnic cleansing, caste atrocities, xenophobia, ethnocentrism (belief that one's culture/race is superior) and genocide. Ethnocentrism and racism have no place in God's household.

Full and Creative Participation in the Church

As leaders of our churches, we have been entrusted with gifts of power and authority, delegated to us by God and the church community. The experiences of the churches' Decade call us to examine our use of that power for the inclusion of all: "In a world of increasing abuse of power, arrogant assumption of authority and misuse of position, we are reminded of Jesus' words, 'that it shall not be so among you.' Unfortunately abuse of power and authority takes place in many church circles. Women can be the victims of such abuse of power."

Women have also been silenced from speaking about God. Their contributions in theology through worship, liturgy, and praise are so clearly needed to strengthen the healing and sense of redemption in our congregations.

As we move from solidarity into accountability, it will be necessary not only to hope for, but to be held accountable for the achievement of full participation of women, including young women, in all levels of the church. This is especially true of the participation and contributions of women of diverse racial, ethnic, and national origins.

Therefore, the 2000 General Conference commits United Methodists to the fulfillment of these recommendations for our congregations, conferences, general boards, and agencies:

1. Use the resources and support of the General Board of Global Ministries and the General Board of Church and Society, to seek the ratification of the UN Convention on the Elimination of All Forms of Discrimination Against Women. United Methodists are urged to work through local and national governments and organizations to implement the Convention.

2. Support the creation of programs, educational materials, networks, and opportunities that continue to empower women in church and society. We call on the General Commission on the Status and Role of Women, the General Board of Discipleship, the General Board of Global Ministries, and the General Board of Church and Society to assist in this implementation.

3. With the support and resources of the General Commission on the Status and Role of Women, strengthen our commitment to study and action for the full voice and participation of women at every level of the church. Increase the time and energy devoted to monitoring church structures and practices so that all forms of exclusion are eradicated, including these strategies:

   a. adopt policies that promote a balance of gender, age, and race in leadership positions and roles, honoring all cultural identities;

   b. collect and analyze data to identify areas needing intensive work to increase the participation of women; and

    c. initiate actions to correct the gender imbalances that exist in our midst, making all levels of power in the church accessible and equitable for women.

4. Work with renewed energy and vigilance for the elimination of all violence, especially as it affects the lives of women and children (sexual, religious, psychological, structural, physical, spiritual, and military). United Methodists in every congregation, community, conference, and nation are encouraged to:

    a. create opportunities and places for women and girls to learn and speak about violence and abuse so the "culture of silence" can be broken;

    b. expose all sexual abuse, especially in positions of church leadership;

    c. create restorative justice processes where victims of violence and perpetrators can experience truth telling and the power of forgiveness and reconciliation;

    d. eliminate the use of biblical and theological justifications for violence;

    e. denounce all initiatives of war, seeking alternative, nonviolent ways to handle conflict; and

    f. denounce sex tourism, trafficking of women and children, and female genital mutilation.

5. Through the advocacy and programs of the General Board of Church and Society and the General Board of Global Ministries, support the development of just economic systems and structures in church and society so all may experience the blessings of justice, equal pay for comparable work, sustainable and livable wages, and honorable labor practices.

6. Study the resources and programs of the UN "Beijing Platform for Action" and the UN Decade of Eradication of Poverty 1997-2007, available through the United Methodist Office at the United Nations (UMOUN). Through the UMOUN, advocate, monitor, and support the continued emphasis on women by the UN, and participate in all UN arenas where nongovernmental organizations have potential for influence.

7. Use the document, "From Solidarity to Accountability" as the basis for studies in local churches, districts and clusters, and annual and central conferences. Boards of Ordained Ministry and cabinets can use this document for reflection and assessment of barriers to women in our church structures and processes. The resources and

programs of the General Board of Global Ministries and the General Board of Higher Education and Ministries can provide support.

8. Give special attention to the eradication of global racism/tribalism and its impact on women and girls. With the support and resources of the General Commission on Religion and Race, the General Commission on the Status and Role of Women, and the collaborative work of the General Board of Global Ministries, General Board of Church and Society, and the General Board of Higher Education and Ministry, United Methodist leaders at every level will work diligently to increase the involvement of racial, ethnic, national minority, indigenous, immigrant and refugee women and young women in leadership, decision making, and policy/program development in our churches.

ADOPTED 1996
REVISED AND READOPTED 2000

See Social Principles, ¶ 162F.

190. Goals and Recommendations for Full Participation of All Women

Recalling Our Historic Commitments

The historic General Conference of 1972 made a significant commitment to strengthening the participation of women at all levels of our church. To support this commitment, it created the General Commission on the Status and Role of Women "to foster an ongoing awareness of the problems and issues related to the status of women and to stimulate progress reports on these issues."

The General Conference called for changes about theological, philosophical, and biblical interpretations and understandings about the role of women. It called for increased sensitivity to expectations for the achievement and contributions of women, and the issues of the rights of women. The General Conference further endorsed overcoming rigid sex role distinctions and discriminatory language, images, and practices in our own church life and work.

At that conference, only 16 years after the approval of full clergy rights and privileges for women (1956), the goals called for an openness and receptivity for women in the professional ministry and the utilization of men and women in elections and appointments at all levels of the church. Action plans included development of programs, evaluation measures, curriculum, doctrinal studies, and analysis of the particular problems and barriers faced by women.

Celebrating the Progress Made

Now, approaching the new millennium, we as United Methodists celebrate significant efforts and progress made toward the goals and recommendations of our forebears in 1972. We have accomplished:

- studies and resources on women's roles in the Bible and in mission;
- programs and curriculum on changes needed in theological, biblical, and language interpretations;
- research and analyses on the barriers and problems facing women in the church;
- participation in the Ecumenical Decade of Churches in Solidarity with Women and growth in our understanding of the issues faced by women and young women worldwide;
- increase in the election of women to roles of leadership in the church, including the election of bishops, general secretaries and agency heads, general and jurisdictional conference delegates; increase in the appointment of women to lead, senior, or co-pastorates;
- significant increase in the number of women enrolling and graduating from seminary;
- studies, resources and training, and advocacy programs on the issue of sexual harassment and sexual misconduct; and establishment of annual conference commissions on the status and role of women providing monitoring and resources, leadership and policy development.

We thank God for the work of countless women, men, and young people carefully and spiritually building a more inclusive community of faith. We stand on their shoulders as we project the work before us into the next century, prayerfully aware of God's vision of justice and mutuality.

Theological Guidance for the Work Ahead

Georgia Harkness in her book, *Women in Church and Society*, said, "The women's movement is more than a struggle for 'women's rights'. It is essentially a struggle for the recognition of women as persons of equal worth and status with men, and with equal opportunities according to their talents, training, and various forms of ability." Although some advances have been made for women's rights in recent years, patriarchy and sexism are still prevalent and much work remains to be done. In society, women continue to struggle for equality in employment, income, education, and leadership. The situation is comparable in the church. In many ways the church, the body of Christ, has followed the world, embracing and institutionalizing patriarchy, with its attendant sexism, rather than living out God's vision of justice and mutuality.

The vision of justice and mutuality is expressed throughout the Judeo-Christian scriptures and in the life and ministry of Jesus Christ. God's intention for partnership and mutuality is evidenced in the creation stories when God made male and female in God's own image and then placed them in harmonious partnership in the garden. The consistent message of the prophets is a call for justice and for speaking out against inequalities, to stand with the oppressed and marginalized. In all the Gospels, Jesus reached out to women with tenderness and compassion. He treated women with dignity and redefined a woman's role. In having women as friends, disciples, and witnesses, Christ challenged the conventional sexism of his time. The apostle Paul affirmed this call of Christ to create and live in a world where the gifts of both women and men are celebrated and utilized, where "there is neither male nor female, but all are one in Christ Jesus" (Galatians 3:28). Christ calls forth each generation to do the same in its time.

Concerns and Issues That Face Us Now

Recalling this vision of justice and mutuality and recognizing the notable progress toward the commitment of that General Conference nearly 30 years ago, we confess the vision of full and equitable participation for all women is not yet realized. We have fallen short of the goals of 1972 and major barriers still exist. Testimony from women, men, and youth throughout the world demands we renew and revitalize our commitment to full and equitable participation of women. Some of those voices identify the concerns and issues now before us:

(1) *Voices from Churches Around the World: From Solidarity to Accountability.* This powerful letter from the closing of the Ecumenical

Decade of Churches in Solidarity with Women (1998) called for initiatives to realize the full participation of all. It urged churches to create programs and opportunities that support and empower women, including monitoring church structures and practices "so that all forms of exclusion are eradicated." It recommended providing theological and educational opportunities for women that honor their voices and experiences, gender studies and training, liturgies and gender language policies that affirm all, and policies that promote a balance of gender, age, and race in leadership and roles, honoring all people's cultural identities.

Participants in the 1998 Decade Festival in Harare, Zimbabwe also identified the barriers to women in theology. The women and men there experienced the healing and redemptive power of women speaking about God through their own experiences of violence, poverty, forgiveness, and empowerment in worship, liturgy, and song. There is a clear need for churches to value the contribution of women doing theology.

(2) *Voices from United Methodist Churches.* Research studies and information collected by our general agencies describe the concerns and experiences of women in leadership in startling detail. A summary of these findings follows and provides a litany of testimony that all is not as it could be:

A. Participation monitored by general agencies:

Clergywomen. The General Board of Higher Education and Ministry, through the Division of Ordained Ministry, works for the full acceptance and empowerment of clergywomen throughout the church. At the end of this century, after 40 years of women having full clergy rights within the UMC, we note: In the U.S., approximately 13 percent of all ordained elders are women and about 13 percent of all ordained women in pastoral ministry are racial ethnic clergywomen. This is a low percentage compared to other professions (doctors = 21 percent women, lawyers = 25 percent women), to The United Methodist Church profile (women = over 50 percent of church membership), and to the society at large (women = 50 percent). Clergywomen, with the same number of years experience as men and with the same type of appointment, make 9 percent less than their male counterparts. This not only affects current economic situations for clergywomen, but also has an impact on their pension and retirement.

Women are beginning to fill leadership positions at the same rate or a little higher than the percentage of women elders. The percentage of women serving as district superintendents is approximately 15 percent and the women serving as bishops make up 8 percent of all bishops, active and retired. Only 2 percent of the clergy serving as lead pastors of churches of 1000 members or more are women.

In the Philippines, Africa, and Europe the percentage of ordained elders who are women varies greatly from conference to conference. While some women are serving as district superintendents there are no women episcopal leaders.

In the 1996 and the 2000 General Conference, clergywomen (elders) make up 20 percent of clergy delegates. Though the percentage did not change, the number of women elders decreased (women deacons make up the difference) and the number of delegations chaired by a clergywoman increased.

Women in the Master of Divinity (M.Div.) degree program at 13 United Methodist seminaries make up over 50 percent of all M.Div. degree students (the statistic has been over 40 percent for over 12 years); and, yet, the number of ordained women is still very low (less than 18 percent).

One of the major obstacles for clergywomen in acceptance and appointments is institutional or systemic sexism-bias against women that is inherent within a system. The United Methodist Church still perpetuates a hierarchical and linear model of ministry. Persons, particularly women, who tend to see ministry as a partnership and cyclical in style, often struggle in this system. Women are often told:

- that they are "leaving" ministry when following a call to ministry outside the local church;
- that they need to "start at the bottom" when they return to local church ministry;
- that women are not accepted as clergy in some churches;
- that it is cheaper for a church and will help a budget if a woman is appointed; and
- that if women are interested in ministry outside the local church, they should consider lay ministry.

The church is called to ask itself the difficult questions about the underlying theology and values that it reinforces and affirms in its policy and practices.

Local Church Participation. In its quadrennial survey of local churches in the U.S., the General Commission on the Status and Role of Women found these indications that more work is needed: Local church lay leaders in the study were 2:1 men to women; churches whose ushers are men or mostly men were 45 percent, 22 percent had all or mostly women ushers.

In the pulpit: 53 percent of the churches had one or no lay women preachers in the last year; of churches with male pastors: 77 percent had no clergywomen preaching in the last year. If lay liturgists were used, 35 percent of these churches use all or mostly males, 39 percent use all or mostly females; in language for God, 80 percent of these churches use all or mostly all-male language for God, in language for people, about 65 percent use inclusive terms like humankind or gender-neutral terms in their own language other than English.

Women fill roles of leadership most frequently in these committees (in order): education, staff parish relations, worship, administrative councils/boards, and evangelism/ witness/ outreach.

Areas where women participate the least in these local churches: finance, treasurer, missions and, lastly, trustees.

Issues important to women in the local church: 20 percent of the pastors responding didn't know. The most common responses pastors did name as important issues were missions, church growth and children. Then came family and parenting, domestic violence, and aging.

B. Indicators from research and experience:

The "United Methodist Clergywomen Retention Study," conducted by the Anna Howard Shaw Center of the Boston University School of Theology[1] and co-sponsored by the Division of Ordained Ministry General Board of Higher Education and Ministry (GBHEM) studied written and interview responses of nearly 1400 UM clergywomen. UM clergywomen leave local church ministry at a 10 percent faster rate than clergymen, despite an overwhelming commitment to local church ministry. The data indicated four major reasons: lack of support from the hierarchical system, being unable to maintain one's integrity in the system, rejection from congregations/parishioners, and the conflict of family and pastoral responsibilities. Clearly this is a serious loss of gifts, graces, and our church's investment in these leaders. Five groups were identified as having responsibility for addressing this crisis in clergy leadership development: the appoint-

1. "United Methodist Clergywomen Retention Study," Anna Howard Shaw Center, Boston University School of Theology, Margaret S. Wiborg, Director; Elizabeth J. Collier, Primary Investigator. October 1997.

ment system, conference leaders and clergy colleagues, congregations, seminaries, and clergywomen themselves.

Several of these points were underscored by two other studies. The University of Florida study of ordained United Methodist clergywomen across the U.S.[2] found that most UM clergywomen surveyed identified the high stress factors of "pettiness, the patriarchy, and the pressures of ministry." The most common challenge to clergywomen is balancing work and family responsibilities given the expectations of congregations for 24-hour availability. The Clergywomen Retention Study stated it well in saying "the church must ask itself why the traditional values and the theology of family do not apply to clergywomen as clergy but are applied to them as women."

A study initiated by the Women in Ministry Task Force of the Virginia Annual Conference[3] found that clergywomen more than their male colleagues prefer nontraditional roles in the church, and are more likely to feel the conference underutilizes their gifts and provides insufficient support. The study, conducted in 1998, found on the whole that clergywomen earn less than clergymen. Half of female clergy responding had salaries less than $30,000 (compared to 25 percent of male clergy), and half of the male clergy had salaries of $40,000 or more (compared to 15 percent of female clergy).

In a significant finding, the United Methodist Clergywomen Retention Study determined that a larger proportion of racial ethnic clergywomen have exited local church ministry (particularly among African and Asian American clergywomen), and their exits are more permanent than those of white clergywomen. Despite the fact that a larger proportion of racial ethnic clergywomen is committed to the church as an institution, almost twice the proportion of racial ethnic women as white women named "lack of support from the hierarchical system" as their primary reason for leaving the local church setting. The study makes the strongest implication that issues of racism are active in this loss of clergy leadership. On the whole, this study identifies details on hostile climates toward clergywomen for which our whole denomination must claim responsibility.

Women's Congress: A Spiritual Journey. During the 1993-1996 quadrennium, the General Commission on the Status and Role of Women

2. Study of 190 UM Clergywomen by Jesse Schultz, Constance Shehan, and Marsha Wiggins Frame in August 1999, Sociological Focus.

3. Study of Clergy in the Virginia Annual Conference. 1997-1998 Virginia Commonwealth University Survey & Evaluation Research Laboratory 1-800-768-6040 ext. 316.

reflected on the status and role of women in The United Methodist Church and identified that progress had been made on behalf of some, but not all women in The United Methodist Church. The Commission recognized the need to be vigilant in working on behalf of all women, particularly those marginalized by race, ethnicity, class, or economic status. What emerged was a vision for the next several years of the Commission's ministry: full and equal responsibility and participation for ALL women in the life and ministry of The United Methodist Church.

In 1999, The Women's Congress: A Spiritual Journey called forth women with potential for leadership who may not otherwise have opportunity for education and development in the church. More than 150 women gathered and were affirmed as daughters created in the image of God and as persons bearing gifts for life and service in God's creation. With the enthusiastic encouragement of those who participated in this spiritual journey, the General Commission on the Status and Role of Women committed itself anew to be a catalyst for similar efforts to call forth women of gift and potential throughout The United Methodist Church.

Racism/Sexism Task Force. For several years, the General Commission on the Status and Role of Women and the General Commission on Religion and Race have convened a Task Force on Racism/Sexism to explore and study the impact of the intersection of racism and sexism on racial ethnic women within the denomination. At the beginning of the 21st century, one might have expected that the issues of racism and sexism would be moot issues, both in the church and in the secular society. Unfortunately, this is not true, for this double-headed sin of racism/sexism still rears its un-Christian head in our lives.

A major three-year study was done by the research advisory group, Catalyst. They issued an article in July 1999 which states "ethnic women view employers as largely ineffective at combating racism and removing barriers in advancement." While this study was done in a secular setting, could not this also be said of United Methodists?

Racism and sexism place immeasurable pain and suffering on racial ethnic women. As a result, we all suffer, for when one of God's children is mistreated, the family is broken. The work of the Joint Task Force on Racism/Sexism is still very much needed to continue to bring awareness, understanding, and sensitivity to racism and sexism which are alive and well in The United Methodist Church. The work of the task force is still needed to enable our church to fully receive the gifts and graces of racial ethnic women as we strive to make the church inclusive and welcoming of all.

United Methodist Women (UMW). Over one million members strong, UMW has outstanding experience preparing women and youth to serve in ministry, and mission. The Women's Division of the General Board of Global Ministries has historically called attention to gaps in the participation of women in the church, especially in positions in finance, treasury, and trusteeship in local congregations. They have also identified the gap in participation of young women in all levels of church life and have embarked on a comprehensive recruitment, training, and mission opportunity program targeting teen, college, and university women.

Congregations' inability to utilize the recruited and trained women may be a barrier to progress in closing these gaps.

A Vision of Parity and Equitable Treatment

In The United Methodist Church we have used various tools to set goals for full and equitable participation of women in all levels of our church. For a time, we used encouragement; then for a time we used numerical participation targets. From the indicators described above, we need more and better tools to reach our commitment for full participation. The tool of "parity" may be such a tool.

Parity in participation is reached when participation of a category of individual is comparable to that category's representation in the group as a whole. For example, if women represent 56 percent of the membership of The United Methodist Church in an annual or central conference, then parity in women in clergy leadership is reached when clergywomen represent 56 percent of that annual or central conference clergy membership. Parity is a flexible measurement that can be applied to General Conference Committee officers, or local church administrative council membership, or to conference delegations to General Conference.

We have learned over the last 30 years in this journey toward full and equitable participation that it is not enough to be present at the table where decisions are made. It is not enough to be a member of a committee or a board where programs and policies are shaped. Inequities and unjust treatment at the table or in the committee room can create barriers to full participation. We must pay special attention to the hospitality and affirmation that are offered to all who are given access. What are the environments of our church systems that could prevent someone's participation and contributions?

Therefore the General Conference recommits The United Methodist Church to these recommendations for strengthening the participation of youth, young adult, and adult women in the church:

1. That conference boards of ordained ministry take action with cabinets to:

  a. reach an increased proportion of women in all levels of professional ministry;
  b. build a more hospitable climate in local churches to receive women as clergy and lay employees; and
  c. create a more favorable setting for the appointment of racial ethnic clergywomen and clergy couples, paying particular attention in clergywomen's appointments to salary range equity, size of congregation and/or worship attendance, and provisions for family leave.

2. That all nominating committees in local churches, and annual, jurisdictional, central and General conferences give attention to the nomination of women for membership and leadership in significant numbers according to parity (participation comparable to representation in the body as a whole).

3. That the General Commission on the Status and Role of Women in cooperation with appropriate general agencies collect data on the participation of laywomen across the church with particular emphasis on racial ethnic women. This data will be used in preparation for analyzing women's participation at various levels of church life and work, and for supporting networks of women seeking ministry settings in which to serve.

4. That the General Commission on the Status and Role of Women advocate that particular attention be given by the appropriate agencies and institutions to the problems and barriers faced by women in racial and ethnic groups within our churches, including clergywomen.

5. That general program agencies develop new avenues of participation for younger adult members of the church, particularly youth and young adult women, and that these efforts include staff time and financial resources needed. And that the conferences support the efforts of these agencies with youth and young adult women.

6. That the General Board of Higher Education and Ministry conduct follow-up study and action to address the reasons clergywomen leave local church ministry. That the General Board of Higher Education and Ministry continue to work toward the full acceptance and empowerment of clergywomen including preparation of resources and action plans for cabinets, annual conference leadership, boards of ordained ministry, and clergywomen that address the reasons women leave local church ministry; and, that the General Board of Higher Education and Ministry specifically:

    a. study the disparities for racial ethnic clergywomen and prepare action plans for the elimination of racism and sexism in regards to clergywomen;

    b. continue to provide resources for clergywomen including national and international gatherings; and,

    c. coordinate with other United Methodist general church agencies and centers in the gathering of oral and written history of clergywomen from 1956 through 2006.

7. That the training for new district superintendents address strategies and awareness needed to support and retain clergywomen in local church ministries, particularly racial ethnic clergywomen in the different cultural traditions in our churches.

8. That central conferences be encouraged to move forward in their efforts to eradicate barriers to full and equitable participation of women in their programs and ministry settings, utilizing structures, channels and methods appropriate to these settings.

9. That the General Council on Finance and Administration include in its annual statistical report requests for information on the participation of persons by gender and race in our local churches and conferences.

10. That the General Commission on the Status and Role of Women and the General Commission on Religion and Race continue to work cooperatively on the issues of the intersection of race and gender.

11. That the General Commission on Religion and Race, the General Commission on the Status and Role of Women, the Women's Division of the General Board of Global Ministries, and the General Board of Higher Education and Ministry Division of Ordained Ministry explore the feasibility of conducting a consultation with lay and clergy women during the 2001-2004 quadrennium on progress and plans toward full and equitable participation of women in The

United Methodist Church, with recommendations from the consultation to be infused into the work of these agencies and units.

ADOPTED 2000

See Social Principles, ¶ 163.

191. The Status of Women

I.

Christianity was born in a world of male preference and dominance. Practices, traditions, and attitudes in almost all societies viewed women as inferior to men, as having few talents and contributions to make to the general well-being of society aside from their biological roles. This was true of the Judaic society of which Jesus was a part.

But the life of Jesus, the Redeemer of human life, stood as a witness against such cultural patterns and prejudices. Consistently, he related to women as persons of intelligence and capabilities. He charged women as well as men to use their talents significantly in the cause of God's kingdom. His acts of healing and ministry were extended without distinction to women and men.

The central theme of Jesus' teaching is love for God and neighbor. Jesus embodied this message in his life, and, in the early church, women held prominent positions of leadership. Christian love as exemplified in the New Testament requires that we relate to others as persons of worth. To regard another as an inferior is to break the covenant of love; denying equality demeans, perpetuates injustice, and falls short of the example of Jesus and the early church.

II.

The movement to improve the status of women is one of the most profoundly hopeful of our times. The United Methodist Church, recognizing that equality between women and men is a matter of social justice, in various ways has sought to support that movement.

Although change is taking place, in most societies women are still not accorded equal rights and responsibilities.

There is increasing awareness that we cannot solve world problems associated with globalization and unequal distribution of resources population growth, poverty, and war so long as the talents and potential of half the world's people are disregarded and even repressed. There are strong interrelationships between all these problems and the status of women.

The International movement for the equality of women formally began in 1975, with the proclamation of International Women's Year by the United Nations General Assembly. The United Nations Decade for Women (1976-1985) which followed was a world-wide effort to examine the status and rights of women at all levels. For Christians, it was a time for repentance and for new dedication to Christ's ideal of equality.

In 1995, the Fourth World Conference on Women succeeded in bringing about a new and international commitment to the goals of equality, development and peace for all women, and moved the global movement for the advancement of women into the twenty-first century. The Beijing Declaration and the Platform for Action constitute a powerful agenda for women's empowerment and gender equality.

The Beijing Platform for Action defined a set of strategic objectives and spelled out actions to be taken by governments and civil society in the following twelve critical areas of concern: poverty, economy, power and decision-making, education, media, health, armed conflict, environment, violence, human rights, the girl child and the institutional mechanisms for the advancement of women.

Economics: As part of the Beijing Platform for Action, statisticians were called upon to develop a more comprehensive knowledge of all forms of work and employment. Often the productive labor of women is ignored in economic statistics, reinforcing the impression that work done by women is peripheral, of secondary importance, even dispensable. For that reason, few studies have actually evaluated the importance of contributions by women. As one example, when women grow food to feed their families, they are "just" tending kitchen gardens, but when men grow cash crops such as tobacco and coffee, they are engaged in agricultural and commercial enterprises. In more industrialized societies, the enormous amount of volunteer work done by women is not counted as adding to the nation's wealth.

Although the gender gap in rates of economic activity is narrowing, the nature of women's and men's participation in the labor force continues to be very different. Women have always engaged in the less formal types of work, working as unpaid workers in a family business, in the informal sector or in various types of household economic activities. They also continue to receive less pay than men. In manufacturing, for example, in 27 of the 39 countries with data available, women's wages were 20 to 50 per cent less than those of men.

Power and Decision-making. In 1945, only 31 countries allowed women to vote; today women have the right in more than 125 nations. Only eight countries exclude women entirely from political processes open to men. Still, many areas of legal discrimination remain. In some nations, women are still considered the chattels of their husbands, with few rights in family law, landholding, inheritance, and guardianship of children.

In the United States, some of the more glaring inequities are being corrected step by step. However, women are still under represented in all branches of the government. The 75 women sworn into the 108th Congress in January 2003, account for only 13.8% of the 540 members.

Education. The perception of women as inferior and dependent is perpetuated through many institutions in society—the media, school textbooks and curricula, political structures, and, often, religious organizations. Education is one of the principal ways of opening doors to wider participation in society. Thus, it is distressing that, while the percentage of literate women is at an all-time high, the absolute number of illiterate women is greater than at any time in the past. The fact that two thirds of the world's 876 million illiterates are female is evidence of continuing disparity in importance given to the education of boys and girls.

Violence Against Women. Traditional perceptions of female qualities also are a factor in the widespread domestic violence against women, now coming to be recognized as a tragically widespread occurrence. Nearly one third of women in the world report being physically or sexually abused by a husband or boyfriend at some point in their lives (according to World Health Organization).

Human Rights in Fertility Decisions. Throughout the centuries, women have been little consulted or involved in the decisions regarding fertility-related laws or practices. For women, particularly, the ability to make choices concerning fertility is a liberating force, helping to safeguard their health and that of their children, to plan for the future, to assume wider roles and responsibilities in society.

The United Nations has declared that education and access to means for determining the number and spacing of children is a human right, yet this is an ideal far from realization.

Coercion is still common, sometimes aimed at increasing births, sometimes at limiting them. Evidence now clearly shows that many poor, particularly ethnic, women have been sterilized without their understanding of what was being done to them and without their informed consent. In many places, safe and legal abortion is denied, in some cases even to save the life of the pregnant woman. In other cases, women are threatened that welfare payments or aid programs will be cut if the pregnancy continues. Such inconsistency reflects lack of value-centered decision making, as well as insensitivity to the personhood of the woman involved.

While societal needs should be considered more and more in fertility matters, this should never be at the price of demeaning the individual or applying restrictive measures only to the poor. Women should be fully informed and fully involved in the decision making.

HIV/AIDS and Women. According to 2004 Joint United Nations Program on HIV/AIDS report, women now account for almost half of the 38 million adults currently living with HIV/AIDS and of the 20 million adults who have died from the disease since the epidemic began. In 1999, 52 per cent of the 2.1 million adults who died from AIDS worldwide were women. The majority of these deaths occurred in sub-Saharan Africa. where women account for 57 per cent of those infected with HIV/AIDS. Women's risk of becoming infected with HIV during unprotected sexual intercourse is also known to be two to four times higher than that of men.

The Beijing Platform for Action recognizes that social and cultural factors often increase women's vulnerability to HIV and may determine the course that the infection takes in their lives. Women too often do not have the power to insist on safe and responsible sex practices and have little access to public health information and services, both of which have been found to be effective in preventing the disease and/or slowing its progress.

Women and Armed Conflict. Although the threat of global conflict has been reduced, wars of aggression, colonial or other forms of alien domination and foreign occupation, civil wars, and terrorism continue to plague the world. Grave violations of the human rights of women occur, particularly in times of armed conflict, and include murder, torture, systematic rape, forced pregnancy and forced abortion, in particular under policies of ethnic cleansing. Women and girls are among those most affected by the violence and economic instability associated with armed conflict Yet, when it comes to negotiating peace and facilitating the reconstruction of societies after war, women are grossly under represented. For example, no Bosnian women were present at the Dayton Peace negotiations in 1995. With Security Council Resolution 1325 on Women, peace and security (2000), the United Nations has affirmed that women's protection in armed conflict and the integration of women's voices and experiences in the process of building peace are a primary concern of the international community.

III.

Across the nations of the world, new movements are growing that address the serious handicaps and harsh realities of the lives of many women. In the context of this increasing momentum for a more just society, we call on local congregations and the agencies of the church:

1. to exert leadership in working, wherever possible, for legal recognition of equal rights for women. In the United States, this means a strengthened determination to secure passage for the Equal Rights Amendment,[1] in line with the United Methodist Conference affirmations of 1972 and 1976. We need to recognize that this measure has become a symbol of the drive for equality. It has meaning far beyond the borders of one nation in the search for equal rights in other societies;

2. to urge governments to ratify the Convention on the Elimination of Discrimination Against Women, which was adopted by the United Nations in December 1979;

3. to encourage support of studies by scientific and governmental bodies of the economic contributions made by women outside the formal economic sector, and to include this information in the gross national product of nations or compilations of national wealth;

1. Proposed 27th Amendment: Section 1. Equality of rights under the law shall not be denied or abridged by the United States or by any State on account of sex. Section 2. The Congress shall have the power to enforce, by appropriate legislation, the provisions of this article.Section 3. This amendment shall take effect two years after the date of ratification.

4. to urge governments to ratify the Statute of the International Criminal Court, adopted in June 1998, which specifically addresses gender-based crimes and crimes against humanity such as rape, sexual slavery, enforced prostitution, forced pregnancy and enforced sterilization;

5. to support the need to enact specific legislation and develop policies to strengthen women's executive and professional abilities, in particular to allow them to manage their own businesses. To this end, governments should develop policies and projects that use local, national and international networks to facilitate information, technology, credit and training for women entrepreneurs, as well as programs that aim to enhance women's education;

6. to examine governmental policies and practices, including development assistance, as to their impact on women's lives; to work to ensure that policies upgrade the status of women and that women are included in decision-making regarding development goals and programs. The key roles of women as workers and consumers and as transmitters of culture must be given adequate weight in national development activities;

7. to examine the impact of transnational corporations on women's lives, and to work to eradicate exploitative practices where identified. One such area is the promotion and selling of inappropriate products and technologies;

8. to encourage steps that promote legal literacy by publicizing and disseminating information on laws relating to the equal rights of men and women;

9. to encourage private charitable organizations, including churches, to initiate and support more programs of leadership education for women and other educational programs that upgrade the status of women; In many parts of the world, illiteracy remains high among adult women because of the lack of access to education in childhood. Strategies to combat female illiteracy must focus on ensuring girls' equal access to, and completion of, basic education. In addition, there is a need to reach out to adult women through massive literacy campaigns using all modern means available;

10. to monitor printed and audio/visual media and other means of communication on their portrayals of the roles and nature of women and men, and to seek ways to eradicate narrow stereotypes that limit the possibilities of useful contributions by both sexes. The church should encourage study of the impact of Western—particularly U.S.—

television, radio, and other media on cultural patterns and national development around the world, and it should draw public attention to cases where such influence is destructive to other cultures;

11. to support programs providing knowledge of the access to resources in the area of family planning and contraception, including that which is Christian based, to encourage abstinence outside of marriage as a method of birth control, and to involve women in the preparation and distribution of these resources. Attention should particularly be given to ensuring access to safe, legal, and noncoercive contraception; well-informed choice regarding abortion and its alternatives (adoptions and so forth); informed consent for sterilization procedures; and safe women's health-care facilities. We also oppose profit-making referral agencies, which charge fees for providing information freely available elsewhere; and

12. to examine the impact of judicial decisions at all levels upon the daily lives of women in such areas as child custody, employment, civil rights, racial and sexual discrimination, credit practices, estate settlements, reproduction and education, and socioeconomic status.

ADOPTED 1992
AMENDED AND READOPTED 1996
AMENDED AND READOPTED 2004

See Social Principles, ¶ 162F.

192. Women's Colleges

WHEREAS, the Methodist movement historically has espoused the unity of "knowledge and vital piety"; and

WHEREAS, The United Methodist Church currently supports and advances higher education as a ministry of the church, giving expression to the commitment so that the faithful may become informed citizens and so that the citizenry may remain faithful; and

WHEREAS, The United Methodist Church has increasingly affirmed the role of women in the church and in society as decision makers, leaders, and active participants in ministry, business, private life, and public life; and

WHEREAS, access to higher education for women is crucial to their success in these important roles; and

WHEREAS, women have not always had access to the same level of higher education as men; and

WHEREAS, Methodist leaders were responsible for creating the first institution of higher learning for women, equivalent to those available to men; and

WHEREAS, graduates of women's colleges excel in private, public, and professional life; and

WHEREAS, in the last twenty years the number of women's colleges in the United States has diminished precipitously, from 298 to 77 with an average of at least two colleges closing per year in the last six years; and

WHEREAS, four of the 77 remaining women's colleges in the nation are affiliated with The United Methodist Church; and

WHEREAS, Wesleyan College in Macon, Georgia was, in 1836, the first college in the world chartered to grant baccalaureate degrees to women and thrives today "affirming its relationship with The United Methodist Church, [emphasizing] a search for knowledge in the Judeo-Christian ethic and the supporting tradition of open inquiry and the pursuit of truth"; and

WHEREAS, Columbia College, in Columbia, South Carolina, was founded in 1854 to "educate young women for fruitful service to church, state, and nation," and continues today to educate women in a vital learning community which emphasizes academic excellence, diversity, technology, globalization, and leadership enhanced by ethics and values; and

WHEREAS, Randolph-Macon Women's College in Lynchburg, Virginia, founded in 1891 and proud of its historic relationship with The United Methodist Church, embodies today a firm grounding in the liberal arts, a residential environment, and an education of academic excellence fully and completely directed toward women to prepare them for leadership, responsibility, and service; and

WHEREAS, Bennett College in Greensboro, North Carolina, founded in 1873 and proud of its heritage as an institution deliberately reorganized to become Bennett College for Women in 1926, provides a strong academic and personal development program in a residential setting, and continues its strong relationship with The United Methodist Church as it produces phenomenal, serious women leaders, primarily African American, grounded in a spiritual value system, for scholarship, citizenship, service, and social justice;

Therefore, be it resolved, that the 2000 General Conference of The United Methodist Church affirm the church's long-standing and faithful ministry in higher education for women with and through the four women's colleges affiliated with The United Methodist Church and listed by the University Senate;

Be it further resolved, that the church encourage each of these institutions to continue to advance its role in the educational ministry of the church and to interpret that ministry to United Methodists worldwide;

Be it further resolved, that the church encourage each of these institutions to continue to advance its role in the educational ministry of the church and to interpret that ministry to United Methodists worldwide;

Be it further resolved, that the General Board of Higher Education and Ministry undertake a study of women in higher education and the role of women's colleges in the education and training of women leaders in an effort to strengthen the church's commitment to the education of women;

Be it finally resolved, that United Methodists learn more about the contributions to the church's ministry and to society made by these four institutions, and that they counter the rapid attrition of women's colleges by fortifying these colleges with prayer and support.

ADOPTED 2000

See Social Principles, ¶ 162F.

THE ECONOMIC COMMUNITY

APPALACHIA

193. Appalachia: A Call to Action

The General Conference of 1972 directed its boards, agencies and conferences to coordinate denominational and ecumenical ministries within the Appalachian region through the United Methodist Appalachian Ministry Network (UMAMN), and the Commission on Religion in Appalachia (CORA). The region encompasses 23 United States Annual Conferences that span more than 400 counties in 13 states.

The United Methodist Church is called upon to reaffirm its commitments to integrated strategies for mission and ministry in the region and to work denominationally and ecumenically to be present with and supportive of the people and churches of Appalachia by directing its boards, commissions, annual conferences and local churches to examine ways that they might address the systemic issues that contribute to the ongoing plight and exploitation of the people and land of Appalachia.

This can be accomplished by studying the history, culture, social and economic realities of the region called Appalachia: developing opportunities for involvement in mission and ministry in Appalachian communities, enhancing spiritual renewal, addressing social recovery, developing leadership opportunities, working toward economic transformation through advocacy and economic development, securing environmental integrity, promoting political involvement and responsibility, and ministering with compassion.

In recent years, bishops in the Appalachian region of The United Methodist Church have joined with other religious leaders and Roman Catholic bishops of Appalachia in producing pastoral letters calling attention to the continued exploitation of the people and of the land.

ADOPTED 2004

See Social Principles, ¶ 163B.

BOYCOTTS

194. Boycott of USA TODAY

Be it resolved that the General Conference of The United Methodist Church reaffirm its witness for justice in the workplace by continuing to refrain from buying the *Detroit News* and *Detroit Free Press* until a just settlement of the newspaper dispute is achieved through collective bargaining. And further, by instituting an economic boycott against *USA TODAY*, the flagship publication of Gannett Co., Inc., to protest the lack of progress in settling the dispute and to press for early resolution.

This action is proposed in compliance with "Guidelines for Instituting an Economic Boycott" as prescribed in the *1996 Book of Resolutions*, pages 458-462. (*See also* pp. 507-511, 2004 edition.)

Rationale

From its earliest history, The United Methodist Church has supported and engaged in activities that promote just working conditions. John Wesley's street ministry responded to the poor treatment of coal miners. He helped create laws against abusive child labor and the inhumane treatment of prisoner workers. Our Social Principles affirm the dignity of the worker and explicitly reject the permanent replacement of a worker who engages in a legal strike (¶ 163b). Federal law also prohibits the replacement of workers in an unfair labor practice strike.

Biblical and theological statement: The creation story of Genesis 1 asserts that human beings are made in God's image. Since in the Ancient Near East it had always been the king who represented the image of God, Israel's assertion was a radical statement of common human dignity, worth, and equality. That same Genesis account, by identifying God's labor and rest in creation, honors all human labor and establishes the justice and spiritual integrity of human rest.

In Exodus, when the brick makers of Egypt cry out to God, Moses is sent with authority to negotiate on their behalf with Pharaoh. With

God's power, Moses then leads the most definitive and exemplary walkout to freedom in history.

When the prophets took measure of the nation's health, they always looked to the least-the widows and orphans and sojourners in the land, but also (as the law spells out—Lev. 19:13; Deut. 24:15) to the fate of workers. King Josiah was challenged by Jeremiah: "Woe to him who builds his house by unrighteousness, and his upper rooms by injustice; who makes his neighbors serve him for nothing, and does not give them their wages" (22:13). And the book of James echoes that same spirit: "Behold, the wages of the laborers who mowed your fields, which you kept back by fraud, cry out; and the cries of the harvesters have reached the ears of the Lord of hosts" (5:4).

The Issue

On July 13, 1995, twenty-five hundred employees—members of six unions of the *Detroit News*, the *Detroit Free Press*, and Detroit newspapers—engaged in a strike over an accumulated list of 12 unfair labor practices which the unions had charged against the newspapers. Three weeks later, workers were threatened with permanent replacement and subsequently were replaced.

The Gannett corporation has controlling interest in Detroit newspapers, an agency created to manage the joint operating agreement between the *Detroit News* and *Detroit Free Press*, and has failed to effect a negotiated settlement with its striking/locked-out employees over four long years. The newspapers have twice been found guilty of unfair labor practices. Twice they were ordered to bargain the contracts and return locked-out workers to their jobs; they have not complied. There is little evidence that serious attempts are being made by the newspapers to resolve outstanding issues. The papers have published incomplete and distorted information regarding the dispute. An economic boycott against *USA TODAY* will bring the strength and power of our body of faith to the effort for resolution. It will demonstrate that people of faith take seriously their commitment to just treatment of employees and in their basic right to collective bargaining.

This dispute has created untold suffering for the workers involved. Because of the lack of reliable information, the dispute with the *Detroit News* and *Detroit Free Press* has caused devastating hardship for the greater community once served by these two newspapers. The *News* and *Free Press* have continued to publish, but hundreds of thousands of readers have canceled subscriptions; and many community, political, and religious leaders have acted out their call for justice by publicly refusing to buy or read the papers. Many progressive leaders refuse to be interviewed or to write opinion articles until a just settlement is reached. Such circumstance creates a serious lack of balanced and accurate news for all of the state.

In the four years since the strike began, numerous attempts have been made by union leaders and striking/locked-out workers to reopen negotiations. And from the beginning, community, political, and religious leaders have tried to help resolve the conflict and bring about a resolution. Offers to assist in mediating have been made by several religious leaders and public officials.

Religious Leaders for Justice at the Detroit newspapers (more than 850 religious leaders from the greater Detroit metropolitan area) joined other groups such as the Interfaith Committee for Worker Justice and Readers United in working toward a resolution. Twenty-six municipal bodies were represented at the May, 1998 summit meeting and also joined in the attempt. The National Labor Relations Board (NLRB), federal mediators, federal courts who have twice found the newspapers guilty of nine unfair labor practices, the UAW, and the International AFL-CIO, have all made efforts to resolve this divisive dispute.

Consider these events among many:

- October 1995—The unions proposed a 30-day period of intensive bargaining. At the end of 30 days, all unresolved issues would be submitted to a community panel to be chosen jointly by the unions and the company for binding arbitration. Detroit Newspapers rejected this offer.
- December 1995—U.S. Senator Carl Levin (Michigan), Cardinal Adam Maida of the Detroit Archdiocese and Detroit Mayor Dennis Archer met with newspaper officials and offered to help arbitrate the dispute. The unions accepted the offer, but the company rejected it. United Methodist Bishop Donald A. Ott of the Detroit Conference and Episcopal Bishop Stewart Wood of the Michigan Diocese also offered to mediate and were rejected.
- January 1996—Many denominations and faiths have definitive statements about the just treatment of workers. Early in 1996, more than 850 religious leaders from the greater Detroit metro-

politan area (Religious Leaders for Justice at the Detroit Newspapers) presented an appeal asking the newspapers to negotiate contracts and settle the strike. They vowed not to buy the *Detroit News* and *Detroit Free Press* until the dispute was resolved, saying, "We consider the permanent replacement of striking workers by the owners of both the *News* and *Free Press* to be morally objectionable and a breach of the ethical teachings of our faith traditions," and that, " . . . workers have a moral right to form unions for the purpose of collective bargaining to achieve justice in the workplace. The permanent replacement of strikers negates that basic right." Hundreds of thousands of readers have joined this refusal to buy the papers.

- March-May, 1996—Community and religious leaders, among them seven United Methodist pastors, undertook weekly symbolic and direct actions at the newspaper headquarters. These non-violent actions, organized by the independent community group, Readers United, resulted in nearly 300 arrests. United Methodist pastor Rev. Bill Wylie-Kellermann led weekly non-violence training of participants and peacekeepers.
- May 1996—Representatives of Readers United met separately with the Metro Council of Newspaper Unions and with Detroit Newspapers executives Frank Vega and Heath Meriwether to discuss both non-violence and the urgency of a settlement. They also offered community mediation to resolve the struggle. The newspapers refused this offer.
- August 1996—Detroit Mayor Dennis Archer met with both sides and offered to give good-paying jobs to all the replacement workers so union members could reclaim their rightful places. The newspapers rejected the offer.
- Spring of 1996, 1997 and 1998—Delegations of religious, political, community and union members attended each annual meeting of the Gannett and Knight-Ridder corporations, appealing for a good faith effort to settle the labor dispute. The meetings took place in Arlington, Va., Miami, Fla., Philadelphia, Pa., and San Jose, Calif. The CEOs and Directors of Gannett and Knight-Ridder rejected requests for private meetings from community leaders, U.S. Congressman John Conyers, Detroit City Council Chair Maryanne Mahaffey, and Reverend Edwin Rowe, pastor of Detroit Central UMC.

- February 1997—The unions ended their strike with an unconditional offer to return to work. Detroit newspapers accepted the offer, but refused to reinstate the workers. Employees were placed on a hiring list to be recalled as positions opened up. Over the course of two years, less than 700 union members have been called back, leaving more than 1,000 workers locked-out. The company has eliminated entire job categories, locking out dozens of employees with more than 30 years service. They have reduced wages by 50 percent for some positions, turned full-time jobs into part-time work and made massive changes in the terms of employment without regard for employee representation. Following these unilateral actions, the NLRB instituted new charges of unfair labor practices against the newspapers.
- June 1997—After a yearlong trial, an administrative law judge found the Detroit newspapers guilty of 10 of 12 unfair labor practices. The judge ordered the company to take back all the locked-out workers immediately, releasing replacement workers if necessary. He also said the company must provide workers with back pay dating back to the day the return to work offer was made.

Among the company's unfair labor practices were: provoking and prolonging the strike, forcing an illegal merit pay system on the Newspaper Guild, refusal to provide the unions with information essential to the collective bargaining process, the illegal destruction of materials ripped down from union bulletin boards, the unlawful use of permanent replacement workers in an unfair labor practice strike.

The day after the judge's decision, 100,000 people marched through downtown Detroit as part of Action Motown, a mobilization called to support locked-out workers and urge the company to negotiate contracts.

- Winter 1998—The National Labor Relations Board charged the newspapers with illegally firing 125 union members for exercising their civil and constitutional rights to strike and picket. Lawyers estimate that with company appeals, many of these cases may take up to five years to resolve.
- March-April, 1998—Religious and community leaders made presentations to more than two dozen city councils in and around Detroit. The municipalities issued resolutions agree-

ing to attend a community summet meeting to explore ways
to urge the ending the labor dispute.

- May 1998—More than 300 people, including city council mem-
bers and mayors from 26 cities in the Detroit area, participated
in the Summit Meeting held at Sacred Heart Seminary in
Detroit. Episcopal Bishop Start Wood of the Michigan Diocese
presided over the meeting. Panelists Rabbi Robert Syme,
United Methodist pastor Rev. Bill Wylie-Kellermann, Baptist
Ministers Conference president Rev. J. J. Perry, Newspaper
Guild President Lou Mleczko, former Free Press columnist
Susan Watson, Roman Catholic Bishop Thomas Gumbleton
and United Methodist Bishop Donald Ott, asked the participants how the labor dispute was affecting their communities.
Many cited the absence of basic information so necessary in
the democratic process. Hundreds of thousands of people
refuse to buy or read the papers because they believe employees were treated unfairly. Public officials and progressive
voices of the area refuse to be interviewed by the newspapers
while the lockout continues. Such absences create unbalanced
and incomplete news. Others cited the bad feelings and divi-
siveness created by the community's perception of being overcome by a media giant who operates from hundreds of miles
away and appears to care little about Detroit's problems.
Detroit newspaper officials were invited to participate in the
summit but declined to send a representative. They agreed,
however, to receive information gathered at the meeting.
- July 1998—A delegation led by United Methodist Bishop Jesse
DeWitt representing elected officials, Religious Leaders for
Justice, and the Inter-faith Committee for Worker Justice met
with union leadership and Detroit newspaper management separately to report the conclusions of the Summit. Both the news-
papers and the unions agreed to begin bargaining in good faith.
- August 1998—After more than three years of the strike/lock-
out, negotiations resumed under the supervision of the
Federal Mediation Service.
- September 1998—After a year of deliberation, the National
Labor Relations Board upheld the administrative law judge's
decision that the company is guilty of provoking and prolonging the strike through nine unfair labor practices. The
NLRB, comprised of both Republicans and Democrats,

reached a unanimous decision. Once again, the company was ordered to take back all workers who were illegally replaced. The company still refused to abide by the order, instead asking the NLRB to reconsider its unanimous decision.

- February 1999—Sporadic negotiations continue, while both sides wait for the NLRB to announce its decision on the motion to reconsider its ruling.

During all this time of community distress, endless appeals and economic hardship for striking/locked-out workers, hundreds of prayer vigils, marches, rallies, picket lines, and demonstrations have taken place in support of a just settlement and protesting the permanent replacement of workers. All these efforts have failed to resolve this dispute.

Much has been made of the violence of the strike, yet observers are surprised at how restrained frustrated workers have been. Security guards, admittedly trained to instigate violence and then photograph reaction to it, have injured many workers who were legally picketing. No incidence of injury against replacement workers or managers has been documented.

Decision Making

The act of instituting an economic boycott is a sobering one and is approached with all seriousness. We have thoughtfully considered the implications of a boycott in light of the disciplinary requirements in *The Book of Resolutions*. We believe an economic boycott of *USA TODAY*, the flagship publication of the Gannett corporation, is necessary to: achieve a just resolution before the suffering of the workers and the community becomes more acute; and, before the process of collective bargaining is further eroded. A fair resolution to this dispute will also have profound effects on newspaper employees in other cities who struggle for fair treatment and just wages.

Monitoring

Upon approval by the Detroit Annual Conference, information regarding this issue will be dispersed through established agencies. The Gannett Company will be informed of the boycott and its intended purpose. A monitoring team with broad representation of clergy, lay, political, and business members will be established to keep our constituencies informed. The annual conference, districts, and pastors will be informed of the circumstances and reasons for the action.

Suspension/Termination Procedure

The boycott will be terminated as soon as bargained contracts with the six unions are achieved.

ADOPTED 2000

See Social Principles, ¶ 163B.

195. Guidelines for Initiating or Joining an Economic Boycott

Preamble

An economic boycott is understood to be a combined effort to abstain from the purchase or use of products or services provided by a targeted firm, government, or other agency. The purpose of a boycott is to persuade the targeted body to cease from certain practices judged to be unjust, and/or to perform certain practices deemed to be just.

Acknowledging the boycott as a legitimate Christian response to an identified social or economic injustice, we recommend the following criteria as a process for guiding the church and its agencies in decisions regarding boycott. This process includes the following steps:

- preparation
- decision making
- monitoring
- suspension/termination

The decision-making body shall designate those persons who will perform the tasks of each step.

The twelve criteria are the minimal concerns to be addressed as a decision-making body secures information and data upon which to determine its action.

The questions following the criteria statements are not part of the criteria but are given to help a decision-making body address specific areas of concern and secure information that will assist in its decision.

The gathered information and data are to be written and distributed to the decision-making body.

Clarifying Who May Call

Any local church, district, annual conference, or general church board or agency shall be able to join a boycott if it ascertains that another part of The United Methodist Church, or an ecumenical agency that the church is a member of, has completed the initiation process described below. Any of the above may request the General Conference to join it in the boycott in the name of The United Methodist Church. Only the General Conference shall be empowered to initiate a boycott in the name of The United Methodist Church. It shall designate responsibility for monitoring and suspending and/or terminating such a boycott.

Preparation

I. Identify in writing the biblical and theological imperatives that address the issues involved in this particular conflict. How are the issues involved related to the purposes and mission of the decision-making body?

II. Document the social-justice issues in the dispute through on-site investigation, interviews, and hearings and study of literature, including input from:

A. each of the major parties in the dispute;

B. United Methodist sources, including the presiding bishop(s), leadership of the annual conferences, superintendent(s), and local church leadership (laity and clergy) in the region where the dispute or alleged injustice is occurring; and

C. objective third parties.

1. How do the social justice issues affect various segments of society and the communities in the area?

2. What sources of political, economic, or social power does each party in the dispute or alleged injustice have?

3. How will a boycott affect a potential resolution of the situation?

4. Are the leaders in the dispute or grievance supported by the persons for whom they speak, and are they committed to nonviolent action?

5. What denominational reviews have been made on this issue?

6. What groups, agencies, or governmental bodies have been seeking resolution in the conflict?

III. Evaluate the conflict described by the gathered information in relation to the theological, ethical, and social principles of Christian tradition and The United Methodist Church.
  1. Is intervention needed, and what magnitude of response is appropriate to the scope of the injustice?
  2. Is the desired end clearly specified?
IV. Generate a list of potential public and private means of intervention in the situation, and evaluate the probable results of each.
  1. What methods of mediation, dialogue, and negotiations have been attempted and evaluated?
  2. Have these means of intervention been publicized and shared with connectional leadership in the region of the conflict and other constituencies?
  3. Is the injustice of sufficient scope to warrant the mobilization of a boycott?
  4. Is a boycott a more constructive and effective means of achieving justice than more coercive means?
  5. What are likely to be the positive and negative consequences of a boycott?
  6. What will the effects likely be in the local community?
  7. Are the issues adequately clarified so as to provide support for a boycott?
  8. How can negative stereotyping of contending parties be avoided?
V. Clearly state in writing the objectives the potential boycott is intended to achieve.
  1. How will these objectives be shared with the disputing parties?
  2. Is it clear as to how the objectives of the potential boycott relate to other strategies being used by this or other church bodies?
  3. Are these objectives in harmony with the theological, ethical, and social principles? (*See* criteria I and III.)
VI. Develop a plan and identify resources for carrying out a potential boycott, including mechanisms for:
  1. communicating to church constituencies the objectives of the boycott; the issues as seen by the various parties; and the biblical, theological, and ethical imperatives for involvement;

2. informing disputing parties of an intention to call or participate in a boycott;
3. coordinating efforts with other United Methodist bodies, interfaith coalitions, and groups dealing with the issues;
4. monitoring the progress of the boycott (*see* VIII);
5. suspending/terminating the boycott when objectives are met (*see* IX, X, XI);
6. developing ministries of reconciliation between aggrieved parties, during and following the boycott action.
7. deciding what resources and plans have been made to ensure that the potential boycott will be carried out effectively and responsibly; and
8. providing the presiding bishop(s), council director(s), superintendent(s), pastors, and membership in the region with the opportunity to participate in the development of this plan.

Decision

VII. On the basis of the information obtained in I and II above, decide whether a boycott action is merited.
1. What opportunity has been or will be provided for thorough consideration and debate of the issues?
2. Why is this the best time for this decision-making body to enter the boycott?
3. Is the boycott likely to achieve the stated objectives and assist in resolution of the dispute?

Monitoring

VIII. Designate a group of persons, including church representatives from the local area affected, who will monitor the boycott. Monitoring shall include:
1. regular evaluation and reporting of progress toward the stated objective;
2. regular written reporting of such progress to the local area affected and to the constituencies of the decision-making bodies through appropriate denominational channels;
3. reporting substantial changes in the conditions under which the boycott is being carried out;
4. a process for issuing public statements; and

5. coordination with designated coalitions and interfaith groups.

Suspension/Termination

IX. In those cases where circumstances have changed, making it unclear whether the objectives of the boycott are being met, in consultation with the designated coalition and/or participating groups that are coordinating the boycott action, the decision-making body, or its designate, may call for suspension of the boycott while monitoring and evaluation continues.

X. When the clearly stated written objectives of the boycott have been met, in consultation with the designated coalition and/or participating groups that are coordinating boycott action, the decision-making body or its designate shall terminate boycott participation.

XI. Notification of suspension/termination shall be made in writing to all parties in the dispute and to all constituencies of the decision-making body.

XII. Following this notification, monitoring of compliance with objectives and ministries of reconciliation shall be continued by the decision-making body for a responsible period of time.

ADOPTED 1988
REVISED AND ADOPTED 2000

See Social Principles, ¶ 163B.

196. Taco Bell Boycott

WHEREAS, all people have been created in the image of God, redeemed through Jesus Christ, and called to share in a ministry of reconciliation that shapes our world according to God's intention of shalom;

WHEREAS, fasting is a sign of repentance as well as a spiritual practice that helps us to see God's vision for our world more clearly and to identify the grave injustices around us, refraining from patronage in response to unjust practices can likewise be an act of repentance through which we acknowledge and take responsibility for our participation and complicity in such injustice and act with God to transform our world;

WHEREAS, in Globalization and its Impact on Human Dignity and Human Rights, our church has stated that "[m]igrant workers continue to be discriminated against and abused, especially those who are undocumented in their host countries. Women migrants are particularly vulnerable to exploitation especially when they work in gender-specific jobs that consign them to various forms of sexual, domestic, and menial work. Studies show that the majority of migrants are uprooted because of the lack of jobs at home or because jobs pay extremely low wages. While globalization has spawned more capital and spurred greater production, workers' wages have been kept low and below a livable wage even in those countries whose governments have a prescribed minimum wage";

WHEREAS, "[m]igrants' rights are human rights. It is tragic when migrants, whose rights

have already been violated in their home countries, find their human rights also violated in their foreign host countries. Invoking host country laws rarely works in their favor;

WHEREAS, we have urged governments to ratify and implement the United Nations International Convention on the Protection of the Rights of All Migrant Workers and Members of Their Families. This Convention will be an instrument to protect, secure, and ensure the human rights of migrant workers and their families;

WHEREAS, the Immokalee farm workers earn sub-poverty wages for picking tomatoes used in Taco Bell food products. According to the Department of Labor, their average wage (40 cents per 32 pound bucket) has not changed in more than twenty years;

WHEREAS, some farm workers picking tomatoes have been held in debt-bondage slavery;

WHEREAS, farm workers are not covered by the National Labor Relations Act, which means that unemployment and workers' compensation benefits have been systematically denied to them. Farm labor policies, such as the current guestworker/H2A visa program, which allows agricultural workers temporary entrance into the U.S., have severely diminished the limited protections afforded farm workers. This type of program keeps real wages down; maintains substandard working conditions; eliminates workers' rights to voice grievances; and denies workers their civil rights, including the fundamental right of freedom of movement. Farm work is one of the most hazardous occupations in the United States, placing workers at a higher risk of injury and therefore blocking access to the means other workers have for addressing workplace problems;

WHEREAS, the Coalition of Immokalee Workers (CIW) has called for a consumer boycott of Taco Bell restaurants and products;

WHEREAS, the 214th General Assembly of the Presbyterian Church (U.S.A.) and the Twenty-third General Synod of the United Church of Christ have endorsed this consumer boycott;

WHEREAS, the NCCC through its policy statements, resolutions and the accompaniment of the National Farm Worker Ministry has consistently supported the right of farm workers in their efforts to win just wages and working conditions and a voice in the workplace;

WHEREAS, at the November 2002 meeting of the NCCC Executive Board unanimously called for the issues behind the Taco Bell boycott to be reviewed and reported to the next meeting of the Executive Board;

WHEREAS, at the February 2003 meeting the NCCC Executive Board voted to study the issues behind the boycott and invite the member communions similarly to study the issues by: (a) using resources prepared by the Presbyterian Church (U.S.A.), the United Church of Christ, the National Farm Worker Ministry, and the Coalition of Immokalee Workers; (b) speaking with the Coalition of Immokalee Workers and with Emil Brolick, president of Taco Bell; and (c) prayerfully engaging these issues from their own tradition's teachings and witness so as to be prepared to make a recommendation on the boycott to the General Assembly for action at the November 2003 meeting;

WHEREAS, in February 2003 the Executive Board of the National Council of Churches of Christ, of which The United Methodist Church is an active member, unanimously adopted a resolution of support of and pastoral concern for the CIW workers who were on a hunger strike outside of Taco Bell's worldwide office in Irvine, CA;

WHEREAS, General Secretary Robert Edgar designated Noelle Damico of the Presbyterian Church (U.S.A.) to dialogue on his behalf with the Coalition of Immokalee Workers and with Emil Brolick, president of Taco Bell about the NCCC's Executive Board's resolution;

WHEREAS, Mr. Brolick has not until now responded to either Rev. Edgar's verbal request for a meeting with Noelle Damico nor has he responded to Rev. Edgar's written request of February 2003, requesting an appointment for himself and the heads of the Council's member denominations at Mr. Brolick's earliest convenience to discuss issues related to the boycott;

WHEREAS, on Ash Wednesday 2003 the General Secretary, President, and President Elect of the NCC sent a letter respectfully requesting that the workers cease their hunger strike and allow the church to carry forward their struggle that was copied to Mr. Brolick;

WHEREAS, member communions have been prayerfully engaging this issue from their own traditions' teachings and witness and with information provided by the NCCC;

Therefore be it resolved, that 2004 General Conference of The United Methodist Church joins the CIW's boycott of Taco Bell restaurants and products until such time as Taco Bell

1. convenes serious three-way talks between the Coalition of Immokalee Workers, representatives of Taco Bell, and their tomato suppliers to address exploitation and slavery in the fields,

2. contributes to an immediate increase in farm worker wages through an increase in the per pound rate it pays for tomatoes, and

3. works with the CIW, tomato industry representatives, and tomato suppliers to establish a code of conduct that would ensure workers' fundamental labor rights by defining strict wage and working condition standards required of all Taco Bell suppliers.

Be it further resolved, that the Council of Bishops in consultation with the General Board of Church and Society, name a monitoring committee that will be responsible to assess the progress and the status of the negotiations between Taco Bell and CIW.

Be it finally resolved, that the monitoring committee be empowered to recommend the end of the boycott when the above-mentioned criteria are met or the workers call for an end to the boycott.

ADOPTED 2004

See Social Principles, ¶163B.

197. Mt. Olive Pickle Company Boycott

WHEREAS, Agricultural Missions Inc. of the National Council of the Churches of Christ in the USA, and the General Board of Church and Society of The United Methdist Church have completed the process outlined in "Guidelines for Instituting an Economic Boycott," *2000 Book of Resolutions,* and endorsed the Farm Labor Organizing

Committee AFL-CIO Boycott* of Mt. Olive Products on the basis of its findings; and,

WHEREAS, the National Council of Churches of Christ in the USA has endorsed the boycott of Mt. Olive Products; and

WHEREAS other boards or divisions of The United Methodist Church are members of Agricultural Missions Inc. and the National Council of Churches of Christ in the USA; and

Therefore be it resolved, the General Conference of The United Methodist Church reaffirms its justice witness for migrant farm workers by supporting the boycott of Mt. Olive Pickle Co. products until the Farm Labor Organizing Committee and the Mt. Olive Pickle Company reach a collective bargaining agreement.

ADOPTED 2004

See Social Principles, ¶ 163*B*.

CONSUMPTION

198. Tobacco Marketing by Altria/Philip Morris and RJR Nabisco

As people of faith in the living God, we are reminded that Jesus spoke out for justice for the poor, the disenfranchised and the powerless and called us to love one another. The Bible reminds us that our bodies are "temples of the living God" (1 Corinthians 6:13-20) and since we are created in God's own image, we are then called by God to perfect our bodies in God's image. Moreover, we are called by God to ensure that all of God's creation has access to the knowledge of God's love and God's concern for our well-being and welfare. Through our historic Wesleyan heritage and by John Wesley's words, we are reminded as United Methodists that "the world is our parish," and we are called to minister in and throughout the whole world.

The United Methodist Church and its predecessor denominations have a long history of witness against the use and marketing of tobacco products. There is overwhelming evidence linking cigarette smoking with lung cancer, cardiovascular diseases, emphysema, chronic bronchitis, and related illnesses.

*On September 15, 2004, the Farm Labor Organizing Committee signed an agreement with the North Carolina Growers Association, which the Mt. Olive Pickle Company endorsed, ending the boycott. For more information on the original findings see "Report on the Mt. Olive Boycott by the Farm Labor Organizing Committee and Migrant Farm Worker Conditions in North Carolina and in the United States," Agricultural Missions Inc., National Council of Churches of Christ in the USA, September 18, 2000, at www.nccusa.org/publicwitness/mtolive.

We are outraged by the use of marketing techniques aimed at children by leading cigarette manufacturers. Specific companies using marketing strategies aimed at children are Altria/Philip Morris, which sells Marlboro cigarettes, and RJR Nabisco, which sells Camel cigarettes.

Therefore, as people of faith who believe our bodies are temples of the living God (1 Corinthians 6:13-20), we:

1. direct the General Board of Church and Society to maintain and publish a current list of consumer products produced by Altria/Philip Morris and RJR Naboscp so that United Methodists are made aware of their indirect support of the tobacco industry;

2. commend the General Board of Pensions and Health Benefits for its long-standing exclusion of tobacco manufacturers from its investment portfolio and ask it to challenge public media in its portfolio not to carry advertisements and promotion of tobacco products;

3. ask all United Methodist agencies and related institutions to take into account the church's Social Principles and tobacco concerns and, specifically, to consider the role of Altria/Philip Morris and RJR Nabisco in tobacco marketing as a factor in any decision concerning purchasing food products manufactured by them;

4. request the United Methodist general agencies to communicate, interpret, and advocate for this concern with their affiliated institutions;

5. ask all local churches and annual conferences to educate their membership about the tobacco industry's marketing tactics aimed at children. It is equally important we understand the connection between our purchasing food products and our indirect support of the tobacco industry;

6. request the General Board of Church and Society to explore productive measures aimed at stopping tobacco companies from marketing cigarettes and other tobacco products to children and, if necessary, organize a boycott; and

7. direct the General Board of Church and Society to communicate this resolution to the tobacco companies, serve as a continuing advocate of the United Methodist position within The United Methodist Church and with the companies, and monitor the implementation of this resolution for report at the next General Conference.

ADOPTED 1996
AMENDED AND READOPTED 2004

See Social Principles, ¶ 163D.

199. United Methodist Church Use of Fair Trade Coffee

WHEREAS, coffee is one of the world's most heavily traded commodities; it originates from either large plantations that are traditionally run and owned by wealthy landowners or small operations that are primarily owned by impoverished farmers. These small farmers frequently live in isolated communities relying on middlemen to buy their coffee invariably at the lowest price possible. The way the system is set up, the farmers' inability to get a just return for their labor is essentially guaranteed and they are condemned to a life of extreme poverty; and,

WHEREAS, biblical justice brings all into the economic community, with a share in productive power as seen in the provision of land to every family unit (Numbers 26; Leviticus 25); and,

WHEREAS, our Social Principles state that "we support measures that would reduce the concentration of wealth in the hands of the few," that "we advocate for the rights of people to possess property and to earn a living by tilling the soil"; and that "we call upon our churches to do all in their power to speak prophetically to the matters of food supply and the people who grow the food for the world" (¶ 163); and,

WHEREAS, the United Methodist Committee on Relief (UMCOR) partnered in April 2002 with Equal Exchange to launch a denomination-wide coffee program and through the partnership, any United Methodist church or individual buying coffee through Equal Exchange's Interfaith Program can now order coffee through UMCOR (at the Equal Exchange Web site), and who, for every case of coffee ordered, receives approximately 5 percent of purchase price from Equal Exchange to be used in UMCOR's small farmer economic development programs; and,

WHEREAS, the annual conferences of New England, East Ohio, and Nebraska have resolutions and programs to foster purchase of fair trade coffee by their member churches to support impoverished family farmers in the developing world provide for their families; and

WHEREAS, many of our agencies and congregations, their administrations and their committee organizations serve coffee at meetings, programs, and fund-raising events; and,

WHEREAS, purchasing domestic coffee brands at the least expensive price makes us unintentional participants in an exploitative system that has trapped thousands of developing world farmers, their families and children in an inescapable cycle of poverty; and,

WHEREAS, economic justice can be fostered by consumers exercising their economic power to avoid purchasing products in conditions where workers are being exploited; and,

WHEREAS, the International Standards of Fair Trade focus on ensuring that small farmers are compensated with a fair and true living wage, working with democratically run farming cooperatives that are owned and governed by and for the farmers themselves, buying directly from the co-ops so that the benefits and profits from the trade actually reach the farmers and their communities, providing vital advance credit to farmers and encouraging sustainable farming practices; and,

WHEREAS, the General Conference of The United Methodist Church seeks to address the underlying systemic justice issues throughout the world and to provide opportunities for supporting systems based on the values of justice, cooperation, sustainability, and the common good, we therefore create a partnership with a key U. S. Fair Trade organization, Equal Exchange, and join over 5,000 places of worship and faith-based organizations who support small coffee farmers in developing nations.

Therefore, be it resolved, that in seeking an authentic Christian response to the plight of developing world small individual coffee farmers, their families, and their communities, the General Conference of The United Methodist Church urges all agencies of the church, local congregations and their affiliated organizations that use coffee to purchase coffee for corporate and personal use through the fair trade partner, Equal Exchange, or through another fair trade organization.

ADOPTED 2004

See Social Principles, ¶ 163D.

EDUCATION

200. Endowment Funds for Black Colleges and Universities

WHEREAS, The United Methodist Church and its predecessor denomination, the Methodist Episcopal Church, from its inception in 1784, has been deeply rooted in the social order; and

WHEREAS, The United Methodist Church has actively identified with the problems of society and this has been one source of its strength and spiritual life; and

WHEREAS, after slavery, the establishment of schools for African-Americans immediately after the Civil War was a powerful expression of the very nature of the denomination's doctrine derived from John Wesley; and

WHEREAS, The United Methodist Church today supports the largest number of historically Black colleges and universities of any denomination in the United States; and

WHEREAS, these eleven institutions provide access to higher education for thousands of young women and men of promise; and

WHEREAS, the historically Black colleges and universities are preparing a new generation of leaders, lay and clerical for the next millennium; and

WHEREAS, the Black College Fund, created by the 1972 General Conference, is essential to the ongoing life of these eleven academic institutions; and

WHEREAS, technological demands, library resources, and faculty development are critical driving forces for continual accreditation and academic excellence, be it resolved that The United Methodist Church build sufficient permanent endowment funds to enable these academic institutions to sustain their long term institutional viability and effectiveness and to advance their mission in partnership with The United Methodist Church in preparing a new generation of leaders for our church and society; and

WHEREAS, the General Council on Finance and Administration (GCFA) made a unanimous decision at its December 1-4, 1998, meeting that "GCFA encourage the General Board of Higher Education and Ministry to consider creation of an endowment fund for the colleges" in addition to the church's continuing support of the Black College Fund,

Therefore, be it resolved, that the General Board of Higher Education and Ministry request that the 2000 General Conference authorize the General Board of Higher Education and Ministry to develop and implement a twenty-five-year plan to raise $300 million in endowment funds, to be managed by GBHEM, that will increase and strengthen the $205-million endowment now held collectively by the eleven historically Black colleges and universities of The United Methodist Church.

Be it further resolved, that said endowment funds will be raised by private programs under the leadership of the General Board of Higher Education and Ministry.

ADOPTED 2000

See Social Principles, ¶ 163.

FAMILY FARMS

201. Ask the United States Attorney General to Investigate Violations of Sherman Anti-Trust Act in Order to Protect Family Farms

WHEREAS, it has been established that the potential for monopoly control of an industry begins as a threshold share of 40 percent of the market in the respective industry; and

WHEREAS, it has been established that an alternative form of monopoly control of an industry begins when a small group of firms passes the 40-percent threshold market share thereby creating an oligopoly; and

WHEREAS, a January 1999 report of the Concentration of Agricultural Markets by Heffernan, Gronski, and Hendrickson of the University of Missouri documents that oligopoly control of food processing exists at 40 percent or higher in 7 out of 8 major food commodities; and

WHEREAS, that same report reveals those same processing firms are now moving into production at greater levels; and

WHEREAS, all major commodity prices that family farmers have received since the fall of 1998 do not reach the break-even point; and

WHEREAS, the number of family farms has shrunk from 6 million to 2 million over the last three decades; and

WHEREAS, two thirds of local United Methodist Churches in the United States serve rural parishes; and

WHEREAS, 2 Timothy 2:6 advises, *It is the hard-working farmer who ought to have the first share of the crops,*

Therefore, be it resolved, that the 2000 General Conference of The United Methodist Church call upon the attorney general of the United States to begin an immediate and comprehensive investigation of all matters pertaining to the effects of industry concentration on production, marketing, processing, and pricing of all major farm commodities.

Be it further resolved, that this investigation be conducted with the express purpose of determining if the current, documented oligopoly in agriculture has indeed been operating in violation of the Sherman Anti-trust Act.

ADOPTED 2000

See Social Principles, ¶ 163H.

202. Family Farm Justice

WHEREAS, John Wesley preached that the renewal of the image of God in creation is a goal of Christianity, and it is the Christian's vocation to assist in that renewal; and

WHEREAS, the majority of producers and farmers caring for creation today understand themselves to be stewards holding a sacred trust from God, and as such are conservators of the land within that trust; and

WHEREAS, we are in the midst of a financial crisis in rural and agricultural areas; and

WHEREAS, the root cause of this financial crisis appears to be the sin of greed, which manifests itself at all levels, from the producers up to and especially including the multinational corporations in the agricultural-related industries; and

WHEREAS, this crisis promotes on the farm decision making based not in conservatorship or stewardship, but in profit making, which may result in harm to God's creation; and

WHEREAS, God's producers, farmers, and conservators of creation are not receiving a just and fair amount for the goods they produce; and

WHEREAS, we believe that rural persons/families should be able to enjoy the just fruits of their labor, as much as any of the rest of us; and

WHEREAS, this financial crisis has also created a spiritual crisis in many rural families,

Therefore, because we believe this to be a justice issue which affects our sacred trust of God's creation, we resolve to respond to this need on both the general church and local church level in the following ways:

(1) We resolve to direct the appropriate agencies of the general church to lobby both our national government and multinational corporations, to do all they can to bring justice to the local producers, by lobbying for fair and equitable prices for goods and services produced.

(2) We resolve that the General, jurisdictional, annual conferences, and local churches encourage every pastor whose congregation is touched by these issues to invite caring laypersons to join her or him in making a personal visit to the home of every farm family in our parishes.

ADOPTED 2000

See Social Principles, ¶ 163H.

GAMBLING

203. Gambling

The Social Principles state that, "Gambling is a menace to society, deadly to the best interests of moral, social, economic, and spiritual life, and destructive of good government. As an act of faith and concern, Christians should abstain from gambling and should strive to minister to those victimized by the practice. Where gambling has become addictive, the church will encourage such individuals to receive therapeutic assistance so that the individual's energies may be redirected into positive and constructive ends. The church should promote standards and personal lifestyles that would make unnecessary and undesirable the resort to commercial gambling—including public lotteries—as a recreation, as an escape, or as a means of producing public revenue or funds for support of charities or government" (¶ 163G).

When asked which commandment is first of all, Jesus answered, "Hear, O Israel: the Lord our God, the Lord is one; you shall love the Lord your God with all your heart, and with all your soul, and with all your mind, and with all your strength" (Mark 12:29-30). Gambling feeds on human greed and invites persons to place their trust in possessions rather than in God. It represents a form of idolatry that contradicts the first commandment. Jesus continued: "The second is this, `You shall love your neighbor as yourself' " (Mark 12:31). In relating with compassion to our sisters and brothers, we are called to resist those practices and systems that exploit them and leave them impoverished and demeaned. The apostle Paul wrote in 1 Timothy 6:9-10a: "People who want to get rich fall into temptation and a trap and into many foolish and harmful desires that plunge men into ruin and destruction. For the love of money is a root of all kinds of evil."

Gambling, as a means of acquiring material gain by chance and at the neighbor's expense, is a menace to personal character and social morality. Gambling fosters greed and stimulates the fatalistic faith in chance. Organized and commercial gambling is a threat to business, breeds crime and poverty, and is destructive to the interests of good government. It encourages the belief that work is unimportant, that money can solve all our problems, and that greed is the norm for achievement. It serves as a "regressive tax" on those with lower income. In summary, gambling is bad economics; gambling is bad public policy; and gambling does not improve the quality of life.

We oppose the growing legalization and state promotion of gambling.

Dependence on gambling revenue has led many states to exploit the weakness of their own citizens, neglect the development of more equitable forms of taxation, and thereby further erode the citizens' confidence in government.

We oppose the legalization of pari-mutuel betting, for it has been the opening wedge in the legalization of other forms of gambling within the states and has stimulated illegal bookmaking. We deplore the establishment of state lotteries and their use as a means of raising public revenues. The constant promotion and the wide advertising of lotteries have encouraged large numbers of persons to gamble for the first time.

We express an even more serious concern for the increasing development of the casino enterprise in the United States, for it has taken captive entire communities and has infiltrated many levels of government with its fiscal and political power.

Public apathy and a lack of awareness that petty gambling feeds organized crime have opened the door to the spread of numerous forms of legal and illegal gambling.

We support the strong enforcement of antigambling laws, the repeal of all laws that give gambling an acceptable and even advantageous place in our society, and the rehabilitation of compulsive gamblers.

The church has a key role in fostering responsible government and in developing health and moral maturity that free persons from dependence on damaging social customs. We urge national, tribal, state and local governments to read, analyze and implement the recommendations of the National Gambling Impact Study report released by the United States in 1999. It is expected that United Methodist churches abstain from the use of raffles, lotteries, bingo, door prizes, other drawing schemes, and games of chance for the purpose of gambling or fundraising. United Methodists should refrain from all forms of gambling practices carried on in our communities and should work to influence community organizations to develop forms of funding that do not depend upon gambling.

The General Board of Church and Society shall provide materials to local churches and annual conferences for study and action to combat gambling and to aid persons addicted to gambling. The,General Board of Church and Society, annual conferences, and local churches shall work with the National Coalition Against Legalized Gambling and grassroots organizations opposing gambling to stop and reverse legalized gambling. The General Board of Church and Society shall report to the 2008 General Conference which stock market and securities practices might be considered forms of gambling. The Board shall consult with the General Board of Pensions and Health Benefits and other agencies with investment portfolios in developing this report.

ADOPTED 1980
AMENDED AND READOPTED 1996
AMENDED AND READOPTED 2004

See Social Principles, ¶ 163G.

204. Gambling Impact Report

WHEREAS, Congress charged nine persons to serve in the task of a very broad and difficult-to-conduct comprehensive legal and factual study of the social and economic implications of gambling in the U.S.; and

WHEREAS, these commissioners, in dedicated service to the truest demonstration of democracy, did present for our good use an executive summary of their conclusions and recommendations, strongly suggested that the public follow as guidelines in evaluating the impact on which this phenomena—gambling—is sweeping the nation; and

WHEREAS, the recommendations are in place for all to see on the Web site www.ngisc.gov and in the hands of every congressperson,

Therefore, be it resolved, that every delegate of the 2000 General Conference be persuaded to obtain a copy from each one's respective representative, read it completely, and make the contents known to those they, in turn, represent at this conference so as to make their states more knowledgeable of the dangers of addiction, the preludes, and consequences and pledge leadership in using their knowledge, duly received as soon as possible.

ADOPTED 2000

See Social Principles, ¶ 163G.

GLOBAL ECONOMIC JUSTICE

205. The United Methodist Church, Justice, and World Hunger

Is not this the fast that I choose: to loose the bonds of injustice, to undo the thongs of the yoke, to let the oppressed go free, and to break every yoke? Is it not to share your bread with the hungry, and bring the homeless poor into your house; when you see the naked, to cover them, and not to hide yourself from your own kin? Then your light shall break forth like the dawn, and your healing shall spring up quickly; your vindicator shall go before you, the glory of the LORD *shall be your rear guard* (Isaiah 58:6-8, NRSV).

I. Introduction

In 1996, the World Food Summit held in Rome, Italy, reaffirmed "the right of everyone to have access to safe and nutritious food, consistent with the right to adequate food and the fundamental right of everyone to be free from hunger." It declared that urgent action must be taken to create food security. "Food security exists when all people, at all times, have physical and economic access to sufficient, safe and nutritious food to meet their dietary needs and food preferences for an active and healthy life."[1]

Although globally enough food is produced to feed everyone, 840 million people are undernourished, 799 million of them in the developing world. Children and elderly are particularly at risk. Each year, six million children die as a result of hunger. Although hunger is also a problem in cities, seventy-five percent of the world's hungry people live in rural areas.[2]

The reasons for this continuing tragedy are complex and interrelated. Some causes of world hunger are:

- drought and other weather-related problems;
- poverty and greed;
- inequitable distribution of wealth and unjust economic systems;
- insufficient food production in developing nations;
- use of arable land for non-food and cash crops such as tobacco;
- increasing emphasis on export-oriented agriculture;
- over-fishing of the oceans;
- population growth;
- internal displacement of people;
- wasteful consumerism in richer countries;
- militarism, war, and civil unrest;
- HIV/AIDS pandemic;
- corruption in governments;
- lending policies of the World Bank (IBRD) and the International Monetary Fund (IMF);
- production of unnecessary goods and services that waste resources;
- environmental degradation;
- use of farm subsidies in richer nations that export to poor countries causing them to reject their own products;

1. "Rome Declaration on Food Security," World Food Summit 13-17 November, 1996, http://www.fao.org/docrep/003/w3613e/w3613e00.htm 8 May, 2003
2. *Agriculture in the Global Economy* (Washington, D.C.: Bread for the World Institute, 2003), pp. 2-5; Bread for the World Hunger Basics: International Facts on Hunger and Poverty, http://www.bread.org/hungerbasics/international.html; *The State of Food Insecurity in the World 2002* (Rome: Food and Agriculture Organization of the United Nations, 2002), 8 May http://www.fao.org/docrep/005/y7352e/y7352e00.htm 8 May, 2003.

- lack of participation in decision-making processes and access to land by women;
- poor regulations on multi-national corporations; and
- dwindling water resources.

(Refer to 2000 *Book of Resolutions*, "Global Economic Justice," #195, section III, for more detailed information.)

It is especially important to note that the causes of hunger are intricately related to the problems of poverty and greed. Hunger cannot be dissociated from people and systems that keep people in poverty.

II. Theological Bases for Action

The Bible reveals that, from the earliest times, God's faithful community has been concerned about hunger and poverty. Helping those in need was not simply a matter of charity, but of responsibility, righteousness, and justice (Isaiah 58:6-8; Jeremiah 22:3; Matthew 25:31-46). For example, the Israelites were commanded to leave the corners of their fields and the gleanings of harvests for the poor and aliens (Leviticus 19:9-10). Jesus taught that whatever people do to "the least of these," they also do him (Matthew 25:31-46). That Jesus was born to a poor, unmarried woman who was living in a small nation, occupied and oppressed by a mighty foreign empire, concretely reveals God's full identification with poor, powerless, and oppressed people.

As Christians, a key question that we must ask ourselves is: What does God require and enable us individually and corporately to do? We know that God loves and cares for all creation. Jesus stressed that the two greatest commandments were to love God and to love our neighbors as ourselves (Matthew 22:34-40). He also challenged the rich young ruler who said he was keeping all of the commandments to sell all of his possessions and give his money to the poor (Matthew 19:16-26).

In the incarnation, life, death, and resurrection of Jesus Christ, the promise and the first fruits of redemption were brought to sinful and selfish humanity. Jesus' own concern for human need in his ministry is a model for the church's concern. His opposition to those who would ignore the needs of the neighbor makes clear that we grossly misunderstand and fail to grasp God's grace if we imagine that God overlooks, condones, or easily tolerates our indifference to the plight of our neighbors, our greed and selfishness, or our systems of injustice and oppression.

We believe that God's Holy Spirit continues to move today, re-fashioning lives, tearing down unjust structures, restoring community, and engendering faith, hope, and love. The work of the Holy Spirit impels us to take action, even when perfect solutions are not apparent. We engage in the struggle for bread and justice for all in the confidence that God goes before us and guides us. That struggle includes examination of our personal and congregational lives in the light of God's love and concern for all and Jesus' question, "Who is your neighbor?"

As United Methodists, we also look to our ongoing tradition of social concern. Methodism's founder, John Wesley, preached and wrote about the importance of simpler lifestyles. He emphasized ethical stewardship of time, money, and resources as important means to enable ministry with those suffering from hunger and poverty. Wesley preached the gospel to people who were poor, visited them, and lived with them. He donated *most* of the money that he earned—not just a tithe (ten percent of his income)—to the church and charitable ends.

Wesley's teachings about ministry and frugal lifestyle stand in stark contrast to today's reality. According to the United Nations Development Program (UNDP), 20 percent of the world's people in the highest-income countries account for 86 percent of total private consumption expenditures, whereas the poorest 20 percent account for only 1.3 percent (1998). For example:

- The richest fifth consumes 45 percent of all meat and fish—the poorest fifth, 5 percent.
- The richest fifth consumes 58 percent of total energy—the poorest fifth, less than 4 percent.
- The richest fifth consumes 84 percent of all paper—the poorest fifth, 1.1 percent. [3]

In faithfulness to our understanding of God's good intentions for all peoples, we, as members of The United Methodist Church, set for ourselves, our congregations, institutions, and agencies no lesser goals than repentance for the existence of human hunger and increased commitment to end world hunger and poverty.

III. A Call for United Methodists

Change is not easy. Movement toward the abolishment of hunger and poverty requires commitment and stamina. All nations, particu-

---

3. United Nations Development Programme, "Overview," *Human Development Report 1998: Comsumption for Human Development* http://hdr.undp.org/reports/global/1998/en/ 8 May, 2003.

larly the developed nations, must examine and modify those values, attitudes, and institutions that are the basic causes of poverty and underdevelopment, the primary sources of world and economic hunger. United Methodists must act corporately and individually.

1. We call for The United Methodist Church to engage in an educational effort that would provide information about the scale of world and domestic hunger and its causes, and to engage in study and effort to integrate the church's missional programs into a coherent policy with respect to a just, sustainable, and participatory development.

2. We call for The United Methodist Church to develop effective public policy strategies and educate the constituency on hunger issues, through its appropriate agencies, that would enable church members to participate in efforts to:

    a. decrease mother/child mortality;

    b. promote environmental justice and sustainable practices for using and restoring natural resources;

    c. provide safe drinking water and sustainable water-management systems;

    d. support community organizing to effect change in systems that keep people poor and powerless;

    e. organize and work to retain programs such as Women, Infants, and Children (WIC), food stamps, and food co-ops;

    f. develop and implement policies that enable family farms to compete in the global market, provide just wages and working conditions for farm workers, and provide incentives that enable and promote sutainable agriculture and equitable access to land by all;

    g. become advocates for reduction of military spending and reallocation of resources to programs that provide human services, convert military facilities to provide for civilian needs, and protect and restore the environment;

    h. become advocates of trade policies that alleviate economic disparities between rich and poor countries while protecting labor and human rights; environmental, health, and safety standards; and respecting the need for agricultural and food security;

    i. protect craftspeople and artisans from exploitative trade practices; and

    j. support community-based economic development that provides jobs; recycles money within communities; provides low-cost, high-quality services to meet basic human needs; and combats unemployment and underemployment.

3. We specifically call upon each local church, cooperative parish, district, and conference to:

    a. increase sharing resources through support of church and community agencies dedicated to eliminating hunger and poverty at home and abroad;

    b. become involved in Fair Trade activism through efforts such as purchasing fair trade products from fair trade companies such as SERVV International, asking grocery and specialty stores to carry fair trade coffee and other fair trade items, and participating in UMCOR's Coffee Project. (More ideas are on Global Exchange's Web site at: http://www.globalex-change.org)); and

    c. promote World Food Day, which is observed on October 16 (*see* http://www.worldfooddayusa.org) and National Hunger Awareness Day observed on June 5 (*see* http://www.hungerday.org).

4. We call on United Methodists to strive for "Christian perfection" and to recover the Wesleyan tradition of simpler lifestyles and generosity in personal service and financial giving. Therefore, individuals are encouraged to:

    a. study and discuss John Wesley's sermons (and related scripture passages) that address "acts of mercy" and Christian stewardship, including "The More Excellent Way," "The Use of Money," "On the Danger of Riches," "On the Danger of Increasing Riches," "On Dress," and "On Visiting the Sick;"[4]

    b. simplify their lifestyles, moving away from consumerism and toward caring;

    c. compost, recycle, conserve energy, practice or support organic gardening, and participate in other environment-friendly practices;

    d. commit themselves to give more of their time and money to programs that address hunger and poverty, including United Methodist Advance projects and UMCOR's World Hunger/Poverty Advance (#982920); and

    e. participate in projects such as "The Souper Bowl of Caring" and Bread for the World's annual "Offering of Letters."

4. These sermons are available in books and online at: http://gbgm-umc.org/umhistory/wesley/sermons/.

5. We urge the General Board of Church and Society and the General Board of Global Ministries to:

a. work with the Food and Agriculture Organization, the International Fund for Agricultural Development, and grass-roots small farmer and peasant organizations for the right of everyone to have access to safe and nutritious food acceptable within their culture. This would require many countries to implement genuine agrarian reforms that allow for the fair distribution of incomes, new management models which place human needs before profits, and access for the poor to land, natural resources, capital, and markets. Many developed countries would have to reform their agricultural subsidies programs.

b. work with other churches and agencies in the United States and internationally:

1) for the achievement of the United Nations Millennium Development Goals (MDGs) which set targets for 2015 in the areas of basic education, infant and maternal mortality, clean water supplies and poverty reduction throughout the developing nations;

and, because progress is currently not fast enough to meet those targets by 2015,

2) to urge governments to support any proposals for an International Finance Facility (IFF). The concept is that, in addition to regular aid flows, donor governments in rich countries should guarantee additional flows of funds from the private sector to the developing world. These would allow investments by developing economies to enable them to converge more closely onto the MDGs. This private sector finance would be a liability of the rich country governments and therefore not increase the debt burden of the poorer nations. It would eventually be repaid out of rich country aid budgets but mostly after 2015. The IFF is therefore a means of bringing forward potential investment money to enable much earlier progress towards the MDGs.

ADOPTED 2004

See Social Principles, ¶ 164A.

206. Economic Justice for a New Millennium

I. Wesleyan Tradition and The United Methodist Church Witness for Economic Justice

The United Methodist Church and its predecessor bodies have a long history of public witness on matters of economic justice. John Wesley set the example in his famous sermon on "The Use of Money," his public stand against slavery, and his witness among England's working class. The 1908 "Social Creed" committed The Methodist Episcopal Church to work for the protection and rights of people disadvantaged by society. The Evangelical United Brethren Church made a comparable commitment to personal, social, and international justice in its *Discipline* statement, "Moral Standards of The Evangelical United Brethren Church" (Section IX). As United Methodists at the dawn of a new millennium, "We claim all economic systems to be under the judgment of God no less than other facets of the created order" (Social Principles, ¶ 163).

II. Biblical/Theological Background

In Luke 4:18-19, Jesus began his public ministry with these words from Isaiah:

The Spirit of the Lord is upon me, because the Lord has anointed me to preach good news to the poor. God has sent me to proclaim release to the captives and recovery of sight to the blind, to let the oppressed go free, to proclaim the year of the Lord's favor (New Revised Standard Version, adapted)

Christ teaches that faith requires action for social and spiritual well-being and especially care for the poor and the oppressed. The early church understood that all were to share all that they had and especially care for the widows and orphans (Acts 2:44-45; 2 Corinthians 8:13-15). Israel's early law codes required persons to meet human needs and guarantee basic economic and legal rights: food (Leviticus 19:9-10; Deuteronomy 23:21-22; 24:19-22), clothing (Exodus 26–27), just business dealings (Deuteronomy 25:13-16), and access to just juridical process (Exodus 23:6-8). Special concern is expressed for the marginalized in society: the poor (Exodus 23:6; Deuteronomy 15:7-11), the disabled (Mark 2:1-12), the stranger (Exodus 22:21-24; 23:9), the sojourner (Deuteronomy 10:19), the widow and the orphan (Deuteronomy 24:19-22).

The covenant community was called to observe sabbatical years in which the land was not worked and its produce was available to the poor

(Exodus 23:10-11), and slaves were set free (Exodus 21:2). In the fiftieth year the Jubilee is to be celebrated (Leviticus 25:8-55) as the year of God's release, when prisoners are set free, debts are canceled, and land is returned to families. But throughout the ages people elected to break covenant with God and instead worship the idols of greed, privilege, materialism, and oppressive power. Likewise, our age worships economic privileges that benefit the rich and powerful. Still, the prophets warn us that an economic system based on greed, economic exploitation, and indifference to the needs of the poor is contrary to God's will and leads to ruin for the society (Amos 8:4-6; Jeremiah 22:13-17).

III. *Structures of Injustice*

Today, the world economy continues to change dramatically. The results of rapid consolidation of wealth and power by fewer individuals, corporations, and banks, the shift in government priorities from social to military expenditures, and the growing interconnections between national economies have led to increases in poverty, hunger, and despair in the human family. Technology, which has the potential to benefit all humanity, is being developed, produced, and marketed to serve rich nations. Materialism and selfishness are undermining the values of community and mutual sharing. Within this context, The United Methodist Church, in following its traditional commitment to justice, must analyze economic systems and work for ministries rooted in justice.

A. *Concentration of Wealth and Power*

"We support measures that would reduce the concentration of wealth in the hands of a few" (¶ 67, *1996 Book of Discipline*).

As transnational corporations and banks have extended their ownership and control of agriculture, industry, land, finances, and communications, two consequences have emerged:

1. The separation between the rich and the poor has become greater. The United Nations 1997 Human Development Report found that of the world's 100 largest economies, 50 are transnational corporations. The 1998 Human Development Report found that the combined gross domestic product of 48 of the world's poorest countries is worth less than the assets of the world's three wealthiest people.

2. Many corporations have become increasingly anonymous and unaccountable to their employees, to the communities in which they operate, and to governments.

B. Production and Work

"Every person has the right and responsibility to work for the benefit of himself or herself and the enhancement of human life and community to receive adequate remuneration" (¶ 73C, *1984 Book of Discipline*; ¶ 67C, with different language, *1996 Discipline*).

Around the world, working people share many of the same concerns: unjust hours and wages; unsafe workplaces; sexual harassment; and discrimination because of race, age, disability, and sexual orientation. Some workers encounter harassment, violence, or job loss for even raising issues of concern with their employer; aging workers are quickly `let go' from their jobs for having reached a company-imposed `senior' status and are suddenly replaced with `more energetic,' younger persons; young workers accept lower wages more readily; and many workers are employed full-time but are unable to live above poverty conditions. Women are profoundly vulnerable to poverty because women's labor, whether in the home or community, has traditionally gone unrecognized, undervalued, unpaid, or underpaid. Overall, women have yet to attain pay equity for their time, dexterity, or expertise in the workplace. According to the 1997 Human Development Report, 500 companies account for 2/3 of international trade. Most transnational corporations have transferred much of the manufacturing base of industrial countries to developing countries, seeking cheap labor and less stringent environmental practices, consumer protection, and occupational safety and health codes. They have taken advantage of favorable tax treatment for overseas investment, employer or government suppression of labor organizing, and the employment of the most vulnerable persons for the lowest of wages. Women, especially young women, indigenous persons, and even children toil for long hours under harsh and unsafe conditions.

C. Development, Debt, and Structural Adjustment

"We affirm the right and duty of the people of developing nations to determine their own destiny. We urge the major political powers to use their power to maximize the political, social, and economic self-determination of developing nations rather than to further their own special interests . . . We urge Christians in every society to encourage the governments under which they live and the economic entities within their societies to aid and work for the development of more just economic orders" (¶ 75B, *1984 Discipline*; ¶ 69B, with different language, *1996 Discipline*).

The global economic system and external debts continue to force developing countries to allocate major resources to produce goods with heavy emphasis on production for export rather than for domestic use. Many of these countries are locked into exporting primary commodities at widely fluctuating prices. Few manage to export manufactured goods and most face uncertain markets due to rapid changes in the terms of trade.

Encouraged by Western banks, many developing countries found that by the early 1980s (when interest rates rose and raw material prices collapsed), they could no longer meet the service payments on their debts. The creditor banks and governments turned to the World Bank and International Monetary Fund (IMF), which makes loans contingent on strict austerity or `structural adjustment' programs. The Bank and IMF remedies have placed the burden of debt repayment squarely on the shoulders of poor and working people by devaluing currencies, freezing wages, curbing government price subsidies (on rice, cooking oil, beans, and other essential items), and cutting subsidized credits in rural areas. In addition, the corruption by some government officials has made it impossible to provide an adequate food supply, health care, education, and other services. Compelled to commit their natural and human resources to compete in world markets, the irony is that developing nations may have no other options, but to sacrifice their domestic economy, social welfare programs, and possibly the life and spirit of the people.

D. Military Spending

"Human values must outweigh military claims as governments determine their priorities; . . . the militarization of society must be challenged;. . . the manufacture, sale, and deployment of armaments must be reduced and controlled" (¶ 69C, *1996 Discipline*).

Many governments, in shifting major resources to the military, have hurt the most vulnerable people in their societies: women, children, and youth. Some economies, such as that of the United States, increasingly depend on the military for jobs, exports, and economic growth. Among developing countries, some produce weapons to pay their foreign debt, while others import military equipment to control their own populations. And in so doing, the basic needs of the average residents go unmet or are severely diminished.

IV. The Effects of the Global Economic System

Injustices are imposed upon the people of the world by economies characterized by a concentration of wealth and power, an export-based development, heavy indebtedness, and reliance on a militarized national security system. The belief that competition results in greater economic growth underlies much of the emerging global economic order. In the production and consumption of goods, corporations are to compete with corporations, individuals with one another, and societies with other societies. The central value is "more." Greed and the corporate culture of materialism, of "more is better," have permeated our world. It is a culture that has little use for those who lack the means to consume. The following evidence shows the effects of the global economy:

1. Worldwide, poverty and hunger have increased, especially among women and children. Human rights have become untenable. Homelessness remains rampant in major cities, while many rural communities are in rapid decline as family farms go bankrupt in record numbers. In developing countries, shanty-towns surround major cities as people leave rural areas in search of jobs. These resulting poor populations, with a disproportionate share being of a different ethnic racial heritage of a nation's elites, are also faced with discriminatory obstacles to overcome.

2. As transnational corporations shift centers of production, unemployment and underemployment is increasing in some parts of the world, while education and job training have not kept pace with the global economy. According to the 1998-99 International Labor Organization (ILO) World Employment Report, some one billion workers, one third of the world labor force, remain unemployed or underemployed. In a 1996 report, the ILO reported that at least 120 million children between the ages of five to 14 were fully at work which leaves them little time for school education.

3. The increasing ability of large corporations to shift their resources around the globe has contributed to an erosion of worker rights everywhere. Sweatshops and child labor have increased. Many corporations have shifted to the use of temporary and part-time workers in order to avoid paying benefits, such as insurance, health care, and pensions. As wages and benefits decline, the number of full-time employees living in poverty increases.

4. Beyond business owners, employers, and contractors, the international stock markets and corporate traders are not accountable for the wages and workplace conditions of workers. Usually, workers are excluded from profit-sharing schemes. Women and some racial and ethnic groups are denied promotions to high-level positions.

5. The unrestrained business and development pursuits have negative social, economic, and ecological ramifications: shifts in agricultural production have led to indigenous seed crops being replaced by chemically dependent cash crops or genetically engineered seeds; destruction of fragile environments and exploitation of non-renewable natural resources have occurred; and the forced dislocation of people and indigenous cultures has devalued human dignity and life.

6. Churches and social-service agencies have struggled to meet the spiritual and psychological needs caused by economic injustice. But they are not able to keep up with the problems. In communities under economic stress, there is a rising incidence of crime, family breakdown, child and spouse abuse, suicide, substance abuse, gambling, and other worrisome behavior.

V. Call to Action

The United Methodist Church, as a covenant community committed to God's justice, must work toward a just global economy. Our Social Principles remind us that "in spite of general affluence in the industrialized nations, most of the persons in the world live in poverty. To provide basic needs such as food, clothing, shelter, education, health care, and other necessities, ways must be found to share more equitably the resources of the world" (¶ 163E). Faced with securing economic justice for a new millennium, the General Conference calls upon:

1. each local congregation and every central and annual conference to use this resolution and related resources as a foundation to initiate a study curriculum and social actions on global economic justice issues;

2. the whole church to work with people in local communities to identify specific economic issues that affect families, communities, and individuals, especially the impacts upon the lives of women.These issues include jobs with livable wages and benefits, debt, plant closings and relocation, public education, homelessness, affordable housing, and meeting sanitation, clean water, and energy needs. These issues

should be addressed through the strategies of prayer, study, service, advocacy, community organizing, and economic development;

3. the General Board of Church and Society and the General Board of Global Ministries to engage in ongoing searches for and study of alternative and sustainable systems of economic order, shall work with local congregations, central and annual conferences to initiate and support legislative efforts at the local, state, national, and international levels that will address "Structures of Injustice" (Section III). Attention should be given to marginalized and indigenous people; the accountability or reform of transnational corporations and banks; personal and corporate investment responsibility; land reform, and the dependency of national economies on the military;

4. the general program agencies of the church and the General Board of Pension and Health Benefits to work with the Interfaith Center on Corporate Responsibility and support its *Principles for Global Corporate Responsibility*; and

5. all bodies of the church to be more intentional in using their investment portfolios to strengthen developing national economies and global economic justice. We also encourage central and annual conferences, local churches and individuals in wealthy nations to live a simpler, more modest lifestyle.

In order to be God's real community, we must realize that people are not here to serve an economic system, but economic systems must serve all people so all live in God's abundance.

ADOPTED 1988
REVISED AND ADOPTED 2000

See Social Principles, ¶ 163D and E.

207. Global Debt Crisis: A Call for Jubilee

I. Introduction

As the 21st century begins, the global debt crisis continues to cripple poor countries. Countries in Africa, Asia, the Pacific, Latin America, and the Caribbean owe over $2 trillion to rich nations and international financial institutions like the World Bank and the International Monetary Fund (IMF). The poorest countries in the world are the most heavily indebted, owing around $370 billion. For many countries, the burden of repaying the debt has prevented them from providing adequate health care, education, and food for the masses. This debt burden inhibits the social and economic development that is needed to lift people out of poverty. Throughout the world there is a call for Jubilee, a call for debt cancellation.

II. Biblical Foundation

Scriptures mandate periodically overcoming structural injustice and poverty and for restoring right relationships by forgiving debt and reforming land holding. In the earliest Sabbath traditions, consumption and exploitation of the land were limited by the Sabbath and the Sabbath year. People and animals were to rest every seventh day (Exodus 23:10-12). In the Sabbath year, there was to be release from debts and slavery and during the jubilee year—every 50th year—a restoration of all family lands (Leviticus 25). Fulfilling these commandments proclaims "the year of the Lord's favor" (Isaiah 61:1-2) and anticipates "new heavens and a new earth" (Isaiah 65:17-25). Jesus emphasized this jubilee vision of proclaiming good news to the poor, release of the captives, sight to the blind, and liberation of the oppressed (Luke 4:16-19). He taught his disciples to pray for the forgiveness of debts (as we forgive our debtors) (Matthew 6:12). Pentecost results in the voluntary sharing of possessions, so that "there was not a needy person among them" (Acts 4:34; Deuteronomy 15:4).

The Sabbath tradition of the jubilee vision is as relevant today as it was thousands of years ago. Debt bondage by the poorest countries to rich nations and financial institutions is today's new slavery. The accelerating concentration of wealth for a few in the richest countries and the devastating decline in living standards in the poorest countries call for correction along the lines of the ancient Sabbath and jubilee cycles. The social, political, and ecological costs of the debt crisis are intolerable and must be challenged and stopped. Only when we have implemented the Sabbath-jubilee mandate can we "turn to God" and "rejoice in hope."

III. Causes of the Debt Crisis

The causes of the debt crisis are complex. Colonialism has tied the developing world's economies to the export of agricultural, mineral, and other raw materials while creating a dependence on imported goods. This export-oriented and import-dependent economic arrangement sunk poor and debtor countries even more into debt. For decades, prices for agricultural, mineral, and most raw materials have steadily declined in relation to the cost of manufactured goods. Poor countries that still depend on these exports find themselves increasingly disadvantaged in the global marketplace and often deeper in debt. Declining commodity prices between 1986 and 1990 alone cost Africa $50 billion in export earnings, more than double the funds received in foreign assistance from all nations.

In the 1970s, the oil-producing nations deposited billions of dollars in Western commercial banks. In turn, many banks aggressively marketed their loans to developing countries who were short of cash, facing high oil costs, and eager to borrow. Banks' normal loan-review procedures were often abandoned in the rush to lend large amounts of money quickly. Some of the loans went to productive uses, such as water purification and sewage systems, education and health programs, and subsidies for basic food staples. However, a large percentage of the money has supported militarization and, sometimes, repressive regimes and corrupt leadership.

By the mid 1970s, developing countries, encouraged by the West to grow cash crops, suddenly found that they were not getting the prices they used to for the raw materials they sold. The reason: too many countries—advised by the West—were producing the same crops, so prices fell. Soon after, U.S. interest rates began to rise dramatically and oil prices rose again. This led to a global recession that depressed demand and commodity prices of products from developing countries. Receiving less for their exports and forced to pay more on loans and imports, indebted countries had to borrow more money just to pay off the interest.

In 1982, Mexico, Brazil, and other middle-income countries announced that they were about to default on billions of dollars in loans. Banks suddenly stopped new lending to developing countries. By late 1980s, the crisis had eased for most middle-income countries, as a result of some debt restructuring by commercial banks, intervention by international financial institutions, and export growth. However, the poorest countries continue to struggle under heavy unpayable debt burden and are essentially bankrupt.

IV. Consequences of the Global Crisis—Everyone Loses

The World Bank and International Monetary Fund (IMF)—the two main international financial institutions—lend money and reschedule the debt of poor countries. However, these loans to highly indebted poor countries come with conditions known as Structural Adjustment Programs (SAPs). SAPs consist of measures designed to help a country repay its debts by earning more hard currency (i.e., increasing exports and decreasing imports). While a few countries appear to have been helped by SAPs, poverty and inequality have increased in most countries due to the externally imposed programs. This is because, in order to obtain more foreign currency, governments implementing SAPs usually must:

- reduce government spending, resulting in cuts in health care, education, and social services—many people are forced to go without;
- devalue the national currency, which increases the cost of imported goods and increases taxes, especially regressive sales taxes;
- reduce or eliminate transportation and food subsidies— because of this, prices of essentials soar out of the financial reach of many citizens;
- reduce jobs and wages for workers in government industries and services;
- encourage privatization of public industries which benefits the country's business elite and foreign investors; and
- shift agricultural and industrial production from food staples and basic goods for domestic use to commodities for export, which results in a transfer of land holdings from small subsistence farmers to large-scale agribusiness leaving many farmers with no land to grow their own food and few are employed on these new cash crop farms.

Children and women bear the full costs of debt repayment. In addition, by concentrating on exports in order to repay their debts, poor countries strip forests and overexploit land and nonrenewable resources, further aggravating serious environmental problems. Reports on the impact of debt repayment show that many indebted governments spend two to four times as much money "servicing"— that is, making timely interest and principal payments—their international debt as they spend on health care (such as basic medicines and clean water) and education combined. These IMF and World Bank policies, by taking away indebted country's sovereignty, undermine accountability by debtor governments, which in turn erodes local democratic institutions. In short, IMF and World Bank policies do more harm than good. The debt burden carried by impoverished nations hurts everyone—including citizens of rich nations such as the United States. The environmental damage magnified by indebtedness, such as destruction of forests, has global repercussions. Growing poverty—worsened by the debt—is linked to the spread of disease. Indebted countries are forced to use scarce dollars for debt payments instead of importing goods and services. This directly affects jobs and incomes in the rich countries. Indebtedness creates the climate that fosters the production and trafficking of illicit drugs. Debt also causes an increase of economic migration. It should trouble the conscience of citizens of rich nations that people living in misery have to spend their money for debt servicing that they need for their own survival.

V. Principles to Guide Debt-Crisis Solutions

As Christians, our love of God and neighbor must be reflected by our actions within the global family. Thus, we affirm the following policies and principles as necessary to ensure a just resolution to the debt crisis:

- We need to examine patterns of greed that may cause us as individuals and nations to become debtors and lenders. Debt cancellation and relief should be fashioned in a way that benefits the poor and helps move debtor nations to sustainable human development.
- The poor should not bear the burden of repayment and structural adjustment. Living standards of those least responsible and most vulnerable should not be sacrificed in order to meet external obligations. Developing countries have the right to choose their own development paths without military or economic interference from outside. They should not be forced to surrender their right to political or economic self-determination in exchange for relief.
- The debt burden should be shared equitably among credit institutions and the debtor governments, corporations, banks, and elites that incurred the debt. Factors adding to and perpetuating the debt problem but beyond the control of debtor countries—such as previous U.S. budget deficits, high interest rates, unfair commodity prices, and trade barriers—should be alleviated.

- Long-term solutions should promote a more just international economic system in order to prevent such crises from recurring. New structures and mechanisms, involving participation and dialogue between creditors and debtors, including civil society groups such as community and faith-based organizations are critically needed.
- There is a need for a new just process of arbitration for international debt cancellation, such as the introduction of an international insolvency law, which ensures that losses and gains are equally shared.
- New mechanisms involving civil society must produce ethical, mutually responsible and transparent solutions, which not only satisfy requirements for economic efficiency, but also for the protection of basic human needs and rights as well as protecting of the environment.
- Where funds are released through debt cancellation or other relief measures, civil society organizations must be enabled to take part in determining how monies are reallocated for social priorities.

VI. Recommended Actions for The United Methodist Church

The United Methodist Church, as a covenant community committed to Christian discipleship and advocacy with the poor, must work toward "measures that would reduce the concentration of wealth in the hands of a few" (¶ 67, *1996 Discipline*). Thus, the General Conference of The United Methodist Church:

1. celebrates the worldwide Jubilee 2000 Campaign, a movement to cancel the crushing debt of the world's poorest countries in the year 2000, and the participation of the General Board of Church and Society and the General Board of Global Ministries in the campaign;

2. calls for the United States, governments of other leading industrial nations, private commercial lending institutions, and international financial institutions such as the World Bank and IMF to:

   a. cancel the debts of the poorest countries to enable them to enter the new millennium with a fresh start;

   b. substantially reduce the debts of the middle-income countries within the same time frame;

    c. introduce a new, independent, and transparent arbitration process for negotiating and agreeing upon international debt cancellation;

    d. implement measures to promote accountability of debtor countries when debts are relieved; these measures must be determined and monitored by local community organizations, including churches, and other communities of faith, and representative organizations of civil society, to ensure that debt cancellation leads to a more just distribution of wealth;

    e. use their powers to ensure that funds illegitimately transferred to secret foreign bank accounts are returned to debtor nations; and

    f. engage, in consultation with civil society, in a process of global economic reform towards a more just distribution of wealth and prevention of new cycles of debt.

3. urges the General Board of Church and Society and the General Board of Global Ministries to:

    a. work with annual and central conferences to become advocates for debt cancellation and relief, for new structures and mechanisms involving participation and dialogue between creditors and debtors, that is open and transparent and includes civil society;

    b. advocate for the introduction of an international insolvency law which ensures that losses and gains are equally shared, new terms of trade that insure poor nations can trade on an equal footing with rich nations, and other equitable resolutions of the global debt crisis that will protect the poor through public policy and corporate responsibility;

    c. develop and distribute appropriate curriculum and study materials to annual conferences and local congregations; and

    d. organize and assist speaking tours on the human impact of the global debt crisis.

4. urges United Methodist theological seminaries to include Christian responsibility for economic justice, including the global debt crisis, as a necessary part of education for ministry; and

5. urges the General Board of Church and Society and the General Board of Global Ministries to continue public policy work for major reforms of the International Monetary Fund, the World Bank, the World Trade Organization, and other international financial institutions to

promote equitable development through poverty alleviation, protection of the environment, openness, democracy, and human rights.

ADOPTED 1988
REVISED AND ADOPTED 2000

See Social Principles, ¶ 163D and E.

208. Pathways to Economic Justice

The church is set in a world of growing inequality. Even in the United States where there are 268 billionaires, a large percentage of all children live below the poverty line. The richest 1 percent of Americans had as much income in 1999 as the bottom 38 percent combined. In many poor countries in Africa and Asia, the poverty is deeper and the gap between rich and poor exceeds the gap that existed in life between Dives and Lazarus. In such a situation, the church must decide whether its mission to preach good news to the poor is good news only for their spiritual life or whether it is good news to the whole person.

From the beginnings of Methodism, we have always been a movement that sees the whole person, body and soul. Wesley's class meetings emphasized both acts of piety and acts of mercy. He organized and used the class meetings to support groups like sewing collectives, that helped those who didn't have much money, bring their resources together to start small businesses that would be a witness to God's abundance in the midst of poverty. The church has many opportunities to continue that witness if we make the commitment that Wesley made: every congregation not only gives to mission, but has an opportunity to use its assets for the building of a more just economy.

Drawing on the teachings of Jesus and the prophets, the writings and example of our founder John Wesley, and on an analysis of current economic conditions, we can discern pathways leading to a more just and equitable sharing of the riches which God has given us as a human family. These pathways are personal, local, and global.

Personal Pathways to Economic Justice

- Support locally based businesses.
- Recycle waste products and avoid use of disposable products where possible.

- Buy organic, locally produced foods as much as possible.
- Invest personal savings in stocks and mutual funds which are socially screened.
- Buy only clothing and other articles that you know are not manufactured by child labor, sweatshop, or slave labor.
- Engage in Bible study on economic justice.
- Take part in study groups on economic issues, using materials from groups like the People of Faith Network.

Local Paths to Economic Justice

- Support local initiatives for moderate and low income housing.
- Support policies of Affirmative Action and Equal Opportunity employment.
- Open your church to house the homeless and feed the hungry.
- Each congregation commit a tithe (10 percent) of its budget to helping the poor and working for economic justice.
- Support full rights for farm workers, especially the right to organize and bargain collectively.

National and Global Paths to Economic Justice

- Conference United Methodist Women organizations take up at least one specific action project for economic justice in the next quadrennium.
- Make every annual conference staff racially and ethnically diverse at all levels.
- Support the right of governments to limit the international flow of capital.
- Deny Most Favored Nation Trade Status to nations which permit sweatshop, child, or slave labor, do not permit workers to organize, and do not guarantee workers a living wage by accepted international standards.
- Enact campaign finance reform that prevents corporations and special interest groups buying legislators and dominating the legislative process.
- Support public sector job creation to build highways, schools, and housing when the private sector is unable to provide jobs for all who need them.

- Support policies that encourage the use of renewable resources and limit the destruction of nonrenewable resources, leading to a sustainable environment.
- End the fiction that the corporation is a "person," a doctrine never envisioned by the founding fathers.
- Support Jubilee 2000 through living out its spirit and principles in the life of the community.

The church has too often neglected the full call of the gospel and left economics in the hands of government and business. The kingdom of God is a form of economy that calls forth from each of us a commitment to the abundance of God in our midst. It is a call to renounce the politics of greed and acquisitiveness which dominate the institutions of government and business and reclaim their true calling in the service of people. Economy is how we order our lives, our politics, our world. It is time that we manifest gospel values in the economic order. It is after all, our calling.

ADOPTED 2000

See Social Principles, ¶ 163D and E.

209. Seek Pardon for Latin American Debt

WHEREAS, the end of the century finds us thrusting forward in the creation of a so-called "world order" that is exclusionary of great populations of the Third World, the same ones that will end up being even poorer as other people in developed countries are becoming richer; and

WHEREAS, in Latin America, with 468 million people, in spite of the efforts of their governments to diminish poverty, the number of poor people continues to grow; and

WHEREAS, the global village, called to be a village of solidarity, has demonstrated very few signs of that kind of fellowship, an exception being the positive example of the European governments that are willing to forgive the external debt of the countries affected by hurricanes George and Mitch; and

WHEREAS, the "external" debt of Latin American countries has become an "eternal" debt and a modern form of slavery, given the fact that the payment of just the interest on this debt is made in detriment of human life itself; and

WHEREAS, Christian people are called by Christ to realize the Reign of God, which is a reign of life, justice and love of God and neighbor,

Therefore, be it resolved, that the 2000 General Conference of The United Methodist Church condemn this travesty of justice against human life and dignity and that it commit itself to support the Council of Evangelical Methodist Churches in Latin America and the Caribbean (CIEMAL) and Methodists Associated to Represent the Cause of Hispanic Americans (MARCHA) in our request that this external debt of Latin American countries, especially those affected by the hurricanes George and Mitch be pardoned,

Be it further resolved, that the 2000 General Conference petition this pardoning from the President of the United States of American and instruct all our churches, particularly the Hispanic/Latin churches, to write their representatives and senators in Washington, D.C. about this issue.

ADOPTED 2000

See Social Principles, ¶ 163D and E.

210. Bread for the World Covenant Church

In developing countries, 1.3 billion people (equaling the entire population of China) live in absolute poverty, with individual purchasing power equivalent to less than one U.S. dollar a day and 70 percent of childhood deaths are associated with malnutrition and preventable diseases. Approximately 35,000 children worldwide die each day from hunger-related causes, and another 841 million other people will suffer from malnutrition (Bread for the World Institute).There is significantly more hunger-related pain, suffering and death in the world than that caused by all the wars in the world. Approximately 18 million people die each year from hunger, malnutrition and resulting diseases. In the U.S., approximately 31 million people go to bed hungry a part of each month.

The prophets promised a messiah who would establish justice and the knowledge of God, and Jesus later announced himself as the fulfillment of those promises: "The Spirit of the Lord is upon me, because he has anointed me to preach the good news to the poor. He has sent me to proclaim release to the captives. . .to set at liberty those who are oppressed . . ." (Luke 4:18-21). Jesus asked that we see that the hungry are fed (Matt. 25:35), and Jesus also said "in as much as you have done it unto the least of these, you have done it unto me" (Matt. 25:40). Jesus fed hungry people, befriended outcasts and called for radical sharing. He embodied forgiveness and mercy. Those of us who have been embraced by this "good news" are drawn to be concerned about people in need and we are compelled to work to make our society's laws fair and helpful toward poor and hungry people.

The Social Principles of The United Methodist Church state that, "In order to provide basic needs such as food, clothing, shelter, education, health care, and other necessities, ways must be found to share more equitably the resources of the world. Increasing technology, when accompanied by exploitative economic practices, impoverishes many persons and makes poverty self-perpetuating" (¶ 163 E).

Our General Conference resolution, "Call for a Rebirth of Compassion," reinforces this sentiment when it states that "we call upon United Methodists throughout the land not only to feed the hungry and house the homeless, but also to work for policies that will end hunger and homelessness."

Bread for the World (BFW), established in 1974, is a nonprofit, nonpartisan Christian citizens' movement which performs a unique and critical role within the faith community by working to eradicate hunger from the face of the earth by using their network of thousands of local Covenant Churches across America to lobby elected officials to change policies to provide opportunities to establish a sustainable livelihood for all people. BFW's main campaign is an annual nationwide "Offering of Letters," which not only provides church members with the opportunity to write members of Congress concerning hunger-related issues, but also enables congregations to incorporate into their worship experience, their passionate concerns for those that are starving and suffering from malnutrition.

Covenant Church membership includes training, Bible study and worship aids (resources/materials) on the Christian response to world hunger. The BFW Covenant Church network (www.bread.org) is an essential component of the hunger program of The United Methodist Church, and its efforts complement UMCOR's (http://gbgm-umc.org/umcor) and the General Board of Church and Society's ministry (http://umc-gbcs.org) in alleviating the root causes of hunger/poverty. Direct feeding (soup kitchens) provides relief one day at a time (and may always be needed) but does little to eradicate causes of hunger. Holistic spirituality and development (putting love in action) prepares persons for sustainable livelihoods, but only if government policies are changed to permit this. The Bread for the World Covenant Church program provides opportunities to change government policies. Bread for the World works, but more grassroots initiative is needed. Otherwise, at the current rate of change, between 1.5 and 2 billion people will die during the next 75 years due to hunger/malnutrition.

BFW's Covenant Church program focuses on an annual nationwide "Offering of Letters" and helps prepare United Methodists to effectively change public policy through new legislation each year.

The United Methodist Church, along with more than 45 denominations and church agencies, generously supports BFW, and in fact, The United Methodist Church has a 25-year history of collaboration with BFW's fight against the root causes of both global and domestic hunger. The United Methodist Advance Special Number is: 982325-3. BFW has said that, "[It] owes much to Methodism's historic commitment to social justice and active concern for the poor and downtrodden. John Wesley's conviction that `the world is my parish' is at the heart of BFW's work,"

Therefore, be it resolved, that The United Methodist Church significantly enhance its efforts to END HUNGER by increasing participation in the Bread for the World (BFW) Covenant Church program. We further urge that The United Methodist Church achieve a minimum of a 5 percent increase in the number of churches participating in the BFW Covenant Church program each year.

ADOPTED 2000
AMENDED AND READOPTED 2004

See Social Principles, ¶ 163D and E.

211. Greed

God's vision of abundant living is a world where we live out of a theology of "enough," a theology based in the knowledge that we are grounded in Christ, that our sense of personal value and esteem grows from our Christ-centered life. (*Book of Resolutions 2000*, #188)

Scripture calls us to be compassionate and just stewards of our wealth and warns us of the sin of greed and its devastating effects.

The Law ensured that the basic needs and rights of the poor were protected from the greedy (Exodus 23:6-11; Leviticus 25:35-55). The prophets warned that an economic system based on greed is contrary to God's will and leads to ruin of the society (Amos 8:4-7; Jeremiah 22:13-17). Echoing the Law and the prophets, Jesus condemned the rich for the hypocrisy of greed and the barriers greed creates to salvation (Luke 6:24; 16:1-15; Matthew 18:16-22). He taught that in the Reign of God everyone would have enough (Matthew 13:31-32; 20:1-16). The early church rejected greed by sharing their wealth among their members (Acts 2:44-45). When their salvation was jeopardized by greed, Paul warned them that "the love of money is the root of all kinds of evil" (I Timothy 6:6-10).

In our Wesleyan tradition, greed is an impediment to holiness. John Wesley taught and practiced that excessive wealth, absent of effective stewardship and radical charity, prevents a believer from growing in grace and cultivates sinful actions and attitudes. Wesley said that greed is "destructive of that faith which is of the operation of God; of that hope which is full of immortality; of love of God and of our neighbor, and of every good word and work. ("The Danger of Riches" I.11). Wesley also believed that stewardship that centers on care for the poor is a means of Grace. "O let your heart be whole with God. Sit as loose to all things here below as if you was a poor beggar. Be a good steward of the manifold gifts of God." ("On Riches" II.12).

Furthermore, John Wesley encouraged government leaders to develop public policies that provided for the well-being of the poor and the just distribution of wealth through taxation. For example, he praised the mayor of Cork for public policies which curbed the negative effects of greed on the poor. In his tract, "Thoughts on the Present Scarcity of Provisions" he described the widespread suffering of the poor due to changes in the English economy. Among his solutions was a call for the wealthy to pay taxes on their carriages and for the government to regulate the amount the poor could be charged for land rent.

Therefore, we support measures that would reduce the concentration of wealth in the hands of the few. We encourage personal lifestyles that embody good stewardship of wealth on behalf of the poor. We further support efforts to revise tax structures and to eliminate governmental support programs that now benefit the wealthy at the expense of other persons. (Social Principles, ¶ 163; *see also Book of*

Resolutions, #206, "Economic Justice for a New Millennium") Gandhi predicted: "There is enough in the world for everyone's need; there is not enough for everyone's greed."

Call to Action:

At the General Church Level:

That the General Board of Global Ministries and General Board of Church and Society study and support measures in the U.S. Congress that would reject new trade agreements that allow continuing subsidies to the richest nations and multinational corporations of the world and restrict the possibilities of advancement of the poorest nations and individuals including family farmers everywhere.

That The United Methodist Church oppose tax reduction measures that would increase the concentration of wealth in the hands of the few and support progressive income taxes.

That The United Methodist Church advocate for revisions of tax structures to reduce the regressive taxes paid by the poor worldwide and redouble our efforts toward debt cancellation for the poorest nations.

That the General Board of Global Ministries and the General Board of Church and Society research public policy solutions to practices in global financial markets which create currency speculation that destroys the ability of countries to protect their currency from devastating ruin

At the Local Church Level:

That local congregations organize "simple-living" seminars in our churches and UMW units.

That local congregations examine their investments and endowment funds to determine how they can be better utilized for the poor.

That local congregations expand their stewardship programs to include education about the effects of materialism on discipleship.

That local congregations advocate for fairness in local taxes that ensure the well-being of the poor.

Be it resolved, that the people called United Methodists search the scriptures concerning greed and pray for forgiveness.

ADOPTED 2004

See Social Principles, ¶ 163*A*, *D*, and *E*.

212. Protecting Health Care, Labor, and Environment in Trade Negotiations

Under the World Trade Organization (WTO) and its General Agreement on Trade in Services (GATS) first negotiated in 1994, the concept of free trade has moved beyond the lowering of trade barriers at a country's borders, focusing now on what are called "internal barriers to trade." But what appear to trade interests to be barriers to trade are often laws and regulations passed by national, regional, and local legislatures to protect health care, labor, and the environment. Past WTO decisions have compromised Ontario's ability to discourage the sale of alcoholic beverages, Guatemala's ability to promote breast feeding in preference to use of infant formula, and Europe's ability to support public health by restricting the sale of hormone-treated beef. In the future, GATS rules under discussion could prevent member countries, including the United States, from considering a full range of solutions to problems in their health-care systems or from protecting standards for working conditions. Countries could be challenged under GATS for subsidizing hospitals that disproportionately serve the poor or that seek to extend current "monopolies" such as the U.S. Medicare program to include additional services, such as prescription drugs. Proposed GATS rules could allow foreign corporations and governments to challenge laws requiring reasonable staffing ratios, use of safe needles, and professional licensing as "more burdensome than necessary." The United Methodist Church supports economic development around the globe, but we insist that economic development be sustainable, safeguard human beings and the environment, support the health of workers and communities, and provide a safety net for the most vulnerable among us.

We call upon governments around the world to take steps to protect the right of legislatures at all levels—national, regional and local—to safeguard the health care, environment, and labor of their citizens. In countries like the United States where "fast track" legislation permits Congress to only give a yes or no to new trade legislation, Congressional leaders must involve themselves more in the trade negotiations or be prepared to vote no to the entire trade package when it is presented.

We call upon the General Board of Church and Society to represent these concerns before the U.S. Congress, the United Nations, and the WTO, and to assist United Methodists in all nations to seek attention of their own governments to health care, labor, and environmental issues when trade issues are negotiated.

ADOPTED 2004

See Social Principles, ¶ 163*I* and *J*.

INVESTMENTS

213. Investment Ethics

The United Methodist Church and its predecessor denominations have a long history of witness for justice in the economic order. John Wesley and early Methodists, for instance, were staunchly opposed to the slave trade, to smuggling, and to conspicuous consumption. In fact, John Wesley refused to drink tea because of its relationship to the slave trade. Social creeds adopted by our predecessor churches, beginning in 1908, stressed social justice in the economic world, with special attention to the exploitation of child labor and inhumanely long working hours.

Throughout this century our church has promoted decent working conditions and the right to organize and bargain collectively, and it has opposed discrimination in the workplace on the basis of race, ethnic background, gender, age, or disability. Historically our tradition has opposed church investments in companies manufacturing liquor or tobacco products or promoting gambling.

Since the 1960s, our denomination and its predecessors have built a solid record expressing our ethics in our investment decisions. United Methodist agencies and conferences fought against the manufacture of napalm and were involved in the social-justice issues raised by religious shareholders. In the mid-1970s, the General Council on Finance and Administration (GCFA) began official social responsibility guidelines for general church investments.

While the issue of economic sanction against *apartheid* in South Africa engaged us more than any other, United Methodist agencies, affiliated institutions, conferences, congregations, and individual members have brought the church's Christian witness to business on numerous issues, including employment discrimination, environmental preservation, militarism, nuclear weapons production, reevaluation of infant formula use and addressing the HIV/AIDS pandemic. The church also continues to advocate on such issues as: international fair labor practice; domestic and global human rights; lending practices or policies for lesser developed communities and nations; and issues of violence to persons, firearms sales, gun policies; best corporate governance practices, unethical corporate practices, environmental reporting, public disclosure on financial risks of global warming and climate change, genetically modified organisms and food safety.

We affirm that all financial resources of the church and its members are God-given resources, to be held in trust for use or investment in ways that promote the reign of God on earth.

Further, we recognize that every investment has ethical dimensions. Financial investments have consequences that are both fiscal and social. We believe social justice and social usefulness must be given consideration together with financial security and financial yield in the investment of funds by United Methodist Church agencies and affiliated institutions, and by congregations as well as individual United Methodists. Socially responsible investing by Christian institutions and individuals must take account of both sets of considerations.

Our church's witness through investments has taken four forms, each of which may be employed with the others. They are:

1. *Avoidance by Divestment.* This policy prohibits investment in enterprises that have policies or practices that are so morally reprehensible that investment in these companies is not tolerated by the church. Our denomination traditionally has avoided investments in liquor, tobacco, and gambling. Historically many church investors have refused to invest in major military contractors, companies with nuclear weapons contracts, or companies when they were doing business in South Africa under *apartheid*. In some cases, they have divested of such companies, making public their action as a moral statement.

2. *Affirmative Choice.* This strategy is to choose intentionally enterprises for investment based on careful consideration of return, both in social values and in social justice, as well as financial security and monetary profit. For United Methodist investors, the Social Principles and *The Book of Resolutions* delineate the social goals to which we expect all our investments to make a positive contribution. But with certain affirmative investments we may seek a very specific social

outcome, such as the construction of affordable housing, the renewal of a particular neighborhood, or the expansion of business ownership to those traditionally excluded.

3. *Shareholder Advocacy.* The practices of corporations in which the church invests may fall short of the moral standards expressed in the Social Principles and *The Book of Resolutions.* Responsible Christian investing includes seeking to change company policies and practices for the better. Church investors have, as shareholders of corporations, engaged corporate management in a great variety of ways—from gentle persuasion to public pressure, from dialogue to voting proxies to filing shareholder resolutions, and building coalitions. In many cases, corporate policies have changed as a result.

4. *Strategic Partnerships.* This is the practice of working in collaboration with others to utilize synergy of strategies and resources to engage corporations on issues of governance, environmental and social importance. Such partnerships may include: United Methodist boards, agencies, foundations, universities, concerned socially responsible investors, domestic and global faith-based and non-governmental organizations.

Policy and Implementation of Policy

The policy goals of the General Conference of The United Methodist Church, its general agencies, and entities under its control shall be:

1. to invest as much as possible in entities that are making a positive contribution to the communities, societies, and world on which they have impact and to the realization of the goals outlined in the Social Principles and *The Book of Resolutions* of our church;

2. to employ this combination of socially responsible approaches that contribute to economic justice and corporate responsibility:

Avoidance by nonpurchase or divestment of holdings in companies that:

   a. produce tobacco products or alcoholic beverages, or manage or own gambling enterprises, or have as their primary business the production, distribution, or sale of pornographic material;
   b. rank among the top 100 Department of Defense (DOD) contractors (those receiving the largest volume of prime contract awards) for the past three years; and have DOD contracts larger than 10 percent of sales for voting securities and 5 percent of sales for nonvoting securities; the GCFA shall publish

the listing of the top 100 DOD contractors annually; provided, however, health care providers and humanitarian relief providers are not intended to be excluded even if they rank in the top 100 DOD contractors.

c. make components for nuclear explosive devices;
d. manufacture chemical or biological warfare materials;
e. make components for anti-personnel weapons;
f. have as their primary business the production, distribution or sale of handguns and assault-type weapons or ammunition for such weapons; or
g. manufacture, or purchase through subcontracting, a significant amount of products made with sweatshop or forced labor.

Affirmative investing in companies, banks, funds, or ventures that are seeing specific targeted social goals upon which the church places high value, such as those that:

a. encourage recycling and use recycled products;
b. work within legally imposed discharge limits for toxic chemicals, noise, and water temperature;
c. do not sell chemicals that would be banned in the company's country of origin;
d. obtain future power supplies from renewable resources that do not have undue adverse environmental, socioeconomic and human rights impacts upon indigenous peoples;
e. invest in low-income housing, affordable housing, and community development in urban and rural areas;
f. invest in companies that have positive records in hiring and promoting women and racial and ethnic persons;
g. are companies owned by women and by racial and ethnic persons;
h. have programs, benefits and wages that assure quality of life for employees and their families; and
i. have policies and practices that preclude predatory or harmful lending practices.

Shareholder advocacy through which the agency exercises its rights as shareholder to persuade corporations to end irresponsible behavior or live up to high ethicalstandards by using any combination of the following approaches:

- letter of inquiry or expression of its position to management;
- dialogue with management;

- voting proxies;
- soliciting votes from other investors for a particular reason;
- sponsoring resolutions for votes at stockholder meetings;
- speaking at stockholder meetings;
- legal action;
- publicity;
- working in coalitions with other concerned shareholders;
- petitioning the SEC or Congress for changes in the proxy rules;

3. To seek opportunites to invest in companies, banks, funds, or ventures that invest or have operations in African and other poor countries, provided that those countries respect human and labor rights and have a record of trying to raise living standards of their people and work to maintain ecological integrity.

4. To encourage companies to adopt, implement and monitor for compliance a supplier code of conduct consistent with the International Labor Organization's core labor standards that will prevent the manufacture or purchase through subcontracting of products made with sweatshop or forced labor.

5. To seek opportunities to commend corporations publicly for greater transparency and disclosure, socially responsible behavior, and for endeavors to raise industry standards on social issues that are major concerns of The United Methodist Church.

6. To consider using investment-portfolio managers and funds that specialize in corporate social responsibility screening.

    a. The General Council on Finance and Administration is assigned responsibility by *The Book of Discipline* for preparing and distributing the Investment Guidelines that must be used by all general agencies receiving general church funds, including social responsibility guidelines. The council shall periodically review and update these guidelines as needed, inviting the counsel of the agencies and other interested sectors of the church. The council encourages the active involvement of investing agencies in the overview of socially responsible investing described in this policy.

    b. All general agencies receiving general church funds shall file a copy of their investment policy with the General Council of Finance and Administration. It shall be available upon request to any interested member of the church.

c. These policy goals are strongly recommended to all the institutions affiliated with The United Methodist Church and any of their entities, and to the annual conferences and local churches and any funds of foundations related to them. It is also recommended that a copy of their social responsibility investment guidelines be available upon request by any United Methodist Church member.

d. Where financial considerations preclude immediate divestment of securities held in violation of the above policy goals, boards, agencies, and institutions of The United Methodist Church shall develop a plan for meeting the criteria that will bring them into compliance no later than the 2008 General Conference.

e. These policy goals are also strongly recommended to all individual United Methodist investors and users of financial services.

ADOPTED 1992
AMENDED AND ADOPTED 2000
AMENDED AND READOPTED 2004

See Social Principles, ¶ 163D.

NATIVE AMERICANS

214. Native Americans—A Study of Economic Strategies

WHEREAS, for more than five hundred years, Native Americans have lived and survived in the context of first, colonialism and then, capitalism; and

WHEREAS, Native Americans have been impacted by this economics of greed and were forced to live in poverty; and

WHEREAS, a small part of the Native American population are now surviving through tribal economic development based on gambling, which has many negative social consequences; and

WHEREAS, the next century will see new economic realities, such as "one world economies" and the "mega-mergers," that will have a negative impact on both the rich and poor of this world; and

WHEREAS, Native American spirituality is one voice than can speak to and challenge this issue with its understanding of how to care for the whole family of God; and

WHEREAS, Native American United Methodists believe that our God-given stewardship talents have been warped from their intended purpose and that we have used God's creation with greed rather than care; and

WHEREAS, Native Americans in The United Methodist Church believe that The United Methodist Church must take a proactive stand for a reform of church and society that will introduce a radically different model of economic relationships into the new century; a model that is God-centered; and

WHEREAS, Native Americans in The United Methodist Church are hopeful that this will include new models of economic development for Native Americans that will not impact Native people negatively,

Therefore be it resolved, that the 2000 General Conference mandate the following:

1. that The United Methodist Church sponsor a four-year study of the economic impact of colonialism and capitalism on the Native people of the Americas and the manner of their influence on contemporary mission and ministry with Native people;

2. that the Native American Comprehensive Plan be the lead entity, working with program agencies of The United Methodist Church and other Native American entities both within and without the church; and

3. that the Native American Comprehensive Plan (NACP) and the Native American Economic Development and Empowerment Task Force under the leadership of the General Board of Church and Society develop an innovative and economically strategic report for a God-centered alternative to gambling-centered economic development for Native American communities with recommendations that will be brought back to the 2004 General Conference.

ADOPTED 2000

See Social Principles, ¶ 163G.

215. Economic Development for Native American People

Christians are called to celebrate and protect the worth and dignity of every human being and to struggle against oppression and exploitation. We are called to "proclaim release to the captives . . . to set at liberty those who are oppressed" (Luke 4:18, RSV).

The need for economic development and growth is critically acute in most Native American communities across the United States. Economic conditions are appalling, with some reservations facing upwards of 80 percent unemployment and poverty rates at many times the national average.

Native American reservations have the highest poverty rate in America. Health, education, and income statistics are the worst in the country. There is virtually no tax base on many reservations. Equity for investment is practically nonexistent, and capital for development is nearly impossible to obtain. Some tribes have resorted to gambling enterprises in an effort to transform their economies. The vast majority of tribes remain in desperate need of meaningful, diversified economic development.

Economic development encompasses everything from job creation to reform in tax codes, from the creation of banking institutions to the expansion of tribal authority. Development of basic physical infrastructure such as roads and sewers, telecommunications to bridge the digital divide, and fiscal literacy development for Native American people must all occur for successful economic development.

With due recognition of tribal sovereignty and the self-determining aspirations of Native Americans, we affirm economic development as a critical means by which Native American communities will truly be empowered to pursue their own priorities for their people and their lands and the only means to successfully weave tribal economies into the larger economic fabric of the Americas. The ultimate goal of economic development is to create economic self-sufficiency in Native American communities. The primary economic decisions must be made by tribes. Tribes must control their own affairs and resources.

The U.S. Department of the Interior has grossly mismanaged tribal lands and has lost track of billions of dollars in mining, logging, and other royalties that should have gone to benefit Native American tribes. Cleaning up the accounting and management of trust funds is critical.

The General Conference of The United Methodist Church urges:

1. United Methodists to support the efforts of sovereign Native American nations to create means and methods of economic development that do not depend on gambling and do not disrupt or destroy sacred sites;

2. the U.S. government to end its domination and paternalism and work with Native American tribes in a genuine partnership to support economic development and trust reform;

3. the General Board of Church and Society and the Native American Comprehensive Plan of the General Board of Global Ministries to cosponsor the Native American Economic Development and Empowerment Task Force. The responsibilities of the task force are to provide ways for United Methodist boards, agencies, and annual conferences to work with Native American tribes on economic development; to develop collaborative models for economic empowerment; to consider convening a summit with socially responsible investors, community development organizations, religious representatives, and government officials on Native American economic development; and to monitor public programs and holding decision-makers accountable;

4. the General Board of Church and Society to work with the National Congress of American Indians and other Native American organizations in advocating for federal economic development programs and initiatives;

5. the General Board of Global Ministries to support funding of economic development projects of Native American tribes;

6. the General Board of Pension and Health Benefits to invest funds in Native American financial institutions and community organizations such as the First Nations Development Institute, the Montana Native American Finance and Development Initiative, and the Blackfeet Reservation Development Fund;

7. the General Board of Church and Society to facilitate participation of United Methodist Native Americans in the work of the United Nations Permanent Forum on Indigenous Issues.

ADOPTED 2004

See Social Principles, ¶ 163.

STEWARDSHIP ISSUES IN THE CHURCH

216. Clergy Compensation Packages
to Be Above National Poverty Level

WHEREAS, all United Methodist clergy are in covenant with one another; and

WHEREAS, equity in compensation is part of that covenant; and

WHEREAS, compensation packages in churches are often low and inadequate,

Therefore, be it resolved, that it is recommended that the compensation packages of all full-time United Methodist clergy be, at least, above the national poverty level.

ADOPTED 2000

See Social Principles, ¶ 163E.

217. Living Wage Model

WHEREAS, The United Methodist Church supports a living wage, as outlined in ¶ 67 of the *1996 Book of Discipline*; and

WHEREAS, "all church agencies shall respect their employees' rights to good working conditions, fair compensation and collective action" ("Rights of Workers," resolution adopted by the United Methodist General Conference 1988); and

WHEREAS, church office workers, over 95 percent of whom are female, work in low-paying jobs, which "keep people and families in poverty and women and children are increasingly employed in (low paying) jobs, thus perpetuating a poverty class with sex (and race) characteristics" ("The Economic Community: Economic Justice," *1996 Book of Resolutions,* p. 440),

Therefore be it resolved, that The United Methodist Church adopt the living wage as a model for justice in the world and in the household of faith, specifically challenging all levels of the church—local United Methodist congregations, annual conferences, and their agencies, the general church and its agencies, to adjust compensation for all employees, including support staff, to effect the following:
- reflect the local cost of living;
- provide for adequate health coverage for employees and their dependents;
- provide mechanisms for training, promotion, and advancement for all United Methodist employees at all levels; and
- establish checks and balances to ensure that fair and consistently applied personnel policies pertain to all employees of The United Methodist Church and its agencies.

ADOPTED 2000

See Social Principles, ¶ 163B and C.

218. Financial Help for Seminary Students

WHEREAS, many seminarians and course-of-study students graduate with high levels of debt as they begin ministry; and

WHEREAS, the cost of seminary education and course-of-study school strains normal family expenses, and most annual and missionary conferences are unable to provide sufficient scholarship funds through the Ministerial Educational Fund (MEF),

Therefore, there is a great need for clergy trained for mission and ministry in churches with small memberships and/or in town and rural settings, but many of these small-membership churches are able to pay only minimum compensation.

Therefore, be it resolved, that General Conference:

1. encourages each annual conference to develop a plan to help seminary graduates and course-of-study graduates retire their educational debts; and

2. strongly urges United Methodist seminaries to provide annual workshops on financial planning and/or a financial planner to work with their students.

ADOPTED 2000

See Social Principles, ¶ 163D and E.

219. Pay Equity in General Agencies

WHEREAS, the General Conference of The United Methodist Church has, through the Social Principles and previous action, affirmed the inherent value and equal worth in God's sight of every person, and

WHEREAS, the General Conference has directed the General Council on Finance and Administration to evaluate internal wage structures and practices of general agencies of The United Methodist Church in light of the principle of pay equity and to include this assessment in its regular monitoring of equal employment opportunity compliance under *The Book of Discipline,*

Therefore, be it resolved, that the General Council on Finance and Administration be and hereby is directed to continue to evaluate internal wage structures and practices of general agencies of The United Methodist Church in light of the principle of pay equity and to include this assessment in its regular monitoring of equal employment opportunity compliance under *The Book of Discipline*, and

Be it further resolved, that this evaluation and monitoring during the next quadrennium include but not be limited to the development of a uniform cross-agency job evaluation system that results in a common data base for obtaining information, development of a uniform cross-agency job classification/description system that results in a common data base for obtaining information, development of a uniform cross-agency performance appraisal system, which would facilitate the evaluation of job performance on an ongoing basis, provide a common data base of information about job performance, and reduce the opportunity for bias based on gender or ethnic status, development of uniform cross-agency salary administration procedures designed to reduce the opportunity for bias based on gender or ethnic status, and development of an ongoing pay equity monitoring program using these new systems and processes, and

Be it further resolved, that these new systems and processes include all staff, exempt and nonexempt, at all general agencies receiving general church funds, and

Be it further resolved, that the general agencies not receiving general church funds at their own expense shall participate and cooperate with the General Council on Finance and Administration and its consultants pursuant to these resolutions, to devise a mechanism for collecting and reporting information as to their own job classification, description, salary, and job evaluation processes which will provide the General Council on Finance and Administration with adequate data to monitor, assess, and report on each agency's achievement of pay equity, and

Be it further resolved, that these resolutions are not intended to expand the role and authority of the General Council on Finance and Administration to address or administer pay scales for general agencies that do not receive general church funds, and

Be it further resolved, that the quadrennial budget for the General Council on Finance and Administration be increased by $880,000 for this project, with any unused funds at the completion of this project to be held in short-term reserves and available to reduce apportionments in the 2005-2008 quadrennium, and

Be it further resolved, that the General Council on Finance and Administration provide the 2004 General Conference with an informational report on the new systems and processes and progress with the new monitoring functions, and

Be it further resolved, that the General Council on Finance and Administration provide the 2008 General Conference with an evaluative report on pay equity in the general agencies, based on the monitoring of pay equity that has been conducted since implementation of the new systems and processes, and

Be it further resolved, that the General Council on Finance and Administration be and hereby is empowered to do such other things and take such other actions as may be necessary and expedient in order to carry out the spirit and intent of this directive.

ADOPTED 2000

See Social Principles, ¶ 163D.

220. Pension Agency to Examine Policies

WHEREAS, the General Board of Pensions and Health Benefits has two different rules that apply to the three types of employer contributions and how the employee may have access to the contributions that the employer made to the employee account; and

WHEREAS, laypeople throughout the church, upon retirement, have the option of withdrawing any percentage of their employer's contributions of up to 100 percent if they so desire; and

WHEREAS, clergy who are employed by any general board or agency, upon retirement, also have the option of leaving their employer's contributions with the General Board of Pensions or withdrawing any portion of those funds up to 100 percent, if they so desire; and

WHEREAS, clergy who have employer contributions made for them by a local church, district or annual conference entity currently have the option of withdrawing only up to 25 percent of these funds, and the local churches believe they are contributing funds for their pastor's use and do not know that these funds are not totally available to these pastors,

Therefore, be it resolved, that the General Conference instruct the Board of Pensions to examine its policies relating to the employer contributions to an employee's account. They shall take into consideration the two methods used to administer three types of employer contributions and try to combine the two methods into one and make a report on their findings and reasons for changes or reasons for no changes to the 2004 General Conference.

ADOPTED 2000

See Social Principles, ¶ 163D.

221. Provide Financial Incentives for Clergy in Churches with Small Membership

WHEREAS, churches with small memberships require clergy with specialized training and skills; and

WHEREAS, such training is available at various times/places involving personal costs; and

WHEREAS, clergy with such training are often influenced by financial concerns to move to churches that provide higher salaries,

Therefore, be it resolved, that annual conferences be creative and intentional in providing clergy in churches with small memberships salary increments for each continuous year of service in churches with small membership; and/or in town and country settings; and

Be it further resolved, that annual conferences be creative and intentional in providing financial support to clergy who desire specialized training for ministry in churches with small memberships, and/or town and country settings.

ADOPTED 2000

See Social Principles, ¶ 163D and E.

222. Scrutinize/Establish Policies for Use/Retention of Unrestricted Reserves by Boards/Agencies of The United Methodist Church

WHEREAS, First United Methodist Church of Marietta, Georgia, a part of the body of Christ, experienced a split in its congregation resulting in the loss of approximately one-third of its active membership due to real and/or perceived concerns with the denomination; and

WHEREAS, the majority of those leaving were young adults with families who would have constituted much of the future membership of the church; and

WHEREAS, the division in this body of Christ caused conflict and misunderstanding among friends and within families; and

WHEREAS, those who remained, while recognizing much good in our church and in our denomination, had continuing concerns about The United Methodist Church; and

WHEREAS, they love the church and are committed to resolving issues and solving problems and truly desire to ensure the well-being of our denomination and to avoid similar divisions within other United Methodist churches; and

WHEREAS, financial reserves of boards and agencies have increased in recent years through growth in investments from surpluses; and

WHEREAS, local churches and charges have difficulty in understanding such imbalances in the finances within the church,

Therefore, be it resolved, that policies be considered which would assert ownership by the church over surpluses earned by boards and agencies.

ADOPTED 2000

See Social Principles, ¶ 163D and E.

223. Seminary Student Indebtedness

WHEREAS, the future of The United Methodist Church will, in large part, be shaped by the ordained clergy who will serve our 30,000 congregations; and

WHEREAS, these local congregations cannot call their own pastors, but depend upon the United Methodist connection for the formation, ordination, and appointment of pastors through the action of annual conference and the appointment of the bishop; and

WHEREAS, the United Methodist connection has responsibility for training clergy and has created 13 United Methodist seminaries to assist in fulfilling that responsibility; and

WHEREAS, the church has established the Master of Divinity degree, or its equivalent, as the basic requirement for elder's ordination and has set the appropriate educational requirements for the ordained deacon in full connection; and

WHEREAS, in fulfillment of these requirements many candidates for ordination are incurring significant debt, often between $10,000 and $20,000; and

WHEREAS, this indebtedness has significant impact on the clergyperson's ability to provide effective leadership in the local congregation; and

WHEREAS, the need to attract highly qualified, gifted, and called candidates for ordained ministry will be profoundly influenced by the issue of student indebtedness,

Therefore, be it resolved, that the General Board of Higher Education and Ministry/Division of Ordained Ministry, in cooperation with the Council of Bishops, the United Methodist Foundation for Christian Higher Education, and the Office of Loans and Scholarships, will develop a plan to reduce the seminary indebtedness of candidates for ordained ministry though various means including:

1. assisting annual conferences in addressing the seminary indebtedness of probationary members in their conference;

2. challenging local churches to support candidates for ordination with scholarship assistance during seminary;

3. working with United Methodist seminaries to minimize student borrowing and the potential for indebtedness; and

4. raising endowment funds to provide tuition scholarships for United Methodist candidates for ordination attending United Methodist seminaries, and

Be it further resolved, that the General Board of Higher Education and Ministry set aside funds, as they become available, to assist students and annual conferences in addressing the issue of seminarian indebtedness, for the sake of effective clergy leadership for the future of the church.

ADOPTED 2000

See Social Principles, ¶ 163D and E.

224. Stewardship Education for Small Membership Churches

WHEREAS, there is a general absence of financial development and stewardship education in small membership and rural churches; and

WHEREAS, there is a need to guide small membership and rural churches to change the concept of stewardship from "meeting the budget" to "sharing the resources God has given to us"; and

WHEREAS, *A Tithing Church* was approved for inclusion in *The Book of Resolutions, 1996* (p. 715); and

WHEREAS, stewardship responsibilities are outlined in *The 2000 Book of Discipline,* ¶¶ 258.4, 627.5 and 1113,

Therefore, be it resolved, that the General Board of Discipleship, through the Office of Small Membership Church and Shared Ministries and the Office of Stewardship, and the General Board of Global Ministries, through the Office of Field Service and Finance, be called on to network with the United Methodist Rural Fellowship on the issue of financial development and stewardship education; and

Be it further resolved, that we encourage a new resource packet on stewardship be developed for today's small membership and rural churches; and

Be it further resolved, that we encourage resources be developed for training pastors and lay leadership regarding personal tithing, speaking about stewardship and finances, and negotiating pastoral compensation; and

Be it further resolved, that a leadership team be formed with individuals from the above-named groups to follow through on these concerns.

ADOPTED 2000

See Social Principles, ¶ 163D.

225. Stewardship Emphasis

WHEREAS, the Bible speaks of responsible stewardship of money and possession; and

WHEREAS, most clergy and laity have forgotten that giving is a vital part of Christian discipleship and is a strong indication of a person's commitment to God; and

WHEREAS, the concept of tithing has not been taught in most congregations during the past few decades, meaning that many have been denied the knowledge of how to grow spiritually in their stewardship of giving; and

WHEREAS, statistics show that giving by persons in The United Methodist Church is somewhere below two percent; and

WHEREAS, many programs of ministry have been eliminated or not even started in many conferences or national United Methodist agencies because of lack of funds,

Therefore, be it resolved, that the 2000 General Conference adopt as a high priority for the next four years a program for teaching and preaching about spiritual growth in giving with an emphasis of setting tithing as a goal for every person in The United Methodist Church; and

Be it further resolved, that the Board of Discipleship be directed to develop a program that can be used by annual conferences to train clergy and laity how to develop within their congregations an attitude of spiritual discipleship related to giving, which includes the teaching of tithing.

ADOPTED 2000

See Social Principles, ¶ 163D.

226. Tithing

WHEREAS, the earth and all that is in it belongs to God; and

WHEREAS, Jesus spoke about money and possessions; and

WHEREAS, God has promised many blessings if people will live by biblical standards as it involves the management of that which God has given us; and

WHEREAS, those blessings would include the following: God will fill your barns with plenty, when you honor the Lord with your possessions and with the first fruits of all your increase (Proverbs 3:9-10); God gives back to you in the same measure that you use to give to God (Luke 6:38); God will pour out so much blessing you will not have enough room for it (Malachi 3:10); and

WHEREAS, the concept of tithing has not been taught in most congregations during the past few decades, which means many people have been denied the knowledge of how to grow spiritually in their stewardship of giving; and

WHEREAS, this is confirmed by statisticians that giving by people in The United Methodist Church is somewhere below two percent, and

WHEREAS, programs of ministry have been eliminated or not even started because of the lack of funds; and

WHEREAS, annual conferences have had to eliminate or not start programs because of the lack of funds; and

WHEREAS, general boards at the national level have had to curtail their programs because of the lack of funds,

Therefore, the 2000 General Conference adopts as a high priority for the next eight years a program for teaching and preaching for spiritual growth in giving, with an emphasis of setting tithing as a goal for every person in The United Methodist Church.

ADOPTED 2000

See Social Principles, ¶ 163D.

UNITED STATES ECONOMIC ISSUES

227. Enabling Financial Support for Domestic Programs

In Genesis 4:3-9 Cain displays the selfishness that exploits and destroys and God calls him into accountability for his treatment of his brother. Acts 2: 44-45 provides us with an early glimpse of the transformation in community that is the gift of the Holy Spirit, especially in our responsibility to each other. It is apparent that God calls us to be responsible for how we live and share the resources of community with others.

The United Methodist Church has declared war to be "incompatible with the teachings of Jesus Christ"; and

Dr. Martin Luther King Jr. wrote that "racism and its perennial ally," economic exploitation, "provide the key to understanding most of the international complications of this generation."

While unemployment is increasing among minority groups, tens of thousands of African American, Hispanic, and Native American male and female young adults have never been employed and are, therefore, not counted in current unemployment statistics; and

Many public school districts (especially those that serve the masses of urban Black, Hispanic, and poor people) find themselves facing severe financial shortfalls, staff cuts, the elimination of vital programs, and school closings.

Those same communities are experiencing social trauma due to plant closings and the relocation of industry to countries where the wages are from fifty cents to one dollar an hour. All of these are examples that we have not heard God's answer to Cain, that we are our sisters' and brothers' keepers and have not sought to usher in the community that is blessed by the Spirit.

We petition the President and Congress of the United States to reduce the U.S. military presence by recognizing principles of sovereignty in every region of the world.

We petition the President and Congress of the United States to reapportion dollars, saved by reduced military spending and base closings, for domestic programs that will enable the financial support for an increase in quality educational offerings in the public school systems of the country, adequate health care, affordable housing, the creation of sufficient employment opportunities, and a new comprehensive employment training act, that will appropriate federal dollars into elements of the private sector that are currently in compliance with affirmative action guidelines for the purpose of encouraging their participation in the retraining of U.S. workers and for redevelopment of plants within the continental United States.

ADOPTED 1992
AMENDED AND READOPTED 2004

See Social Principles, ¶ 164.

228. Establish Annual Conference State Taxation Task Force

WHEREAS, the Bible enjoins all Christians to establish a just society, called "the Kingdom of God" by our Lord Jesus; the Hebrew prophets condemn in no uncertain terms depriving the poor of fair treatment and Jesus described his mission as liberating the oppressed and preaching good news to the poor and further identified with "the least of these"; and

WHEREAS, tax laws are necessary to raise revenues to meet the minimum health, safety, educational, and welfare needs of the community, the Judeo-Christian standards of justice require that the taxes imposed be fair to poor and low-income citizens and raise adequate revenues for the society's common good; and

WHEREAS, Susan Pace Hamill, United Methodist layperson and professor of law at the University of Alabama School of Law in Tuscaloosa, has convincingly documented in her thesis "An Argument for Tax Reform Based on Judeo-Christian Ethics" http://www.law.ua.edu/pdf/hamill-taxreform.pdf that the State of Alabama tax code, by oppressively burdening poor and low-income Alabamians and failing to raise adequate revenues for basic services, does not meet the Judeo-Christian standards of justice; and

WHEREAS, the North Alabama Conference and the Alabama-West Florida Conference both organized to work to reform their state's regressive tax code;

Be it hereby resolved that, State Taxation Task Forces are established in each annual conference at their next session to examine the tax codes of their states, following the guidelines in Professor Hamill's book *The Least of These (Fair Taxes and the Moral Duty of Christians);*

and that the task forces in each Conference prepare a strategy for action to promote and establish a just tax code in every state;

and that strategies seek to enlist the cooperation and support of all local churches through tax education and advocacy;

and that their results are communicated annually to the General Board of Church and Society in Washington D.C.;

and that the General Board of Church and Society report on the effectiveness of these strategies and recommend continued action to the General Conference of 2008.

ADOPTED 2004

See Social Principles, ¶ 163 *D* and *E*.

229. Welfare Reform

There have been many changes in recent years to programs of public assistance and welfare. These programs resulted in significant reductions in the number of persons and families on the welfare rolls. However, there is considerable confusion over where people who left the rolls have gone. Some have gone to work, but there is much evidence that many others have not found employment and have had to move in with relatives or even become homeless.

In addition, many that may have initially found work have since become unemployed.

The purpose of welfare reform was not only to reduce the welfare rolls, but to move people from dependence on public assistance to economic independence and a better life, especially for children of welfare families. Too often, this has not happened. So-called "workfare" programs are not a permanent solution. Studies have shown that one third of the people who were enrolled in these programs are now back where they started. In addition, these programs, paying minimum wage with no benefits, have also eliminated many good-paying jobs in the public sector, putting even more people out of work. What is required are bold new programs of training and public sector job creation. Training is needed to equip people for jobs that pay well, such as manufacturing and the information economy, to assist them in completing their formal education, and to provide assistance in parenting while making the transition.

Funds are available now to achieve these goals. One result of the reduction in the number of persons on welfare has been the accumulation of funds allocated to the states for their welfare programs. These funds are available to the states, but in most cases have not been drawn down. In November 1999 these unused surpluses amounted to more than $4.3 billion. Amounts vary from state to state and grow larger each month. For example, in Pennsylvania alone, the surpluses are in excess of $350 million. With only half that amount, the state could create 10,000 public sector jobs with 18 months training. These funds are a "welfare surplus" accrued as states drop people from the rolls. They cannot be spent for any other purpose and should not be confused with a "state surplus."

Therefore, we call on annual conference boards of church and society or their equivalents to urge their state and county governments to create programs of training, public sector job creation, child care and resources for parenting, to assist current and former welfare recipients in making the transition from dependence to economic health. We urge local churches to familiarize themselves with the issue and to ask their legislators to act immediately to free up surplus welfare funds, in order that people who leave welfare can "have life, and have it more abundantly."

ADOPTED 2000

See Social Principles, ¶ 163D *and* E.

230. Women and Social Security in the United States

The Old and New Testaments share prophetic-messianic traditions in which God stands with the oppressed against a dehumanizing and destructive social order. The emphasis on the protection of those in deepest need was a theme of the events of Exodus. And Jesus, drawing on intimate knowledge of the Hebrew Scriptures, inaugurated his ministry with a quotation from Isaiah:

"The spirit of the Lord . . . has anointed me to preach good news to the poor . . . to set at liberty those who are oppressed" (Luke 4:18-19, RSV; cf. Isaiah 61:1-2).

The early Christian church in Jerusalem, following this tradition, established a community in which all things were held in common. Special attention was given to those who were the neediest-widows, the elderly, the disabled. Israel and the early church exemplified the role of the community of faith as they addressed concern for the welfare of the poor and establishment of a just social order.

The Social Security system in the United States, with its disability, survivors and retirement benefits, has historically functioned as a basic insurance program to provide income and medical expenses for those persons who are retired or disabled or are the survivors of deceased workers. It has helped to hold families together by maintaining income in times of personal hardship and has relieved younger persons of the necessity of total care for aging parents. Social Security also allows older persons, most of whom are women, the independence and dignity of their own income by providing basic benefits. The Social Security Act's enactment in 1935,has been a cornerstone of the social policy of the United States and remains the most successful antipoverty program in U.S. history.

Because of the important role of Social Security, people of faith have a special interest in ensuring that it is operated fairly and securely. Its benefits must continue to be designed to overcome disadvantages of age, race, gender, sexual orientation or disability and regularly reviewed to ensure that it is flexible enough to adjust to the changing needs of society.

In the United States, Social Security is a woman's issue. Since its inception, Social Security has often been the only income source keeping women from living in poverty. Today, while women's lives have changed, women are still over-represented in the lowest wage jobs and earn only 74 percent of what men earn. Women leave the labor force for an average of 15 percent of their working careers, primarily to fulfill responsibilities as caregivers to their children, spouses, or elderly family members. In addition, women live an average of seven years longer than their male counterparts.

Current proposals begun by the fractious report of the Advisory Council on Social Security have caused turmoil in the debate over the future of Social Security in the United States. Especially pernicious were the proposals to divert workers' current payments from the Social Security system into individually held private accounts, which would significantly damage women's retirement income. The returns on individual accounts would be dependent on the risks of volatile investment markets and would not be guaranteed to keep pace with inflation nor provide spousal benefits, widow's benefits, or benefits for divorced spouses—all of which are special features of the current Social Security system. Since Social Security provides the core of women's retirement income, without the guarantees of a shared insurance pool, cost-of-living increases, and spousal and lifetime benefits, many women could easily outlive their assets.

The United Methodist Church has always affirmed that Social Security's central role in family income protection must not be compromised. We believe that all proposals to address the future solvency of the Social Security Trust Fund must be viewed through the eyes of women who are the majority of Social Security recipients. Remaining inadequacies for women in the current system also must be addressed. If we strengthen the Social Security system so that it works well for women, we will have a system that works well for all persons in the United States.

Therefore, we affirm that the following principles on Social Security in the United States must guide our work on this critical issue:

Continue to Help Those With Lower Lifetime Earnings, Who Are Disproportionately Women

Social Security's benefit formula is structured so that the lowest-paid workers receive benefits that replace a higher proportion of their preretirement earnings than higher-wage workers. Many of the lowest-paid workers also have no pensions from their jobs. Any reform must retain this feature benefiting lower-paid workers.

Maintain Full Cost of Living Adjustments

Social Security's annual cost-of-living adjustment (COLA), which is indexed to inflation, is a crucial protection against the erosion of benefits. Because women, on average, live longer than men and rely more on Social Security, and also often lack other sources of retirement income, this provision is particularly important to women. Even when employment-based pension income is available, it is rarely inflation-protected.

Protect and Strengthen Benefits for Wives, Widows, and Divorced Women

Social Security's family protection provisions help women the most. Social Security provides guaranteed, inflation-protected, lifetime benefits for the wives of retired workers, widows, and divorced women, many of whom did not work enough at high enough wages to earn adequate benefits on their own accounts.

Preserve Disability and Survivor Benefits

Social Security provides benefits to three million children (Social Security Administration, 1998) and the remaining caretaking parent in the event of the premature death or disability of either working parent. Spouses of disabled workers and the widows (or widowers) of workers who died prematurely also receive guaranteed lifetime retirement benefits. Two out of five of today's 20-year-olds will face premature death or disability before reaching retirement age.

Protect the Most Disadvantaged Workers from "Across-the-Board" Benefits Cuts

Some proposed "across-the-board" benefit cuts such as raising the retirement age or the numbers of years of work history used in calculating benefits would disproportionately hurt those with the most physically demanding or stressful jobs who cannot work more years, as well as those who have low lifetime earnings, including many women, minorities, temporary, seasonal and part-time workers, agricultural workers, and the chronically under and unemployed. These workers are also unlikely to have other employer-provided retirement benefits.

Ensure That Women's Guaranteed Benefits Are Not Reduced by Individual Account Plans That Are Subject to the Uncertainties of the Stock Market

Proposals to divert worker's current payments from the Social Security system into individually held, private accounts, whose returns would be dependent on volatile investment markets and would not be guaranteed to keep pace with inflation nor provide spousal benefits, would reduce the retirement income of many women. Without the guarantees of a shared insurance pool, cost-of-living increases, and spousal and lifetime benefits, many women could easily outlive their assets.

Address the Care-Giving and Labor Force Experiences of Women

The Social Security system is based on marriage and work patterns that have changed. Currently, the benefit formula, which generally helps those with low lifetime earning, also favors those with 35 years of labor force participation, years which many women lack because of family care-giving. Moreover, the effects of sex-based wage discrimination during their working years are not fully offset by the more generous treatment low earners receive. Such issues as divorce, taking time out of the workforce for care-giving, the differences in current benefits between one and two-earner couples, and the inadequacies in benefits for surviving spouses must be considered at the same time that solutions to strengthening the financial soundness of the system are being sought.

Further Reduce the Number of Elderly Women Living in Poverty

Social Security has helped reduce poverty rates for the elderly, from 35 percent in 1959 to less than 11 percent in 1996. In 1995, the poverty rate for all women over the age of 65 was 13.6 percent while the poverty rate among women age 65 or older who lived alone was 23.6 percent. Without Social Security, the poverty rate for women over 65 would have been an astonishing 52.9 percent. Nevertheless, unmarried women still suffer disproportionately; single, divorced, and widowed women age 65 or older have a poverty rate of 22 percent, compared with 15 percent for unmarried men and 5 percent for women and men in married couples.

The United Methodist Church, in its Social Principles, urges social policies and programs that ensure to the aging the respect and dignity that is their right as senior members of society; affirms the need to support those in distress; and calls for the equal treatment of men and women in every aspect of their common life.

Therefore, be it resolved:

1. that the 2000 General Conference support the above principles recognizing Social Security's central role in family income protection and in the special needs of women;

2. that the secretary of the General Conference shall communicate this support to the appropriate officials in the executive and legislative branches of the U.S. government;

3. that the General Boards of Church and Society and Global Ministries shall continue to research and document Social Security issues, advocating on behalf of these principles; and

4. that The United Methodist Church shall continue to educate its constituents so that churches and individual United Methodists can encourage their legislators to support a strong Social Security system in the U.S. throughout the 21st Century.

ADOPTED 1984
REVISED AND READOPTED 2000

See Social Principles, ¶ 163D and E.

231. Support of Employment Retirement Income Security Act (ERISA)

WHEREAS, as United Methodists, we have a long history of public witness on matters of economic justice. As we view questionable business practices in our world, we must speak out for ethical behavior and call our Congress to action; and

WHEREAS, hundreds of thousands of people have lost their jobs and life savings to illegal, corrupt, or questionable business practices that manipulate short term stock prices and tend to benefit the very few individuals in upper management positions, and we see that the brunt of this mismanagement is borne by employees who have been downsized, forced into early retirement, or forced to work longer hours; and

WHEREAS, loyal employees have seen their retirement savings eroded in an atmosphere of growing bankruptcy and a more skewed distribution of wealth and income throughout the nation, we realize we must call for action to protect the futures of these peoples; and

WHEREAS, procedures of corporations such as Enron, Tyco, WorldCom, and others enabled financial officers aware of financial difficulties within their structures to divest themselves of stock during freeze-out periods, creating steep drops in stock prices. When employees were finally able to sell stock, stock prices had plummeted because of the "dumping" of stock by managers, thus leaving employees with great losses in the value of their Employment Retirement Income Security Act (ERISA) managed plan.

Therefore, we United Methodists as employees, investors, and consumers in the Kansas East Conference adopt and petition the General Conference to petition Congress to enact legislation that would protect ERISA managed plan participants through limitation of company-owned stock, through eliminating freeze-out periods restricting sale of company stock, and by increasing investment options available to ERISA managed plan participants;

Further, we petition Congress to tighten the requirements for converting traditional pension plans to cash balance plans, especially for long-term employees.

ADOPTED 2004

See Social Principles, ¶¶ 162E and 163E and I.

232. Negative Implication of U.S. Deficit Spending

All expenditures by governments are funded either by current taxation or by borrowing from future revenues. Experience has shown that when governments borrow from the future by making expenditures for which no current source of income exists, frequently the effect is inflation. Inflation erodes the purchasing value of funds held by common people of the country, sometimes dramatically. While inflation affects all persons, it especially affects those persons, primarily retired, whose incomes, such as pensions, annuities, and interest from savings, are fixed.

We note with consternation the willingness of the U.S. Congress to essentially fund foreign conflicts by printing currency not backed by income at the same time it is legislating tax reductions. In effect, without so stating, the government is confiscating the financial security of the vulnerable poor and elderly in order to fund the military costs of foreign conflicts.

We call upon all United Methodists to contact their legislators to remind them of the negative implications of deficit spending. We especially call upon United Methodists in the United States to request that their senators and representatives assure an adequate tax base for all expenditures for military conflicts. We call upon the General Board of Church and Society to provide all appropriate resources in support of this resolution.

ADOPTED 2004

See Social Principles, ¶ 163.

WORK/LEISURE

233. Concern for Workers Task Force

WHEREAS, Scripture and Wesleyan tradition call us to do justice and demonstrate mercy for workers as an expression of our witness for Jesus Christ;

WHEREAS, transitions in the global economy and local communities have created systems and practices of unfairness and persecution of workers; and

WHEREAS, The United Methodist Church continues to need guidance and support in developing ministries of justice for workers,

Therefore, be it resolved, that the 2004 General Conference authorize the continuation of the Concern for Workers Task Force for the next four years. The General Conference shall direct the General Board of Global Ministries and the General Board of Church and Society to appoint a task force composed of clergy and laity. All appointees will be persons who are informed about the issues and are presently engaged in ministry to working people, the unemployed, and the underemployed. The task force will be gender, racial, and class inclusive.

Be it further resolved, that the task force shall fulfill the following goals:

A. Educate the church about the integration of justice for workers with the Christian faith by:

1. providing resources and opportunities for United Methodists who are employers and directors of church-related institutions to become aware of workers' concerns and to integrate our social teachings on workers' rights into their vocations. The task force may organize a forum for United Methodist employers and directors for this purpose;

2. providing resources and opportunities for United Methodists who are leaders of labor unions and workers' rights organizations to integrate our social teachings on workers' rights into their vocations. The task force may, for example, organize a forum for such persons;.

3. providing resources and training for United Methodist clergy and seminarians to engage in ministry to and advocacy with workers who are engaged in labor struggles; and

4. providing congregations and lay members with resources and opportunities to develop their awareness of workers' concerns and our social teachings.

B. Empower the church to advocate for workers' rights in local and international struggles by:

1. guiding the development of the United Methodist Concern for Workers Network, through the General Boards of Church and Society and Global Ministries. The purpose of the network will be:
   a. to help United Methodists connect with local struggles for workplace peace and justice;
   b. to provide information about national and international campaigns and legislation that are endorsed by the General Boards of Church and Society and Global Ministries;
   c. to promote the observance of Labor Sunday; and
   d. to receive and share information from members of the network;

2. exploring collaborations with labor unions, Pan Methodist denominations, ecumenical organizations and other workers' rights organizations.

3. assisting the General Boards in the implementation of General Conference resolutions related to the rights of workers.

ADOPTED 2000
AMENDED AND READOPTED 2004

See Social Principles, ¶ 163*B* and *C*.

234. Environmental Health and Safety
in Workplace and Community

God's covenant with humanity affirms that God is involved in the healing of individuals (Proverbs 3:7-8) and includes the mandate to protect the community from dangers that threaten the health and safety of the people. At the beginning of Methodism, John Wesley provided medicine and medical treatment at no cost to the poor in London and Bristol. In addition to pioneering free dispensaries in England, Wesley emphasized prevention of illness. In his book *Primitive Physic,* he dealt with nutrition and hygiene, as well as treatment of the sick. The first Social Creed, adopted by the 1908 General Conference of The Methodist Episcopal Church, declared that workers must be protected "from dangerous machinery, occupational disease, injuries, and mortality," and that working conditions must be regulated to safeguard the physical and moral health of the community. Today as well, the church is called to declare that the health of every individual is part of community health, including safe and healthy conditions in places where people work. The church has a responsibility to pronounce clearly the implications of God's law of love for human health. Where human life and health are at stake, economic gain must not take precedence.

A. Public Health and Safety Hazards

Public health hazards originate from a variety of sources, including organisms (e.g., bacteria, fungi, and viruses), physical conditions (e.g., hazardous machinery, excessive noise, repetitive motion), toxic chemicals, and radiation. Such hazards can produce infectious diseases, disabling injuries, incapacitating illnesses, and death. Toxic substances and related hazards such as ionizing radiation threaten the exposed individual to additional hazards such as cancer and sterility, and they also threaten future generations with birth defects and gene mutations.[1]

1. *Estimates of the Fraction of Cancer in the United States Related to Occupational Factors,* prepared by the National Cancer Institute, National Institute of Environmental Health Sciences, National Institute for Occupational Safety and Health, mimeographed report, September 14, 1978; page 24. One substance alone, asbestos, is expected to claim the lives of 1.6 million of the 4 million individuals heavily exposed since World War II, including a substantial number of shipyard workers.

B. Declaration

Public health and safety is dependent on effective prevention and active protection before illness or injury have occurred. To fulfill God's commandment to love our neighbor as ourselves, we should support action to protect each individual's health and to preserve the health of the community. To this end, we declare:

1. Every individual, including those with disabilities, has a right to a safe and healthful environment unendangered by a polluted natural world, a hazardous workplace, an unsanitary community, dangerous household products, unsafe drugs, and contaminated food. This human right must take precedence over property rights. Moreover, the necessary preservation of human life and health must not be sacrificed or diminished for economic gain. It is unconscionable that anyone should profit from conditions that lead to the disease, disability, or death of another.

Furthermore, the essential protection of the physical and moral quality of human life must not be compromised by competing considerations of capital investment and return, or diminished by society's insistence on affluence, luxury, and convenience. Environmental health and safety regulations must not be compromised by private property rights or risk-benefit analysis.

2. Public health hazards must be prevented in order to avoid the serious individual and community consequences of injury, illness, and untimely death, including disability, physical pain, mental anguish, lost human potential, family stress, and the diversion of scarce medical resources.

3. Public health hazards to future generations, such as toxic substances and wastes that produce birth defects and gene mutations, must be prevented in order to avoid a legacy of disease, disability, and untimely death. No generation has the right to assume risks that potentially endanger the viability of future life.

4. The public health risks of technological development must be fully researched and openly assessed before new technologies are introduced into the home, the workplace, the community, or the environment. Consumers and workers have the right to know what technologies and substances are used in the workplace, in foods, and other products.

5. The preservation and protection of human life from public and environmental health hazards is a fundamental responsibility of gov-

ernment that must be maintained by active public support and adequate public funds. All levels of government must enforce public and environmental health and safety laws.

6. Preventive health care should be taught in educational institutions to persons in every age group at every level of society. Health professionals in all branches of medicine and public health, and those in related fields, should be encouraged to practice preventive medicine, implementing community preventive health strategies, and assist patients in the adoption of healthy lifestyles. Programs should be implemented that educate and inform consumers and workers about physical, chemical, biological, and radiological hazards of products, services, working conditions, and environmental contaminants.

7. The right to a healthy and safe workplace is a fundamental right. Employers must assume responsibility to eliminate hazards in their workplaces which cause death, injury, and disease and to work together with their employees and employee organizations to achieve this objective.

C. General Recommendations

We call upon all local churches, annual and central conferences, and general boards and agencies of The United Methodist Church to provide for the safety and health of persons in their meeting places and work places; and to educate and to encourage advocacy for public and environmental health and safety in the community as indicated in the declarations above.

ADOPTED 1988
REVISED AND ADOPTED 2000

See Social Principles, ¶ 163C.

235. Rights of African American Farmers

The 1996 Social Principles state, "We support the right of persons and families to live and prosper as farmers . . ."Unfortunately, this has not been the reality for African American farmers. Since the landmark 1982 Civil Rights Commission report the situation facing Black farmers remains dismal. That report found that the United States Department of Agriculture had not placed adequate emphasis on dealing with the crisis facing black farmers and that if the current rate of land loss continues there will not be any Black farmers left by the year 2000.

A November 1990 Report of the U.S. House of Representatives Committee on Government Operations confirms that conditions have not improved. The report states, "By 1978 the rate of loss for blacks increased to 57.3 percent, 2 and 1/2 times the rate of loss for whites. Between census years 1982 and 1987, the number of black operated farms declined 30.9 percent compared with 6.6 percent for white operated farms. A 1992 U.S. Department of Commerce Bureau of Census of Agriculture found that between 1920 and 1978, the number of white-operated farms declined 63 percent in the United States. Between 1920 and 1992, the number of Black farmers in the United States declined from 925,710 to 18,816, or by 98 percent. Presently, according to the U.S. Department of Agriculture, Black farmers now own less than 1 percent of the farmland in the United States; at the turn of the 20th century that figure was 14 percent. In 1920 nearly 1 million Black farmers tilled American soil; 70 years later, that number had dropped to fewer than 20,000.

The continuing loss of ownership and control of agricultural land by African American farmers has reduced their ability to achieve economic viability and financial independence. This loss has been accelerated by the Black landowners' lack of access to capital, technical information, and legal resources needed to train and develop agricultural land holdings into stable, income-producing, self-sustaining operations. The U.S. Department of Agriculture (USDA), the institution designed to help all farmers, practiced widespread discrimination. These discriminatory practices have cost Black farmers loan approval, loan servicing, and farm management assistance. Many Black farmers never learned of the many support services available to them, including low-interest rates for socially disadvantaged farmers. Black farmers in financial distress often do not receive reliable and comprehensive advice from USDA officials in time to prevent foreclosure. Many times Black farmers who go to apply for various conservation and credit programs are told that applications are not available for another several weeks. When they return, they are then told that all resources are committed. A 1997 USDA Civil Rights Report has confirmed these practices.

In 1999, USDA reached a settlement of a class action suit by African American farmers who have experienced discrimination. The Agriculture Department will provide $50,000 in cash settlement plus debt forgiveness to qualified Black farmers who were denied government loans and other assistance because of their race. Farmers who have strong documentation of their case may receive more than the $50,000. Unfortunately, for many Black farmers the settlement is too little, too late. Many have lost their land and opportunities to prosper in the vocation of their choice. The United Methodist Church takes seriously Paul's advice: "If one member suffers, all suffer together." Thus, the General Conference:

1. condemns the discriminatory policies against African American farmers by the private lenders and the U.S. Department of Agriculture (USDA);

2. strongly supports the crucial need for the church, the government and the private sector to provide financial, technical, and management assistance to help stop the decline of Black-owned farmland in America;

3. applauds the settlement of the class action suit by Black farmers against USDA;

4. calls on USDA to put into place stringent regulations to guard against discrimination; to fully implement, without delay, the recommendations of the 1997 USDA Civil Rights Report and the National Commission on Small Farms Report; and to include Black and other minority farmers on county committees that oversee USDA loan and other programs;

5. calls on the U.S. Congress to fully fund the Minority Farm Outreach and Technical Assistance Program; and

6. calls on the General Board of Church and Society and the General Board of Global Ministries to work with the Federation of Southern Cooperatives/Land Assistance Fund and other community-based organizations to address the needs of Black farmers and to improve access to USDA programs.

ADOPTED 2000

See Social Principles, ¶ 163*A* and *H.*

236. Rights of Farm Workers in the U.S.

As we embark on a new century, the gap between the wealthy and poor in the United States continues to widen. The church is called to take an active role in advocating for social justice.

Farm workers are essential to the economic well-being of U.S. society, but they continue to live and work under conditions which deprive them of what is decent and adequate to survive. They are among the poorest paid workers in this country and have struggled to be included under the minimum wage laws. The wages they receive (an average annual income of $8000) result in farm workers and their families living in conditions of poverty. At their workplace and in communities in which they live, they face discrimination and exploitation based on ethnicity, country of origin, socioeconomic status, immigrant status, and educational level. U.S. national labor laws exclude farm workers from their protection. Intentional exclusion from these protections denies farm workers such rights as overtime pay or the protected right to organize. The few state and federal laws established to protect farm worker rights, such as the Migrant and Seasonal Agricultural Worker Protection Act, have not been adequately enforced. Instead these laws have continued to be weakened at every level. This places farm workers and their families in jeopardy of abuse, serious injury, and even death. In addition, unemployment and workers' compensation benefits have been systematically denied to farm workers. Farm labor policies, such as the current guest-worker/H2A visa program which allows agricultural workers temporary entrance into the U.S., have severely diminished the limited protections afforded farm workers. This type of program keeps real wages down; maintains substandard working conditions; eliminates workers' rights to voice grievances; and denies workers their civil rights, including the fundamental right of freedom of movement. Farm work is one of the most hazardous occupations in the United States, placing workers at a higher risk of injury. Farm workers and their families exhibit a variety of severe health problems at a rate well above the national average. Health insurance benefits for most workers are nonexistent and access to adequate health care services is extremely limited. They cope with both a lack of toilets and drinking water in the fields, and daily exposure to pesticides. The U.S. Environmental Protection Agency estimates that as many as 300,000 farm workers are poisoned each year by pesticides. They suffer the highest rate of chemically-related illness of any occupational group. Farm workers' ability to protect themselves from pesticide poisoning is minimized by their lack of access to the necessary information, and the fear of retaliation for filing complaints when violations occur. The agricultural industry continually attempts to dilute the law and render it useless.

Children of farm workers are often forced by their parents' poverty into the fields at ages as young as 10. Educational systems have almost universally failed to provide for their needs, resulting in extremely high dropout rates of farm worker children and perpetuating the poverty of farm worker families. Immigration and welfare reform laws attempted to exclude many farm worker children from access to education.

In a 1994 report entitled "Farmworker Women Speak Out," the Farmworker Justice Fund found that:

1. farm worker women do nearly every kind of farm labor on every kind of farm;

2. they routinely receive less pay than men for the same work;

3. employers frequently attribute and give women's earnings to the male head of the household as a way of meeting federal or state minimum wage requirements;

4. they are subjected to sexual harassment, assault, and rape by crew leaders and male farm workers (Crew leaders are paid by growers to recruit, transport, house, and supervise farm workers); and

5. crew leaders often demand sexual favors in return for giving them places on work crews—and on the buses that take them to the fields.

We Christians are called to be in solidarity with the least of these our brothers and sisters (Matthew 25). In response to the plight of farm workers and their families, The United Methodist Church:

- publicly denounces any and all mistreatment of farm workers and strongly demands that the employers treat farm workers and their families with dignity and respect;
- commits itself to work in cooperation with the National Farm Worker Ministry and community-based farm worker organizations, whose primary mission is promoting the self-organization and self-determination of farm workers;
- calls on the General Board of Church and Society, the General Board of Global Ministries, and annual conferences to support state and federal legislation that would strengthen the laws protecting farm workers' rights and provide the funding necessary for adequate enforcement of the laws;

- urges the United Methodist Committee on Relief to especially consider the needs of farm workers when administering relief efforts;
- urges annual conferences, especially where farm workers live and work, to monitor situations where farm workers have won union elections but have not been able to negotiate effective collective agreements and to use their personal and institutional resources to encourage bargaining in good faith; and
- urges local churches to consider a farm worker Sabbath as a day of study, prayer, and action, including legislative advocacy, and to develop ministries of mercy and justice to and with farm workers in cooperation with community organizations, government agencies, and labor unions.

ADOPTED 2000

See Social Principles, ¶ 163H.

237. Rights of Workers

I. Biblical/Theological Background

Scripture teaches that human beings, created in the image of God, have an innate dignity (Genesis 1:27). God grants dignity to work by commanding human beings to be stewards of the land and to till and keep the earth (Genesis 1:28, 2:15). Work is one way through which human beings exercise their God-given creativity. Scripture also teaches that an economic system should be ordered so that employees receive justice at their place of work. It mandates that society and its institutions are to be structured so that marginalized persons participate fully in the shaping of society and their own future. This requires respect for the right to organize and bargain collectively without fear of reprisal, to receive a living wage, to be free from discrimination or any form of forced or bonded labor, and the right to a safe and healthy workplace.

The concern of The United Methodist Church for the dignity of workers and the rights of employees to act collectively is stated in the Social Principles. Both employer and union are called to "bargain in good faith within the frame work of the public interest" (¶ 163B). The increasing globalization of the economic system requires the church to reaffirm again our position.

II. Characteristics of the International Economy and Working Conditions

National economies are being integrated into one global system. This system extends the means of production, financial investments, and employment opportunities around the world to poor and rich countries alike. The ability of workers, governments or other social forces to counter the power of corporations is weakened by the ability of capital to move rapidly from one place to another.

Because of capitalist globalization, multinational companies compete with each other on a worldwide scale. This has encouraged third world countries like the Philippines and those in southeast Asia to offer skilled yet cheap labor by practicing contractualization and subcontractualization. Under this scheme, workers are hired and are asked to sign a contract for three or five months. After the contract has expired, the worker is either asked to leave or sign another contract. Contractual employees, also known as casuals, are not covered by the collective bargaining agreement of the local union because he/she is not a member. Only regular employees become members of the union, and in the Philippines, one has to be an employee for at least 6 months in a company in order to be accepted as a regular worker. Casuals [temporary workers] do not receive bonuses, other cash benefits, social security, minimum wage, and security of employment, among other things.

Subcontracting is similar to contractualization. Manufacturing companies work with subcontractors who, in turn, hire contractualized employees. The main company provides the subcontractor with raw materials, and the subcontractor's temporary workers do their job usually in sweatshop conditions without the legal benefits of regular workers. Besides that, they are paid very low wages. It is sad that some United Methodist business people are involved in these unfair labor practices. These practices are allowed by the government and must be stopped. The adoption of this amendment in the resolution for "Rights of Workers" will help United Methodists in the Philippines to lobby against this scheme with the moral backing of our church.

These practices threaten to perpetuate injustice on a global scale:

1. Workers are not paid for how much value they put into the products they produce. They are paid according to the wage scales where they live. This is often not a livable wage.

2. Working conditions, hours, and safety are not regulated by local public authorities, but increasingly by corporations. These corporations can threaten to move if authorities push to change working conditions.

3. Child labor is widely used in many parts of the world. Minorities, migrants, and women still suffer from discrimination in employment.

4. Corporations still reject workers' rights of free association, collective bargaining, collective actions. They discriminate against workers who try to organize for these rights. They use the threat of transferring production to defeat organizing efforts and to bargain away rights.

5. Millions of workers are mired in poverty as the global economy becomes more stratified.

6. Big and small industries in developing countries, in an effort to attract investors with cheap labor, practice contractualization and subcontractualization which are schemes to deny workers social security benefits, minimum wage, security of tenure, and membership in a union.

III. Witness of The United Methodist Church

Since The United Methodist Church is a participant in the global economy, we should witness for justice in the international labor arena. The following actions are proposed:

1. The General Board of Church and Society and the General Board of Global Ministries will use a Concern for Workers Task Force in conjunction with annual conference and local church leaders to sponsor religion and labor programs that: (1) study the theological significance of work and employment, (2) initiate cooperation with workers, labor unions, employers, and other organizations about how best to protect and enhance the rights of all workers, especially those of women, children, migrants and people of color and (3) promote Labor Sunday.

2. The church and its agencies, annual conferences, and local congregations will actively support the universally accepted human right of workers to join or support a union or other worker association; call on employers to exercise neutrality toward organizing efforts, recog-

nize the union chosen by the workforce as their bargaining representative and to negotiate a fair agreement with them; and work within the community to prevent employers from taking adverse action against employees who support unions, other worker associations, and other groups trying to bring justice to the workplace.

3. All church agencies, related institutions and organizations, annual conferences, and local congregations should respect their employees' rights to good working conditions, fair compensation, and collective action. This includes the right to form a union or other association and participate in its activities without fear of reprisal. Church employers should affirm the Social Principles and support the right of their employees to engage in collective bargaining.

4. The church and its agencies should encourage unions to: (1) accept union responsibility to look beyond their own organizational benefit and be more active in organizing women, temporary employees, people of color, and others disadvantaged in the labor market; (2) promote full participation of rank-and-file members in union decision making; and (3) defend the rights of organized and unorganized workers and develop global solidarity across nations and industries.

5. The church and its agencies should support the conventions of the International Labor Organizations that advance safety in the workplace; freedom from bonded or forced labor; the elimination of discrimination in respect to employment and occupation; effective abolition of child labor; fair compensation; just supervision; and the right of collective action for employees in all nations. The church and its agencies should call for the ratification and enforcement of these conventions.

6. The church and its agencies should join efforts to reform national labor laws that inadequately protect or enable workers to form unions and negotiate terms of employment. These reforms should, at a minimum: (1) enable workers to form unions when a majority have indicated their desires for representation; (2) correct slow administrative or judicial procedures that unduly delay representation decisions; and 3) eliminate exclusions of any class of workers from coverage.

7. The church and its agencies to address the global crisis of unemployment will support development efforts that enhance job creation, effective vocational training, and transitional security measures during periods of economic turmoil.

8. The General Board of Church and Society and the General Board of Global Ministries should urge the United States government to pro-

tect the rights of migrant workers through the ratification of the International Convention on the Rights of Migrant Workers and their Families.

ADOPTED 1988
AMENDED AND ADOPTED 2000

See Social Principles, ¶ 163*B* and C.

238. The Right to Organize and Bargain Collectively

The United Methodist Church through its Social Principles recognizes and supports the right of workers to organize into unions of their own choosing and to bargain collectively regarding hours, wages and conditions of employment. The theological basis for this has been presented in the resolution on the *"Rights of Workers."*

The national policy of the United States since 1935 has codified procedures through the National Labor Relations Act for the selection of labor unions by workers, for the recognition of these unions by management, and for collective bargaining. However, at the start of the new millennium, workers are finding it harder and harder to form labor unions to achieve economic and social justice in the workplace. Many employers interfere with employees' efforts to exercise their right to unionize by threatening to close their facilities, to fire union activists, or otherwise retaliate against them.

Therefore, The United Methodist Church:

1. uges all employers to allow their employees to freely choose whether to unionize or not, without intimidation or coercion;

2. urges all employers to clearly communicate to their employees that they are neutral on their employees' choice, and will deal fairly with any union they select;

3. calls all employers to abide by their employees' decision when a majority has signed union authorization cards or otherwise indicated their desire to be represented by a union, and to refrain from using National Labor Relations Board hearings, elections, and appeals as a means for delaying or avoiding representation for their employees;

4. supports efforts in the U.S. Congress to amend the National Labor Relations Act to (a) expedite workers' efforts to organize and bargain collectively and (b) cover workers, such as farm workers, who are presently excluded; and

5. urges annual conferences, local congregations, and clergy to actively affirm the right of workers to organize for collective bargaining by involving themselves in efforts to support workers who desire to exercise this right. United Methodist institutions and organizations have a Christian responsibility to exemplify the teachings found in the Social Principles and to support the right of their employees to organize for collective bargaining. The United Methodist Church through its boards and agencies, conferences, and local congregations will publicize this resolution among members of the church.

ADOPTED 2000

See Social Principles, ¶ 163B and C.

THE POLITICAL COMMUNITY

BASIC FREEDOMS

239. Religious Liberty

The United Methodist Church, as a worldwide denomination, declares religious liberty, the freedom of belief, to be a basic human right that has its roots in the Bible. Paul admonished Christians with these words: "Who are you to pass judgment on servants of another?" (Romans 14:4 NRSV). This understanding is fundamental to our religious heritage, which requires that we honor God, not by placing our demands on all persons, but by making true account of our own selves.

The preamble to the Universal Declaration of Human Rights states that "the advent of a world in which human beings shall enjoy freedom of speech and belief has been proclaimed as the highest aspiration of the common people."

Minimal standards of the right of belief are amplified by the international community in the Declaration on the Elimination of All Forms of Intolerance and of Discrimination Based on Religion or Belief, adopted by the General Assembly of the United Nations on November 25, 1981. It declares that the right to freedom of thought, conscience, religion, or belief is basic to the following freedoms:

1. to assemble and to worship;

2. to establish and maintain places for those purposes;

3. to establish and maintain charitable, humanitarian, and social outreach institutions;

4. to produce and possess articles necessary to the rites and customs of a religion or belief;

5. to write, to issue, and to disseminate relevant publications;

6. to teach religious beliefs;

7. to solicit and receive voluntary financial and other contributions from individuals and institutions;

8. to train, to appoint, to elect, or to designate by succession necessary leaders;

9. to observe days of rest and to celebrate holidays and ceremonies in accordance with the precepts of one's religion or belief; and

10. to establish and maintain communications with individuals and religious communities in matters of religion and belief at the national and international levels.

The declaration further establishes the rights of parents to provide religious training for their children.

Our test of religious liberty is not limited by these standards. We also believe that religious liberty includes the freedom to doubt or to deny the existence of God, and to refrain from observing religious practices. Further, we believe that persons of faith have the right to propagate their faith through evangelistic outreach. Persons must be allowed to live within the constraints and the demands of their convictions. We believe it is the right of a person to be allowed to follow the call of conscience when it becomes impossible to live by both the dictates of the state and the decisions of faith.

Threats to Religious Liberty

Religious liberty involves much more than the right to worship within the walls of a house of worship. Religious individuals, institutions, and their members have the right—indeed, the obligation—to be engaged in faith-based witness on issues of state and society. Broad latitude must be allowed in defining this religious function.

Theocracies or other governments and societies that give special privileges to adherents of one religion or ideology have a particular responsibility to ensure and guarantee not only the religious rights and spirituality of indigenous groups, but also the political, economic, social, and cultural rights of those who are not members of the favored group.

A grave threat to religious liberty exists in nation states where all forms of voluntary association—even for purposes of private religious worship—are limited or prohibited. In such situations, special accommodation that uses the United Nations Declaration as a minimum standard must be made for the observance of religious functions.

Religious liberty is menaced in other ways. Governments or political movements have used religious institutions or organizations for their own purposes by compromising their personnel through offering power, or by manipulation, infiltration, or control. Governments also subvert religious organizations by means of surveillance of their legitimate activities through use of informers, covert searches of religious property, and politically motivated threats to the safety of religious leaders or the financial operation of religious institutions. We pledge our continual efforts to protect against these activities.

We recognize that situations exist where religious observances seem to threaten the health or safety of a society. However, the importance of religious liberty dictates that restrictions of religious observances that are alleged to be contrary to government policy on the presumption that health or safety is threatened must be carefully examined. Governments must present a compelling interests test (i.e., public health and safety could be affected by a particular religious observance) to any government action that places a substantial burden on sincere religious practices. That is, government should have to prove a compelling reason for burdening a religious practice as well as proving that it is pursuing its compelling reason in a way that places the most minimal burden on religion.

Denominational Action to Expand Religious Liberty

The United Methodist Church places a high priority on the struggle to maintain freedom of religious belief and practice in the world. Religiously observant persons in some societies are denied the rights on which there have been international agreements. Our members have an obligation to speak out on behalf of those for whom such freedoms are abridged.

In carrying out their responsibilities, United Methodist agencies and institutions, shall:

1. affirm and support these concerns for religious liberty in the ecumenical groups in which we participate;

2. pursue application of these minimal standards of the human rights of religious liberty in all societies and work toward conditions where governmental units neither inhibit nor encourage religion;

3. advocate, through education and political action, to gain religious liberty in all places where it is lacking;

4. extend the compassionate ministry of the church to persons who suffer because either religious or governmental authorities seek to deny these rights to them, assuming a special responsibility to work on behalf of "unregistered," in addition to governmentally sanctioned, religious institutions;

5. educate ourselves so that we will be able to identify and respond to violations of religious liberty both in our own and in other societies; and

6. offer support to the mandate of the United Nations Special Rapporteur on Religious Intolerance.

ADOPTED 1988
AMENDED AND READOPTED 2000

See Social Principles, ¶ 164B.

240. Taking Liberties: On the Stifling of Dissent

The Social Principles affirm, "We hold governments responsible for the protection of the rights of the people" (¶ 164A). Yet governments often use wartime and/or perceived threats to national security to justify restrictions on civil rights, immigrant rights, and the right to express political dissent.

In ancient Egypt, Pharaoh appealed to a mixture of patriotic loyalty and national security fears to justify the repression of immigrants: "Come let us deal shrewdly with them, or they will . . . in the event of war, join our enemies and fight against us and escape from the land" (Exodus 1:10).

The prophet Jeremiah, like many of the other biblical prophets, voiced his dissent to the unjust practices of his government during war. The powers-that-be repeatedly condemned Jeremiah, charging him with "desertion" (Jer. 37:13-15). The prophets invariably faced beatings, imprisonment, and death threats for their political dissent in times of national crisis (*See* 1 Kings 22:13-27, Jeremiah 20:10; 26:11; 37:13-18; 38:4; Psalm 120).

The early church often faced beatings, imprisonment, and death for their religious and political dissent. The early church, as a religious minority, was frequently accused of being a political opposition group that must be suppressed: *see* Acts 6:11 on charges brought against

Stephen. In Acts 17, early Christians are accused: "They are all acting contrary to the decrees of the emperor"(17:7).

Yet in the midst of repression, Paul affirms the importance of due process respect for civil liberties. He insists that government officials acknowledge their own human rights violations:" 'They have beaten us in public, uncondemned, men who are Roman citizens . . . and now are they going to discharge us in secret? Certainly not! Let them come and take us out themselves.' So they came and apologized to them" (Acts 16:37, 39).

The recent U.S.-led "war on terrorism," the USA PATRIOT Act ("Uniting and Strengthening America by Providing Appropriate Tools Required to Intercept and Obstruct Terrorism") legislation, the creation of military tribunals which lack due process or independent means of appeal, as well as draft legislation known as PATRIOT Act II, or the Domestic Security Enhancement Act, have created a political climate in which an increasing number of governments have adopted executive orders and legislation restricting the rights of immigrants and opposition groups. Such measures include:

- use of 'unlawful combatants' to designate political opposition
- detention without charges or a trial
- use of secret evidence and secret hearings
- expanded wiretap and government surveillance
- denial of access to legal counsel
- deportation of asylum seekers, refugees and others who face persecution in their home country
- use of racial and religious profiling
- threatening to strip someone's citizenship
- denying rights of peaceable assembly and freedom of speech based on political beliefs
- use of military tribunals that lack due process and independent judicial review
- the combination of restrictive government measures with appeals to unquestioning patriotic loyalty often foster a climate of mounting intolerance and repression against foreigners and any who voice peaceful political dissent.

The international human rights organization, Human Rights Watch, has compiled a report entitled, "Opportunism in the Face of Tragedy: Repression in the name of anti-terrorism." (www.hrw.org) The report analyzes various repressive laws and measures adopted by 17 nations in the name of fighting terrorism. In reality, most of these measures seek to stifle internal political and religious dissent, as well as restrict the rights of refugees, asylum seekers, and foreigners. Those who are targeted are often the most vulnerable and violated in a society.

Legitimate security concerns of any nation are best met by upholding and protecting the full human rights of all, including the rights of political opposition, immigrants, and minority groups. The church has a long history of advocating and protecting the rights of religious and political dissent.

Even in a context of heightened fears and violence, The Social Principles clearly declare, "We also strongly reject domestic surveillance and intimidation of political opponents by governments in power. . . . The use of detention and imprisonment for the harassment and elimination of political opponents or other dissidents violates fundamental human rights" (¶ 164A).

We affirm the prophetic tradition of dissent and call on all United Methodists to publicly speak out for the protection of all human rights for all—including the right to dissent through peaceable assembly, freedom of the press, freedom of speech and other nonviolent means.

We call for the following actions:

- Local congregations undertake educational efforts (studying the Social Principles ¶ 164, the Universal Declaration of Human Rights, and the U.S. Bill of Rights) to promote greater understanding of international human rights and civil liberties, especially the rights of immigrants, political opposition groups and religious minorities, and that these educational programs build toward the 60th anniversary of the Universal Declaration of Human Rights on December 10, 2008;
- General Board of Global Ministries and General Board of Church and Society, working with national and international civil liberties and human rights organizations, such as the Center for Constitutional Rights, Amnesty International, Human Rights Watch, and American Civil Liberties Union, develop resources and advocacy materials for use in local congregations, to: 1) monitor potentially restrictive government measures that effect people's civil liberties; 2) challenge repressive legislation and executive orders already in place (such as ones listed above); and 3) protect the rights of peaceful dissent;
- call on the U.S. government and all other national governments to submit timely reports on their compliance with the

International Covenant on Civil and Political Rights and the UN Convention Against Torture, and that governments especially document steps taken to insure full civil liberties to religious and political minority groups, immigrants, and the right to peaceful dissent; and

• local congregations, working with others in their communities, organize to defend civil liberties by encouraging local authorities to adopt Civil Liberties Safe Zone resolutions, and by forming local Bill of Rights (or Human Rights) defense committees to create a climate of tolerance and respect for different views.

ADOPTED 2004

See Social Principles, ¶ 164*A* and *F.*

CHURCH AND STATE

241. Church Is a Weapon-Free Zone

WHEREAS, in keeping with the spirit of Isaiah 2:4: God shall judge between the nations, and shall arbitrate for many peoples; they shall beat their swords into plowshares, and their spears into pruning hooks; nation shall not lift up sword against nation, neither shall they learn war any more;

WHEREAS, reflecting the church's traditional role as a place of safety and sanctuary,

Therefore, every United Methodist church is officially declared a weapon-free zone.

ADOPTED 2000

See Social Principles, ¶ 164.

242. Church-Government Relations

In response to a question about paying taxes, Jesus said: "Then give to Caesar what is Caesar's and to God the things that are God's" (Luke 20:25). Although this statement refers specifically to taxation, its apparent implications are that there are separate obligations and responsibilities to government and to religion.

The Social Principles of The United Methodist Church assert: "We believe that the state should not attempt to control the church, nor should the church seek to dominate the state. `Separation of church and state' means no organic union of the two, but it does permit interaction. The church should continually exert a strong ethical influence upon the state, supporting policies and programs deemed to be just and opposing policies and programs that are unjust" (¶ 164B).

As we consider the religious protections of the First Amendment—the free exercise and non-establishment of religion—we are profoundly grateful for the major statement made by the 1968 General Conference on "Church/Government Relations." In recognizing that debt, we reaffirm the substance of that declaration.

A Statement Concerning Church-Government Relations and Education

The fundamental purpose of universal public education at the elementary and secondary levels is to provide equal and adequate educational opportunities for all children and young people, and thereby ensure the nation an enlightened citizenry.

We believe in the principle of universal public education, and we reaffirm our support of public educational institutions. At the same time, we recognize and pledge our continued allegiance to the U.S. constitutional principle that citizens have a right to establish and maintain private schools from private resources so long as such schools meet public standards of quality. Such schools have made a genuine contribution to society. We do not support the expansion or the strengthening of private schools with public funds. Furthermore, we oppose the establishment or strengthening of private schools that jeopardize the public school system or thwart valid public policy.

We specifically oppose tuition tax credits, school vouchers, or any other mechanism that directly or indirectly allows government funds to support religious schools at the primary and secondary level. Persons of one particular faith should be free to use their own funds to strengthen the belief system of their particular religious group. They should not, however, expect all taxpayers, including those who adhere to other religious belief systems, to provide funds to teach religious views with which they do not agree.

To fulfill the government's responsibility in education, sometimes government and nonpublic educational institutions need to enter a cooperative relationship. But public funds should be used only in the best interests of the whole society. Extreme caution must be exercised to ensure that religious institutions do not receive any aid directly or indirectly for the maintenance of their religious expression or the expansion of their institutional resources. Such funds must be used for the express purpose of fulfilling a strictly public responsibility, and should be subject to public accountability.

By providing a setting for contact at an early age between children of vastly different backgrounds, public schools have often been an important unifying force in modern pluralistic society. We recognize in particular that persons of all religious backgrounds may have insight into the nature of ultimate reality, which will help to enrich the common life. It is therefore essential that the public schools take seriously the religious integrity of each child entrusted to their care. Public schools may not properly establish any preferred form of religion for common exercises of worship, religious observance, or study. At the same time, however, education should provide an opportunity for the examination of the various religious traditions of humankind.

We believe that every person has a right to an education, including higher education, commensurate with his or her ability. It is society's responsibility to enable every person to enjoy this right. Public and private institutions should cooperate to provide for these educational opportunities.

Freedom of inquiry poses a risk for established ideas, beliefs, programs, and institutions. We accept that risk in the faith that all truth is of God. Colleges and universities can best perform their vital tasks of adding to knowledge and to the perception of truth in an atmosphere of genuine academic freedom.

We affirm the principle that freedom to inquire, to discuss, and to teach should be regulated by the self-discipline of scholarship and the critical examination of ideas in the context of free public dialogue, rather than by censorship by supervisors, school boards, or any control imposed by churches, governments, or other organizations. In the educational process, individuals have the right to appropriate freely for themselves what they believe is real, important, useful, and satisfying.

Experience has demonstrated that freedom to inquire, to discuss, and to teach is best preserved when colleges and universities are not dependent upon a single base or a few sources of support. When an educational institution relies upon multiple sources of financial support, and where those sources tend to balance one another, the institution is in a position to resist undue pressures toward control exerted from any one source of support. In the case of church-related colleges and universities, we believe that tuitions; scholarships; investment return; bequests; payments for services rendered; loans; government grants; and gifts from individuals, business corporations, foundations, and churches should be sought and accepted in as great a variety as possible. Care must be exercised to ensure that all support from any of these sources is free from conditions that hinder the college or university in the maintenance of freedom of inquiry and expression for its faculty and students.

We are very much aware of the dangers of church-sponsored colleges and universities being overly dependent upon government funding. However, we are also aware that given the independent thought of most college students today, there is little danger of using government funds to indoctrinate students with religious beliefs. Therefore, institutions of higher learning should feel free to receive government funds (except for religious teaching and structures for worship). At the same time, they should be eternally cognizant of the dangers of accompanying government oversight that might threaten the religious atmosphere or special independent character of church-sponsored educational institutions.

No church-sponsored higher education institution should become so dependent upon government grants, research projects, or support programs, that its academic freedom is jeopardized, its responsibility for social criticism (including criticism of governments) inhibited, or its spiritual values denied.

We recognize that the freedom necessary to the existence of a college or university in the classical sense may be threatened by forces other than those involved in the nature and source of the institution's financial support. Institutional freedom may be adversely affected by governmental requirements of loyalty oaths from teachers and students, by public interference with the free flow of information, or by accreditation and certification procedures and requirements aimed at dictating the content of college and university curricula.

With respect to church-related institutions of higher education, we deplore any ecclesiastical attempts to manipulate inquiry or the dissemination of knowledge, to use the academic community for the promotion of any particular point of view, to require ecclesiastical loyalty oaths designed to protect cherished truth claims, or to inhibit the social action activities of members of the academic community. We call upon all members of The United Methodist Church, in whatever capacity they may serve, to be especially sensitive to the need to protect individual and institutional freedom and responsibility in the context of the academic community.

We are persuaded that there may be circumstances or conditions in which the traditional forms of tax immunities granted to colleges and universities may be a necessary requirement for their freedom. Therefore, we urge a continuation of the public policy of granting reasonable and nondiscriminatory tax immunities to all private colleges and universities, including those that are related to churches.

We believe that colleges and universities should consider the benefits, services, and protections that they receive from the community and its governmental agencies and should examine their obligations to the community in the light of this support. We believe it is imperative that all church-related institutions of higher education determine on their own initiative what benefits, services, and opportunities they ought to provide for the community as a whole, as distinct from their usual campus constituencies.

A Statement Concerning Church-Government Relations and Governmental Chaplaincies

We recognize that military and public institutional chaplaincies represent efforts to provide for the religious needs of people for whom both churches and governments are responsible. We recognize that in such a broad and complex undertaking there are bound to exist real and serious tensions that produce genuine uneasiness on the part of government officials as well as church leaders. Great patience and skill are required to effect necessary accommodations with understanding and without compromising religious liberty.

We believe that there are both ethical and constitutional standards that must be observed by governments in the establishment and operation of public chaplaincies. At a minimum, those standards are as follows:

First, the only obligation that governments have is to ensure the provision of opportunities for military personnel, patients of hospitals, and inmates of correctional institutions to engage in religious worship or have access to religious nurture.

Second, participation in religious activities must be on a purely voluntary basis; there must be neither penalties for nonparticipation nor any rewards for participation.

Third, no preferential treatment should be given any particular church, denomination, or religious group in the establishment and administration of governmental chaplaincies.

Fourth, considerable care should be exercised in the role assignments of chaplains so they are not identified as the enforcers of morals. Precaution should also be taken to avoid chaplains' being given duties not clearly related to their primary tasks.

Standards should be maintained to protect the integrity of both churches and governments. The practice of staffing governmental chaplaincies with clergy personnel who have ecclesiastical endorsement should be continued. The practice of terminating the services of such personnel in any instance where it becomes necessary for ecclesiastical endorsement to be withdrawn should also be continued. Supervision of clergy personnel in the performance of their religious services in governmental chaplaincies should be clearly effected through ecclesiastical channels with the cooperation of the public agencies and institutions involved. In the performance of these administrative functions, churches and agencies of government have an obligation to be fair and responsible and to ensure that due process is observed in all proceedings.

The role of a governmental chaplain should be primarily pastoral but with important priestly, prophetic, and teaching roles. The chaplain has an obligation to perform these ministries in as broad an ecumenical context as possible. A chaplain is responsible for the spiritual welfare and religious life of all the personnel of the military unit or the public institution to which he or she is assigned.

There are many persons, and some groups, whose personal religious practices or whose church's rules make it impossible for them to accept the direct ministry of a particular chaplain. In such instances, the chaplain, to the full extent of his or her powers, has an obligation to make provision for worship by these persons or groups. A chaplain is expected to answer specific questions by members of faith groups other than his or her own. Chaplains must know the basic tenets of their denominations in order to protect such members in the expression and development of their faith. The absence of parochialism on the part of a chaplain is more than an attitude; it necessitates specific, detailed, and accurate knowledge regarding many religions.

The churches should strive to make public chaplaincies integral expressions of their ministry and to face the implications of this for supervision and budget. The chaplain represents the church by affirming the dignity of all persons in military service through the chaplain's function in upholding their freedom of religion and conscience. Every person exists within a broader set of values than those of the military, and within a broader spectrum of responsibilities than those created by military orders. The chaplain is a bearer of the gospel to affirm the freedom of the individual and represents The United Methodist Church at that point of tension. Whether the freedom of the gospel is compromised or limited may be a result of either external pressures or internal submission, or both. Failure to sustain the freedom of the gospel lies within any human system or any individual. It is the task of the church to confront prophetically institutions or chaplains who compromise the gospel. The United Methodist Church provides presence, oversight, and support to chaplains who risk ministry in such a setting.

There are degrees of tension in present arrangements whereby a chaplain is a commissioned officer of the armed forces or an employee of a public institution. As such, he or she is a member of the staff of the military commander or of the director of the public institution involved. Government regulations and manuals describe him or her as the adviser on religion, morals, morale, and welfare. Therefore, we believe it is the chaplain's duty in faithfulness to his or her religious commitments to act in accordance with his or her conscience and to make such viewpoints known in organizational matters affecting the total welfare of the people for whom the chaplain has any responsibility. The chaplain has the obligation and should have the opportunity to express his or her dissent within the structures in which the chaplain works, in instances where he or she feels this is necessary. With respect to such matters, it is the obligation of religious bodies to give the chaplain full support.

Churches must encourage chaplains who serve in the armed forces to resist the exaltation of power and its exercise for its own sake. They must also encourage chaplains who serve in public institutions to maintain sensitivity to human anguish. Churches and chaplains have an obligation to speak out conscientiously against the unforgiving and intransigent spirit in people and nations wherever and whenever it appears.

A Statement Concerning Church-Government Relations and Tax Exemption

We believe that governments recognize the unique category of religious institutions. To be in this unique category is not a privilege held by these institutions for their own benefit or self-glorification but is an acknowledgment of their special identity designed to protect their independence and to enable them to serve humankind in a way not expected of other types of institutions.

We urge churches to consider at least the following factors in determining their response to the granting of immunity from property taxes:

1. responsibility to make appropriate contributions for essential services provided by government; and

2. the danger that churches become so dependent upon government that they compromise their integrity or fail to exert their critical influence upon public policy.

We support the abolition of all special privileges accorded to members of the clergy in U.S. tax laws and regulations and call upon the churches to deal with the consequent financial implications for their ministers. Conversely, we believe that all forms of discrimination against members of the clergy in U.S. tax legislation and administrative regulations should be discontinued. We believe that the status of an individual under ecclesiastical law or practice ought not to be the basis of governmental action either granting or withholding a special tax benefit.

A Statement Concerning Church Participation in Providing Social Services

We believe that all the organizations and resources of the private sector, as well as those of governments, should be taken into account in the formulation and execution of social welfare policies.

We recognize that appropriate government bodies have the right to prescribe minimum standards for all public and private social welfare agencies. We believe that no private agency, because of its religious affiliations, ought to be exempted from any of the requirements of such standards.

Governmental provision of material support for church-related agencies inevitably raises important questions of religious establishment. In recognition, however, that some health, education, and welfare agencies have been founded by churches without regard to religious proselytizing, we consider that such agencies may, under certain circumstances, be proper channels for public programs in these fields. When government provides support for programs administered by private agencies, it has the most serious obligation to establish and enforce standards guaranteeing the equitable administration of such programs and the accountability of such agencies to the public authority. In particular, we believe that government resources should not be provided to any church-related agency unless it meets the following minimum criteria:

1. The services to be provided by the church-related agency shall meet a genuine community need.

2. The services of the agency shall be designed and administered in such a way as to avoid serving a sectarian purpose or interest.

3. The services to be provided by the agency shall be available to all persons without regard to race, color, national origin, creed, or political persuasion.

4. The services to be rendered by the agency shall be performed in accordance with accepted professional and administrative standards.

5. Skill, competence, and integrity in the performance of duties shall be the principal considerations in the employment of personnel and shall not be superseded by any requirement of religious affiliation.

6. The right to collective bargaining shall be recognized by the agency.

We recognize that all of the values involved in the sponsorship of a social welfare agency by a church may not be fully expressed if that agency has to rely permanently on access to government resources for its existence. We are also aware that under certain circumstances, sponsorship of a social welfare agency by a church may inhibit the development of comprehensive welfare services in the community. Therefore, the church and the agency should choose which pattern of service to offer: (1) channeling standardized and conventional services supplied or supported by government, or (2) attempting experimental or unconventional ministries and criticizing government programs when they prove inadequate. We believe that these two patterns are difficult, if not impossible, to combine in the same agency, and that the choice between them should be made before dependence upon government resources makes commitment to the first pattern irreversible. In their efforts to meet human needs, churches should never allow their preoccupation with remedial programs under their own direction to divert them or the larger community from a common search for basic solutions. In dealing with the elimination of the conditions of poverty and hunger, churches should have no stake in programs that contribute to promote dependency or embody attitudes and practices that fail to promote self-sufficiency.

We believe that churches have a moral obligation to challenge violations of the civil rights of the poor and marginalized. They should direct their efforts toward helping the poor overcome the powerlessness that makes such violations of civil rights possible. Specifically, churches should protest such policies and practices by welfare personnel as unwarranted invasions of privacy and oppose any requirement of attendance at church activities in order to qualify for social services.

A Statement Concerning Church Participation in Public Affairs

We recognize that churches exist within the body politic, along with numerous other forms of human association. Like other social groups, their existence affects, and is affected by, governments. We believe that churches have the right and the duty to speak and act corporately on those matters of public policy that involve basic moral or ethical issues and questions. Any concept of, or action regarding, church-government relations that denies churches this role in the body politic strikes at the very core of religious liberty.

The attempt to influence the formation and execution of public policy at all levels of government is often the most effective means available to churches to keep before humanity the ideal of a society in which power and order are made to serve the ends of justice and freedom for all people. Through such social action churches generate new ideas, challenge certain goals and methods, and help rearrange the emphasis on particular values in ways that facilitate the adoption and implementation of specific policies and programs that promote the goals of a responsible society.

We believe that any action that would deny the church the right to act corporately on public policy matters threatens religious liberty. We therefore oppose inclusion of churches in any lobby disclosure legislation.

This does not mean, in any way, that we wish to hide actions taken by the church on public issues. On the contrary, we are usually proud of such actions. It does recognize, however, that the church is already responding to members who request information with respect to church action on public policy questions. In effect, in accordance with legislation enacted by the 1976 General Conference, The United Methodist Church already has its own lobby disclosure provisions in place.

It is quite another matter, however, for the government to insist that it must know everything about what a church is saying in its private communications with its own members.

When the U.S. Supreme Court acted in the 1971 landmark case of *Lemon v. Kartzman* (403 U.S. 602, 612-13), the Court applied a test to determine the constitutionality of legislation on First Amendment grounds as it deals with religion. Among its three criteria were these two: (1) its principal or primary effect must neither advance nor inhibit religion; (2) the statute must not foster an excessive government entanglement with religion.

Lobby disclosure legislation before the U.S. Congress over the last several years has required: (1) extremely burdensome record keeping and reporting of all legislative activity; (2) reporting of contributions of churches giving $3,000 or more annually to a national body if a part of this is used for legislative action; (3) criminal penalties with up to two years in jail for violations; and (4) unwarranted subpoena powers to investigate church records.

Legislation that passed the House in 1978 would have required detailed records of expenditures of twenty-two items. As such, it would have been burdensome and would inhibit religion in that The United Methodist Church would have been severely handicapped in implementing its Social Principles due to being neutralized by minutia.

Furthermore, if the government insists on knowing everything the church is doing on public policy questions over a five-year period (as was required) and imposes a criminal sentence for violations, this could inhibit religion to the extent that the church might be tempted to limit severely its activity to avoid noncompliance.

If the government is going to require that religious groups keep burdensome records and make voluminous reports, and there is some question as to whether the churches are complying, federal authorities would be authorized to step in and check church records and files.

Such action would undoubtedly represent an unconstitutional excessive government entanglement with religion.

The United Methodist Church would have great difficulty in complying with the provision that all organizational contributions of $3,000 annually be reported if some of these funds are used for lobbying. Since local churches contribute generously to the World Service Fund, and a small portion of those funds is used for legislative action, this brings our church under coverage of this provision. Such a requirement could mean that reports of contributions of some 30,000 United Methodist churches would have to be made to the government shortly after the close of each year. This could not be done, and we would be in violation, having knowingly omitted material facts required to be disclosed. As a result, church officials would be subject to criminal penalties of up to two years in prison.

For these reasons, we oppose lobby disclosure measures for the churches. In its most stringent form, legislation such as this would inhibit our free exercise of religion. It would be impossible for the church to comply with certain provisions, thus subjecting our church leaders to criminal penalties.

We believe that churches must behave responsibly in the arena of public affairs. Responsible behavior requires adherence to ethically sound substantive and procedural norms.

We live in a pluralistic society. In such a society, churches should not seek to use the authority of government to make the whole community conform to their particular moral codes. Rather, churches should seek to enlarge and clarify the ethical grounds of public discourse and to identify and define the foreseeable consequences of available choices of public policy.

In participating in the arena of public affairs, churches are not inherently superior to other participants; hence the stands that they take on particular issues of public policy are not above question or criticism.

Responsible behavior in the arena of public affairs requires churches to accept the fact that in dealing with complex issues of public policy, good intentions and high ideals need to be combined with as much practical and technical knowledge of politics and economics as possible.

Another norm of responsible behavior derives from the fact that no particular public policy that may be endorsed by churches at a given point in time should be regarded as an ultimate expression of Christian ethics in society. Churches should not assume that any particular social pattern, political order, or economic ideology represents a complete embodiment of the Christian ethic.

When churches speak to government, they also bear the responsibility to speak to their own memberships. Cultivation of ethically informed public opinion is particularly crucial in local congregations. It is essential to responsible behavior that procedures be established and maintained to ensure full, frank, and informed discussion by religious groups within the arena of public affairs. In the present period of human history, attention should be given to the dignity of every person, and appeal should be made to the consciences of all persons. Churches must acknowledge and respect the role of the laity as well as the clergy in determining their behavior in the arena of public affairs.

Because of their commitment to unity, and in the interest of an effective strategy, churches should, to the maximum extent feasible, coordinate their own efforts and, where appropriate, cooperate with other organizations when they seek to influence properly the formation and execution of public policy at all levels of government.

Finally, churches should not seek to utilize the processes of public affairs to further their own institutional interests or to obtain special privileges for themselves.

United Methodism is a part of the universal church. In the formulation and expression of the United Methodist voice in public affairs, we must listen to the concerns and insights of church members and churches in all nations. It is imperative that our expressions and actions be informed by participation in the universal church.

With particular reference to The United Methodist Church and public affairs, we express the following convictions: Connectional units of the denomination (such as General Conference, jurisdictional conference, annual conference, local congregation, or general board or agency) should continue to exercise the right to advocate government policies that involve basic moral or ethical issues or questions. In exercising this right, each such connectional unit, or any other official group within The United Methodist Church, should always make explicit for whom or in whose name it speaks or acts in the arena of public affairs. Only the General Conference is competent to speak or act in the name of The United Methodist Church.

ADOPTED 1980
AMENDED AND READOPTED 2000

See Social Principles, ¶ 164*A* and *D*.

243. Separation of Church and State

We believe in the Christian church, the community of God's people founded on the confession of Christ. Jesus is the head of the body, the universal church, which is united by its common faith in Him. The church participates in the worship of God, the fellowship and training of believers, and the spread of God's love in the world. This ministry of God's love continues in the church as people are called to love and to bring together those who are separated from God and each other (Matthew 16:16-18; John 3:16-17; 2 Corinthians 5:14-20). On the other hand, we believe that government is an institution established by God for the welfare of society. Government, as many other things in creation, is a part of God's common grace to humanity. This is a grace where all members of society benefit, whether they are Christians or not. Wayne Grudem has said, "Human government is also a result of common grace. . . . One of the primary means God uses to restrain evil in the world is human government."

There are several places in Scripture that help us understand this gracious act of God. In the Flood story (Genesis 9:6ff) God reestablishes God's covenant with Noah and sets forth the truth of the sanctity of life. The Bible does not speak much of the role of civil government; however, when it does it gives us a clear idea as to the reason God has for the establishment of governments and its leaders (*see* 1 Samuel 10:17-25). For the biblical tradition the role of the government (as seen through the work of the kings and leaders) was very clear.

The psalmist says regarding kings and rulers: "Endow the king with your justice, O God, / the royal son with your righteousness. / He will judge your people in righteousness, / your afflicted ones with justice. . . . / He will defend the afflicted among the people / and save the children of the needy; / he will crush the oppressor" (Psalm 72:1-2, 4, New International Version). Thus the prayer for the king continued by describing the task of the rulers (i.e., governments): "For [they] will deliver the needy who cry out, / the afflicted who have no one to help. / [They] will take pity on the weak and the needy / and save the needy from death. / [They] will rescue them from oppression and violence, / for precious is their blood in [their] sight" (Psalm 72: 12-14, NIV). And, thus, adds Isaiah regarding the ruler whom God will bring: "But with righteousness [they] will judge the needy, / with justice [they] will give decisions for the poor of the earth. . . . /

Righteousness will be [their] belt / and faithfulness the sash around [their] waist" (Isaiah 11:4-5, NIV; *see also* Isaiah 3:14; 1Kings 3:8-9; Proverbs 8:14-16; Daniel 4:32).

The fact that God allows for the establishment of governments cannot be interpreted to mean that they are all good, as we can see in Scripture. As a matter of fact many governments act contradicting God's will. The reality is that governments fail as human beings fail to live according to God's will. Nevertheless, God uses governments for God's purposes. In the New Testament we also see the important role that governments play according to Paul. When Paul speaks of those in authority he states: "For he is God's servant to do you good. But if you do wrong, be afraid, for he does not bear the sword for nothing. He is God's servant, an agent of wrath to bring punishment on the wrongdoer. Therefore, it is necessary to submit to the authorities, not only because of possible punishment but also because of conscience. This is also why you pay taxes, for the authorities are God's servants, who give their full time to governing" (Romans 13:4-7, NIV).

The above in no way equates God and government, on the contrary there is no way to reconcile God's purpose for government with a government that acts contrary to God's will. There are many examples where governments pervert this God-given authority. It is in situations such as this where the prophetic voice of the church best honors its responsibility to the state, and its faithfulness to the gospel, by calling the state to accountability. Christians must become the conscience of government, in the best sense of the prophetic tradition. As Martin Luther King, Jr. once stated: "The church must be reminded that it is not the master or the servant of the state, but rather the conscience of the state. It must be the guide and the critic of the state, and never its tool." Over the years The United Methodist Church has come to a clearer understanding of this relationship. Hence, our church has historically supported the separation of church and state and the free exercise of religion because of our direct experience of exclusion and persecution, due to religious intolerance and bigotry. During the early years of the republic The Methodist Church was seen as a group of outsiders and as an inconsequential religious body that was not part of the Protestant establishment, thus resulting in the exclusion of the Methodist preachers from many towns and pulpits in many places around the new nation.

This experience, which the Methodists shared with the Baptists, Moravians, and a few other nonestablishment religious groups of the time, helped the Methodists to affirm the need to support the first constitutional amendment: "Congress shall make no laws respecting an establishment of religion or prohibiting the free exercise thereof" (also known as the establishment clause).

The Social Principles of The United Methodist Church assert: "We believe that the state should not attempt to control the church, nor should the church seek to dominate the state. 'Separation of church and state' means no organic union of the two, but it does permit interaction. The church should continually exert a strong ethical influence upon the state, supporting policies and programs deemed to be just and opposing policies and programs that are unjust" (Social Principles, ¶ 164B). The notion of the separation of the state from the church deals with the relationship of institutions that are independent of each other, although interrelated. Religion and politics are two spheres of activities in the life of Christians that cannot be separated. Citizens who belong to religious groups are also members of the secular society, and this dual association generates tensions. Religious beliefs have moral and social implications, and it is appropriate and necessary for people of faith to express these through their activities as citizens in the political arena. The fact that ethical convictions are rooted in religious faith, does not disqualify them from the political realm.

On the other hand these ethical convictions do not have secular validity merely because they are thought by their exponents to be religiously authoritative. They must be argued for in appropriate social and political terms in harmony with broad social values, including competing   values.

The appropriate place of religion in our society has been in a constant flux, its nature and relations have been clarified in ongoing social debates. "It may not be easy," James Madison wrote, "in every possible case, to trace the line of separation between the rights of religion and civil authority with such distinctness as to avoid collisions." Clearly, collisions are what provide opportunities for careful deliberations of religious liberty issues, helping us to fine-tune this important pillar, in an increasingly pluralistic society.

Therefore, we should be prepared to deal with the complexities, ambiguities, and overlapping interests of church and state. We must discern workable principles that are compatible with fundamental constitutional imperatives, as well as our theological imperatives, in order to act morally and in accordance with God's will. As the Book of Acts reminds us: "We must obey God rather than any human authority" (5:29, New Revised Standard Version).

Thus, The United Methodist Church has supported that "[e]veryone has the right to freedom of thought, conscience and religion; this right includes freedom to change his [or her] religion or belief, and freedom, either alone or in community with others and in public or private, to manifest his [or her] religion or belief in teaching, practice, worship and observance" (The Universal Declaration of Human Rights, Article 18).

In addition, The United Methodist Church also agrees with the Universal Declaration of Human Rights (Article 18), which is not limited in its application to traditional religions or to religions and beliefs with institutional characteristics or practices analogous to those of traditional religions. Given our Church's history, the Church views with concern any tendency to discriminate against any religion or belief for any reasons, including the fact that they might be newly established or represent a religious minority that may be the subject of hostility by a predominant religious community.

The United Methodist Church, in agreement with the International Covenant on Civil and Political Rights, affirms that the freedom to manifest one's religion or beliefs may be subject only to such limitations as are necessary to protect public safety, order, health, or morals or the fundamental rights and freedoms of others (Article 18, Paragraph 3).

Furthermore, The United Methodist Church has understood this to mean that government must be neutral in matters of religion and may not show preference of one religion over others, for religion in general, for religion over nonreligion, or for nonreligion over religion.

Therefore, be it resolved, that the General Conference of The United Methodist Church continue to affirm its historical position that government may not engage in, sponsor, supervise, aid, or lend its authority to religious expressions or religious observances.

Be it further resolved, that the General Conference urge rejection of any attempt of legislative bodies at the federal and state levels to bridge this important separation between church and state by providing direct financial assistance to houses of worship and religiously affiliated organizations in order for them to evangelize or proselytize. The state should not support any religious group's interest to evangelize or proselytize, the state is not the defender of the faith, whichever that faith might be.

Be it further resolved, that the General Conference reaffirms its historical position in opposition to any government legislation or constitutional amendment that would allow the use of public funds to support nonpublic elementary and secondary schools, or in regards to religious observances in public schools.

ADOPTED 2004

See Social Principles, ¶ 164C.

244. Guidelines for "Charitable Choice" Programs

WHEREAS, the term "charitable choice" entered the vocabulary of human service delivery in the United States of America (USA) in social welfare reform legislation in 1996, with particular reference to religious provider access to and utilization of public funds; and

WHEREAS, the term has come to be widely used in USA legislation, government regulations, and public discourse on the role of religious organizations as providers of publicly funded programs; and

WHEREAS, the term and its implications have become the source of ongoing debate on appropriate relations between religious organizations and governments, including the issue of church-state separation and religious nondiscrimination in hiring by religious service providers using public funds; and

WHEREAS, many United Methodist congregations, church-related institutions, and programs in the USA, are potentially or actually affected by charitable choice issues; and

WHEREAS, United Methodist agencies, related institutions, and some congregations have long histories of partnership with government in the delivery of human services; and,

WHEREAS, The United Methodist Church, through policy and practice, has developed sound and practical guidelines on the use of public funds by churches and church-related entities;

Therefore, be it resolved, that the 2004 General Conference urge congregations, agencies, related institutions, and programs in the USA to:

- adhere to the minimum nondiscrimination criteria to be met by church and church-related recipients of public funds;
- abide by the historical and prudent principle of separate nonprofit incorporation for organizations and programs receiving public service funds, including the setting up of separate service corporations by congregations so engaged, in large measure as a means of protecting the Church from liability claims;

- carefully investigate the terms and implications of all public grants and contracts to ensure that the tasks undertaken and expected outcomes are consistent with the United Methodist Social Principles; and
- engage in informed dialogue on the public policy and religious liberty implications of charitable choice.

ADOPTED 2004

See Social Principles, ¶ 164C.

CRIMINAL JUSTICE

245. Bishops Urged to Uphold Opposition to Capital Punishment

WHEREAS, more than 600 persons will have been executed in the United States since the death penalty was resumed in 1977; and

WHEREAS, total executions for 1999 in the U.S. will reach 100 or more for the first time in more than half a century; and

WHEREAS, the U.S. ranked fourth in the world for executions in 1997; and

WHEREAS, the U.S. is the only nation in the West which has not abolished the death penalty; and

WHEREAS, the then Methodist Church officially opposed the death penalty as early as General Conference, 1956; and

WHEREAS, the 1980 General Conference resolution represents one of the most eloquent and prophetic of all religious expressions of opposition to the death penalty,

Therefore, be it resolved, that the Council of Bishops be encouraged to honor and uphold the teachings of United Methodism as expressed in ¶ 164A of *The 2000 Book of Discipline*, opposing and calling for the abolition of capital punishment, requesting all clergy and lay officials to preach, teach, and exemplify its sacred intent—especially by calling upon governors and state legislators in capital punishment states to commute present death sentences to life imprisonment and work for the abolition of capital punishment as historically advocated by The United Methodist Church.

ADOPTED 2000

See Social Principles, ¶ 164A.

246. Capital Punishment

In spite of a common assumption to the contrary, "an eye for an eye and a tooth for a tooth" does not give justification for the imposing of the penalty of death. Jesus explicitly repudiated the *lex talionis* (Matthew 5:38-39), and the Talmud denies its literal meaning and holds that it refers to financial indemnities.

When a woman was brought before Jesus having committed a crime for which the death penalty was commonly imposed, our Lord so persisted in questioning the moral authority of those who were ready to conduct the execution that they finally dismissed the charges (John 8:31 f.).

The Social Principles of The United Methodist Church condemn the "torture of persons by governments for any purpose" and assert that it violates Christian teachings. The church, through its Social Principles, further declares, "We oppose capital punishment and urge its elimination from all criminal codes" (¶ 164A).

After a moratorium of a full decade, the use of the death penalty in the United States has resumed. Other Western nations have largely abolished it during the twentieth century. But a rapidly rising rate of crime and an even greater increase in the fear of crime has generated support within the American society for the institution of death as the punishment for certain forms of homicide. It is now being asserted, as it was often in the past, that capital punishment would deter criminals and would protect law-abiding citizens.

The United States Supreme Court, in *Gregg* v. *Georgia,* in permitting use of the death penalty, conceded the lack of evidence that it reduced violent crime, but permitted its use for purpose of sheer retribution.

The United Methodist Church cannot accept retribution or social vengeance as a reason for taking human life. It violates our deepest belief in God as the Creator and the Redeemer of humankind. In this respect, there can be no assertion that human life can be taken humanely by the state. Indeed, in the long run, the use of the death penalty by the state will increase the acceptance of revenge in our society and will give official sanction to a climate of violence.

The United Methodist Church is deeply concerned about the present high rate of crime in the United States and about the value of a life taken in murder or homicide. When another life is taken through capital punishment, the life of the victim is further devalued. Moreover, the church is convinced that the use of the death penalty would result in neither a net reduction of crime in general nor a lessening of the particular kinds of crime against which it was directed. Homicide—the crime for which the death penalty has been used almost exclusively in recent decades—increased far less than other major crimes during the period of the moratorium. Progressively rigorous scientific studies, conducted over more than forty years, overwhelmingly failed to support the thesis that capital punishment deters homicide more effectively than does imprisonment. The most careful comparisons of homicide rates in similar states with and without use of the death penalty, and also of homicide rates in the same state in periods with and without it, have found as many or slightly more criminal homicides in states with use of the death penalty.

The death penalty also falls unfairly and unequally upon an outcast minority. Recent methods for selecting the few persons sentenced to die from among the larger number who are convicted of comparable offenses have not cured the arbitrariness and discrimination that have historically marked the administration of capital punishment in this country.

The United Methodist Church is convinced that the nation's leaders should give attention to the improvement of the total criminal justice system and to the elimination of social conditions that breed crime and cause disorder, rather than foster a false confidence in the effectiveness of the death penalty.

The United Methodist Church declares its opposition to the retention and use of capital punishment in any form or carried out by any means; the church urges the abolition of capital punishment.

The United Methodist Church recommends the following specific actions:

1. Congregations, districts, conferences, and ecumenical coalitions in sovereign nations and lesser political entities where the death penalty is currently practiced are called to take overt action to change the laws and social conditions which produce this violent act.

2. Persons and groups who take this moral issue into the public arena (such as addressing elected officials, vigils, letter-writing campaigns, paid advertising, and other responsible direct action) will be supported by the church.

3. The General Boards of Global Ministries and Church and Society and their affiliates throughout the denomination and ecumenical partnerships are called to develop strategies of education and political action to overcome the evil of capital punishment.

4. The global scope of the protest summons the people of the church to seriously oppose this abhorrent practice, and for United Methodist persons to incorporate this protest into their personal social conscience.

5. The United Methodist Church commends the people who have provided moral judgment, prophetic insight, pastoral care for those who suffer from this practice, and have borne the pain of hostility and indifference to this advocacy.

ADOPTED 1980
REVISED AND READOPTED 2000

See Social Principles, ¶ 164A *and* G.

247. Juvenile Death Penalty

The United Methodist Church's position on the death penalty, based on explicit biblical and theological grounds, is clear and unequivocal: This Church "declares its opposition to the retention and use of capital punishment in any form or carried out by any means . . . [and] urges the abolition of capital punishment."[1]

In view of its consistent position on this issue since being first stated in 1956, The United Methodist Church is deeply grieved by the continued use of the death penalty in the United States and profoundly so by its use against juvenile offenders. Since its first recognized execution of a juvenile offender in 1642, the United States has executed at least 366 persons for crimes committed as juveniles and has, since 1990, executed more juvenile offenders than all other countries combined.[2]

Today the United States stands practically alone among the nations of the world in executing persons for crimes committed as juveniles, with all countries except the United States and Iran now forbidding such executions.[3] Among all the signatories to three major interna-

1. "Capital Punishment," *The Book of Resolutions of The United Methodist Church 2000* (Nashville: United Methodist Publishing House, 2000), 578.

2. National Coalition to Abolish the Death Penalty, *Human Rights Human Wrongs. Sentencing Children to Death* (Washington, D.C., National Coalition to Abolish the Death Penalty, 2003), 2, 20 (hereafter, *HRHW*); American Bar Association (ABA), "Overview of the Juvenile Death Penalty Today," 2 of 2, http://www.abanet.org/crimjust/juvjus/juvdp.html (29 October 2003).

3. Out of all countries that continue to use the death penalty, since 1990 the United States is one of only six countries that have executed persons for crimes committed as juveniles (the others are China, Iran, Pakistan, Yeman and Zimbabwe); since 2000 only the United States and Iran have executed persons for crimes committed as juveniles, and in 2002 only the United States carried out such executions. In 1994 Yeman and Zimbabwe enacted legislation to forbid the execution of persons for crimes committed as juveniles; China did so in 1997, and was followed by Pakistan in 2000. ABA, "Evolving Standards of Decency," 4 of 4, http://www.abanet.org/crimjust/ juvjus/juvdp.html (29 October 2003); *HRHW*, 20.

tional human rights treaties—the International Covenant on Civil and Political Rights, the American Convention on Human Rights, and the Convention on the Rights of the Child—only the United States has reserved for itself the right to kill juvenile offenders.[4]

Appallingly, racial disparities in the application of the death penalty are even greater among juvenile offenders than among adult offenders.[5] There are also major regional disparities, with the juvenile death penalty being applied almost exclusively in the South, which accounts for 84 percent of the 224 death sentences imposed on juveniles since 1973, and 95 percent of the 22 executions of juvenile offenders carried out during the same period.[6]

4. The *International Covenant on Civil and Political Rights (ICCPR)* was adopted by the U.N. General Assembly in 1966, came into force in 1976, and as of June 2003 had 149 states as signatories; the *American Convention on Human Rights (ACHR)* was adopted by the Organization of American States in 1969, came into force in 1978, and as of June 2003 had 24 states as signatories, and the *Convention on the Rights of the Child (CRC)* was adopted by the U.N. General Assembly in 1989, came into force in 1990, and as of June 2003 had 192 states as signatories.

The United States is a signatory to all three treaties. But it was not until 1992 that the USA ratified the *ICCPR* and in doing so made a reservation to Article 6(5), stating "[t]hat the United States reserves the right, subject to its Constitutional constraints, to impose capital punishment on any person (other than a pregnant woman) duly convicted under existing or future laws permitting the imposition of capital punishment, including such punishment for crimes committed by persons below eighteen years of age." Article 6(5), to which exception is taken, states that "Sentence of death shall not be imposed for crimes committed by persons below eighteen years of age and shall not be carried out on pregnant women. The United States has not yet ratified the *ACHR*, and all countries except the United States and Somalia have ratified the *CRC*.

Amnesty International, "The Exclusion of Child Offenders from the Death Penalty under General International Law," 2, http:// www.amnestyusa.org/abolish/reports/exclusion child offenders.html (29 October 2003); American Convention on Human Rights, 1 of 18, http://www.oas.org/juridico/english/Sigs/b-32.html (5 November 2002); Convention on the Rights of the Child, 1 of 20, http://www.unhchr.ch/html/menu3/b/k2crc. htm (5 November 2003); Amnesty International, International Bill of Human Rights (Colombo: Amnesty International, 1978), 11, 27.

5. For example, "Between 1642 and 1899, approximately 52% of persons executed for juvenile offenses were African-American. During the twentieth century that proportion rose to nearly 75%." *HRHW*, 12. Out of 224 death sentences imposed on juvenile offenders since 1976, over 60 percent have been either African American or Latino. As of June, 2003, 67 percent of the 75 persons on death row for juvenile crimes were persons of color (African American—45%; Latino—19%; Asian— 2%, and Native American—1%), while only 55 percent of all offenders on death row were persons of color. Of the 22 juvenile offenders executed since 1976, 55 percent were either African American or Latino. Death Penalty Information Center, "Juvenile Offenders on Death Row," 2 of 5, http://www.deathpenalty-info.org/article.php?did=204&scid=27; National Coalition to Abolish the Death Penalty, "Fact Sheet: The Juvenile Death Penalty," 1-2 of 3, http://www.ncadp.org/html/juvenile fact sheet.html (29 October 2003); Victor L. Streib, "The Juvenile Death Penalty Today: Death Sentences and Executions for Juvenile Crimes, January 1, 1973 - September 30, 2003," 4, http://www.law. onu.edu/faculty/streib/JuvDeath Sept2003.htm (4 November 2003).

6. ABA, "Factsheet: The Juvenile Death . . . ," 2 of 2; *HRHW*, 6-7, 29.

Significant recent studies have found that the majority of juveniles on death row had terrible childhoods, with backgrounds of physical or sexual abuse, "profound psychological disorders, low IQ, indigence, and/or intensive substance abuse."[7] Moreover, recent studies using magnetic resonance imaging (MRI) have found that adolescent brains are far less developed than previously thought; that the brain development process continues into the early 20's; that "the parts of the brain that govern judgment, reasoning and impulse control are not fully developed until the early twenties"; that due to the underdevelopment of this portion of the brain teenagers rely heavily on another part of the brain responsible for "gut reactions"; that this reliance continues until the early twenties and is found more among males than females.[8]

These studies confirm the long-accepted view in our society about the lesser maturity of juveniles—the main reason for which our society, by law, excludes persons below 18 years from a range of activities such as voting, serving on juries or in the military, marrying, entering into contracts, purchasing alcohol and tobacco products, and executing wills and holds that minors should not be held accountable for their actions to the same degree as adults.

The "evolving standards of decency" cited by the U.S. Supreme Court in Atkins v. Virginia (2002) for prohibiting execution of mentally retarded offenders apply also to juvenile offenders—namely, considerations such as a national consensus against the practice, lesser capacity to control their impulses, and the risk of wrongful exe-

7. ABA, "Adolescent Brain Development and Legal Culpability," 3-4 of 4, http://www.abanet.org/crimjust/juvjus/ juvdp/html (29 October 2003).

8. ABA, "Factsheet . . . ," 1 of 2. The reference is to studies by Harvard Medical School, the National Institute of Mental health, and UCLA's Department of Neuroscience. These studies have found that the part of the brain in the frontal lobe that provides us with our advanced level of consciousness—enabling us to "prioritize thoughts, imagine, think in the abstract, anticipate consequences, plan, and control impulses"—undergoes the most change in adolescence and is the last part of the brain to develop. ABA, "Adolescent Brain Development . . . ," 3-4 of 4. MIR scans have shown that due to the underdevelopment of this part of the frontal lobe, teenagers rely heavily upon the amygdala, another part of the brain that is responsible for 'gut reactions'; that this reliance continues until early adulthood (early 20's), and is found more among males than females as the frontal lobe develops more slowly in males than in females. It has also been found that the rate of brain maturation "can be severely retarded by abuse and neglect—conditions that affect most juvenile offenders on death row," and that "abuse and traumas during childhood and adolescence may permanently alter one's brain structure . . . [and] physically damage brain tissue." ABA, "Adolescent Brain . . . ," 2 of 4; HRHW, 14-15; NCADP, "Factsheet . . . ," 3 of 3.

cution due to greater vulnerability "to giving false confessions and [being] less able to provide meaningful assistance to counsel."[9]

The United Methodist Church is glad to note that there is now a growing national consensus against the juvenile death penalty, as evidenced by an increasing majority of states and jurisdictions in the United States holding that the death penalty should not be applied to persons for crimes committed as juveniles, with 44 states, plus the U.S. military and the federal government, by either law or practice, not executing any juvenile offender since reinstatement of the death penalty in 1976,[10] and by strong opposition to the practice from a large number of child advocacy and educational organizations; medical and social service organizations; legal, human, and civil rights groups;

9. ABA, "Overview . . . ," 2 of 2; NCADP, "Factsheet . . . ," 3 of 3. When last considering the juvenile death penalty issue in *Stanford v. Kentucky* (1989), the U.S. Supreme Court held that state legislation did not indicate a consensus against the practice. However, as indicated in note 9 below, since then six additional states have rejected the execution of juvenile offenders, thereby bringing the total number of states which by law have rejected the juvenile death penalty to 29— which is very close to the 30 states prohibiting execution of the mentally retarded at the time of the Atkins decision (2002). Moreover, as indicated in note 9 below, 15 additional states which by law permit the death penalty to be applied to juvenile offenders have not since 1973 executed any person for offenses committed while a juvenile. This means that 44 states, either by law or in practice, have not executed any juvenile offender since reinstatement of the death penalty in 1976. This strongly suggests that there is now a widespread consensus that the death penalty should not be applied to juvenile offenders. ABA, "Evolving Standards of Decency," 1 of 4, http://www.abanet.org/crimjust/juvjus/juvdp.html (29 October 2003).

10. Since reinstatement of the death penalty was permitted by the U.S. Supreme Court in 1976, 12 states have chosen not to reinstate the death penalty. Among the 38 states that have reinstated the death penalty, 17 do not permit the death penalty to be applied to juvenile offenders. Hence, 29 states, plus the Federal Government and U.S. Military, by law, do not allow the juvenile death penalty.

Additionally, among the 21 states which by law permit the death penalty to be applied to juvenile offenders, 15 have not executed any person for a crime committed while a juvenile. Hence, a total of 44 states, either by law or by practice, have not executed any juvenile offenders since reinstatement of the death penalty in 1976.

The Federal Government and U.S. Military set the minimum age at 18 when reinstating the death penalty in 1984. Over the past decade, six states have rejected the juvenile death penalty: Washington (1993), by State Supreme Court action; Kansas (1994) and New York (1995) by setting the minimum age at 18 when reinstating the death penalty; Montana (1999) and Indiana (2002) by legislatively raising the minimum age to 18, and Missouri (2003) by State Supreme Court action. During the same period, legislation to ban the juvenile death penalty was introduced in at least 12 states, and progressed partway to adoption in 4. During this period, no state or jurisdiction having chosen not to have the juvenile death penalty has reinstated the execution of juvenile offenders. The 12 states in which legislation to abolish the juvenile death penalty has been introduced are: Arizona, Arkansas, Florida, Kentucky, Mississippi, Missouri, Nevada, Oklahoma, Pennsylvania, South Dakota, Texas and Wyoming. States in which such legislation has advanced partway to adoption are: Arkansas, Florida, South Dakota, and Texas.

ABA, "Overview . . . ," 1-2 of 2; *HRHW*, 7-10; Streib, "The Juvenile Death Penalty . . . ," 6-7.

at least thirty-three religious and ethical organizations calling for abolition of the juvenile death penalty on the grounds of juvenile justice and regard for the sanctity of human life, and by polls indicating that two out of every three persons in the U.S. are opposed.[11]

While juvenile offenders must be punished for wrongs committed, their lesser maturity lessens their culpability, their potential for growth provides promise for rehabilitation, the sanctity of human life calls us to never give up hope for what each child of God can become, the juvenile death penalty is at odds with the emerging consensus in the U.S. and the rest of the world, and the abolition of the juvenile death penalty in the United States is long overdue.

The United Methodist Church therefore recommends the following specific actions:

11. These organizations include: *Child Advocacy and Educational Organizations*—Children's Defense Fund, Child Welfare League of America, Coalition for Juvenile Justice, National Association for Children's Behavioral Health, National Education Association, and Youth Advocate International;

Medical and Social Service Organizations—American Academy of Child & Adolescent Psychiatry, American Academy of Pediatrics, American Medical Association, American Society for Adolescent Psychiatry, American Psychiatric Association, American Psychological Association, National Association of Social Workers, National Alliance for the Mentally Ill, National Mental Health Association, and Physicians for Human Rights;

Legal, Human and Civil Rights groups:—American Bar Association, American Civil Liberties Union, Amnesty International USA, Constitution Project, Human Rights Watch, International Human Rights Law Group, National Association for the Advancement of Colored People, National Bar Association, National Council on Crime and Delinquency, National Legal Aid and Defender Association, and World Organization Against Torture, USA;

Religious and Ethical Organizations—American Baptist Churches in the U.S.A., American Ethical Union, American Friends Service Committee, American Humane Association, American Humanist Association, American Jewish Committee, Bruderhof Communities, Central Conference of American Rabbis, Christian Church (Disciples of Christ), Church of the Brethren, Church Women United, Episcopal Church, Evangelical Lutheran Church of America, Fellowship of Reconciliation, Friends Committee on National Legislation, Friends United Meeting, General Conference of General Baptists, General Conference Mennonite Church, Mennonite Central Committee, Murder Victims' Families for Reconciliation, Mennonite Church, Moravian Church in America, Mormons for Equality and Social Justice, National Board YMCA of the U.S.A., National Council of Churches of Christ, Orthodox Church in America, Presbyterian Church (U.S.A.), Rabbinical Assembly, Reformed Church in America, Reorganized Church of Jesus Christ of Latter Day Saints, Union of American Hebrew Congregations, Unitarian Universalist Association, United Church of Christ, United Methodist Church, and the U.S. Catholic Conference.

ABA, "National Organizations that Oppose the Juvenile Death Penalty," 1 of 1, http://abanet.org/crimjust/ juvjus/juvdp.html (6 November 2003); Religious Organizing Against the Death Penalty, "Statements of Opposition to Capital Punishment from Faith Groups," www.deathpenaltyreligious.org/education.html (6 November 2003).

A May 2002 Gallup Poll found 69 percent of Americans opposed to the death penalty for juvenile offenders. ABA, "Overview . . . ," 2 of 2.

1. Members, congregations, districts, and conferences in states where the juvenile death penalty is currently upheld by law take overt action to change these laws.[12]

2. The General Boards of Global Ministries and Church and Society, and their affiliates in states where current law supports the juvenile death penalty, develop strategies of education and political action to overcome the evil of states killing persons for crimes committed when juveniles.

3. The United Methodist Church, through its episcopal leadership, agencies, constituent entities, clergy and individual members, commend and uphold persons and groups who take this moral issue into the public arena.

ADOPTED 2004

See Social Principles ¶ 164*A* and G.

248. Equal Justice

It must be remembered that the advice "Let every person be subject to the governing authorities" (Romans 13:1, NRSV) is preceded by "Live in harmony with one another; do not be haughty, but associate with the lowly; never be conceited. Repay no one evil for evil, but take thought for what is noble in the sight of all" (Romans 12:16-17, NRSV). The admonition is directed to the authorities who govern as well as those who may be subject.

The Social Principles of The United Methodist Church state (¶ 164*B* and *F*): "The church should continually exert a strong ethical influence upon the state, supporting policies and programs deemed to be just and opposing policies and programs that are unjust. . . . In the

12. States with laws which provide for the imposition of the death penalty on juvenile offenders are:

States having executed juvenile offenders since reinstatement of the death penalty in the U.S. in 1976: Georgia (1), Louisiana (1), Oklahoma (2), South Carolina (1), Texas (13), and Virginia (3). The death penalty for juvenile offenders was rejected in Missouri (1) in 2003.

States currently with juvenile offenders on death row: Alabama (13), Arizona (5), Florida (2), Georgia (2), Kentucky (1), Louisiana (7), Mississippi (5), Nevada (1), North Carolina (5), Pennsylvania (3), South Carolina (3), Texas (28), and Virginia (1).

Other states whose laws provide for imposition of the death penalty on juvenile offenders, but which have not imposed this punishment since reinstatement of the death penalty (have not executed any juvenile offender and currently do not have any juvenile offenders on death row): Arkansas, Delaware, Idaho, New Hampshire, South Dakota, Utah, and Wyoming.

ABA, "Factsheet: The Juvenile Death Penalty . . . ," 2 of 2.

love of Christ, who came to save those who are lost and vulnerable, we urge the creation of a genuinely new system for the care and restoration of victims, offenders, criminal justice officials, and the community as a whole."

The Police

In a democratic society, the police fill a position of extraordinary trust and power. Usually the decision of whether a citizen is to be taken into custody rests solely with the police. For these reasons, law enforcement officers must be persons who possess good judgment, sound discretion, proper temperament, and are physically and mentally alert.

Unusual care must be exercised in the selection of those persons to serve as police officers. We recommend psychological testing prior to employment of police officers and periodically thereafter. During the period of training and continually thereafter, police must be instilled with the knowledge that the rights of many will never be secured if the government, through its police powers, is permitted to prefer some of its citizens over others. The practice of citizen preference in the enforcement of our criminal laws must not be tolerated. Our laws must be fairly enforced and impartially administered. No one is immune from the requirements of the law because of power, position, or economic station in life. Further, the power of the police must never be used to harass and provoke the young, the poor, the unpopular, and the members of racial and cultural minorities.

Where there is heavy pressure upon police officers by police departments to regularly make a large number of arrests as a demonstration of their initiative and professional performance, we urge that such practice be discontinued.

In a democratic society, however, a large majority of police work encompasses peacekeeping and social services rather than crime control functions. Police routinely use more than 85 percent of their duty time in giving assistance to citizens and making referrals to other governmental agencies. It is important for police to be recognized and promoted for their effectiveness in such roles as diverting youths from disorderly activities, peacefully intervening in domestic quarrels, anticipating disturbances through the channeling of grievances, and the building of good community relationships.

The United Methodist Church recommends that police departments publicly establish standards of police conduct and policies for promotion. To this end, congregations should encourage the police to conduct public hearings among all classes of citizens, giving adequate weight to peacekeeping, life-protecting, and other service roles, as well as the bringing of criminal offenders to justice. The standards must include strict limits on the police use of guns.

We further recommend that police officers live within the jurisdiction in which they are employed.

We make these recommendations not only in concern about the frequent abuses of people by the police, but also because we are concerned for more effective control of crime. We observe that only about one half the victims of serious crime, and a far smaller proportion of witnesses, report to the police. If offenders are to be apprehended and convicted, police and law-abiding citizens must work closely together. Such cooperation can occur only when the police are fair and humane and when they are publicly known to be sensitive and considerate.

The United Methodist Church urges that communities establish adequate salary scales for police officers and develop high standards for recruiting both men and women, and members of all ethnic groups. Recruitment must be followed by adequate training in social relations and dispute settlement as well as in law and the skills of crime detection investigation and the apprehension of offenders. As police officers continue to meet those improved qualifications, we will recognize law enforcement as a profession with status and respect.

Criminal Laws and the Courts

Restorative justice practices should be utilized within the community as a first response to any criminal behavior. Justice can only prevail when there is healing of the victim, repentance of the offender, and when forgiveness and reconciliation are shared throughout the community. Victim-offender mediation, family group conferencing, and various other restorative justice techniques are urged to be considered as an alternative to the criminal courts.

Overwhelmingly, criminal convictions are by guilty pleas, a large proportion of those by plea bargaining. Where the law recognizes and permits plea-bargaining, and in those instances where the ends of justice dictate that a renegotiated plea be considered, we recommend it should be permitted and approved only after full disclosure in open court of the terms and conditions of such plea-bargaining agreement.

Equal justice requires that all trials and the sentencing of those convicted under our criminal laws must be conducted in the public courtroom.

However, that work should be correspondingly eased by changes in the law, such as the moving of most traffic offenses out of criminal court to administrative procedures, and by relieving the court of great numbers of civil cases through the adoption of genuine no-fault motor-vehicle insurance laws. The courts must also organize their work efficiently, employing modern management procedures. Many improvements could be made by the use of administrative volunteers, including retirees who can furnish professional services to the court at minimal costs.

Other changes needed to obtain equal justice in the courts include:

1. the repeal of some criminal laws against certain personal conditions or individual misconduct. Examples are criminal prohibitions of vagrancy, personal gambling, public drunkenness, drug use, and prostitution. Together, these charges alone account for more than half of all arrests in some jurisdictions. They result in little social good, but great evil in class discrimination, alienation, and waste of resources needed for other purposes. Some related laws such as those against drunken driving and those limiting and controlling the operation of gambling establishments need to be tightened;

2. the adoption of systematic new penal codes prescribing penalties proportionate to the predictable damage done by the various kinds of crime, without regard to the race or class of the offender. For example, in the United States, there are discriminatory high penalties for the use of crack cocaine (most often used by blacks) as opposed to powder cocaine (most often used by whites);

3. the training of judges of juvenile and criminal courts in the use of non-incarcerating community sanctions wherever the offense does not involve persistent violence;

4. the adoption of systematic new penal codes prescribing a range of penalties without regard to the race or class of the offender, but utilizing non-incarceration community sanctions wherever consistent with community protection;

5. the provision for court-fixed sentences, rather than mandatory ones, in order to draw upon the skill and the training of qualified judges;

6. a statement by the sentencing judge of the reason or reasons why he or she is selecting from the range permitted by the law the particular sentence being pronounced;

7. the development of appropriate jury selection procedures that would ensure the most inclusive representation, including representatives of the socioeconomic class and ethnic group of the defendants and of the crime victims, as well as balance between male and female jurors;

8. the adoption by all courts of: (a) speedy trial provisions, which the Constitution guarantees; and (b) that degree of personal recognizance and supervision which each defendant's situation warrants, regardless of race and class identity, in place of the present, inherently discriminatory bail-bond, pretrial release process that exists in some courts;

9. when fines are assessed, they should be scaled to the magnitude of the crime and the ability of the offender to pay. In suitable cases, fines should be made payable in installments; and

10. governmentally regulated programs of compensation for reimbursement of financial loss incurred by innocent victims of crime should be encouraged, with preference being given for programs in which specific offenders provide restitution to their specific victims as an alternative to incarceration; and

11. changes in state self-defense laws to allow for cases in which persistently battered persons, especially women and children, are driven to violence against their batterers, when they believe with good reason, that another attack is forthcoming.

We recommend that local churches consider setting up court monitoring panels to observe court operations and proceedings. Such panels may well adopt a role of friends of the court or of advocacy on behalf of accused persons and/or on behalf of crime victims. They may adopt other appropriate procedures in the interest of restorative justice, including close scrutiny of plea-bargaining and/or evidence of unequal imposition of sentences.

ADOPTED 1980
AMENDED AND READOPTED 2000

See Social Principles, ¶ 164F.

249. Transforming Injustices in Criminal Justice Systems

The Social Principles of The United Methodist Church state: "In the love of Christ, who came to save those who are lost and vulnerable, we urge the creation of a genuinely new system for the care and restoration of victims, offenders, criminal justice officials and the community as a whole." Deeply rooted racial and economic injustices in most nations' criminal justice systems form barriers to the realization of this vision. These problems include:

- media's disproportionate portrayal of poor people and people of color as criminals;
- legislation that results in ever-increasing rates of arrests and longer sentencing of the poor and people of color;
- disproportionate rates of incarceration of poor people and people of color;
- racial profiling and arrest quota systems;
- prosecutors and judges who have too much discretion and too few unbiased guidelines on whom they will prosecute and incarcerate;
- court-appointed legal representation for poor people that is often inferior to that available to those who can afford private representation;
- prisons that have become warehouses for the poor and people of color;
- privatization of prisons;
- prisons that fail to provide educational programs and/or employment training to prisoners, thus contributing to recidivism.

We call upon The United Methodist Church at all levels to:

- increase awareness, through resources and educational opportunities, of the realities outlined above, as well as possibilities for just alternatives;
- create and sustain new ministries of justice and involve United Methodist churches in advocacy for the elimination of racism and classism in the criminal justice system; and
- work in states and local communities for specific systemic changes, including:
  * reducing poverty by improving educational systems, creating affordable housing and dignified employment opportunities;
  * promoting equity in courts by legal representation of equal quality regardless of financial ability;
  * calling for a moratorium on building prisons;

* re-assessing incarceration guidelines and reducing incarceration of persons guilty of non-violent crimes;
* reversing the trend toward privatization and profit-making of prisons;
* developing high-quality education and training programs in prisons;
* creating laws against discrimination against ex-offenders;
* re-instating voting rights for ex-offenders;
* eliminating mandatory sentences for drug-related crimes;
* developing guidelines for police officers, prosecutors, and judges that result in less subjective exercise of authority; and
* educating media and the public about realities of poverty and race, so that the poor and people of color cease being portrayed as criminals and potential criminals.

We further call upon the General Board of Global Ministries, through the Restorative Justice Ministries program, to give leadership to the above actions through educational and training opportunities and resources, and to promote these concerns and activities throughout the denomination's general agencies, annual conferences, districts, and local churches.

ADOPTED 2004

See Social Principles, ¶ 164G and *H*.

250. Grand Jury Abuse

Jesus' words, "Do not judge, so that you may not be judged" (Matthew 7:1 NRSV), surely imply that all judgments are made in the light of God's truth. The Social Principles of The United Methodist Church state boldly that "governments, no less than individuals, are subject to the judgment of God" (¶ 164E). Such a social principle causes us, appropriately, to view with concern the government's use of the grand jury to control dissent and to harass those who act under the constraint of conscience.

The grand jury is envisioned in American law as a protector of citizens from unwarranted prosecutions. It is for this reason that its proceedings are secret and it has the power to subpoena witnesses.

Evidence indicates that in recent years, the extraordinary powers of the grand jury often have been used not for the *protection* of citizens, but in subjecting them to harassment and intimidation. Historically, political dissidents, antiwar activists, and leaders of minority groups and religious organizations have been particularly vulnerable to these abuses.

A government prosecutor can control the grand jury, thus distorting the grand jury's power to monitor and moderate the actions of the prosecution. The prosecutor can use the subpoena powers of the grand jury to conduct investigations that are the responsibility of law enforcement agencies. As an example, the United States Congress has never given the Federal Bureau of Investigation subpoena powers, yet agents routinely threaten uncooperative persons with subpoenas from a grand jury. In fact, subpoenas are often served at the request of the Federal Bureau of Investigation.

The use of the powers of the grand jury to harass and pursue political dissidents is a departure from its proper constitutional function, and it is a threat to public order, lawful government, and true domestic security.

Witnesses called before a grand jury may be given little or no warning of their subpoenas, may be forced to travel to court at distances from their homes, may not know whether they are targets of prosecution, may have little understanding of their rights, and cannot have legal counsel in the chambers.

Comprehensive grand jury reform legislation is needed to restore the constitutional guarantees of protection for citizens. The United States Constitution's Fifth Amendment right against self-incrimination and false accusation must be reestablished and reinforced.

The United Methodist Church, therefore, supports legislation designed to enhance the rights to due process of law, freedom of association, effective legal counsel, the presumption of innocence, and the privilege against self-incrimination of persons subpoenaed to testify before grand juries.

ADOPTED 1980
AMENDED AND READOPTED 2000

See Social Principles, ¶ 164E and F.

251. Gun Violence

Violence and, more particularly, violence to children and youth is a primary concern for United Methodists. We recognize and deplore violence which kills and injures children and youth. In the name of Christ, who came so that persons might know abundant life, we call upon the church to affirm its faith through vigorous efforts to curb and eliminate gun violence.

Gun violence is killing America's children. Based on statistics from the Bureau of Alcohol, Tobacco and Firearms, there are an estimated 223 million firearms in the United States. Approximately one out of every four households owns a handgun. The risk of handgun violence to children and youth is more prevalent in the United States today than in any previous generation. Our communities and schools are so exposed to large numbers of privately owned guns that no mere attempts at providing slightly better security can match the awful threat of guns finding their way through our well-intentioned safety systems.

A significant total reduction in the numbers of guns in our communities is our goal in ministry. We serve and our society's children go to school amidst passionately violent segments of current youth culture. No appeals to individual autonomy are sufficient to justify our church's ignorance of this threat. The need to prevent the incidence of firearm-related injury and death is an issue of increasing concern and a priority U.S. public health issue. The United Methodist Church is among those religious communions calling for social policies and personal lifestyles that bring an end to senseless gun violence.

Gun violence in America's schools has emerged as a growing and disturbing trend. The United Methodist Church supports ministries that address the issue of violence and crime prevention for children/youth in urban areas through the Communities of Shalom. Violence is no longer confined to the streets of urban areas but has occurred at an increasing rate in suburban communities. Over the past several years, high-profile cases of school shootings involving suburban youth killing and injuring teachers and peers alike have once again brought the issue of guns and youth to the forefront of national attention.

These acts of senseless violence should not be an acceptable occurrence in any community: suburban, urban, or rural. The church must continue to address these issues of violence and develop programs to enrich the lives of all children/youth.

In light of the increase of gun violence affecting the lives of children and youth, we call upon The United Methodist Church to:

1. convene workshops of clergy and other mental health care professionals from communities (urban, rural, and suburban) in which gun violence has had a significant impact in order to discuss ways by which The United Methodist Church should respond to this growing tragedy, and to determine what role the church should take in facilitating dialogue to address the issue of gun violence in our schools and among our children;

2. educate the United Methodist community (parents, children, and youth) on gun safety, violence prevention, adult responsibility around gun violence prevention, and the public health impact of gun violence;

3. identify community-based, state, and national organizations working on the issue of gun violence and seek their assistance to design education and prevention workshops around the issue of gun violence and its effect on children and youth;

4. develop advocacy groups within local congregations to advocate for the eventual reduction of the availability of guns in society with a particular emphasis upon handguns, handgun ammunition, assault weapons, automatic weapons, automatic weapon conversion kits, and guns that cannot be detected by traditionally used metal detection devices. These groups can be linked to community-based, state, and national organizations working on gun and violence issues;

5. support federal legislation to regulate the importation, manufacturing, sale, and possession of guns and ammunition by the general public. Such legislation should include provisions for the registration and licensing of gun purchasers and owners, appropriate background investigation and waiting periods prior to gun purchase, and regulation of subsequent sale;

6. call upon all governments of the world in which there is a United Methodist presence to establish national bans on ownership by the general public of handguns, assault weapons, automatic weapon conversion kits, and weapons that cannot be detected by traditionally used metal-detection devices;

7. call upon the print, broadcasting, and electronic media, as well as the entertainment industry, to refrain from promoting gun usage to children;

8. discourage the graphic depiction and glorification of violence by the entertainment industry, which greatly influences our society, and recommend that these issues be addressed through education and consciousness raising;

9. call upon the federal and state governments to provide significant assistance to victims of gun violence and their families; and

10. recommend that annual conferences make visible public witness to the sin of gun violence and to the hope of community healing.

ADOPTED 2000

See Social Principles, ¶ 164F.

252. Human Rights

God created human beings,
in the image of God they were created;
male and female were created.
    (Genesis 1:26-27, adapted)

We affirm that all persons are of equal worth in the sight of God, because all are created in the image of God. Biblical tradition demands that we live in an interdependent relationship with God and our neighbor. We must respond to human need at every community level.

As covenant people of God, we are called to responsibility rather than privilege.

God's vision for humanity as revealed in the life, death, and resurrection of Jesus Christ demands the total fulfillment of human rights in an interdependent global community. It is a vision of life where needs of the community have priority over individual fears and where redemption and reconciliation are available to all. Human rights are holistic in nature and therefore indivisible in their economic, social, cultural, civil, and political aspects. The omission of any of these aspects denies our God-given human dignity.

As Christians, we receive and carry a mandate to seek justice and liberation. Isaiah calls us to

loose the bonds of injustice,
to undo the thongs of the yoke,
to let the oppressed go free,
and to break every yoke.
    (Isaiah 58:6)

The United Methodist Church continues its commitment to human rights as grounded in God's covenant by critically assessing and safeguarding the following principles as defined in the Universal Declaration of Human Rights:

1. All persons are of equal worth and dignity.
2. All persons have the right to the basic necessities of life.
3. All persons have the right to self-determination, cultural identity, and minority distinction.
4. All persons have the right to religious expression and practice.

The United Nations has spoken strongly against racism as a human rights violation in the United Nations Declaration on the Elimination of All Forms of Racial Discrimination:

> Discrimination between human beings on the ground of race, color or ethnic origin is an offense to human dignity and shall be condemned as a denial of the principles of the Charter of the United Nations, as a violation of the human rights and fundamental freedoms proclaimed in the Universal Declaration of Human Rights, as an obstacle to friendly and peaceful relations among nations and as a fact capable of disturbing peace and security among peoples.

In addition, the United Nations has also defined sexism as a violation of human rights in the Declaration on the Elimination of Discrimination Against Women:

> Discrimination against women, denying or limiting as it does their equality of rights with men, is fundamentally unjust and constitutes an offense against human dignity.

Furthermore, Amnesty International has proposed to "end abuses based on sexual orientation" and to "defend the rights of lesbians, gay men, and bisexuals to live lives free from stigmatization and violence."

We call upon citizens within the church and society to analyze critically trends and developments that adversely affect human rights. These include:

1. the increase of capital-intensive technology that destroys opportunities for productive and meaningful employment;
2. the intentional use of data banks to undermine rather than enhance abundant living;
3. the growing phenomenon of an "underclass" of persons domestically and internationally excluded from full participation in society due to educational, cultural, economic, and political conditions;

4. the possible economic and political scapegoating of such an underclass for technological and social displacement;

5. increasing extrajudicial executions; torture; and disappearances of dissenters, their families, and communities;

6. the growth of militarism and the imposition of military-like control over civilians;

7. the increase of terrorism and the growth of white supremacist and racial hate groups, neo-Nazi groups, paramilitary units, and extreme ultranationalistic groups;

8. in many countries, the decreasing civilian control of domestic and international policing and intelligence units as well as increasing surveillance of their own citizenry, imposed under the guise of a potential threat to national security; and

9. the conflict between meeting the basic needs of developing countries and the disproportionate sharing of global resources.

We are increasingly aware that militarism and greed can overwhelm and undermine movements to secure human rights. The church is called to be an advocate for the human rights of all persons in the political, social, and economic quest for justice and peace.

As people of faith and hope, we commend those trends that contribute positively to the human rights movement. Among them:

- the growing acceptance of universal standards for human rights;
- the establishment of organizations such as Amnesty International, which documents, verifies, and publicizes political imprisonment, torture, killings, and crimes against humanity;
- the increasing consensus against war as a viable solution to international conflicts;
- movement toward the inclusion of "basic human needs" criteria in international aid packages and financial aid programming;
- the growing importance of human rights offices in governments around the world; and
- the growing emphasis on technology appropriate to the cultural setting.

We uphold the requirements advocated by the National Council of Churches to preserve and protect human rights:

1. Human rights require world peace.
2. Human rights require a secure and sustainable environment.

3. Human rights require sustainable human development.

4. Human rights require the preservation of communities.

5. Human rights require the preservation of religious liberty and freedom of conscience.

We call upon all governments to accept their obligation to uphold human rights by refraining from repression, torture, and violence against any person. We further call upon all governments to ratify and implement international conventions, covenants, and protocols addressing human rights in the context of justice and peace.

We call the church to be a place of refuge for those who experience the violation of their human rights. It is the duty of Christians "to help create a worldwide community in which governments and people treat each other compassionately as members of one human family."

ADOPTED 1996
AMENDED AND READOPTED 2000

See Social Principles, ¶ 164A.

253. Opposition to USA PATRIOT ACT to Violate Human Rights

WHEREAS the United States Constitution guarantees rights to everyone living in the United States, including temporary and permanent aliens as well as citizens; and

WHEREAS these rights are threatened by the October 2001 USA PATRIOT ACT that includes provision for indefinite detention or deportation of non-citizens, even if they have not committed a crime; grants the FBI access to medical, financial, and educational records without a court order; creates a new crime, "domestic terrorism," which is so broadly defined it could apply to acts of civil disobedience; and

WHEREAS the PATRIOT ACT includes Federal Executive Orders that establish secret military tribunals for terrorism suspects; permit wiretapping of conversations between federal prisoners and their lawyer; lift Justice Department regulations against covert, illegal counterintelligence operations by the FBI; and limit the disclosure of public documents under the Freedom of Information Act; and

WHEREAS, despite the fact that this law and these executive orders particularly target foreign nationals and people of color, anyone in the

USA could be affected even when acting and speaking legally in opposition to government policy; and

WHEREAS this law has resulted in the detention and arrest of at least 2,000 Muslims, Arabs, and Southeast Asians in the United States without due process of law; and

WHEREAS at the outbreak of WW II, the United States government interned 120,000 persons of Japanese ancestry, two-thirds of whom were American citizens, in just such a manner without semblance of due process of law; and

WHEREAS, after extensive investigation, a Presidential Commission in 1982 concluded that such internment was the result of "war hysteria, racial prejudice and a failure of political leadership," and

WHEREAS a token monetary award and an apology signed by Presidents Bush (first) and Clinton on behalf of the USA was made to those affected as a result of this finding;

Therefore, be it resolved, that the 2004 General Conference of The United Methodist Church go on record as opposed to the use of the USA PATRIOT ACT to violate fundamental rights guaranteed by the United States Constitution; and

Be it further resolved, that all members of the General Conference be encouraged to ask their elected representatives to work toward the repeal of those portions of the USA PATRIOT ACT that could be used to violate fundamental rights guaranteed by the United States Constitution; and

Be it further resolved, that the General Conference Secretary be directed to immediately forward a copy of this resolution to the President of the United States, members of Congress; and

Be it further resolved, that the 2004 General Conference incorporate the language of this resolution into *The Book of Resolutions of The United Methodist Church.*

ADOPTED 2004

See Social Principles, ¶ 164*A, B, D,* and *F.*

254. Juvenile Delinquency and Prevention

Let the little children come to me; do not stop them; for it is to such as these that the kingdom of God belongs (Mark 10:14, NRSV).

Our Lord particularly identified with children and illustrated the loving care which they need to grow and mature.

The Social Principles of The United Methodist Church calls for special attention to the rights of children and youth. From these perspectives we are concerned that in many states, children are arrested and incarcerated for truancy, incorrigibility, stubborn altercations with parents, and other conduct which would not be criminal if performed by an adult. Such status offenses should not be considered as grounds for involving a juvenile in processes of criminal or delinquency procedures. Rather, a child in trouble should be helped by caring communities, such as churches, mentoring programs, and boys/girls clubs.

There is considerable evidence that the methods of dealing with children play a major part in developing criminal tendencies. Most adults who repeat violent crimes began their conflict with law and order as children ten to fourteen years old. If treatment by the state or local agencies leads the child to think of him or herself as a tough young criminal, he or she is likely to act out that role.

The United Methodist Church urges that all status offenses be eliminated from the juvenile codes and from the processes for determining juvenile delinquency. We urge further that all offenses by children and youth be handled with extreme reluctance to incarcerate the offender. We especially oppose solitary confinement of children and youths in official detention. Institutions where juveniles classified as delinquent often are segregated from the general population often become schools of crime. As an alternative, we encourage greater use of supportive and restorative services for parents and children in their home settings; foster child care; neighborhood group homes, Parents Anonymous, and other alternatives.

There are communities within the states in which children are routinely locked up in jails because of a lack of temporary shelter, care or an unwillingness to use home detention. We urge the prohibition of placing dependent and neglected children in jails or facilities for juvenile delinquents.

For many children, the quality of life continually declines due to poverty, gangs, school violence, emotional, sexual and physical abuse, and other social ills that have yet to be recognized. The United Methodist Church must take a stand against juvenile delinquency and work to prevent it.

The church can witness to children in a restorative and prophetic way. The church must continue to address the social issues that children and adolescents face and become a safe haven where the children can come. By addressing the issues that children face, we help bring God's children back to their Creator.

Therefore, be it resolved, that General Conference of The United Methodist Church takes a stand against juvenile delinquency and works to strengthen prevention programs.

Be it further resolved, that The United Methodist Church, through the appropriate churches, annual conferences, agencies, or coalitions work to prevent juvenile delinquency and treat offenders by:

- updating the Urban and Rural Life Youth Mentoring Guide;
- continuing to develop and distribute peer mentoring guides to local churches;
- continuing to develop and distribute up-to-date information on juvenile delinquency and strategies on how local churches can help prevent juvenile delinquency;
- encouraging local churches to create ministry partnerships with local juvenile justice officials and juvenile justice agencies;
- forming alliances with other international, national, state, and local civic and religious groups that work on juvenile justice issues; and
- encouraging conference council on youth ministries or other similar boards to create ministry teams and/or programs for their peers.

ADOPTED 2000

See Social Principles, ¶ 164F.

255. In Opposition to Capital Punishment

The United Methodist Church declares its opposition to the retention and use of capital punishment and urges its abolition. In spite of a common assumption to the contrary, "an eye for an eye and a tooth for a tooth," does not give justification for the imposing of the penalty of death. Jesus explicitly repudiated retaliation (Matthew 5:38-39), and the Talmud denies its literal meaning and holds that it refers to financial indemnities.

Christ came among us and suffered death. Christ also rose to new life for the sake of all. His suffering, death, and resurrection brought a new dimension to human life, the possibility of reconciliation with God through repentance. This gift is offered to all without exception, and human life was given new dignity and sacredness through it. The death penalty, however, denies Christ's power to transform and restore all human beings. In the New Testament, when a woman having committed a crime was brought before Jesus, He persisted in questioning her accusers, so that they walked away (John 8:1-11).

The Social Principles of The United Methodist Church condemn ". . . torture of persons by governments for any purpose," (¶ 164A) and assert that it violates Christian teachings. The church, through its Social Principles, further declares, "we oppose capital punishment and urge its elimination from all criminal codes" (¶ 164A).

During the 1970s and 1980s a rapidly rising rate of violent crime and an even greater increase in the fear of crime generated support in some countries and within the American society, for the institution of death as the punishment for certain forms of homicide. It continues to be wrongly asserted, that capital punishment uniquely deters criminals and protects law-abiding citizens from violent crime.

Studies conducted over more than sixty years have overwhelmingly failed to support the thesis that capital punishment deters homicide more effectively than does imprisonment. Careful comparisons of homicide rates in similar states with and without use of the death penalty have revealed that homicide rates remained the same or slightly greater regardless of the use of the death penalty in those states. Governments that have enacted the death penalty continue to have higher civilian murder rates that those that do not. The five countries with the highest homicide rates that do not impose the death penalty average 21.6 murders per every 100,000 people, whereas the five countries with the highest homicide rate that do impose the death penalty average 41.6 murders every 100,000 people. The United Methodist Church is deeply concerned with the rate of crime throughout the world, and the value of a life taken by murder or homicide. When another life is taken through capital punishment, the life of the victim is further devalued. Moreover, the church is convinced that the use of the death penalty would result in neither a net reduction of crime nor a lessening of the particular kinds of crime against which it was directed.

In the 1980s and 1990s, the use of the death penalty in the United States reached almost unprecedented proportions. The rate of homicide, the crime for which the death penalty has been used almost exclusively, increased very little during the 1980s and declined during the 1990s. As United Methodist Christians, part of our mission is to give attention to the improvement of the total criminal justice system and to the elimination of social conditions which breed crime and cause disorder, rather than foster a false confidence in the effectiveness of the death penalty.

Sixty-seven percent of law enforcement officials do not think capital punishment decreases the rate of homicide. A poll of police chiefs found that they ranked the death penalty least effective in reducing violent crime.

In 1993, the U.S. Supreme Court ruled that executing an innocent person was not "cruel and unusual" if all the proper and legal procedures were followed. The court thus does not have to reopen a case if new evidence, exonerating the defendant, comes to light after a legally established deadline for new information. Between 1972 and 1999 more than seventy people have been released from death row as a result of being wrongly convicted. On average, for every seven people executed, one person under a death sentence is found innocent.

The United States is the world leader in sentencing children to death. Since 1990 only Iran, Pakistan, Yemen, Saudi Arabia, Nigeria and the U.S. are known to have executed persons for crimes they committed as children. Of these, the U.S. has executed more juvenile offenders than any other nation. This practice has been condemned in nearly every major human rights treaty. Canada, Italy, and South Africa are among the many countries that abolished the death penalty in the 20th century.

The death penalty falls unfairly and unequally upon marginalized persons including the poor, the uneducated, ethnic and religious minorities, and persons with mental and emotional illnesses. In the United States, persons who receive the death penalty are usually convicted of killing middle or upper class white persons, are almost always poor and unable to afford a lawyer, and often suffer from brain damage associated with previous head injuries, often in childhood. In the U.S. methods for selecting the few persons sentenced to die from among the large number who are sentenced for comparable offenses are entirely arbitrary. What warrants the death penalty and what sentencing options are available vary among the few countries that impose capital punishment and even among the states in the United States.

The United States Supreme Court, in *Gregg v. Georgia* (1976), in permitting use of the death penalty, conceded the lack of evidence that it reduced violent crime, but permitted its use for purpose of sheer retribution.

The United Methodist Church cannot accept retribution or social vengeance as a reason for taking human life. It violates our deepest belief in God as the Creator and the Redeemer of humankind. In this respect, there can be no assertion that human life can be taken humanely by the state. Indeed, in the long run, the use of the death penalty by the state will increase the acceptance of revenge in our society and will give official sanction to a climate of violence.

Therefore, we call upon United Methodists individually, at the district and conference level and through general boards and agencies to:

- work in collaboration with other ecumenical and abolitionist groups for the abolition of the death penalty in those states which currently have capital punishment statutes, and against efforts to reinstate such statutes in those which do not;
- speak out against the death penalty to state governors, state and federal representatives;
- develop education materials on capital punishment; and
- oppose all executions through prayer and vigils.

ADOPTED 2000

See Social Principles, ¶ 164*A*.

256. Prisons and Criminal Justice

Today the United States has 1.8 million people behind bars—more people than any other country in the world—perhaps half a million more than China. One out of every 100 adult males in the USA is behind bars. The inmate population is growing by 50,000 to 80,000 per year. Prison construction is booming and a new "prison industrial complex" now costs taxpayers $35 billion a year. All this despite the fact that since 1991 the rate of violent crime in the U.S. has fallen by about 20 percent, while the number of people in prison or jail has risen by 50 percent.

Viewed through a racial lens, the statistics are even more disturbing. About half the inmates in the U.S. are African-American; one out of every 14 black men is now in prison or jail. One out of every four is likely to be imprisoned at some point during his lifetime. While women still comprise a distinct minority of those in prison, the number of women sentenced to 1 year or more of prison has grown twelve-fold since 1970. Seventy percent of women now in prison are nonviolent offenders. Prisons have ceased to be places of rehabilitation and have become rather human warehouses. "All across this country new cellblocks rise. And every one of them, every brand new prison, becomes another lasting monument, concrete and ringed with deadly razor wire, to the fear and greed and political cowardice that now pervade American society" (Eric Schlosser in the December 1998 issue of the *Atlantic Monthly*, the source for much of the above information).

The prison system in the U.S.A. is oppressive, racist and a major contributing cause of crime and poverty. Recent trends toward privatizing prisons have raised the specter of prisons operated not for rehabilitation but only to maximize profit for shareholders, with all the possibilities of overcrowding, harsh conditions, and denial of basic necessities that such a motivation encourages. In addition, many prisons are now contracting convict labor to public agencies and private corporations at substandard wages and working conditions, often resulting in a loss of jobs in the general economy.

The prison industrial complex includes some of the nation's largest architecture and construction firms, Wall Street investment banks, and companies that sell everything from security cameras to padded cells.

The increasing use of the death penalty compounds the racism already inherent in a criminal justice system in which adequate representation is often dependent on the wealth of the accused. The abolition in many states of college programs and work release eviscerates efforts at rehabilitation and increasingly restrictive parole policies deny parole to those inmates who have been rehabilitated. The whole emphasis in the prison system has moved away from rehabilitation to custody and punishment.

The prison system of his time was one of Mr. Wesley's primary concerns and has remained a concern of the people called Methodist into this century. The prison system in the U.S. today cries out for a major church-wide emphasis. The General Board of Global Ministries is already planning a major program in this area.

The Humanity of the Imprisoned

We call for a renewed emphasis on ¶ 164F of the Social Principles: "In the love of Christ, who came to save those who are lost and vulnerable, we urge the creation of genuinely new systems for the care and support of the victims of crime and for rehabilitation that will restore, preserve, and nurture the humanity of the imprisoned. For the same reason, we oppose capital punishment and urge its elimination from all criminal codes."

Policy

We call for:
- a renewed churchwide focus on removing the death penalty;
- opposition to privatization of prisons;
- incarceration within reasonable proximity of the place of conviction to promote visitation;
- support for programs of rehabilitation: parole, college programs, drug programs, work release, conjugal and family visits, and offense related counseling programs;
- improved prison conditions to eliminate overcrowding and provide recreational opportunities;
- restoration of voting rights to ex-offenders.

Evangelization

For John Wesley, visiting those who were sick and in prison was an essential element of the Christian life. The prison population in the U.S. today is the most isolated, alienated and forgotten segment of our population, and it is growing even as crime rates decrease. There is no greater mission field in the United States than the prison system. We call on the General Conference to establish a comprehensive initiative to encourage and assist local congregations to reach out to those in prison. Goals of such an emphasis should include:

1. Ten percent of the churches in each annual conference with programs of prison visitation on a regular basis. These programs should focus first on establishing relationships with inmates without regard

to their religious affiliation and only then on programs of bible study and worship for those who wish them. Wesley visited the imprisoned both for his own spiritual well being and to work for the spiritual and material well being of those in prison.

2. Encouraging churches with primarily white congregations to link up with ethnic churches to do prison ministry together, especially in areas where the prison population is predominantly ethnic.

3. Assisting men and women coming out of prison to find housing and employment and in making the adjustment to society on the outside. This might include receiving inmates on release into local congregations.

4. Formation of a Prison Missional Task Force in each annual conference with the mission of studying the prison system in their state. These task forces shall make prison visits and meet with correctional administrators and former inmates and prepare recommendations for the amelioration of prison conditions where indicated. They shall address such issues as resources for parenting of children of incarcerated persons, transportation needs of families of prisoners.

5. Identifying former inmates with special skills to act as consultants to the Prison Missional Task Force and where appropriate, to local church prison ministries.

6. Linking death row inmates with UM congregations for visitation and prayer.

7. Support the Karios and Epiphany movements within Emmaus communities as they minister to youth and adults placed in prisons or detention centers. The Racial Justice Interagency Task Force shall assist in the development of the prison emphasis.

ADOPTED 2000

See Social Principles, ¶ 164F.

257. Prison Industrial Complex

There are a number of penal systems in the United States which take upon themselves the job of confinement or supervision of persons charged with, or convicted of crimes. For the most part, these systems are capable neither of rehabilitating criminals nor of protecting society, much less restoring crime victims. They are, in fact, institutions where persons are further conditioned in criminal conduct and where advanced skills in crime are taught. More often than not, penal institutions have created more crime rather than deterred criminals. They represent an indescribable failure and have been subjected to gross neglect by the rest of society and by the church. They do not deserve the designation of correctional institutions, for they correct nothing for the crime victim, the offender, or the community.

Despite their massive failure, prisons and jails and the numbers of persons confined within them are growing rapidly in the United States, leading some to speak of a "Prison Industrial Complex." This concept refers to the extent to which corporate interests and the profit motive—not concerns of public safety, equal justice, offender rehabilitation, or victim restoration—are increasingly driving and determining criminal justice policy in the United States.

Private Prisons

International attention has been given to the long and rapid rise in the United States prison population over the last 25 years. The United States imprisons a higher proportion of its people than all but one other country in the world, Russia. Incarceration has become a very expensive growth industry in the United States.

This industry of warehousing people has presented a temptation to those who would profit from the punishment of human beings, leading to perhaps the most ominous illustration of the prison industrial complex at work: the privatization of prison operation and/or ownership. Sometimes governments contract with corporations to operate prisons. A recent trend is for private corporations to design, build, and own prisons to be privately operated and to house prisoners from anywhere in the United States or its territories. Often this takes the form of companies' building prisons on spec, or as speculation, assuming that prisoners will be found, somewhere, to fill their beds.

There is a long history in the United States especially in the South, of exploitation of prison labor through the convict lease system and other arrangements whereby private industry has been allowed to have control over prisoners' lives. The 13th Amendment to the United States Constitution allows for legal exploitation of prisoners. Today, private prison entrepreneurs seek areas which have a surplus of prisoners and areas of high unemployment which often welcome prisons as a new form of economic development. Typically, this means that it tends to be the poor and ethnic minorities who find their labor, their spirits, and their lives exploited, whether as the keepers or as the kept.

Private prison companies typically are paid on a per-capita and per-diem basis. Therefore they have little incentive to rehabilitate prisoners or to prevent recidivism. Indeed, it is in their economic interest to have more crime, more incarceration, and more recidivism, all of which lead to more profits. The logic of the profit motive is to cut costs. In privately operated prisons, this is usually achieved by cutting staff, payroll, benefits, supplies, security, and rehabilitation programming for prisoners. Such cuts lead to a decreased sense of professionalism and a higher rate of turnover among employees, greater hopelessness and bitterness among prisoners, and greater threats to the safety of staff, prisoners, and the general public, especially in the local community.

Many states where private prisons are now operating have no laws regulating their operations (including health, safety, security, legal access for prisoners, and disciplinary policies). Many private prisons are under no obligation to ensure access to information about prisoners held in them or how they are classified, and often regard this as proprietary information. Private prisons hurt local and state economies. Contracting out operations exports taxpayer monies from local communities to corporations often headquartered out of state. For existing prisons, communities lose public sector jobs with family-supporting wages and benefits, and civil service job security. Local communities which provide supplies, services, or equipment to government agencies lose out when a large contractor, usually based out of state, wins a contract to operate a former government facility. Finally, when private prisons contract out bed space to prisoners from distant states, it makes it more difficult for families, friends, ministers, attorneys, and advocates to visit them for support, or counsel. This also increases their chances of recidivism when they are released.

Our Lord began his ministry by declaring "release to the captives . . ." (Luke 4:18, NRSV), and he distinguished those who would receive a blessing at the Last Judgment by saying, "I was in prison and you visited me." (Matthew 25:36b, NRSV). Jesus also declared that one cannot serve two masters and condemned the idolatry of mammon, or wealth (Luke 16:13).

Christians, therefore, must have a special concern for those who are captive in any way, especially for those who are imprisoned, and for the human conditions under which persons are incarcerated. Individual Christians and churches must also oppose those policies and practices which reflect greater allegiance to the profit motive than to public safety and to restorative justice for offenders, crime victims, and local communities.

Therefore, The United Methodist Church declares its opposition to the privatization of prisons and jails and to profit making from the punishment of human beings.

ADOPTED 2000

See Social Principles, ¶ 164F.

258. Mission Plan for Restorative Justice Ministries

I. Biblical/Theological Grounding

> The words of Micah ring out clearly, setting the tone for justice ministries in the church: "He has told you, O Mortal, what is good; and what does the Lord require of you but to do justice, and to love kindness, and to walk humbly with your God?"
>
> (Micah 6:8)

Justice is the basic principle upon which God's creation has been established. It is an integral and uncompromising part in God's redemptive process, which assures wholeness. Compassion is characterized by sensitivity to God's justice and, therefore, sensitivity to God's people.

The gospel, through the example of Jesus Christ, conveys the message for Christians to be healers, peacemakers, and reconcilers when faced with brokenness, violence, and vengeance. Through love, caring and forgiveness, Jesus Christ is able to transform lives and restore dignity and purpose in those who are willing to abide by his principle.

Jesus was concerned about victims of crime. In the story of the Good Samaritan, Jesus explored the responsibility we have for those who have been victimized: " 'Which of these three, do you think, was neighbor to the man who fell into the hands of the robbers?' He said,

654

'The one who showed him mercy.' Jesus said to him, 'Go and do likewise'" (Luke 10:36-37).

Jesus was concerned about offenders, those who victimize others. He rejected vengeance and retribution as the model of justice to being used for relating to offenders: "You have heard that it was said, 'An eye for an eye and a tooth for a tooth.' But I say to you, Do not resist an evildoer. But if anyone strikes you on the right cheek, turn the other also; . . . " (Matthew 5:38ff). Jesus also indicated the responsibility Christians have for offenders: "I was sick and you took care of me. I was in prison and you visited me . . . Truly I tell you, just as you did it to one of the least of these . . . you did it to me" (Matthew 25:36, 40).

The apostle Paul believed that this biblical concept of justice which was reflected in the life of Christ was a primary molder of Christian community and responsibility: "All this is from God, who reconciled us to himself through Christ, and has given us the ministry of reconciliation; that is, in Christ God was reconciling the world to himself, not counting their trespasses against them, and entrusting the message of reconciliation to us" (2 Corinthians 5:18-19).

While acknowledging that the biblical concept of justice focuses on the victim, the offender, and the community in the hope of restoring all to a sense of God's wholeness, it is also important to understand that our Methodist heritage is rich with examples of ministries carried out in jails and prisons. John Wesley (and others in his inner circle, including a brother, Charles) had a passion for those in prison. As early as 1778, the Methodist Conference adopted action making it the duty of every Methodist preacher to minister to those who were incarcerated. United Methodists have reaffirmed and expanded the mandate for prison ministry and reform in many different chapters of our denominational history. This is a part of our identity and call.

Criminal justice in our world rarely focuses on the biblical initiatives of restoration, mercy, wholeness, and shalom. Out of a desire to punish rather than restore, governments around the world have made retribution the heart of their criminal justice systems, believing that this will deter crime and violence. The statistics indicate the colossal failure of retributive justice. Therefore, we call on the church to embrace the biblical concept of restorative justice as a hopeful alternative to our present criminal justice codes. Restorative justice focuses on the victim, the offender, and the community in the desire to bring healing and wholeness to all.

II. Our Current Criminal Justice System: A Retributive Justice System

A. Victims

When crime is defined as the breaking of a law, the state (rather than the victim) is posited as the primary victim. Criminal justice, as we know it, focuses little or no attention on the needs of the victim. Legal proceedings inadvertently cause crime victims, including loved ones, to experience shock and a sense of helplessness which is further exacerbated by financial loss, spiritual or emotional trauma and, often, a lack of support and direction. Many victims feel frustrated because, in most cases, there seems to be little or no provision for them to be heard or to be notified of court proceedings. Victims, moreover, are seldom given the opportunity to meet with their offenders, face to face, in order to personally resolve their conflicts and to move toward healing, authentic reconciliation, and closure.

B. Offenders

Our criminal justice systems around the world have become increasingly based on retribution. Although it is often cloaked or justified in the language of accountability, this focus on punishment has resulted in massive increases in the number of incarcerated persons across the globe. In the United States, for example, the prison population doubled between 1990 and 2000, even as the crime rate decreased during this period. Because prisons are often places where dehumanizing conditions reinforce negative behavior, present criminal justice systems actually perpetuate a cycle of violence, crime, and incarceration, especially among those whose race, appearance, lifestyle, economic conditions, or beliefs differ from those in authority.

Incarceration is costly. In the United States, the cost of incarcerating someone for a year ranges between $15,000 and $30,000. Citizens are, therefore, paying billions of dollars for the support of systems that consistently engender a grossly dehumanizing experience characterized by the loss of freedom, the loss of contact with family and friends, the loss of self-determination, the loss of education, the loss of adequate medical care, and the loss of religious freedom and opportunities for spiritual growth.

C. Community

Criminal justice, as we know it, is retributive justice. It is consumed with blame and pain. It is a system of retribution that pays little or no consideration to the root causes of criminal behavior. It does not aim at solutions that will benefit the whole community by helping the community to repair the breach and often fails to come to terms with the social conditions that breed crime. Retributive justice permanently stigmatizes the offender for past actions, thereby creating such a sense of alienation from the community that social reintegration is virtually impossible. An offender who is held in exile away from the community cannot be held accountable to the community for his or her wrongdoing. An ex-offender who is ostracized and kept in exile after paying his or her debt to society is further violated. He or she is stripped of the opportunity to fully understand the consequences of the crime committed, to make restitution to the victim, to be reconciled with the community, or to heal and become a viable member of the community.

III. Our Vision of Restorative Justice

The gospel, through the example of Jesus Christ, conveys the message for Christians to be healers, peacemakers, and reconcilers when faced with brokenness, violence, and vengeance. The concept of restorative justice shows us specific ways by which to transform lives and effect healing.

Restorative justice asks: Who has been hurt? What are their needs? Whose obligations are they?

We label the person who has been hurt "the victim." But the victim is essentially a survivor who need not remain a victim for his or her entire life. The victim needs healing and emotional support. Victims (survivors) want people to recognize the trauma they have endured and how this trauma has affected their lives and the lives of their loved ones. Often survivors/victims need counseling, assistance, compensation, information, and services. Victims/survivors need to participate in their own healing. They may need reparations from the offender, or the victim may want to meet the offender and have input during the trial, sentencing, and rehabilitation process.

During the healing process, the victim often asks: Why me? What kind of person could do such a thing? Therefore, they may want to meet their offender to receive answers to such questions. Victims deserve to have these questions answered and to hear that the offender is truly sorry.

Victims suffer real pain; however, encouraging vengeance does not heal pain. The community needs to aid in the recovery of the victim. The community can help the victim by not ostracizing him or her, by learning how to accept him or her as a person and not just a victim.

Offenders are harmed as well. An offender is harmed by being labeled for life as an offender. One or more bad decision or action sometimes measures the total of an offender's life. Offenders are further harmed when they are denied the opportunity to make amends, to have respectful interaction with others, and to develop healthy social skills before, during, or after incarceration. Often young offenders do not have constructive guidance or a good role model in the community. Sometimes they need treatment for a disorder, life skills development, or mentoring with clear and achievable expectations of heightened self-awareness and accountability.

The victim and the community need to identify ways the offender can remedy hurt and harm caused. The offender needs to understand how his or her behavior affected others, and acknowledge that the behavior was indeed harmful. The offender needs to be transformed into a contributing citizen of the community with a system of limits and support.

Crime hurts the community. When crime occurs, the neighborhood is disrupted; people become more isolated, fearful, distrusting, and uninterested in the community. Restorative justice helps to release the community members from their fear of crime; it empowers them with the knowledge that circumstances are not out of their control. The community needs to express pain and anger to the one or ones who caused the harm. However, we need to take one step further by helping in the healing process. We need to understand and address the causes of crime to prevent future occurrences. The victim, community, and offender (when possible) need to help others who face similar struggles.

Restorative justice opens the opportunities for personal and community transformation. This transformation cannot be mapped, planned, or put into a program or structure. Nevertheless, it can be encouraged and nurtured.

United Methodists have the will, the vision, the opportunity and the responsibility to be advocates for systemic change. We are called to minister with all parties affected by crime: the victim, the offender, and the community.

Expectations are high for the faith community to lead the way in practicing restorative justice. We need to own and advocate a vision for restorative justice. We need to be supportive to members of the congregation who are victims, offenders, and their families, and especially to those who work toward restoration in the criminal justice system.

The church must initiate models of restorative justice with service providers, policy makers, and law enforcement. We need to work in partnership with the criminal justice system to make it more open, accessible, humane, effective, rehabilitative, and less costly. We need to see our own capacity in community breakdowns and in the racism and classism present in the enactment and enforcement of criminal law. We must also advocate for social and economic justice to see the restoration and strengthening of our communities.

IV. A Call to Action

As United Methodists we are called to:
- repent of the sin we have committed that has fostered retributive justice;
- speak prophetically and consistently against dehumanization in the criminal justice system;
- establish restorative justice as the theological ground for ministries in The United Methodist Church and build bridges of collaboration and cooperation to advance the practice of restorative justice with boards and agencies within The United Methodist Church, with United Methodist and other Methodist communions around the globe, with other faith communities in the United States and worldwide, and with nonprofit organizations and/or governmental organizations; and
- intensify our redemptive ministries with those who work within criminal justice, victims of crime and their families, those who are incarcerated in jails and prisons and their families, and communities traumatized by crime.

1. At the General Church Level:
Restorative Justice Ministries Committee:

Continue and expand the work of The United Methodist Church's Restorative Justice Ministries through the Restorative Justice Ministries Committee, which serves as the global coordinating committee for criminal justice and mercy ministries mandated by the 1996 General Conference of The United Methodist Church. The members should include:

- two bishops named by the Council of Bishops, attending with funds from the Episcopal Fund;
- one elected board member and one staff person (responsible for Restorative Justice Ministries within the named agency) from each of the General Board of Global Ministries, the General Board of Church and Society, the General Board of Discipleship, the General Board of Higher Education and Ministry, the General Council on Ministries and the General Commission on Religion and Race—all to be selected and funded by their respective agencies;
- one member from United Methodist Women and one member from United Methodist Men—each selected and funded by their respective agency; and
- up to seven members-at-large selected by the Council of Bishops in order to ensure that the committee as a whole reflects the varied constituency of the church by gender, age, laity, and clergy; and that the committee have persons who can contribute to Restorative Justice Ministries.

Fulfill these specific functions:

- Provide a biblical/theological basis for a restorative justice approach to criminal justice.
- Be a center for resourcing, teaching, learning, and networking.
- Work collegially with other groups and organizations whether they are inside or outside the denomination, religious or secular, by finding common ground to bring about systemic change in the spirit of mediation (even when there is disagreement about theological rationale).
- Coordinate the training, networking, and advocacy for Restorative Justice Ministries of The United Methodist Church by working with jurisdictions, annual conferences, central conferences, districts, local United Methodist churches and their communities.

- Serve as the primary advocate and interpreter of Restorative Justice Ministries.
- Identify and expand critical models and facilitate the development of Restorative Justice Ministries, on a global basis, at all levels of The United Methodist Church.

2. Specific General Church Agencies:

As The United Methodist Church moves into the 2005-2008 quadrennium, we reaffirm the 1996 and 2000 General Conference mandate which led to a program of Restorative Justice Ministries and recommend that the church continue to support and strengthen its commitment. We recommend the following:

- that the Restorative Justice Ministries Committee continue to give guidance and oversight to the operation of the Restorative Justice Ministries with each board/agency providing the funds to continue the work of Restorative Ministries as outlined below;
- that the General Board of Global Ministries provide resources to annual and central conferences to enable them to develop Restorative Justice Ministries with victims, offenders, prisoners, their families, and communities;
- that the General Board of Global Ministries provide funding to enable the assignment of missionaries, including youth and young adults, to serve in restorative justice ministries with victims, offenders, prisoners, and communities;
- that the General Board of Global Ministries provide funding to support gatherings of United Methodists working in the fields of criminal justice, community corrections, and restorative justice. The events will be focused on the relationship between faith and work;
- that the General Board of Global Ministries provide funding to organize global consultations on restorative justice to be held in central conferences, bringing together United Methodist leaders from across the globe who are using restorative justice ministry strategies and techniques to transform and resolve social, political, religious, economic, racial, and ethnic conflicts and end violence within their churches and communities;
- that the General Board of Global Ministries work with annual and central conferences and their ecumenical, interfaith, and community partners to develop victim offender reconciliation

programs and neighborhood conflict resolution programs based on restorative justice ministries models to serve the church and community;

- that the General Board of Global Ministries, in consultation with annual and central conferences, continue to organize training events in restorative justice ministries;
- that the General Board of Global Ministries continue to work to evaluate and identify model programs of restorative justice ministries and develop the network for these ministries;
- that the General Board of Global Ministries work with the boards and agencies to develop written resources to assist the church in their work in these ministries;
- that the General Board of Global Ministries work with the DISCIPLE Bible Study Ministries in order to increase the involvement of annual conferences and local congregations in ministries with prisoners, ex-offenders and juvenile offenders;
- that the General Board of Global Ministries develop a group of United Methodist trained mediators who can respond to conflicts in the community and who can assist in training other United Methodists to serve as mediators in their communities;
- that the General Board of Global Ministries develop electronic resources and a quarterly newsletter to provide information and updates on new developments in restorative justice ministries around the world to serve The United Methodist Church;
- that the General Board of Church and Society intensify their advocacy for social and economic justice in order to restore and strengthen communities;
- that the General Board of Church and Society continue to advocate for a criminal justice system that is not racist, less costly, more humane, effectively rehabilitative and accessible to family members of victims and offenders;
- that the General Board of Church and Society provide training and resourcing to annual and central conferences and local churches that intend to advocate for a more just system of justice;
- that the General Board of Church and Society intensify its advocacy for the abolition of the death penalty throughout the world;

- that the General Board of Discipleship work to develop print and training resources, including Sunday school resources, for local churches to use as they embrace restorative justice ministries. This directive includes: the development of resources and training for reconciling parents and youth offenders; the development of small group resources that support victim and offender reconciliation; and the provision of material for small groups that wish to explore restorative justice issues within the local church;
- that the General Board of Discipleship work to explore the development of a training and certification process for laity and local church pastors carrying out restorative justice ministries;
- that the General Board of Higher Education and Ministry continue to provide certification for chaplains and explore the development of certification for others interested in professional ministry with restorative justice ministries;
- that the General Board of Higher Education and Ministry work with United Methodist seminaries to promote curriculum and practicum offerings in those seminaries in areas of violence, crime, and criminal justice from a restorative justice perspective;
- that United Methodist Women continue to start units within jails and prisons to promote restorative justice;
- that United Methodist Women continue ministries with families of prisoners;
- that United Methodist Men work jointly with the General Board of Church and Society to resource UMM to become involved in the various aspects of Restorative Justice; and
- that United Methodist Women and United Methodist Men consider working with DISCIPLE Bible Study Ministries, KAIROS, and other Bible studies/retreats to start units of Christian disciple making with prisoners, ex-offenders and juvenile offenders.

3. At Jurisdictional/Central Conference and Annual Conference Levels:

- Support jurisdictional/central conference and annual conference networking as modeled by the Southeastern Jurisdiction's and South Central Jurisdiction's Restorative Justice Network Group, or bring together clusters of contiguous conferences or expedite processes of training and resource sharing.

- Encourage conferences to establish inter-agency restorative justice task forces to coordinate Restorative Justice Ministries within their bounds, with special emphasis on partnership with the Restorative Justice Ministries Inter-agency Task Force and the facilitation and resourcing of local church ministries.

4. At the Local Level:

- Encourage local congregations to provide adult and youth education programs on restorative justice: theory, practice, issues, models, and use of resources (utilizing curriculum resources, printed and audiovisual, provided through the above-mentioned connectional sources).
- Encourage congregations to provide safe space to enable people to share real experiences of victimization, incarceration, or other direct encounters with the criminal justice system and/or restorative justice processes.
- Encourage congregations to schedule a "Restorative Justice Ministries Sunday" to generate deeper awareness by the entire congregation regarding the contrasting paradigms of retributive justice and restorative justice—and their different outcomes.
- Encourage congregations to organize or form direct service and/or advocacy efforts to support the work of restorative justice.
- Work with local ecumenical and/or interfaith agencies and other community agencies to:
  * Convene consultations of representatives of the restorative justice community to define policy/legislative needs and strategies.
  * Encourage/resource congregations to work on restorative justice through regional judicatories and media.
  * Encourage/initiate dialogue with correctional/criminal justice system officials.
  * Identify and nurture criminal justice system leaders (e.g., judges, attorneys, wardens, police, etc.) regarding restorative justice.
  * Involve local congregations in ministries with juvenile detention centers and domestic violence centers.

* Build covenant discipleship groups at the local level for restorative justice advocates, as well as for other persons involved in the criminal justice system.
* Provide victim-offender mediation and other restorative justice processes.
* Identify and develop coalition partnerships with victim assistance groups, advocacy groups, jail and prison ministry groups, ex-offender assistance groups, etc.
* Plan and implement strategies for advocacy that encourage legislative support for restorative justice programs.

ADOPTED 2004

See Social Principles, ¶ 164*A* and *F.*

259. Seek Moratorium on Capital Punishment

WHEREAS, United Methodists value the sanctity of human life, and desire that no human being be executed by capital punishment; and

WHEREAS, 75 innocent persons have been released from death row due to wrongful conviction and imprisonment since 1976, according to the National Conference on Wrongful Convictions and The Death Penalty at Northwestern University Law School; and

WHEREAS, the American Bar Association has called for a moratorium on the death penalty until flaws in the criminal justice system related to capital cases are corrected, so that innocent people are not put to death; and

WHEREAS, thorough investigations and competent experienced capital case lawyers are often not appointed to defend poor defendants in capital cases; and

WHEREAS, highly publicized capital cases seem often to be decided in an emotionally charged atmosphere; and

WHEREAS, DNA evidence was not available when most current death row prisoners were convicted; and

WHEREAS, by October 1, 1998, the work of privately paid lawyers (by those who could afford them), DNA evidence, and legal corrections had exonerated 75 of the over 3,500 people currently on death row in the United States,

Therefore, the General Conference of The United Methodist Church calls upon the government to enact an immediate moratorium on carrying out of the death penalty sentence.

Be it further resolved, that the secretary of the General Conference, the Council of Bishops, and the general secretary of the Board of Church and Society invite the governors and senators from the 50 U.S.A. states and the president, vice president, and major candidates for president of the U.S.A. to take a strong stand for this moratorium.

Be it further resolved, such a request or invitation to government officials should be made within 40 days of the end of the 2000 General Conference and should be publicized in the major newspapers around the world.

ADOPTED 2000

See Social Principles, ¶ 164A.

260. Victims of Crime

In answering the question "Who is my neighbor?" by telling the parable of the Good Samaritan (Luke 10:25-37 NRSV), Jesus formulated a new question, to whom are we a neighbor? In this parable the neighbor was the victim of crime.

Many people become victims of crime. Victims and their families suffer shock and a sense of helplessness. In addition to financial loss, there is a spiritual and emotional trauma and often a lack of support and direction. Many victims feel frustrated because there often seems to be no provision for them to be heard. Their injuries are not redressed, and they are not always notified of the court procedures. This is an area where the church has an opportunity to be a neighbor and to minister with the victims. We often assume victims and offenders are two separate groups of people. It has been noted that offenders are often victims as well. A focus on prevention will break this cycle.

Therefore, we call upon the members of The United Methodist Church to minister with the victims and to be advocates for them. We also call upon the General Conference:

1. to direct the General Board of Church and Society to work for the recognition of the needs and rights of victims and survivors of crime;

2. to support laws at both the federal and state levels whereby offenders make restitution to their crime victims, to work for restorative justice and for the adoption of laws where there are no such provisions;

3. to recognize that the constitutional rights of the victim must be provided. Victims of crime or their lawful representatives, including the next of kin of homicide victims, are entitled to be kept informed during criminal proceedings, to be present at the trial, and to be heard at the sentencing hearing as well as to be given an opportunity to make an impact statement at the time of the parole consideration;

4. to encourage seminaries to develop continuing education programs on this subject;

5. to direct the General Board of Discipleship to develop guidelines, programs, and study materials for pastors and others in providing spiritual support and understanding for victims and families; and

6. to urge all members of The United Methodist Church to initiate prayers, presence, and support for victims and survivors as well as strategies to bring about necessary changes in the criminal justice system and to assure and advocate for the fair treatment of victims and survivors.

ADOPTED 1988
AMENDED AND READOPTED 2000

See Social Principles, ¶ 164F.

EDUCATION

261. Bilingual Education

The United States is a country based on the contributions of different races, ethnic groups, languages, and traditions. The fabric of the U.S. society thus is a mosaic of diversity that has enriched its history and its common life as a nation.

Education has played a very important role in the development of this nation. To have access to it and to receive a sound education are considered inalienable rights of all children. Bilingual education has been and is a critical tool to ensure these rights for non-English-speaking children living now in this country. It has been an instrument of education for children to make the transition from their native tongues to English (without abandoning their native tongues) while at the same time staying at the level correspondent to their age. Bilingual education does work. There are thousands of living examples of bilingual education successes. They are students who learned English in bilingual classrooms and who continue to achieve to the highest of academic and professional standards. Additionally, the overwhelming majority of scientific research studies clearly show that bilingual education is effective. In fact, not only do children in well-designed bilingual programs acquire academic English as well or better than children in English-only programs (Willig, 1985; Cummins, 1989; Krashen, 1996; Greene, 1997), they do much better in academic content subjects such as math and science.

WHEREAS, we believe that these values are part of the trust of this nation; and

WHEREAS, most educators have confirmed that non-English-speaking children benefit from good bilingual programs; and

WHEREAS, the growth of the non-English-speaking population continues to increase through immigration, and it is estimated to be even larger in the next few decades; and

WHEREAS the percentage of Hispanic Latino/adropouts from school is one of the largest in the country, thus challenging the nation to provide resources for this segment of the population more effectively in both elementary and high schools; and

WHEREAS projections of the future envision a larger demand in the fields of mathematics and sciences, precisely where women, Hispanics Latinos/as, African Americans, and Native Americans are currently underrepresented; and

WHEREAS, more intentional efforts must be made to bring children and youth from these groups to the same level as the rest of the student population;

Therefore, be it resolved, that the 2004 General Conference proclaim bilingual education to be an educational program needed for this country that must be not only continued but also strengthened; and

Be it further resolved, that the General Conference affirm in writing to the President of the United States, the United States Congress, and the Department of Education that bilingual education is a right for all children and that by strengthening such a program the nation will in reality be laying the foundations for a better future in this land; and

Be it further resolved, to commend this resolution to all annual conferences for promotion and interpretation, and to ask the General Board of Church and Society to make this resolution an important item in its program and work agenda.

ADOPTED 1992
AMENDED AND READOPTED 2004

See Social Principles, ¶ 164D.

262. Community Life and Public Education

At the heart of the Christian faith is an abiding concern for persons. This concern is evidenced by the Christian's sensitivity to all factors that affect a person's life. In our society, the community has become known as a gathering of people who nurture one another and create an atmosphere for general enhancement. The community should be characterized by good schools, adequate housing, spirit-filled churches, and creative community organizations.

The church has always been interested in communities as arenas where people engage in the common experiences of life. It is in community that men, women, youth, and children discover and enhance their identity. And it is in community that all persons learn to appreciate social, religious, and ethical values.

Communities are undergoing serious changes. Perhaps the most serious of these changes are destructive to the forces that have built communities in the past. Integrated housing patterns are beginning to prevail in many sections all across America. The previous pattern was accentuated by massive flight of white residents to the suburbs and an entrenchment of African Americans in the inner city. This polarization along class and racial lines serves to destroy the idea of a democratic community and has brought into being hostile entities along political, social, economic, and educational lines.

The development of federal and state housing authorities with a democratic pattern for housing development has restored the faith of many that the possibilities of a new community are there. We affirm The United Methodist Church's Statement on Housing.

The Local Church and the Local Public School

In innumerable and concrete ways, the local church serves as interpreter of and witness to the gospel in the life of its community. Therefore, it is the primary channel through which the demands of the gospel are made known in society. By virtue of the nature of the church, there is nothing in the community outside its concern or beyond its ability to affect. This is why we can affirm with John Wesley: "the world is [our] parish."

The church teaches that all are created in the image of God and blessed by the Creator with the gifts of creativity, morality, and reason. In a pluralistic and democratic society, a quality public education system is the best means whereby these gifts can be nurtured and a community of equality, transcending differences of race, ethnic origins, and gender can be built.

Public schools historically represent one of the fundamental focal points in American communities. This is as it should be, because the democratic approach to education is the bedrock of democratic, political, and economic systems. The local public schools also represent one of the largest financial outlays in any given community. In these days, many public school systems have been caught in the whirling social and educational changes of the times and have fallen victim to influences and powers that have not kept the fundamental purposes of the public schools as highest priorities.

Some of the many challenging issues confronting the schools are: financial inadequacies, school vouchers, historic racial attitudes, lack of cultural and language sensitivity, school violence, curriculum, growing professionalism of teachers and administrators, lack of parental involvement and well-informed and sensitive school board members. Many times these issues are combined, making the problems that much more acute.

The issues confronting public schools may be different in the respective communities, as the church is different in its respective communities. Yet by the virtue of its calling, the church must lead the communities in exploring the issues and in identifying and seeking solutions to their particular problems.

In each community, the local United Methodist church is responsible for being a catalyst in helping the entire community become sensitive to the issues of public education.

We believe that our country must again recommit itself to public education and be willing to pay taxes sufficient to develop quality education, and attract and retain quality teachers. We support the continuing education and training of teachers to better prepare them to deal with the cultural diversity of students. Priority should be placed on recruitment of ethnic minorities in a national training plan, for these teachers serve as positive role models and instill cultural pride in minority students. Living within a global society, it is important that our children be bilingual and that this is facilitated through the public school system. Though state and local governments have a primary responsibility for public education, the federal government's responsibility is also to be affirmed. In such areas as racial integration and education for the disadvantaged, the involvement of the federal government is crucial. As the nation seeks to increase excellence in education, it must continue to provide quality education for all. New immigrants, persons with handicapping conditions, poor persons, racial minorities, and women must have equal access to quality education. A democratic and pluralistic society is built on the foundation of commonly shared values such as honesty, truthfulness, fairness, and responsibility. The schools also have the task of teaching the social values of equality amid diversity, civic participation, and justice for all.

We encourage each local church to recognize the importance of the language, culture, history, and important contributions of ethnic minorities to the educational process and the resulting loss when these are omitted from the curriculum. Local churches should take the initiative to be certain that local school boards in their area or communities at every level of education include in the total curricula all contributions of all peoples to the growth and development of the United States.

The lack of opportunities to learn and understand the history and cultures of all ethnic groups and nationalities is reflected in our present problems in human relations.

Our theological tradition of holy living reveals clearly our personal accountability to Almighty God in relation to our personal responsibility to and for our fellow human beings.

Where problems exist, it is especially important that the local United Methodist church support and work with existing community groups and organizations in bringing solutions. It is also recommended that each local United Methodist church develop a committee or an informal group of members to keep the congregation and community aware of public school issues and their obligation to assist in finding meaningful solutions.

The continuation of a democratic and pluralistic society in the United States requires a public education system that produces quality education for every student, so that all might contribute to the building of community. We encourage state government to budget adequately for quality education, with special attention given to low income areas, rather than to tie this important function to risky funding such as lotteries. We urge general boards and agencies to support and work toward legislation that could bring meaningful solutions to the challenges facing public education.

ADOPTED 1976
REVISED AND READOPTED 2000

See Social Principles, ¶ 164D.

263. Public Education and the Church

I. Historic Church Support for Public Education

The United Methodist Church has issued statements supportive of public education, and now at a time when public education has become a political battleground, the church is called to remember, first and foremost, the well-being of all God's children. Education is a right of all children and is affirmed by Scripture which calls us to "train them in the right way" (Proverbs 22:6). Furthermore, the Social Principles affirm that education "can best be fulfilled through public policies that ensure access for all persons to free public elementary and secondary schools and to post-secondary schools of their choice" (¶ 164D).

The public school is the primary route for most children into full participation in our economic, political, and community life. As a consequence of inequities in our society, we have a moral responsibility to support, strengthen, and reform public schools. They have been, and continue to be, both an avenue of opportunity and a major cohesive force in our society, a society becoming daily more diverse racially, culturally, and religiously.

Historically, education has been held to contribute to the development of religious faith. To that end, the great figures of the Reformation called for the establishment of schools. Our founder, John Wesley, was dedicated to the education of poor and underprivileged children. The Sunday School Movement of the latter 18th century was an outgrowth of this ministry and largely established a model for access to public education, regardless of social or economic status. Our heritage should lead us to defend the public schools, and to rejoice that they now more nearly reflect the racial, ethnic, and religious diversity of our country than they have ever done before.

II. The Larger Social Context

We welcome the fact that many public schools now teach about diversity and the role of religion in human life and history; and we applaud the schools' efforts to promote those virtues necessary for good citizenship in a pluralistic democracy. These reforms help to accommodate the constitutional rights of all students and their parents. Just as we encourage schools to ensure that all religions are treated with fairness and respect, so we urge parents and others to refrain from the temptation to use public schools to advance the cause of any one religion or ethnic tradition, whether through curriculum or through efforts to attach religious personnel to the public schools. We believe that parents have the right to select home schooling or private or parochial schools for their children. But with that personal right comes an obligation to support quality public education for all children. The long-range solution is to improve all schools so that families will not be forced to seek other educational alternatives.

At a moment when childhood poverty is shamefully widespread, when many families are under constant stress, and when schools are limited by lack of funds or resources, criticism of the public schools often ignores an essential truth: we cannot improve public schools by concentrating on the schools alone. In this context, we must address with prayerful determination the issues of race and class that threaten both public education and democracy in America.

III. Public Funding Issues

By almost any standard of judgment, the schools our children attend can be described in contradictory terms. Some are academically excellent; others are a virtual disgrace. Some are oases of safety for their students; others are dangerous to student and teacher alike. Some teachers are exceptionally well qualified; others are assigned to areas in which they have little or no expertise. Some school facilities are a fantasy land of modern technology; others are so dilapidated that they impede learning.

The wide disparities among public schools exist largely because schools reflect the affluence and/or the political power of the communities in which they are found. Within virtually every state, there are school districts that lavish on their students three or four times the amount of money spent on other children in the same state. A new phenomenon in our society is "re-segregating of communities" which further diminishes the effectiveness of public schools. Most tellingly, the schools that offer the least to their students are those serving poor children, among which children of color figure disproportionately, as they do in all the shortfalls of our common life. Indeed, the coexistence of neglect of schools and neglect of other aspects of the life of people who are poor makes it clear that no effort to improve education in the United States can ignore the realities of racial and class discrimination in our society as a whole.

We acknowledge the debate over whether public funds might appropriately be used to remedy the lingering effects of racial injustice in our nation's educational system. We do not purport to resolve our differences over this issue, but we do affirm our conviction that public funds should be used for public purposes. We also caution that government aid to primary and secondary religious schools raises constitutional problems and could undermine the private schools' independence and/or compromise their religious message.

IV. What the Church Can Do

Local churches and all communities of faith must become better informed about the needs of the public schools in their communities and in the country as a whole. Only through adequate information can we defend public education and the democratic heritage which it supports. Full knowledge of our religious and democratic traditions helps us ensure that those elected to school boards are strongly committed to both public education and religious liberty.

Therefore, we call upon local churches, annual conferences, and the general agencies of The United Methodist Church to support public education by:

1. establishing partnerships with local public schools such as providing after-school and vacation enrichment programs, adopt-a-school programs, and literacy and reading emphases;

2. monitoring reform efforts in public schools, including the creation of charter and magnet schools, of schools-within-schools, and of classes sized to best serve all children;

3. honoring teachers for the crucial work they do with young People; and advocating for appropriate salaries commensurate with their vital role in society;

4. encouraging young people of our congregations to enter the teaching profession;

5. encouraging school libraries to provide quality materials, including those of religious perspectives, that will broaden students' understanding of human life all over the world;

6. insisting that all curricula present the best textbooks and teaching at all levels acknowledging that we encourage children to read, to imagine, and to understand the many wonders of God's creation;

7. encouraging teaching about religion as an essential dimension in the development of civilization;

8. encouraging teaching basic character and civic virtues such as honesty, truthfulness, and respect for life and property;

9. providing parenting classes to emphasize the special responsibilities of families to schools and school-aged children;

10. encouraging the use of curricula in all schools that reflect the role of the many racial, ethnic, and religious groups in the history and culture of the United States;

11. rejecting racial-and gender-biased curricula and testing which limit career options of children and youth;

12. advocating for quality, age-appropriate, comprehensive health education in the public schools;

13. advocating for the inclusion of differently-abled students in our classrooms, and ensuring that teachers have the special training needed to meet these children's needs;

14. supporting thoughtful reform and innovation in local schools to improve teaching and learning at all levels;

15. advocating at the state and local level for adequate public school funding and equitable distribution of state funds; and supporting efforts to end unjust educational disparities between rich and poor communities;

16. learning about public school issues, offering candidate forums during school board elections, and educating church members about local funding ballot issues and about the historical role of churches in creating and supporting public schools;

17. advocating for strengthened teacher training, for enhanced professional development for teachers and administrators, and for policies that assign teachers only to disciplines in which they are fully prepared, to classes whose size encourages individualized assistance, and to schedules that give teachers time to prepare or consult with other teachers, students, and parents;

18. supporting standards-based school reforms and working in districts and states until the country as a whole has reasonable and challenging standards by which to assess students and schools;

19. encouraging the development of smaller schools (including "schools within schools") to provide a caring environment;

20. calling upon the United States Congress to pass and fully fund legislation to repair and modernize school facilities and to create new facilities as needed;

21. advocating for universal, early, and quality preschool education for all children; and

22. advocating for public education as a basic human right; and not relying solely on school fund raising and state alternative revenues, such as gambling, for financial support.

ADOPTED 2000
AMENDED AND READOPTED 2004

See Social Principles, ¶ 164D.

IMMIGRATION

264. Assistance, Sanctuary, and Deportation Relief for Central American, Caribbean, Salvadorean, and Other Refugees

As Christians we are called by God to show compassion for refugees. The Bible directs us to care for the "foreigners" in our midst (Exodus 23:9, King James Version) and reminds us that we too are "sojourners" (Leviticus 25:23, Revised Standard Version). Jesus and his family had to flee to Egypt to escape persecution (Matthew 2:13-15). We are told in Hebrews 13:2 (RSV), "Do not neglect to show hospitality to strangers for thereby some have entertained angels unawares."

According to the terms of the Refugee Act of 1980, the United States accords refugee or asylum status to persons who cannot return to their countries of origin because of persecution or fear of persecution, for reasons of race, religion, nationality, membership in a particular social group, or political opinion. Refugees from Central America and other areas of Latin America and the Caribbean are fleeing to the United States to escape the persecution, torture, and murder of their civil-war-torn homelands. Many of these refugees have been tortured and murdered when forced to return to their homelands.

We call upon The United Methodist Church to:

1. strongly oppose the deportation of Central American, Caribbean, Salvadorean, and other refugees from the United States; and call on the President of the United States, the United States attorney general, the Department of State, and the Congress to grant "permanent resi-

dent" legal status to Central American, Caribbean, Salvadorean, and other refugees;

2. request that annual conferences and local churches assist in ministries to Central American, Caribbean, Salvadorean, African, and other refugees by providing them with legal assistance, bail bond funds, food, housing, and medical care;

3. encourage congregations to resist the policy of the Immigration and Naturalization Service by declaring their churches as "sanctuaries" for refugees from El Salvador, Guatemala, and other areas of the Caribbean and Latin America; and

4. urge the United States government to follow the United Nations definition of refugees.

ADOPTED 1984
REVISED AND ADOPTED 2000

See Social Principles, ¶ 164A.

265. Immigrants and Refugees: To Love the Sojourner

I. Biblical/Theological Basis

The Bible is full of stories of sojourners, strangers without homes, whom God called people to protect. The Israelites were themselves sojourners for forty years after the exodus from Egypt, as they sought the Promised Land. God did not let the Israelites forget that they had been without a homeland for such a long time; the ethic of welcoming the sojourner was woven into the very fabric of the Israelite confederacy. It was more than an ethic, it was a command of God. "Do not mistreat or oppress a stranger; you know how it feels to be a stranger, because you were sojourners in the land of Egypt" (Exodus 23:9, Revised Standard Version, adapted).

A *sojourn* implies uprootedness; sojourners are uprooted people. At times uprooted people in the Bible were looking for a home, but other times they were not. Often they were telling those who would listen that the real home was a spiritual home-with God providing accompaniment. Sojourners were messengers. The message they sent then as well as today is that the Spirit of God is with each of us as we sojourn through life. We are all on a journey, and God is with us. Such was the message of Moses and many of the prophets; such was the message of John the Baptist, a voice crying in the wilderness; and such was the message of Jesus Christ, whose own life was characterized by uprootedness. The infant Jesus and his family had to flee to Egypt to avoid persecution and death; they became refugees, sojourning in Egypt until they could come home. Jesus was a person on the move. Jesus' ministry occurred throughout the countryside of Judea, and his life was marked by uprootedness: "Foxes have holes, and birds of the air have nests; but the Son of Man has nowhere to lay his head" (Matthew 8:20). Jesus made a point of spending time with the poor, the powerless, the despised and rejected. Jesus did so while spreading the word of God's steadfast love, the same love spoken of in the Book of Hosea: "I will betroth you to me forever; yes, I will betroth you unto me in righteousness and justice, and in loving kindness and mercy" (Hosea 2:19, New King James Version).

Jesus embodied the love of God to the world and modeled how we are to act with love and compassion for the sojourner. In fact, Jesus' most pointed description of how human beings should behave once they are aware of God's love is in the story of the good Samaritan, in which the love of God is expressed through the compassion of a stranger: "But a certain Samaritan, as he journeyed, came where he was: and when he saw him, he had compassion on him, and went to him, and bound up his wounds, pouring in oil and wine, and set him on his own beast, and brought him to an inn, and took care of him" (Luke 10:33-34, King James Version). This is the radical love of God as expressed by Jesus Christ. It transcends race, nationality, and religion and is a love that cries for justice and peace; it is a love that is sorely needed today.

II. Global Uprootedness

We live in a world where there are over 13 million people who are refugees, another 26 million who are internally displaced persons (IDPs), and millions more who seek asylum or are migrants looking to find a way out of poverty. No nation can afford to turn a blind eye toward these realities. People who must flee their land because they have no choice are today's uprooted populations. They are given different labels depending on their circumstances: *refugees*—persons who have been officially recognized by the United Nations as having a well-founded fear of persecution because of their political affiliation, religion, race, nationality, or membership in a particular social group or opinion; *asylum seekers*—those who have left their homeland and are applying for political asylum in the country to which they have fled (in the United States, applying for asylum is a right that can be exercised); *internally displaced*—people who are displaced within the borders of their own lands because of civil strife but who cannot receive the protection of the international community because of the principle of national sovereignty; *economic migrants*—those who flee dire poverty in search of employment and a way to feed their families. No matter what label they are given, they are usually vulnerable people in need of compassion and protection. Most of them are women and children; often, the women are subjected to the brutality of sexual violence.

Many issues emerge from violent conflict. Even when refugees feel they can return home safely, they face immense problems in restarting their lives, including possible injury or death from landmines strewn wantonly during periods of conflict. Refugees now returning to Sri Lanka, Democratic Republic of Congo, Sierra Leone, and Angola, face these horrors, and landmines still remain in parts of Mozambique, Cambodia and Bosnia, even after years of de-mining efforts.

Other issues are political and economical. A potent mix of unstable governments, political and economic injustice, and ethnic and religious strife combine to produce violence, terror, and refugee flight. More people are displaced every day. Uprooted peopled need the protection of the international community in the months and years before they can safely return home.

Nations of the Global South are particularly concerned about the migration of people from rural to urban areas and the loss of young generations of strong leaders to other countries. These people often do not want to migrate; they feel pressured to do so by the promise of education, job opportunities, and economic security for themselves and their families at home. Underlying their need to migrate is an unjust global economic system that drains their countries' resources, and thereby undermines local and national economies. These economic patterns combine with war in some areas and colonialism in others to increase migration.

In Europe, many governments are implementing policies that are designed to prevent asylum seekers from successfully finding refuge within their borders. The recent increase in the number of uprooted persons demonstrates that the international community, including the churches, must focus more attention on understanding and alleviating the causes of forced human uprootedness, as well as responding to the consequences.

Most refugees and IDPs, are temporarily accommodated in stark situations in camps or urban centers, then wait an average of ten years before conditions in their homeland stabilize and permit a safe return. For refugees whose lives are in imminent danger, their last hope is often to seek asylum in North America, Europe, or Australia. Yet these wealthy nations lack the political and moral will to provide safe havens in the face of other demands. Uprootedness is seen by the governments of the industrialized nations as a problem to be dealt with by leaving other countries to solve their own problems or by exercising force, rather than grasping the complex phenomena that need coherent and human solutions on a global scale.

III. Immigration and Asylum in the United States

In the wake of September 11, 2001 (9/11), uprooted people in the United States are not only looked upon as the cause of societal problems, but are often seen also as threats to national security. The effect on asylum seekers arriving in the United States has been to set back hopes for reform of the asylum process. Since 1997, most asylum seekers are detained until their case is adjudicated and they are either granted asylum or deported. They are denied due process and held in conditions as bad or worse than those of convicted felons—conditions which heap further suffering on those who have fled persecution and even torture. Additionally, the response to September 11 was not only a setback for asylum seekers in the United States but seriously damaged the U.S. Refugee Resettlement Program for which refugees are interviewed and approved overseas.

In the four years prior to September 11, the United States accepted an average 70,000 refugees for resettlement each year. Refugees approved for the U.S. program had always been the most thoroughly scrutinized of any persons coming into the United States. No refugee had been involved in the events of September 11, and the lengthy scrutiny involved in entering the U.S. as a refugee would deter any terrorist from attempting that route. Yet it was the Refugee Program—designed to provide refuge to persons who had themselves been victims of terror—that the government targeted with some of its first anti-terrorism measures.

The consequences of these actions were to halt refugee flights through December 2001, stop all refugee interviews for four months, require all refugees to be fingerprinted, impose a maximum number of 35 refugees to a flight, and limit them to four ports of entry (now eight). A new security rule requiring an FBI check for all males from Africa and the Middle East between the ages of 15 and 45 can hold up an entire family for eight months until the member in that category is cleared. By adding to this the simultaneous introduction of an improved procedure for verifying the relationship of refugees joining family already in the U.S., the government developed a protracted process resulting in only 28,000 of the 70,000 possible refugee visa slots being filled in Fiscal Year 2002 and a loss of 40,000 refugee places; these slots do not carry over into the next year.

The commitment of the U.S. to the resettlement of refugees speaks to its concern for the plight of victims of persecution and terror and serves as an example for other nations. Refugees should be the last people to be the target of anti-terrorism policies—yet, since September 11, at least 50,000 refugees have lost a chance to restart their lives in the U.S. A restored generous refugee admissions policy would not jeopardize national security and would add to the benefit of the nation and its relationships with nations across the world.

The reduction in refugee admissions adds urgency the United States and international community, including the churches, to address the causes of uprootedness and endeavor to restore the commitment to the protection of refugees.

Nearly all the citizens of the United States have ancestors who emigrated from other parts of the world. Since the seventeenth century, millions of immigrants have come to the United States, often to seek freedom from religious persecution and broader opportunities in a new land. No other nation has welcomed so many immigrants from so many parts of the world, and no other nation has taken such pride in its immigrant roots. Nevertheless, the history of immigration policy in the United States has been heavily influenced by economic and labor-force needs, as well as by systemic racism. The United States has at times encouraged the presence of immigrants who could provide the cheap hard labor to build canals and railroads, help with the harvesting of crops, and supply industry with needed workers. At other times, however, U.S. laws have systematically excluded immigrants because of racial, ethnic, religious, or other prejudicial reasons. Examples are the Chinese Exclusion Act of 1882, the Immigration Act of 1924, the

Immigration Act of 1965, and the Immigration, Reform, and Control Act of 1986.

The 1980s and early 1990s witnessed an influx of persons seeking asylum in the United States from Central America, including Haiti and Cuba. All of these groups fled a combination of dire poverty, government repression or persecution, and general strife in their homelands. This influx of refugees to the United States was unexpected, and many—particularly the Haitian, Salvadoran, and Guatemalan people—were denied the protection of asylum they so desperately needed. Recent laws enabled many of these people to adjust to permanent residency, although many others are still undocumented.

Since 1996, the United States immigration law and policies have been moving toward greater restriction on immigration and less protection of immigrants' and refugees' rights. Immigrants are singled out for harsh punishment under immigration law for minor and even very old criminal violations. Their eligibility for the social safety net is limited. Immigrants' rights to due process of the law are increasingly being circumscribed by nearly all the branches of government, using tactics ranging from judicial review to detention without bond.

The USA PATRIOT ACT of 2001 mandates the development of a technological system that will ensure the inter-agency sharing of information and tracking and monitoring of foreign visitors' entry and exit. However, it was the then Immigration and Naturalization Service (INS) under the current administration that had shaped and developed policies beyond the expressed mandate of Congress. In the wake of 9/11, the INS increased its use of secret evidence in immigration hearings, citing threats to national security and barring the immigrants from proceedings or access to evidence against them. It instituted a "Special Registration" program, requiring male nationals of certain countries—predominantly Muslim—to register by providing fingerprints and all key information such as addresses, bank accounts, and credit cards. This program has resulted in the arrest and prosecution of many undocumented immigrants, even those with pending applications for immigration benefits.

In another area of policy, the U.S. Attorney General has issued a directive that is resulting in serious abridgement of immigrants' rights to due process. The Board of Immigration Appeals (BIA) has been ordered to clear its backlog of immigration appeals, and it has attempted to do so by increasing the use of one-judge review, instead of a panel of three, and dispensing with opinions supported with analysis, issuing instead one-sentence boilerplate decisions. Coupled with the drastic limitations on judicial review imposed by the 1996 law, this means that immigrants' rights to appeal are severely curtailed. In many of the above instances of legal and policy shifts, the government has cited national security as justification. As history has demonstrated, however, when a measure is adopted which affects a broad base of the population without regard to individual circumstances, and where preservation of national security comes at the cost of human dignity and civil rights, such laws or policies often prove unjustified and unjustifiable in the final analysis. The Japanese internment during WWII and the McCarthy investigations are two prime examples.

In a time when our nation and world is desperate for peace, security, and community, people of faith and good will are needed to encourage leadership at home and abroad and, especially, in our churches; and to have the courage to speak up for the newly vulnerable people put at risk in the rush to provide for our own safety. We must remember that God's household is bigger than our own.

Therefore, we call upon The United Methodist Church, in collaboration with other ecumenical and interdenominational organizations, to urge the government of the United States as well as all other governments:

1. to encourage and support international economic policies that promote sustainable development and that use capital, technology, labor, and land in a manner that gives priority to employment for all people and the production of basic human necessities, thereby reducing migration pressures;

2. to alleviate conditions of uprootedness by working toward the elimination of all forms of warfare and by supporting agrarian reform, social justice, and an adequate measure of economic security for all peoples;

3. to take decisive action to eliminate the sale and international trade in land mines and provide technical assistance to facilitate their removal from lands to which refugees are returning;

4. to withhold all support—military and financial—to governments with a documented recent history of abuses and disregard for human rights, particularly the right of asylum;

5. to provide a fair and generous resettlement policy as one of the ways of ensuring meaningful protection and a durable solution for refugees;

6. to adopt reasonable standards for consideration as refugees for those seeking asylum and to prevent and/or eliminate within the Bureau of Immigration and Customs Enforcement, the Bureau for Customs and Border Control, and the Bureau of Citizenship and Immigrant Services of the Department of Homeland Security all abuses of civil and human rights, including such practices as the violation of due process, denial of bond, detention of noncriminal asylum seekers, and hasty deportation of people who are undocumented or overstayed;

7. to insure that the rights and dignity of all immigrants and foreign visitors are fully respected in all national security measures developed to combat terrorism, and to end Special Registration requirements;

8. to monitor all attempted reforms on immigration and refugee policy and practices in order to ensure fair and adequate process in regard to asylum petitions, judicial review, refugee resettlement priorities, and immigrant categories;

9. to review and reject all legislative measures that propose summary exclusion for *bona fide* asylum seekers, to end the practice of detaining asylum seekers during the asylum process, and to ensure access to counsel and meaningful review of asylum claims by an immigration judge; and

10. to ensure protection of the basic human rights of immigrants and refugees, such as the right to an education, adequate health care, due process and redress of law, protection against social and economic exploitation, the right to a cultural and social identity, and access to the social and economic life of the nation whether in documented or undocumented status.

As people of faith, we are called to do justice, love kindness, and walk humbly with God (Micah 6:8). We must work for justice and peace for all people and envision a world where institutions are transformed into true servants of the people, full of the compassion exemplified by Jesus Christ.

Therefore, in addition to advocating for the above measures, we call upon United Methodist churches and agencies:

1. to support international efforts to promote sustainable development policies designed to alleviate human suffering and counteract some of the root causes of forced migration;

2. to advocate for protection of uprooted women and children against all forms of violence and to call for full legal protection of uprooted children in the midst of armed conflict;

3. to provide assistance for projects of relief to refugees and displaced persons;

4. to provide assistance for projects of economic development for refugees and returnees;

5. to provide sponsorships for refugees through local congregations;

6. to denounce and oppose the rise of xenophobic and racist reactions against newcomers in the United States and elsewhere, and to support any and all efforts to build bridges between people of diverse ethnicities and cultures;

7. to denounce and oppose government policies that use the threat of terror to target people who are in violation of minor immigration regulations, and criminalizes them as threats to national security—actions which amount to racial and ethnic profiling;

8. to continue to work with community-based organizations to provide forums for citizens to voice concerns, educate one another, and confront the problems of racism and xenophobia as obstacles to building community;

9. to work with civic and legal organizations to support communities that are now or will be affected by harsh immigration laws passed since 1996 and the heavy-handed national security measures such as the USA PATRIOT ACT of 2001;

10. to provide pastoral care and crisis intervention to individuals and families who are refugees and asylum seekers; and

11. to speak out, make declarations, and adopt resolutions to condemn and delegitimize violence against foreigners.

We recommend that the General Board of Church and Society and the General Board of Global Ministries:

1. monitor cases of possible human-rights violations in the area of immigration and give guidance to United Methodists in responding to such cases;

2. advocate for human rights (including political, economic, and civil) for all people, and especially for the strangers who sojourn in the land;

3. advocate for repeal of the harsh provisions of the immigration laws and policies passed since 1996;

4. continue explorations of solutions to the problems of asylum seekers and undocumented people;

5. lead United Methodists throughout the United States in the fight against nativism and continue to respond to the current threat against refugees and immigrants;

6. lead the churches throughout the United States and the world in recognizing the contributions newcomers have made that have culturally and economically enriched that nation;

7. provide technical and financial assistance to local churches in active ministry with refugees and asylum seekers;

8. continue the task of educating United Methodists about issues related to refugees, immigrants, and migrants;

9. develop materials to educate churches on immigration and refuge issues as well as encourage churches to be in ministry with refugees and asylum seekers; and

10. assist the churches in advocating for fair and just immigration laws and practices.

ADOPTED 1996
AMENDED AND READOPTED 2000
AMENDED AND READOPTED 2004

See Social Principles, ¶ 164A.

266. Immigrants in the United States:
Ministries of Hospitality, Advocacy, and Justice

Our Christian roots are centered among people who were sojourners in the land. Throughout history, people have been uprooted under conditions similar to that of Mary and Joseph, who were forced to flee to save the life of their son. Most of our own forefathers and foremothers were immigrants to this country. The Bible is clear about how we should treat these wanderers:

> *When strangers sojourn with you in your land, you shall not do them wrong. The strangers who sojourn with you shall be to you as the natives among you, and you shall love them as yourself; for you were strangers in the land of Egypt. . . .* (Leviticus 19:33-34, Revised Standard Version)

Immigrants come to the United States because communities throughout our world are suffering from war, civil conflict, economic hardships, environmental destruction, and persecution for political, religious, ethnic, or social reasons. They come seeking food and shelter-refuge, but instead they are met with closed doors and detention centers fueled by attitudes of racism, fear or hatred of foreigners and hostility. Immigrants with or without legal status are vulnerable to human rights abuses starting with coyotes, or people who provide illegal transportation into the United States to the sub-standard working conditions and low-wages that swell business profits. Often immigrants are forced into prostitution and other forms of illegal work in order to pay their transportation debt.

For these reasons, we stand firmly opposed to state or federal legislative action such as the federal Illegal Immigration Reform and Immigrant Responsibility Act of 1996, California's Proposition 187, or any similar legislation which discriminates against immigrants and that may have the following effects:

- *Public Schools*: Districts are required to verify the legal status of students enrolling for the first time. The status of parents or guardians of students must also be verified.
- *Higher Education*: Undocumented immigrants are barred from community colleges and public institutions of higher learning.
- *Health*: Undocumented immigrants as well as legal immigrants are ineligible for public health services, except for emergency care.
- *Welfare*: Undocumented immigrants as well as legal immigrants are already ineligible for major welfare programs. Most child-welfare and foster-care benefits are also eliminated.
- *Law Enforcement*: Service providers are required to report suspected undocumented immigrants. Law-enforcement agencies must verify the residency status of individuals arrested or suspected of being in the United States illegally. When legal residency cannot be proved, the person will be reported to the United States Immigration and Naturalization Service.

With grace and concern, the church must address the legal, economic, social, and human rights conditions of people who are legal or undocumented immigrants, and it must oppose the introduction of legislation by Congress or any state that would cause human suffering and a denial of such individual's rights as interpreted through our biblical understanding of God's grace to all peoples, but especially to the sojourner. Our faith, grounded in Christ and in the Wesleyan call to work for prophetic justice, calls us to follow our Social Principles and respond in appropriate and direct ways to prevent harm to the sojourner. Jesus teaches us to show special concern for the poor and oppressed who come to our land seeking survival and peace. We call upon United Methodist individuals and churches in the United States and through general boards and agencies throughout The United Methodist Church to do the following: (1) actively oppose anti-immigrant legislative action and support legislative action that protects the poor and oppressed in their quest for survival and peace; (2) urge stringent policing and penalties for coyotes (illegal transporters); (3) urge that humane and fair treatment be extended to all immigrants by business and agricultural groups; (4) advocate human rights (political, economic, and civil) for all people, including the strangers who sojourn in our land; (5) support communities and congregations by prayer and action where anti-immigrant measures are implemented; (6) continue to work with community organizations to provide forums for citizens to voice concerns, educate one another, and confront the problems of racism and fear or hatred of foreigners as obstacles to building community; (7) continue to work with civic and legal organizations to support communities who are now, or will be, affected by the destructive, deteriorating social issues raised by anti-immigrant measures; (8) support the legal needs of immigrants through church-based immigration clinics.

Finally, we call upon United Methodists to practice hospitality and express our commitment to an inclusive church and society through all our ministries in the spirit of our biblical tradition:

Do not oppress an alien; you yourselves know how it feels to be aliens, because you were aliens in Egypt. (Exodus 23:9, New International Version)

ADOPTED 1996
AMENDED AND READOPTED 2000

See Social Principles, ¶ 164A.

267. Civil Rights of Undocumented Workers and Employee Benefits

It is a well known fact that the economy of this country depends on the labor of both documented and undocumented workers. They work in industries such as: agriculture, manufacturing, sweatshops, etc., and their contribution is indispensible. They deserve the right to a safe, secure, just working and living environment. Such a just working environment should include equitable living wages, health care, and other social benefits provided by public and private agencies.

WHEREAS, a great number of Hispano/Latino and other immigrants contribute significantly to the economy of the country and engage in the most difficult jobs; and,

WHEREAS, a great number of Hispano/Latino and other laborers are undocumented and are not paid equitable salaries; and,

WHEREAS, we recognize the work of those Hispano/Latino and other undocumented workers as essential for the economic growth of the nation; and

WHEREAS, the USA PATRIOT ACT has created more fear and unjustly oppresses undocumented workers; and

WHEREAS, we recognize that injustices are committed against Hispano/Latino and other undocumented workers and that it is against God's will;

Be it resolved, that the General Conference requests the General Board of Church and Society to strongly advocate the United States government for the establishment of more just laws to protect and enforce the human and civil rights of undocumented workers.

Be it further resolved, that the General Conference demand, by way of the General Board of Church and Society, that the government require employers provide adequate health care and encourage employers to provide other social benefits provided by public and private agencies.

ADOPTED 2004

See Social Principles, ¶ 164A.

MILITARY SERVICE

268. Support Men and Women in the Military

General Conference honors, supports, and upholds in our prayers those men and women who serve in our armed services and, in addition, honor and support those United Methodist clergy who serve as chaplains.

ADOPTED 2000

See Social Principles, ¶ 164G.

POLITICAL RESPONSIBILITY

269. Campaign Finance Reform in the United States

Campaign finance reform is a moral matter for the religious community. The temptation to buy unjust favors is an ancient one that is addressed often in Scripture. The prophet Amos thundered against those merchants in Israel who "sell the righteous for silver and the needy for a pair of sandals ... and push the afflicted out of the way..." (Amos 2:6-7, NRSV). Psalm 15 defines upright persons as those who "... stand by their oath even to their hurt ... and do not take a bribe against the innocent."

The pouring of tens of millions of dollars into political campaigns in order to buy special influence with legislators has become a scandal. Citizens forsake participation in the political process because they believe policies are shaped by money from special interests—not by the national interest or the needs of the people.

The issue of campaign financing is far more than a political matter. It goes to the heart of the ethical and moral life of a nation.

Many elected officials continually court monied special interests in order to finance their next election campaign. It is time to free electoral politics from this corrupting pressure—through a system of public campaign financing that would take government away from special interests and return it to the people.

If politicians are to focus on the well-being of the people and the nation, they must be able to depend on public financing rather than pursuing special-interest money.

We commend those politicians of all parties who are working to achieve real campaign financing reform.

We call upon all United Methodists to work within their own countries to build support for measures that would end the flood of special-interest monies to political campaigns and restore integrity to decision making.

In 2002, the bipartisan Campaign Reform Act was enacted in the United States. The long-term goal of campaign finance reform is the public financing of campaigns at the national level. The next short-term steps for reform are strengthening the oversight of the Federal Election Commission, changing the presidential public financing system, and establishing a system that will enable federal candidates and parties to air on television and radio stations a limited amount of free advertising. Similar legislation is ongoing in Germany and other countries. Candidates for public office should focus their campaigns on the issues and on their own qualifications to serve in office. They should refrain from personal attacks and name-calling of opponents, not distort an opponent's views by taking quotes out of context or misrepresenting the opponent's positions or voting record, and set an example of truthfulness and integrity for the public. Similar legislation is ongoing in Germany and other countries. See Social Principles, ¶ 164A and B.

ADOPTED 1996
AMENDED AND READOPTED 2004

See Social Principles, ¶ 164A and B.

270. Encouragement to Vote in Elections

WHEREAS, members of The United Methodist Church have a history of being pro-active in all levels of governmental activity; and

WHEREAS, the first sentence of ¶ 164 of the Social Principles states, ". . . we acknowledge the vital function of government as the principal vehicle for the ordering of society"; and

WHEREAS, Resolution # 228 in *The Book of Resolutions of The United Methodist Church, 2000* entitled "Church-Government Relations" presents a broad discussion of the relationship that is or should exist between the church and the government; and

WHEREAS, the decision-making power and administrative leadership of the government is vested primarily in elected officials; and

WHEREAS, in many jurisdictions within the United States there may be propositions, amendments and/or resolutions appearing on the election day ballot; and

Whereas, in some jurisdictions within the United States there is provision for initiative and referendum, the consideration of which may appear on the election day ballot;

Therefore, it is resolved, to urge churches in our global community to encourage their members to take advantage of the opportunities to vote; and

Be it further resolved, those registered voters be encouraged to inform themselves concerning the qualifications of persons running for office and the merit(s) of items requiring decision(s) that are to appear on the election day ballot, and, after thoughtful and prayerful consideration, to vote their choices on the various election days.

ADOPTED 2004

See Social Principles, ¶ 164*A* and *B*.

UNITED STATES LEGISLATIVE ISSUES

271. Enlarge the Cabinet of the President of the United States to Include a Secretary of Peace

The United Methodist Church resolves that the cabinet of the President of the United States be enlarged to include a Secretary of Peace, and that a Peace Academy be established comparable to the Army, Navy, and Air Force academies.

ADOPTED 2000

See Social Principles, ¶ 164.

272. Support for Development of U. S. Department of Peace

WHEREAS, the people of the United States overwhelmingly support peace in the world; and

WHEREAS, the current structure of our government has not been designed to research and advocate new strategies for peace; and

WHEREAS, the Department of Defense consumes an increasingly large portion of our national budget (currently 40 percent of outlays — Friends Committee on National Legislation, March 24, 2003); and

WHEREAS, Congressman Dennis Kucinich (D-OH), Congresswoman Barbara Lee (D-CA) and Congressman John Conyers Jr. (D-MI), and others have advocated for a Department of Peace, and have introduced H.R. 2459 for the establishment of a Department of Peace; and

WHEREAS, the bill defines the mission of the Department of Peace such that it shall: 1) hold peace as an organizing principle, coordinating service to every level of American society; 2) endeavor to promote justice and democratic principles to expand human rights; 3) strengthen nonmilitary means of peacemaking; 4) promote the development of human potential; 5) work to create peace, prevent violence, divert from armed conflict, use field-tested programs, and develop new structures in nonviolent dispute resolution; 6) take a proactive, strategic approach in the development of policies that promote national and international conflict prevention, nonviolent intervention, mediation, peaceful resolution of conflict, and structured mediation of conflict; 7) address matters both domestic and international in scope; and 8) encourage the development of initiatives from local communities, religious groups, and nongovernmental organizations; and

WHEREAS, the Social Principles of The United Methodist Church states that "we deplore war and urge the peaceful settlement of all disputes among nations" (¶ 164G of the *Book of Discipline, 2000*); and

WHEREAS, Jesus taught us that "blessed are the peacemakers," and valued all human life;

Therefore, be it resolved, that The United Methodist Church supports the development of a Department of Peace.

ADOPTED 2004

See Social Principles, ¶ 164B, and *I*.

273. Justice for Filipino WWII Veterans

Filipinos who fought in the Armed Forces of the United States during World War II were American soldiers. On July 26, 1941, President Franklin D. Roosevelt ordered the Army of the Philippine Commonwealth to serve under the American flag and under the command of General Douglas MacArthur. One hundred and forty two thousand Filipino soldiers fought courageously, served faithfully, suffered inhumane treatment and received the wrath of Japanese Imperial Army captors. These Filipino soldiers fought alongside soldiers from the United States in the battles of Bataan and Corregidor and were forced to take part in the Bataan Death March. They delayed and disrupted Japan's effort to conquer the Western Pacific and bought time for the United States to prepare the military to defeat Japan.

President Harry Truman promised veterans' benefits to the Filipinos who had fought in the United States Armed Forces.

However, on February 18, 1946, the United States Congress passed the Rescission Act which denied Filipino WWII veterans any benefits unless they had died in service or had been seriously wounded. Thus, Filipino WWII veterans were singled out not to receive benefits which were given to the French, Canadian and other allied nationals who, like the Filipinos, had served under the U.S. flag. Although President Roosevelt promised American citizenship to the Filipino soldiers who fought in the United States Armed Forces, it was not until 1990 that the U.S. Congress passed a law to allow them to become U.S. citizens.

Today, there are 72,000 surviving Filipino WWII veterans in their 70's and 80's who are still waiting for justice after more than fifty years. Many in the United States live in poverty. Often, four to six veterans share a studio apartment or live in a converted garage without heat during winter. They must continue to work in order to survive, because they don't get veterans' benefits. Although some Filipino WWII veterans living in the U.S. eventually qualify for SSI, those living in the Philippines do not receive any benefits of any kind. A number of Filipino WWII veterans, both living in the United States and in the Philippines, are active members of United Methodist churches. The Filipino WWII veterans are fighting the last battle of their lives, to receive justice and veterans benefits in their lifetime.

The Bible says, "You shall not wrong or oppress a resident alien, for you were aliens in the land of Egypt" (Exodus 22:21) and "You shall not deprive a resident alien or an orphan of justice" (Deuteronomy 24:17). The Social Principles state, "To begin to alleviate poverty, we support such policies as: adequate income maintenance, quality education, decent housing, job training, meaningful employment opportunities, adequate medical and hospital care, . . ." (¶ 163E) which includes, veterans' benefits for those who are entitled to them because of past service to the United States.

Every American deserves to know the important contribution of the Filipino veterans to the outcome of WWII. It is demeaning to Americans as well as to the Filipinos, for the United States to continue denying full benefits pledged by the President of the United States to Filipino WWII veterans. These benefits are not a gift or a favor, they were earned on the battlefield defending the United States.

The United Methodist Church and its members therefore resolve to support the Filipino WWII veterans in their fight for justice and equal benefits, and individual members and churches are urged to: (1) write to their senators and representatives urging them to co-sponsor legislation giving full benefits for Filipino WWII veterans; (2) write the President of the United States at The White House, 1600 Pennsylvania Ave. NW, Washington, DC 20500, urging him to include a budget line item in the budget to fund full veterans benefits for Filipino WWII veterans; (3) contact Filipino WWII veteran-support groups to see how local churches can help indigent veterans who are so sick that they can no longer work to support themselves; and (4) invite Filipino WWII veterans to come and speak of their experiences to groups such as United Methodist Women, United Methodist Men, United Methodist Youth Fellowship, and the United Methodist Young Adult Fellowship.

ADOPTED 2000

See Social Principles, ¶ 164F.

274. Puerto Rican Political Prisoners

WHEREAS, Methodists Associated to Represent the Cause of Hispanic Americans (MARCHA) celebrates the partial victory of the release of eleven Puerto Rican political prisoners; and

WHEREAS, there are six Puerto Rican political prisoners still unjustly incarcerated in federal prisons for terms unrealistic to their alleged crimes,

Therefore, be it resolved, that MARCHA and The United Methodist Church rededicate their efforts to continue the work towards the unconditional freedom and release of the six remaining Puerto Rican political prisoners;

Be it further resolved, that the General Conference 2000 of The United Methodist Church adopt the existing resolution regarding the Puerto Rican political prisoners with this amendment.

These men and women received sentences that are excessive and geared toward punishing political activity more than the stated crimes and for refusing to participate in the U.S. judicial system process based on their own conscientious objection. A total of thirty Puerto Rican prisoners refused to participate in the U.S. court system because of their belief that the U.S. government was the colonial and enemy power. They requested a war court trial and were denied. Some of these thirty have served their sentences; others were let go because no valid case could be brought against them.

The United Nations' resolutions on decolonization have clearly established that colonialism is a crime, and they recognize a colonized people's right to end colonialism. The United Nations also recognizes that these resolutions and laws apply to Puerto Rico. For many years, the United Nations Decolonization Committee has approved resolutions recognizing the inalienable right of Puerto Rico's people to independence and self-determination. The injustice suffered under Puerto Rico's colonial reality cannot be overlooked. President Bush admitted that the people of Puerto Rico have never been consulted as equals on their political status.

The call for the release of these prisoners enjoys wide support in the U.S., Puerto Rico, and internationally. Many civic, religious, and international organizations have also joined in the effort.

We, as Christians, have been called to identify with the prisoners and their needs. We have been called to bring justice to them when injustice has taken place (Luke 4:18; Matthew 25:36).

Therefore, be it resolved, that the General Conference of The United Methodist Church advocate for justice and freedom for the Puerto Rican political prisoners; *furthermore,* that a letter from the General Conference secretary be sent to the President of the United States asking him to grant pardon, because they have more than sufficiently served their sentences, to all fourteen Puerto Rican political prisoners who are presently found in federal and state prisons; and *in addition,* that a copy of the letter be forwarded to Dr. Luis Nieves Falcon, coordinator of the effort to free the Puerto Rican political prisoners.

ADOPTED 1996
AMENDED AND READOPTED 2000

See Social Principles, ¶ 164A and E.

275. Justice for Cuban Prisoners

WHEREAS, in Matthew 25, Jesus tells us that those who care for those in need are his true disciples (verses 31-46). By the same token, the Lord reminds us that to do justice, and mercy are the most important aspects of the Law, that anyone who forgets these points has forgotten God's purposes for them. Thus, the author of Hebrews urges us to "[r]emember those in prison as if you were their fellow prisoners, and those who are mistreated as if you yourselves were suffering" (13:3).

WHEREAS, taking the scriptural witness to heart we must respond to the injustice suffered today by five Cuban political prisoners in U.S. federal prisons. Since their arrest in 1998 and incarceration following sentencing, they have received inhumane and cruel treatment.

WHEREAS, they are not allowed to visit with their families, and in many occasions their families have been denied visas to come to the US to see them, or have been allowed to come to the U.S. and returned to their country without seen their loved one, and

The following are their names and their sentences:

1. Gerardo Hernández Nordelo: Two lives in prison plus 15 years.
2. Ramón Labañino Salazar: Life in prison plus 18 years
3. Antonio Guerrero Rodríguez: Life in prison plus 10 years
4. Fernando González Llort: 19 years in prison

Therefore, be it resolved that, the 2004 General Conference of The United Methodist Church meeting in Pittsburgh, Pennsylvania, request the U.S. government: the State Department, the federal prison system, to allow the families of these prisoners access to their loved ones; to allow them to see their children and their spouses in prison.

Therefore, be it further resolved, that The United Methodist Church support these prisoners' families with their prayers and supplications before God, and that the Church through its leadership may accompany these families to visit their loved ones in prison.

Finally, be it further resolved, that, given that there have been concerns about the impartiality of their trials, The United Methodist Church gathered in Pittsburgh, Pennsylvania, considers that it would be appropriate for the Justice Department to address these concerns and to truly do justice to these prisoners.

ADOPTED 2004

See Social Principles, ¶ 164A.

276. Repression and the Right to Privacy

The Social Principles of The United Methodist Church affirm that "illegal and unconscionable activities directed against persons or groups by their own governments must not be justified or kept secret, even under the guise of national security" (¶ 164C). "We strongly reject domestic surveillance and intimidation of political opponents by governments in power and all other misuses of elective or appointive offices" (¶ 164A). Citizens of all countries should have access to all essential information regarding their government and its policies.

Openness is a redemptive gift of God, calling for trust and honesty between various segments of the community. Justice is the cornerstone of that trust we have come to expect in our elective and appointive representatives of the community. Communal wholeness is attained through the concerted use of these elements.

The prophets of Israel denounced the repression of the poor, widows, orphans, and others of their society, and our Lord's ministry began with the announced purpose to set at liberty the poor and disadvantaged. In our biblical tradition, we raise the following issues:

Repression

We have lived in a time when the accumulated hopes of racial and cultural minorities, combined with a growing dissent in the United States, were met by mounting fears and rising anxieties of the dominant group within the population. Institutions of this society began to reflect these fears and established policies and procedures that, in the short range, provided expedient control. These policies, however, were seen as repressive measures by those who sought legitimate rights and new opportunities.

In the immediate past, we sounded a call of concern because we recognized that society can become repressive in nature with hardly a trace of consciousness by the mass of the people, particularly if that people is feverishly fearful and has developed the readiness to accept any measure that seems to offer a new form of protection.

It is deplorable that in a society that is democratic in theory and structure there are signs of increasing repression: dragnet arrests; police and the intelligence community's harassment of minority leaders; charges of conspiracy; summary acquittals of police accused of brutality; the rising militancy of rank-and-file police; support for the use of preventive detention; the utilization of wiretaps; censorship of journalism in educational and correctional institutions; heavy punitive action against dissidents; the confinement of those who protested within the military forces; the utilization of grand juries for the purpose of harassment rather than indictment; and the use of church members, clergy, and missionaries for secret intelligence purposes by local police departments, the Federal Bureau of Investigation, and the Central Intelligence Agency.

We affirm the many civil, school, and church authorities who are working toward the elimination of these abuses through their work and example; and we note that many of the most flagrant of these acts of repression no longer occur. Congress, the press, and the American people have begun watching agency activities more closely and with a greater demand for public accountability.

This vigilance must not be relaxed, for if it is, there may be renewed acts of repression and fresh attempts to curtail the rights of citizens whenever redress is sought for economic and social grievances.

Therefore, we urge that all church members and leaders continue to be sensitive to this situation in their local community and in the nation by:

1. seeking to understand and undergird responsible institutions and agencies of the community and being supportive of measurements that will improve them and upgrade their personnel; and

2. establishing programs in the community sponsored by local churches to:

   a. educate church members and their wider community about the potential for repression in the institutions of society;

   b. study and affirm the biblical and constitutional basis for justice under law;

   c. work in state and federal legislatures to bring about just and responsible criminal code revisions that do not reinforce repressive elements in our nation's life;

   d. oppose forms of legislation that would legalize repression; support legislation that would prohibit intelligence agencies from conducting surveillance or disruption of lawful political activities or otherwise violating constitutional rights;

   e. develop an awareness of the rights and protection citizens should expect; and

   f. work for institutional change in situations where rights are not respeced and protection is not furnished.

The Right to Privacy

The Christian faith stresses the dignity of and respect for human personality. Invasion of the privacy of an ordinary citizen of society negates this dignity and respect. Further, the Christian faith is supportive of a society that elicits hope and trust, not a society that foments fear and threatens with oppression.

The revelation that intelligence agencies, local police, the Internal Revenue Service, and the United States Army have, over a number of years, developed a domestic espionage apparatus involving the gathering of information about the lawful political activities of millions of citizens is a cause for concern.

Although it is now illegal for any governmental unit to engage in any kind of wiretapping without a warrant of a court, we urge restraint in the use of wiretapping and electronic surveillance, for its prevalence creates an air of suspicion throughout the whole society and contributes to the insecurity of law-abiding American citizens.

Therefore, we respectfully request the Congress of the United States to:

1. enact comprehensive charter legislation for all of the intelligence agencies that would prohibit them from engaging in surveillance or disruption of lawful political activity. We oppose any charter provision that permits intelligence agencies to recruit and use as agents clergy or missionaries;

2. place statutory limitations upon the demand by governmental bureaus and agencies for personal information about any citizen or family for statistical purposes. When such requests by agencies are for information not required by law, the respondent should be informed that compliance is voluntary. Restrictions should be placed by law on private agencies in gathering, storing, and disseminating personal information; and

3. retain the Freedom of Information Act as it is, in support of the right of all citizens to know the actions of their government.

ADOPTED 1980
AMENDED AND READOPTED 2000

See Social Principles, ¶ 164A.

277. Support Legislation Prohibiting Malicious Harassments

The United Methodist Church encourages and supports the introduction, passage, and funding of legislation that prohibits malicious and intimidating actions that are reasonably related to, associated with, or directed toward a person's race, color, religion, ancestry, national origin, sexual orientation, age, gender, or disability.

ADOPTED 1992
READOPTED 2004

See Social Principles, ¶ 164A.

278. The U.S. Campaign for a Tax Fund

We have long supported those persons who cannot in conscience pay taxes in support of war. We believe they should be granted the same legal recognition as that granted to conscientious objectors to military service. Toward that end, we recognize the work of the National Campaign for a Peace Tax Fund (NCPTF). The NCPTF advocates for legislation by the United States Congress to establish a Peace Tax Fund.

The purpose of Peace Tax Fund legislation is to:
- provide each individual the right not to be coerced into any form of participation in killing other human beings—whether that participation is physical or financial;
- offer conscientious objectors the right to pay their full tax obligation without violating deeply held religious or ethical beliefs; and
- give those who are conscientiously opposed to war because of religious or ethical beliefs the right not to have legal penalties imposed because of those beliefs.

We believe all persons have these rights based in the freedom to exercise their beliefs according to the dictates of conscience. To that end, we support the National Campaign for a Peace Tax Fund and affirm the work it does on behalf of those who conscientiously object to payment of taxes for war.

ADOPTED 1996
READOPTED 2004

See Social Principles, ¶ 164E.

279. Urge State Legislatures to Allow Candidates Without Large Bank Accounts to Appear on Ballots

WHEREAS, equal access to the ballot is important in a free republic; and

WHEREAS, no one group should be permitted to have exclusive access to the ballot; and

WHEREAS, over the past quarter century election laws have been passed that make it difficult if not impossible for anyone other than the Democratic or Republican parties to have the names of their candidates printed on the general election ballot; and

WHEREAS, it is manifestly unfair to make ballot access so difficult (30,000 signatures in Texas) that a political party has to have a very large bank account to get on the ballot; and

WHEREAS, some states have "low requirements" (Colorado has a $500 filing fee, Mississippi requires a filed petition to have 1,000 names, New Jersey requires a filed petition to have 800 names, Utah requires only 500 names) to get on the ballot without having their ballot filled with spurious parties and candidates,

Therefore, be it resolved by the 2000 General Conference of The United Methodist Church that we urge all state legislatures to review their requirements for a political party to appear on their ballot and, if necessary, change their statutes to make it possible for a political party to have its candidates appear on the ballot without the party needing an enormous bank account just to appear on the ballot.

ADOPTED 2000

See Social Principles, ¶ 164B.

280. Voting Representation for People in the District of Columbia

WHEREAS, the District of Columbia was established on the first Monday in December, 1800, by an Act of Congress as a seat for the national government under authority granted to the Congress by Article 1, Section 8, of the U.S. Constitution, under which the Congress has the power to "exercise exclusive legislation in all cases whatsoever, over such District . . ."; and

WHEREAS, no provision for voting representation in the Federal Legislature for the residents of this Federal District was made in the Constitution or has been made at any time since; and

WHEREAS, throughout our nation's history, citizens of the District of Columbia have given their undivided allegiance to the United States: fighting and dying in wars, paying their full measure of taxes, and providing labor and resources to the federal government; and

WHEREAS, we recognize that governments derive their "just powers from the consent of the governed" in order to secure the people's rights "endowed by their Creator"; and

WHEREAS, the Social Principles contained in the United Methodist *Book of Discipline* state that the "form and the leaders of all governments should be determined by exercise of the right to vote guaranteed to all adult citizens," and further, that "the strength of a political system depends on the full and willing participation of its citizens"; and

WHEREAS, it has been the enduring tradition and history of The United Methodist Church, from the time of Wesley to the present day, to support the rights of the individual, to provide relief to the disenfranchised, and to champion the equality of all persons before God and before the law; and

WHEREAS, we are agreed that the continuing disenfranchisement of the citizens of the District of Columbia is an egregious moral wrong which must be rectified,

Therefore, be it resolved, that the General Conference of The United Methodist Church declares its full support, on moral grounds, for the provision of full democratic rights to the people of the District of Columbia. We affirm that district citizens are entitled to political rights equal to those of other Americans, including voting representation in both houses of Congress. We call on the President and the Congress of the United States of America to take action to provide congressional representation to the citizens of Washington, D.C., by whatever means they should find suitable and appropriate, and

Be it further resolved, that we call on all United Methodist congregations throughout the United States, to support the people of the District of Columbia in this cause. We call on the United States members of The United Methodist Church to call upon their elected representatives in Congress to demand democratic rights for the District of Columbia, and

Be it further resolved, that we call on other communities of faith, locally and throughout the nation, to join with us in advocating for the provision of these rights to Washington, D.C., so that at last the citizens of the District of Columbia are provided with the same democratic rights available to all other Americans.

ADOPTED 1980
REVISED AND ADOPTED 2000

See Social Principles, ¶ 162

281. Food and Drug Administration (FDA) Regulation of Tobacco

WHEREAS, The United Methodist Church historically has opposed the use of tobacco products and their devices in the Social Principles ¶ 162K:

"We affirm our historic tradition of high standards of personal discipline and social responsibility. In light of the overwhelming evidence that tobacco smoking and the use of smokeless tobacco are hazardous to the health of all ages, we recommend total abstinence from the use of tobacco. We urge that our educational and communication resources be utilized to support and encourage such abstinence. Further, we recognize the harmful effects of passive smoke and support the restriction of smoking in public areas and workplaces."

WHEREAS, the sixth commandment says, "Thou shalt not kill";

WHEREAS, the medical community and surgeon general have known the causal effects of tobacco and disease and death for over fifty years;

WHEREAS, annually more than 450,000 people in the United States die because of the over 240 cancer-causing ingredients in tobacco products and their devices and their products of combustion. This is equivalent to all the American casualties in all the wars of the 20th century occurring every eighteen months and the same number of casualties of Sept. 11, 2001 occurring every three days;

WHEREAS, the Congress of the United States has intentionally maintained for itself the authority to regulate the ingredients in tobacco products, their devices, and their products of combustion;

Therefore, be it resolved, that the General Conference of The United Methodist Church strongly urges the members of Congress to provide the authority to the Food and Drug Administration to regulate the ingredients of tobacco products, their devices, and their products of combustion in order to render harmless the greatest menace to human life in our country's history.

ADOPTED 2004

See Social Principles, ¶¶ 162J and K and 164.

282. U.S. Federal Single-Payer Health Insurance Program

WHEREAS more than forty million Americans are without health care insurance and countless others are under-insured, and

WHEREAS there already exists within the present federal government a fractured and disjointed set of national health care insurance plans in the form of Medicare, CHAMPUS, Federal Employees Health

Benefit Program, Railroad Employees Health Benefit Plan, Medicaid, and possibly others,

Therefore, be it resolved, that The United Methodist Church exert influence through all its structures and means to connectionally advocate and fervently lobby the federal government for the adoption and implementation of a totally nonprofit health insurance system, a single-payer system administered by the federal government, and

Be it further resolved, that the General Board of Church and Society be charged with initiating conversations with, and developing strategies for, working with other nonprofit groups, such as AARP, the United Health Care Action Network, the Physicians for a National Health Care Program, and other denominations to lobby members of the federal government to develop a national health insurance plan that embodies the principles spelled out in Resolutions 118 and 120.

Be it further resolved, that the General Board of Church and Society communicate annually to its annual conference counterparts what actions it has taken on General Conference resolutions pertaining to health care.

ADOPTED 2004

See Social Principles, ¶¶ 162*T* and 164*A*.

THE WORLD COMMUNITY

JUSTICE AND LAW

283. Church Supports Global Efforts to End Slavery

WHEREAS, the institution of slavery controls the lives of over 27 million persons worldwide, in lands including Sudan, Mauritania, India, Pakistan, Brazil, and Thailand; and

WHEREAS, slavery is a crime against humanity, and is expressly prohibited by international law and a number of international treaties; and

WHEREAS, the United Nations, the United States Congress, the United States State Department, the American Anti-Slavery Group, Christian Solidarity International, as well as a host of other organizations, have recognized and officially documented the current existence of slavery; and

WHEREAS, founder of Methodism, John Wesley, in numerous instances, including a tract entitled "Thoughts on Slavery" and sermon entitled "The Use of Money," condemned slavery as wrong and incompatible with Christ's teachings; and

WHEREAS, The United Methodist Church regards the institution of slavery as an "infamous evil" and recognizing that "All forms of enslavement are totally prohibited and shall no way be tolerated by the church" (*Book of Discipline*, ¶ 164A); and

WHEREAS, the General Board on Global Ministries, through the United Methodist Committee on Relief Sudan Emergency campaign, as well as other United Methodist organizations, has worked to aid enslaved and freed slaves,

Therefore, be it resolved, that The United Methodist Church officially support efforts to end slavery.

Be it further resolved, that The United Methodist Church actively champion anti-slavery efforts by petitioning the United Nations, United

States Congress and State Department, and the legislative bodies of all countries in which The United Methodist Church has an organized ecclesiastical structure, to demand the freeing of all modern-day slaves.

Be it further resolved, that The United Methodist Church petition the United Nations and the United States Congress and State Department to abolish slavery through the use of nonmilitary options such as negotiations and sanctions.

Be it further resolved, that The United Methodist Church officially support stock/mutual fund divestment campaigns that urge people to remove funds from organizations whose actions contribute to slavery's existence.

Be it further resolved, that The United Methodist Church inform all members of the church, via news publications and other communication channels of the connectional system, that slavery currently exists and that The United Methodist Church officially opposes its existence.

Be it further resolved, that this document be sent to the Secretary-General of the United Nations, the President of the United States, the United States Congress, and the legislative bodies of countries in which The United Methodist Church has an established ecclesiastical structure..

ADOPTED 2000

See Social Principles, ¶ 165B.

284. Compensation for Comfort Women

"So if anyone is in Christ, there is a new creation: Everything old has passed away; see, everything has become new! All this is from God, who reconciled us to himself through Christ, and has given us the ministry of reconciliation; that is, in Christ God was reconciling the world to himself, not counting their trespasses against them, and entrusting the message of reconciliation to us. So we are ambassadors for Christ" (2 Corinthians 5:17-20).

The United Methodist Church affirms all persons as equally valuable in the sight of God. We therefore work toward societies in which each person's value is recognized, maintained, and strengthened. We support the basic rights of all persons to equal access to legal redress for grievances, and physical protection. We deplore acts of hate and violence against groups or persons based on race, ethnicity, gender, sexual orientation, religious affiliation, or economic status (Social Principles, ¶ 162).

The United Methodist Church also regards nations as accountable for unjust treatment of their citizens and others living within their borders. While recognizing valid differences in culture and political philosophy, we stand for justice and peace in every nation (Social Principles, ¶ 165).

The urgency for the ministry of reconciliation has never been greater. For over fifty years the sexual enslavement of more than 200,000 women from Korea (80 percent), Malaysia, Burma, China, Taiwan, East Timor, Indonesia, and the Pacific Islands by the Japanese military and government, remains one of the greatest unresolved injustices of the Second World War as stated by the judges of the Women's War Crimes Tribunal. They further stated, there are no museums, no graves of the unknown comfort women, no education of future generations, and no judgment days, for the victims of Japan's military sexual slavery. Many of the women who have come forward to fight injustice have died unsung heroes. While the names inscribed in history's pages are often those of the men that commit the crimes, rather than the women that suffer them, this judgment bears the names of the survivors that took the stage to tell their stories, and thereby, for four days at least, put wrong on the scaffold and truth on the throne (The Hague, December 4, 2001). The urgency is the need to find justice before the survivors of Japan's sexual slavery die, never knowing whether the Japanese government agreed to be accountable for their monstrous treatment of women inside and outside their borders. David J. Scheffer, United States Ambassador-at-Large for War Crimes suggested that a conservative estimate (based on each woman being raped five times a day for five years) would amount to 125 million rapes. Thousands of women were raped up to 60 times a day.

The United Nations Commission on Human Rights accepted the Final Judgment of the Women's International War Crimes Tribunal of Japan's Military Sexual Slavery (held in Tokyo in 2000) as an official document of its 58th Session and reminded Japan to do the honorable thing and recognize its state responsibility.

We call on The United Methodist Church to:
- urge United Methodists to become informed about and supportive of the continuing struggle of the survivors of sexual slavery and urge the General Board of Global Ministries to make resources available; and,
- urge United Methodists to be supportive of the remedial measures recommended by the Women's International War Crimes Tribunal.

Therefore, be it resolved, that the 2004 General Conference calls upon the General Board of Global Ministries to develop a strategy to urge the government of Japan to do the following:

- acknowledge fully its responsibility and liability for the establishment of the comfort system and that this system was in violation of international law;
- issue a full and frank apology, taking legal responsibility and giving guarantees of non-repetition;
- compensate the victims and survivors and those entitled to recover as a result of the violations declared herein through the government and in amounts adequate to redress the harm and deter its future occurrence;
- establish a mechanism for the thorough investigation into the system of military sexual slavery, for public access and historical preservation of the materials;
- consider, in consultation with the survivors, the establishment of a Truth and Reconciliation Commission that will create a historical record of the gender-based crimes committed during the war, transition, and occupation.
- recognize and honor the victims and survivors through the creation of memorials, a museum, and a library dedicated to their memory and the promise of never again;
- sponsor both formal and informal educational initiatives, including meaningful inclusion in textbooks at all levels and support for scholars and writers, to ensure the education of the population and, particularly, the youth and future generations concerning the violations committed and the harm suffered.

Be it further resolved, that the General Board of Global Ministries report its efforts and the response of the government of Japan to the 2008 General Conference.

ADOPTED 2004

See Social Principles, ¶ 165.

285. Abolition of Sex Trafficking

"Again I looked and saw all the oppression that was taking place under the sun: I saw the tears of the oppressed—and they have no comforter; power was on the side of their oppressors—and they have no comforter."

Ecclesiastes 4:1

"But this is a people plundered and looted, all of them trapped in pits or hidden in prisons. They have become plunder, with no one to rescue them; they have been made loot, with no one to say, "Send them back."

Isaiah 42:22

These are hard words of Scripture. Yet, even harder is this Scripture's contemporary reality, daily reflected in the tears of millions of women and children who are trafficked into sexual slavery. Secretary of State Colin Powell asserts, "It is appalling that in the twenty-first century hundreds of thousands of women, children, and men made vulnerable by civil conflict, dire economic circumstances, natural disasters or just their own desire for a better life, are trafficked and exploited for the purposes of sex or forced labor. The deprivation of a human being's basic right to freedom is an affront to the ideals of liberty and human dignity cherished by people around the world."[1]

This resolution addresses a gaping hole that exists in The United Methodist Church's advocacy concerning sexual violence—sex trafficking. The United Methodist Church has never recoiled in the face of controversial and painful issues such as the myriad ways in which human sexuality is abused.[2] It would be wrong to suggest that this hole exists purposefully. Rather, one can rightly assume that the pervasive existence and deep gravity of the sex trafficking industry has only recently begun to be uncovered.[3] Sex trafficking was briefly raised as a concern for "Responsible Travel" in the 2000 BOR. However, the daunting statistics have not been discussed, nor has the

1. U.S. Department of State, Trafficking in Persons Report, June 2003. Trafficking Victims Protection Act of 2000. www.state.gov/g/tip/rls/tiprpt/2003/ http://www.state.gov/g/tip/rls/tiprpt/2003/

2. See previous BOR 2000 statements regarding issues such as sexual abuse in the Church and in the home, sexual harassment, pornography, and on the Federal level, the support of reparations made for the use and abuse of military "comfort women" in WWII.

3. The first trafficking case in the U.S. was prosecuted in 1998 and the State Department Office to Monitor and Combat Trafficking in Persons was created in 2001. For more information on the recent press given to sex trafficking, see http://usinfo.state.gov/topical/pol/usandun/03092305.htm. Excerpt: *"There's another humanitarian crisis spreading, yet hidden from view. Each year an estimated 800,000 to 900,000 human beings are bought, sold, or forced across the world's borders. Among them are hundreds of thousands of teenage girls, and others as young as five, who fall victim to the sex trade. This commerce in human life generates billions of dollars each year—much of which is used to finance organized crime . . . The American government is committing $50 million to support the good work of organizations that are rescuing women and children from exploitation, and giving them shelter and medical treatment and the hope of a new life . . . Other governments [are urged] to do their part . . . The trade in human beings for any purpose must not be allowed to thrive in our time."* For a comprehensive overview of trafficking on the global scale and current efforts toward its abolition, see the aforementioned State Department *Trafficking in Persons Report.*

direct and indirect compliance of U.S. citizenry and businesses in this matter been exposed to the members of the Church. In its prophetic role, The United Methodist Church is called to inform its members and the public at large that an estimated 700,000 to 4,000,000 people worldwide are trafficked each year. Furthermore, the most overlooked aspect of these statistics is the fact that 18,000 to 20,000 people are trafficked into the United States each year. [4]

Sexual violence in the twenty-first century, through many and varied manifestations, destructively permeates the whole of society. Not only must the Church denounce these issues, such as sex trafficking, both in and outside its own walls, but also, it must embrace its crucial responsibility to witness to the only One who is truly able to offer lasting hope, refuge, restoration, and redemption. The United Methodist Church is called to model that the church universal is the very first place to which people can turn in their hunger for justice, wholeness, and sanctuary. This calling comprises an essential element of the church's identity as the body of Jesus Christ, and, for The United Methodist Church specifically, the identity of being a community that carries the Wesleyan legacy of seeking justice and proclaiming the healing that can only come from our reconciling, Incarnate God. The church is given by God to be a place in which broken people—both victims and perpetrators of sexual violence—can be welcomed, heard, embraced with the gospel, and even healed.

WHEREAS, the United Nations defines trafficking to be "the recruitment, transportation, transfer, harboring, or receipt of persons, by means of the threat or use of force or other forms of coercion, of abduction, of fraud, of deception, of the abuse of power or of a position of vulnerability or of the giving or receiving of payments or benefits to achieve the consent of a person having control over another person, for the purpose of exploitation. Exploitation shall include, at a minimum, the exploitation of the prostitution of others or other forms of sexual exploitation, forced labour or services, slavery or practices similar to slavery, servitude...";[5]

---

4. According to estimates by the CIA and the State Department. http://usinfo.state.gov/gi/Archive/2003/Jun/10-239681.html.

5. FACT SHEET from the Trafficking in Persons National Security Presidential Directive, http://usinfo.state.gov/gi/Archive/2003/Jun/10-239581.html.

WHEREAS, there are currently an estimated 20,000 women and children trafficked yearly into the United States, and an estimated 700,000 to four million worldwide; and

WHEREAS, the church has a difficult and awesome responsibility, by the power of the Holy Spirit, to seek justice and Christ's healing in the face of structures of oppression; and

WHEREAS, such structures of oppression are well-embedded in the institution of sex trafficking,

Therefore, be it resolved, that The United Methodist Church, through education, financial resources, publication, lobbying, and the use of every relevant gift of God, shall join in the active battle against the modern-day enslavement of humans for commercial sexual exploitation, i.e., sex trafficking.

Be it further resolved, that the General Board of Church and Society shall lead The United Methodist Church's efforts toward the abolition of sex trafficking for the 2005-2008 quadrennium. On this issue, the GBCS shall work in cooperation with the General Commission on the Status and Role of Women and the Women's Division of the General Board of Global Ministries. The United Methodist Church shall recognize the urgency and gravity of this issue through a substantial monetary investment toward the galvanization of the Church at all levels to live out her gifts and calling in relation to the abolition of modern day slavery. To this end, the General Board of Church and Society shall receive sufficient funding toward the concrete implementation of a specific anti-sex trafficking program, which would include the empowerment of victims to support themselves and the prevention of their return to sex-related industries.

ADOPTED 2004

See Social Principles, ¶ 165.

286. Global Racism and Xenophobia: Impact on Women, Children, and Youth

The General Conference of The United Methodist Church affirms the United Nations principles relating to global racism and xenophobia.[1]

1. Principles can be found on the United Nations Web site in various reports including "Declarations World Conference against Racism, Racial Discrimination, Xenophobia and Related Intolerance, Durban, South Africa, 31 August to 8 September 2001."

The General Conference reaffirms the principles of equality and nondiscrimination in the Universal Declaration of Human Rights and encourages respect for human rights and fundamental freedoms for all without distinction of any kind such as race, color, sex, language, religion, political, or other opinion, national or social origin, property, birth, or other status.

We, the General Conference, affirm that all peoples and individuals constitute one human family, rich in diversity. "So then you are no longer strangers and aliens, but you are citizens with the saints and also members of the household of God" (Ephesians 2:19).

We recognize the fundamental importance of nations in combating racism, racial discrimination, xenophobia, and related intolerance [hereinafter referred to as racism]; and, the need to consider signing, ratifying or acceding to all relevant international human rights instruments, with a view to international adherence.

We recognize that religion, spirituality, and belief can contribute to the promotion of the inherent dignity and worth of the human person and to the eradication of racism.

We recognize that racism reveals itself in a different manner for women and girls and can be among the factors leading to deterioration in their living conditions, poverty, violence, multiple forms of discrimination, and the limitation or denial of their human rights.

We recognize the need to develop a more systematic and consistent approach to evaluating and monitoring racial discrimination against women, children, and youth.

Therefore, we, the General Conference, urge:

- that, in light of these affirmations and principles, each nation in which The United Methodist Church is established to adhere to the principles and programs contained in the opening statements;
- that the United States, all nations and The United Methodist Church incorporate a gender perspective in all programs of action against racism;
- that the United States, all nations, and The United Methodist Church undertake detailed research on racism, especially in respect to its effect on women, children, and youth;
- that the United States, all nations, and The United Methodist Church address the burden of such discrimination on women, children, and youth and promote their participation in the economic and productive development of their communities, especially in respect to:

* the increased proportion of women migrant workers, human rights violations perpetrated against them, and the contribution they make to the economies of their countries or their host countries;
* the large number of children and young people, particularly girls, who are victims of racism;
* the rights of children belonging to an ethnic, religious, linguistic minority or indigenous community and their right individually or in community to enjoy their own culture, their own religion, and their own language;
* child labor and its links to poverty, lack of development, and related socioeconomic conditions that can perpetuate poverty and racial discrimination disproportionately, denying children a productive life and economic growth;
* education at all levels and all ages.

• that the United States, all nations and the appropriate structures of The United Methodist Church involve women, children, and youth in decision-making at all levels related to the eradication of racism;
• that the General Commission on Religion and Race, the General Commission on the Status and Role of Women, in consultation with the Women's Division of the General Board of Global Ministries, create a monitoring instrument for assessing evidences of racism in programs for and with women, children, and youth;
• that all national mission institutions, schools, and institutions of higher education, annual conferences, and general agencies evaluate current and projected programs to determine their impact in reducing racism in programs for women, children, and youth; and
• that a report be prepared and presented to each General Conference by the General Commission on Religion and Race, the General Commission on the Status and Role of Women, in consultation with the Women's Division of the General Board of Global Ministries, related to the status of women, children, and youth impacted by racism.

ADOPTED 2004

See Social Principles, ¶ 165.

287. Responsible Travel

The travel and tourism industry has become one of the fastest growing and largest sectors in the global economy. The annual revenues are second only to the weapons industry and, according to the United Nations, earnings from tourism are expected to triple in the next 20 years. The impact of travel and tourism on local economies, disadvantaged communities, women and children, indigenous peoples, and the environment has become a serious concern. This necessitates a critical examination of the travel and tourism activities in which United Methodists engage.

We are called by Scripture to be sojourners in ways which promote justice: *Exodus 12:48-49—Sojourners are to abide by one law for both the native and for the stranger.*

Exodus 22:21—You shall not wrong a stranger or oppress [him/her], for you were a sojourner in the land of Egypt.

Leviticus 19:34—When a stranger sojourns with you in your land, you shall not do [him/her] wrong. The stranger who sojourns with you shall be as a native among you. You shall love [him/her] as yourself.

1 Peter 1:17—Conduct yourselves with reverent fear throughout the time of your exile (sojourning).

To travel is not to take a vacation from our faith. Just as we are called to express hospitality by welcoming the stranger, we are also called to abide in love and justice with our neighbors when we visit them, whether near or far away. When sojourning in a strange land, travelers should behave with reverence and respect for the people, their culture, and the land upon which they live.

Too often travel and tourism is exploitative as a result of the globalization of local economies in ways that transform self-sufficient communities into consumer-oriented and dependent societies. The impact of the travel industry can be viewed as a new form of colonialism in which local people are displaced and priced out of their own communities. Local people are most commonly employed in low-wage service positions without benefits. They are also faced with rising prices for basic needs such as food, transportation, and housing to meet the demand of tourists, hotels, and resorts. This disintegration of the local economy often leads to devastating social impacts such as the rise of alcoholism, drug abuse, prostitution, and sexually transmitted diseases. In the wake of this transformation, traditional knowledge and skills are forgotten, and the natural environment is exploited to meet the needs of a tourist economy.

Exploitative travel and tourism also impacts women and children who become victims in sex trade or trafficking, child prostitution, and/or pornography. The sex tourism industry seeks out young girls, offering payments to their families under a guise to better their lives, and takes them away to brothels in large cities where traveling businessmen are approached as potential customers. Women may also be trafficked across international borders for use in sex trade. Children are caught in the sex trade at a young age, thus depriving them of schooling and opportunities to become active participants in society. These women and children are at high risk of acquiring sexually transmitted diseases and suffer long-term emotional pain.

The impact of tourism is of particular concern to indigenous peoples. Tourism may exploit sacred sites such as burial grounds, ritual areas, and other places which hold significance in the cultural traditions of the indigenous peoples. Tourists may be offered tour packages which visit these sites, where the approval of indigenous peoples has not been sought. During such tours, tourists may trample over ancestral burial grounds or other such sacred sites, irrespective of the traditions of the indigenous peoples.

God's creation, the natural environment, can also be a victim of exploitative tourism when the local resources are viewed as a commodity to be consumed by the tourist industry as resources, entertainment, or merely as a dumping ground for the waste products they produce. For example:

- cruise lines that dump waste into the ocean;
- resort areas which do not comply with environmental standards by practicing energy and water conservation, as well as recycling and minimizing waste; and
- golf course development around the world that results in deforestation, erosion, overconsumption of water, and pollution of ground water through the extensive use of pesticides and chemical fertilizers. If these exploitative practices continue, there will be no "paradise" left to which to travel.

A just alternative to exploitative travel and tourism is "sustainable tourism." Sustainable tourism development in the travel industry should include the following principles:

- support for community and indigenous involvement in the planning, implementation, and monitoring of any tourism

717

policies or development plans; and, wherever possible, ownership or joint venture of destination sites/travel programs;

- creation of tourist/travel programs that combat poverty by ensuring that a larger share of the profits and jobs generated by tourism remain in the local communities through purchases of local crafts, foods, and supplies;
- practice of travel behaviors that are respectful of cultural norms and traditions within the society; and
- development of forms of tourism that are not destructive to the local or global environment. As United Methodists, we reaffirm our commitments to care for the environment, promote economic justice, advocate for women and children, support the economic sustainability of disadvantaged communities, and uphold the rights of indigenous peoples to preserve their culture regarding our own travel, patronage of the tourist industry, or the travel of fellow United Methodists, including that of the general agencies.

We call upon The United Methodist Church, its general agencies, annual conferences, and members of local churches to do the following:

- Learn about and respect the codes of conduct and cultural practices of the destination country or community.
- Ask travel agents / agencies whether local people are involved in the development of the "tour packages"; i.e., whether local people set the conditions under which travelers may come to visit.
- Purchase souvenirs that are locally produced and not made from endangered species of plants or animals.
- Patronize cruise ships that do not pollute the environment or exploit their workers.
- Practice "low impact" travel and tourism, which do minimal damage to local culture and the ecology.
- Support tour packages and hotels that are rated "green," which are committed to causing minimal waste and damage to the environment. Ask critical questions of tour packages that promote themselves as "eco-tourism."
- Raise awareness and affect policies regarding sex tourism and trafficking of women and children. Advocate for laws which prohibit sex trade/tourism and call for prosecution of offenders. Educate businesses and travelers about their legal responsibilities to these laws.

- Support HIV/AIDS education among women and children who are at risk due to involvement in sex trade/tourism. Promote programs of alternative employment for women and educational opportunities for children.
- Take action against companies, agencies, and tour packages that have been shown to exploit their workers, pollute the environment, or impact local economies in destructive ways. Investigate investments in such companies for possible shareholder actions.
- Monitor advertising and the Internet Web sites on travel with respect to race, gender, or age discrimination.
- Support ratification and implementation of United Nations Conventions on sex, tourism, and exploitation of women and children (i.e., United Nations Convention on the Rights of the Child; the Convention on the Elimination of All Forms of Discrimination Against Women; and the Convention on the Elimination of All Form of Racial Discrimination).
- Advocate for international policies that hold the travel industry and related companies accountable for their impacts on the environment, local economies, and local traditions.
- Affirm the work of organizations which advocate the end of child prostitution, child pornography, and trafficking of children for sexual purposes.
- Develop educational resources for local churches on ethical and responsible travel.
- Monitor ethical, responsible travel practices of conferences, board and agencies of The United Methodist Church.

ADOPTED 2000

See Social Principles ¶ 165*A, B,* and *D.*

NATIONAL POWER AND RESPONSIBILITY

288. Atomic Testing on the Marshall Islands—A Legacy

WHEREAS, in the Old Testament the Lord spoke to Moses saying: "Speak to the Israelites: When a man or a woman wrongs another, breaking faith with the Lord that person incurs guilt and shall confess the sin that has been committed. The person shall make full restitution for the wrong, adding one fifth to it, and giving it all to the one who was wronged" (Numbers 5:5-7). And in the New Testament Zacchaeus stood there and said to the Lord, "Look, half of my possessions, Lord, I will give to the poor, and if I have defrauded anyone of anything, I will pay back four times as much." (Luke 19:8, NRSV)

WHEREAS, The Marshall Islands government has indicated that new information on the health of its people exposed to radiation from atomic and nuclear testing by the United States in the Marshalls requires more just compensation and expansion of medical care than the $150 million trust fund provided in the Compact of Free Association; and

WHEREAS, evidence from recently declassified U.S. government reports and studies shows that many more Marshall Islanders were exposed to nuclear fallout from the 67 U.S. atomic and nuclear tests than American negotiators admitted when the compensation package in the compact was negotiated in the early 1980s; and

WHEREAS, many questions are arising about the accuracy of medical research done by U.S. Government labs on Marshall Islanders who were exposed to fallout from atomic and nuclear testing; and

WHEREAS, although the U.S. Government provided full compensation to American citizens living downwind of the Nevada Test Site, Marshall Islanders have not received more than sixty-one percent of their total awards because the compensation level is inadequate; and

WHEREAS, fully one-third of the 1,074 Marshall Islands recipients of nuclear test awards have died without receiving full compensation; and

WHEREAS, the U.S. government provided full compensation to American citizens living in a significantly larger area compared to the Marshall Islands, despite the fact that the total tonnage of U.S. tests in the Marshall Islands was almost 100 times greater than the yield of tests at the Nevada test site; and

WHEREAS, documents now show that the people of Ailuk and other nearby islands were exposed to dangerous amounts of radiation, yet purposely were not evacuated; and

WHEREAS, the Marshall Islanders are increasingly becoming aware that islanders were not evacuated *despite* information that prevailing wind would blow fallout over a number of inhabited islands and that they were likely being used as "guinea pigs" in radiation studies; and

WHEREAS, U.S. government representatives deceived the people of Bikini Atoll by telling that their island would be used "for the benefit of mankind"; and

WHEREAS, the March 1, 1954 "Bravo" hydrogen bomb test at Bikini Atoll was detonated despite weather reports the previous day that winds were blowing to the east toward the inhabited atolls of Rongelap, Utrik, Ailuk and others; and

WHEREAS, a 1985-1989 health survey in the Marshall Islands revealed cancer rates 2-30 times higher among Marshall Islanders than in the U.S.; and

WHEREAS, a nationwide survey of thyroid problems in the Marshall Islands in the mid-1990s by doctors from Tohoku University in Japan confirmed a high rate of thyroid disorders among Marshall Islanders; and

WHEREAS, the economic provisions of a Compact of Free Association implemented in 1986 will expire in 2001 and are up for renegotiation in 1999; and

WHEREAS, the U.S. government has not yet apologized to the Marshallese people for the death of Marshallese citizens and for the damage done to their homeland, waters and people; and

WHEREAS, the $150 million trust fund provided in a Compact of Free Association with the Marshall Islands is woefully inadequate and not just compensation for the health injuries and deaths caused by U.S. nuclear testing to the population, and the loss of the use of their atolls because of radiation contamination since 1946; and

WHEREAS, U.S. funding for medical surveillance and treatment programs is inadequate to meet the needs of the exposed population in the Marshall Islands,

Therefore, be it resolved, that this General Conference of The United Methodist Church call upon The United Methodist Church through the General Board of Church and Society and the General Board of Global Ministries to work closely with the Marshallese people and our ecumenical partners, to bring about an official apology and full redress including all necessary funding from the U.S. Government; and

Be it further resolved, that copies of this resolution be sent to the U.S. attorney general, the secretary of the department of energy, the secretary of defense, the secretary of state, with copies to the Republic of the Marshall Islands Embassy Office in Washington, D.C., and to the people in the Marshall Islands.

ADOPTED 2000

See Social Principles, ¶ 165B.

289. Close the United States Army School of the Americas

The United Methodist Church calls upon the U.S. President and the U.S. Congress to close the U.S. Army School of the Americas (SOA) at Ft. Benning, Georgia.

History

The SOA was established by the U.S. in 1946 in Panama to promote stability and combat communism in the region. It moved to Ft. Benning, Georgia in 1984 under terms of the Panama Canal Treaty. Panama's President Jorge Illueca called it the "biggest base for destabilization in Latin America," and a major Panamanian newspaper called it "The School of the Assassins." The school trains 900-2,000 soldiers a year from Latin America and the Caribbean. In its 50-year history, the SOA has trained more than 60,000 military personnel.

Controversy about the school continued with the release in March 1993, of the United Nations Truth Commission Report on El Salvador. This report indicated that 48 military officers cited for human rights violations were trained at the SOA. Other findings in the report about SOA graduates:

- nineteen of the twenty-six officers involved in the 1989 murders of Jesuit priests and the subsequent cover-up;
- two of the three soldiers involved in the 1980 murder of Archbishop Oscar Romero;
- three of the five soldiers involved in the 1980 murder of U.S. church women;
- all three soldiers cited for the 1981 murder of union leaders;
- two of three cited for the 1981 El Junquillo massacre;
- ten of twelve cited for the 1981 El Mozote massacre;
- three of six cited for the 1983 Las Hojas massacre; and
- six of seven cited for the 1988 San Sebastian massacre.

In September 1996, the Department of Defense (DoD) released copies and translations of seven Spanish-language training manuals taken out of circulation in 1991 when the DoD discovered material and passages condoning murder, torture, kidnapping, and extortion. According to the DoD, the manuals had been used from 1982 to 1991 by instructors at the SOA and by mobile training teams of the U.S. Southern Command. The material in these manuals violated

U.S. law. The DoD ordered the manuals and their source material destroyed.

U.S. Foreign Policy Context

According to Jeffrey Davidow, assistant secretary of state for inter-American affairs, U.S. foreign policy objectives for Latin America and the Caribbean are:

- to promote free trade and economic integration in order to enhance economic development and assist American business;
- to strengthen democracy and the rule of law to ensure that the values and principles that have guided the U.S. thrive throughout the hemisphere;
- to combat drug trafficking, migrant smuggling and environmental degradation to minimize the impact of these transnational problems; and
- to encourage sustainable development and poverty alleviation programs to improve living standards for all citizens of the region (testimony by Jeffrey Davidow before the House International Relations Committee, Subcommittee on Western Hemisphere, 3/19/97).

Davidow also stated that, "Disparities in income, inadequate health and education, fragile democracies and the narcotics trade create conditions of tremendous cost and risk to U.S. national interests." The two Summits of the Americas (Miami, 1994 and Santiago, 1998) put forward the vision of a hemisphere of free trade, strong democratic institutions, and fewer problems with drugs, environmental degradation and poverty. But the reality is that U.S. assistance to the region is at an all-time low.

The SOA is not the kind of assistance Latin America needs. The school's original goal of fighting communism in the region is not valid. The real security "threat" to the U.S. from Latin America is the poverty that exists there, forcing people to migrate to already overcrowded cities, or further north. Faced with starvation, some Latin American people have become involved in the drug trade.

U.S. foreign policy objectives do not take into consideration the needs of the people of Latin America. Where they appear to do so, these objectives in practice contradict each other. Through our continued military training in Latin America, we have maintained a relationship of control and obligation to the power elite. We have traded our focus on fighting communism to free trade and economic expansion. Access to resources has been restricted to the few business, government, and military elite. This reality has kept most of the Latin American population in poverty. Most of the people do not see the benefits of free trade and economic development. Military rulers and rulers supported by the military have prevailed at the expense of human rights and freedoms. Expanding the principles which have guided the U.S. may not be greeted warmly by the people of Latin America. Continuing to favor military institutions over democratic movements is not the route to sustainable communities in Latin America. The principles which result in our policy have led to the oppression and suffering of many people in Latin America. If given a choice, many citizens in Latin America would probably opt for the prevalence of their own rich culture, allowed to flourish unimpeded by selfish, outside interests, and not for an imported version of what the U.S. has decided is best for them. As Christians, we cannot support such condescension. The United Methodist Bishops have stated, "It is not the function of Christian witness to 'westernize,' 'easternize,' 'Americanize,' or in other ways acculturate human attitudes and responses. It is the function of the Christian to bring the full dimensions of a gospel of love and justice to bear upon the human situation." An enemy of peace, as outlined by the bishops, is economic exploitation. "With networks of economic and military interests intruding into almost every land, [the "superpowers"] frustrate authentic self-determination, manipulate power relationships, and disturb the essential ingredients of international community." (Both quoted statements are from the "Bishops' Call for Peace and Self-Development of Peoples.")

The government's most recent justification for the SOA is to train soldiers to combat narco-terrorism in Latin America. This allows the SOA to accuse its opponents of being "soft" on fighting the international drug trade.This sudden shift in public relations strategy has occurred at a time when some Latin American military officers training at the school have been accused of laundering drug money and participating in the drug trade.

Closing the SOA may seem like a small step in the overall U.S. foreign policy scheme, but it is an important symbol of U.S. policy toward Latin America. Closing the school would send a message to the people of Latin America and encourage the emergence of policies that create real security in the region. At a time when we are looking for real assistance for Latin America, the SOA should not be seen as a substitute for that.

Though the percentage of its students who have been implicated in atrocities is small, the question must not be what number or percentage of SOA trained soldiers have been involved in atrocities, but how people have been victimized by SOA-trained soldiers. The question must be how to best use limited natural, economic and human resources to create real security in the hemisphere. U.S. foreign policy must be guided by an ethic that is based on long-range objectives and real security. Advancing policies that continue to impoverish most Latin American citizens, or even maintaining the status quo is unacceptable to us as Christians. From a security and foreign policy standpoint they don't make sense either. Establishing acceptable living conditions for all the people of the Americas should be our goal. The SOA is not a means to that end. As the United Methodist bishops stated in the 1992 episcopal address:

"Peacemakers of the world must insist that the arms trade and all military assistance programs for poor nations must cease . . . The common enemy of humanity is militarism . . . We will have no peace on or with the earth until the people of the earth live together in the harmony of a just social order."

Action

Based on our historical advocacy for human rights and against the militarization of societies, The United Methodist Church urges the U.S. President and the Congress to act immediately to close the U.S. Army School of the Americas at Ft. Benning, Georgia. The $20 million in funding provided to the school annually should be used to support sustainable living and conflict resolution in Latin America, not to further militarize societies.

We urge all United Methodists in the United States to work actively to close the School of the Americas and to educate and inform others about closing the school. United Methodists are encouraged to contact the President, their senators and representatives to support legislation to close the school.

ADOPTED 2000

See Social Principles, ¶ 165.

290. Ending the Colonial Status of Puerto Rico

We direct the secretary of the General Conference of The United Methodist Church to send a copy of this resolution to the President of the United States and to all members of Congress.

The Christian tradition has stood clearly against colonialism, believing instead in God's promise of human liberation, found again and again in the Bible. God breaks the bars of the yoke of oppression and feeds the people with justice (Ezekiel 34:27-30). Moses led the Hebrew people out of Egypt to the promised land, and the Hebrew prophets call us to a world in which all people are secure in their own land and on their own mountains (Ezekiel 36:8-15; Amos 9:14-15). In the synagogue, our savior proclaimed the acceptable year of the Lord (Luke 4:16-19). Jesus calls us to be peacemakers, and to seek justice and peace with one other (Matthew 5:1-12).

We, in The United Methodist Church, need to be part of the struggle against colonialism, dependence, and discrimination. Puerto Ricans have resisted, for more than one hundred years, being assimilated into the American "melting pot" because they are proud of their culture, their language, and their heritage. They are proud of their national identity. The God of Israel, who saw, heard, and descended to liberate God's people from oppression in Egypt (Exodus 3:16-18; Isaiah 49:24-26) is calling upon us to acknowledge the colonial status of Puerto Rico and to advocate strongly for a decolonization and self determination process following international law and U.N. guidelines.

Puerto Rico's Colonial Experience

The control of the political life of Puerto Rico (a "U.S. territory") has never been in the hands of the Puerto Rican government, nor the Puerto Rican people, but in the hands of the U.S. Congress. To put it more bluntly, Puerto Rico has never ceased to be a colony of the U.S.

At the end of the Spanish-American War in 1898, the island and the people of Puerto Rico were given to the United States government as war booty. This was the direct result of the Treaty of Paris, a peace agreement signed in Paris on December 10, 1898 between the Spanish government and the United States.

Under the 1917 Jones Act, the United States imposed American citizenship over all citizens of Puerto Rico, making them eligible for the

726

draft and forcing Puerto Ricans to serve in U.S. wars. When the U.S. Congress approved the current political definition of the island in Public Law 447 on July 7, 1952, Puerto Rico became the "Commonwealth of Puerto Rico," recently redefined by Congress as a territory not incorporated of the USA. Although this measure was meant to end the colonial status of Puerto Rico, it in fact enabled the U.S. to adopt the Constitution of Puerto Rico, which had to be approved and framed by the Constitution of the U.S.

In a recent case before the 11th Circuit Court of Appeals (*U.S. vs. Sanchez*, 992F2d 1143, June 4, 1994), the court concluded that Puerto Rico remains a territory of the United States of America. The court sustained that Congress has the power to unilaterally revoke or derogate the Constitution of Puerto Rico and the statutes that regulate the relationship between the U.S. and its territory. And, more recently, the subcommittee on Indian and Insular Affairs of the House of Representatives rejected the inclusion of the current political status of Puerto Rico in a new referendum for considering that the current formula is "clearly colonial," the same formula Congress adopted in 1952.

Even former U.S. President George Bush admitted that the Puerto Rican people have never been consulted as equals on their political status. In pursuit of President Bush's idea, Congressman Don Young (R-AL) introduced the "United States-Puerto Rico Political Status Act" (H.R. 3024), which was passed by the House of Representatives on March 1998. The supporters of this bill affirmed that: "for the first time since the Treaty of Paris entered into force" Puerto Ricans will freely express their wishes regarding their political status. Therefore, they were acknowledging that Puerto Rico is still a colony today under congressional rule.

In July of 1999, the governor of Puerto Rico, the Honorable Pedro Rosello (a pro-statehood advocate), asked the UN Committee on Decolonization to urge the United States to solve the colonial status of Puerto Rico. He argued that the U.S. has the moral and international obligation of solving the colonial status of Puerto Rico.

Why Won't the U.S. Let Puerto Rico Go?

The United States maintains control over Puerto Rico for military and economic reasons. During the 1898 Spanish American War, Puerto Rico was acquired as one of the "militarily strategic" areas of the Pacific, Central America, and the Caribbean—along with Panama, Cuba

(Guantanamo), and others. Captain Alfred T. Mahan, U.S. Naval Strategic Adviser, argued that acquiring Puerto Rico would guarantee the United States' safety from enemy countries: ". . . [I]t would be very difficult for a transatlantic state to maintain operations in the western Caribbean with a United States fleet based upon Puerto Rico and the adjacent islands." Clearly, military necessity was determined by the ideology of "Manifest Destiny," dressed up in religious symbolism. Today, the U.S. controls and uses thousands of acres of Puerto Rican land for military bases (about 10 percent of Puerto Rico's national territory).

Puerto Rico has also remained under U.S. domination for political and economic reasons. After the invasion of the island, Philip C. Hana, the last U.S. consul in Puerto Rico, stated clearly, "The trade of Puerto Rico is of more value to the United States than is the trade of many of the South and Central American countries." The above strategy offered the U.S. economy the possibility of an ample market for a growing capitalist economy. What Puerto Rico had to offer to the United States politically, militarily, and economically, was of too great value to let it pass. As President Theodore Roosevelt wrote, on March 1898, to his good friend, Senator Henry Cabot Lodge: "Do not make peace until we get Puerto Rico. . . ." One can clearly see that this clashes dramatically with General Miles' promise of liberty and equality, a promise suggested in the first official proclamation presented once he was in control of the island.

Today, the U.S. continues to control the island's political and economic policies, leaving the people vulnerable to policies that adversely affect them. As a result, unemployment is disproportionately higher in Puerto Rico than any state of the union (between 10 to 15 percent higher than any state of the union). Puerto Rico is completely dependent on the U.S. economy. It does not have the right (as other nations around the world) to trade with other nations without the consent of the U.S.

Puerto Ricans have to abide by laws and rules that are established by a Congress where they have but one representative who cannot vote, so that the island's destiny and future are in the hands of people for whom Puerto Ricans are just a problem.

A Call to Action

All of the island's political parties, in recent years, have expressed their dissatisfaction with Puerto Rico's political status. However, those Puerto Ricans that struggled for the independence of Puerto Rico have been victims of discrimination, persecution, and imprisonment. The injustices suffered under Puerto Rico's colonial reality cannot be overlooked. The U.N. has clearly established that colonialism is a crime, and recognizes a colonized people's right to end colonialism. The United Nations' Decolonization Committee has approved resolutions recognizing the inalienable right of the people of Puerto Rico to independence and self-determination.

At their 1998 meeting this committee adopted a resolution requesting that steps be taken by the U.S. in order to solve the case of Puerto Rico in accordance with the General Assembly Resolution 1514 (XV). This resolution requires that for self-determination to take place colonial rule has to cease and political and economic powers be returned to the country under colonial domination.

The United Methodist Church has long stood for an end to colonialism and for the self-determination of all peoples. "We affirm the right and duty of people of all nations to determine their destiny" (Social Principles ¶ 165B). We have categorically opposed interventions by more powerful nations against weaker ones. Such actions violate our Social Principles and are contrary to the United Nations Charter and international laws and treaties. As a result of these historical positions, the General Conference asks that United Methodists advocate before the President of the U.S. and Congress for the people of Puerto Rico to be accorded full opportunity for true self determination in accordance with the General Assembly Resolution 1514 (XV), and in accordance with the United Nations Charter, and international laws and treaties.

ADOPTED 2000

See Social Principles, ¶ 165A, B, and D.

291. Haitian Asylum Seekers

WHEREAS, successive governments in Haiti, whether democratically elected or not, have failed to ensure the proper functioning of political, judicial, police, and civil institutions and normal economic and commercial activity, which has led to escalating violence and deepening poverty; and

WHEREAS, thousands of persons have been displaced in Haiti and thousands more have sought refuge in the Dominican Republic, in other countries of the Caribbean, and in the United States; and

WHEREAS, United States law offers opportunity for asylum for those with a well-founded risk of persecution; and

WHEREAS, the United States viewed Haitian refugees as economic migrants and, therefore, not eligible for asylum, and Haiti alone has been subject to an interdiction policy whereby the U.S. Coast Guard turns back refugee boats on the high seas with no offer of protection such as is offered to both interdicted Chinese and Cubans; and

WHEREAS, until December 2002, all asylum seekers arriving in Florida by sea were allowed to remain with family or friends during their asylum application process with the exception of Haitians, all of whom were detained; and

WHEREAS, Haitian families who are detained have been separated, the women and men have been placed for months in jails, in deplorable conditions, and alongside criminals, and others (including small children) have been held in overcrowded hotels unsuitable for detention, without exercise or fresh air; and

WHEREAS, when a boat filled with refugees reached shore in Miami, they were eligible for parole from detention on bond, the Immigration and Naturalization Service (now the Bureau for Customs and Border Control of the Department of Homeland Security), using the authority granted it since 9/11, obtained a stay on bonds granted to Haitians on grounds of "security risk"; and

WHEREAS, the United States, in denying Haitians a full and fair hearing and deporting them, is putting them at great risk on their return, as exemplified in the case of the 200 Haitians who arrived in Miami, December 2002, were given expedited hearings of 30 minutes (including translation time) for their asylum cases with no opportunity to consult with their attorneys, and faced deportation;

WHEREAS, the U.S., in subjecting Haitian asylum seekers to interdiction, summary return, expedited removal, prolonged detention and accelerated asylum adjudications, violates U.S. obligations under the Geneva Convention of 1951 and of U.S. asylum law; and

WHEREAS, the U.S., by its own admission, is detaining Haitian asylum seekers in order to deter a mass exodus from Haiti, and so has a policy contrary to international law and applies it in a discriminatory fashion;

Therefore, the United Methodist Committee on Relief, in cooperation with other appropriate structures of The United Methodist Church:

A. calls upon the government of the United States to:

1. end the practice of interdiction of Haitian refugees and make provision instead for a full and fair opportunity for those who have a credible fear to present it;

2. end the practice of detaining Haitian asylum seekers without parole and/or returning them, and instead to provide for their parole in the same way as the (former) Miami INS District provided for parole of asylum seekers of other nationalities;

3. grant Haitian asylum seekers full access to refugee determination proceedings and offer protection to those who qualify;

4. extend Temporary Protected Status (TPS), which would allow Haitians who had arrived in the country prior to the date announced for the start of the TPS period, to remain in the U.S. legally until the political situation in Haiti improves;

5. increase resettlement opportunities for Haitian refugees;

6. monitor conditions of return for rejected refugees;

7. take the leadership in calling for the Organization of American States (OAS), especially the countries of the Caribbean, to develop a policy for Haitian refugees in which the U.S. assumes its share of the responsibility for their protection.

B. calls upon the United Nations High Commissioner for Refugees to:

1. place an international staff person in the Dominican Republic to respond to the asylum seekers already there and to provide an existing presence given a possible increased exodus from Haiti;

2. increase this presence so as to be able to meet the needs of refugees and asylum seekers in the region;

3. work with the United States government to implement a more just policy for Haitian refugees that will conform with U.S. asylum law, as well as international law.

C. calls upon The United Methodist Church through its boards and agencies to:

1. advocate for an end to the discriminatory treatment of Haitian refugees that runs counter to the laws of the United States and of the international community;

2. involve itself in the coalition of national organizations that are in process of formation under the leadership of Church World Service and that will advocate for Haitian refugees;

3. monitor government actions with respect to Haitian asylum seekers and be ready to respond in advocacy to them; and

4. work to establish ministries of hospitality and development for Haitian refugees.

ADOPTED 2004

See Social Principles, ¶ 165.

292. Holy Land Tours

Concern has been raised across the church about special opportunities that are often being missed by United Methodists traveling to Israel/Palestine, often called the Holy Land. Christians indigenous to the area have also sharpened the question by wondering why they are so often ignored by Christian pilgrims to the region. Why, they ask, do travelers tend to honor the inanimate stones that testify to Jesus' life and ministry while ignoring the "living stones," the indigenous Christians who represent an unbroken line of discipleship to Jesus in the land that he called home?

Travelers to this land have the opportunity to be ambassadors of unity and concern to the churches and Christians in a troubled land. They also have an opportunity to learn from the spiritual traditions of the churches indigenous to the Middle East. Further, they have a special opportunity to discover firsthand the realities of a region of deep meaning and vital importance to Christians, as well as to Jews and Muslims,

Therefore, The United Methodist Church:

1. strongly affirms the resolution of the 1984 General Conference, offering "encouragement of all leaders of and participants in `Holy Land tours' to contact indigenous Christian leaders in the Middle East, and to hear the concerns of both the Israelis and Palestinians who live there, as well as visit the biblical and historical sites" ("The Arab-Israeli Conflict," *The Book of Resolutions, 1984;* page 280);

2. asks the bishops, clergy, members, agencies, and congregations of The United Methodist Church, as they plan visits to the Holy Land, to devote at least 20 percent of the program time to contact with indigenous Christian leaders and to hearing the concerns of Palestinians and Israelis on the current crisis of Palestinian self-determination;

3. recommends that United Methodists planning individual or group tours to Israel/Palestine consult with the United Methodist liaison in Jerusalem and the Middle East Council of Churches Ecumenical Travel Office to seek opportunities to worship with indigenous Christian congregations and to visit United Methodist-supported mission sites;

4. asks the General Board of Global Ministries and the General Board of Church and Society to prepare specific recommendations for United Methodists traveling in the Middle East and other sensitive regions of the world;

5. recommends that United Methodist-sponsored tours use the denomination's joint seminar program in pre-departure seminars for the travelers;

6. urges that travelers use, as advance study materials, positions adopted by General Conference and by general church agencies relating to the Middle East;

7. extends sincere appreciation to those United Methodists who have facilitated the implementation of the above recommendations in tours they have sponsored or participated in during the first quadrennium following adoption of this resolution;

8. expresses deep concern that many tours sponsored or arranged by United Methodist bishops, pastors, and laity do not schedule opportunity for all participants to enter into partnership with the indigenous Christians for the recommended program time and, therefore, fail to "Walk With the Living Stones" in their strides toward Palestinian self-determination, their rich spiritual heritage, and their faithful contemporary witness;

9. expresses deep concern that evidence continues to accumulate that Christianity is dying in the land of Jesus through economic, social, and political pressures, which have greatly diminished the numbers and percentage of Christians in the Holy Land. United Methodist bishops and other organizers of Holy Land tours have a special responsibility to adhere to these recommendations to strengthen the witness of the remaining Palestinian disciples of the Living Lord;

10. affirms the presence of The United Methodist Church in Jerusalem through our liaison office;

11. encourages tour leaders to consult with the United Methodist liaison office in Jerusalem in order to facilitate adherence to these recommendations;

12. instructs the Joint Panel on International Affairs of our general agencies to monitor and report to the General Conference regarding the implementation of this resolution;

13. underscores the significance of Bethlehem 2000, which celebrated two millennia of Christianity in the land of Jesus;

14. urges close cooperation with the Middle East Council of Churches and other indigenous Christian groups to facilitate informed, alternative travel opportunities to the region; and

15. commends the General Board of Global Ministries for initiating visits to the Bible lands that explore issues of justice and peace among all participants in the region, with special emphasis upon the concerns of our Palestinian Christian colleagues.

ADOPTED 1992
AMENDED AND READOPTED 1996
AMENDED AND READOPTED 2000

See Social Principles, ¶ 165A, B, and D.

293. Oppose Food and Medicine Blockades or Embargoes

WHEREAS, as Christians we have a moral obligation to support life and stand against any force or action that causes suffering and death; and

WHEREAS, some groups of nations, governments, and /or factions within a country have stopped the flow and free marketing of food and medicines, seeking political gains; and

WHEREAS, such practices cause pain and suffering, malnutrition, or starvation with all its detrimental consequences to the innocent civilian population, especially the children; and

WHEREAS, the blockade of food and medicines is used many times to force riots in the general population, putting them in greater danger; and

WHEREAS, the media have brought to us the terrible images of children and women suffering, sick, and starving due to the blockade of food and medicines in recent conflicts;

Therefore, be it resolved, that as United Methodists, we request the United Nations to declare the practice of impeding the flow or free commerce of food and medicines to be a crime against humanity; and, as such, not to be permitted in or by the Security Council; and

Be it further resolved, that as United Methodists, we request the President of the United States and the United States Congress to abstain from using embargoes or blockades of food and medicines, with no exceptions, as an instrument of foreign policy;

And we, as Christians, call upon world leaders to affirm life, to affirm and guarantee the right of all human beings to have access to food and adequate health care, regardless of their political or ideological views.

ADOPTED 1992
AMENDED AND READOPTED 2004

See Social Principles, ¶ 165B and C.

294. Opposition to U.S. Policy in Vieques

The Exodus story of liberation speaks volumes about the experience of the people of Vieques, Puerto Rico. Exodus Chapter 3 describes very well the experience of this courageous people who have confronted the power of the U.S. military and have come out victorious. "And the LORD said: 'I have surely seen the oppression of My people who are in Egypt, and have heard their cry because of their taskmasters, for I know their sorrows. So I have come down to deliver them out of the hand of the Egyptians, and to bring them up from that land to a good and large land, to a land flowing with milk and honey..." (3:7-8, NKJV). God has surely seen the oppression experienced by the people of Vieques, and today we can celebrate their journey of no more bombs in Vieques and no more military maneuvers.

Historical Background

Vieques is a small island about eight miles east of the island nation of Puerto Rico. In 1938 the U.S. Navy began using the island-municipality of Vieques for military practices. In 1941, during the height of WWII, the United States initiated a campaign of expropriation of territory (evicting over 3,000 people), which ended in the Navy's control of over two thirds of the island's most arable land. Thousands of families were displaced and those remaining were jeopardized in their basic means of subsistence. The net effect of these policies was the clustering of the entire civilian population into a small strip of land right in the middle of the island. Only 25 percent of the island remained under civilian control.

One of the effects of 60 years of bombing has been the degradation, and in some cases destruction, of Vieques' delicate ecosystems. Hundreds of species of plants and animals have been killed as a result of the direct impact of projectiles during military practices. These bombings and military maneuvers have led to serious contamination of the environment due to toxic residues and other contaminants.

In an article published in 1988, engineer and environmental consultant Rafael Cruz-Pérez identified three ways that the military bombs pollute the environment in Vieques: (1) chemicals in the missiles' explosive payloads, (2) dust and rock particles released into the air from the missile impact and/or detonation, and (3) metallic residues left by missiles after they detonate and the junk and scrap heap they use for target practice. "According to information provided by the Navy, this material has never been removed...Under the effects of additional explosions and sea breezes, metals are oxidized or decomposed, turning in accelerated fashion into leachates that pollute the environment," wrote Cruz-Pérez. He also cited a scientific study by the U.S. Navy that found the drinking water sources in Vieques' Isabel Segunda village and Barrio Esperanza are polluted with toxic chemicals, including TNT, tetryl and RDX. Cruz-Pérez wrote that "the study doesn't explain how these substances got to the water sources, located more than fourteen kilometers away from the shooting area."

In the 1970s, the U.S. Environmental Protection Agency sampled Vieques' air and soil. After studying the samples, the EPA determined that the air has unhealthy levels of particulate matter and the ground has iron levels above normal.

The net result of this environmental pollution is high levels of cancer and other serious health problems that Viequenes have been experiencing for years. Studies carried out by the Puerto Rico Department of Health have shown that from 1985 to 1989 the cancer rate in Vieques was 26 percent higher than the rest of Puerto Rico's already high levels of cancer.

Dr. Rafael Rivera-Castaño, a retired professor from the University of Puerto Rico's Medical Sciences Campus, has documented the increase in extremely rare diseases, including scleroderma, lupus, thyroid deficiencies, as well as more common ailments like asthma, which are significantly affecting Vieques' children.

According to Dr. Rivera-Castaño there is no reason for the children of a small island like Vieques to develop asthma. "The winds that blow in from the ocean are rich in iodine, which prevents asthma. The only possible cause for this high incidence of asthma is air pollution," he stated. Vieques does not have factories or any large industry that could cause the high incidence of asthma; the only source of air pollution on the island has been the Navy.

Economic development on the island has also been drastically affected by the Navy's presence. About 9,400 people live on Vieques and the unemployment rate is almost fifty percent by most conservative estimates.

General Electric, the only large company in Vieques, ended its operations in the summer of 2003. One of the few viable industries in Vieques today is commercial fishing. The bombing, however, has left this industry barely profitable.

Agriculture, the largest industry in Vieques before the Navy expropriated the most fertile land, is today almost non-existent. Now the economic inheritance of the people and the children of Vieques is economic stagnation.

Conclusion

The United Methodist Church has been a key supporter of the struggle in Vieques. The voice of our Church joined with the voices of many organizations in Puerto Rico and around the world to halt the Navy's maneuvers on the island. The Navy's military presence finally ended on May 1, 2003. Justice, however, is not complete. Now the people of Vieques need the Church to call for restoration for their island, urging environmental clean-up of the damage left behind by the U.S. Navy and restoration of the economy through the creation of new jobs and new industry.

Reconstruction in Vieques is only just beginning. It is important that renewal principally benefit the resident people of the island and not the hotel interests, politicians or other powerful forces. Equally important is that restoring agriculture, fishing, eco-tourism, housing, archaeologic-historic investigation and environmental study, will be the backbone of a new model of cooperative, community and sustainable development.

Community participation in all steps of reconstruction (the environmental cleanup, return of the lands, future development) is necessary to ensure a process of genuine healing and reconstruction.

The land cannot be developed if they are not returned—and demilitarized. The use proposed by the Navy for some of the land will determine the level of cleanup. The Navy looks to bypass the Viequenses' demands by "passing" the lands to the U.S. Department of the Interior and Fish and Wildlife Service, so that cleanup is not an essential part of the end of military use process.

Be it resolved that, The United Methodist Church:

1. urge the U.S. Navy to clean up the contamination caused by its practices and maneuvers;

2. urge the U.S. Congress to appropriate sufficient funds to decontaminate Vieques such that the land is again suitable for agriculture, environmental tourism and other social uses, to address the health problems resulting from that contamination;

3. urge Congress and the government of Puerto Rico to establish mechanisms to promote the reconstruction and sustainable economic development of Vieques;

4. urge that civil and religious leaders in Vieques be involved in every decision regarding the future of the island;

5. develop educational resources through the General Boards of Church and Society, Global Ministries and Discipleship, to help United Methodists and others understand the issues affecting the people of Vieques;

6. send a copy of this resolution to the U. S. House and Senate Armed Services Committees, the governor of Puerto Rico and the secretary general of the United Nations; and

7. send a copy of this resolution to the bishop of the Puerto Rico Methodist Autonomous Affiliated Church.

ADOPTED 2004

See Social Principles, ¶ 165B.

295. Puerto Rico—in Opposition to Building a Radar Station In Juana Diaz and the Town of Vieques

WHEREAS, the United States Department of Defense has decided to build a radar station in Juana Diaz and the town of Vieques, Puerto Rico; and

WHEREAS, the use of this radar station is not clear at the present time, the information being that it will be used to detect planes coming from South America with drug cargo; and

WHEREAS, all the diverse political, social, and religious communities of Puerto Rico have spoken against the establishment of such a radar station in Puerto Rico; and

WHEREAS, studies made in the United States have proven the ineffectuality of this kind of installation for the purpose designated; and

WHEREAS, the problem of drug addiction and drug trafficking is by nature moral and social problems needing that kind of approach for a solution instead of a technological one; and

WHEREAS, the bishop of the Affiliated Autonomous Methodist Church of Puerto Rico, pastors, and lay leaders of the church are actively participating, from their faith perspective, in this effort to oppose the building of this radar station,

Therefore, be it resolved, that the General Conference support Methodists Associated Representing the Cause of Hispanic Americans (MARCHA) and those sectors of the Puerto Rican society that oppose the building of the aforementioned radar station, and that copies of this resolution be sent to the President of the United States of America, the governor of Puerto Rico, the media, and the Methodist Church in Puerto Rico.

ADOPTED 1996
AMENDED AND READOPTED 2000

See Social Principles, ¶ 165*B* and *D*.

296. Guidelines for the Imposition of Sanctions

The parable of the good Samaritan invites us to see the fundamental character of God's love as unconditional and overflowing. In the face of death and in death-dealing situations, aid and succor are the hallmarks of Christian response. The neighbor in need and the good neighbor were not known for their friendly relations. They were strangers and historical enemies to one another. In the time of need, however, care was made available—unconditioned by tribe, class, kinship, gender, religion, race, and economic or political status.

Sanctions, in whatever form, lay conditions upon love and on the extension of humanitarian aid and succor; they fall short of the gospel imperative for unconditional love. Yet sanctions as political and economic tools of pressure and leverage can play a critical role in the mitigation and deterioration of conflicts. It is in this sense that sanctions are sometimes seen as a more tolerable alternative to war.

A Church World Service and Witness (CWSW) study defines sanctions as "a menu of possible diplomatic, communications and economic measures used by governments, intergovernmental bodies, and non-governmental entities to force changes in policies and behavior (usually but not exclusively on the part of a government). Sanctions cover a wide variety of measures from moratoria on diplomatic contacts to trade embargoes. Consumer boycotts and disinvestments programs are related measures."

The CWSW study notes that "sanctions can be limited and targeted, such as sports boycotts or restrictions on air travel, or they can be comprehensive, as in the case of trade embargoes. Sanctions can be unilateral (involving a single government) or multilateral (involving more than one)." The term *sanction* is most frequently associated with economic measures intended to inflict economic damage and thereby force a government or other entity to change its behavior and its policies. The effective use of sanctions lies in the political will of the imposer and is to be measured by the positive response of the sanctioned on the desired outcomes.

At the heart of the conflictive character of sanctions is the debate over when or when not to use and impose them. The caution in the use of sanctions arises out of a fundamental ethical and moral dilemma: the impact of sanctions on the innocent, and in situations of armed conflict, on noncombatants. Imposed in any way, those who impose sanctions must always take care to protect the suffering and the innocents with the basic modicum of international and humanitarian laws, uncompromised. This means the minimum guarantee of the right to the protection of human life and of human rights and civil liberties. The Christian community must insist that any and all sanctions include humanitarian exceptions—food, medicine, medical supplies and equipment, basic school supplies, and agricultural inputs and implements.

The CWSW study on the effectiveness of sanctions as an alternative to war concluded with recommendations that include the establishment of decision-making criteria for the imposition of sanctions based on the following guidelines:

- Sanctions must be a part of a broader strategy of peacemaking and an alternative to warfare.
- Sanctions should be adopted only in circumstances of flagrant and persistent violations of international law.
- Sanctions should have a clearly defined purpose.
- Sanctions have their greatest legitimacy and moral authority when authorized by a competent multilateral authority.
- The good achieved must not be exceeded by anticipated harm.
- There must be a reasonable prospect that their stated purpose of effecting political change will be achieved.
- Sanctions are effective only to the extent that they are consistently and thoroughly applied.

There must also be operational criteria to sanction impositions:

- Sanctions should be directed as precisely as possible to those bodies and leaders most responsible for the violation. Humanitarian assistance should be made available to the general population.
- The progress and effects of sanctions should be continually monitored by an independent and impartial multilateral monitoring body.
- Enforcers should be prepared to address the hurts and needs of victims in the sanctioned country and affected third countries.
- Open communication should be maintained with government leaders and civic groups in the sanctioned country.

Therefore, be it resolved, that United Methodists

- request the United Nations and the United States ascribe to and use indicators to assess potential humanitarian impacts prior to imposing sanctions and for monitoring impacts once sanctions are in place;
- request the United Nations and the United States to develop a list of humanitarian exceptions and call upon these bodies to incorporate those exemptions in any and all sanctions regimes;
- call for systematic monitoring of sanctions by independent observers;
- call for consensus to be required on a regular basis, before the United Nations imposes and/or continues Security Council sanctions;

- ensure in our advocacy efforts that sanctions and embargoes meet the requirements of available international human rights and humanitarian laws, including the provisions of the Statute of the International Criminal Court; and
- commit ourselves and our humanitarian aid efforts as United Methodists to be carried out with awareness of this understanding of sanctions, especially because sanctions, especially trade embargoes have been shown to be of limited effectiveness in achieving their stated political goals while resulting in severe hardship for the general population, especially the most vulnerable.

ADOPTED 2004

See Social Principles, ¶ 165A, B, and D.

297. Support for Self-Determination and Nonintervention

Interventions of nations into the affairs of other nations, frustrating justice and self-determination, are a reality of our time. The United Methodist Church stands unequivocally against such interventions.

The Hebrew prophets call us to a world in which all peoples are secure in their own land and on their own mountains. God breaks the bars of the yoke of oppression and feeds the people in justice (Ezekiel 34). Our Savior, Jesus Christ, calls us to be peacemakers, to live in justice and in peace with one another (Matthew 5).

The Social Principles of our church offer guidance:

- "The first moral duty of all nations is to resolve by peaceful means every dispute that arises between or among them. . . ." (¶ 165C)
- "We affirm the right and duty of people of all nations to determine their own destiny. . . ." (¶ 165B)
- "Upon the powerful [nations] rests responsibility to exercise their wealth and influence with restraint. . . ." (¶ 165B)

The United Nations Charter provides mandates. All member states shall:

- settle international disputes by peaceful means;
- respect the principle of equal rights and self-determination of peoples;

- refrain from the threat or use of force against the territorial integrity or political independence of any other state; and
- undertake to comply with the decision of the International Court of Justice in any case to which it is a party.

The Charter of the Organization of American States offers an additional directive:

"No state has the right to intervene in any way, directly or indirectly in the internal or external affairs of any other state. Interventionist actions continue to undermine international law, breed injustice, frustrate the self-determination of peoples, and are responsible for untold human suffering."

Intervention, as used in this resolution, is defined as the knowing and willful intrusion by one nation into the affairs of another country with the purpose of changing its policies or its culture. It includes any covert or overt activity—military, economic, political, social, cultural—designed to stabilize or destabilize an existing government.

We are guided in our activities for self-determination and nonintervention by our biblical faith, the Social Principles, and the principles of international law. Specifically, we adopt the following guidelines:

1. The United Methodist Church categorically opposes interventions by more powerful nations against weaker ones.

2. We oppose clandestine operations, such as political assassinations; political and military coups; sabotage; guerrilla activities; atrocities, particularly those directed at children; paramilitary efforts; military training; weapons support and supply; mining of navigable waters; economic pressures; political or economic blackmail; and propaganda aimed at destabilizing other governments. We oppose activities where national or international intelligence agencies engage in political or military operations beyond the gathering of information.

3. We support multilateral diplomatic efforts—for example, the Contadora peace process and the Afrias Initiative (Esquipulas II), which have been used as a means of settling disputes among nations. We support regional and international negotiations arranged in cooperation with the United Nations and held without resort to political rhetoric and public posturing.

4. To deepen understanding among nations and to affirm the diversity among peoples, their politics and culture, we support increased contacts between peoples—between East and West, North and South. These contacts could include cultural exchanges, tourism, educational and sci-

entific seminars, and church visitations. We applaud and encourage the development of covenant relationships between United Methodist congregations in countries with differing social or economic systems.

5. We support affirmative United Nations policies and actions to assist peoples of the world, particularly of developing nations, in achieving self-determination. We support the development and implementation of United Nations sanctions against those nations that intervene unilaterally in the affairs of other nations in violation of international law.

6. We support United Nations and regional policies and actions designed to isolate and quarantine any nation that consistently denies fundamental human rights, as enumerated in the Universal Declaration of Human Rights, to any segment of its people. Through collective action, wars fought to achieve justice might be averted or diminished. Such measures include: "complete or partial interruption of economic relations and of rail, sea, air, postal, telegraphic, radio, and other means of communication, and the severance of diplomatic relations" (Article 41, United Nations Charter). If we have failed in all these measures and there is clear evidence of genocide, then intervention by the United Nations may be necessary.

Therefore, we call upon all United Methodists, United Methodist agencies and institutions, to:

1. study the issue of intervention and to hold their own governments accountable to the United Nations Charter and other international laws and treaties;

2. deliver this resolution to their government leaders and to discuss its contents with them, urging its support and implementation; and

3. monitor their own governments and to support appropriate actions to hold their governments accountable to the United Nations Charter and international laws and treaties.

ADOPTED 1988
AMENDED AND READOPTED 2000

See Social Principles, ¶ 165*B* and *D*.

298. The Church and the Global HIV/AIDS Pandemic

In response to the global HIV/AIDS pandemic, The United Methodist Church will work cooperatively with colleague churches in every region. The Bible is replete with calls to nations, religious leaders, and faithful people to address the needs of those who are suffering, ill, and in distress. Jesus Christ reached out and healed those who came to him, including people who were despised and rejected because of their illnesses and afflictions. His identification with suffering people was made clear when he said that "whatsoever you do to the least of these, you also do to me" (Matthew 25:40, paraphrased). His commandment to "do to others as you would have them do to you" (Matthew 7:12) is a basis for the church for full involvement and compassionate response.

The Global Impact of HIV/AIDS

The global statistics are grim. At the end of 2002, 42 million adults and children were living with HIV/AIDS in the world; of these 38.6 million were adults and 3.2 million were children under 15 years. In 2002 alone, 3.1 million people died from AIDS-related causes, including 1.2 million women and 610,000 children under the age of 15. Sub-Saharan Africa has the highest number of people with HIV/AIDS: 29.4 million adults and children, with 58 percent of those infected being women. Although the region has 30 percent of the world's population, it has 70 percent of those living with HIV/AIDS. Between 2002 and 2010, an additional 42 million people are expected to become infected with HIV in 126 low and middle-income countries. More than 40 percent of the projected new cases of HIV will be people living in the Asia and Pacific regions.[1]

At this time, there is no cure for HIV/AIDS. It is mainly spread through intimate sexual contact with an infected person, by needle-sharing among injecting drug users, and, less commonly, through transfusions of infected blood or blood clotting factors. HIV can also be contracted if unsterilized needles tainted with infected blood are used by health care workers, tattooists, and acupuncturists. Other routes of transmission are through transplantation of organs from infected individuals, donated semen, and skin piercing instruments used in cosmetic, traditional, and ceremonial practices. AIDS is not caused by witchcraft, mosquito bites, or nonsexual contact such as shaking hands or hugs.

1. UNAIDS, AIDS Epidemic Update, December 2002, http://www.unaids.org/worldaidsday/2002/press/Epiupdate.html, March 3, 2003.

The HIV/AIDS pandemic compounds the strain on institutions and resources, while at the same time undermining social systems that enable people to cope with adversity. In seriously affected nations, HIV/AIDS compromises education and health systems, shrinks economic output and undermines socio-political stability. With life expectancy falling and the labor force becoming decimated, many countries are facing low economic growth rates. In parts of southern Africa, a food shortage has added to the woes. Agricultural productivity is declining as more and more women and young people are infected and become unable to work in the fields. The ramifications of HIV/AIDS are particularly grave for societies where the extended family is the system of social security for the care of elderly people, those who are ill, and orphans.

Women and children have been affected in increasing numbers. Deaths from AIDS have left 13 million orphans in Africa; the number is expected to rise to 25 million by 2010. These children are being looked after by extended families, older siblings in child-headed households, and orphan trusts. Older relatives, especially women, have to bear an enormous burden of taking care of the orphans. In countries that are also affected by war and civil strife, children and young people are more vulnerable to becoming infected with HIV because they are at the higher risk of sexual abuse, forced military recruitment and prostitution.

This burden is increased when women are also faced with stigma and discrimination and the hardships of civil strife, war, and famine. Women often have less status and less access to education, health care, and economic security than men, which in turn affect their ability to protect themselves from infection. Many cannot say "no" or negotiate the use of condoms because they fear they will be divorced or that their husband or other male partner will respond by battering them. Pregnant women who are HIV positive may be subjected to forced sterilizations or abortions. The use of rape and sexual violence as instruments of war adds a further serious dimension.

Health budgets and resources are being adversely affected in countries that have to care for increasing numbers of citizens afflicted with HIV/AIDS. For example, it costs $300 to treat a person for a year using the cheapest form of generic antiretroviral drugs, but very few can afford this medicine in sub-Saharan Africa. Antiretroviral drugs and other medicines must be made available at an affordable cost, especially in sub-Saharan Africa. Until effective preventive strategies are implemented, helpful medicines are made universally available, and an effective vaccine is introduced, the future is bleak for deterring the spread of HIV/AIDS.

The suffering borne by individuals, families, and communities and the strain placed on health-care facilities and national economies, call for intensified cooperative efforts by every sector of society, including the church, to slow and prevent the spread of HIV, provide appropriate care of those already ill and speed the development of an effective and affordable vaccine. Those caring for AIDS patients need support too. Communities, health-care workers, and home-care programs must be equipped to meet the challenge.

The Role of United Methodists

The global AIDS pandemic provides a nearly unparalleled opportunity for witness to the gospel through service, advocacy, and other healing ministries. United Methodist public health specialists, health workers, social workers, teachers, missionaries, clergy, and laity live and work in areas where the AIDS pandemic is spreading. United Methodist congregations, schools, health facilities, women's, men's, and youth groups can play a major role by providing awareness, support, education, and care to those affected by HIV/AIDS.

The United Methodist Church Urges:

A. Local congregations worldwide to:

1. be places of openness where persons whose lives have been touched by HIV/AIDS can name their pain and reach out for compassion, understanding, and acceptance in the presence of persons who bear Christ's name;

2. provide care and support to individuals and families whose lives have been touched by HIV/AIDS;

3. be centers of education and provide group support and encouragement to help men, women, and youth refrain from activities and behaviors associated with transmission of HIV infection;

4. advocate for increased levels of funding for HIV/AIDS. In the United States, persons should contact their U.S. Congresspersons and urge adequate funding for the Global Fund for AIDS, Tuberculosis, and Malaria as well as the United States' bilateral initiatives on AIDS. Additionally, funding for the United Nations Population Fund

(UNFPA) must be guaranteed from the United States each year. UNFPA works diligently to provide resources for reproductive health of women and girls as well as HIV/AIDS prevention; and

5. observe World AIDS Day on or around December 1 each year. Materials for World AIDS Day are available from the Web sites of UNAIDS (http:/www.unaids.org), the General Board of Global Ministries (http:/gbgm-umc.org/health/), and the General Board of Church and Society (http:/www.umc-gbcs.org).

B. General program agencies to:

1. assist related health institutions to obtain supplies and equipment to screen donated blood and provide voluntary HIV testing;

2. support efforts by churches, projects, and mission personnel within regions to promote disease prevention and to respond to the needs of family care providers and extended families;

3. facilitate partnership relationships between institutions and personnel from region to region, as appropriate, to share models and effective approaches regarding prevention, education, care, and support for individuals and families with HIV/AIDS;

4. assist health workers to obtain regional specific, timely updates on the diagnosis, treatment, and prevention of HIV/AIDS;

5. facilitate the sharing of pastoral-care resources and materials dedicated to the care of persons and families whose lives have been touched by HIV;

6. respond to requests from the regions to develop training seminars and workshops for church-related personnel in cooperation with ecumenical efforts, private voluntary organizations, and programs already existing in the regions;

7. advocate national, regional, and international cooperation in the development, availability, and transport of appropriate/relevant equipment and supplies for infection control, disease prevention, and treatment; and

8. support programs that focus on the enhancement of women through economic justice and education as well as programs that provide comprehensive reproductive health services, family planning, and HIV/AIDS prevention information.

C. Annual Conferences to:

1. explore HIV prevention and care needs within their areas and to develop conference-wide plans for appropriate, effective responses;

2. promote pastoral responses to persons with HIV/AIDS that affirm the presence of God's love, grace, and healing mercies;

3. encourage every local church to reach out through proclamation and education to help prevent the spread of HIV infection and to utilize and strengthen the efforts and leadership potential of men's, women's, and youth groups; and

4. support denominational global AIDS programs by encouraging congregations to prepare Healthy Homes Healthy Families Kits (http://gbgm-umc.org/health/hfk/) and contribute to Advance Specials such as Global HIV/AIDS Program Development #982345-7, Home-Based Care: Caring for HIV/AIDS Orphans #199545-2, AIDS Orphans Trust #982842-6.[2]

D. Episcopal leaders to:

1. issue pastoral letters calling for compassionate ministries and the development of educational programs that recognize the HIV/AIDS epidemic as a public health threat of major global and regional significance; and

2. provide a level of leadership equal to the suffering and desperation that individuals, families, and communities are experiencing.

God's Unconditional Love and Christ's Healing Ministry

The unconditional love of God, witnessed to and manifested through Christ's healing ministry, provides an ever-present sign and call to the church and all persons of faith to join efforts to prevent the spread of HIV, provide care and treatment to those who are already infected and ill, uphold the preciousness of God's creation through proclamation and affirmation, and be harbingers of hope, mercy, goodness, forgiveness, and reconciliation within the world.

The United Methodist Church unequivocally condemns stigmatization and discrimination of persons with HIV/AIDS and violence perpetrated against persons who are or presumed to be infected with HIV. The United Methodist Church advocates the full involvement of the church at all levels to be in ministry with, and to respond fully to the needs of, persons, families, and communities whose lives have

2. For more information about these programs and HIV/AIDS Ministries, contact Health and Welfare Ministries, General Board of Global Ministries, Room 330, 475 Riverside Drive, New York, New York 10115; Voice phone: 212-870-3871; FAX: 212-870-3624; TDD: 212-870-3709; E-Mail: aidsmin@gbgm-umc.org.

been affected by HIV/AIDS. In keeping with our faith in the risen Christ, we confess our belief that God has received those who have died, that the wounds of living loved ones will be healed, and that Christ, through the Holy Spirit, is present among us as we strive to exemplify what it means to be bearers of Christ's name in the midst of the global HIV/AIDS pandemic.

ADOPTED 2004

See Social Principles, ¶¶ 165B and 162S.

299. Understanding Globality in the United Methodist Tradition

WHEREAS, modern developments in transportation, communications, and technology have brought peoples and nations closer together; and

WHEREAS, globality tends to be understood in The United Methodist Church basically in terms of the United Methodist presence beyond the boundaries of the United States and almost exclusively in relation to those sections of the church that are structurally within it; and

WHEREAS, there are a number of churches in the Methodist family that out of a sense of calling by the Holy Spirit, a desire to affirm their own identity, and their need for self-determination have elected to become autonomous,

Therefore, be it resolved, that The United Methodist Church:

1. celebrate the God-given diversity of race, culture, and people at every level of church life in our worship and other activities;

2. celebrate the international dimension of The United Methodist Church consisting of sisters and brothers from different parts of the world including sisters and brothers from indigenous communities;

3. celebrate the autonomous affiliated Methodist churches as important expressions of the diversity of cultures and peoples called by God to be the church universal;

4. work for a future where The United Methodist Church and the autonomous Methodist churches throughout the world, expressing their faith through their unique, God-given culture, will share resources, personnel, and perspectives as equals in their common task of evangelizing all the world;

5. continue and strengthen its ecumenical commitment; and
6. embody this vision as possible in all United Methodist programs.

ADOPTED 1992
AMENDED AND READOPTED 2000

See Social Principles, ¶ 165.

300. United States Role in Colombia

For many years the nation of Colombia has suffered from internal conflict caused in part by the United States-sponsored "war on drugs." Large areas of land have been rendered unusable and crops destroyed by indiscriminate spraying of chemicals intended to destroy coca plants.

The land rights of indigenous peoples have been violated by Colombian and American corporations exploring and drilling for oil in rain forests.

Paramilitary death squads that receive support from the United States spread fear among the Colombian people. Internal civil war has left 1.4 million internally displaced people in Colombia.

The war against drugs has not succeeded in curbing the production and export of drugs from Colombia. Instead, it has created sharp political and military divisions in that country.

The present policy of the United States has only exacerbated the basic problem in Colombia which is poverty.

Therefore, The United Methodist Church urges the United States government to:

- stop all current and future United States military aid to Colombia;
- support negotiations between the Colombian government and the guerrillas to end the civil war;
- divert funds used for DEA military raids and crop fumigation to provide viable economic alternatives to coca production; and
- support indigenous peoples' rights to self-determination and control over resources in their traditional homelands.

ADOPTED 2000

See Social Principles, ¶ 165B.

301. United States-China Political Relations

Our Political Understandings

In late 1978, the governments of the United States and the People's Republic of China (PRC) reached agreement establishing full diplomatic relations. The United States ended official relations—diplomatic and military—with the authorities on Taiwan. (In March 1979, the U.S. Congress passed the Taiwan Relations Act, putting U.S. relations with Taiwan on an unofficial basis.) The United States recognized the People's Republic of China as the "sole legal government of China" but reserved the right, over PRC objections, to sell "defensive" weapons to Taiwan. At the time of normalization, the PRC refused to rule out the possibility of reunifying with the island of Taiwan by force but offered to allow Taiwan to maintain the political, economic, and military status quo if Taiwan were to recognize PRC sovereignty.

This normalization agreement ended a thirty-year period in which formal American commitments to the authorities on Taiwan blocked closer relations with the People's Republic of China. It laid the foundations for a framework of cooperation and exchanges that continues to develop. Highlights include:

- government-to-government agreements covering consular relations and embassies, civil aviation, scientific and technical cooperation, educational exchange, trade and credit, fisheries, and a wide range of other fields;
- substantial expansion of tourism and specialized visits;
- educational programs facilitating nearly 10,500 scholars and teachers (10,000 Chinese, 500 Americans) to be resident in the other country;
- numerous governmental and private institutional exchange agreements in education, the fine and performing arts, cinema, publishing, and so forth; and
- sister state-province and city-to-city agreements calling for various kinds of cooperation.

The rapid growth and elaboration of these bilateral relations has been unusual and, to many, unexpected. While the direction is generally positive and the initial results heartening, the relationship is still in its early stages. Because the PRC and U.S. systems are so different, translating worthwhile goals into concrete practice has often been difficult.

Fundamentally, the two countries have yet to determine what kind of long-term relationship they want. Misperceptions and misunderstandings are all too common on both sides, even on basic principles.

As a case in point, the two sides had sharp disagreements during 1981 and 1982 over the issue of continuing U.S. arms sales to Taiwan. By August 1982, Washington and Beijing had clarified their understanding on this question: The PRC stated that its "fundamental policy" was to "strive for peaceful reunification" with Taiwan. In that context, the U.S. government pledged not to increase and in fact to reduce its sale of arms to Taiwan. But this agreement only holds in abeyance a resolution of the Taiwan issue.

Recommendations on U.S.-China Political Relations

The United Methodist Church:

1. recognizes the necessity for China to continue its economic and social development and urges U.S. cooperation to that end within the context of Chinese independence and selfhood;

2. feels the long-term basis of U.S.-China relations should emphasize people-to-people, educational, social, and economic short-term or expedient military or strategic interests; opposes the sale of U.S. military equipment to the PRC;

3. endorses a peaceful approach to ending the long-standing conflict between the governments in the People's Republic of China and in Taiwan while recognizing that the resolution of the status of Taiwan is a matter for the People's Republic of China and for Taiwan and in that context supports the continued reduction and early cessation of U.S. arms sales in Taiwan;

4. declares our continuing concern regarding the human rights of all people on both sides of the Taiwan Straits; and

5. recognizes that U.S.-PRC relations have an important influence on the peace and stability of the Asian region, particularly in Southeast Asia; and urges the United States and the People's Republic of China and Taiwan to seek peaceful means to contribute to the peace and stability of the region.

ADOPTED 1984
AMENDED AND READOPTED 2000

See Social Principles, ¶ 165C and *D.*

302. United States-Mexico Border

The United States-Mexico border is a 2,000-mile-long area where the socio-economic dynamics of two interacting cultures have a negative impact on the quality of life of adjoining populations. This adverse situation has been exacerbated by domestic and international policies espoused by the U.S. and Mexican governments.

The border region is characterized by:

- political domination by a minority of rich and powerful families;
- drastic economic disparity between segments of the population;
- constant deterioration of the health conditions, particularly those affecting the poor;
- high incidence of crime, drug trafficking, and human trafficking for the exploitation of children and adults; and
- high rates of unemployment and underemployment, These detrimental conditions also affect the constant influx of thousands of refugees and undocumented persons coming to the United States seeking safe haven or better economic conditions. This situation of pain and suffering affects millions of women, children, and men residing on both sides of the border. The impact of these dynamics reaches well into the interiors of both countries.

Confronted by this human suffering along the United States-Mexico border region, we recognize that the vision of the "new heaven and new earth" (Revelation 21) will be only an illusion as long as "one of the least" (Matthew 25) continues to suffer.

We are particularly concerned about the following conditions:

1. *Environmental:*

    a. the constant indiscriminate use of pesticides in the growing and harvesting of agricultural products, a problem on both sides of the border; and the export of banned or restricted pesticides across the border;
    b. water contamination caused by corporations dumping industrial toxic waste and the flushing of poisonous compounds into the Rio Grande, the Colorado, and other rivers; and
    c. growing air pollution on both sides of the border.

2. *Health:*

    a. a high rate of birth defects and other health problems among industrial workers, many of whom have neither been given proper equipment nor been informed of the hazards of the toxic materials they have been exposed to;

    b. the high incidence of dysentery, tuberculosis, and hepatitis especially among children in the Colonias (rural unincorporated areas), caused by lack of adequate water treatment facilities and a lack of food and fresh water;

    c. the growing number of unsafe, crowded barracks and shanty towns without sanitation and other basic facilities due to a lack of adequate, affordable housing for workers; and

    d. the lack of access to health, education and welfare services, already overburdened by the volume of need, perpetuating the cycle of poverty and dehumanization.

3. *Economic:*

    a. wages kept low by repressing workers' bargaining rights, which keeps the border region below the average of Mexican industrial wage levels, despite the fact that the Maquiladoras are the second largest producers of export income (after oil), and the largest source of income for the Mexican border region;

    b. the lack of long-range economic and industrial development strategies, making both the U.S. and the Mexican economies more dependent on quick economic fixes such as Maquiladoras, quick cash crops, tourism, and services that can help temporarily and superficially, but ignore the needs of most of the present and future generations;

    c. the trade agreements (such as the North American Free Trade Agreement), which worsen existing economic dependencies and foster the exploitation of human and natural resources; and

    d. the region's low level of educational attainment, high incidence of illiteracy, the high dropout rate, and the availability and influx of drugs, which have a greater impact on the low-income population along the border.

4. *Civil and Human Rights:*

    a. heightened anxieties of Americans who perceive immigrants as unwelcomed foreigners who threaten U.S. social, political, and economic security;

b. strategies devised by U.S. governmental agencies and groups to harass, intimidate, and repress legal and foreign entrants into the U.S. territory; and

c. the poor administration of justice; the cultural insensitivity of border patrol agents; the high incidence of illegal use of force; and the constant violation of the civil and human rights of those detained or deported. These situations create an atmosphere of tension and distrust that adds to the polarization between Mexicans and U.S. residents and transients.

These detrimental conditions create pain and suffering among millions of women, children, and men residing on both sides of the border. The impact of these dynamics reaches well into the interiors of both countries. As Christians and United Methodists, we express our sorrow and indignation about this human suffering and accept the responsibility to use our resources toward the elimination of the root causes creating this tragic human problem. We are urged by God through Christ to love our neighbor and to do what we must to bring healing in the midst of pain, and to restore to wholeness those whose lives are shattered by injustice and oppression.

Therefore, we recommend and urge the Mexican and U.S. governments to:

- develop national and international policies that bring more economic parity between the two countries, as an integral part of any trade agreement;
- develop bi-national and multilateral agreements that improve the quality of life; safeguard water rights; and prevent the contamination of air, water, and land of both sides of the border;
- develop binding and enforceable mechanisms with respect to: labor and human rights; agriculture, including farm workers; environmental standards; and health and safety standards for both nations and in any agreements to which they are a party;
- develop and support national and international policies, such as the UN Convention on the Protection of the Rights of all Migrant Workers and Members of their Families, that facilitate the migration and immigration of peoples across the border while respecting their rights and aspirations; and
- find alternative and creative ways to reduce the foreign debt of Mexico.

We further recommend that the General Board of Church and Society, with churches in Mexico, the United States, and Canada, seek ways to network on fair trade, labor and human rights, agricultural, and environmental concerns.

ADOPTED 1992
AMENDED AND READOPTED 2004

See Social Principles, ¶ 165.

NATIONS AND CULTURES

303. Africa Reconstruction and Development

We applaud international efforts to develop a more just international economic order in which the limited resources of the earth will be used to the maximum benefit of all nations and peoples. We urge Christians in every society to encourage the governments under which they live and the economic entities within their societies to aid and work for the development of more just economic orders. (Social Principles, ¶ 165B)

The continent of Africa is in crisis. A century of colonial rule, preceded by two centuries of a vicious slave trade and followed by a generation of neo-colonialism, has left much of Africa's social, political, and economic life in a shambles. The scale of poverty and suffering is daunting. More than 300 million people survive on under $1 per day. Life expectancy remains lower than 60 in 41 of the 53 countries. Africa is now the epicenter of the greatest catastrophe in recorded human history—the HIV/AIDS pandemic—with women making up 58 percent of those infected and more than 11 million children orphaned since the pandemic started. Corruption and bribery in many African countries places unbearable burdens on the most vulnerable people and blocks progress towards poverty reduction. More than one-third of all children are malnourished, and more than 40 percent have no access to education and are far more likely to die before the age of five than children in any other region. Famine and starvation continue to devastate women, children and men. In December 2002, the United Nation's World Food Programme issued an "African Hunger Alert" appealing for emergency assistance to care for 38 million Africans threatened by famine. Almost half the continent does not have access to safe water.

Conflicts affect one in five people living in Africa. There are more than 3 million refugees throughout the continent. Arms merchants, worldwide, find ready markets for weapons and their components among African governments and the combatant movements that oppose them. Massive numbers of ruinous land mines and explosive traps are installed by both offenders and defenders but, even after the combatants have moved on, the potential for dismemberment and death remains. Demobilized child soldiers have represented a particular challenge to communities. Young people who have proven their murderous effectiveness must be nurtured into positive social productivity.

In 1995, at the United Nations World Summit for Social Development in Copenhagen, Denmark, Africa was singled out as a region requiring special attention by the international community to address the urgent need to develop the economic, social, and human resources of the continent. In the 2000 review of the implementation of the goals set by the Summit the following observations were reported:

"African countries have made real efforts to implement the commitments made at Copenhagen, but internal and external constraints continue to make progress extremely difficult. The mobilization of resources at the national and international levels to accelerate the economic and social development of Africa…through a holistic approach is needed for the full implementation of the commitments. Equitable access to education and health services, income earning opportunities, land, credit, infrastructure and technology, as well as official development assistance and debt reduction are vital to social development in Africa….

"In a rapidly globalizing economic world, Africa continues to be marginalized. A persistent decline in the international terms of trade for commodities exported from African countries has reduced real national income and savings for finance investment. The external debt burden has drastically reduced resources available for social development. Furthermore, promises made to provide official development assistance to developing countries in general and the least developed countries in particular have not been fulfilled. More concerted efforts and an internationally enabling environment are necessary to integrate Africa as well as the least developed countries into the world economy." (World Summit for Social Development and Beyond:

Achieving Social Development for all in a Globalizing World—24th Special Session of the UN General Assembly)

Africa is blessed with people of remarkable energy, spirit, and ingenuity. The continent is rich in natural resources needed by the entire world. The spread of democracy and the growing strength of African civil society offer a real chance to tackle the root causes of poverty and conflict. Social movements and organizations throughout the continent have developed to hold governments accountable and to build societies where public institutions and policies will guarantee cultural, economic, political, and social rights of all citizens. There is a call for alternative development programs based on the fundamental principles of democracy, human rights, gender equality and social justice. African leaders have developed their own initiative for establishing new relationships between Africa and the world—New Partnership for Africa's Development (NEPAD) focuses on the eradication of poverty and support for sustainable development. Key priorities of NEPAD are to attract investment in energy, agriculture, communications and human resources as well as to request increased aid and debt relief to build the infrastructure to attract investment. The African Union (replacing the Organization of African Unity) was established in 2002 and endorsed NEPAD at its first meeting in July 2002. The United Nations General Assembly officially endorsed NEPAD in November 2002. African civil society (including the faith communities), which has not been consulted on NEPAD, is organizing to study and offer their suggestions to the initiative. The debate has been heated across the continent.

The United Methodist Church in Africa is continuing to grow rapidly and is a transforming presence in many countries, influential beyond its numbers, engaging in a holistic Wesleyan ministry of outreach, evangelism, and humanitarian service. The church in Africa is part of civil society and has a strong witness to make in participating in the eradication of poverty; in promoting reconciliation, conflict resolution and justice ministries; in humanitarian assistance and refugee resettlement programs; and in pastoral training in HIV/AIDS. The church in the United States and in Europe has a strong role to play in advocating respect for the rights of African governments and peoples to define their economic policies and priorities and for continuing to support—among other things—debt cancellation, increased humanitarian and development aid, removal of trade barriers which discourage African exports, funding to overcome HIV/AIDS, ratification of the Treaty to Ban Landmines, as well as discouraging the militarization of the continent.

As Christians, our faith is in the God of Jesus Christ, who stands with the most vulnerable and oppressed people in our societies. Their well-being must serve as a guidepost for justice. God, sovereign over all nations, has made of one blood all the peoples of the earth. United Methodists, therefore, remain ever-vigilant, listening more attentively than ever to churches and movements around the world, as they struggle for social, political, economic, and spiritual development.

Therefore, we call upon the United Methodist people, local churches, and agencies to:

1. encourage United Methodist churches to increase their participation in programs of missionary support, pastors' salary supplementation, emergency relief, aid to refugees, reconstruction, and development through the appropriate units of the General Board of Global Ministries, regional councils of churches and the World Council of Churches;

2. encourage United Methodists to participate in Volunteers in Mission programs and other volunteer-based projects; and educate themselves (through orientation, cultural sensitivity, and contingency planning) for working alongside African brothers and sisters to, for example, reconstruct schools, clinics and churches. There is a need to emphasize the importance of preparation for the cross-cultural experience by volunteers and receiving partners. Orientation and training for both are available through the Jurisdictional VIM Coordinators and the Mission Volunteers Program of the General Board of Global Ministries. In addition, the United Methodist Seminar Program on National and International Affairs in Washington, DC, and New York City provides educational opportunities for United Methodists to learn about significant issues affecting Africa;

3. urge United Methodist churches in Africa to advocate with government leaders in every country as to the need for people and justice to be at the center of any concerted national and international efforts toward the eradication of poverty, sustainable and equitable development, and reconstruction on the continent of Africa. Urge United Methodist churches to become knowledgeable about the Copenhagen Commitments, the continuing United Nations plans of action and commitments to Africa and other bilateral and multilateral initiatives—including the Special Program of Assistance to Africa (SPA) and the U.N. System-Wide Initiative on Africa; Urge the United

Methodist Office for the United Nations in New York to be ready with resources regarding the United Nations and Africa;

4. urge United Methodists to persuade their governments to ratify the United Nations Convention to Combat Desertification in Those Countries Experiencing Serious Drought and/or Desertification;

5. be supportive of civil society in Africa as it seeks to continually review, assess and offer constructive suggestions to government leaders implementing the objectives of the New Partnership for Africa's Development (NEPAD). Urge the General Board of Global Ministries and the General Board of Church and Society to stay abreast of the issues involved, be ready to offer resources and opportunities for United Methodist churches and the ecumenical movement in Africa to gather, study and debate the concerns;

6. urge the General Board of Church and Society to develop a grassroots public policy action network to:

   a. address peacemaking concerns including the end of arms sales and landmines sales to government and non-government combatants;
   b. urge the reduction of foreign assistance to countries that rely on African arms sales for their own hard currency;
   c. support efforts to end the international trade in stolen diamonds and other minerals to fund chronic African wars. Support the General Board of Global Ministries' efforts to remove landmines safely and in sufficient numbers to return land to productive agriculture.

7. continue and further develop the General Board of Global Ministries' commitment to health care in Africa through comprehensive, community-based primary health care, recognizing the role that poverty and poor sanitation play in the spread of communicable diseases across the continent; the collapse of the health-care systems in many countries; and the ineffectiveness of total reliance on institutional medical models. Support the revitalization of mission hospitals as critical adjuncts to community-based care. Support AIDS prevention training through the African Churches, AIDS orphan trusts, prevention of mother to child transmission of HIV and equipped and informed home care for terminally ill family members;

8. monitor all programs of relief and development, with special attention to these criteria:

   a. give priority to women and children, who suffer the most during times of social unrest and war;

b. involve full consultation with African United Methodists relying upon their experience, wisdom, and resourcefulness;

c. design programs to alleviate the root causes of poverty, oppression, and social unrest;

d. seek resources for program support from beyond the church to augment the church's contribution to African social development;

e. implement methods to demonstrate financial transparency and accountability in all development programs and projects; and

f. program for sustainability, both in terms of ecological integrity and appropriate technologies that do not require continuing input of resources from other countries, capacity building for local hand-off of sustainable size and scale of projects.

> *God bless Africa*
> *Guard her children*
> *Guide her leaders*
> *And give her peace*

ADOPTED 2004

See Social Principles, ¶ 165A.

304. Africa University

WHEREAS, the Africa University initiative formally began by the inspiring address delivered by Bishop Emilio de Carvalho of Angola at the General Board of Higher Education and Ministry of The United Methodist Church in October, 1984; and

WHEREAS, Bishop de Carvalho was joined by Bishop Arthur Kulah of Liberia, Bishop F. Herbert Skeete, then president of the General Board of Higher Education and Ministry, Bishop Felton E. May, then president of the General Council on Ministries, and other members in discussing the educational needs of Africa and ways the denomination might respond to this challenge; and

WHEREAS, the African central conferences of The United Methodist Church asked the General Board of Higher Education and Ministry and the General Board of Global Ministries to assist them in developing significant post-secondary institutions of learning for the churches of Africa; and

WHEREAS, in St. Louis, Missouri, the 1988 General Conference of The United Methodist Church overwhelmingly approved the establishment of a university on the continent of Africa to be built in Zimbabwe and authorized an apportionment of $10 million over a four-year period and an additional $10 million to be raised through World Service Special Gifts; and

WHEREAS, the official groundbreaking for the university occurred on site in Old Mutare in 1991, and Africa University opened in 1992 with two faculties and forty students representing six nations on the African continent; and

WHEREAS, Africa University celebrated its tenth anniversary November 13-17, 2002, during which celebrations the Council of Presidents of the denomination's eleven historically Black colleges and universities met on the University's campus for the first time; the Association of United Methodist Theological Schools met on the University's campus for the first time; Ms. Graca Simbine Machel, wife of President Nelson Mandela, delivered the keynote anniversary address and was bestowed an honorary Doctor of Law degree; the Faculty of Theology building built by the South Carolina Annual Conference was dedicated and named in honor of its resident bishop, Bishop J. Lawrence McCleskey; two dormitories built by the South Indiana Annual Conference (Bishop Woodie W. White resident bishop) were dedicated and one named in honor of Vice-Chancellor Rukudzo Murapa and his wife Helen, and the second named in honor of the Associate Vice-Chancellor for Institutional Advancement, James H. Salley; and the United Methodist Volunteers in Mission Program was recognized and commended for its ministry in building ten staff houses in ten years; and

WHEREAS, Africa University's enrollment reached a significant milestone in 2002 with its student population reaching 1,123 representing 22 African nations; and

WHEREAS, the number of faculties has grown from two in 1992 to five in 2002 with the sixth faculty scheduled to open in the fall of 2003; and

WHEREAS, in February 2003, Africa University launched its Institute of Peace, Leadership and Governance with an initial enrollment of 15 students, each of whom will earn a masters degree in Peace and Governance (MPG); and

WHEREAS, 880 Africa University alumni have been deployed across the African continent in fulfillment of the University's mission to train new leaders for the nations of Africa—new leaders like Walter Manyangawirwa, who was in the first graduating class at Africa University and who is now a leader in the field of study of fungi, viruses, bacteria, and other plant diseases; and

WHEREAS, Africa University is the only private institution of higher learning on the African continent that may fly the international flag of the United Nations; and

WHEREAS, Africa University has been called "...one of the great success stories of Christian missions in the world today" by Millard Fuller, founder and president of Habitat for Humanity International; and

WHEREAS, the General Council on Ministries at its fall meeting held in Pittsburgh, Pennsylvania, on October 28, 2002, unanimously adopted a resolution expressing "its sincere congratulations and warm best wishes to Africa University on the occasion of its Tenth Anniversary," and avowing to "continue to stand in solidarity with Africa University and the United Methodist churches of Africa in educating for the right, speaking out against the wrong, and faithfully responding to the call of God to proclaim the Good News of the Gospel"; and

WHEREAS, the support and enthusiasm of United Methodists worldwide for Africa University are demonstrated in the apportionments remitted annually, the second-mile givings, and contributions from churches and individuals for the Africa University Endowment Fund; and

WHEREAS, the South Carolina Annual Conference calls upon each local church in the annual conference to pay the full Africa University apportioned line item and give generously to the Africa University Endowment Fund;

Therefore, be it resolved, that the General Conference affirms that Africa University is a dynamic and important mission project of The United Methodist Church; affirms the leadership of all those involved in the continuing development and day-to-day operations of the university; commends the Africa University Board of Directors and advisory Development Committee for their persistence, diligence, and visionary leadership in overcoming the obstacles and barriers to fulfilling the dream; and,

Be it further resolved, that the 2004 General Conference make Africa University a priority and allocate an apportionment of $10 million over a four-year period and an additional $10 million to be raised through World Service Special Gifts to continue development, construction, and endowment of Africa University as outlined in the planning process determined by the General Board of Higher Education and Ministry and the Africa University Board of Directors.

ADOPTED 2004

See Social Principles, ¶ 165A.

305. Aid for Taiwan

WHEREAS, a catastrophic earthquake struck the Island of Taiwan on September 21, 1999, killing over 3,000, and injuring more than 10,000 people, destroying hundreds of high-rise buildings and thousands of homes in the affected areas; and

WHEREAS, amid the shock, grief, and turmoil in the aftermath of the earthquake disaster, the people of Taiwan stood in solidarity; government, military, emergency services, local organizations, religious groups, and others worked tirelessly, side by side, united in common purpose, and the response of the international community was overwhelmingly supportive; and

WHEREAS, China behaved in a most imperious way while Taiwan was trying to cope with this national tragedy, hindering international humanitarian response; while words of condolences and offer of aid from China was being reported, the arrival of the Russian rescue team was delayed because the government of China would not grant them permission to use their airspace, and the Red Cross of China warned the Red Cross of the world community not to help Taiwan unless they went through their "official" channels, thus adding insult to injury; and

WHEREAS, the UN Secretary-General announced it sought "permission" from China to enter and aid one of its provinces—Taiwan—and consequently, the UN's international organization's disaster-response coordinating effort was delayed while UN officials arranged to discuss the matter with the Chinese diplomats; and

WHEREAS, the Chinese government pointedly expressed thanks to the countries for helping "their people" in "the Taiwan province." These actions contradicted China's public expression of sympathy towards a country devastated by the earthquake, proving to be an affront to Taiwan and the international communities' expressions of pain and grief,

Therefore, be it resolved, that The United Methodist Church:

1. expresses deep disappointment that China sought to assert its political right over Taiwan, when the latter was suffering from devastation caused by the earthquake in September, 1999;

2. expresses its profound sympathy for the victims of the earthquake in Taiwan and affirms its willingness to render assistance towards their reconstruction efforts; and

3. affirms its strong support for the security of Taiwan and for the self-determination of the people for Taiwan's political future.

ADOPTED 2000

See Social Principles, ¶ 165B and C.

306. Continuance of Funding to the Evangelical Seminary of Puerto Rico

WHEREAS, The Methodist Episcopal Church, one of the predecessors of The United Methodist Church, was one of the founders of the Evangelical Seminary of Puerto Rico through the Board of Home Missions and Church Extension in 1919; and

WHEREAS, many graduates of the Evangelical Seminary of Puerto Rico are serving The United Methodist Church in the United States, and it is expected that the flow of pastors coming from Puerto Rico to serve in The United Methodist Church will continue;

Therefore, be it resolved, that the General Conference of The United Methodist Church requests the General Board of Global Ministries and the General Board of Higher Education and Ministry to consult with the Evangelical Seminary of Puerto Rico, and consider the continuation of financial support to the seminary through the year 2004, and explore what financial assistance is possible beyond the beforementioned period in the light of our ecumenical and moral responsibilities as founders. Both agencies shall report their findings and recommendations to the 2004 General Conference.

ADOPTED 2000

See Social Principles, ¶ 165A.

307. East Timor

This year will mark 25 years since Indonesia's invasion and occupation of East Timor first took place. The invasion and occupation resulted in the death of over 200,000 people (one-third of the population) according to Amnesty International and Roman Catholic Church estimates. The United States government provided crucial military and diplomatic support for Indonesia's invasion and occupation of East Timor.

On November 12, 1991, the Indonesian army massacred over 270 Timorese mourners at the Santa Cruz cemetery in Dili, East Timor. Western journalists witnessed that massacre, and their reports to the outside world resulted in the renewal of a worldwide effort to free East Timor from Indonesian domination and repression.

In January 1995, a delegation from the National Council of the Churches of Christ in the USA and a representative of the Canadian Council of Churches visited East Timor to express solidarity with the churches and people of East Timor. Following that visit, the delegation recommended an advocacy effort that endorsed demilitarization of East Timor and determination of East Timor's political status with the full participation of the East Timorese people.

A resolution of The United Methodist Church, adopted in 1996, deplored the continuing occupation of East Timor and the resultant oppression and abuse of human rights. That resolution supported the rights of the East Timorese to self-determination, calling for an end to the Indonesian occupation, intensified United Nations efforts to resolve East Timor's political status, and full participation of the East Timorese in the just resolution of that status. The resolution urged the United States to cease military aid, military training, and arms sales to Indonesia during its de facto military occupation of East Timor. The resolution also exhorted the United States government and other governments to take legislative and administrative action to pressure Indonesia to end its occupation and cooperate with the United Nations in bringing about East Timorese self-determination.

In July 1998, the United States Senate unanimously passed a resolution affirming the right of the East Timorese to self-determination, and in October 1998, the full Congress went on record as supporting East Timor's right to self-determination. In November 1998, Congress passed into law an effective ban on the use of all weapons in East Timor.

In late January 1999, for the first time since the 1975 invasion of the territory, the Indonesian government publicly raised the possibility of independence for East Timor. In February 1999, the Indonesian government moved East Timorese national resistance leader, Xanana Gusmao, from Cipinang Prison in Jakarta to a form of house arrest.

In May 1999, United Nations-sponsored talks between Indonesia and Portugal on the future of East Timor resulted in Indonesia agreeing to allow a United Nations-sponsored referendum, ultimately held on August 30, 1999, on whether the East Timorese supported or rejected the Indonesian government's autonomy proposal. The Indonesian government also stated that if the East Timorese rejected that autonomy proposal in this popular consultation, it would set East Timor free.

In the years prior to the August 30, 1999, referendum on East Timor's independence, the Indonesian National Army (TNI) in East Timor created and armed paramilitary groups and vigilante gangs for the purpose of terrorizing pro-independence civilians, thereby creating a severe refugee crisis and threatening to undermine this historic opportunity to achieve a peaceful resolution of the conflict in East Timor.

East Timorese 1996 Nobel Peace Prize laureate, Bishop Carlos Filipe Ximenes Belo, called repeatedly for United Nations peacekeepers to be sent to East Timor to prevent further bloodshed and monitor the rapidly deteriorating human rights situation. Those warnings went unheeded during the period prior to the referendum.

Despite the violence and intimidation directed against East Timorese supporters of independence, 78.5 percent of East Timor's voters rejected Indonesia's autonomy proposal and, thereby, supported independence from Indonesia in the United Nations-sponsored referendum. International observers monitored the election and verified the results, which reflected a voter turnout for the referendum of 98 percent of registered voters.

Following the announcement of the results of the August 30, 1999, election, Indonesian armed forces and their proxies in anti-independence paramilitary groups and vigilante gangs engaged in the systematic destruction of East Timor, including the burning and leveling of Dili and numerous towns and villages, the forced deportation of thousands of civilians, and widespread killing and torture. Those targeted for assassinations included religious leaders, student leaders, relief workers, and countless others who were perceived as supporting independence.

Not even East Timor's most internationally prominent figures were spared from the wave of terror that followed the vote for independence. Bishop Belo was forced into exile after anti-independence forces attacked and burned his residence. Following his release from captivity, East Timor's national resistance leader, Xanana Gusmao, decried the systematic efforts to eliminate community leaders and other supporters of independence for East Timor, and to destroy the places where they lived and worked.

In September 1999, the Vatican deplored the violence directed against the East Timorese people and urged the United Nations to send international peacekeepers to East Timor. The Vatican's foreign minister described the circumstances in East Timor as "another genocide."

Statements of United Nations officials in September 1999 confirmed numerous accounts from the East Timorese people and international observers of a close connection between the Indonesian military and the anti-independence militias. The United Nations High Commissioner on Human Rights concluded that Indonesian forces were "orchestrating" the violence and that it appeared to be "systematic." United Nations Secretary-General Kofi Annan called for an investigation of possible "crimes against humanity." United Nations officials have raised the prospect of a future war crimes tribunal.

The destruction of East Timor in September 1999 also produced a refugee crisis of staggering proportions, forcing hundreds of thousands of East Timorese people into hiding within that country or into refugee camps in Indonesian West Timor. The United Nations High Commissioner for Refugees expressed grave concern for the status of refugees in West Timor citing "mounting evidence" of forced deportations to West Timor and forcible separation of men from women and children.

In response to the destruction of East Timor, the President of the United States announced the suspension of military ties and other assistance to Indonesia in September 1999. Military transfers and commercial weapons sales were suspended, as were bilateral economic assistance and multilateral assistance from the International Monetary Fund and World Bank. Economic assistance has been resumed, despite the fact that more than 100,000 East Timorese were still in camps in West Timor, many against their will. The Clinton Administration is also moving toward a resumption of U.S. military training for Indonesian forces. The United Nations Security Council unanimously passed a resolution in September 1999 approving an international force for East Timor empowered under Chapter VII of the United Nations Charter, and authorized to take all necessary measures to restore peace and security and facilitate humanitarian assistance. The resolution directed Indonesia to take immediate measures for the safe return of refugees and called for United Nations administration of East Timor during the transition to East Timorese self-rule. But months later it remained uncertain whether Indonesian forces would cooperate in allowing full access to refugees in West Timor and elsewhere in Indonesia.

Therefore, be it resolved, that The United Methodist Church, its members, local churches, annual conferences, central conferences, and general agencies:

1. recognize our continuing moral and religious duty to respond to acts of inhumanity and genocide, and to rescue a people, a nation, and a culture from annihilation;

2. reaffirm their call to the United States government and other governments to act within their powers to ensure that the Indonesian government fully complies with all United Nations efforts on East Timor in the years to come;

3. deplore the systematic destruction of East Timor orchestrated by Indonesian forces and allied paramilitary groups in the wake of East Timor's vote for independence in the United Nations-sponsored referendum of August 30, 1999, including the killing and torture of civilians, targeted assassinations of religious and community leaders, burning and leveling of communities, forcible mass deportations, and separation of families;

4. exhort the executive and legislative branches of the United States government and the United Nations to take all steps within their respective powers to reduce the suffering of the East Timorese people, ensure that the forces responsible for their slaughter be brought to justice in an international war crimes tribunal, immediately safeguard and account for all refugees within East and West Timor and elsewhere in Indonesia, provide for the safe return of refugees, and facilitate the rebuilding of East Timor as an independent nation;

5. commend the President of the United States and the United States Congress for taking steps in 1999 to suspend military aid and assistance and weapons sales to Indonesia;

6. emphasize that the termination of United States and multilateral assistance to Indonesia (including government-to-government and

commercial arms sales) must be comprehensive and continuing in order to achieve effective results, and that additional pressure on the Indonesian military and allied militia remains necessary to ensure that the refugees in West Timor and elsewhere are able to return to East Timor;

7. commend the United Nations Security Council for unanimously approving an international force to stop the destruction of East Timor and its people, protect its refugees and secure their return, provide immediate humanitarian assistance, and implement the transition from Indonesian occupation to East Timorese self-determination;

8. express concern that further vigilance will be necessary to achieve these objectives, and that the Indonesian military and allied militia may continue to frustrate these efforts even after their withdrawal from East Timor;

9. urge the United Methodists, including the General Board of Global Ministries and the General Board of Church and Society, to make the issue of East Timor a priority for social justice and mission purposes, and to support constituency education, emergency assistance, direct relief efforts, and related projects on East Timor; and

10. direct that The United Methodist Church, immediately following 2000 General Conference, send copies of this resolution to the secretary-general of the United Nations, the president of the UN General Assembly, the President of the United States, all U.S. senators and congressional representatives, the president of Indonesia, president of Portugal and all appropriate ecumenical colleagues.

ADOPTED 1996
REVISED AND ADOPTED 2000

See Social Principles, ¶165A, B, and C.

308. Global Economy and the Environment

The United Methodist Church has been rightly concerned about the environment and its sustainability, given the rapid depletion of natural resources and the contamination of the air, water, and land. However, we have been slow to recognize the impact of the emerging global economy and its impact upon the environment.

When the economic institutions were contained within the boundaries of countries, governments had the power to regulate.

Particularly, in the area of the environment, communities could exercise control so that pollution and waste could be regulated and conservation encouraged. Of course, this adds costs to doing business. However, if everyone is under the same constraints, no one is at a disadvantage.

As countries rush to open up markets in the name of free trade, it is obvious that those countries that have strict environmental regulations are going to be at a competitive disadvantage in attracting and keeping business. Business will seek countries in which to operate that have lower environmental standards and, therefore, lower operating costs. Pressures will increase on countries with higher standards to lower them, and developing countries will be hesitant to enact environmental legislation.

The United Methodist Church therefore recommends:

1. that every country, including the United States, require that there be roughly equivalent environmental standards between itself and any other country with which it enters into a free-trade agreement, so that there is not a competitive disadvantage for the country with the stricter standards. Mechanisms should also be included in the agreement that will allow for further new standards of environmental regulations in the future;

2. that the General Board of Church and Society develop a statement outlining the relationship of the world economy to the environment and communicate this to appropriate governmental agencies and the church;

3. that the General Board of Church and Society develop study materials for local congregations; and

4. that local congregations study the implications of the global economy on the environment. Study materials might include: *For the Common Good: Redirecting the Economy Toward Community, The Environment, and a Sustainable Future,* by Herman E. Daly and John B. Cobb; *Sustaining the Common Good, A Christian Perspective on the Global Economy;* or materials to be developed by the General Board of Church and Society.

ADOPTED 1996
READOPTED 2004

See Social Principles, ¶165B and D.

309. Globalization and Its Impact on Human Dignity and Human Rights

What are human beings that you are mindful of them, mortals that you care for them? Yet you have made them a little lower than God (or divine beings, or angels), and crowned them with glory and honor.

—Psalm 8:4-5 NRSV

Human rights are what make us human. They are the principles by which we create the sacred home for human dignity. Human rights are what reason requires and conscience commands.

—Kofi Annan, United Nations Secretary General

Our Globalized World

In an age of globalization, the struggle for human rights has become more complex and challenging. While protections for human rights are increasingly passed by governments and international bodies like the United Nations, grave threats to and gross violations of human rights are also on the rise.

The world's financial capital is ever more integrated, and wealth is ever more centralized in the hands of financial elites and institutions. Realizing social and economic rights, especially eradicating hunger and unemployment, is becoming increasingly difficult. Bringing conflicts to a just and durable resolution is more daunting with the increased capacity of individuals, governments and their military forces, and other groups, including paramilitary, to organize and unleash violence. These groups have access to more sophisticated communications technology and more deadly instruments of war than ever before.

Ending violence and wars, and checking impunity and disregard for international human rights and humanitarian laws, will require more than political will and moral courage. Concrete programs and mechanisms are needed to realize the totality of human rights—civil, political, social, economic, and cultural.

Our Christian tradition shows us an alternative to globalization. It is a "counter-globalization" that empowers God's people to "do justice, and to love kindness, and to walk humbly" (Micah 6:8b) with God. What must be globalized is a culture of peace that institutes peace with justice in ways that are visible and tangible in the lives of peoples and communities. We are challenged to globalize an ethos that respects and protects human life with human rights so that all "may have life, and have it abundantly" (John 10:10b) as God intends.

Biblical and Theological Grounding

The Psalmist exclaims: "What are human beings that you are mindful of them, mortals that you care for them? Yet you have made them a little lower than God" [or divine beings, or angels], and crowned them with glory and honor." (Psalm 8:4-5). Every human being bears the likeness of our just, gracious, and loving God: "God created human beings, in the image of God they were created; male and female were created" (Genesis 1:27, adapted).

Human dignity is the foundation of all human rights. It is inherent and inborn. Human dignity is the image of God in each human being. Human dignity is the sum total of all human rights. We protect human dignity with human rights. Human rights are the building blocks of human dignity. They are indivisible and interdependent. It is God's gift of love for everyone. Human rights, being the expression of the wholeness and fullness of human dignity, are indivisible and interdependent.

Human rights—expressed in affirmations and declarations, treaties and conventions, laws and statutes—are products of struggles to affirm and fulfill the wholeness and fullness of life. As peoples and governments increase the catalogue of rights that are recognized and protected, protections not only increase, but so do our approximation of and striving for human dignity. To be engaged in the human rights struggle is to accept God's gift of love in Jesus Christ who has come to affirm all God's people as they are—as individuals and people in community together.

But human rights do not affect humanity alone. The integrity of God's creation is possible only with the affirmation of both the dignity of all persons and the integrity of the whole ecological order. Human rights cannot be enjoyed in an environment of pillage and decay.

Human dignity is the common bond that affirms the individuality of each human being while celebrating the plurality and variety of communities to which each belongs, including the diverse economic, political, religious, ideological, racial, class, gender, and ethnic identities each represents.

The United Methodist Church and Human Rights

The United Methodist Church's Social Principles provide foundational understanding of rights and freedoms. These principles affirm both the sovereignty of God over all of creation and the duties and responsibilities of each person for the natural and nurturing world, and the social, economic, political, and world communities. At their spring 1998 meeting, and on the occasion of the 50th anniversary of the *Universal Declaration of Human Rights*, the Council of Bishops called on "United Methodists across the connection worldwide [to] join in . . . safeguarding the worth and dignity of peoples and the integrity and sacredness of all of God's creation."

"As Christians," the bishops said, "loving our God and loving our neighbor together advance the imperatives of human rights. Human rights enable us to express in concrete ways our love for one another by assuring that each person's value is recognized, maintained, and strengthened."

Human rights are safeguards of peoples and communities against violations of their rights and infringements on their freedoms. To this end, the General Conference called on "all governments to accept their obligation to uphold human rights by refraining from repression, torture, and violence against any person" and "to ratify and implement international conventions, covenants, and protocols addressing human rights in the context of justice and peace" (¶ 164 , Social Principles).

Arenas for Human Rights Work

An emerging feature of the new global context is the rise and increasing participation of peoples' and citizens' organizations in leading the establishment of just, participatory, and sustainable communities. This new context must be celebrated; it is one venue of counter-globalization. The so-called "civil society," especially through non-governmental organizations, is increasingly present in forums where grassroots advocacy and global governance are at stake. Through the presence of non-governmental organizations in all levels of governance—local, national, regional, global—globalization is challenged in multiple ways, from the local and the global. Human rights monitors, themselves a threatened group of defenders, have increased in the ranks of civil society. As a new millennium is ushered in, we lift the following arenas for human rights work to all United Methodists worldwide, and to the attention of all general agencies, particularly the General Board of Church and Society and the General Board of Global Ministries of The United Methodist Church.

A. Children's Rights and Well-Being: Receiving the Reign of God as a Little Child

Let the little children come to me, and do not stop them; for it is to such as these that the kingdom of heaven belongs (Matthew 19:14).

The Social Principles strongly support children and children's rights. It says: "Once considered the property of their parents, children are now acknowledged to be full human beings in their own right, but beings to whom adults and society in general have special obligations. All children have the right to quality education. . . . Moreover, children have the rights to food, shelter, clothing, health care, and emotional well-being as do adults, and these rights we affirm as theirs regardless of actions or inaction of their parents or guardians. In particular, children must be protected from economic, physical, and sexual exploitation and abuse." (¶ 162C).

The *United Nations Convention on the Rights of the Child* expresses this same concern for the child. The convention extends the basic concept of protection to the level of human rights. The Convention affirms that the rights described in the *Universal Declaration of Human Rights* are rights that belong also to children.

Children's rights are human rights. United Methodists worldwide must continue to urge their governments to implement the convention, and for the United States to ratify it.

The proliferation of and easy access to small arms have a devastating effect on our children. Children must never have access to or opportunity to use guns. Both the children killed and those wounded by small arms are victims of a culture of violence which denies human rights, snuffs out precious human life, and debases human dignity.

The United Methodist Church is called to join the international campaign to prevent the proliferation and unlawful use of small arms. The campaign raises our awareness of the need for emergency measures to save the lives of children, in our schools, in inner cities, and in many parts of the world, particularly those countries and communities that are highly militarized and governed by national security laws.

Children in situations of conflict and war test our commitment to the future. There is something wrong in our sense of the moral when children are put in harm's way. No boy or girl must be sent to the front lines of war, battles, and conflict. The field of play must not be replaced with the field of combat. War games are not child games. Playgrounds are for children; battlegrounds are not.

The United Methodist Church must oppose the recruitment and use of child soldiers. We must support the call of the United Nations Commission on Human Rights (Resolution 1999/80) to raise the current minimum age limit set by Article 38 of the *Convention on the Rights of the Child* on the recruitment into the armed forces or participation of any person in armed conflicts from 15 to 18. The General Conference of the International Labor Organization (ILO), through Convention 182 (1999), prohibits forced or compulsory recruitment of children under the age of 18 for use in armed conflict. ILO also recommends (Recommendation 190) that governments prohibit the use, procuring or offering of a child for activities which involve the unlawful carrying or use of firearms or other weapons.

B. Migrant Workers: Entertaining Angels Unawares

"Let mutual love continue. Do not neglect to show hospitality to strangers, for by doing that some have entertained angels without knowing it" (Hebrews 13:1-2).

A complex of factors—civil conflicts, human rights abuse, extreme poverty, and misguided development schemes—have produced in many countries around the world an unprecedented number of migrant workers and people looking for jobs beyond their national borders.

While globalization heralded the swift movement of capital across national borders, the movement of laborers seeking work in richer countries of the world has been slow and increasingly restricted. Transnational corporations have moved to poor countries where labor is much cheaper and workers' organizing is either weak, suppressed, or altogether banned.

The underlying causes of migration are twofold: first, economic competition which forces industrial economies to hire cheap labor in order to remain competitive in the global market, and second, to resolve structural imbalances in the local labor force on the part of the labor-sending countries.

Migrant workers continue to be discriminated against and abused, especially those who are undocumented in their host countries. Women migrants are particularly vulnerable to exploitation especially when they work in gender-specific jobs that consign them to various forms of sexual, domestic, and menial work. Studies show that the majority of migrants are uprooted because of the lack of jobs at home, or because jobs pay extremely low wages. While globalization has spawned more capital and spurred greater production, workers' wages have been kept low and below a livable wage even in those countries whose governments have a prescribed minimum wage.

Migrants' rights are human rights. It is tragic when migrants, whose rights have already been violated in their home countries, find their human rights also violated in their foreign host countries. Invoking host country laws rarely works in their favor. United Methodists should urge their governments to ratify and implement the *United Nations International Convention on the Protection of the Rights of All Migrant Workers and Members of Their Families.* This Convention will be an instrument to protect, secure, and ensure the human rights of migrant workers and their families.

C. Indigenous Peoples: Toward Self-Determination

But they shall all sit under their own vines and under their own fig trees, and no one shall make them afraid; for the mouth of the Lord of hosts has spoken (Micah 4:4).

Globalization threatens the human rights of indigenous peoples, including their aspirations for self-determination. Exploration and colonization have led to rapid appropriation of indigenous peoples' lands and natural resources, and the destruction of their sciences, ideas, arts, and cultures.

Indigenous peoples struggle against the industries encroaching on their sacred lands. They are fighting for sovereignty over their ancestral lands in the face of systematic campaigns of extermination. They face population transfers, forced relocation, and assimilation, often because of the aggressive development interests of big business.

Indigenous peoples demand respect of their right to their culture, spirituality, language, tradition, forms of organization, ways of knowing and doing, and their intellectual properties. Indeed, it will be hard for indigenous peoples all over the world to exercise their fundamental human rights as distinct nations, societies, and peoples without the ability to control the knowledge they have inherited from their ancestors.

The 1992 General Conference urged The United Methodist Church to "place itself at the vanguard of the efforts to undo and correct the injustices and the misunderstandings of the last 500 years" of colonialism. It raised the church's awareness of "the shameful stealing of the Native's land and other goods and the cruel destruction of their culture, arts, religion, the environment, and other living things on which their lives depended."

Religious intolerance is one form of human rights violation perpetrated on indigenous peoples around the world. The experience of forced relocation by the Dineh (Navajo) of Black Mesa in Arizona is an example of religious intolerance. The Dineh consider their ancestral lands as sacred. For them, to be uprooted is to be exterminated as a people. Big mining companies have been responsible in the destruction of livelihood, sacred sites, and ancestral homelands of indigenous peoples. Indigenous peoples' rights are human rights. United Methodists are urged to support the ongoing drafting and the eventual adoption of the *United Nations Declaration on the Rights of Indigenous Peoples*. United Methodists must also support the establishment of a Permanent Forum of Indigenous Peoples and the appointment of a Special Rapporteur on Indigenous Populations, both within the aegis of the United Nations. We must also continue support for the work and the mandate of the United Nations Special Rapporteur on Religious Intolerance.

D. Impunity: The Case for an International Criminal Court

You shall not render an unjust judgment; you shall not be partial to the poor or defer to the great: with justice you shall judge your neighbor (Leviticus 19:15).

A culture of peace must be globalized today. The prevailing culture of repression, oppression, and exploitation has no place in this culture of peace. Only the pursuit of a just peace, which includes the search for truth and justice for victims, will bring about forgiveness, reconciliation, and healing in many rural villages, towns, cities, nations, and regions of the world that are scarred by conflict and war.

The establishment of an International Criminal Court (ICC), as provided for in a treaty adopted in Rome in June 1998 by the United Nations Diplomatic Conference of Plenipotentiaries on the

Establishment of an International Criminal Court, provides an important step in ending impunity. This court will hear cases against war crimes, genocide, crimes against humanity, and crimes of aggression. Faith-based and religious groups, working together with the Coalition for an International Criminal Court (CICC), identified several moral and ethical imperatives and included these in a draft preamble they offered the Rome Conference to consider. The draft stated: "Desirous that the quest for justice includes retributive justice whose purpose is the prosecution and punishment of offenders while insuring the rights of the accused to fair trials, restorative justice whose purpose is that of reparation, restitution and rehabilitation for the victims, and redemptive justice which must be seen as the enablement of communities to deal with the truths of the past in ways which will allow and enable social reconstruction and reconciliation, and the ending of cycles of violence;

"Recognizing that adjudication of crimes of international concerns that have transcended national boundaries are often beyond the scope of national criminal justice systems, and that crimes whose immediate victims have occurred within national contexts are often beyond the competence or ability of national judicial systems; *Noting the basic principles of justice for victims of crime and the abuse of power approved by the United Nations General Assembly; therefore, establish the International Criminal Court . . .*"

As Pope John Paul II stated, "A positive sign of the growing will of the States to acknowledge their responsibility in the protection of the victims of [crimes against humanity], and their commitment to prevent them, is the recent initiative of the Diplomatic Conference of the United Nations that distinctly adopted the Statute for an International Criminal Court that will assess the guilt and punish those responsible of genocide, crimes against humanity and war crimes."

United Methodists all over the world must urge all governments, especially the United States of America, to sign and ratify the treaty to establish the court. The work of the CICC and the Washington Working Group on the International Criminal Court (which focuses on getting the U.S. to ratify the treaty) must be supported. In their support, United Methodists must preserve and strengthen the unprecedented provisions of the Rome Statute calling for an end to impunity for crimes committed against women and children. Also, the ancestral and sacred sites of indigenous peoples must be included in the Court's definition of protected sites.

E. Religious Liberty: The Case Against Intolerance

Religious liberty forms part of the pantheon of human rights. The *Universal Declaration of Human Rights* provides that "Everyone has the right to freedom of thought, conscience and religion: this right includes freedom to change his religion or belief, freedom, either alone or in community with others and in public or private, to manifest his religion or belief in teaching, practice, worship and observance" (Art. 18). Religious liberty, according to The United Methodist Church, includes the belief that "it is the right of a person to be allowed to follow the call of conscience when it becomes impossible to live by both the dictates of the State and the decisions of faith" (Religious Liberty, *1996 Book of Resolutions*, p. 571).

Religious liberty continues to be denied and violated in many parts of the world. Concerns about religious persecution have been raised by almost every religious group especially in places where one particular religion or belief is in a minority position. Religious intolerance, of both the established as well as "nontraditional" religions, is growing both in new and established democracies. The rise in religious extremism, of all sorts, and from all of the established and nontraditional religions, have been convenient pretexts for the curtailment of the exercise of religious liberty by many governments around the world.

The United Methodist Church must continue to foster further cooperation among spiritual, religious, and ecumenical bodies for the protection of religious freedom and belief. It must enter into healthy dialogues with peoples of differing faiths and ideologies, including Native and indigenous peoples, in the search for shared spiritual, social, and ethical principles that engender peace and justice.

The United Methodist Church is already committed to uphold the minimum standards of the right of belief that are contained in the provisions of the *United Nations Declaration on the Elimination of All Forms of Intolerance and of Discrimination Based on Religion or Belief* adopted by the United Nations General Assembly on November 25, 1981. This declaration enunciates that "freedom of religion and belief should also contribute to the attainment of the goals of world peace, social justice and friendship between peoples and to the elimination of ideologies or practices of colonialism and racial discrimination."

United Methodists must urge their governments and encourage civil society to enter into dialogues about racism and discrimination and resolve to address especially those concerns that have religious bases. The United Methodist Church must also support and participate in the World Conference on Racism and Discrimination in 2001 organized by the United Nations.

F. Peace and Peace-building: The Case for a Culture of Peace

[God] shall judge between many peoples, and shall arbitrate between strong nations far away; they shall beat their swords into plowshares, and their spears into pruning hooks; nation shall not lift up sword against nation, neither shall they learn war anymore (Micah 4:3).

In this era of globalization, the icons of war are more prominent and the arsenal of killing machines is more lethal than ever before. Our images of peace and the implements that make for a just peace most often are stymied by these icons and arsenals.

The resolution of conflicts and the establishment of a just and durable peace proceed from a just and liberating practice of governance on all levels of life-local and global. Just governance thrives not on wars and rumors of wars, but in the advancement of a world order that protects human rights, develops sustainable communities, cultivates a culture of peace, empowers people and their associations, and promotes a just and participatory democracy. It is imperative for human rights to be the foundational principle for a just and durable peace. The United Methodist Church must participate in building communities that prioritize the eradication of poverty and the elimination of hunger; the ending of wars and the resolution of conflicts; and the overcoming of ignorance, curing of diseases, and healing of enmities. The United Nations remains the single most important international institution to achieve these ends. The United Methodist Church must continue to support the United Nations. Our participation in its many activities allows us to participate in making it a responsible and effective global force in peacemaking and human rights.

The United Methodist Church must also support The Hague Agenda for Peace and Justice for the 21st Century. This agenda, produced by a historic conference in The Hague in May of 1999, and encompassing fifty areas of concern with:

1. root causes of war and the culture of peace;
2. international humanitarian and human rights law and institutions;
3. the prevention, resolution, and transformation of violent conflict; and
4. disarmament and human security.

The United Methodist Church must also support the Pillars of Peace for the 21st Century, written as a policy statement in support of the United Nations for the National Council of the Churches of Christ in the USA. The seven pillars state that peace rooted in justice requires:

1. increased political collaboration and accountability among governments within the United Nations system, among regional bodies, governments, local authorities, people's organizations, and global economic structures to seek the common good and equality for all;

2. increased moral, ethical, and legal accountability at all levels from governments, financial institutions, multilateral organizations, transnational corporations, and all other economic actors to seek a just, participatory, and sustainable economic order for the welfare and well-being of all people and all creation;

3. a comprehensive international legal system, capable of change as conditions require, in order to prevent and resolve conflicts, to protect rights, to hold accountable those who disturb peace and violate international law, and to provide fair and effective review and enforcement mechanisms;

4. the participation of vulnerable and marginalized groups, seeking to promote justice and peace, in those mechanisms capable of redressing the causes and consequences of injustice and oppression;

5. the nurturing of a culture of peace in homes, communities, religious institutions, and nations across the world, including the use of nonviolent means of resolving conflict, appropriate systems of common security, and the end of the unrestrained production, sale, and use of weapons worldwide;

6. respect for the inherent dignity of all persons and the recognition, protection, and implementation of the principles of the International Bill of Human Rights so that communities and individuals may claim and enjoy their universal, indivisible, and inalienable rights; and

7. a commitment to the long-term sustainability of the means of life, and profound reorientation of economic systems and individual lifestyles to support ecological justice for human communities in harmony with the whole of creation.

The United Methodist Church must also continue its support for the campaign to ban land mines by urging all governments to ratify and implement the landmine ban treaty which prohibits the use, production, stockpiling and transfer of antipersonnel land mines. This treaty also calls on parties to increase mine clearance and victim assistance efforts around the world.

United Methodists must also urge their governments to ratify the Comprehensive Nuclear Test Ban Treaty. Counterglobalization happens when we ban land mines, abolish nuclear weapons, and prevent wars from happening.

G. Economic, Social, and Cultural Rights: That the Hungry May Be Filled

When you give a banquet, invite the poor, the crippled, the lame and the blind (Luke 14:13).

The Lord our God commanded us "to do justice, and to love kindness, and to walk humbly." Justice, kindness, and humility underscore society's obligations to its people. But even with the indivisibility of civil, political, economic, social, and cultural rights, global hunger and poverty challenge our priorities. It is a challenge that confronts and addresses our concern for lifting the poor and marginalized among us. In this era of globalization, poverty is defined as the inability of a human being to take advantage of global and market opportunities that are supposed to be booming and soaring. This globalization process deifies the market even as it commodifies the earth and its resources, if not even people themselves who become pawns to economic production. One's worth and dignity in this globalization process is measured by one's ability to contribute to the gains of the market.

But gain or loss, in this era of globalization, it is the poor, the marginalized, and the vulnerable who suffer from price increases, reductions in government support for needed social and environmental programs, business disruptions, higher unemployment levels, and increased human rights violations.

The sudden devaluation and large outflow of capital from countries such as recent ones in Mexico, Thailand, Indonesia, and South Korea resulted in severe economic downturns, political instability, widespread social turmoil, job loss, and human suffering. The proposal by Professor James Tobin, Nobel laureate in economics, to levy taxes on cross-border speculative financial and currency exchange transactions deserves our support. The so-called "Tobin Tax" aims to:

1. shrink the volume of the currency market;
2. help to restore national control of currency; and
3. generate sizable revenue that would provide resources urgently needed to wipe out extreme poverty.

The indivisibility of human rights underscores the understanding that freedom is hollow without food, that justice without jobs is like a clanging cymbal, and that liberty is a sham when people do not have land to inhabit and farm. The right to food and the right to employment are fundamental economic human rights. Societies become peaceful when the demands of justice are met. Justice becomes not only a dream but a reality when implements of war give way to implements of peace. Food and jobs, also, are implements of peace. Would that indeed, at the end of the day, no child, no woman, and no one, goes to bed with an empty stomach.

United Methodists must continue to urge their governments to ratify the *International Covenant on Economic, Social, and Cultural Rights* and for these governments to make these rights a reality.

We also urge United Methodists worldwide to call on their governments to implement the Millennium Development Compact. Adopted as part of the UN Millennium Declaration in 2000 at the largest-ever gathering at the United Nations of Heads of State, these government leaders pledged together to eradicate poverty, promote human dignity and equality, and achieve peace, democracy, and environmental sustainability.

The compact declared eight goals (known as the Millennium Development Goals) with specific targets to which governments have pledged to implement by the year 2015. These goals include: 1) eradicating extreme poverty and hunger, 2) achieving universal primary education, 3) promoting gender equality and empowering women, 4) reducing child mortality, 5) improving maternal health, 6) combating HIV/AIDS, malaria, and other diseases, 7) ensuring environmental sustainability, and 8) developing a global partnership for development.

In this era of globalization—where profit and profit making at the expense of the needs and welfare of the poor and the vulnerable, and where unbridled pursuit of wealth and power have trampled upon and denied human rights of peoples—peace rooted in God's justice brings about the true globalization that will heal the wounds and scars of wars and conflict peoples and nations have engaged with each other. Peace rooted in God's justice will help bring about forgiveness and wholeness for all God's people and the whole of creation. God's reign on earth, as it is in heaven, is, in the end, the true globalization we must long and work for.

ADOPTED 2000
AMENDED AND READOPTED 2004

See Social Principles, ¶ 165.

310. Human Rights of Religious Minorities in India

WHEREAS, ever since the Bahartiya Jauta Party (BJP) came to power in India a year ago, there has been a tremendous increase in systematic persecution of religious minority groups in India. Both the religious and secular media report that the BJP Party and its leaders incite and sponsor their young and active party members to engage in terrorizing and intimidating the Christian and minority groups in India; and

WHEREAS, the India media reported recently that Christian nuns were raped, churches demolished and in some cases pastors and priests humiliated, tortured and paraded nude through the streets in some places of the northern part of India. In some instances, Christian schools were broken into while the schools were in session and the students were intimidated by burning of the Bibles and Christian literature; and

WHEREAS, the members of National Federation of Asian American United Methodists join in solidarity with the Indian minority religious communities and other advocacy groups in condemning the human rights violations against people who practice religions other than Hinduism,

Therefore, we call upon the General Board of Church and Society and the General Board of Global Ministries to work with our ecumenical partners and human rights organizations such as Amnesty International to communicate our displeasure and disappointment on the part of the Indian government in failing to protect and promote the constitutional rights of the religious minorities, and to promote peace, harmony, and mutual respect for all religious faiths; and

Be it further resolved, that these agencies be requested to urge the Prime Minister and his cabinet to take immediate executive measures to not only protect the constitutional rights of the religious minorities but also to ensure Articles 7 and 18 of the *Universal Declaration of Human Rights,* which state:

Article 7—All are equal before the law and are entitled without any discrimination to equal protection of the law. All are entitled to equal protection against any discrimination in violation of this Declaration and against any incitement to such discrimination.

Article 18—Everyone has the right to freedom of thought, conscience and religion; this right includes freedom to change his/her religion or belief, and freedom, either alone or in community with others and in public or private, to manifest his/her religion or belief in teaching, practice, ownership and observance.

ADOPTED 2000

See Social Principles, ¶ 165D.

311. International Day of Prayer

WHEREAS, many societies are intolerant of religious people, and deny them human rights; and

WHEREAS, according to the U.S. State Department, the governments of over 60 nations around the world condone the persecution of Christians; and

WHEREAS, the people called Methodist have traditionally taken the lead in opposing injustice, intolerance, and bigotry; and

WHEREAS, Methodists believe in the power of prayer,

Therefore, be it resolved, that the United Methodist congregations observe an International Day of Prayer for the Persecuted Church.

Be it further resolved, that through our earnest prayers we may grow in our sense of unity with Christians around the world and become more aware of the needs of our brothers and sisters who suffer because of their Christian faith.

ADOPTED 2000

See Social Principles, ¶ 165A.

312. Opposition to Israeli Settlements in Palestinian Land

We join with Palestinian Christians as well as our Jewish and Muslim brothers and sisters in feeling a deep sense of rootedness to the land that has special meaning for our three religious traditions. We celebrate the diversity of religious customs and traditions throughout the Middle East.

Jerusalem is sacred to all the children of Abraham: Jews, Muslims, and Christians. We have a vision of a shared Jerusalem as a city of peace and reconciliation, where indigenous Palestinians and Israelis can live as neighbors and, along with visitors and tourists, have access to holy sites and exercise freedom of religious expression. The peaceful resolution of Jerusalem's status is crucial to the success of the whole process of making a just and lasting peace between Palestinians and Israelis.

We seek for all people in the region an end to military occupation, freedom from violence, and full respect for the human rights of all under international law.

WHEREAS, the prophet Isaiah cautioned against coveting the lands and homes of one's neighbors: "Ah, you who join house to house, who add field to field, until there is room for no one but you, and you are left to live alone in the midst of the land!" (Isaiah 5:8); and

WHEREAS, the continuing confiscation of Palestinian land for construction of settlements and the building of a separation wall violates basic understanding of human rights, subverts the peace process, destroys the hope of both Israelis and Palestinians who are working for and longing for peace, and fosters a sense of desperation that can only lead to further violence; and

WHEREAS, continued and often intensified closures, curfews, dehumanizing check points, home demolitions, uprooted trees, bulldozed fields, and confiscation of Palestinian land and water by the government of Israel have devastated economic infrastructure and development in the West Bank and Gaza, have caused a massive deterioration of the living standards of all Palestinians... and an increasing sense of hopelessness and frustration; and

WHEREAS, targeted assassinations, suicide bombings, and attacks against civilians by both Israelis and Palestinians heighten the fear and suffering of all; and

WHEREAS, people in the United States, through their taxes, provide several billion dollars in economic and military assistance to the State of Israel each year, which allows for the building of bypass roads and settlements that are illegal according to the Fourth Geneva Convention;

WHEREAS, the church continues to work with ecumenical and interfaith bodies to advocate for Palestinian self-determination and an end to Israeli occupation; to affirm Israel's right to exist within secure borders; to affirm the right of return for Palestinian refugees under international law; to call for region-wide disarmament; to urge Israelis and Palestinians to stop human rights violations and attacks on civilians, such as targeted assassinations and suicide bombings; and to urge the U.S. government to initiate an arms embargo on the entire Middle East region;

Therefore, be it resolved, that The United Methodist Church opposes continued military occupation of the West Bank, Gaza, and East Jerusalem, the confiscation of Palestinian land and water resources, the destruction of Palestinian homes, the continued building of illegal Jewish settlements, and any vision of a "Greater Israel" that includes the occupied territories and the whole of Jerusalem and its surroundings.

Be it further resolved, that we urge the U.S. government to end all military aid to the region, and second to redistribute the large amount of aid now given to Israel and Egypt; to support economic development efforts of nongovernmental organizations throughout the region, including religious institutions, human rights groups, labor unions, and professional groups within Palestinian communities.

The United Methodist Church requests that the government of the United States, working in cooperation with the United Nations and other nations, urge the state of Israel to:

1. cease the confiscation of Palestinian lands and water for any reason;

2. cease the building of new, or expansion of existing, settlements and/or bypass roads in the occupied territories including East Jerusalem;

3. lift the closures and curfews on all Palestinian towns by completely withdrawing Israeli military forces to the Green Line (the 1948 ceasefire line between Israel and the West Bank);

4. dismantle that segment of the Wall of Separation constructed since May 2002 that is not being built on the Green Line but on Palestinian land that is separating Palestinian farmers from their fields.

We also urge the Palestinian Authority and all Palestinian religious leaders to continue to publicly condemn violence against Israeli civilians and to use nonviolent acts of disobedience to resist the occupation and the illegal settlements.

We urge all United Methodists in the U.S. to:

1. advocate with the U.S. administration and Congress to implement the above steps;

2. encourage members of each congregation to study the Israeli-Palestinian conflict from all perspectives by inviting speakers to church events, reading books, using audio-visual resources in educational forums, and getting information from Web sites.

3. provide financial support to the Palestinian people through contributions to the General Board of Global Ministries;

4. support, and participate in, the work of international peace and human rights organizations to provide protection for Palestinians and Israelis seeking nonviolently to end the occupation; and

5. reach out to local synagogues, mosques, and Christian faith groups by engaging in interfaith and ecumenical dialogue on how to promote justice and peace in the Holy Land; and

That the General Board of Global Ministries, working together with the General Board of Church & Society and interfaith organizations, develop advocacy packets for use in local congregations to promote a just and lasting peace and human rights for all in the region.

ADOPTED 2004

See Social Principle, ¶ 165.

313. Mission and Aging of the Global Population

Throughout the world, many older persons look to religion for meaning in life, for opportunities to serve, and for a way to address human suffering. The achievement of long life among increasing numbers of global citizens holds possibilities for an invigorated ministry by, for, and with older persons. In taking action, older people challenge discriminatory perceptions of the aged and reveal abundant talents and capacities.

From the earliest days reported in our Scripture, the stories of our faith have looked at aging realistically but positively. Ecclesiastes 12 catalogues the physical miseries of old age with the warning to "remember your creator in the days of your youth, before the days of trouble come" (12:1, NRSV). Nevertheless, the patriarchal stories, depicting individuals who lived hundreds of years, expressed the belief that life itself was good and, therefore, extended life was very good. Age was presumed to bring wisdom, and the elders of Israel were looked to for guidance (Exodus 12:21, etc.), as were, later, the elders of the church (Acts 20:17). Age brings its own pleasures, including grandchildren (Proverbs 17:6), and is marked by the beauty of gray hair (Proverbs 20:29). A life well lived, that is righteous in the sight of God, gives purpose to our aging; Psalm 92 vividly pictures the righteous elderly, "who flourish like the palm tree...in old age they still produce fruit; they are always green and full of sap" (92:12, 14, NRSV). Those who survive to old age are, therefore, to be honored, especially one's father and mother (Deuteronomy 5:16; Mark 10:19). It can be assumed that when Paul spoke of giving "honor to whom honor is due" (Romans 13:7), he meant to include respect for older persons. A sign of the coming of the Lord is that not only young but also old shall be merry (Jeremiah 31:13). Zechariah's vision of a truly restored Jerusalem was one in which not only would once again the streets be full of boys and girls playing, but of old men and old women sitting, "each with staff in hand because of their great age" (Zechariah 8:4-5, NRSV).

Through the centuries, the church has held varying attitudes toward older persons, but the prevailing tradition accords dignity to persons in old age. This tradition underpins our United Methodist Social Principles statement on rights of the aging, in which social policies and programs are called for "that ensure to the aging the respect and dignity that is their right as senior members of the human community" (¶ 162E).

In 2002, the United Nations' World Assembly on Ageing stated clearly the demographic facts that confront this century: "The world is experiencing an unprecedented demographic transformation. By 2050, the number of persons aged 60 years and over will increase from 600 million to almost 2 billion; the proportion of persons aged 60 years and over is expected to double from 10 percent to 21 percent. The increase will be greatest and most rapid in developing countries where the older population is expected to quadruple during the next fifty years. This demographic transformation challenges all societies to promote increased opportunities, in particular, for older persons to realize their potential to participate fully in all aspects of life."

Advances in public health and education, as well as control of infectious diseases, have contributed to these changes. Nevertheless, the extreme conditions of poverty, war and hunger, and the HIV/AIDS pandemic prevent realization of the biblical hope for a blessed old age. In situations of armed conflict, combatants increasingly target older persons. All too frequently, families and other caregivers abuse older persons in domestic and institutional settings. Income support and access to health care in old age apply only to a small minority in many countries. Age and gender discrimination often blocks access to the participation and involvement throughout the world. In these challenging situations, a greater proportion of older persons now take their own lives.

Many older persons live in vulnerable situations. They live in rural areas, working the land, and are predominantly female. Older persons are heavily concentrated in agriculture, with manufacturing jobs ranking a distant second. Women outlive men in virtually all countries. Most women past age sixty-five are widows, a trend likely to continue. They suffer low incomes and chronic illnesses. Less than 10 percent of older women in many poor societies read or write. Across the globe, traditional social support based on family structures continues to erode, leaving many elders in isolation with no one to care for them in their last years.

In some developing countries, older persons attract love and respect precisely because of their experience and their place as wise leaders and survivors within the community. Contrast this love and respect with some attitudes in the United States and other Western nations that deprecates old age because it is less "productive," or because physical energy and commercial images of beauty replace spiritual energy and the beauty of the inner soul. For this reason, the United States and other developed societies can learn much from other societies.

Responding to these challenges, the United Nations, in its 2002 International Plan of Action on Ageing, recommends action in three directions: assuring older persons right to social and economic development; advancing health and well being into old age; and ensuring enabling and supportive environments.

In the United States, the great majority of older persons have access to public social insurance through Social Security and Medicare. Those in The United Methodist Church celebrate the inclusion of older persons in decision-making structures throughout the church. Appreciation for these advances does not blind us to misguided efforts to depict older persons as benefiting, at the expense of the young, to the low quality of care in many nursing homes and to outright abuse in families, institutions, and organizations that employ older persons. We must remain vigilant to keep government programs publicly available to all, free of privatized substitutes that sharply limit many older persons' access to income support and health care.

The United Methodist Church calls upon

A. Local churches to:

    1. involve older adults inter-generationally and in ways that empower and encourage them to use resources for skills,

knowledge, experience, and spiritual insight; and

2. use resources from general agencies of The United Methodist Church that suggest actions and models for learning from other cultures and countries in their understanding of and appreciation of older persons.

B. Annual conferences to:

1. involve older adults in the full range of programs of the conference, including Volunteer in Mission (VIM) projects; health ministries in which able older adults care for the frail elderly; public advocacy; and use of resources and action suggestions from the Committee of Older Adult Ministries of The United Methodist Church;

2. ask itinerating missionaries to speak to constructive ways churches in the United States can: (a) learn from the customs, values, and practices of churches in other countries and cultures; and (b) support older persons in other countries and cultures through Advance Specials, VIM projects, and mission support; and

3. study the United Nations International Plan of Action on Ageing adopted in 2002 as a basis for action initiatives and guide to programming.

C. All general program agencies of The United Methodist Church to:

1. develop resources and programs that support and undergird the faith development of older adults and encourage their full participation in ministry;

2. identify specific actions in their ongoing programs and ministries by which families on a global basis can be assisted in caring for their frail elderly;

3. include older persons in training for care-giving in relation to mission and ministry globally; and

4. provide analysis and advocacy training to equip older adults to defend and expand public policies and programs that serve all elders.

D. The General Board of Church and Society and the General Board of Global Ministries to:

1. advocate support for older persons' needs and capacities in governmental and non-governmental organizations, including the United Nations, the U.S. government, and ecumenical and other nongovernmental international organizations; and

2. study and share with the whole church pertinent issues related to the well-being of older persons, such as allocation of governmental resources for support and care, end-of-life issues, and avoidance of age discrimination in employment and community life.

E. The General Board of Global Ministries to include in mission education:

1. positive images of older persons in all countries and cultures, along with images realistically depicting the difficulties many of these persons have under conditions of poverty and isolation;

2. information about the "double bind" in which many poor societies find themselves by virtue of the demands of a growing young population and the demands of a growing older population; and

3. resources for annual conferences and local churches that provide models for appropriate mission and ministry on the local level, and specific action and program suggestions.

F. All general agencies and all episcopal leadership to:

1. include older persons as full participants in programs and ministries from planning through decision making and evaluation;

2. seek opportunities by which The United Methodist Church can affirm its aging members, and offer ways that older members can collaborate with younger persons in evangelism and renewal of the whole church, to the end that persons of all ages are called to the discipleship of Jesus Christ; and

3. lift the prophetic voice of Christian faith to proclaim a vision of human community in which older persons are accorded respect and dignity as those made in the image of God and part of the human family.

ADOPTED 2004

See Social Principles, ¶ 165.

314. United Methodists Sharing the Vulnerability in the Process of Alteration

Paul reminded the divided Corinthians, "If one part (of the body) suffers, every part suffers with it; if one part is honored, every part rejoices with it" (1 Corinthians 12:25). It is in this spirit that the European community, its peoples and its churches, are gathering together to respond to a time of change and transformation—a time of alteration in Europe.

The fall of the Berlin wall (1989) was a symbol of a new political order in Europe. Ever since, Europe has been in a process of alteration which has led to both improvements and new challenges.

The United Methodist Church recognizes with gratitude a trend to democratisation and increased freedom in many countries as well as a development towards a larger community of European nations. We affirm that many people, among them numerous Christians, including United Methodists, are now more vigilant in the journey of Europe towards "An Area of Freedom, Security and Justice" (expression from European Community Law).

After September 11, 2001, people all over the world are more than ever experiencing a profound sense of vulnerability. As a people of faith we are recognizing that a shared vulnerabililty may become more important for mutual understanding and caring than privileged security of some. This shared vulnerability has helped to see the European Process of Alteration in the context of an encompassing global transformation which in particular includes the continents of Africa, Asia and Latin America.

A decade ago we rejoiced as we experienced great political changes in Central and Eastern Europe.

Today it is clear that the magnitude and the content of the problems encountered have been underestimated by governments, the media, the general public as well as the churches. Rising unemployment and the falling value of pensions and wages has plunged millions of people into poverty. United Nations Development Reports for Central and Eastern Europe show that in 1989 about 14 million people in the former communist block lived with less than four dollars a day. By the mid-nineties that number had risen to 147 million people. Only a small minority has participated in economic growth and development. In many places health care, schooling and education standards declined dramatically whilst commerce-based criminality grew rapidly.

Given this situation, the United Methodist Minorities in Europe together with the other denominations emphasises the need for human development through witness for Jesus Christ and through working towards justice for the poor and vulnerable like women, children, gypsies and other ethnic minorities. United Methodists are together in mission to safeguard the local initiatives and the dignity of clergy and lay missionaries, women and men, faithfully responding to the calling of Jesus, our Lord and Saviour. We therefore affirm that church-planting, evangelism and social initiatives in Eastern Europe, Russia, the Baltics and the Balkans require continued support by the larger Methodist family, spiritually and fiancially. Even if local churches may become financially self-sustaining and strong enough to continue the mission among the vulnerable and the poor on their own it should not be forgotten that the Lord's commandment to mission is addressed to the whole Church.

We are thankful for the "Fund Mission in Europe," a solidarity initiative of the European Methodist Council to collect financial means among Methodist congregations in Western and Northern Europe for newly emerging churches and congregations in the East and in the South. The financial and spiritual support generated by local churches and conferences in the USA during the last ten years was an act of rescuing.

The Process of European Integration—Hopes and Challenges

The process of change has been strengthened especially by the European Union which aims to work for peace, stability and welfare. The initiation of an unprecedented enlargement involving 13 new candidate countries is an ambition on a new level and on a new scale. Unfortunately, it has become clear that there is a widening gap between the expectations of tangible results on the one hand and loss of patience resulting from dissatisfaction with the actual process on the other hand.

Particular challenges in this context are:
- transparency in the negotiating process;
- free movement of persons / migration;
- human and social costs of the integration process;
- protection of the rights of minorities;
- preservation of indigenous (regional) cultures and identities;
- future borders of the European Union and the relations to the new neighbours;
- commitment to common (Christian) values.

As United Methodists, we affirm that the European integration process is a sign of hope. We support efforts for the creation and development of independent regional cooperation and communities of nations, such as the European Union and the OSCE including USA and Canada. At the same time, we are also aware of the dangers that continue to threaten the process toward a new Europe such as self-serving nationalism, serious economic problems and social upheavel. Against this background, the current priorities of the United Methodist Church's human rights program are as follows:

- protection of refugees, migrants, asylum seekers and displaced people;
- social policy questions in the transformation that nations make into market economics;
- social rights for all, in particular respect and justice for women, children and minorities;
- religious freedom;
- environmental and energy policies for a sustainable way of life.

The Churches are not left untouched by the processes of political, economic and cultural integration. The Conference of European Churches, together with the Roman Catholic Council of European Bishops Conferences, the Leuenberg Church Fellowship and the European Methodist Council, are very actively involved in internal and external processes of integration. In particular, the European Churches developed a "Charta Oecumenica" which is meant to be a helpful tool for dialogue and advocacy for the practical life together of the Orthodox, Protestant, Anglican and Roman Catholic Churches.

We believe and affirm that the Churches in Europe have a message of hope. The new Europe can not be built without them. The United Methodist Church is not nationally bound and is, therefore, particularly called upon to advance the goal of integration in the present European process of alteration on the way to a true Area of Freedom, Security and Justice.

Zurich and Budapest, March 5, 2003

ADOPTED 2004

See, Social Principles, ¶ 165.

315. Our Muslim Neighbors

Christians are called to initiate and promote better relationships between Christians and Muslims on the basis of informed understanding, critical appreciation, and balanced perspective of one another's basic beliefs.

The Historical Context

United Methodists, seeking to be faithful neighbors and witnesses to other members of the human family, recognize with respect peoples of the religion of Islam.

Christians and Muslims acknowledge common roots, along with Jews, in the faith of Abraham, Sarah, and Hagar. As members of one of the monotheistic world religions, Muslims worship and serve the one God with disciplined devotion. Both Christians and Muslims believe that God is ever-inclined toward humankind in justice and mercy. Based on this common ground, we celebrate where Christians and Muslims are working together to make God's justice a reality for all people. The two faiths sometimes understand differently the particular ways in which God deals with human beings, but they agree that the proper human response to the Almighty is a life of humble obedience, including repentance, faith, and good works. Muslims believe that the Qur'an sets forth the principles for righteous conduct and a harmonious life in society. The following verses from the Qur'an show that these principles are similar to the ones found in the Christian Scriptures:

O believers, be steadfast witnesses for God with justice. Do not let the hatred of a people make you act unjustly. Be just, for justice is next to piety (5:8).

Worship only God; be good to parents and kindred, to orphans and the poor; speak kindly to others (92:83).

Do not mix truth with falsehood, nor knowingly conceal the truth (2:42).

O believers, fulfill your obligations (5:1).

Hold to forgiveness and enjoin good; turn aside from the foolish (7:199).

It may be that God will bring about friendship between you and those whom you hold to be your enemies (60:7).

The Need for Understanding

United Methodists live together with Muslims in many countries of the world and in a variety of social environments. Indeed, in the United States of America, Muslims comprise one of the most rapidly growing religious communities. In places around the world, Muslims may constitute the majority of the population, and in other places,

Christians may be the majority. As believers of the two religions build their lives in the same general area, they are often affected by patterns of religious antagonism inherited from the past history of disputes and misunderstanding between the two.

Also, Muslims and Christians experience varying degrees of political and social discrimination, depending on the particular circumstances of each country. In certain areas of tension believers in the two faiths are caught up in struggles for economic, political, and human rights.

We believe that sustained and ever-renewed initiatives of open discussion and sharing of concerns in interfaith settings contribute to the achievement of social justice.

By this statement, we express solidarity with those of either religion who suffer oppression or discrimination.

By this statement, we make a step toward more hospitable and cooperative relationships and encourage dialogical relations.

Basic United Methodist Documents

A. Called to Be Neighbors

A clear biblical basis for discussion in interfaith settings is set forth in *Guidelines for Interreligious Relationships*:

> In conversation with a lawyer (Luke 10:25), Jesus reminded him that his neighbor, the one to whom he should show love and compassion, included a stranger, a Samaritan. Today, Christ's call to neighborliness (Luke 10:27) includes the "stranger" of other faiths. It is not just that historical events have forced us together. The Christian faith itself impels us to love our neighbors of other faiths and to seek to live in contact and mutually beneficial relationship, in community with them.

B. The Social Community

In our United Methodist Social Principles, we affirm all persons as equally valuable in the sight of God and determine to work toward societies in which each person's value is recognized, maintained, and strengthened.

Religious persecution has been common in the history of civilization. We urge policies and practices that ensure the right of every religious group to exercise its faith free from legal, political, or economic restrictions. In particular, we condemn anti-Semite, anti-Muslim, and anti-Christian attitudes and practices in both their overt and covert forms, being especially sensitive to their expression in media stereotyping.

C. Our Theological Task

In our United Methodist Doctrinal Standards, our relationship with adherents of other living faiths of the world is set in the context of our ecumenical commitment. We are encouraged to enter into serious interfaith encounters and explorations between Christians and adherents of other living faiths of the world. Scripture calls us to be both neighbors and witnesses to all people. Such encounters require us to reflect anew on our faith and to seek guidance for our witness among neighbors of other faiths.

When Christians enter into such dialogue, they come to it consciously as they seek to live as one people, under the living God who is the Creator of all humankind, the One "who is above all and through all and in all" (Ephesians 4:6).

This theological understanding compels us to a particular kind of dialogue, one in which we reflect critically upon our Christian tradition, gain accurate appreciation of the traditions of others, and engage with love and generosity of spirit as we seek "to raise all such relationships to the highest possible level of human fellowship and understanding."

Christian-Muslim Discussions

The long-standing commitment of The United Methodist Church to social justice, to theological inquiry, and to just and open relationships places a particular responsibility on its members to develop discussions between Christians and Muslims. Mutual respect requires the church to recognize and affirm that, although individuals may move from one religion to another, we do not enter into formal interfaith dialogue with the intent to convert the Muslim community to Christianity. Although the movement is still small, there is increasing evidence that groups of Christians and Muslims are coming together to witness to their faith and acknowledge the power of God in their lives, to identify problems that challenge all on the deepest theological and moral level, and to try to understand better the complex factors that determine the crucial decisions being made by governments around the world.

Through such interactions, Christians and Muslims are finding that working for better exchange of information and for ways to cooperate in solving mutual problems and concerns often leads to discovery and growth, adding to the depth and understanding of each tradition.

If we observe the unfolding of events in today's world and assess Islamic movement as only reactionary and threatening, we will hinder the advancement of justice and peace and neither gain from nor contribute to mutual understanding.

If we develop friendships with Muslims as members of the human community from whom and with whom we have much to learn, we will increase our respect for Islam as a way of life that calls its millions of followers to the highest moral ideals and satisfies their deepest spiritual aspirations.

In the aftermath of September 11, 2001, The United Methodist Church has intentionally explored what it means to be in relationship with the Muslim community. The United Methodist Church stands in solidarity with Muslims in the struggles for economic, political and human rights.

Action Statement

Local congregations and United Methodist agencies are encouraged to develop ongoing relationships with Muslims and their respective organizations. They are urged to initiate conversations, programs, and dialogues leading to the understanding of both Islam and Christianity, and appreciation of their particular gifts, while discovering commonalities and differences; and seeking areas of mutual cooperation. They are also urged to exchange information and discuss ways to cooperate when they address common problems and concerns.

Recommendations

We request the Council of Bishops to support, participate in, and assist United Methodists in implementing this resolution.

We call upon the General Board of Global Ministries, and particularly its Women's Division, to promote a program of ongoing relationships with Muslim women, seeking areas of mutual concern about how to live ethically, morally, and responsibly in today's world and to join in common struggles for peace and justice.

We urge the General Board of Church and Society to work with Muslims in activities designed to achieve common political, social, economic, and ecological goals.

We urge that the General Board of Global Ministries and the General Board of Church and Society develop advocacy programs on behalf of religious freedom and minority rights, particularly regarding nations that are experiencing crisis in Christian-Muslim conflict in which religious minorities are harassed or persecuted. These advocacy programs should be directed toward, among others, the U.S. Department of State, U.S. Embassies, and the United Nations Human Rights Commission.

We recommend that the General Commission on Christian Unity and Interreligious Concerns, as it initiates and engages in dialogue with representatives of Islam, remain mindful of the evangelism imperatives of the gospel and the gospel mandate to seek justice for those who are oppressed.

We recommend that United Methodist Communications, through its Division of Public Media and News Service, monitor and call attention to discrimination against Muslims in both the religious and secular media.

We urge United Methodist members, local churches, and agencies to take the following specific actions:

1. Study Islam, using resources such as: Brochures, "Basic Facts about Islam," "Guidelines for Interfaith Dialogue," (GCCUIC, 2001) "Called to be Neighbors and Witnesses" (General Conference, 2000); *Guidelines on Dialogue with People of Living Faiths and Ideologies,* World Council of Churches (Geneva: 1990); *God Is One: The Way of Islam,* by R. Marston Speight (New York: Friendship Press, updated/revised 2001); *The Holy Qur'an,* New Revised Edition, trans. 'Abdullah Yusuf' Alli (Brentwood, MD: Amana Corp., 2001); National Council of Churches Interfaith Policy Statement 2000; *Silent No More: Confronting America's False Images of Islam,* by Paul Findley (Amana Publications, Beltsville Maryland, 2001); *A New Religious America,* by Diana Eck (Harper Collins, New York, 2001); *Creating Interfaith Community,* by Marston Speight (GBGM, Service Center, 2003); magazines such as *Minaret* (MultiMedia Vera International, 434 South Vermont, Los Angeles, CA 90020).

2. Initiate dialogue with Muslims, utilizing as our guide the resolution of the 2000 General Conference entitled "Called to Be Neighbors and Witnesses, Guidelines for Interreligious Relationships," and models of dialogue developed by the General Commission on Christian Unity and Interreligious Concerns. The dialogue will address theological and justice issues, related to the particular contexts in which those dialogues occur.

3. Develop awareness of the concerns of particular Muslim populations through implementation of other applicable General Conference Resolutions in the 2000 *Book of Resolutions*, such as "Prejudice Against Muslims and Arabs in the U.S.A."

4. Promote understanding between Christians and Muslims in local communities through:

- arranging visits to local mosques;
- developing and participating in cultural exchanges with Muslims;
- inviting Muslims to social occasions;
- seeking Muslim participation in local interfaith councils and interfaith worship;
- sending messages of greeting and good will to Muslims upon the occasion of their religious festivals;
- encouraging authorities of schools, hospitals, prisons, factories, and places of business and government to respect particular features of Muslim life;
- upholding the dignity of individuals, families, and communities; and
- seeking to remedy situations in which Muslims encounter misunderstanding, prejudice, stereotyping, or even hostility from the neighborhood or population when they desire to express their faith in everyday life.

ADOPTED 1992
AMENDED AND READOPTED 2004

See Social Principles, ¶ 165*A, B,* and *C.*

316. End the U.S. Embargo of Cuba

The United Methodist Church is linked in Christ with The Methodist Church of Cuba. We share a common heritage and mission.

We are mutually responsible for the proclamation of God's love and the nurturing of neighbor love. We celebrate the continued growth of The Methodist Church of Cuba. We acknowledge the difficulties that our two churches continue to face in their mission partnership due to the U.S. embargo and the lack of diplomatic relationships between the two countries.

For over 44 years, the government of the United States has not maintained diplomatic relations with the Cuban government and has, instead, pursued an economic embargo prohibiting trade with Cuba and controlling very tightly travel to that country. The Democracy Act of 1992 (22 U.S.C. 6001) and the 1996 Helms/Burton Act tightened the embargo and brought about additional suffering to the people of Cuba. In addition to that, the embargo has failed its stated purpose of bringing political change to Cuba after all these years.

The United Methodist Church has long advocated for an improved relationship between Cuba and the U.S. The Methodist Church in 1964 made a historical statement entitled "The Re-examination of Policy Toward Mainline China, Cuba and Other Countries," which said: "The Christian gospel involves reconciliation by encounter and by communication regardless of political considerations. Therefore, we cannot accept the expression of hostility by any country, its policies, or its ideologies as excuses for the failure of Christians to press persistently, realistically, and creatively toward a growing understanding among the peoples of all countries."

There are many groups in the United States desiring the end of the United States embargo against Cuba. Among them, U.S. farmers and other business concerns that went through the recently allowed, but very cumbersome, licensing process imposed by the U.S. government to permit sales of food products to Cuba resulting in sales of over $125,000,000.00 by the end of 2002. This development was a step in the right direction, which we celebrate on the basis of the United Methodist-stated position that embargoes of food and medicines should not be part of any country's policies. Individuals and organizations—religious, academic, business—want to exercise their constitutional right to travel freely to Cuba. In 2001 alone, over 176,000 U.S. citizens traveled to Cuba, and some are facing steep fines for not adhering to the embargo travel restrictions.

The General Assembly of the United Nations has overwhelmingly approved, every year since 1992, a resolution called "The Necessity of Ending the Economic, Commercial, and Financial Embargo Imposed by the United States of America Against Cuba." The latest of these, in December 2002, passed by a vote of 173 to 3, demonstrating the international community's concern for what it calls the "adverse effects of the embargo on the Cuban people and on Cuban nationals living in other countries" (UN resolution 57/11 of December 16, 2002).

WHEREAS, the Council of Churches of Cuba, of which The Methodist Church of Cuba is a member; the Cuban Conference of Roman Catholic Bishops; and several other international religious groups and leaders such as CIEMAL [Council of Evangelical Methodist Churches of Latin America and the Caribbean], the Caribbean Conference of Churches, and Pope John Paul II, as well as U.S. religious bodies such as the United Church of Christ, the Presbyterian Church (USA), and the American Baptist Churches have stated or passed resolutions in favor of lifting the embargo; and

WHEREAS, we acknowledge that the embargo also curtails religious freedom by making very difficult the relationship between churches in the United States and churches in Cuba; and

WHEREAS, we believe that stopping the hostility generated by the U.S. embargo policies would facilitate improvements in democratic reforms and human rights in Cuba; and

WHEREAS, we reaffirm the Bible teachings and mandate to "love one another, because love is from God" (1 John 4:7), and to practice mercy as the good Samaritan did (Luke 10:25-37);

Therefore, be it resolved, that The United Methodist Church, from its Christian and humanitarian perspective, inspired by the love of God and the historic Methodist commitment to peace and social justice, and in light of historic changes with the end of the Cold War, hereby petitions the President and Congress of the United States to lift its economic embargo against Cuba and any other regulations, practices or measures enforcing the embargo law and to seek negotiations with the Cuban government for the purpose of resuming normal diplomatic relations.

Note: The United States broke diplomatic relations with Cuba on January 3, 1961. A partial trade embargo against Cuba by the U.S. government was declared on October 19, 1960. On July 8, 1963, "the Treasury Department, using its authority under the Trading with the Enemy Act of 1917, issued more restrictive Cuba Assets Control Regulations."

(Cuban Foreign Relations, A Chronology, 1959-1982).

ADOPTED 2004

See Social Principles, ¶ 165*A* and *D*.

317. Call for Free Speech in Cuba

WHEREAS, the Scripture calls us to raise our voice for those who have no voice, judge with justice those who have no voice (Proverbs 31:8-9); and

WHEREAS, the right of free expression is one of the most basic rights recognized in the Universal Declaration of Human Rights; and

WHEREAS, over seventy-five (75) Cuban dissidents, among them independent journalists, economists, and human rights activists, were condemned to sentences up to twenty-eight (28) years in prison, for exercising their freedom of expression, and according to the Cuban government, because they were receiving compensations and expensed reimbursements by the U.S.;

Therefore, be it resolved, that the 2004 General Conference of The United Methodist Church supports the right of all people to express themselves freely, regardless of where they live, and

Be it further resolved, that The United Methodist Church, through the General Board of Church and Society, calls upon the Cuban government to review their sentences and consider their release from prison, seeking reconciliation and understanding among all people in Cuba.

ADOPTED 2004

See Social Principles, ¶ 165A and D.

318. Support Methodists in Portugal, Spain, and Italy

WHEREAS, the Methodist communities of the Iberian-Mediterranean countries of Portugal, Spain and Italy had their ongoing historical relationship with their respective founding Methodist bodies severed by events produced by the Second World War and its aftermath; and

WHEREAS, in each of these countries, the state government in response to the interests of the Roman Catholic Church, declared illegal the presence and ministries of these Methodist churches, thereby disrupting their relationship with their founding bodies; and

WHEREAS, the commitment of these faithful few made possible the survival of Methodist Christians under this religiously adverse environment in Western Europe and struggle today to find new vitality and renewal,

Therefore, be it resolved, that this General Conference of The United Methodist Church reaffirm our common history and mission with these churches, and celebrate their important and brave witness during the troubled times of this century in Western Europe. We call on the Council of Bishops, as well as the executive, program, and service staff of the general boards and agencies to develop a strategic approach to affirm, support, and strengthen the life of the Methodist Church of Portugal, The Evangelical Church of Spain, and the Methodist Church of Italy, by exploring jointly with the leadership of these respective churches (Bishop Ireneu da Silva Cunha, Portugal; President Enrique Capú, the Evangelical Church of Spain; President Valdo Benecchi, the Evangelical Methodist Church of Italy) ways to collaborate in those opportunities where common efforts will help usher in this new millennium, fresh vitality and renewed hope to these faith communities of our Methodist family.

ADOPTED 2000

See Social Principles, ¶ 165A.

319. The Philippines

We rejoice with the reported release of 15 hostages previously held by extremist Muslim rebels. We share the agony of those twenty-one hostages from Sipadan Island in Malaysia, among them French, German, Lebanese, South African, Finnish, and Malaysian nationals who face continuing uncertainties. We condemn the outbreak of violent conflict involving the rebels and the Philippine government in fourteen localities in Mindanao, including those in Sulo and Basilan Islands.

Therefore, be it resolved, the 2000 General Conference of The United Methodist Church express its prayer: that hostilities immediately cease; that food, medicines, clothing, and safe refuge be insured by all parties to those whose lives are in their hands; and that humanitarian agencies be allowed to care for them until ultimate return of peace in their lands; that we join all who desire a solution of the conflicts and the struggles that will build a just and durable peace; that we call upon all peoples to recognize one another to be in community with each other in the hope of a just world order, upholding how all persons and groups must feel secure in their life and right to live within society if order is to be achieved and maintained by law; and that we especially express this hope to both Christian and non-Christian alike, who live the rigors of southern Philippines community.

ADOPTED 2000

See Social Principles, ¶ 165D.

320. Resourcing Missions, Evangelism, and Congregational Development in Indochina

WHEREAS, Cambodia, Laos, and Vietnam have been ravaged by war, natural disasters, poverty, and deprivation; and women, children, and the disabled have been the most disadvantaged in society and continue to be victims of discrimination, violence, and exploitation,

WHEREAS, defying dangers and difficulties, Methodist men and women from around the world responded to God's call and sacrificed their time, money, and lives to bring the message of hope and salvation to the poor and marginalized in these countries,

WHEREAS, by the grace of God congregational development and missions work in Indochina led to encouraging results, as there are currently one hundred twenty-five (125) congregations in Cambodia—Methodism being the largest Christian denomination in the country—sixty (60) congregations in Laos, fourteen (14) congregations in Vietnam, one (1) Cambodian missionary couple, ten (10) Cambodians ordained in Jan 2003; a Bible College in Cambodia with forty-five (45) students, the Wesley Theological College in Vietnam training seventy-two (72) students, and one (1) Vietnamese missionary couple,

WHEREAS, the rapid growth in all three countries in evangelism, congregational development, and theological training for pastors and lay leaders has dramatically increased the need for literature, resources, Bibles, and hymnals, medical and social services, and has created many opportunities for The United Methodist Church to provide help and support,

Therefore, be it resolved, that the General Conference of the United Methodist commend local churches, annual conferences, general boards, and agencies in their efforts to promote social justice, missions, evangelism, and congregational development in Cambodia, Laos, and Vietnam,

Be it further resolved, that the 2004 General Conference highly recommend annual conferences, general boards and agencies to allocate funds, personnel, and resources to empower the United Methodist Mission Initiatives in Cambodia, Laos, and Vietnam in their efforts to promote the inherent dignity and right of the Indochinese peoples to religious freedom, economic and cultural development, and to continue and expand the work in their home countries.

Indochinese National Caucus
November 2003

ADOPTED 2004

See Social Principles, ¶165.

321. Empowering and Equipping Young Indochinese Americans for the Future

WHEREAS, since the end of the Vietnam War in 1975, the United States has joined many countries around the world to open their homes and their lands to the refugees from Indochina. There are 450,000 Cambodian, 350,000 Hmong and Laotian, and over 1.5 million Vietnamese Americans in the United States at the present time; and as of November 2003, there are nine (9) Cambodian fellowships and congregations, twelve (12) Hmong fellowships and congregations, three (3) Laotian fellowships, and twenty-one (21) Vietnamese fellowships and congregations; and there are only nine (9) Cambodian pastors with one (1) ordained; fourteen (12) Hmong pastors with seven (5) ordained; three (3) Laotian pastors with two (2) ordained; and twenty-seven (27) Vietnamese pastors and eighteen (18) ordained United Methodist clergy,

WHEREAS, the children of Indochinese immigrants who were born or grew up in America do not sufficiently understand the language and culture of the parents and their local churches; and lack of communication and understanding between children and parents, and youths and adults in the church has had a negative impact on the spiritual, emotional and intellectual development of the younger generations;

WHEREAS, many Indochinese youths and young adults left the church due to the linguistic, cultural and generational gaps, and a sense of disempowerment; a significant number of teenagers and young adults with unmet needs are looking for support and nurture outside the church, with some dropping out of school, joining youth gangs, engaging in criminal activities or becoming drug addicts,

Therefore, be it resolved, that the General Conference of The United Methodist Church celebrate God's wonderful grace, blessings, and providence through this emerging Indochinese American ministries in the last twenty-nine years and acknowledge the urgent needs of English-speaking ministries to the Indochinese youths and young adults and the importance of continuing leadership training in order to mobilize, disciple, empower, and equip the young people to become influential leaders in church and society,

Be it further resolved, that the 2004 General Conference commend local churches, annual conferences, general boards and agencies in their efforts to reach out to Indochinese youths and young adults.

Be it further resolved, that the 2004 General Conference highly recommend annual conferences, general boards and agencies to allocate funds, personnel, and resources to empower the Indochinese National Caucus and local churches in their efforts to minister to, disciple and train the young people for the future.

Indochinese National Caucus
November 2003

ADOPTED 2004

See Social Principles, ¶ 165.

322. Theological Education in Europe

WHEREAS, The United Methodist Church in post-communist Europe has been growing in witness and strength since the collapse of communism in eastern Europe and the former Soviet Union; and

WHEREAS, the Baltic Methodist Theological Seminary in Estonia, the first United Methodist seminary founded in post-communist Europe by the only Methodist group to survive in the former Soviet Union, has recently moved into a new facility and is currently the largest Methodist seminary in Europe; and

WHEREAS, Russia Methodist Theological Seminary, the newest United Methodist educational institution in the world, was established by the revived United Methodist Church in Russia to serve the vast expanse and population of Russia, and has recently purchased a new facility; and

WHEREAS, the seminary in Poland has continued to serve the Polish church with limited funding throughout the years of communist rule; and

WHEREAS, a new Theological Training Center for the Balkans has been established in Graz, Austria, to provide training for pastors and church leaders in the Balkans; and

WHEREAS, the Course of Study has emerged as an effective program for pastoral training in Bulgaria, the Czech and Slovak Republics, and Hungary; and

WHEREAS, there is an urgent need for trained pastoral leadership in the emerging church in order to effectively proclaim the gospel; and

WHEREAS, with limited funding and in the face of conflict and war, The United Methodist Church in post-communist Europe has continued to grow, establish new churches, and reach youth and young adults with the gospel, creating an urgent need for trained pastoral clergy leadership,

Therefore, be it resolved, that the General Conference of The United Methodist Church establish a new "Fund for Theological Education in Post-Communist Europe." Specific funding amounts will be determined by the General Board of Higher Education and Ministry Division of Ordained Ministry in consultation with the bishops, seminary leadership, and leaders of programs of theological education in Eastern Europe.

ADOPTED 2000

See Social Principles, ¶ 165.

323. United Nations Resolutions on the Israel-Palestine Conflict

WHEREAS, negotiations between the State of Israel and the Palestinian National Authority still have not achieved a just and lasting peace for the Palestinian people; and

WHEREAS, the United Nations Security Council has passed numerous resolutions, including Resolutions 242 and 338, that outline a framework for a just and lasting peace; and

WHEREAS, the UMC recognizes and affirms the role of the United Nations in the resolution of this conflict and has already affirmed that the "principles embodied in United Nations Security Council Resolutions 242 and 338 provide an agreed upon formula to achieve security and peace for all states in the area" (see "The Current Arab-Israeli Crisis"),

Therefore, be it resolved, that The United Methodist Church calls upon the United States, as a permanent member of the UN Security Council, to accept the authority of Security Council resolutions and abide by Resolutions 242 and 338, as well as all other relevant Security Council resolutions, that provide a framework for bringing this conflict to a just and permanent end.

ADOPTED 2000

See Social Principles, ¶ 165*A, B, C,* and *D.*

324. Violence Against Children in Latin America and the Caribbean

WHEREAS, millions of children in Latin America and the Caribbean struggle daily to survive in the midst of violence:
- the violence of armed conflict;
- the violence of scarce resources taken from children's health and educational needs to support inordinately large military budgets;
- the violence of poverty linked to the massive external debt burdening every nation of the region;
- the violence of hunger;
- the culture of violence permeating television and other mass media;
- widespread domestic violence;
- ecological violence that is destroying and polluting the natural world and all live creatures;
- the violence of HIV-Aids, with the second highest incidence in the world in many Caribbean nations, destroying children's lives from birth;
- the violence of very high infant mortality.

Therefore, be it resolved, that the General Commission on Religion and Race endorses MARCHA's petition to the 2004 General Conference to establish a special program to address, in cooperation with the member churches of CIEMAL, the grave crisis of children struggling to survive in the midst of violence and poverty by communicating this concern to the Council of Bishops and be referred to the General Board of Global Ministries (GBGM) and the General Council on Finance and Administration (GCFA) for the implementation of a program.

ADOPTED 2004

See Social Principles, ¶¶ 162C, 164A, and 165.

325. Support for Covenant of the Commonwealth of the Northern Mariana Islands

WHEREAS from 1972 to 1976, the United States government and the people of the Northern Mariana Islands negotiated in phased implementation the "Covenant of the Commonwealth of the Northern Mariana Islands" (CNMI)
in Political Union with the United States of America"; and

WHEREAS the Northern Mariana Islands district previously was part of the United Nations Trust Territory of the Pacific Islands; and

WHEREAS under the terms of the covenant, citizens of the self-governing commonwealth do not participate in federal elections but enjoy all the other benefits of U.S. citizenship; and

WHEREAS unlike the other Insular Areas of Puerto Rico, the US Virgin Islands, American Samoa, and the territory of Guam, the CNMI do not have a delegate in the United States Congress; and

WHEREAS the Commonwealth of Northern Mariana Islands has always elected a representative to Washington DC; and

WHEREAS in solidarity with the aspirations of the people of the CNMI, members of the Immanuel United Methodist Church of Saipan publicly declared their support for delegate representation in the United States Congress;

Therefore be it resolved that the 2004 General Conference direct the General Board of Church and Society to win congressional representation for CNMI in the United States Congress with committee level membership that includes voice and seat.

ADOPTED 2004

See Social Principles, ¶165.

WAR AND PEACE

326. In Support of the United Nations

Preamble

The world needs a new vision, a vision of peace rooted in justice, a vision of a world bound together in intentional community dedicated to the well-being of all people and all creation. The United Nations, however limited, represents the best efforts made so far by governments and peoples of the world toward such a vision.

The Christian faith and community are rooted in theological understanding that is global by its very nature. The foundation for the church's involvement in the quest for world peace and justice can be found in the following biblically based beliefs: (1) the transcending sovereignty and love of God for all creation and the expression of that love in the Incarnation of Jesus Christ, whose mission was to reveal understanding about that divine presence, to proclaim a message of salvation, and to bring justice and peace; (2) the unity of creation and the equality of all races and peoples; (3) the dignity and worth of each person as a child of God; and (4) the church, the body of believers, whose global mission of witness, peacemaking, and reconciliation testifies to God's action in history.

The world is the responsibility of each of our communities where the securing of justice for one individual, one community, one nation contributes to the securing of justice and peace for all. To work for justice and peace for all is to affirm God's promise of the fullness of life: "The earth is the Lord's and the fullness thereof" (Psalm 24:1); "I came that they may have life, and have it abundantly" (John 10:10b).

The United Methodist Church, therefore, reaffirms its support for the United Nations and calls upon all governments to fully support the United Nations in the fulfillment of its charter and in its highest calling to work for peace and justice for all the world's people. Furthermore, The United Methodist Church affirms the following principles as *Pillars of Peace for the 21st Century*:

1. *Political Accountability*. Peace rooted in justice requires increased political collaboration and accountability within the United Nations system, and among regional bodies, governments, local authorities, peoples' organizations, and global economic structures to seek the common good and equality for all.

2. *Economic Accountability*. Peace rooted in justice requires increased moral, ethical, and legal accountability at all levels from governments, financial institutions, multilateral organizations, transnational corporations, and all other economic actors to seek a just, participatory, and sustainable economic order for the welfare and well-being of all people and all creation.

3. *Legal Accountability*. Peace rooted in justice requires a comprehensive international legal system, capable of change as conditions require, in order to prevent and resolve conflicts, to protect rights, to hold accountable those who disturb peace and violate international law, and to provide fair and effective review and enforcement mechanisms.

4. *Liberation and Empowerment*. Peace rooted in justice requires the participation of vulnerable and marginalized groups who are seeking to promote justice and peace in those mechanisms capable of redressing the causes and consequences of injustice and oppression.

5. *Peace and Conflict Resolution*. Peace rooted in justice requires the nurturing of a culture of peace in homes, communities, religious institutions, nations, and across the world; the use of non-violent means of resolving conflict; appropriate systems of common security; and the end of the unrestrained production, sale and use of weapons worldwide.

6. *Human Dignity and Rights*. Peace rooted in justice requires respect for the inherent dignity of all persons and the recognition, protection, and implementation of the principles of the International Bill of Human Rights so that communities and individuals may claim and enjoy their universal, indivisible, and inalienable rights.

7. *Preservation of the Environment*. Peace rooted in justice requires a commitment to long-term sustainability of the means of life, and profound reorientation of economic systems and individual lifestyles to support ecological justice for human communities in harmony with the whole of creation.

Policy Base

1. NCCC Policy Statement: "The United Nations and the World Community," adopted May 4, 1977.
2. NCCC Policy Statement: "The National Council of Churches Views Its Task in Christian Life and Work," adopted May 16, 1951.
3. NCCC Policy Statement: "Statement on the International Situation, " adopted January 17, 1951.
Federal Council of Churches Statement: "Six Pillars of Peace," 1943.

ADOPTED 1992
REVISED AND READOPTED 2000

See Social Principles, ¶ 165A, B, C, and D.

327. Justice, Peace, and the Integrity of Creation

A World Council of Churches Convocation on "Justice, Peace and the Integrity of Creation" was held in Seoul, Republic of Korea, in March 1990 "to engage member churches in a conciliar process of mutual commitment to justice, peace and the integrity of creation." A set of ten affirmations was approved by the convocation for a process of covenanting:

1. We affirm that all forms of human power and authority are subject to God and accountable to people. This means the right of people to full participation. In Christ, God decisively revealed the meaning of power as compassionate love that prevails over the forces of death.

2. We affirm God's preferential option for the poor and state that as Christians our duty is to embrace God's action in the struggles of the poor in the liberation of us all.

3. We affirm that people of every race, caste, and ethnic group are of equal value. In the very diversity of their cultures and traditions, they reflect the rich plurality of God's creation.

4. We affirm the creative power given to women to stand for life whenever there is death. In Jesus' community women find acceptance and dignity, and with them he shared the imperative to carry the good news.

5. We affirm that access to truth and education, information, and means of communication are basic human rights. All people have the right to be educated, to tell their own stories, to speak their own con-

victions and beliefs, to be heard by others, and to have the power to distinguish truth from falsehood.

6. We affirm the full meaning of God's peace. We are called to seek every possible means of establishing justice, achieving peace, and solving conflicts by active nonviolence.

7. We affirm that the world, as God's handiwork, has its own inherent integrity; that land, waters, air, forests, mountains, and all creatures, including humanity, are "good" in God's sight. The integrity of creation has a social aspect, which we recognize as peace with justice, and an ecological aspect, which we recognize in the self-renewing, sustainable character of natural ecosystems.

8. We affirm that the land belongs to God. Human use of land and waters should release the earth to replenish regularly its life-giving power, protecting its integrity and providing spaces for its creatures.

9. We affirm the dignity of children that derives from their particular vulnerability and need for nurturing love; the creative and sacrificial role that the young people are playing in building a new society, recognizing their right to have a prophetic voice in the structures that affect their life and their community; the rights and needs of the younger generation as basic for establishing educational and developmental priorities.

10. We affirm that human rights are God-given and that their promotion and protection are essential for freedom, justice, and peace. To protect and defend human rights, an independent judicial system is necessary.

The Social Principles of The United Methodist Church clearly reflect our commitment to justice, peace, and the integrity of creation. In addition, The United Methodist Church has demonstrated its support for justice, peace, and the integrity of creation through its complementary Peace with Justice Program.

In affirming its participation in the justice, peace, and the integrity of creation process of the World Council of Churches, The United Methodist Church specifically pledges to:

1. encourage local churches and individuals to study the documents of "Justice, Peace, and the Integrity of Creation" in order to develop greater understanding and support for those movements of people who struggle for human dignity, liberation, and for just and participatory forms of government and economic structures;

2. join the worldwide ecumenical movement to articulate its vision for all people living on earth and caring for creation;

3. urge the General Board of Global Ministries and the General Board of Church and Society to give priority to integrated programs supportive of the four covenants affirmed by the convocation in Seoul, Korea, which advocate:

- a just economic order and liberation from the bondage of foreign debt;
- true security of all nations and people;
- the building of a culture that can live in harmony with creation's integrity; and
- the eradication of racism and discrimination on national and international levels for all people;

4. urge all United Methodists to implement the Social Principles and General Conference resolutions that address these issues, especially "Economic Justice," "The United Methodist Church and Peace," "Environmental Stewardship," "Global Racism," and "Ecumenical Decade: Churches in Solidarity with Women"; and

5. urge all United Methodists to join in covenant with Christians around the world to work to fulfill the goals of justice, peace, and the integrity of creation.

ADOPTED 1992
AMENDED AND ADOPTED 2004

See Social Principles, ¶ 165.

328. Korea—Peace, Justice, and Reunification

Christians in Korea have spoken about the urgency of the reunification of their nation. Celebrating one hundred years of Korean Methodism in 1985, the Korean Methodist Church, in its Centennial Statement, said:

"Faced as we are with the forty years' tragic division of the Korean peninsula, we express our longing for unification of the nation in any form possible through peaceful means in the earliest possible time. This must be done through establishing a democratic political structure based upon freedom and human rights, and must be fulfilled by working toward the establishment of a just society built for the sake of the people. Therefore, we reject any form whatever of dictatorship. Deploring the long history of our nation in which the reality has been the sacrifice of our country's political life, and now with a definite sense of national self-determination which rejects any domination by the superpowers, we disavow any form of war or the taking of life, and commit the whole strength of the Korean Methodist Church to the peaceful reunification of our country."

For the nation of Korea, divided for more than fifty years, justice, peace, and reconciliation are tragically overdue. In 1945 just before the end of World War II, the United States proposed and the Soviet Union agreed to the division of Korea. The division was to have been temporary to facilitate the surrender of Japanese troops in Korea. More than four decades later the country is still divided into the Republic of Korea (ROK) and the Democratic Peoples Republic of Korea (DPRK). The enmity between the superpowers has been played out in the Korean tragedy of war and death, dictatorship and militarization, separation of one people into two hostile camps and divided families with no contact at all. All members of the body of Christ, but especially Christians in the United States, have a special responsibility to support the Korean people in their attempts to build democracy, reduce tension, create trust on the Korean peninsula, heal the divisions, and reunite their country. The threat to peace remains critical with the world's fifth and sixth largest armies facing each other across the Demilitarized Zone.

In many ways, the Korean people, north and south, have expressed their strong desire for reunification. Since 1984, there have been official contacts and conversations on economic and humanitarian issues between ROK and DPRK. Emergency assistance by the DPRK and the ROK following devastating floods in the south and floods and drought in the north was offered and accepted by each other. The first government-sponsored exchange of visits between divided family members occurred in 1985. Thousands of overseas Koreans were able to visit their family members in the DPRK. Christians from north and south met in 1986 in Glion, Switzerland, as part of an ecumenical process on peace and the reunification of Korea led by the World Council of Churches. In 1987, both sides offered proposals to lower military tensions on the peninsula. In June 2000, an unprecedented historic summit between North and South Korean leaders took place in Pyongyang, DPRK. President Kim Dae Jung and Chairman Kim Jong Il pledged themselves to work toward Korean reunification. Since the summit, both Koreas have had numerous exchanges such as reunions of separated families, ministerial level talks, and other economic, social, cultural, and sports exchanges including reconnection of railways and roads through the Demilitarized Zone.

The relationship between the United States and the DPRK, however, has deteriorated due to the issues related to the DPRK's violation of nuclear proliferation since 2001. It has turned out that both signatories of the 1994 Agreed Framework have violated the mandates of the agreement. It is most desirable that the United States and the DPRK, through direct negotiations, redraft or update the 1994 Agreement encompassing all vital matters of interest to both sides including DPRK's nuclear proliferation issues and U.S. recognition of the sovereignty and security of the DPRK.

In 1991, the Agreement on Cooperation of Non-aggression and Exchange was adopted; and in 1992, a Non-nuclearization of the Peninsula was signed by both sides. In 1994, the United States and DPRK signed the Agreed Framework in reference to the DPRK nuclear programs and bilateral US-DPRK issues. The agreement stipulated that funds would be provided to the DPRK from the United States, Japan, and the Republic of Korea (South Korea) for the construction of two light-water electric power reactors. In addition, the U.S. agreed to provide 500,000 tons of heavy oil annually to the DPRK. In return, the DPRK agreed to forego any further accumulation of fuel rods which could be used to produce atomic bombs. The Agreed Framework remains an important stabilizing element in the US-DPRK relations. It is one of the key tools of engagement by which DPRK uses incentives rather than threats to build inter-Korean and regional cooperation.

In 1986, as a result of consultations in Korea, north and south, with Christians and government representatives, the National Council of the Churches of Christ in the U.S.A. (NCCCUSA) adopted an important policy statement on "Peace and the Reunification of Korea." United Methodist representatives participated fully in the development of this statement, in consultations on peace and reunification, and in an official ecumenical delegation to North and South Korea in the summer of 1987.

In support of the Korean people and in cooperation with partner Christian groups, it is recommended that The United Methodist Church, its members, local churches, annual conferences, and agencies undertake the following actions through intercession, education, public advocacy, and support of programs furthering justice, peace, and reconciliation:

1. Engage in prayer of penitence and petition with the Korean people and with Christians in the north and south, scarred and pained by the division of their nation and yearning for reunion, and support the efforts of the Korean Methodist Church, the National Council of Churches of Korea (ROK), and the Korean Christian Federation (DPRK) to seek peace and reconciliation.

2. Commend the policy statement on "Peace and the Reunification of Korea" of the National Council of the Churches of Christ in the U.S.A. (NCCCUSA), November 1986, to annual conferences and local churches for study and action. The policy statement affirms the desire of the Korean people for restoration of national unity and reunion of separated families, traces the history of division and hopeful steps toward change, and outlines Recommendations for Advocacy and Action in the areas of "Healing and Reconciliation," "Peace With Justice," and "New Directions for U.S. Policy." Recommendations 3, 4, and 5, which follow, are in line with the policy statement.

3. Participate in the ecumenical effort of the World Council of Churches (WCC) and NCCCUSA to facilitate the reunion of separated Korean families, including Korean residents in the U.S. and their family members in the DPRK;

4. Urge all governments that have relations with the ROK or the DPRK, or both, to exercise their influence to further mediation, interchange, peace, and reunification.

5. Urge all governments involved to forthright commitment to the following policy directions in support of Korean efforts for peace and reunification:

    a. The peaceful reunification of Korea should be a formal U.S. policy goal.

    b. A peace treaty should be signed among the nations involved to eliminate the threat of war, establish an enduring peace, and minimize tension in the Korean peninsula. The Peace treaty, replacing the existing armistice treaty, should be based on the conditions of a Non-aggression Pact between the Republic of Korea and the Democratic People's Republic of Korea, with the full participation of the United States and the People's Republic of China, as well as other related countries.

    c. ROK and DPRK contacts should be encouraged;

    d. Bilateral diplomatic and human contacts between the United States and the DPRK should be enhanced.

e. The U.S. should negotiate to end the war and to seek a comprehensive peace settlement in Korea.

6. Continue to provide humanitarian aid to the DPRK through the World Food Program (WFP). This aid is directed to those persons most at risk, and is monitored carefully. The WFP has developed productive working relationships with its DPRK counterparts and continues to push for more open access to the food distribution process.

7. Increase communication with the DPRK. Since 1986, the General Board of Global Ministries, in cooperation with the NCCCUSA, has been exchanging delegations with the ROK and DPRK for dialogue and support. Political, economic, social, and religious delegations are a high priority with the DPRK leadership. They provide Korean middle management with experience outside their country and a greater perspective regarding the situation between Korea and the rest of the developed world. Delegations from the DPRK can also be matched with exchange delegations to the DPRK which allows U.S. residents and others to see and understand what the country is like, share ideas, and have personal contact with Korean people.

8. Remove economic sanctions against the DPRK. Sanctions limit the engagement of the DPRK with the global market economy. Removing sanctions will also facilitate foreign investment in improving the DPRK production infrastructure. Because of economic and legal obstacles, development of foreign investment will be a difficult and long-term process, even without sanctions. Removing sanctions is a high priority with the DPRK leadership.

9. Continue to redraft or update policies to comply with the Agreed Framework, of which the most positive element is the US-DPRK relations, by supplying heavy fuel oil and supporting the ROK and Japanese financing for the Korea Peninsula Energy Development Office (KEDO) light-water reactors.

10. Encourage a consistent, bipartisan, and long-range U.S. policy formulation regarding both North and South Korea. Policies that engage the ROK and DPRK governments effectively and promote change and moderation will stand a greater chance of resolving the present crisis and bringing the DPRK into the world community.

11. Urge the United Nations to look into the North Korean refugee situations arising from political and economic needs, as thousands of North Koreans are crossing the border seeking asylum in the neighboring countries. The United Nations should declare them refugees,

assist them as they seek asylum and, also, provide humanitarian assistance.

When these approaches can be taken, and most of them depend on U.S. government policy decisions, there are still no guarantees that the crisis can be resolved. But it is quite clear that a U.S. policy of isolation, sanctions and military buildup directed against the DPRK will stimulate North Korea to rely more on its military, even at the expense of the lives of its population, and may lead to another catastrophic war on the Korean peninsula. Continued engagement, steadfast negotiation, and careful cultivation of cooperative relationships with the appropriate DPRK organizations provide the only real opportunity for a positive resolution of the Korean stalemate.

ADOPTED 1988
AMENDED AND ADOPTED 2000
AMENDED AND READOPTED 2004

See Social Principles,¶ 165B and C.

329. Nuclear-Free Pacific

The United Methodist Church affirms its commitment to a nuclear-free Pacific. As Christian people committed to stewardship, justice, and peacemaking, we oppose and condemn the use of the Pacific for tests, storage, and transportation of nuclear weapons and weapons-delivery systems and the disposal of radioactive wastes. We further affirm the right of all indigenous people to control their health and well-being.

ADOPTED 1984
READOPTED 2000

See Social Principles, ¶ 165B and C.

330. Okinawa—Removal or Reduction of U.S. Military Bases

Be it resolved, that the 2004 General Conference support the strong and unceasing efforts of the Okinawan government and its people to achieve the complete removal or substantial reduction of U.S. military bases and U.S. military personnel on the island of Okinawa and other islands in Okinawa Prefecture of Japan, and the return of those lands for peaceful, constructive purposes; and that a copy of this petition be sent to the President of the United States, the U.S. secretary of state, and the U.S. secretary of defense for consideration and action, and that a copy be sent to the governor of Okinawa and the prime minister of Japan for their information.

ADOPTED 1996
AMENDED AND READOPTED 2004

See Social Principles, ¶ 165B and C.

331. Reduction of U.S. Military Personnel in Okinawa

In recognition of the great investment that The United Methodist Church has made in the mission of the Church in Okinawa (Japan) since the turn of the century, with the arrival of the first Methodist missionary, this resolution is presented to request the support of United Methodist congregations for one of the urgent issues in mission of the Okinawa District of The United Church of Christ in Japan, the Christian body with which The United Methodist Church has a cooperative mission relationship.

In accordance with the U.S.-Japan Mutual Security Treaty, which grants the U.S. use of facilities and areas in Japan, the United States military forces occupy a substantial amount of the land area of Okinawa Island, in addition to having exclusive use of designated air and sea space for military training. This vast military presence greatly hinders the development of Okinawa and threatens the livelihood of Okinawan citizens.

Even after Allied occupation ended on the Japanese mainland in 1952, Okinawa remained under complete U.S. military administration for twenty years, until 1972, when the islands reverted to Japanese jurisdiction

Private property requisitioned by the U.S. military to construct the vast military bases after the war is still held today, denying some 30,000 families the right to live on and utilize their own land. Military aircraft produce ear-splitting noise on a daily basis. Military drills endanger the lives of citizens and destroy the natural environment.

Since 1972, the date of Okinawa's reversion to Japan, U.S. military personnel have committed thousands of crimes. These crimes, which include robbery, murder, and rape, imperil the fundamental human rights of the Okinawan people.

The September 4, 1995, rape of an elementary school girl by three American military personnel and the June 29, 2001, rape of another young woman are not extraordinary cases. Such structural violence is inherent in the enforced "presence of military bases and armed forces which create environment for such incidents" (Okinawa District's July 8, 2001, Statement in Protest Against Rape Incident). The residents of Okinawa living around the bases become the primary targets of this violence, with women and children being especially vulnerable.

This latest rape is only the spark igniting the Okinawans' anger over this and past crimes perpetuated upon them by the U.S. military. In its July 8, 2001, statement, the Okinawa District of the United Church of Christ in Japan demanded "1) apology, mental and physical care, and compensation to the victim, and 2) removal of military bases from Okinawa in order to establish sovereignty and to protect dignity of Okinawan people."

The Okinawa District considers militarization to be an issue that the church is called on to address in its mission of peacemaking.

In light of the above, this resolution requests the General Conference of The United Methodist Church to join with Okinawan Christians in urging the following four appeals to the governments of the United States and Japan:

1. a thorough investigation of all crimes and acts of violence committed by U.S. military personnel stationed on U.S. military bases in Okinawa, and an apology and compensation to the victims of the crimes;

2. an immediate cessation of all military exercises that destroy the environment and threaten the daily life of Okinawans;

3. an immediate review of the U.S.-Japan Mutual Security Treaty (AMPO) which completely ignores the laws of Japan, imposing great hardship on the people of Okinawa; and

4. establishment of a peace not based on military power, and the removal of all U.S. bases from Okinawa.

Therefore, be it resolved, that the 2004 General Conference support the prefectural government of Okinawa and the vast majority of the Okinawan people in their strong, unceasing efforts to achieve the complete removal or substantial reduction of U.S. military bases and U.S. military personnel on the island of Okinawa and other islands in

Okinawa Prefecture of Japan, and the return of those lands for peaceful, constructive purposes; and that a copy of this petition be sent to the President of the United States, the U.S. Secretary of State, and the U.S. Secretary of Defense for consideration and action, as well as to the Governor of Okinawa and the Prime Minister of Japan for their information.

ADOPTED 2004

See Social Principles ¶ 165B and C.

332. Peace with Justice Sunday and Special Offering

Background: From Despair to Hope

The world today has seen unprecedented worsening of economic conditions all over the world. Economically debilitating conditions have sunk the poor of the world further in the quagmire of exploitation and despair. While we have seen the globalization of financial capital that has made possible the unprecedented creation of wealth, we have not seen the globalization of economic justice that would have spread this wealth equitably and sustainably. While there has been increased movement of capital in the world, unemployment and labor conditions remain appalling.

The world, also, has seen unprecedented worsening of political conditions that have mired many countries in ever escalating political tensions, especially those brought about by conflict and wars, genocide and terrorism, and political repression. The wanton disrespect for basic modicums of international cooperation has led to violations of already agreed principles of international law. Human rights continue to be violated and disregarded. Changes taking place in our global community diminish our hope for potential future reductions in military expenditures. These military expenditures drain resources of money and talent to be used for meeting urgent social needs.

Living together on this planet, we have realized that the many threads that connect both fragile and solid foundations of human life and of God's whole creation are endangered. The cultural conditions under which we undergird our citizenship on planet earth continue to be challenged by acts of intolerance and aggression, by acts of racism and xenophobia, by acts of classism, sexism, ageism, and gender discrimination. God's beautiful universe, and all that was good in creation, is in danger of extinction by the unsafe and unsound environmental practices that all too daily governments and peoples around the world inflict upon it. HIV/AIDS continues to escalate to pandemic proportions.

We must renew our call for a social transformation, for the quest to open the doors of opportunity for all, to distribute resources more equitably, and to provide better care for persons in need.

Biblical Basis for Response

The United Methodist Church, with its historic commitment to peace and justice, can and should provide leadership to this social transformation. This heritage is expressed in the Social Principles and the Social Creed. It gained eloquent articulation by the United Methodist Council of Bishops in the foundation document *In Defense of Creation: The Nuclear Crisis and a Just Peace*, which offers a well-grounded biblical analysis for peace with justice. The bishops wrote:

> At the heart of the Old Testament is the testimony to *shalom*, that marvelous Hebrew word that means peace. But the peace that is *shalom* is not negative or one-dimensional. It is much more than the absence of war. *Shalom* is positive peace: harmony, wholeness, health, and well-being in all human relationships. It is the natural state of humanity as birthed by God. It is harmony between humanity and all of God's good creation. All of creation is interrelated. Every creature, every element, every force of nature participates in the whole of creation. If any person is denied *shalom*, all are thereby diminished. . . .

The Old Testament speaks of God's sovereignty in terms of *covenant*, more particularly the "covenant of peace" with Israel, which binds that people to God's *shalom* (Isaiah 54:10; Ezekiel 37:26). In the covenant of *shalom*, there is no contradiction between justice and peace or between peace and security or between love and justice (Jeremiah 29:7). In Isaiah's prophecy, when "the Spirit is poured upon us from on high," we will know that these laws of God are one and indivisible:

> *Then justice will dwell in the wilderness, and the effect of righteousness will be peace, and the result of righteousness, quietness and trust forever. My people will abide in a peaceful habitation, in secure dwellings, and in quiet resting places* (Isaiah 32:16-18).

Shalom, then, is the sum total of moral and spiritual qualities in a community whose life is in harmony with God's good creation. . . .

In Defense of Creation, pp. 24, 25-26

In their analysis, the United Methodist bishops pointed out that when the elders of Israel forsook their moral covenant for warrior-kings, the nation descended into generations of exploitation, repression, and aggression—then into chaos, captivity, and exile in Babylon. Yet we must look to the great prophets of that bitter period of Exile for the renewed vision of *shalom*. If Exodus is liberation, Exile is renewal. Ezekiel and Isaiah (40-66) reaffirm God's creation and redemption as universal in scope. Narrow nationalism is repudiated. Servanthood is exalted as the hopeful path to *shalom* (page 27).

And the prophets' images—swords into plowshares, peaceable kingdoms, new covenants written on the heart—forecast the coming of One who will be the Prince of Peace."

And so he comes. He comes heralded by angels who sing: "Glory to God in the highest, and on earth peace!" He invokes the most special blessings upon peacemakers. He exalts the humanity of aliens. He commands us to love our enemies; for he knows, even if we do not, that if we hate our enemies, we blind and destroy ourselves. *Shalom*, after all, is the heart of God and the law of creation. It cannot be broken with impunity.

New Testament faith presupposes a radical break between the follies, or much so-called conventional wisdom about power and security, on the one hand, and the transcendent wisdom of *shalom*, on the other. Ultimately, New Testament faith is a message of hope about God's plan and purpose for human destiny. It is a redemptive vision that refuses to wallow in doom.

Paul's letters announce that Jesus Christ is "our peace." It is Christ who has "broken down the dividing wall of hostility," creating one humanity, overcoming enmity, so making peace (Ephesians 2:14-19). It is Christ who ordains a ministry of reconciliation. Repentance prepares us for reconciliation. Then we shall open ourselves to the transforming power of God's grace in Christ. Then we shall know what it means to be "in Christ." Then we are to become ambassadors of a new creation, a new Kingdom, a new order of love and justice (2 Corinthians 5:17-20).

The promise of peace envisioned by Israel's prophets of the Exile at the climax of the Old Testament is celebrated once more at the climax of the New Testament. The Revelation of John, in the darkest night of despair, sings of a new earth, radiant with infinite love and compassion, in which all nations and peoples come together peaceably before the Lord God and in which hunger and hurt and sorrow are no more (Revelation 7) (pp. 27-30).

This is the foundation of faith that enables us in The United Methodist Church to offer hope to those who despair and to bring forth joy to replace sadness. As Saint Francis of Assisi prayed to act in the spirit of Christ, so we too can sow love where there is hatred; where injury, pardon; where darkness, light. As instruments of peace and justice, we can seek to replace discord with harmony and to repair the brokenness that shatters the wholeness of *shalom*.

Program Activities

The General Board of Church and Society will carry out the following "Peace with Justice" activities:

1. implement "Policies for a Just Peace" as specified in the Council of Bishops' Foundation Document, The United Methodist Church and Peace, Globalization and Its Impact on Human Dignity and Human Rights, and other resolutions on war, peace, disarmament, and terrorism;

2. implement the process of "Justice, Peace, and the Integrity of Creation" as adopted by the 1990 World Convocation for Justice, Peace, and the Integrity of Creation in Seoul, Republic of Korea;

3. work for social-justice policies and programs that seek the wholeness of *shalom* for all of God's people, and

4. work to eradicate attitudinal and systemic behavior patterns that perpetuate the sin of racism as it is lived out in the areas of peace, justice, and the integrity of creation.

To achieve these objectives, the General Board of Church and Society may:

a. assist annual conferences, districts, and local churches to organize and carry out peace with justice activities, and to promote the Peace with Justice Special Sunday Offering;

b. provide a regular flow of information on public issues to local churches, districts, and annual conferences;

c. strengthen its capacity to act as a public-policy advocate of measures that improve global relations and move toward nuclear disarmament and measures that provide jobs, housing, education, food, health care, income support, and clean water to all;

d. assist annual conferences and/or local churches to assess and respond to the disproportionate effect of injustices on racial and ethnic persons in the United States, and that of people around the world; and

e. assist annual conference Peace with Justice coordinators to carry out their duties.

For the purpose of financing activities (a) to achieve the "Policies for a Just Peace" contained in the Council of Bishops' Foundation Document *In Defense of Creation*, and (b) to pursue other justice and peace objectives contained within the vision of *shalom* in this same document, revenue shall come from the Peace with Justice offering and other possible sources in accordance with ¶ 264.5 and World Service Special gifts.

Assignment

The Peace with Justice Sunday and Special Offering shall be assigned to the General Board of Church and Society.

ADOPTED 1992
AMENDED AND READOPTED 2004

See Social Principles, ¶ 165C.

333. Rape in Times of Conflict and War

Their infants will be dashed to pieces
before their eyes;
their houses will be plundered,
and their wives ravished (Isaiah 13:16).

Women are raped in Zion,
virgins in the towns of Judah (Lamentations 5:11).

For I will gather all the nations against Jerusalem to battle, and the city shall be taken and the houses looted and the women raped; half the city shall go into exile, but the rest of the people shall not be cut off from the city (Zechariah 14:2).

"We believe war is incompatible with the teachings and example of Christ. We therefore reject war as an instrument of national foreign policy, to be employed only as a last resort in the prevention of such evils as genocide, brutal suppression of human rights, and unprovoked international aggression. We insist that the first moral duty of all nations is to resolve by peaceful means every dispute that rises between or among them; that human values must outweigh military claims as governments determine their priorities; that the militarization of society must be challenged and stopped; that the manufacture, sale, and deployment of armaments must be reduced and controlled; and that the production, possession, or use of nuclear weapons be condemned" (Social Principles, ¶ 165C).

For centuries, women have been raped as an act of violence and a demonstration of power—most especially in times of conflict and wars. Rape has been and is sanctioned by military organizations for the gratification of soldiers as was seen in several Asian countries during World War II. The comfort women from Korea (some 80%) and from China, Taiwan, Malaysia, Burma, Indonesia, East Timor, the Philippines and the Pacific Islands are a most blatant example of this practice. Rape during wartime constitutes many individual and group acts of violence perpetrated by soldiers against girls and women of enemy countries or opposing sides, often under orders. Thus rape, in effect, is used as an extension of warfare. But rape is rarely mentioned in resolutions and statements on war and peace. And the conquest of women as spoils of war continues to be tolerated in times of conflict.

Mass rape is an increasingly sophisticated weapon of war, used in the Bosnia-Herzegovina conflict and in other conflicts—such as Haiti, Georgia (CIS), Rwanda, and in other parts of the world today.

Survivors of conflicts speak of rape on the frontline and third-party rape; these rapes are carried out publicly by soldiers to demoralize family members and opposition forces compelled to witness them.

Many stories refer to village communities being rounded up in camps—perhaps a school or community center—where a space is cleared in the middle. It is in this space that public raping takes place. It is reported as repeated and violent and procedural. It is claimed that many of the victims and witnesses know the rapists.

Destruction and violation of women is one way of attacking male opponents who regard the women as their property—and whose male identity is therefore bound to protection of their property.

The United Methodist Church affirms the sacredness of all persons and their right to safety, nurture, and care. And, together with the international community, it is challenged to respond to the rape of women in military conflicts. The extent and frequency of the violation of women in war must not be allowed to deaden sensitivity to this as gross injustice. There must be greater understanding of the use of rape in this manner (as a weapon of warfare). Documentation and analysis of such planned violation of human rights and its root causes must be developed. Strategizing to confront systems that give rise to it and the needs of those who are its victims must be undertaken.

International instruments such as The Hague Conventions and the Geneva Conventions included prohibitions on rape and sexual violence but these crimes were not codified in their charters. And while, evidence on sexual violence was presented at the International Military Tribunals after World War II, the crime did not get singled out but was included in the accusations of Crimes Against Humanity-Inhumane Treatment. Not until the International Criminal Tribunals for the Former Yugoslavia and for Rwanda did the crimes of sexual violence become recognized and prosecuted. In February 2001, in the Hague, three Bosnian Serbs were convicted of rape and sexual enslavement of Muslim women and girls. This was the first time in history that defendants had been condemned exclusively for sexual violence. In addition the judges asserted that the rape was used as an "instrument of terror" and as a "systematic attack "on the Muslim populations. The judgment declared rape as a crime against humanity.

"...crimes against international law are committed by men, not by abstract entities, and only by punishing individuals who commit such crimes can the provisions of international law be enforced." The Judgment of the Nuremberg Tribunal

In 2002, the International Criminal Court was established in The Hague. Unlike the International Court of Justice (also in the Hague) which handles issues between states, the

International Criminal Court deals with individual responsibility for acts of genocide and egregious violations of human rights, crimes against humanity. No longer will there be the need for setting up International Criminal Tribunals. The Treaty setting up the Court has been ratified by more that 90 Countries and represents an international community which will no longer tolerate genocide, ethnic cleansing, murder, rape and brutalization of civilians trapped in military conflicts.

We call on The United Methodist Church:

1. to condemn all forms of rape as incompatible with the church's understanding of the sacredness of life; and to affirm the right of all persons to safety, nurture, and care;

2. to urge United Methodists to work towards the ratification by their country of the Treaty establishing the International Criminal Court;

3. to urge the General Board of Global Ministries to develop an anthology of theological and biblical perspectives of rape in times of war, written by survivors and other women who have observed and reflected on this grave concern;

4. to urge both the General Board of Global Ministries and the General Board of Church and Society to act as resources for churches who wish to pressure for legal and political redress for victims of rape in times of war; and

5. to urge the United Methodist Committee on Relief to continue developing assistance and support for women victims of war and their families, to meet their physical and emotional needs. This may mean supporting, as wartime refugees, women who cannot return to their homes because of fear of rape, violence, and condemnation.

ADOPTED 1996
AMENDED AND READOPTED 2004

See Social Principles, ¶ 165C.

334. Saying No to Nuclear Deterrence

In 1986, the United Methodist Council of Bishops, after nearly two years of prayerful and penitent study, adopted a pastoral letter and foundation document entitled *In Defense of Creation: The Nuclear Crisis and a Just Peace.*[1]

The bishops' statement was deeply rooted in biblical faith. They wrote:

At the heart of the Old Testament is the testimony of shalom, that marvelous Hebrew word that means peace. But the peace that is shalom is

1. *In Defense of Creation: The Nuclear Crisis and a Just Peace,* the United Methodist Council of Bishops (Nashville: Graded Press, 1986).

not negative or one dimensional. It is much more than the absence of war. Shalom is positive peace: harmony, wholeness, health, and well-being in all human relationships. It is the natural state of humanity as birthed by God. It is harmony between humanity and all of God's good creation. All of creation is interrelated. Every creature, every element, every force of nature participates in the whole of creation. If any person is denied shalom, all are thereby diminished. . . .[2] New Testament faith presupposes a radical break between the follies, or much so-called conventional wisdom about power and security, on the one hand, and the transcendent wisdom of shalom, on the other. Ultimately, New Testament faith is a message of hope about God's plan and purpose for human destiny. It is a redemptive vision that refuses to wallow in doom.[3]

Based upon this faith, the bishops in their pastoral letter stated unequivocally that "we say a clear and unconditional *No* to nuclear war and to any use of nuclear weapons. We conclude that nuclear deterrence is a position that cannot receive the church's blessing."[4]

The implication is clear. If nuclear weapons cannot be legitimately used for either deterrence or war fighting, no nation should possess them. Accordingly, in the foundation document the bishops indicated:

We support the earliest possible negotiation of phased but rapid reduction of nuclear arsenals, while calling upon all other nuclear-weapon states to agree to parallel arms reductions, to the eventual goal of a mutual and verifiable dismantling of all nuclear armaments.[5]

In 1988, the United Methodist General Conference affirmed and supported the statements of the Council of Bishops contained in *In Defense of Creation*.[6] Four years later, in a resolution entitled "Nuclear Disarmament: The Zero Option," the 1992 General Conference stated that "now is the time to exercise the zero option: to eliminate all nuclear weapons throughout the globe,"[7] and the conference offered a series of concrete actions for achieving this goal.

2. Ibid., page 24.
3. Ibid., page 28.
4. Ibid., page 92.
5. Ibid., page 76
6. *The Book of Resolutions of The United Methodist Church, 1988*, page 503.
7. Ibid., page 601.

Our Commitment

We reaffirm the finding that nuclear weapons, whether used or threatened, are grossly evil and morally wrong. As an instrument of mass destruction, nuclear weapons slaughter the innocent and ravage the environment. When used as instruments of deterrence, nuclear weapons hold innocent people hostage for political and military purposes. Therefore, the doctrine of nuclear deterrence is morally corrupt and spiritually bankrupt.

In contrast to the goal of total nuclear disarmament, policy of the United States government has moved in the opposite direction in recent years. A series of policy documents—"Nuclear Posture Review" (January 2002), "National Security Strategy" (September 2002), "National Security Presidential Directive 17" (September 2002), and "National Strategy to Combat Weapons of Mass Destruction" (December 2002)—have called for the development of new nuclear weapons, preparation for renewal of nuclear testing, targeting non-nuclear states with nuclear weapons, and using nuclear weapons in response to biological and chemical weapons. Policy statements have asserted the right to take unilateral, pre-emptive action, including the use of nuclear weapons, against emerging threats by states and terrorist groups before they are fully formed.

These policies undermine the intent of the Nuclear Non-Proliferation Treaty and increase the risk that nuclear weapons will actually be used. We deplore these dangerous and retrogressive policies.

Therefore, we reaffirm the goal of total abolition of all nuclear weapons throughout Earth and space.

Recommended Actions

Because we unequivocally reject the use or threatened use of nuclear weapons, we call upon all possessors of nuclear weapons to carry out the following actions as soon as possible:

1. renounce unconditionally the use of nuclear weapons for deterrence and war-fighting purposes;

2. pledge never to use nuclear weapons against any adversary under any circumstance;

3. immediately take all nuclear weapons off alert by separating warheads from delivery vehicles and by other means;

4. embark upon a program to systematically dismantle all nuclear warheads and delivery vehicles as soon as possible with adequate safeguards and verification, carried out under multilateral treaties and through reciprocal national initiatives;

5. ratify and implement the Comprehensive Test Ban Treaty;

6. cease all research, development, testing, production, and deployment of new nuclear weapons and refrain from modernizing the existing nuclear arsenal;

7. halt all efforts to develop and deploy strategic antimissile defense systems because they are illusory, unnecessary, and wasteful;

8. respect the requirements of nuclear weapon-free zones where they exist;

9. enter into a multilateral process to develop, adopt, and carry out a nuclear weapons convention that outlaws and abolishes all nuclear weapons under strict and effective international control; and

10. develop and implement a system for control of all fissile material with international accounting, monitoring, and safeguards.

We call upon all nations that do not possess nuclear weapons to:

1. cease all efforts to develop these instruments of mass destruction and their delivery systems;

2. ratify and carry out the provisions of the Comprehensive Test Ban Treaty;

3. adhere to all provisions of the Non-Proliferation Treaty; and

4. respect the requirements of nuclear weapon-free zones and extend this approach to other nations and continents.

Implementation

To promote the achievement of goals and objectives specified in this resolution:

1. We ask the Council of Bishops to transmit a copy of the resolution to the heads of state of all nations possessing nuclear weapons.

2. We ask the General Board of Church and Society to publicize the resolution with appropriate governmental officials, legislators, the media, and the general public.

3. We call upon the Council of Bishops and the General Board of Church and Society to provide leadership, guidance, and educational material to United Methodists, congregations, and conferences in

order to assist them in understanding and working for the goal and objectives of nuclear abolition.

4. We request that the General Board of Church and Society prepare an annual "report card" to be included with Peace With Justice Sunday materials in relation to: a) countries that possess nuclear weapons and their compliance with the recommended actions in this resolution, and b) countries that do not posses nuclear weapons and their compliance with the recommended actions in this resolution.

Conclusion

We fervently believe that these recommendations will greatly enhance global security by eliminating the possibility of nuclear war. Furthermore, the resources of human talent, production capacity, and money released can become available to deal with urgent human problems around the globe. Nuclear abolition provides great hope for global peace and prosperity.

ADOPTED 1996
AMENDED AND READOPTED 2000
AMENDED AND READOPTED 2004

See Social Principles, ¶ 164C.

335. Support for the Land Mine Treaty

Antipersonnel land mines are weapons of mass destruction that claim life or limb of another innocent victim every 20 minutes. Peacekeepers, humanitarian workers, and missionaries daily risk death and injury from land mines. Today, 135 countries have signed the 1997 Mine Ban Treaty. Religious leaders, physicians, veterans, humanitarian activists, environmentalists, and human-rights advocates have called upon the United States to sign the Mine Ban Treaty.

Antipersonnel land mines are a growing threat to human community and the environment, kill or maim hundreds of people every week, bring untold suffering and casualties to mostly innocent and defenseless civilians and especially children, obstruct economic development and reconstruction, inhibit the repatriation of refugees and internally displaced persons, and have other severe consequences for years after emplacement.

Therefore, the General Conference of The United Methodist Church, calls upon the President of the United States and, if need be, his successor, to endorse the "Convention on the Prohibition of the Use, Stockpiling, Production and Transfer of Anti-Personnel Mines and on Their Destruction," commonly called the Mine Ban Treaty; and further, that our Council of Bishops, the general superintendents of The United Methodist Church, send representation of that body to deliver this heartfelt call to the President as soon as possible after the adjournment of the year 2000 General Conference.

We commit ourselves to strategies of advocacy against the deployment of land mines, de-mining, and caring for persons who have been wounded by land mines.

We call upon U.S. citizens and the U.S. Government to increase resources for humanitarian de-mining, mine awareness programs, and increased resources for landmine victim rehabilitation and assistance; and we ask that the secretary of the General Conference to send this resolution to the President of the United States Senate and to the speaker of the U. S. House of Representatives as soon as possible after the adjournment of the year 2000 General Conference.

ADOPTED 2000

See Social Principles, ¶ 165*B* and C.

336. Plan to Eliminate Terrorism

Biblical visions of a new heaven and a new earth speak of a time when there will be no more death and suffering (Revelation 21) and of a time when swords shall be turned into plowshares and none shall be afraid (Micah 4: 3-5). Toward this end, all biblically based codes of ethics, beginning with the Ten Commandments, prohibit the killing of others.

Horrific terrorist attacks of recent years have caused fear and desperation among many people around the world, contributing to feelings of hopelessness and powerlessness. During the past four decades, many nations have suffered acts of terror perpetrated by diverse political and religious groups. In the past several years, however, this tragic global phenomenon has assumed an even greater prominence, and debates over "fighting terrorism" have taken on broader and more varied meanings.

The September 11, 2001 attacks in the United States perpetrated by the al-Qaeda terrorist network that killed more than 3,000 persons from at least 78 countries were a terrible watershed in the world's experience with international terrorism. The attacks galvanized a strong response from the United Nations and the international community, which joined together to fight terrorism through enhanced law enforcement, diplomatic and intelligence cooperation, and actions to restrict terrorist financing. Despite such cooperation, however, thousands of additional persons have been killed since September 11 by acts of terror in the Middle East, Southeast Asia, South Asia, North Africa, East Africa, and Europe; and the threat of other catastrophic attacks continues to challenge governments and societies around the world.

Global terrorism reminds us of how fragile our global community is and points up the continuing weaknesses in the international system. As God's children, all of us are united in an increasingly interdependent world linked in myriad ways, both good and harmful.

The church has a prophetic message to proclaim in what some have called an age of global terror. The image of God and the sacrifice of Christ bestow a worth and dignity on each human being that cannot be rightfully ignored or violated by any human institution or social movement. For this reason, we condemn all acts of terrorism, with no exception for the target or the source.

There is no significant difference between "state terrorism," as the disproportionate response of a state, and group terrorism, whether in the international arena or on the home front. The killing of innocent persons in horrific bombings, hijackings and other malicious acts of violence cannot be justified by any political or other objective.

Working to prevent further acts of terror clearly is a central responsibility of governments and the international community. Unilateral and preemptive actions and policies of nations including the "doctrine of preemption" and the U.S. invasion of Iraq, are disproportionate, deeply disturbing and counter-productive, as they undermine the international cooperation that is key to preventing further terrorist attacks.

We are equally concerned about repressive governments that brand those who oppose them as "terrorists;" this label should not be an excuse to justify government oppression or to support colonial or repressive rule.

Therefore, The United Methodist Church:

1. stands against acts of terror of all kinds and condemns them unequivocally;

2. urges all world leaders to repudiate violence and the killing and victimizing of innocent people;

3. pledges to examine critically the causes of terrorism and affirm the primacy of international cooperation to confront terrorism effectively;

4. firmly supports the United Nations as an agency for conflict resolution, as a viable alternative to resorting to war or terrorism, and as an effective body to promote cooperation against terrorism, through the Security Council and its Counter-Terrorism Committee;

5. urges support of United Nations Security Council Resolution 1373 and other UN resolutions that urge greater international cooperation to prevent acts of terror, and commends the cooperation of many nations to take steps to halt financing for terrorist organizations, to prevent movement of terrorists across borders, and to take other steps to help prevent further destruction by terrorists;

6. commends the hard work and dedication of persons across the globe who engage in appropriate law enforcement actions, consistent with internationally recognized human rights standards and due process, to prevent further acts of terror;

7. opposes the use of indiscriminate military force to combat terrorism, especially where the use of such force results in casualties among noncombatant persons who are not themselves perpetrators of acts of terror;

8. calls for tolerance toward and dialogue with Muslims to prevent the "war on terrorism" and actions against al-Qaeda from poisoning relations between Christians and Muslims;

9. urges that concerns about acts of terror not be used to impose discriminatory restrictions on immigration and freedom of movement among countries; such restrictions cause unnecessary harm and suffering to many individuals and families and can prove counter-productive;

10. Oppose governmental policies or actions which, in the name of combating terrorism, violate civil and human rights protected by national and international laws and conventions.

11. condemns the use of extremist tactics by groups around the world that resort to violence because of ideological differences, racism, and anti-Arab and anti-Jewish attitudes; and

12. urges churches and United Methodist Christians to support the activities and program of the "Decade to Overcome Violence" led by the World Council of Churches.

To further these objectives, we urge United Methodist Church members and congregations to utilize the study on terrorism produced by the General Board of Church and Society. In an "age of terror" the church needs—more than ever—to respond prophetically and pastorally to this critical issue of our time.

ADOPTED 2004

See Social Principles, ¶ 165B and *D.*

337. Prayer for Military Personnel and for Peace in Iraq

WHEREAS, the Church is called to proclaim the peace of our Lord Jesus Christ and to work for God's kingdom in which all people live together in peace;

Therefore, be it resolved, that we will pray for all military personnel and their families, international leaders and the Iraqi people; and furthermore,

Be it further resolved, that we call upon the United States government and The United Methodist Church to work cooperatively with the international community and the worldwide Body of Christ for a just and peaceful rebuilding of Iraq that provides for Iraq's self-determination as a nation with intentional focus on the needs and concerns of the Iraqi people; and furthermore,

Be it finally resolved, that we exemplify Christ's peace through the words and actions of each of our daily lives.

ADOPTED 2004

See Social Principles, ¶ 165B and *C.*

338. The United Methodist Church and Peace

"Peace is not simply the absence of war, a nuclear stalemate or combination of uneasy cease-fires. It is that emerging dynamic reality envisioned by prophets where spears and swords give way to implements of peace (Isaiah 2:1-4); where historic antagonists dwell together in trust (Isaiah 11:4-11); and where righteousness and justice prevail. There will be no peace with justice until unselfish and informed life is structured into political processes and international arrangements" (Bishops' Call for Peace and the Self-Development of Peoples).

The mission of Jesus Christ and his church is to serve all peoples regardless of their government, ideology, place of residence, or status. Surely the welfare of humanity is more important in God's sight than the power or even the continued existence of any state. Therefore, the church is called to look beyond human boundaries of nation, race, class, sex, political ideology, or economic theory and to proclaim the demands of social righteousness essential to peace.

The following are interrelated areas that must be dealt with concurrently in a quest for lasting peace in a world community.

I. Disarmament

The arms race goes on. However, the danger of a holocaust remains as long as nations maintain nuclear weapons. Meanwhile, millions starve, and development stagnates. Again and again, regional tensions grow, conflicts erupt, and outside forces intervene to advance or protect their interests without regard to international law or human rights.

True priorities in national budgeting are distorted by present expenditures on weapons. Because of fear of unemployment, desire for profits, and contributions to the national balance of payments, the arms industry engenders great political power. Arms-producing nations seek to create markets, then vie with one another to become champion among the arms merchants of the world. Food, health, social services, jobs, and education are vital to the welfare of nations. Yet their availability is constantly threatened by the overriding priority given by governments to what is called "defense."

We support initiatives in every part of the world that move toward the goal of disarmament. This demands a radical reordering of priorities coupled with an effective system of international peacemaking, peacekeeping, and peace building. The church must constantly keep that goal before peoples and governments. In particular, we support the abolition of nuclear weapons. We affirm the prophetic position of our bishops who said in their statement In Defense of Creation: "We say a clear and unconditional 'NO' to nuclear war and to any use of nuclear weapons. We conclude that nuclear deterrence is a position that cannot receive the church's blessing." Accordingly, we reject the possession of nuclear weapons as a permanent basis for securing and maintaining peace. Possession can no longer be tolerated, even as a temporary expedient. We call upon all nations that possess nuclear weapons to renounce these vile instruments of mass destruction and to move expeditiously to dismantle all nuclear warheads and delivery vehicles. As a first step, we support all movement to ban the "first strike" policy from all North Atlantic Treaty Organization (NATO) doctrine.

We support the Comprehensive Nuclear Test Ban Treaty and the Nuclear Non-Proliferation Treaty. We call upon all nations to become signatories of these important treaties and to abide by their provisions.

At the same time, nations must provide for more secure control of weapons-grade nuclear materials. It is clear deterrence comes from international controls on materials from which bombs are made. We support the concept of nuclear-free zones where governments or peoples in a specific region band together to bar nuclear weapons from the area either by treaty or declaration. The United Methodist Church affirms its commitment to a nuclear-free Pacific. As Christian people committed to stewardship, justice, and peacemaking, we oppose and condemn the use of the Pacific for tests, storage, and transportation of nuclear weapons and weapons-delivery systems and the disposal of radioactive wastes. We further affirm the right of all indigenous people to control their health and well-being.

World public opinion justly condemns the use of chemical or biological weapons. Governments must renounce the use of these particularly inhumane weapons as part of their national policy. We support universal application of the Chemical Weapons Convention and the Biological Weapons Convention.

We support treaty efforts to ban the development, trade, and use of weapons that are inhumane, are excessively injurious, and have indiscriminate effects. Such weapons include land mines, booby traps, weapons with nondetectable fragments, incendiary weapons, and blinding laser weapons. We call upon all nations to sign and abide by the Convention on the Prohibition of the Use, Stockpiling, Production, and Transfer of Anti-Personnel Mines and on Their Destruction.

We are also concerned about the use of inhumane weapons by civilian or military police. Hollow-point ("dumdum") or other bullets designed to maim are not acceptable weapons for use by civilian or military forces. We support measures that outlaw use of such weapons at all levels. We affirm peoples' movements directed to abolition of the tools of war. Governments must not impede public debate on this issue of universal concern.

II. Democracy and Freedom

Millions of people still live under oppressive rule and various forms of exploitation. Millions more live under deplorable conditions of racial, sexual, and class discrimination. In many countries, many persons, including Christians, are suffering repression, imprisonment, and torture as a result of their efforts to speak truth to those in power. Action by governments to encourage liberation and economic justice is essential but must be supported by parallel action on the part of private citizens and institutions, including the churches, if peaceful measures are to succeed. Unless oppression and denial of basic human rights are ended, violence on an increasing scale will continue to erupt in many nations and may spread throughout the world. The human toll in such conflicts is enormous, for they result in new oppression and further dehumanization. We are concerned for areas where oppression and discrimination take place. We, as United Methodist Christians, must build the conditions for peace through development of confidence and trust between peoples and governments. We are unalterably opposed to those who instill hate in one group for another. Governments or political factions must not use religious, class, racial, or other differences as the means to achieve heinous political purposes. This concern extends to all situations where external commercial, industrial, and military interests are related to national oligarchies that resist justice and liberation for the masses of people. It is essential that governments which support or condone these activities alter their policies to permit and enable people to achieve genuine self-determination.

III. The United Nations

International justice requires the participation and determination of all peoples. We are called to look beyond the "limited and competing boundaries of nation-states to the larger and more inclusive community of humanity" (Bishops' Call for Peace and the Self-Development of Peoples).

There has been unprecedented international cooperation through the United Nations and its specialized agencies as they have worked to solve international problems of health, education, and the welfare of people. The United Nations Children's Fund (UNICEF) is one of the agencies that has been successful in this area.

These achievements are to be commended. However, in other areas, political considerations have diminished the support needed for the United Nations to achieve its goals. Many nations, including the most powerful, participate in some programs only when such action does not interfere with their national advantage.

We believe the United Nations and its agencies must be supported, strengthened, and improved. We recommend that Christians work for the following actions in their respective nations:

- The Universal Declaration of Human Rights is a standard of achievement for all peoples and nations. International covenants and conventions that seek to implement the Declaration must be universally ratified.
- Peace and world order require the development of an effective and enforceable framework of international law that provides protection for human rights and guarantees of justice for all people.
- Greater use should be made of the International Court of Justice. Nations should remove any restrictions they have adopted that impair the court's effective functioning.
- The industrialized world must not dominate development agencies. We support efforts to make controlling bodies of such agencies more representative.
- We support the development and strengthening of international agencies designed to help nations or peoples escape from domination by other nations or transnational enterprises.
- Economic and political considerations greatly affect issues of food, energy, raw materials, and other commodities. We support efforts in the United Nations to achieve new levels of justice in the world economic order.
- We support the concept of collective action against threats to peace. Wars fought in the search for justice might well be averted or diminished if the nations of the world would work

vigorously and in concert to seek changes in oppressive political and economic systems.

IV. World Trade and Economic Development

The gap between rich and poor countries continues to widen. Human rights are denied when the surpluses of some arise in part as a result of continued deprivation of others. This growing inequity exists in our own communities and in all our nations. Our past efforts to alleviate these conditions have failed. Too often these efforts have been limited by our own unwillingness to act or have been frustrated by private interests and governments striving to protect the wealthy and the powerful.

In order to eliminate inequities in the control and distribution of the common goods of humanity, we are called to join the search for more just and equitable international economic structures and relationships. We seek a society that will assure all persons and nations the opportunity to achieve their maximum potential.

In working toward that purpose, we believe these steps are needed:

- Economic systems structured to cope with the needs of the world's peoples must be conceived and developed.
- Measures that will free peoples and nations from reliance on financial arrangements that place them in economic bondage must be implemented.
- Policies and practices for the exchange of commodities and raw materials that establish just prices and avoid damaging fluctuations in price must be developed.
- Control of international monetary facilities must be more equitably shared by all the nations, including the needy and less powerful.
- Agreements that affirm the common heritage principle (that resources of the seabed, subsoil, outer space, and those outside national jurisdiction are the heritage of humanity) should be accepted by all nations.
- Multilateral, rather than bilateral, assistance programs should be encouraged for secular as well as religious bodies. They must be designed to respond to the growing desire of the "developing world" to become self-reliant.
- Nations that possess less military and economic power than others must be protected, through international agreements, from loss of control of their own resources and means of pro-

duction to either transnational enterprises or other governments.

These international policies will not narrow the rich-poor gap within nations unless the powerless poor are enabled to take control of their own political and economic destinies. We support people's organizations designed to enable the discovery of local areas of exploitation and development of methods to alleviate these problems.

Economic and political turmoil within many developing nations has been promoted and used by other powers as an excuse to intervene through subversive activities or military force in furtherance of their own national interests. We condemn this version of imperialism that often parades as international responsibility.

We support the United Nations' efforts to develop international law to govern the sea and to ensure that the world's common resources will be used cooperatively and equitably for the welfare of humankind.

We urge the appropriate boards and agencies of The United Methodist Church to continue and expand efforts to bring about justice in cooperative action between peoples of all countries.

V. Military Conscription, Training, and Service

1. *Conscription.* We affirm our historic opposition to compulsory military training and service. We urge that military conscription laws be repealed; we also warn that elements of compulsion in any national service program will jeopardize seriously the service motive and introduce new forms of coercion into national life. We advocate and will continue to work for the inclusion of the abolition of military conscription in disarmament agreements.

2. *Conscientious objection.* Each person must face conscientiously the dilemmas of conscription, military training, and service and decide his or her own responsible course of action. We affirm the historic statement: "What the Christian citizen may not do is to obey persons rather than God, or overlook the degree of compromise in even our best acts, or gloss over the sinfulness of war. The church must hold within its fellowship persons who sincerely differ at this point of critical decision, call all to repentance, mediate to all God's mercy, minister to all in Christ's name" ("The United Methodist Church and Peace," 1968 General Conference).

Christian teaching supports conscientious objection to all war as an ethically valid position. It also asserts that ethical decisions on political matters must be made in the context of the competing claims of biblical revelation, church doctrine, civil law, and one's own understanding of what God calls him or her to do.

We therefore support all those who conscientiously object to preparation for or participation in any specific war or all wars, to cooperation with military conscription, or to the payment of taxes for military purposes, and we ask that they be granted legal recognition.

Since 1936, The United Methodist Church or one of its predecessors has provided to those of its members who claim to be conscientious objectors the opportunity to register. Certified copies of such registration are supplied for use with the draft authorities. It is the responsibility of the church at all levels to inform its members of the fact that conscientious objection, as well as conscientious participation, is a valid option for Christians and is recognized in many countries as a legal alternative for persons liable to military conscription.

The local church's support of an individual participating in this process does not express agreement or disagreement with the convictions of the applicant member. Rather, the church's task is to record which of its members are opposed to participation in military service on grounds of conscience and to assist them in securing proper counsel. When a member has registered as a conscientious objector and his or her registration has been certified by the proper authorities, that action should be recorded with the conference and the General Board of Church and Society.

The United Methodist Church also supports those persons who refuse to register for the draft and deplore discrimination against those persons by any institution.

3. *Amnesty and reconciliation.* We urge understanding of and full amnesty or pardon for persons in all countries whose refusal to participate in war has placed them in legal jeopardy. We urge governments to grant political asylum to persons whose countries fail to recognize their conscientious objection to war.

VI. Peace Research, Education, and Action

The 1960 General Conference established the landmark study "The Christian Faith and War in the Nuclear Age." That study said, "The Christian Church and the individual must accept responsibility for the creation of a climate of opinion in which creative changes can occur." It called work for these creative alternatives "our mission field as we live as disciples of the Prince of Peace." In order to create such a climate of conciliation and compromise, we call upon The United Methodist Church, including its agencies and institutions of higher education, in the light of its historical teachings and its commitment to peace and self-development of peoples, to:

1. seek the establishment of educational institutions devoted to the study of peace;

2. develop alternatives to vocations that work against peace, and support individuals in their quest;

3. explore and apply ways of resolving domestic and international differences that affirm human fulfillment rather than exploitation and violence;

4. affirm and employ methods that build confidence and trust between peoples and countries, including training in multicultural understanding and appreciation of differences, rejecting all promotion of hatred and mistrust;

5. continue to develop and implement the search for peace through educational experiences, including church school classes, schools of Christian mission, and other settings throughout the church; and

6. encourage local churches and members to take actions that make for peace and to act in concert with other peoples and groups of goodwill toward the achievement of a peaceful world.

ADOPTED 1984
AMENDED AND READOPTED 2000

See Social Principles, ¶ 165B and C.

339. Rejection of Unilateral First-Strike Actions and Strategies

WHEREAS, the United Methodist Council of Bishops has stated its opposition to the first-strike use of nuclear weapons (Resolution 334);

WHEREAS, our denomination is on record for opposing war as a usual instrument of foreign policy and insists that the first moral duty of all nations is to resolve by peaceful means every dispute that arises among them (*Discipline* ¶ 165C); and that it may only be waged "when peaceful alternatives have failed" (*Discipline* ¶ 164G).

WHEREAS, our denomination is on record that "We urge the establishment of the rule of law in international affairs," and whereas, policies of unilateral first strike military actions without United Nations approval violate established international law;

WHEREAS, by attacking Iraq without the approval and participation of the United Nations, the United States has squandered its positive reputation as a responsible member of the global community in the effort to make the world safe for democracy, instigating instead, a wide-spread mood of resentment and an attitude of mistrust toward Americans;

Therefore, The United Methodist Church strongly protests all unilateral first-strike actions and strategies on the part of any government or military force and calls on the President and Congress of the United States to cease and desist from such actions without ratification by, and collaboration with, the United Nations.

ADOPTED 2004

See Social Principles, ¶165.

340. In Defense of International Law and Cooperation: Cornerstone of Multilateralism

"Those who say, 'I love God,' and hate their brothers and sisters, are liars; for those who do not love a brother or sister whom they have seen, cannot love God whom they have not seen. The commandment we have from him is this: those who love God must love their brothers and sisters also" (1 John 4:20-21).

Justice and Law—Persons and groups must feel secure in their life and right to live within a society if order is to be achieved and maintained by law. We denounce as immoral an ordering of life that perpetuates injustice. Nations, too, must feel secure in the world if world community is to become a fact. We commend the efforts of all people in all countries who pursue world peace through law. We endorse international aid and cooperation on all matters of need and conflict . . . Bilateral or multilateral efforts outside of the United Nations should work in concert with, and not contrary to, its purposes. Social Principles, ¶ 165D.

At the beginning of the 21st century, the world is faced with an unprecedented global environmental crisis and a devastated global economy increasingly unequal and exploitative, the pandemic of

HIV/AIDS, the spread of weapons of mass destruction, terrorist actions which recognize no borders and gross violations of human rights and humanitarian law. No country can develop solutions to these grave concerns alone. Unfortunately, the United States has time and again insisted that they can act alone. A leading US columnist, Anna Guindlen (Newsweek, March 10, 2003), asks the question "What is required of a nation that is not only the greatest democracy but the nation by which all other democratic attempts have been measured?" and one of her answers is "The danger in having enormous power is that the ambition to use it for good can so often be subverted by the temptation to use it for dominance." The United States has embarked on such a foreign policy (spelled out in its National Security Strategy) which assumes its supremacy in the world. The United States maintains global military dominance and the right of a preemptive military attack against any country it regards as a current or even a potential future threat. In addition the USA is manipulating international law, weakening international cooperation and using multilateralism only if its self-interest is preserved. The USA:

1. accounts for 50 percent of the worlds military spending, devotes more than $1 billion a day to military spending and has the largest number of military bases around the world. The USA has abrogated the Anti-Ballistic Missile (ABM) Treaty and squanders billions in chasing the illusion of national missile defense. It has refused to ratify the Treaty to Ban Landmines;

2. has the largest nuclear arsenal and has undermined the Nuclear Non-Proliferation Treaty and the Comprehensive Test Ban Treaty while expressing support for testing new nuclear weapons and refusing to rule out a nuclear first strike against non nuclear nations;

3. derailed negotiations to improve international inspection systems to monitor and prevent the production of biological and chemical weapons. Dismissed the need for broad international cooperation in its war on terrorism, preferring to act alone or with selected allies. Renounced the U.S. signature on the treaty to create an International Criminal Court and campaigned aggressively to exempt all U.S. personnel from its jurisdiction;

4. treated human rights as an obstacle to rather than an essential component of civic security at home and abroad. Suspended U.S. support for the UN's family planning programs and balked at supporting the Convention on the Elimination of All Forms against Women

(CEDAW) and the Convention on the Rights of the Child. Walked out on the World Summit against Racism, Racial Discrimination and Xenophobia.

5. withdrew from global efforts to curb global warming thru the Kyoto Protocol on reducing carbon emissions. Continued to pursue a global economic agenda that is of, by, and for transnational corporations. Has blocked efforts to build international rules to enforce labor and consumer rights and environmental protections. Slighted global efforts to mobilize an offensive against the spread of AIDS, instead privileged the financial interests of pharmaceutical companies over the need for affordable life-saving medicines.

6. undermined the Oslo peace process, condoned the Israeli reoccupation of Palestinian territory, and rejected UN Security Council resolutions supported by previous administrations that provide a framework for conflict resolution containing strict security guarantees for both Israel and the Palestinians.

Therefore, the United Methodist Church urges United Methodists to take seriously the question, "How does Gods love abide in anyone who has the worlds goods and sees a brother or sister in need and yet refuses to help?" and agree that for the followers of Christ there is but one answer, " . . . let us love, not in word or speech, but in truth and action" (1 John 3: 17 and 18).

While this resolution addresses primarily the United States because it is the greatest power in the world, the United Methodist Church recognizes that several other nations such as the other members of the G8 (France, Germany, United Kingdom, Japan, Italy, Russia, and Canada) as well as China and other less powerful nations should not be forgotten when implementing the following recommendations:

1. The United Methodist Church including its agencies and institutions of higher education must find ways to implement the following resolutions from *The Book of Resolutions of The United Methodist Church:* a) The United Methodist Church and Peace #338, particularly to encourage local churches and members to take actions that make for peace and to act in concert with other peoples and groups of goodwill toward the achievement of a peaceful world and b) Globalization and Its Impact on Human Dignity and Human Rights #309, which reminds United Methodists that "The indivisibility of human rights underscores the understanding that freedom is hollow without food,

that justice without jobs is like a clanging cymbal, and liberty is a sham when people do not have land to inhabit and farm."

The United Methodist Church must urge the USA to:

a. to commit itself to the fundamental principle of international justice—that no country is above international law;

b. to increase its commitment to multilateralism including the UN security system, while urging UN action against threats to peace;

c. to renew efforts to mobilize a global consensus and global action against all forms of terrorism at home and around the world;

d. to strengthen multilateral, verifiable arms control regimes that aim to curb weapons of mass destruction and their delivery systems, while at the same time promoting nuclear disarmament and international demilitarization. Extend treaties to ban cluster bombs, carbon filament bombs, depleted uranium and herbicides;

e. to exercise leadership for protection of the environment through the ratification of the Kyoto Protocol and other international environmental agreements while protecting existing multilateral environmental agreements from challenges by free trade agreements;

f. to increase the Global Fund to fight AIDS, Tuberculosis and Malaria as well as other efforts to respond to the AIDS Pandemic;

g. to ratify and enforce the new International Criminal Court which judges individuals and groups of individuals who commit crimes against humanity; and

h. to expand the international human rights regime by ratifying such key international human rights treaties such as the Covenant on Economic, Social and Cultural Rights; the International Labor Organizations core labor rights conventions; the Convention on the Elimination of All Forms of Discrimination Against Women and the Convention on the Rights of the Child.

That the General Board of Global Ministries and the General Board of Church and Society, in consultation with each other, develop resources on the concerns described above, including a theological perspective and strategies for advocacy by United Methodists.

That United Methodist Churches, in all countries who belong to the G8, work in their own countries and together to advocate for their countries to work in defense of international law and cooperation, through multilateral efforts to be witnesses of God's love for all humanity by promoting the eradication of poverty, sustainable development, justice, human rights and peace around the world.

ADOPTED 2004

See Social Principles, ¶ 165.

341. Prohibition of Arms Sales to Foreign Countries for Purposes of War

WHEREAS, the United States sells more armaments around the world than any other country ($18.6 billion in sales in 2000, of $36.9 billion worldwide—Frida Berrigan, World Policy Institute, August 21, 2001); and

WHEREAS, these arms are frequently used in conflicts which we do not support and have even been used against our own troops in combat; and

WHEREAS, prohibitions against the resale of such arms have proven to be unenforceable in the world market; and

WHEREAS, President Jimmy Carter has said, "We cannot have it both ways. We can't be both the world's leading champion of peace and the world's leading supplier of arms"; and

WHEREAS, the Social Principles of The United Methodist Church states that " . . . the manufacture, sale, and deployment of armaments must be reduced and controlled; and that the production, possession, or use of nuclear weapons be condemned;" (¶ 165 C of the *Book of Discipline, 2000*); and

WHEREAS, Jesus taught us that "blessed are the peacemakers," and valued all human life;

Now, therefore, be it resolved, that The United Methodist Church supports the strict prohibition of sales of arms for purposes of war to foreign countries.

ADOPTED 2004

See Social Principles, ¶ 165B and C.

342. "Just 1 Day" Ministry of Peace

WHEREAS since the birth of humankind, war and threats of war between nations, religions and ethnic backgrounds have kept the world from knowing a true and lasting peace; and

WHEREAS unfathomable pain, suffering, and grief have come about from the battles humankind has waged throughout history continuing today with humankind having devoted more wealth to weapons of war than any other cause, resulting in parallel pain and suffering from hunger, disease, loss of habitat, and other sins against humanity as well as our environment and wildlife that have no say in our world; and

WHEREAS the fellowship ministry A Circle of Friends, working with other churches around the globe, has set August 22, 2004, for Just 1 Day, 24 hours, of peace requesting that every nation lay down their arms for a period of reflection.

Be it resolved by this General Conference that The United Methodist Church supports the initiative brought forth by the ministry of peace at Peoples United Methodist Church and all of its fellowship churches in A Circle of Friends called Just 1 Day and in doing so:

- request that all UM churches support the spirit of Just 1 Day through prayer and active participation, as they see fit, through discussion within each church;
- call upon the leaders of the United States of America and the world to commit to this step toward a permanent world peace;
- invite all faiths and denominations of the world to set forth a common doctrine together with us of peaceful coexistence, understanding of, and respect for each other's beliefs beginning on August 22, 2004.

Be it further resolved, that with this vote of support today, The United Methodist Church takes this initiative as an expression of hope for those who live in a world without hope today.

ADOPTED 2004

See Social Principles ¶ 165B and C.

OTHER RESOLUTIONS

UNITED METHODIST GUIDELINES

343. By Water and the Spirit:
A United Methodist Understanding of Baptism

A Report of the Baptism Study Committee

Contemporary United Methodism is attempting to recover and revitalize its understanding of baptism. To do this, we must look to our heritage as Methodists and Evangelical United Brethren and, indeed, to the foundations of Christian tradition. Throughout our history, baptism has been viewed in diverse and even contradictory ways. An enriched understanding of baptism, restoring the Wesleyan blend of sacramental and evangelical aspects, will enable United Methodists to participate in the sacrament with renewed appreciation for this gift of God's grace.

Within the Methodist tradition, baptism has long been a subject of much concern, even controversy. John Wesley retained the sacramental theology which he received from his Anglican heritage. He taught that in baptism a child was cleansed of the guilt of original sin, initiated into the covenant with God, admitted into the church, made an heir of the divine kingdom, and spiritually born anew. He said that while baptism was neither essential to nor sufficient for salvation, it was the "ordinary means" that God designated for applying the benefits of the work of Christ in human lives.

On the other hand, although he affirmed the regenerating grace of infant baptism, he also insisted upon the necessity of adult conversion for those who have fallen from grace. A person who matures into moral accountability must respond to God's grace in repentance and faith. Without personal decision and commitment to Christ, the baptismal gift is rendered ineffective.

Baptism for Wesley, therefore, was a part of the lifelong process of salvation. He saw spiritual rebirth as a twofold experience in the normal process of Christian development—to be received through baptism in infancy and through commitment to Christ later in life. Salvation included both God's initiating activity of grace and a willing human response.

In its development in the United States, Methodism was unable to maintain this Wesleyan balance of sacramental and evangelical emphases. Access to the sacraments was limited during the late eighteenth and early nineteenth centuries when the Methodist movement was largely under the leadership of laypersons who were not authorized to administer them. On the American frontier where human ability and action were stressed, the revivalistic call for individual decision making, though important, was subject to exaggeration. The sacramental teachings of Wesley tended to be ignored. In this setting, while infant baptism continued not only to be practiced, but also to be vigorously defended, its significance became weakened and ambiguous. Later toward the end of the nineteenth century, the theological views of much of Methodism were influenced by a new set of ideas which had become dominant in American culture. These ideas included optimism about the progressive improvement of humankind and confidence in the social benefits of scientific discovery, technology, and education. Assumptions of original sin gave way before the assertion that human nature was essentially unspoiled. In this intellectual milieu, the old evangelical insistence upon conversion and spiritual rebirth seemed quaint and unnecessary.

Thus the creative Wesleyan synthesis of sacramentalism and evangelicalism was torn asunder and both its elements devalued. As a result, infant baptism was variously interpreted and often reduced to a ceremony of dedication. Adult baptism was sometimes interpreted as a profession of faith and public acknowledgment of God's grace, but was more often viewed simply as an act of joining the church. By the middle of the twentieth century, Methodism in general had ceased to understand baptism as authentically sacramental. Rather than an act of divine grace, it was seen as an expression of human choice.

Baptism was also a subject of concern and controversy in the Evangelical and United Brethren traditions that were brought together in 1946 in The Evangelical United Brethren Church. Their early pietistic revivalism, based upon belief in the availability of divine grace and the freedom of human choice, emphasized bringing people to salvation through Christian experience. In the late nineteenth and early twentieth centuries, both Evangelical and United Brethren theologians stressed the importance of baptism as integral to the proclamation of the gospel, as a rite initiating persons into the covenant community (paralleling circumcision), and as a sign of the new birth, that gracious divine act by which persons are redeemed from sin and reconciled to God. The former Evangelical Church consistently favored the baptism of infants. The United Brethren provided for the baptism of both infants and adults. Following the union of 1946, The Evangelical United Brethren Church adopted a ritual that included services of baptism for infants and adults, and also a newly created service for the dedication of infants that had little precedent in official rituals of either of the former churches.

The 1960-64 revision of *The Methodist Hymnal,* including rituals, gave denominational leaders an opportunity to begin to recover the sacramental nature of baptism in contemporary Methodism. The General Commission on Worship sounded this note quite explicitly in its introduction to the new ritual in 1964:

> In revising the Order for the Administration of Baptism, the Commission on Worship has endeavored to keep in mind that baptism is a sacrament, and to restore it to the Evangelical-Methodist concept set forth in our Articles of Religion. . . . Due recognition was taken of the critical reexamination of the theology of the Sacrament of Baptism which is currently taking place in ecumenical circles, and of its theological content and implications.

The commission provided a brief historical perspective demonstrating that the understanding of baptism as a sacrament had been weakened, if not discarded altogether, over the years. Many in the church regarded baptism, both of infants and adults, as a dedication rather than as a sacrament. The commission pointed out that in a dedication we make a gift of a life to God for God to accept, while in a sacrament God offers the gift of God's unfailing grace for us to accept. The 1964 revision of the ritual of the sacrament of baptism began to restore the rite to its original and historic meaning as a sacrament.

In the 1989 *United Methodist Hymnal,* the Services of the Baptismal Covenant I, II, and IV (taken from the 1984 official ritual of the denomination as printed in *The Book of Services*) continue this effort to reemphasize the historic significance of baptism. These rituals, in accenting the reality of sin and of regeneration, the initiating of divine grace, and the necessity of repentance and faith, are consistent with the Wesleyan combination of sacramentalism and evangelicalism.

United Methodism is not alone in the need to recover the significance of baptism nor in its work to do so. Other Christian communions are also reclaiming the importance of this sacrament for Christian faith and life. To reach the core of the meaning and practice of baptism, all have found themselves led back through the life of the church to the Apostolic Age. An ecumenical convergence has emerged from this effort, as can be seen in the widely acclaimed document *Baptism, Eucharist, and Ministry* (1982).

Established by the General Conference of 1988 and authorized to continue its work by the General Conference of 1992, the Committee to Study Baptism is participating in this process by offering a theological and functional understanding of baptism as embodied in the ritual of The United Methodist Church. In so doing, the broad spectrum of resources of Scripture, Christian tradition, and the Methodist-Evangelical United Brethren experience has been taken into account. The growing ecumenical consensus has assisted us in our thinking.

We Are Saved by God's Grace

The Human Condition. As told in the first chapters of Genesis, in creation God made human beings in the image of God—a relationship of intimacy, dependence, and trust. We are open to the indwelling presence of God and given freedom to work with God to accomplish the divine will and purpose for all of creation and history. To be human as God intended is to have loving fellowship with God and to reflect the divine nature in our lives as fully as possible.

Tragically, as Genesis 3 recounts, we are unfaithful to that relationship. The result is a thorough distortion of the image of God in us and the degrading of the whole of creation. Through prideful overreach or denial of our God-given responsibilities, we exalt our own will, invent our own values, and rebel against God. Our very being is dominated by an inherent inclination toward evil which has traditionally been called original sin. It is a universal human condition and affects all aspects of life. Because of our condition of sin, we are separated from God, alienated from one another, hostile to the natural world, and even at odds with our own best selves. Sin may be expressed as errant priorities, as deliberate wrongdoing, as apathy in the face of need, as cooperation with oppression and injustice. Evil is cosmic as well as personal; it afflicts both individuals and the institutions of our human society. The nature of sin is represented in Baptismal Covenants I, II, and IV in *The United Methodist Hymnal* by the phrases "the spiritual forces of wickedness" and "the evil powers of this world," as well as "your sin." Before God all persons are lost, helpless to save themselves, and in need of divine mercy and forgiveness.

The Divine Initiative of Grace. While we have turned from God, God has not abandoned us. Instead, God graciously and continuously seeks to restore us to that loving relationship for which we were created, to make us into the persons that God would have us be. To this end God acts preveniently, that is, before we are aware of it, reaching out to save humankind. The Old Testament records the story of God's acts in the history of the covenant community of Israel to work out the divine will and purpose. In the New Testament story, we learn that God came into this sinful world in the person of Jesus Christ to reveal all that the human mind can comprehend about who God is and who God would have us be. Through Christ's death and resurrection, the power of sin and death was overcome and we are set free to again be God's own people (1 Peter 2:9). Since God is the only initiator and source of grace, all grace is prevenient in that it precedes and enables any movement that we can make toward God. Grace brings us to an awareness of our sinful predicament and of our inability to save ourselves; grace motivates us to repentance and gives us the capacity to respond to divine love. In the words of the baptismal ritual: "All this is God's gift, offered to us without price" (*The United Methodist Hymnal*, page 33).

The Necessity of Faith for Salvation. Faith is both a gift of God and a human response to God. It is the ability and willingness to say "yes" to the divine offer of salvation. Faith is our awareness of our utter dependence upon God, the surrender of our selfish wills, the trusting reliance upon divine mercy. The candidate for baptism answers "I do" to the question "Do you confess Jesus Christ as your Savior, put your whole trust in his grace, and promise to serve him as your Lord . . .?" (*The United Methodist Hymnal*, page 34). Our personal response of faith requires conversion in which we turn away from sin and turn instead to God. It entails a decision to commit our lives to the Lordship of Christ, an acceptance of the forgiveness of our sins, the death of our old selves, an entering into a new life of the Spirit-being born again (John 3:3-5, 2 Corinthians 5:17). All persons do not experience this spiritual rebirth in the same way. For some, there is a singular, radical moment of conversion. For others, conversion may be experienced as the dawning and growing realization that one has been constantly loved by God and has a personal reliance upon Christ. John Wesley described his own experience by saying, "I felt my heart strangely warmed. I felt I did trust in Christ, Christ alone for salvation; and an assurance was given me that he had taken away my sins, even mine, and saved me from the law of sin and death."

The Means by Which God's Grace Comes to Us

Divine grace is made available and effective in human lives through a variety of means or "channels," as Wesley called them. While God is radically free to work in many ways, the church has been given by God the special responsibility and privilege of being the body of Christ which carries forth God's purpose of redeeming the world. Wesley recognized the church itself as a means of grace— a grace-filled and grace-sharing community of faithful people. United Methodism shares with other Protestant communions the understanding that the proclamation of the Word through preaching, teaching, and the life of the church is a primary means of God's grace. The origin and rapid growth of Methodism as a revival movement occurred largely through the medium of the proclaimed Gospel. John Wesley also emphasized the importance of prayer, fasting, Bible study, and meetings of persons for support and sharing.

Because God has created and is creating all that is, physical objects of creation can become the bearers of divine presence, power, and meaning, and thus become sacramental means of God's grace. Sacraments are effective means of God's presence mediated through the created world. God becoming incarnate in Jesus Christ is the supreme instance of this kind of divine action. Wesley viewed the sacraments as crucial means of grace and affirmed the Anglican teaching that "a sacrament is 'an outward sign of inward grace, and a means whereby we receive the same.'" Combining words, actions, and physical elements, sacraments are sign-acts that both express and convey God's grace and love. Baptism and the Lord's Supper are sacraments that were instituted or commanded by Christ in the Gospels.

United Methodists believe that these sign-acts are special means of grace. The ritual action of a sacrament does not merely point to God's presence in the world, but also participates in it and becomes a vehicle for conveying that reality. God's presence in the sacraments is real, but it must be accepted by human faith if it is to transform human lives. The sacraments do not convey grace either magically or irrevocably, but they are powerful channels through which God has chosen to make grace available to us. Wesley identified baptism as the initiatory sacrament by which we enter into the covenant with God and are admitted as members of Christ's church. He understood the Lord's Supper as nourishing and empowering the lives of Christians and strongly advocated frequent participation in it. The Wesleyan tradition has continued to practice and cherish the various means through which divine grace is made present to us.

Baptism and the Life of Faith

The New Testament records that Jesus was baptized by John (Matthew 3:13-17), and he commanded his disciples to teach and baptize in the name of the Father, Son, and Holy Spirit (Matthew 28:19). Baptism is grounded in the life, death, and resurrection of Jesus Christ; the grace which baptism makes available is that of the atonement of Christ which makes possible our reconciliation with God. Baptism involves dying to sin, newness of life, union with Christ, receiving the Holy Spirit, and incorporation into Christ's church. United Methodists affirm this understanding in their official documents of faith. Article XVII of the Articles of Religion (Methodist) calls baptism "a sign of regeneration or the new birth"; the Confession of Faith (EUB) states that baptism is "a representation of the new birth in Christ Jesus and a mark of Christian discipleship."

The Baptismal Covenant. In both the Old and New Testaments, God enters into covenant relationship with God's people. A covenant involves promises and responsibilities of both parties; it is instituted through a special ceremony and expressed by a distinguishing sign. By covenant God constituted a servant community of the people of Israel, promising to be their God and giving them the Law to make clear how they were to live. The circumcision of male infants is the sign of this covenant (Genesis 17:1-14; Exodus 24:1-12). In the death and resurrection of Jesus Christ, God fulfilled the prophecy of a new covenant and called forth the church as a servant community

(Jeremiah 31:31-34; 1 Corinthians 11:23-26). The baptism of infants and adults, both male and female, is the sign of this covenant.

Therefore, United Methodists identify our ritual for baptism as "The Services of the Baptismal Covenant" (*The United Methodist Hymnal*, pages 32-54). In baptism the church declares that it is bound in covenant to God; through baptism new persons are initiated into that covenant. The covenant connects God, the community of faith, and the person being baptized; all three are essential to the fulfillment of the baptismal covenant. The faithful grace of God initiates the covenant relationship and enables the community and the person to respond with faith.

Baptism by Water and the Holy Spirit. Through the work of the Holy Spirit—the continuing presence of Christ on earth—the church is instituted to be the community of the new covenant. Within this community, baptism is by water and the Spirit (John 3:5; Acts 2:38). In God's work of salvation, the mystery of Christ's death and resurrection is inseparably linked with the gift of the Holy Spirit given on the Day of Pentecost (Acts 2). Likewise, participation in Christ's death and resurrection is inseparably linked with receiving the Spirit (Romans 6:1-11; 8:9-14). The Holy Spirit who is the power of creation (Genesis 1:2) is also the giver of new life. Working in the lives of people before, during, and after their baptisms, the Spirit is the effective agent of salvation. God bestows upon baptized persons the presence of the Holy Spirit, marks them with an identifying seal as God's own, and implants in their hearts the first installment of their inheritance as sons and daughters of God (2 Corinthians 1:21-22). It is through the Spirit that the life of faith is nourished until the final deliverance when they will enter into the fullness of salvation (Ephesians 1:13-14). Since the Apostolic Age, baptism by water and baptism of the Holy Spirit have been connected (Acts 19:17). Christians are baptized with both, sometimes by different sign-actions. Water is administered in the name of the triune God (specified in the ritual as Father, Son, and Holy Spirit) by an authorized person, and the Holy Spirit is invoked with the laying on of hands in the presence of the congregation. Water provides the central symbolism for baptism. The richness of its meaning for the Christian community is suggested in the baptismal liturgy which speaks of the waters of creation and the flood, the liberation of God's people by passage through the sea, the gift of water in the wilderness, and the passage through the Jordan River to the promised land. In baptism we identify ourselves with this people of God and join the community's journey toward God. The use of water in baptism also symbolizes cleansing from sin, death to old life, and rising to begin new life in Christ. In United Methodist tradition, the water of baptism may be administered by sprinkling, pouring, or immersion. However it is administered, water should be utilized with enough generosity to enhance our appreciation of its symbolic meanings.

The baptismal liturgy includes the biblical symbol of the anointing with the Holy Spirit—the laying on of hands with the optional use of oil. This anointing promises to the baptized person the power to live faithfully the kind of life that water baptism signifies. In the early centuries of the church, the laying on of hands usually followed immediately upon administration of the water and completed the ritual of membership. Because the laying on of hands was, in the Western church, an act to be performed only by a bishop, it was later separated from water baptism and came to be called confirmation (see pp. 729-31). In confirmation the Holy Spirit marked the baptized person as God's own and strengthened him or her for discipleship. In the worship life of the early church, the water and the anointing led directly to the celebration of the Lord's Supper as part of the service of initiation, regardless of the age of the baptized. The current rituals of the baptismal covenant rejoin these three elements into a unified service. Together these symbols point to, anticipate, and offer participation in the life of the community of faith as it embodies God's presence in the world.

Baptism as Incorporation into the Body of Christ. Christ constitutes the church as his Body by the power of the Holy Spirit (1 Corinthians 12:13, 27). The church draws new persons into itself as it seeks to remain faithful to its commission to proclaim and exemplify the gospel. Baptism is the sacrament of initiation and incorporation into the body of Christ. An infant, child, or adult who is baptized becomes a member of the catholic (universal) church, of the denomination, and of the local congregation (*see* pp. 729-31). Therefore, baptism is a rite of the whole church, which ordinarily requires the participation of the gathered, worshiping congregation. In a series of promises within the liturgy of baptism, the community affirms its own faith and pledges to act as spiritual mentor and support for the one who is baptized. Baptism is not merely an individualistic, private, or domestic occasion. When unusual but legitimate circumstances prevent a baptism from taking place in the midst of the gathered community during its regular worship, every effort should be made to assemble representatives of the congregation to participate in the celebration. Later, the baptism should be recognized in the public assembly of worship in order that the congregation may make its appropriate affirmations of commitment and responsibility.

Baptism brings us into union with Christ, with each other, and with the church in every time and place. Through this sign and seal of our common discipleship, our equality in Christ is made manifest (Galatians 3:27-28). We affirm that there is one baptism into Christ, celebrated as our basic bond of unity in the many communions that make up the body of Christ (Ephesians 4:4-6). The power of the Spirit in baptism does not depend upon the mode by which water is administered, the age or psychological disposition of the baptized person, or the character of the minister. It is God's grace that makes the sacrament whole. One baptism calls the various churches to overcome their divisions and visibly manifest their unity. Our oneness in Christ calls for mutual recognition of baptism in these communions as a means of expressing the unity that Christ intends (1 Corinthians 12:12-13).

Baptism as Forgiveness of Sin. In baptism God offers and we accept the forgiveness of our sin (Acts 2:38). With the pardoning of sin which has separated us from God, we are justified—freed from the guilt and penalty of sin and restored to right relationship with God. This reconciliation is made possible through the atonement of Christ and made real in our lives by the work of the Holy Spirit. We respond by confessing and repenting of our sin, and affirming our faith that Jesus Christ has accomplished all that is necessary for our salvation. Faith is the necessary condition for justification; in baptism, that faith is professed. God's forgiveness makes possible the renewal of our spiritual lives and our becoming new beings in Christ.

Baptism as New Life. Baptism is the sacramental sign of new life through and in Christ by the power of the Holy Spirit. Variously identified as regeneration, new birth, and being born again, this work of grace makes us into new spiritual creatures (2 Corinthians 5:17). We die to our old nature which was dominated by sin and enter into the very life of Christ who transforms us. Baptism is the means of entry into new life in Christ (John 3:5; Titus 3:5), but new birth may not always coincide with the moment of the administration of water or the laying on of hands. Our awareness and acceptance of our redemption by Christ and new life in him may vary throughout our lives. But, in whatever way the reality of the new birth is experienced, it carries out the promises God made to us in our baptism.

Baptism and Holy Living. New birth into life in Christ, which is signified by baptism, is the beginning of that process of growth in grace and holiness through which God brings us into closer relationship with Jesus Christ, and shapes our lives increasingly into conformity with the divine will. Sanctification is a gift of the gracious presence of the Holy Spirit, a yielding to the Spirit's power, a deepening of our love for God and neighbor. Holiness of heart and life, in the Wesleyan tradition, always involves both personal and social holiness.

Baptism is the doorway to the sanctified life. The sacrament teaches us to live in the expectation of further gifts of God's grace. It initiates us into a community of faith that prays for holiness; it calls us to life lived in faithfulness to God's gift. Baptized believers and the community of faith are obligated to manifest to the world the new redeemed humanity which lives in loving relationship with God and strives to put an end to all human estrangements. There are no conditions of human life (including age or intellectual ability, race or nationality, gender or sexual identity, class or disability) that exclude persons from the sacrament of baptism. We strive for and look forward to the reign of God on earth, of which baptism is a sign. Baptism is fulfilled only when the believer and the church are wholly conformed to the image of Christ.

Baptism as God's Gift to Persons of Any Age. There is one baptism as there is one source of salvation—the gracious love of God. The baptizing of a person, whether as an infant or an adult, is a sign of God's saving grace. That grace—experienced by us as initiating, enabling, and empowering—is the same for all persons. All stand in need of it, and none can be saved without it. The difference between the baptism of adults and that of infants is that the Christian faith is consciously being professed by an adult who is baptized. A baptized infant comes to profess her or his faith later in life, after having been nurtured and taught by parent(s) or other responsible adults and the community of faith. Infant baptism is the prevailing practice in situations where children are born to believing parents and brought up in Christian homes and communities of faith. Adult baptism is the norm when the church is in a missionary situation, reaching out to persons in a culture which is indifferent or hostile to the faith. While the baptism of infants is appropriate for Christian families, the increasingly minority status of the church in contemporary society demands more attention to evangelizing, nurturing, and baptizing adult converts.

Infant baptism has been the historic practice of the overwhelming majority of the church throughout the Christian centuries. While the New Testament contains no explicit mandate, there is ample evidence for the baptism of infants in Scripture (Acts 2:38-41; 16:15, 33) and in early Christian doctrine and practice. Infant baptism rests firmly on the understanding that God prepares the way of faith before we request or even know that we need help (prevenient grace). The sacrament is a powerful expression of the reality that all persons come before God as no more than helpless infants, unable to do anything to save ourselves, dependent upon the grace of our loving God. The faithful covenant community of the church serves as a means of grace for those whose lives are impacted by its ministry. Through the church, God claims infants as well as adults to be participants in the gracious covenant of which baptism is the sign. This understanding of the workings of divine grace also applies to persons who for reasons of disabilities or other limitations are unable to answer for themselves the questions of the baptismal ritual. While we may not be able to comprehend how God works in their lives, our faith teaches us that God's grace is sufficient for their needs and, thus, they are appropriate recipients of baptism.

The church affirms that children being born into the brokenness of the world should receive the cleansing and renewing forgiveness of God no less than adults. The saving grace made available through Christ's atonement is the only hope of salvation for persons of any age. In baptism infants enter into a new life in Christ as children of God and members of the body of Christ. The baptism of an infant incorporates him or her into the community of faith and nurture, including membership in the local church. The baptism of infants is properly understood and valued if the child is loved and nurtured by the faithful worshiping church and by the child's own family. If a parent or sponsor (godparent) cannot or will not nurture the child in the faith, then baptism is to be postponed until Christian nurture is available. A child who dies without being baptized is received into the love and presence of God because the Spirit has worked in that child to bestow saving grace. If a child has been baptized but her or his family or sponsors do not faithfully nurture the child in the faith, the congregation has a particular responsibility for incorporating the child into its life.

Understanding the practice as an authentic expression of how God works in our lives, The United Methodist Church strongly advocates the baptism of infants within the faith community: "Because the redeeming love of God, revealed in Jesus Christ, extends to all persons and because Jesus explicitly included the children in his kingdom, the pastor of each charge shall earnestly exhort all Christian parents or guardians to present their children to the Lord in Baptism at an early age" (1992 *Book of Discipline*, ¶ 221). We affirm that while thanksgiving to God and dedication of parents to the task of Christian child-raising are aspects of infant baptism, the sacrament is primarily a gift of divine grace. Neither parents nor infants are the chief actors; baptism is an act of God in and through the church.

We respect the sincerity of parents who choose not to have their infants baptized, but we acknowledge that these views do not coincide with the Wesleyan understanding of the nature of the sacrament. The United Methodist Church does not accept either the idea that only believer's baptism is valid or the notion that the baptism of infants magically imparts salvation apart from active personal faith. Pastors are instructed by *The Book of Discipline* to explain our teaching clearly on these matters, so that parent(s) or sponsors might be free of misunderstandings.

The United Methodist Book of Worship contains "An Order of Thanksgiving for the Birth or Adoption of the Child" (pages 585-87), which may be recommended in situations where baptism is inappropriate, but parents wish to take responsibility publicly for the growth of the child in faith. It should be made clear that this rite is in no way equivalent to or a substitute for baptism. Neither is it an act of infant dedication. If the infant has not been baptized, the sacrament should be administered as soon as possible after the Order of Thanksgiving.

God's Faithfulness to the Baptismal Covenant. Since baptism is primarily an act of God in the church, the sacrament is to be received by an individual only once. This position is in accord with the historic teaching of the church universal, originating as early as the second century and having been recently reaffirmed ecumenically in *Baptism, Eucharist, and Ministry.*

The claim that baptism is unrepeatable rests on the steadfast faithfulness of God. God's initiative establishes the covenant of grace into which we are incorporated in baptism. By misusing our God-given freedom, we may live in neglect or defiance of that covenant, but we cannot destroy God's love for us. When we repent and return to God, the covenant does not need to be remade, because God has always remained faithful to it. What is needed is renewal of our commitment and reaffirmation of our side of the covenant.

God's gift of grace in the baptismal covenant does not save us apart from our human response of faith. Baptized persons may have many significant spiritual experiences, which they will desire to celebrate publicly in the worship life of the church. Such experiences may include defining moments of conversion, repentance of sin, gifts of the Spirit, deepening of commitment, changes in Christian vocation, important transitions in the life of discipleship. These occasions call not for repetition of baptism, but for reaffirmations of baptismal vows as a witness to the good news that while we may be unfaithful, God is not. Appropriate services for such events would be "Confirmation or Reaffirmation of Faith" (*see* Baptismal Covenant I in *The United Methodist Hymnal*) or "A Celebration of New Beginnings in Faith" (*The United Methodist Book of Worship*, pages 588-90).

Nurturing Persons in the Life of Faith. If persons are to be enabled to live faithfully the human side of the baptismal covenant, Christian nurture is essential. Christian nurture builds on baptism and is itself a means of grace. For infant baptism, an early step is instruction prior to baptism of parent(s) or sponsors in the gospel message, the meaning of the sacrament, and the responsibilities of a Christian home. The pastor has specific responsibility for this step (the 1992 *Book of Discipline*, ¶ 439.1*b*). Adults who are candidates for baptism need careful preparation for receiving this gift of grace and living out its meaning (the 1992 *Book of Discipline*, ¶ 216.1).

After baptism, the faithful church provides the nurture which makes possible a comprehensive and lifelong process of growing in grace. The content of this nurturing will be appropriate to the stages of life and maturity of faith of individuals. Christian nurture includes both cognitive learning and spiritual formation. A crucial goal is the bringing of persons to recognition of their need for salvation and their acceptance of God's gift in Jesus Christ. Those experiencing conversion and commitment to Christ are to profess their faith in a public ritual. They will need to be guided and supported throughout their lives of discipleship. Through its worship life, its Christian education programs, its spiritual growth emphases, its social action and mission, its examples of Christian discipleship, and its offering of the various means of grace, the church strives to shape persons into the image of Christ. Such nurturing enables Christians to live out the transforming potential of the grace of their baptism.

Profession of Christian Faith and Confirmation. The Christian life is a dynamic process of change and growth, marked at various points by celebrations in rituals of the saving grace of Christ. The Holy Spirit works in the lives of persons prior to their baptism, is at work in their baptism, and continues to work in their lives after their baptism. When persons recognize and accept this activity of the Holy Spirit, they respond with renewed faith and commitment.

In the early church, baptism, the laying on of hands, and Eucharist were a unified rite of initiation and new birth for Christians of all ages. During the Middle Ages in Western Europe, confirmation was separated from baptism in both time and theology. A misunderstanding developed of confirmation as completing baptism, with emphasis upon human vows and initiation into church membership. John Wesley did not recommend confirmation to his preachers or to the new Methodist Church in America. Since 1964 in the former Methodist Church, the first public profession of faith for those baptized as infants has been called Confirmation. In the former Evangelical United Brethren Church, there was no such rite until union with The Methodist Church in 1968. With the restoration of confirmation—as the laying on of hands—to the current baptismal ritual, it should be emphasized that confirmation is what the Holy Spirit does. Confirmation is a divine action, the work of the Spirit empowering a person "born through water and the Spirit" to "live as a faithful disciple of Jesus Christ."

An adult or youth preparing for baptism should be carefully instructed in its life-transforming significance and responsibilities. Such a person professes in the sacrament of baptism his or her faith in Jesus Christ and commitment to discipleship, is offered the gift of assurance, and is confirmed by the power of the Holy Spirit (*see* Baptismal Covenant I, sections 4, 11, and 12). No separate ritual of confirmation is needed for the believing person.

An infant who is baptized cannot make a personal profession of faith as a part of the sacrament. Therefore, as the young person is nurtured and matures so as to be able to respond to God's grace, conscious faith and intentional commitment are necessary. Such a person must come to claim the faith of the church proclaimed in baptism as her or his own faith. Deliberate preparation for this event focuses on the young person's self-understanding and appropriation of Christian doctrines, spiritual disciplines, and life of discipleship. It is a special time for experiencing divine grace and for consciously embracing one's Christian vocation as a part of the priesthood of all believers. Youth who were not baptized as infants share in the same period of preparation for profession of Christian faith. For them, it is nurture for baptism, for becoming members of the church, and for confirmation.

When persons who were baptized as infants are ready to profess their Christian faith, they participate in the service which United Methodism now calls Confirmation. This occasion is not an entrance into church membership, for this was accomplished through baptism. It is the first public affirmation of the grace of God in one's baptism and the acknowledgment of one's acceptance of that grace by faith. This moment includes all the elements of conversion—repentance of sin, surrender and death of self, trust in the saving grace of God, new life in Christ, and becoming an instrument of God's purpose in the world. The profession of Christian faith, to be celebrated in the midst of the worshiping congregation, should include the voicing of baptismal vows as a witness to faith and the opportunity to give testimony to personal Christian experience. Confirmation follows profession of the Christian faith as part of the same service. Confirmation is a dynamic action of the Holy Spirit that can be repeated. In confirmation the outpouring of the Holy Spirit is invoked to provide the one being confirmed with the power to live in the faith that he or she has professed. The basic meaning of confirmation is strengthening and making firm in Christian faith and life. The ritual action in confirmation is the laying on of hands as the sign of God's continuing gift of the grace of Pentecost. Historically, the person being confirmed was also anointed on the forehead with oil in the shape of a cross as a mark of the Spirit's work. The ritual of the baptismal covenant included in The United Methodist Hymnal makes clear that the first and primary confirming act of the Holy Spirit is in connection with and immediately follows baptism.

When a baptized person has professed her or his Christian faith and has been confirmed, that person enters more fully into the responsibilities and privileges of membership in the church. Just as infants are members of their human families, but are unable to participate in all aspects of family life, so baptized infants are members of the church— the family of faith—but are not yet capable of sharing everything involved in membership. For this reason, statistics of church membership are counts of professed/confirmed members rather than of all baptized members.

Reaffirmation of One's Profession of Christian Faith. The life of faith which baptized persons live is like a pilgrimage or journey. On this lifelong journey there are many challenges, changes, and chances. We engage life's experiences on our journey of faith as a part of the redeeming and sanctifying body of Christ. Ongoing Christian nurture teaches, shapes, and strengthens us to live ever more faithfully as we are open to the Spirit's revealing more and more of the way and will of God. As our appreciation of the good news of Jesus Christ deepens and our commitment to Christ's service becomes more profound, we seek occasions to celebrate. Like God's people through the ages, all Christians need to participate in acts of renewal within the covenant community. Such an opportunity is offered in every occasion of baptism when the congregation remembers and affirms the gracious work of God which baptism celebrates. "Baptismal Covenant IV" in *The United Methodist Hymnal* is a powerful ritual of reaffirmation which uses water in ways that remind us of our baptism. The historic "Covenant Renewal Service" and "Love Feast" can also be used for this purpose (*The United Methodist Book of Worship,* pages 288-94 and 581-84). Reaffirmation of faith is a human response to God's grace and therefore may be repeated at many points in our faith journey.

Baptism in Relation to Other Rites of the Church

The grace of God which claims us in our baptism is made available to us in many other ways and, especially, through other rites of the church.

Baptism and the Lord's Supper (Holy Communion or the Eucharist). Through baptism, persons are initiated into the church; by the Lord's Supper, the church is sustained in the life of faith. The services of the baptismal covenant appropriately conclude with Holy Communion, through which the union of the new member with the body of Christ is most fully expressed. Holy Communion is a sacred meal in which the community of faith, in the simple act of eating bread and drinking wine, proclaims and participates in all that God has done, is doing, and will continue to do for us in Christ. In celebrating the Eucharist, we remember the grace given to us in our baptism and partake of the spiritual food necessary for sustaining and fulfilling the promises of salvation. Because the table at which we gather belongs to the Lord, it should be open to all who respond to Christ's love, regardless of age or church membership. The Wesleyan tradition has always recognized that Holy Communion may be an occasion for the reception of converting, justifying, and sanctifying grace. Unbaptized persons who receive communion should be counseled and nurtured toward baptism as soon as possible.

Baptism and Christian Ministry. Through baptism, God calls and commissions persons to the general ministry of all Christian believers (*see* 1992 *Book of Discipline*, ¶¶ 101-07). This ministry, in which we participate both individually and corporately, is the activity of discipleship. It is grounded upon the awareness that we have been called into a new relationship not only with God, but also with the world. The task of Christians is to embody the gospel and the church in the world. We exercise our calling as Christians by prayer, by witnessing to the good news of salvation in Christ, by caring for and serving other people, and by working toward reconciliation, justice, and peace, in the world. This is the universal priesthood of all believers.

From within this general ministry of all believers, God calls and the church authorizes some persons for the task of representative ministry (*see* 1992 *Book of Discipline*, ¶¶ 108-110). The vocation of those in representative ministry includes focusing, modeling, supervising, shepherding, enabling, and empowering the general ministry of the church. Their ordination to Word, Sacrament, and Order or consecration to diaconal ministries of service, justice, and love is grounded in the same baptism that commissions the general priesthood of all believers.

Baptism and Christian Marriage. In the ritual for marriage, the minister addresses the couple: "I ask you now, in the presence of God and these people, to declare your intention to enter into union with one another through the grace of Jesus Christ, who calls you into union with himself as acknowledged in your baptism" (*The United Methodist Hymnal*, page 865). Marriage is to be understood as a covenant of love and commitment with mutual promises and responsibilities. For the church, the marriage covenant is grounded in the covenant between God and God's people into which Christians enter in their baptism. The love and fidelity which are to characterize Christian marriage will be a witness to the gospel, and the couple are to "go to serve God and your neighbor in all that you do."

When ministers officiate at the marriage of a couple who are not both Christians, the ritual needs to be altered to protect the integrity of all involved.

Baptism and Christian Funeral. The Christian gospel is a message of death and resurrection, that of Christ and our own. Baptism signifies our dying and rising with Christ. As death no longer has dominion over Christ, we believe that if we have died with Christ we shall also live with him (Romans 6:8-9). As the liturgy of the "Service of Death and Resurrection" proclaims: "Dying, Christ destroyed our death. Rising, Christ restored our life. Christ will come again in glory. As in baptism *Name* put on Christ, so in Christ may *Name* be clothed with glory" (*The United Methodist Hymnal,* page 870).

If the deceased person was never baptized, the ritual needs to be amended in ways which continue to affirm the truths of the gospel, but are appropriate to the situation.

Committal of the deceased to God and the body to its final resting place recall the act of baptism and derive Christian meaning from God's baptismal covenant with us. We acknowledge the reality of death and the pain of loss, and we give thanks for the life that was lived and shared with us. We worship in the awareness that our gathering includes the whole communion of saints, visible and invisible, and that in Christ the ties of love unite the living and the dead.

Conclusion

Baptism is a crucial threshold that we cross on our journey in faith. But there are many others, including the final transition from death to life eternal. Through baptism we are incorporated into the ongoing history of Christ's mission, and we are identified and made participants in God's new history in Jesus Christ and the new age that Christ is bringing. We await the final moment of grace, when Christ comes in victory at the end of the age to bring all who are in Christ into the glory of that victory. Baptism has significance in time and gives meaning to the end of time. In it we have a vision of a world recreated and humanity transformed and exalted by God's presence. We are told that in this new heaven and new earth there will be no temple, for even our churches and services of worship will have had their time and ceased to be, in the presence of God, "the first and the last, the beginning and the end" (Revelation 21-22).

Until that day, we are charged by Christ to "go therefore and make disciples of all nations, baptizing them in the name of the Father, the

Son, and the Holy Spirit, and teaching them to obey everything that I have commanded you. And remember, I am with you always, to the end of the age" (Matthew 28:19-20).

Baptism is at the heart of the gospel of grace and at the core of the church's mission. When we baptize we say what we understand as Christians about ourselves and our community: that we are loved into being by God, lost because of sin, but redeemed and saved in Jesus Christ to live new lives in anticipation of his coming again in glory. Baptism is an expression of God's love for the world, and the effects of baptism also express God's grace. As baptized people of God, we therefore respond with praise and thanksgiving, praying that God's will be done in our own lives:

We your people stand before you,
Water-washed and Spirit-born.
By your grace, our lives we offer.
Re-create us; God, transform!

—Ruth Duck, "Wash, O God, Our Sons and Daughters"
(*The United Methodist Hymnal*, 605); Used with permission.

ADOPTED 1996
READOPTED FOR 2005-2008
AND 2009-2012 QUADRENNIA

344. Biblical Language

WHEREAS, The United Methodist Church affirms the use of biblical language and images in worship and in our common life together, and affirms the use of language that reflects the long-standing commitment to the inclusiveness and diversity of United Methodist members and constituencies,

Therefore, be it resolved, that United Methodist clergy and laity be encouraged to use diverse metaphorical images from the Bible, including masculine/feminine metaphors; use language for humans that reflects both male and female; use metaphors of color, darkness, ability, and age in positive rather than exclusively negative ways; and

Be it further resolved, that publications, audiovisual media, and other materials of The United Methodist Church shall reflect the diverse biblical metaphors, as well as language that reflects the diversity and inclusiveness of humanity.

ADOPTED 1988
REVISED AND ADOPTED 2000

345. Emphasize Evangelism

WHEREAS, we the remaining members who have served for the past two years on the Task Force on Denominational Concerns of the Marietta First UMC; and

WHEREAS, Marietta First UMC, a part of the body of Christ, experienced a split in its congregation resulting in the loss of approximately one-third of its active membership due to real and/or perceived concerns with the denomination; and

WHEREAS, the majority of those leaving were young adults with families who would have constituted much of the future membership of the church; and

WHEREAS, the division in this body of Christ caused conflict and misunderstanding among friends and within families; and

WHEREAS, we who remain, while recognizing much good in our church and in our denomination, have continuing concerns about The United Methodist Church; and

WHEREAS, we love the church and are committed to resolving issues and solving problems and truly desire to ensure the well-being of our denomination and to avoid similar divisions within other United Methodist churches;

Therefore, we resolve to offer this constructive recommendation to the 2000 General Conference as the result of our experience and research during these tumultuous times in our church, to reaffirm commitment to and financial support of evangelism in United Methodist programs and institutions with evangelism defined as in ¶ 627.1 in *The 2000 Book of Discipline;*

Be it further resolved, that wherever appropriate in United Methodist programs and institutions, emphasis should be placed on evangelism through commitments to and financial support of such programs.

ADOPTED 2000

346. Establish a Unified Date for Easter

Resolve that the General Conference encourage the World Council of Churches to work toward the establishment of a unified date for Easter.

ADOPTED 2000

347. Korean-English Hymnal: Come Let Us Worship

WHEREAS, while Korean United Methodist congregations use the *Tong Il* hymnal, a generic hymnal used by almost all Korean Protestant churches, the Korean Caucus and the National Committee on Korean-American Ministry have expressed the urgent need for a bilingual hymnal and worship book reflective of United Methodism, both its hymnody and song and its general services; and

WHEREAS, the 1.5 and second generations of the Korean-American church are growing, there is an increasing need for a bilingual worship resource so that they and the first generation can more fully share together in worship; and

WHEREAS, the General Board of Discipleship and The United Methodist Publishing House established a Korean-English Bilingual Hymnal Committee in the spring of 1998 to create a one-volume Korean-English bilingual hymnal/worship book; and

WHEREAS, this committee has included in its aim to ensure:

1. inclusion of the most-used hymns from the current hymnals;

2. inclusion of additional and new hymns from Korean, English, and other sources with translations;

3. attention to gender, geographic diversity, age, and theological stances among Korean United Methodists;

4. the use of the new hymnal in the mission and evangelistic witness of Korean congregations;

5. the inclusion of the general services of the church and such other liturgical resources as are needed for Korean-English participation in the worship life of The United Methodist Church,

Therefore, the 2000 General Conference adopts the new hymnal as an official hymnal of The United Methodist Church and its ritual resources be listed in the *Discipline* as part of the ritual of The United Methodist Church, including the services and resources listed in the Korean-English hymnal sampler.

ADOPTED 2000

348. Gideons International Membership Eligibility

WHEREAS, Gideons International provides an important ministry in the distribution of Scripture; and

WHEREAS, many United Methodist congregations and individuals support Gideons International through memberships and financial donations; and

WHEREAS, the membership of Gideons International is limited to Protestant business and professional men; and

WHEREAS, their membership criteria stand in opposition to the Discipline of The United Methodist Church (see Social Principles); and

WHEREAS, the membership criteria of Gidoens International detract from the strength of their ministry;

Therefore, be it resolved, that the General Conference of The United Methodist Church and its member congregations strongly encourage Gideons International to open their membership to all Christians, regardless of gender, socioeconomic class, or denominational background.

ADOPTED 2004

349. Professional Lay Ministry

WHEREAS, we celebrate our brothers and sisters who are professionally certified, commissioned and/or recognized by our general agencies, as well as all laity who faithfully respond to Christ's call to servant ministry.

WHEREAS, church growth experts are continuing to stress that thriving, transformational congregations are ones that are empowering the laity to be actively involved in ministry and ministry leadership roles; and

WHEREAS, some of those laity may, through their involvement in meaningful ministry leadership, sense a call to full-time ministry, but not sense a call to be ordained; and

WHEREAS, many who are already consecrated as diaconal ministers do not feel a call on their lives to be ordained, but strongly believe in the ministry of the laity as a servant ministry encouraging the ministry of all believers; and

WHEREAS, we celebrate our brothers and sisters who formerly were diaconal ministers and did feel the call to be ordained, we now ask for our opportunity to be affirmed in a continuing lay diaconate,

Therefore, let it be resolved, that the 2000 General Conference instruct the General Board of Higher Education and Ministry, working with the General Board of Discipleship, to seek ways of expanding and recognizing any new forms of professional lay ministry and to more clearly acknowledge professional lay ministry as a call to ministry through authenticating acts of recognition and celebration, and that they bring recommendations to the 2004 General Conference.

ADOPTED 2000

350. Affirmation and Celebration of Professional Lay Ministry

WHEREAS, "Christian ministry is the expression of the mind and mission of Christ," and "All Christians are called through their baptism to this ministry" (¶ 125); the forms of this ministry are as diverse as the gifts and talents with which God has graced each life; and "The ministry of all Christians is complementary. No ministry is subservient to another. All United Methodists are summoned and sent by Christ to live and work together in mutual interdependence and to be guided by the Spirit" (¶ 129); and

WHEREAS, "Within The United Methodist Church, there are those called to servant leadership, lay and ordained," and "Such callings are evidenced by special gifts, evidence of God's grace, and promise of usefulness," and "God's call to servant leadership is inward as it comes to the individual and outward through the discernment and validation of the Church" (¶ 136); and

WHEREAS, the General Board of Higher Education and Ministry, Division of Ordained Ministry, in cooperation with other agencies of the church has developed standards and requirements to certify and renew biennially persons in professional ministry careers (¶¶ 1110.11 and 634.2.*t*); and

WHEREAS, the General Board of Higher Education and Ministry, Division of Ordained Ministry and the General Board of Discipleship continue to encourage and resource conference boards of ordained ministry, boards of discipleship, and other appropriate bodies for the ongoing recognition and support of persons in professional careers (¶¶ 634.2*t* and 1102); and

WHEREAS, the General Board of Higher Education and Ministry, Division of Ordained Ministry works with seminaries, graduate schools, universities, and colleges by providing guidance, standards, and technical support for the academic preparation for professional ministry careers; and

WHEREAS, the Discipleship Ministries Unit of the General Board of Discipleship produces training events and resources for continuing leader formation in the church (lay leadership, youth ministry, Christian education, and so forth);

Therefore, be it resolved that in order to recognize, authenticate, and celebrate those serving in professional lay ministry on behalf of The United Methodist Church, the 2004 General Conference affirm the following recommendations:

1. The focus for continuing development of persons in professional ministry will be shared by GBHEM and GBOD in cooperation with colleges, universities, seminaries, and annual conferences as partners in the educational and development process.

2. A more cooperative approach among the appropriate general agencies, professional associations, conference boards and leadership, and United Methodist colleges, universities, and seminaries will be developed to provide a variety of educational avenues and resources for lay persons serving in the church who seek to enhance their learning and increase their knowledge and skills to become more effective workers in their area of service on behalf of the church. Such avenues may include continuing education, certification, professional development, degree programs, conference programs, regional programs, and so forth. (For example: A college will partner with an annual conference to develop and implement a certificate program or course of study program to prepare and credential persons for youth ministry, Christian education, and so forth.)

3. General agencies; colleges, universities, and seminaries; and conferences will cooperate to broaden and make more accessible the delivery systems for the education and development of church workers, for example college/university/seminary settings, extension sites, lay academies, other conference settings, regional settings, distance learning, e-learning, conferencing, and so forth.

4. An intentional cooperative approach will be shared by GBHEM and GBOD in consultation with conference leadership to develop and expand resources, methods, and rituals for acknowledgment and authentication by the church for those serving in professional/specialized lay ministry. These acts of recognition and celebration may take place where appropriate, including:

- recognition ceremonies at annual conference sessions;
- recognition celebrations where study is completed (either by residence or distance learning)—colleges, universities, seminaries, conference lay academies, and so forth;

- acknowledgment of professional certification in annual conference journals (¶ 632.2t);
- district or local church celebrations.

ADOPTED 2004

351. Proper Use of the Name: The United Methodist Church

WHEREAS, The Methodist Church and The Evangelical United Brethren Church were united under the name The United Methodist Church in the year 1968 and that the uniting name has great historical significance for both bodies,

Therefore, be it resolved, that insofar as possible, all materials used in correspondence, advertisements, and signs of the said churches and other denominational organizations use the complete proper name: "The United Methodist Church," capitalizing the word "The" when referring to the denomination as a whole.

ADOPTED 1980
READOPTED 2000

352. Use of the Name: The United Methodist Church in Periodicals and Advertisements

The 1980 United Methodist General Conference, sympathetic toward Evangelical United Brethren moved Heritage Sunday from the anniversary of John Wesley's Aldersgate experience (the former Aldersgate Sunday) to the anniversary of the United Conference and passed a resolution on the "Proper Use of Name: The United Methodist Church."

We call our members to a more thorough understanding of the joint heritage of our Methodist and Evangelical United Brethren forebears, and we call on our members and agencies to implement with energy and enthusiasm, the 1980 resolution on the "Proper Use of Name: The United Methodist Church."

We call on our church periodical editors, where contributors omit the word "United" from "United Methodist" to correct this usage—both in articles and in letters to the editor. With direct quotations, they should insert "United" in brackets. They should further instruct advertisers that advertisements that refer to "Methodist" without "United" are unacceptable.

We further direct the General Commission on Communication, when it becomes aware of the omission of "United" from "United Methodist" in the church or secular press, to notify the responsible parties that this is unacceptable usage and to report to the Church annually in *The Interpreter* of its compliance with this directive.

ADOPTED 2004

353. This Holy Mystery

WHEREAS, the 2000 General Conference directed the General Board of Discipleship in collaboration with the General Board of Higher Education and Ministry, the General Commission on Christian Unity and Interreligious Concerns, and the Council of Bishops, to develop a comprehensive interpretive document on the theology and practice of Holy Communion in United Methodism and report their findings and recommendations to the 2004 General Conference; and

WHEREAS, The United Methodist Church needs an authoritative contemporary statement of its understanding of Holy Communion, both for strengthening its interpretation and practice of the Lord's Supper in its churches and for clarity in its ecumenical conversations with other denominations; and

WHEREAS, in developing its report the Holy Communion Study Committee took intentional steps to heed our United Methodist heritage and history, remain sensitive to the ecumenical church, and hear the voices of United Methodists in the United States as well as in central conferences in the Philippines, Africa, and Europe;

Therefore, be it resolved, that the 2004 General Conference approve *This Holy Mystery: A United Methodist Understanding of Holy Communion,* affixed and, thereby, made part of this petition, as an official interpretive statement of theology and practice in The United Methodist Church; and

Be it further resolved, that *This Holy Mystery* be used by the Council of Bishops, Church School Publications of The United Methodist Publishing House, the General Board of Higher Education and Ministry, and the General Board of Discipleship as a guide for teaching and formation of both clergy and laity in relation to Holy Communion; and

Be it further resolved, that *This Holy Mystery* be used by the General Commission on Christian Unity and Interreligious Concerns and the

Council of Bishops in interpreting United Methodist understandings and practices in ecumenical dialogue; and

Be it further resolved, that the 2004 General Conference commend to the Church the principles, background, and practices in *This Holy Mystery* for the interpretation and use of the services of Word and Table in our hymnals and *The United Methodist Book of Worship*; and

Be it further resolved, that *This Holy Mystery* be published in *The Book of Resolutions*, and that the General Board of Discipleship offer it in study editions with a leader's guide.

THIS HOLY MYSTERY:

A United Methodist Understanding of Holy Communion

Part One: There Is More to the Mystery

The story is told of a little girl whose parents had taken her forward to receive Holy Communion. Disappointed with the small piece of bread she was given to dip in the cup, the child cried loudly, "I want more! I want more!" While embarrassing to her parents and amusing to the pastor and congregation, this little girl's cry accurately expresses the feelings of many contemporary United Methodist people. We want more! We want more than we are receiving from the sacrament of Holy Communion as it is practiced in our churches.

According to the results of a survey conducted by the General Board of Discipleship prior to the 2000 General Conference, there is a strong sense of the importance of Holy Communion in the life of individual Christians and of the church. Unfortunately, there is at least an equally strong sense of the absence of any meaningful understanding of Eucharistic theology and practice. United Methodists recognize that grace and spiritual power are available to them in the sacrament, but too often they do not feel enabled to receive these gifts and apply them in their lives. Many laypeople complain of sloppy practice, questionable theology, and lack of teaching and guidance. Both clergy and laity recognize the crucial need for better education of pastors in sacramental theology and practice. The concern for improved education is coupled with a call for accountability. Bishops, district superintendents, and other annual conference and general church authorities are urged to prepare their pastors better and to hold them accountable for their sacramental theology, practice, and teaching. Many of the people surveyed are plainly resentful of the lack of leadership they believe they are receiving in these areas. These results are troubling and must provoke the church to reexamination and recommitment.

These results are also exciting and challenging! They reveal a deep hunger for the riches of divine grace made available to us through Holy Communion, for real communion with Jesus Christ and with Christian people. They show that United Methodists want our faith to be enlivened and made more relevant to our daily lives. How can our church best respond to the wonderful hunger of its people for "this holy mystery" ("A Service of Word and Table I," *BOW*; page 39)?

United Methodists share with many other Christians an increased interest in the study and celebration of the sacraments. For the last several decades we have been actively seeking to recover and revitalize appreciation of Holy Baptism and Holy Communion. Our current services of the Baptismal Covenant and Word and Table are the fruit of a long process of development that began in the 1960's and culminated in their adoption by the 1984 General Conference and publication in *The United Methodist Hymnal* approved in 1988. The change in location of these sacramental rituals from the back to the front of the *Hymnal* is an intentional expression of their significance in the life of the community of faith. In 1996, the General Conference approved *By Water and the Spirit: A United Methodist Understanding of Baptism* as an official interpretive and teaching document for the church. *This Holy Mystery: A United Methodist Understanding of Holy Communion* is submitted to the 2004 General Conference with the same purpose. Both of these documents reflect United Methodism's efforts to reclaim its sacramental heritage and to be in accord with ecumenical movements in sacramental theology and practice.

This Holy Mystery is characterized by the effort to avoid rigidity on the one hand and indifference on the other. Neither extreme is true to our heritage nor faithful to the Spirit who leads the church forward in the work of making disciples living toward the new creation. The document is made up of two main parts. The expository introduction titled "Part One: There Is More to the Mystery" describes the document's development and provides grounding in historical tradition and sacramental theology. "Part Two: Christ Is Here: Experiencing the Mystery" is organized by principles. Under each principle, "Background" provides an explanation for the principle, while

"Practice" provides guidelines for applying the principle. The principles make assertions that are truthful and doctrinally clear. They honor the historic and ecumenical center of the Christian church's theology and practice. The committee has endeavored to explain in the "Background" sections how the principles are rooted in the theology and practice of Christians past and present, particularly United Methodist Christians. In the "Practice" sections we have applied the principles to contemporary sacramental practices of the church in the various contexts of United Methodism.

The church is always universal and particular, catholic and local, united and diverse. United Methodists vary geographically, racially, and culturally. *This Holy Mystery* invites United Methodists to share common understandings while allowing for appropriate, faithful applications. Some United Methodist practices differ from those of other Christian traditions. Being truthful about these differences recognizes our ties and responsibility to the wider church while claiming God's work in leading us to affirm distinctive understandings and practices. Both within our own United Methodist community and in fellowship with other traditions, we reject cavalier or arrogant attitudes. We seek to strengthen the bond of unity by "speaking the truth in love" (Ephesians 4:15) as, with humility and openness, we acknowledge our principles, explain our backgrounds, and affirm our practices.

Names of the Sacrament

Several terms naming the sacrament are used in past and present Christianity. In *This Holy Mystery* some are used more than others, but all are largely synonymous. *The Lord's Supper* reminds us that Jesus Christ is the host and that we participate at Christ's invitation. This title suggests the eating of a meal, sometimes called the Holy Meal, and makes us think of the meals that Jesus ate with various people both before his death and after his resurrection. The term *the Last Supper* is not appropriately used for the sacrament, but it does encourage us to remember the supper that Jesus ate with his disciples on the night when he was arrested. This emphasis is especially meaningful around Maundy Thursday. The early church appears to have referred to their celebrations as breaking bread (Acts 2:42).

The term *Holy Communion* invites us to focus on the self-giving of the Holy God, which makes the sacrament an occasion of grace, and on the holiness of our communion with God and one another. *Eucharist*, from the Greek word for thanksgiving, reminds us that the sacrament is thanksgiving to God for the gifts of creation and salvation. The term *Mass*, used by the Roman Catholic Church, derives from the Latin word *missio*, literally "sending forth," and indicates that this celebration brings the worship service to a close by sending forth the congregation with God's blessing to live as God's people in the world. *The Divine Liturgy* is a name used mostly by churches in the tradition of Eastern Orthodoxy. All of these names refer to the same practice: the eating and drinking of consecrated bread and wine in the worshiping community.

Background

As early as the Emmaus experience on the day of Resurrection, recorded in Luke 24:13-35, Christians recognized the presence of Jesus Christ in the breaking of bread. The traditional Jewish practice of taking bread, blessing and thanking God, and breaking and sharing the bread took on new meaning for them. When followers of Christ gathered in Jesus' name, the breaking of bread and sharing of the cup was a means of remembering his life, death, and resurrection and of encountering the living Christ. They experienced afresh the presence of their risen Lord and received sustenance for their lives as disciples. As the church organized itself, this custom of Eucharist became the characteristic ritual of the community and the central act of its worship.

Over the centuries, various understandings and practices of Holy Communion have developed. Roman Catholicism teaches that the substance of bread and wine are changed (although not visibly) into the actual body and blood of Christ (sometimes called transubstantiation). Protestant Reformers in the sixteenth century rejected this teaching but had diverse ideas among themselves. Lutherans maintain that Christ's body and blood are truly is present in and with the elements of bread and wine in the celebration (sometimes erroneously called corporeal presence or consubstantiation). Ulrich Zwingli, a Swiss reformer, taught that the Lord's Supper is a memorial or reminder of Christ's sacrifice, an affirmation of faith, and a sign of Christian fellowship. Although his name may be unfamiliar, Zwingli's views are widely shared today, especially within evangelical churches. Denominations in the Reformed tradition, following

John Calvin, maintain that although Christ's body is in heaven, when Holy Communion is received with true faith, the power of the Holy Spirit nourishes those who partake. The Church of England affirmed a somewhat similar view in its Catechism and Articles of Religion. These understandings (stated here very simplistically) suggest the range of ideas that were available to John and Charles Wesley and the early Methodists.

United Methodist Heritage

Early Methodism

The Methodist movement in eighteenth-century England was an evangelical movement that included a revival of emphasis on the sacraments. The Wesleys recognized the power of God available in the Lord's Supper and urged their followers to draw on that power by frequent participation. The grace available in and through the sacrament was active in conviction, repentance and conversion, forgiveness, and sanctification. John Wesley described the Lord's Supper as "the grand channel whereby the grace of his Spirit was conveyed to the souls of all the children of God" ("Sermon on the Mount—Discourse Six," III.11). During the years in which Methodism was beginning and growing, Wesley himself communed an average of four to five times a week. His sermon "The Duty of Constant Communion" emphasizes the role of the sacrament in the lives of Christians in ways that are keenly meaningful today. The Wesley brothers wrote and published a collection of 166 *Hymns on the Lord's Supper*, which was used for meditation as well as for singing. The Wesleys understood and taught the multifaceted nature of the Lord's Supper. They wrote about love, grace, sacrifice, forgiveness, the presence of Christ, mystery, healing, nourishment, holiness, and pledge of heaven. They knew that Holy Communion is a powerful means through which divine grace is given to God's people. Our sacramental understandings and practices today are grounded in this heritage.

Evangelical and United Brethren Roots

The movements that developed into the Church of the United Brethren in Christ and the Evangelical Church began in the late eighteenth century and early nineteenth century in America. From the beginning, relationships between these groups and the Methodists were close and cordial. The beliefs and practices of the three churches were similar. Francis Asbury and Philip William Otterbein were close friends, and Otterbein participated in Asbury's consecration as a Methodist Episcopal bishop. Conversations about possible union began at least as early as 1809 and continued intermittently until the churches finally merged in 1968 to form The United Methodist Church.

Unfortunately, Otterbein and Martin Boehm—founders of the United Brethren—left little written material. The same is true of Evangelical founder Jacob Albright. Therefore, we can make comparatively few references to their theology and practice of Holy Communion. The *Journal* of Christian Newcomer (d. 1830), third United Brethren bishop, records so many occasions of administering and participating in the sacrament that its significance in the life of the church is apparent.

American Methodism

The early American Methodists, who began arriving in the 1760's, were at first able to receive the sacraments from Anglican churches of which they were considered a part. But the situation soon changed, and Methodists began to reject the English church. As rising tensions between the colonies and England led to the Revolutionary War, most Anglican priests left the country. By the mid 1770's, most Methodists had no access to the sacraments. The missionary preachers sent by John Wesley were laymen, as were the Americans who became preachers. They had no authority to baptize or to offer Holy Communion. Methodists were longing for the sacraments, and it was this need that motivated Wesley to take actions to provide ordained elders for America. In 1784, the Methodist Episcopal Church was created and some preachers were ordained. Still, the number of elders was too small to offer the sacraments regularly to the rapidly increasing number of Methodists. During the decades of the circuit riders, most Methodists were able to receive the Lord's Supper quarterly, at best, when the ordained elder came to their community. The camp meetings of the period were also sacramental occasions where large numbers of people communed. By the late nineteenth century and throughout the twentieth, many Methodist churches were served by ordained elders, but the habit of quarterly Holy Communion remained strong.

American Methodists considered Holy Communion a sacred and solemn event. The tone of the ritual was deeply penitential, calling upon people to repent and having less emphasis on celebration of God's grace. During the nineteenth and twentieth centuries the rich Wesleyan understandings of Eucharist were largely lost, and the sacrament became understood only as a memorial of the death of Christ. In many congregations attendance on Communion Sunday was low. Revitalization of the Lord's Supper in Methodism, and in the Evangelical and United Brethren churches, started in the mid-twentieth century when the churches began to reclaim their sacramental heritage and create new rituals to express it.

As Methodism spread to other parts of the world, ritual and practice established in America were followed. Over the years, however, there have been certain influences from surrounding Christian traditions. These are to some extent reflected in Holy Communion practice in the central conferences (those beyond the geographic area of the United States).

Grace and the Means of Grace

Today Holy Communion must be viewed within the larger context of United Methodist theology. In accord with biblical and Christian teaching, we believe that we are sinners, constantly in need of divine grace. We believe that God is gracious and loving, always making available the grace we need. Grace is God's love toward us, God's free and undeserved gift. Several words describe how grace works in our lives. Prevenient grace is that which "comes before" anything we can do to help ourselves. Although we are all bound by our sinful nature, grace gives us enough freedom of will to be able to respond to God. In truth, all grace is prevenient—we cannot move toward God unless God has first moved toward us. God seeks us out, pursues us, calls us to come into the loving relationship that we were created to enjoy. Convicting grace makes us conscious of our sinfulness and urges us to repentance. Justifying grace forgives and puts us into right relationship with God. Sanctifying grace enables us to grow in holiness of life. Perfecting grace molds us into the image of Christ. The grace of God is made available to us through the life, death, and resurrection of Jesus Christ and works in our lives through the presence and power of the Holy Spirit.

While divine grace reaches us any time and in any way that God chooses, God has designated certain means or channels through which grace is most surely and immediately available. John Wesley expressed it this way: "By 'means of grace' I understand outward signs, words, or actions, ordained of God, and appointed for this end, to be the ordinary channels whereby he might convey to men [and women], preventing, justifying, or sanctifying grace" ("The Means of Grace," II.1). In the General Rules, Wesley listed these means of grace as, "The public worship of God. The ministry of the Word, either read or expounded. The Supper of the Lord. Family and private prayer. Searching the Scriptures. Fasting or abstinence" (*BOD*, ¶ 103; page 74). Elsewhere Wesley added Christian conferencing, by which he meant edifying conversation and meeting together in groups for nurture and accountability. These means are not to be understood as ways of earning salvation, for that is an unmerited gift. They are, rather, ways to receive, live in, and grow in divine grace. The Wesleyan tradition has continued to emphasize the practice of these means of grace throughout our salvation process.

The Theology of Sacraments

The Greek word used in the early church for sacrament is *mysterion*, usually translated mystery. It indicates that through sacraments, God discloses things that are beyond human capacity to know through reason alone. In Latin the word used is *sacramentum*, which means a vow or promise. The sacraments were instituted by Christ and given to the church. Jesus Christ is himself the ultimate manifestation of a sacrament. In the coming of Jesus of Nazareth, God's nature and purpose were revealed and active through a human body. The Christian church is also sacramental. It was instituted to continue the work of Christ in redeeming the world. The church is Christ's body—the visible, material instrument through which Christ continues to be made known and the divine plan is fulfilled. Holy Baptism and Holy Communion have been chosen and designated by God as special means through which divine grace comes to us. Holy Baptism is the sacrament that initiates us into the body of Christ "through water and the Spirit" ("The Baptismal Covenant I," *UMH*; page 37). In baptism we receive our identity and mission as Christians. Holy Communion is the sacrament that sustains and nourishes us in our journey of salvation. In a sacrament, God uses tangible, material things as vehicles or instruments of grace. Wesley defines a sacrament, in accord with his Anglican tradition, as "an outward sign of inward grace, and a means whereby we receive the same" ("Means of Grace," II.1). Sacraments are sign—acts, which include words, actions, and physical elements. They both express and convey the gracious love of God. They make God's love both visible and effective. We might even say that sacraments are God's "show and tell," communicating with us in a way that we, in all our brokenness and limitations, can receive and experience God's grace.

The Meaning of Holy Communion

In the New Testament, at least six major ideas about Holy Communion are present: thanksgiving, fellowship, remembrance, sacrifice, action of the Holy Spirit, and eschatology. A brief look at each of these will help us better comprehend the meaning of the sacrament.

Holy Communion is Eucharist, an act of thanksgiving. The early Christians "broke bread in their homes and ate together with glad and sincere hearts, praising God and enjoying the favor of all the people" (Acts 2:46-47a, NIV). As we commune, we express joyful thanks for God's mighty acts throughout history—for creation, covenant, redemption, sanctification. The Great Thanksgiving ("A Service of Word and Table I," UMH; pages 9-10) is a recitation of this salvation history, culminating in the work of Jesus Christ and the ongoing work of the Holy Spirit. It conveys our gratitude for the goodness of God and God's unconditional love for us.

Holy Communion is the communion of the church—the gathered community of the faithful, both local and universal. While deeply meaningful to the individuals participating, the sacrament is much more than a personal event. The first person pronouns throughout the ritual are consistently plural—*we, us, our*. First Corinthians 10:17 explains that "because there is one bread, we who are many are one body, for we all partake of the one bread." "A Service of Word and Table I" uses this text as an explicit statement of Christian unity in the body of Christ (UMH; page 11). The sharing and bonding experienced at the Table exemplify the nature of the church and model the world as God would have it be.

Holy Communion is remembrance, commemoration, and memorial, but this remembrance is much more than simply intellectual recalling. "Do this in remembrance of me" (Luke 22:19; 1 Corinthians 11:24-25) is *anamnesis* (the biblical Greek word). This dynamic action becomes re-presentation of past gracious acts of God in the present, so powerfully as to make them truly present now. Christ is risen and is alive here and now, not just remembered for what was done in the past.

Holy Communion is a type of sacrifice. It is a re-presentation, not a repetition, of the sacrifice of Christ. Hebrews 9:26 makes clear that "he has appeared once for all at the end of the age to remove sin by the sacrifice of himself." Christ's atoning life, death, and resurrection make divine grace available to us. We also present ourselves as sacrifice in union with Christ (Romans 12:1; 1 Peter 2:5) to be used by God in the work of redemption, reconciliation, and justice. In the Great Thanksgiving, the church prays: "We offer ourselves in praise and thanksgiving as a holy and living sacrifice, in union with Christ's offering for us . . ." (*UMH*; page 10).

Holy Communion is a vehicle of God's grace through the action of the Holy Spirit (Acts 1:8), whose work is described in John 14:26: "But the Advocate, the Holy Spirit, whom the Father will send in my name, will teach you everything, and remind you of all that I have said to you." The *epiclesis* (biblical Greek meaning "calling upon") is the part of the Great Thanksgiving that calls the Spirit: "Pour out your Holy Spirit on us gathered here, and on these gifts of bread and wine." The church asks God to "make them be for us the body and blood of Christ, that we may be for the world the body of Christ, redeemed by his blood. By your Spirit make us one with Christ, one with each other, and one in ministry to all the world . . ." (*UMH*; page 10).

Holy Communion is eschatological, meaning that it has to do with the end of history, the outcome of God's purpose for the world— "Christ has died; Christ is risen; Christ will come again" (*UMH*; page 10). We commune not only with the faithful who are physically present but with the saints of the past who join us in the sacrament. To participate is to receive a foretaste of the future, a pledge of heaven "until Christ comes in final victory and we feast at his heavenly banquet" (*UMH*; page 10). Christ himself looked forward to this occasion and promised the disciples, "I will never again drink of this fruit of the vine until that day when I drink it new with you in my Father's kingdom" (Matthew 26:29; Mark 14:25; Luke 22:18). When we eat and drink at the Table, we become partakers of the divine nature in this life and for life eternal (John 6:47-58; Revelation 3:20). We are anticipating the heavenly banquet celebrating God's victory over sin, evil, and death (Matthew 22:1-14; Revelation 19:9; 21:1-7). In the midst of the personal and systemic brokenness in which we live, we yearn for everlasting fellowship with Christ and ultimate fulfillment of the divine plan. Nourished by sacramental grace, we strive to be formed into the image of Christ and to be made instruments for transformation in the world.

Toward a Richer Sacramental Life

Like the little girl who was disappointed with what she received, United Methodist people are looking and hoping for something more in their Eucharistic experience. As we move toward a richer sacramental life, including weekly celebration of Holy Communion, we ask what spiritual benefits we receive from it. What do divine love and power do in and for us through our participation in the sacrament? The answers to this question involve forgiveness, nourishment, healing, transformation, ministry and mission, and eternal life.

We respond to the invitation to the Table by immediately confessing our personal and corporate sin, trusting that, "If we confess our sins, he who is faithful and just will forgive us our sins and cleanse us from all unrighteousness" (1 John 1:9). Our expression of repentance is answered by the absolution in which forgiveness is proclaimed: "In the name of Jesus Christ, you are forgiven!" (UMH; page 8). This assurance is God's gift to sinners, enabling us to continue striving to live faithfully. Wesley wrote, "The grace of God given herein confirms to us the pardon of our sins by enabling us to leave them" ("The Duty of Constant Communion," I.3).

We receive spiritual nourishment through Holy Communion. The Christian life is a journey, one that is challenging and arduous. To continue living faithfully and growing in holiness requires constant sustenance. Wesley wrote, "This is the food of our souls: This gives strength to perform our duty, and leads us on to perfection" ("The Duty of Constant Communion," I.3). God makes such sustenance available through the sacrament of Eucharist. In John 6:35, Jesus tells the crowd: "I am the bread of life. Whoever comes to me will never be hungry, and whoever believes in me will never be thirsty." As we return to the Table again and again, we are strengthened repeatedly. We go out empowered to live as disciples, reconcilers, and witnesses. In the words of the prayer after Communion, "Grant that we may go into the world in the strength of your Spirit, to give ourselves for others . . ." (UMH; page 11).

As we encounter Christ in Holy Communion and are repeatedly touched by divine grace, we are progressively shaped into Christ's image. All of this work is not done in a moment, no matter how dramatic an experience we may enjoy. It is, instead, a lifelong process through which God intends to shape us into people motivated by love, empowered and impassioned to do Christ's work in the world. The identity and ministry that God bestows on us in our baptism are fulfilled as we continue to be transformed into disciples who can respond to God's love by loving God and others (Romans 12:1-2).

Through Eucharist, we receive healing and are enabled to aid in the healing of others. *Sozo*, the root of the Greek word used in the New Testament for "healing," is also translated as "salvation" and "wholeness." Much of this healing is spiritual, but it also includes the healing of our thoughts and emotions, of our minds and bodies, of our attitudes and relationships. The grace received at the Table of the Lord can make us whole. As those who are being saved, we seek to bring healing to a broken world. *The United Methodist Book of Worship* describes this well: "Spiritual healing is God's work of offering persons balance, harmony, and wholeness of body, mind, spirit, and relationships through confession, forgiveness, and reconciliation. Through such healing, God works to bring about reconciliation between God and humanity, among individuals and communities, within each person, and between humanity and the rest of creation" (page 613). Holy Communion can be a powerful aspect of the services of healing provided in the *Book of Worship* (pages 615-623).

The grace we receive at the Lord's Table enables us to perform our ministry and mission, to continue his work in the world—the work of redemption, reconciliation, peace, and justice (2 Corinthians 5:17-21). As we commune, we become aware of the worth and the needs of other people and are reminded of our responsibility. We express the compassion of Christ through acts of caring and kindness toward those we encounter in our daily lives. In our baptism, we have vowed to "accept the freedom and power God gives [us] to resist evil, injustice, and oppression in whatever forms they present themselves" (*UMH*; page 34). But, in the words of the prayer of confession, we acknowledge our failures: "We have rebelled against your love, we have not loved our neighbors, and we have not heard the cry of the needy" (*UMH*; page 8). Remembering the revolutionary Jesus, we are impelled to challenge unjust practices and systems that perpetuate political, economic, and social inequity and discrimination (Matthew 23; Luke 4:16-21; 14:7-11).

The loving God who meets us at the Table gives us the gift of eternal life. Jesus' presentation of himself as the spiritual bread of life in

John's Eucharistic account (6:25-58) makes clear the connection: "Those who eat my flesh and drink my blood have eternal life, and I will raise them up on the last day" (6:54). This life in union with Christ is life eternal. It is not only the promise of our being with Christ after physical death. It is also our being in dynamic loving relationship with Christ here and now. It is life that never ends because it is grounded in the everlasting love of God who comes to us in the sacraments.

> O Thou who this mysterious bread
> didst in Emmaus break,
> return, herewith our souls to feed,
> and to thy followers speak.
>
> Charles Wesley
> The United Methodist Hymnal, 613

Part Two: Christ Is Here: Experiencing the Mystery

The Presence of Christ

Principle:

Jesus Christ, who "is the reflection of God's glory and the exact imprint of God's very being" (Hebrews 1:3), is truly present in Holy Communion. Through Jesus Christ and in the power of the Holy Spirit, God meets us at the Table. God, who has given the sacraments to the church, acts in and through Holy Communion. Christ is present through the community gathered in Jesus' name (Matthew 18:20), through the Word proclaimed and enacted, and through the elements of bread and wine shared (1 Corinthians 11:23-26). The divine presence is a living reality and can be experienced by participants; it is not a remembrance of the Last Supper and the Crucifixion only.

Background:

Christ's presence in the sacrament is a promise to the church and is not dependent upon recognition of this presence by individual members of the congregation. Holy Communion always offers grace. We are reminded of what God has done for us in the past, experience what God is doing now as we partake, and anticipate what God will do in the future work of salvation. "We await the final moment of grace, when Christ comes in victory at the end of the age to bring all who are in Christ into the glory of that victory" (*By Water and the Spirit: A United*

Methodist Understanding of Baptism, in *BOR;* page 875), and we join in feasting at the heavenly banquet table (Luke 22:14-18; Revelation 19:9).

The Christian church has struggled through the centuries to understand just how Christ is present in the Eucharist. Arguments and divisions have occurred over the matter. The Wesleyan tradition affirms the reality of Christ's presence, although it does not claim to be able to explain it fully. John and Charles Wesley's 166 *Hymns on the Lord's Supper* are our richest resource for study in order to appreciate the Wesleyan understanding of the presence of Christ in the Eucharist. One of these hymns expresses well both the reality and the mystery: "O the Depth of Love Divine," stanzas 1 and 4 (*The United Methodist Hymnal,* 627):

O the depth of love divine,
the unfathomable grace!
Who shall say how bread and wine
God into us conveys!
How the bread his flesh imparts,
how the wine transmits his blood,
fills his faithful people's hearts
with all the life of God!

Sure and real is the grace,
the manner be unknown;
only meet us in thy ways
and perfect us in one.
Let us taste the heavenly powers,
Lord, we ask for nothing more.
Thine to bless, 'tis only ours
to wonder and adore.

Article XVI of The Articles of Religion of The Methodist Church describes the sacraments as "certain signs of grace, and God's good will toward us, by which he doth work invisibly in us, and doth not only quicken, but also strengthen and confirm, our faith in him" (*BOD;* page 63).

Article XVIII describes the Lord's Supper as "a sacrament of our redemption by Christ's death; insomuch that, to such as rightly, worthily, and with faith receive the same, the bread which we break is a partaking of the body of Christ; and likewise the cup of blessing is a partaking of the blood of Christ" (*BOD;* page 64). (*See* section "The Communion Elements" in this paper for related material.)

Article VI of The Confession of Faith of The Evangelical United Brethren Church speaks similarly of the sacraments: "They are means of grace by which God works invisibly in us, quickening, strengthening and confirming our faith in him. . . . Those who rightly, worthily and in faith eat the broken bread and drink the blessed cup partake of the body and blood of Christ in a spiritual manner until he comes" (*BOD*; page 68).

United Methodists, along with other Christian traditions, have tried to provide clear and faithful interpretations of Christ's presence in the Holy Meal. Our tradition asserts the real, personal, living presence of Jesus Christ. For United Methodists, the Lord's Supper is anchored in the life of the historical Jesus of Nazareth, but is not primarily a remembrance or memorial. We do not embrace the medieval doctrine of transubstantiation, though we do believe that the elements are essential tangible means through which God works. We understand the divine presence in temporal and relational terms. In the Holy Meal of the church, the past, present, and future of the living Christ come together by the power of the Holy Spirit so that we may receive and embody Jesus Christ as God's saving gift for the whole world.

Practice:

Because Jesus Christ has promised to meet us there (1 Corinthians 11:23-26), Christians approach the Communion Table with desire and expectation, with awe and humility, and with celebration and gratitude.

Pastors need to be trained and formed (in seminary, course of study, licensing school, and continuing education) in the theology, spirituality, history, and tradition of the sacraments and in how to most effectively utilize proclamation, ritual, gestures, postures, and material signs in order to convey their full meaning.

Christ Is Calling You

Invitation to the Lord's Table

Principle:

The invitation to the Table comes from the risen and present Christ. Christ invites to his Table those who love him, repent of sin, and seek to live as Christian disciples. Holy Communion is a gift of God to the church and an act of the community of faith. By responding to this invitation we affirm and deepen our personal relationship with God through Jesus Christ and our commitment to membership and mission in the body of Christ.

Background:

The Invitation to Holy Communion in "A Service of Word and Table I" and "A Service of Word and Table II" proclaims, "Christ our Lord invites to his table all who love him, who earnestly repent of their sin and seek to live in peace with one another" (*UMH*; pages 7, 12). The more traditional wording in "A Service of Word and Table IV" invites, "Ye that do truly and earnestly repent of your sins, and are in love and charity with your neighbors, and intend to lead a new life, following the commandments of God, and walking from henceforth in his holy ways: Draw near with faith . . ." (*UMH*; page 26). "A Service of Word and Table V," for use with people who are sick or homebound, says that Christ invites "all who love him and seek to grow into his likeness" (*BOW*; page 51).

Practice:

When Holy Communion is celebrated, it is important to always begin with the words of Invitation, including Confession and Pardon. If these are omitted, all those present may not understand either the openness of the Table of the Lord or the expectation of repentance, forgiveness, healing, and entrance into new life in Christ.

The church community has a responsibility to provide ongoing age-appropriate nurture and education about the sacrament of Holy Communion to all its people. Those who are baptized as infants need continual teaching as they mature in faith. Those who come into membership later in life also need ongoing instruction about the significance of the sacrament in their personal faith journey and in the life of the congregation and larger Christian community. All who seek to live as Christian disciples need formation in sacramental spirituality.

Bishops, elders, deacons, pastors, Sunday school teachers, parents and guardians, seminary professors, and others have responsibility for faithfully teaching understandings and practices of Holy Communion. Teaching about the sacraments should emphasize United Methodist positions and practices but should also encourage knowledge of and respect for those of other Christian traditions.

Principle:

All who respond in faith to the invitation are to be welcomed. Holy Baptism normally precedes partaking of Holy Communion. Holy Communion is a meal of the community who are in covenant relationship with God through Jesus Christ. As circumcision was the sign of the covenant between God and the Hebrew people, baptism is the sign of the new covenant (Genesis 17:9-14; Exodus 24:1-12; Jeremiah 31:31; Romans 6:1-11; Hebrews 9:15).

Background:

Baptism is the non-repeatable rite of initiation into the body of Christ, while the Lord's Supper is the regularly-repeated celebration of communion of the body of Christ.

Beginning early in its history, the Christian church divided its worship services into the Liturgy of the Word, in which all participated, and the Liturgy of the Faithful, which was the celebration of Holy Communion. Those who were not yet baptized were dismissed before the celebration of the sacrament (*Didache* 9; Justin Martyr, *First Apology*, 66; *The Apostolic Constitutions*, Book VIII; *The Liturgy of St. Basil*).

John Wesley stressed that baptism is only a step in the salvation process and must be followed by justifying faith and personal commitment to Christ when one reaches an age of accountability. He referred to Holy Communion as "a converting ordinance" (Journal from November 1, 1739, to September 3, 1741; Friday, June 27, 1740). In eighteenth-century England, Wesley was addressing people who, for the most part, although baptized as infants and possessing some degree of faith had not yet experienced spiritual rebirth. Therefore, the conversion Wesley spoke of was transformation of lives and assurance of salvation.

Soon after the merger of The Evangelical Church and the United Brethren in Christ, the Evangelical United Brethren *Discipline* of 1947, reads, "We invite to [the Lord's Supper] all disciples of the Lord Jesus Christ who have confessed him before men and desire to serve him with sincere hearts" (page 447).

The United Methodist Book of Worship says, "All who intend to lead a Christian life, together with their children, are invited to receive the bread and cup. We have no tradition of refusing any who present themselves desiring to receive" (page 29). This statement means that in practice there are few, if any, circumstances in which a United

Methodist pastor would refuse to serve the elements of Holy Communion to a person who comes forward to receive.

By Water and the Spirit affirms: "Because the table at which we gather belongs to the Lord, it should be open to all who respond to Christ's love, regardless of age or church membership. The Wesleyan tradition has always recognized that Holy Communion may be an occasion for the reception of converting, justifying, and sanctifying grace" (*BOR*; pages 873-74).

Practice:

Invitation to partake of Holy Communion offers an evangelical opportunity to bring people into a fuller living relationship with the body of Christ. As means of God's unmerited grace, Holy Baptism and Holy Communion are to be seen not as barriers but as pathways. Pastors and congregations must strive for a balance of welcome that is open and gracious and teaching that is clear and faithful to the fullness of discipleship.

Nonbaptized people who respond in faith to the invitation in our liturgy will be welcomed to the Table. They should receive teaching about Holy Baptism as the sacrament of entrance into the community of faith—needed only once by each individual—and Holy Communion as the sacrament of sustenance for the journey of faith and growth in holiness—needed and received frequently. "Unbaptized persons who receive communion should be counseled and nurtured toward baptism as soon as possible" (*By Water and the Spirit*, in *BOR*; page 874).

Principle:

No one will be turned away from the Table because of age or "mental, physical, developmental, and/or psychological and neurological" capacity (*BOD*, ¶ 162G) or because of any other condition that might limit his or her understanding or hinder his or her reception of the sacrament.

Background:

According to *By Water and the Spirit,*
"The services of the baptismal covenant appropriately conclude with Holy Communion, through which the union of the new member with the body of Christ is most fully expressed. Holy Communion is a sacred meal in which the community of faith, in the simple act of

eating bread and drinking wine, proclaims and participates in all that God has done, is doing, and will continue to do for us in Christ. In celebrating the Eucharist, we remember the grace given to us in our baptism and partake of the spiritual food necessary for sustaining and fulfilling the promises of salvation" (BOR; page 873).

The concluding rubrics of the services make clear that this applies to people of all ages.

The theological basis for baptism of infants and people of varying abilities applies as well to their participation in Holy Communion:

"Through the church, God claims infants as well as adults to be participants in the gracious covenant of which baptism is the sign. This understanding of the workings of divine grace also applies to persons who for reasons of disabilities or other limitations are unable to answer for themselves the questions of the baptismal ritual. While we may not be able to comprehend how God works in their lives, our faith teaches us that God's grace is sufficient for their needs and, thus, they are appropriate recipients of baptism" (*By Water and the Spirit*, in BOR; page 868).

Likewise, the grace given through Holy Communion is offered to the entire church, including those who are unable to respond for themselves. Children are members of the covenant community and participants in the Lord's Supper.

Practice:

Young children and people with handicapping or incapacitating conditions may need special consideration as the elements are served. Pastors and congregations should develop plans for providing assistance that maintains the dignity and affirms the worth of those receiving.

Children of all ages are welcome to the Table and are to be taught and led to interpret, appreciate, and participate in Holy Communion. Adults need training to help them explain the sacrament to children.

When worship spaces are constructed or renovated, attention needs to be given to providing physical access to the Communion Table for all.

Principle:

The Lord's Supper in a United Methodist congregation is open to members of other United Methodist congregations and to Christians from other traditions.

Background:

"A baptized or professing member of any local United Methodist church is a member of the global United Methodist connection and a member of the church universal" (*BOD;* ¶ 215).

The United Methodist Church recognizes that it is only one of the bodies that constitute the community of Christians. Despite our differences, all Christians are welcome at the Table of the Lord.

Practice:

As a part of the directions before the invitation, it is customary to announce that all Christians are welcome to participate in the sacrament in United Methodist congregations.

Response to the invitation is always voluntary, and care needs to be taken to ensure that no one feels pressured to participate or conspicuous for not doing so.

When Holy Communion is served as part of a service of Christian marriage or a service of death and resurrection, "It is our tradition to invite all Christians to the Lord's table, and the invitation should be extended to everyone present; but there should be no pressure that would embarrass those who for whatever reason do not choose to receive Holy Communion" (*BOW;* page 152). It is not appropriate for only the couple or family to commune.

The Issue of "Unworthiness"

Principle:

Any person who answers in faith the invitation "Christ our Lord invites to his table all who love him, who earnestly repent of their sin and seek to live in peace with one another" (*UMH;* page 7) is worthy through Christ to partake of Holy Communion. Christians come to the Lord's Table in gratitude for Christ's mercy toward sinners. We do not share in Communion because of our worthiness; no one is truly worthy. We come to the Eucharist out of our hunger to receive God's gracious love, to receive forgiveness and healing.

Background:

Some deeply committed United Methodist people who hesitate or even refuse to partake of Holy Communion do so because of their sense that they are unworthy. This problem is largely based upon mis-interpretation and false fears. Within the United Methodist tradition, people who participate in the sacrament are assured of the forgive-ness of their sins and of pardon through their participation in the Invitation and the Confession and Pardon.

Paul's words of warning in 1 Corinthians 11:27-32 have long been a source of confusion and concern. Some people are fearful of com-muning "in an unworthy manner" and, sometimes out of genuine Christian humility, believe that their participation would be improper. John Wesley addressed this problem in his sermon "The Duty of Constant Communion": "God offers you one of the greatest mercies on this side of heaven, and commands you to accept it. . . . You are unworthy to receive any mercy from God. But is that a reason for refusing all mercy? . . . Why do you not obey God's command? . . . What! unworthy to obey God?" (II.7-8).

Wesley went on to explain that unworthiness does not apply to the people who are to commune, but to the manner in which the consecrated elements are consumed: "Here is not a word said of being unworthy to eat and drink. Indeed he [Paul] does speak of eat-ing and drinking unworthily; but that is quite a different thing. . . . In this very chapter we are told that by eating and drinking unworthily is meant, taking the holy Sacrament in such a rude and disorderly way, that one was 'hungry, and another drunken' [1 Cor. 11:21]" (II.9).

First Corinthians 11:29 is a word of judgment against "all who eat and drink without discerning the body." A footnote to this passage in *The New Oxford Annotated Bible* (NRSV) explains that this is a reference to "the community, one's relation to other Christians" (page 242). Paul is speaking against those who fail to recognize the church—the body of Christ—as a community of faith within which Christians relate to each other in love.

Practice:

Pastors and other leaders can alleviate most of these concerns about worthiness through patient counseling, faithful teaching, and prayers for healing. These efforts can be focused on study of the cited passage in First Corinthians, with clear explanation of what it meant in its first-century context and what it means today.

The Basic Pattern of Worship: A Service of Word and Table

Principle:

The complete pattern of Christian worship for the Lord's Day is Word and Table—the gospel is proclaimed in both Word and sacrament. Word and Table are not in competition; rather they complement each other so as to constitute a whole service of worship. Their separation diminishes the fullness of life in the Spirit offered to us through faith in Jesus Christ.

Background:

In *The United Methodist Book of Worship* (pages 13-14), the Basic Pattern of Worship is traced to its Jewish roots:

The Entrance and the Proclamation and Response—often called the Service of the Word or the Preaching Service—are a Christian adaptation of the ancient synagogue service. The Thanksgiving and Communion, commonly called the Lord's Supper or Holy Communion, is a Christian adaptation of Jewish worship at family meal tables. . . . Christians held an adapted synagogue service and broke bread when they gathered on the first day of the week. (Acts 20:7)

The practice of the Christian church from its earliest years was weekly celebration of the Lord's Supper on the Lord's Day. The *Didache*, a source from the late first century or early second century says, "On every Lord's Day—his special day—come together and break bread and give thanks . . ." (14). Justin Martyr, writing around A.D. 150, relates, "And on the day called Sunday there is a meeting . . . bread is brought, and wine and water, and the president similarly sends up prayers and thanksgivings . . ." (Chapter 67). Most Christian traditions have continued this pattern.

John Wesley was highly critical of the infrequency of Holy Communion in the Church of England of his day. He exhorted his followers to practice "constant communion" because Christ had so commanded and because the spiritual benefits are so great ("The Duty of Constant Communion"). In his 1784 letter to American Methodists, Wesley counseled, "I also advise the elders to administer the supper of the Lord on every Lord's day" ("Letter to Dr. Coke, Mr. Asbury, and Our Brethren in North America").

For decades the scarcity of ordained pastors made it difficult if not impossible for churches in the Wesleyan tradition to observe the Lord's Supper as a part of regular Sunday worship. The custom of celebrating the sacrament at least quarterly, when an ordained elder was present, ensured the opportunity for regular if infrequent participation. With the introduction of new liturgical texts for the Lord's Supper in 1972, United Methodism has been recovering the fullness of Word and Table as the pattern for weekly worship on the Lord's Day.

The *Journal* of Christian Newcomer, third bishop of the United Brethren in Christ, is filled with references to frequent celebrations of Holy Communion. He rejoiced in the "sacramental festivals" that he led and in which he participated.

Recent theology and practice of worship stress both the proclamation of the gospel enacted through Holy Communion and the sacramental power of Christ's presence through preaching. Partaking of Holy Communion is a response to and continued participation in the Word that has been proclaimed. Those seeking to live as Christian disciples have constant need of the nourishment and sustenance made available through both the Word and the sacrament of Holy Communion.

Practice:

Congregations of The United Methodist Church are encouraged to move toward a richer sacramental life, including weekly celebration of the Lord's Supper at the services on the Lord's Day, as advocated by the general orders of Sunday worship in *The United Methodist Hymnal* and *The United Methodist Book of Worship*. The sacrament can also be celebrated appropriately on other occasions in the life of the church from the congregational to the denominational level. However, occasions of worship that might not always include Communion are revivals, services of daily praise and prayer, love feasts, and services on days other than Sunday.

Attention should be given to the special needs of churches whose pastoral leadership is neither ordained nor licensed. Cooperative parishes and ecumenical shared ministries (*BOD*; ¶¶ 206.2 and 207) may offer patterns through which such congregations could receive regular sacramental ministry.

The Gathered Community

The Whole Assembly

Principle:

The whole assembly actively celebrates Holy Communion. All who are baptized into the body of Christ Jesus become servants and ministers within that body, which is the church. The members are claimed by God as a royal priesthood, God's own people (1 Peter 2:9). The one body, drawn together by the one Spirit, is fully realized when all its many parts eat together in love and offer their lives in service at the Table of the Lord.

Background:

Those baptized are called "Christ's royal priesthood" in the United Methodist services of the Baptismal Covenant ("The Baptismal Covenant I," *BOW;* page 92). We are "royal" because we belong to Christ, the sovereign. As priests, each of us can have access to God without any human intermediary. This priesthood means, especially, that we are to be priests to each other as together we seek to live as Christians. The exchange of words of forgiveness between pastor and congregation is an example in the ritual of this role (*UMH;* page 8).

All Christians share in the ministry of the church. Our diverse abilities and callings are gifts from God that together form the unity of the body of Christ and carry out its mission (Romans 12:3-8; 1 Corinthians 12:4-30; Ephesians 4:1-16). There is no more powerful expression of this reality than the participation of the whole gathered community in the celebration of Eucharist.

Practice:

All in the congregation are participants in the ministry of offering praise and worship to God and in the servant work of mutual ministry. The terms *presiding minister* and *assisting minister* describe the work of those who lead and assist the congregation.

The Prayer of Great Thanksgiving

Principle:

The prayer of Great Thanksgiving is addressed to God, is prayed by the whole people, and is led by the presiding minister. The prayer is shaped by our Trinitarian understanding of the nature of God. It includes an introductory dialogue, thankful remembrance of God's mighty acts of creation and the salvation made possible through Jesus Christ, the institution of the Lord's Supper, invoking of the present work of the Holy Spirit, and concluding praise to the Trinity. The prayer recognizes the fullness of God's triune nature, expresses the offering of ourselves in response, and looks toward the joy of sharing in God's eventual victory over sin and death.

Background:

The Trinitarian structure is evident in the Great Thanksgiving in the Word and Table services of *The United Methodist Hymnal* (pages 6-16). Following the introductory exchange between presiding minister and people in the Great Thanksgiving, prayer is addressed to "Father [God] Almighty, creator of heaven and earth." Following the Sanctus ("Holy, holy, holy . . ."), the work of the second person of the Trinity is proclaimed: ". . . and blessed is your Son [Child] Jesus Christ." The presence and work of the Holy Spirit are invoked in the portion beginning "Pour out your Holy Spirit on us gathered here and on these gifts . . . ," words historically known as the *epiclesis*. Throughout the Great Thanksgiving the congregation prays actively but silently and speaks its responses aloud at designated points in the service.

In their *Hymns on the Lord's Supper*, John and Charles Wesley make clear that divine presence and power come into the Eucharistic experience through the action of the Holy Spirit. Hymn 72 in that collection is a good example:

Come, Holy Ghost, Thine influence shed,
And realize [make real] the sign;
Thy life infuse into the bread,
Thy power into the wine.
Effectual let the tokens prove,
And made, by heavenly art,
Fit channels to convey Thy love
To every faithful heart.

Biblical worship was expressed in gestures and bodily movements, including bowing (Micah 6:6), lifting the cup of salvation (Psalm 116:13), lifting hands (Psalm 141:2), clapping (Psalm 47:1), and dancing (Psalm 149:3). The Gospels tell of Jesus' characteristic actions at meals that include taking bread, blessing or giving thanks, breaking the bread, and giving the bread. In Luke, the disciples who walked with Jesus on the way to Emmaus without recognizing him had their eyes opened "when he was at the table with them" and "he took bread, blessed and broke it, and gave it to them" (Luke 24:30).

Practice:

The prayer of Great Thanksgiving includes the voices of both the presiding minister and the people. The congregation's responses, which may be spoken or sung, include adoration, acclamation, and affirmation.

The whole assembly might join in parts of the Great Thanksgiving that speak for them: (a) the memorial acclamation, beginning, "And so, in remembrance . . ."; (b) an expression of intention to serve the world, beginning, "Make them be for us . . ."; (c) the concluding doxology, beginning, "Through your Son Jesus Christ. . . ." Congregational responses of "Amen" are the affirmation by the people of what has been prayed.

Presiding at Holy Communion involves bodily action as well as verbal communication. Gestures evoke and lead physical and visual participation by the congregation and aid worshipers in recognizing that the action at the Lord's Table is more than reading a script. For the presiding ministers, such gestures may include making welcoming gestures with arms or hands during the Invitation, raising arms or hands to God in praise or supplication, opening arms and hands to indicate including the entire body of Christ, and holding arms and hands over the elements as blessing.

Different postures are appropriate at different points in the ritual. The presiding minister and those in the whole assembly who are physically able appropriately stand throughout the Great Thanksgiving (*BOW*; page 28). Those unable to stand might participate with other gestures of praise as they desire. Standing communicates an attitude of respect and reverence; kneeling and bowing signify humility and confession; hands raised and open express praise and receptivity. The sign of the cross affirms our baptismal identity and the centrality of the cross to our faith. The ancient biblical use of hands and arms in expressing prayer and thanksgiving to God (arms uplifted, called *orans*; see 1 Timothy 2:8) and other gestures are recommended in *The United Methodist Book of Worship*, pages 36-39 and 46-79.

The Community Extends Itself

Principle:

The Communion elements are consecrated and consumed in the context of the gathered congregation. The Table may be extended, in a timely manner, to include those unable to attend because of age, illness, or similar conditions. Laypeople may distribute the consecrated elements in the congregation and extend them to members who are unavoidably absent (*BOD*; ¶¶ 340.2.a and 1117.9). An elder or deacon should offer appropriate training, preparation, and supervision for this important task (¶ 340.2.a).

Background:

In his description of worship practices of the early church, second-century writer Justin Martyr noted that consecrated bread and wine were carried to Christians who were unable to attend the service (*First Apology*; 67).

"Since the earliest Christian times, communion has been brought as an extension of the congregation's worship to sick or homebound persons unable to attend congregational worship" (*BOW*; page 51).

Practice:

When Holy Communion is extended to those unable to attend, the liturgy should include the reading of the Scripture Lesson(s), the Invitation, Confession and Pardon, the Peace, the Lord's Prayer, distribution, and post-Communion prayer. Elders, deacons, and laity may use this liturgy. A prayer of Great Thanksgiving should not be repeated, since this service is an extension of the Communion service held earlier (*BOW*; page 51).

If Holy Communion is to be celebrated with people who are homebound on a day when the congregation has not gathered at Table, "A Service of Word and Table V" (*BOW*; pages 51-53), which includes the Great Thanksgiving, should be used by an elder or another who is authorized to preside.

The Lord's Supper is to be made available to people who are in hospitals and hospices; nursing, convalescent, and rehabilitation facilities; correctional and custodial institutions; or other situations that make it impossible for them to gather with the community of faith. If a person is unable to eat or drink, one or both of the elements may be touched to his or her lips.

Both "self-service" Communion, where people help themselves, and "drop-in" Communion, where the elements are available over a period of time, are contrary to the communal nature of the sacrament, which is the celebration of the gathered community of faith.

The Ritual of the Church

Principle:

As stewards of the gifts given by God to the church, pastors have a responsibility to uphold and use the texts for Word and Table of The United Methodist Church found in *The United Methodist Hymnal; Mil Voces Para Celebrar: Himnario Metodista; Come, Let Us Worship: The Korean-English United Methodist Hymnal; The United Methodist Book of Worship;* and other liturgical material approved by central conferences in accordance with the *Book of Discipline,* ¶ 544.13. These liturgies, arising from biblical, historical, and ecumenical sources, are expressions of the Christian faith and the worship of God.

Background:

Article XXII of The Articles of Religion of The Methodist Church affirms some diversity of "rites and ceremonies" but rebukes "whosoever, through his private judgment, willingly and purposely doth openly break the rites and ceremonies of the church" (*BOD;* page 65).

The *Book of Discipline* specifies in ¶ 1114.3 that "the ritual of the Church is that contained in *The United Methodist Hymnal* (1989), *The United Methodist Book of Worship* (1992), *Mil Voces Para Celebrar: Himnario Metodista* (1996), and *Come, Let Us Worship: The Korean-English United Methodist Hymnal* (2000)."

In the Order for the Ordination of Elders, candidates promise to "be loyal to The United Methodist Church, accepting its order, liturgy, doctrine, and discipline" (*BOW;* page 676).

The preface to "An Order of Sunday Worship Using the Basic Pattern" in *The United Methodist Book of Worship* (page 16) states,

While the freedom and diversity of United Methodist worship are greater than can be represented by any single order of worship, United Methodists also affirm a heritage of order and the importance of the specific guidance and modeling that an order of worship provides. . . . Acts of worship that reflect racial, ethnic, regional, and local customs and heritages may be used appropriately throughout this order.

The ritual officially approved by The United Methodist Church represents the decisions of the church about the theology and practice of Holy Communion. This ritual expresses the unity of the universal church of Jesus Christ and exemplifies our connection within The United Methodist Church. It had its origin in the early Christian community and has evolved in the practice of the church through the centuries. Our ritual is in accord with those currently used in most Christian bodies.

At its best, United Methodist liturgy combines the order and beauty of established ritual with the vitality and freshness of creative expression. The richness of tradition developed through two thousand years of Christian history can be faithfully adapted for present times and situations.

Practice:

Bishops, pastors, and congregations are expected to use the services of Word and Table in the official United Methodist hymnals and books of worship. Knowledgeable use of these resources allows for a balance of flexibility to meet contextual needs and order that reflects our unity and connectional accountability.

"An Order of Sunday Worship Using the Basic Pattern" (*UMH*; pages 3-5) offers flexibility for response to the activity of the Holy Spirit as well as the specifics of events and settings. In attending to the season, day, or occasion, presiders may insert words of their own composition or selections taken from fuller ritual texts as indicated in "A Service of Word and Table II" and "A Service of Word and Table III." (See *UMH*, "A Service of Word and Table II," pages 12-15; "A Service of Word and Table III," pages 15-16; musical settings, pages 17-25.) Pastors using *Mil Voces Para Celebrar* or *Come, Let Us Worship* may apply these directions to the use of the respective rituals in those books. Material from different regions and cultures may also enrich our celebrations.

Pastors and congregations in ecumenical shared-ministry settings will necessarily need to incorporate and use the rituals of the denominations comprising those parishes in ways that are responsible and respectful, both of United Methodist understandings and practices and of those of the other traditions represented.

In accord with our commitments to the pursuit of Christian unity and seeking shared Communion, bishops, pastors, and congregations are encouraged to use the Word and Table ritual from other denominations. Such use is to be compatible with our Basic Pattern of Worship and with United Methodist liturgical and theological commitments.

Servants at the Table

Presiding Ministers: Elders and Licensed Local Pastors

Principle:

An ordained elder or a person authorized under the provisions of the *Book of Discipline* presides at all celebrations of Holy Communion.

Background:

In accord with the practice of the church throughout Christian history, God calls and the church sets apart certain people for leadership within the body of Christians. We believe that the Holy Spirit gives to such people the grace and gifts they need for leadership in obedience to their call. The meaning and purpose of ordination are described in ¶¶ 301-303 in the *Book of Discipline*.

Elders are ordained to a lifetime ministry of service, word, sacrament, and order (*BOD*; ¶ 332) and charged to "administer the sacraments of baptism and the Lord's Supper and all the other means of grace" (*BOD*; ¶ 340.2.a).

John Wesley drew a sharp distinction between the preaching ministry, which was open to lay men and women, and the priestly ministry of administering the sacraments, which was to be exercised only by those ordained as elders. Recounting the 1744 preachers' conference, Wesley wrote, "None of them dreamed, that the being called to preach gave them any right to administer sacraments. . . . 'You are to do that part of the work which we appoint.' But what work was this? Did we ever appoint you to administer sacraments; to exercise the priestly office? Such a design never entered into our mind; it was the farthest from our thoughts" ("The Ministerial Office"). Wesley insisted that there could be no sacramental ministry without ordination as elder. This conviction ultimately determined his decision to perform "extraordinary" ordinations himself.

"The authority of the ordained minister," according to *Baptism, Eucharist, and Ministry* (World Council of Churches, 1982), "is rooted in Jesus Christ who has received it from the Father (Matt. 28:18), and who confers it by the Holy Spirit through the act of ordination. This act takes place within a community which accords public recognition to a particular person" (page 22). Elders administer the sacraments as authorized representatives of the church.

Under the terms of the *Book of Discipline*, several groups of people are authorized to preside at Eucharist in the charges to which they are appointed. These include associate member deacons, deacons ordained under the provisions of the 1992 *Book of Discipline*, licensed local pastors, and commissioned ministers licensed for pastoral ministry (*BOD*; ¶¶ 315, 316, 339, 340). Some of these provisions have been in effect since 1976 in order to enable the sacraments to be served regularly in many small congregations that do not have elders as their pastors. The church continues to seek the best ways to meet this need and still uphold the historic linkage of ordination and administration of the sacraments.

Practice:

Bishops and district superintendents are elders who are assigned and appointed to exercise the ministry of superintending (*BOD*; ¶¶ 403 and 404) as an expression of the connectional nature of The United Methodist Church. To embody the connectional nature of the church and its sacramental life, a bishop or district superintendent who is present may be invited to preside at Holy Communion.

An elder or a person authorized under the provisions of the *Book of Discipline* presides at all celebrations of Holy Communion. While some portions of the order of worship may be led by others, an elder or authorized pastor leads the congregation in praying the Great Thanksgiving, in which the whole assembly takes an active role. (*See* the Sanctus, the memorial acclamation, and the Amen, all printed in bold type, in *UMH*, pages 9-10.)

Elders who are in extension ministries and retired elders may be asked to preside when they are needed in local churches or on other sacramental occasions. "All conference members who are elders in full connection, including those in extension ministries, shall be available and on call to administer the sacraments of baptism and the Lord's Supper as required by the *Discipline* (¶ 340.2.a) and requested by the district superintendent of the district in which the appointment is held" (*BOD*; ¶ 344.3.a). Those in the Order of Elders are encouraged to make every effort to be available for presiding when Holy Communion is needed or desired.

All elders or deacons who are present may be invited to participate in leadership of the service, stand with the presider at the table, and assist in distributing the elements.

All who lead Holy Communion should be knowledgeable and prepared in Eucharistic theology, spirituality, and practice, including the roles of those assisting. This ministry is under the supervision of district superintendents and pastoral mentors (*BOD*; ¶ 316.4).

Assisting Ministers: Deacons and Laity

Principle:

Deacons are ordained to the ministry of word and service (*BOD*; ¶ 329) and charged to "give leadership in the Church's life" in, among other ways, "assisting the elders in the administration of the sacraments" and "in the congregation's mission to the world" (¶ 328).

Background:

"Within the church community, there are persons whose gifts, evidence of God's grace, and promise of future usefulness are affirmed by the community, and who respond to God's call by offering themselves in leadership as ordained ministers" (*BOD*; ¶ 301.2). Deacons, as well as elders, are ordained to the ministry of leadership in The United Methodist Church.

This ordination of a deacon is to a life of linking the church's worship to Christ's service in the world. In worship it is appropriate for deacons to lead, or recruit and support others to lead, those parts of the liturgy that manifest the connection between our worship and Christian witness in daily life.

Practice:

In continuity with historic and ecumenical practice (*Baptism, Eucharist, and Ministry*), the role of deacon in services of Word and

Table appropriately includes reading the Gospel lesson; leading the concerns and prayers for the world, the church, and the needy; receiving the elements and preparing the table before the Great Thanksgiving; assisting the elder in serving the Communion elements; setting the table in order; and dismissing the people to serve before the elder offers God's blessing. Further, deacons have a significant role in preparing for the service by organizing, assembling the necessary elements and containers, and making assignments for other participants, including those taking the meal to those unable to attend. Deacons are designated to serve as links between the church and the world. Their ministry appropriately includes taking the consecrated elements from their congregations and serving them in their places of ministry.

Deacons need training and preparation for their diverse roles in Eucharistic ministry.

Principle:

All members of Christ's universal church are, through their baptism, called to share in the Eucharistic ministry that is committed to the whole church (*BOD;* ¶ 220). Lay people assist the presider in leading the whole congregation to celebrate the Lord's Supper.

Background:

In the section titled "The Ministry of All Christians," *The Book of Discipline* says, "All Christians are called through their baptism to this ministry of servanthood in the world to the glory of God and for human fulfillment" (¶ 125).

In depicting the church as a body of many parts, Paul declares in 1 Corinthians 12:7: "To each is given the manifestation of the Spirit for the common good." This diversity of ministry requires cooperation within the body of Christ, since it is only through such cooperation that the body is complete (1 Corinthians 12:12-31). It is important for liturgical celebrations to embody the active participation of all those gathered, as a demonstration of the full ministry of the body of Christ in the world.

As each layperson fulfills his or her vital ministry in worship, some will be called to exercise various leadership roles. "The United Methodist tradition has recognized that laypersons as well as ordained persons are gifted and called by God to lead the Church. The servant leadership of these persons is essential to the mission and ministry of congregations" (¶ 132). The whole of Part III of the *Book of Discipline* elaborates on this idea.

Practice:

Pastors and other leaders facilitate the full and active engagement of the ministry of all laity in celebrations of Holy Communion. As part of this general liturgical ministry of all Christians, laypeople exercise leadership of worship by reading Scripture, leading prayers, preparing the table, providing and preparing the elements, distributing the elements, and helping with other parts of the service.

At the appropriate point in the service, laity representing the whole congregation may bring the elements forward to the Table as a part of the offering. The entire congregation responds in unison as indicated throughout the ritual. Laypeople may take the consecrated elements to members who are unable to attend the congregational celebration.

Laypeople need instruction and training for this leadership, under the supervision of pastors and deacons.

Setting the Table

The Holy Communion Table

Principle:

The people and leaders gather around the elements for Holy Communion. The place where the elements are set is the Holy Communion table.

Background:

In the Old Testament, sacrifice was offered on an altar. In the Gospel narratives of the Last Supper, Jesus "took his place at the table, and the apostles with him" (Luke 22:14). Through time, the church increasingly understood the Eucharist as a repetition of Christ's sacrifice on the cross, and the Table came to be seen as an altar of sacrifice. It was moved against the wall of the sanctuary and priests stood before the altar, with their backs to the congregation, to offer sacrifice to God.

The more radical Protestant reformers abandoned altars, preferring simple tables and reenactment of the Last Supper of Jesus with his disciples. Others, including the Church of England, of which John Wesley was a priest, retained the altar against a wall.

A twentieth-century international liturgical renewal movement, expressed in the changes of the Second Vatican Council of the Roman Catholic Church, made major reforms in worship. These reforms included moving the table into an open space so that the priest could stand behind it, giving the assembly a sense of meeting around it. The United Methodist Church, along with many other mainline churches, adopted revised rituals that call for the presiding minister to stand behind the Lord's Table, facing the people, from the offertory through the breaking of the bread (*BOW*; page 36).

In a church building, the place where the elements are set is sometimes called the altar, but the terms *altar-table* and *Lord's Table* are preferable.

The rail that in some churches is located between the congregation and the chancel area, while not properly called the altar, is a sacred area for kneeling to receive Communion. People may also come to one or more stations where the elements are served and receive them standing, with an option of kneeling at the rail for prayer.

Practice:

In our churches, the Communion table is to be placed in such a way that the presider is able to stand behind it, facing the people, and the people can visually if not physically gather around it. The table should be high enough so that the presider does not need to stoop to handle the bread and cup. Adaptations may be necessary to facilitate gracious leadership.

While architectural integrity should be respected, it is important for churches to carefully adapt or renovate their worship spaces more fully to invite the people to participate in the Holy Meal. If "altars" are for all practical purposes immovable, then congregations should make provisions for creating a table suitable to the space so that the presiding minister may face the people and be closer to them.

The Communion Elements

Principle:

In accordance with the words of Christ and Christian tradition, the church uses bread in celebrations of Holy Communion.

Background:

Bread is used in both the Old and New Testaments to signify God's sustenance of human beings and the importance of our eating together. When God liberated the Hebrew people from slavery in Egypt, they carried their bread with them. The Jews have celebrated this exodus throughout the centuries as Passover. The provision of manna and the showbread (bread of the Presence) kept in the Tabernacle are examples of God's sustenance from the time of Israel's wandering in the wilderness (Exodus 16; 25:23-30). In the New Testament, Jesus shared meals frequently with his disciples and with others (Matthew 9:9-11 and similar passages). He fed the multitudes (Matthew 14:13-21 and parallels) and used bread to signify his identity and mission (John 6). On the eve of his crucifixion, Jesus ate the Last Supper with his disciples (Matthew 26:26-29 and parallels). After his resurrection, he broke bread with the travelers to Emmaus (Luke 24:13-35) and with his disciples on the seashore (John 21:9-14).

Practice:

It is appropriate that the bread eaten in Holy Communion both look and taste like bread. The use of a whole loaf best signifies the unity of the church as the body of Christ and, when it is broken and shared, our fellowship in that body (1 Corinthians 10:16-17).

Historical continuity with the practice of the universal church is important; however, worship planners should be sensitive to local situations. Bread may be made from any grain according to availability. In ecumenical and other settings, wafers may be an appropriate choice.

The loaf should be plain bread (no frostings, nuts, raisins, artificial coloring, or other additions). Leavened or unleavened bread is equally acceptable. In congregations where there are people with gluten allergies, gluten-free bread may be offered. The loaf broken at the table is to be the bread distributed to the people. As appropriate to the dignity of the occasion, care should be taken to avoid excessive crumbling of the bread and to remove large pieces that fall to the floor.

Principle:

In accordance with Scripture and Christian tradition, the historic and ecumenical church uses wine in celebrations of Holy Communion.

Background:

Throughout the Old Testament story of God's relationship with the Hebrew people, blood was the sign of covenant ratification (Exodus 12:12-28; 24:1-8). At his last meal with the disciples, Jesus spoke of the wine as his blood—the blood of the new covenant (Jeremiah 31:31-34) between God and God's people, made possible through Christ's death and resurrection (Revelation 5:9). Jesus also spoke of the wine as a sign of the heavenly banquet that he will celebrate with the church in the future (1 Corinthians 11:23-26; Matthew 26:26-29).

The juice of the red grape in a common cup represents the church's covenant with Christ, established through his atoning death (Hebrews 9:15-28; 13:20-21), and fulfills Christ's commands at the Last Supper (Matthew 26:27-29; Mark 14:23-24; Luke 22:19-20).

Roman Catholicism, Eastern Orthodoxy, and many Protestant denominations have always used wine in the Eucharist. During the movement against beverage alcohol in the late nineteenth century, the predecessor bodies of The United Methodist Church turned to the use of unfermented grape juice. This continues to be the position of the denomination (*BOR*; page 838). (The term *wine* is used in this document because of its biblical and historical antecedents, although United Methodists customarily serve unfermented grape juice in Holy Communion.)

The use of a common cup dates back to the Last Supper where Jesus takes a single cup of wine, blesses it, and gives it to the disciples. It is a powerful symbol of the unity of the body of Christ gathered at the Lord's Table.

Practice:

Variations may be necessary in cultural contexts where the juice of the grape is unavailable or prohibitively expensive.

A single cup or chalice may be used for intinction—dipping the bread into the wine—or for drinking. The use of a common chalice best represents Christian unity, but individual cups are used in many congregations. In these situations, unity can be effectively symbolized if each person's cup is filled from a pouring chalice.

Principle:

The consecrated elements are to be treated with reverent respect and appreciation as gifts of God's creation that have, in the words of the Great Thanksgiving, become "for us the body and blood of Christ" (*UMH*; page 10).

Background:

We do not worship the consecrated elements nor reserve them for adoration. We respect the elements because God is using them for holy purposes—reconstituting the assembly as the body of Christ, conveying grace, forgiving sin, foreshadowing heaven, and strengthening the faithful for the journey of salvation. Although they have undergone no substantive (physical) change, the elements have been consecrated—set apart for sacred use.

While, in the history of the church, reverence for the consecrated elements has sometimes led to superstition, proper respect for the elements helps Christians grow in authentic sacramental piety.

As Article XVIII of The Articles of Religion of the Methodist Church makes clear, United Methodism rejects any suggestion that the bread and wine used in Communion are transformed or transubstantiated into other substances:

"Transubstantiation, or the change of the substance of bread and wine in the Supper of our Lord, cannot be proved by Holy Writ, but is repugnant to the plain words of Scripture, overthroweth the nature of a sacrament, and hath given occasion to many superstitions. The body of Christ is given, taken, and eaten in the Supper, only after a heavenly and spiritual manner. And the mean whereby the body of Christ is received and eaten in the Supper is faith" (*BOD*; page 64).

(The United Methodist Church notes that the anti-Roman Catholic tone of Article XVIII reflects the "bitterly polemical" relationships of past centuries and "rejoice[s] in the positive contemporary relationships that are being developed . . . at levels both official and unofficial" [*BOR*; pages 272-273].)

The Book of Worship directs, "What is done with the remaining bread and wine should express our stewardship of God's gifts and our respect for the holy purpose they have served" (page 30).

Practice:

The practice of consecrating elements ahead of time for the convenience of the pastor not having to go to small or remote congregations, weekend camps, or other such occasions is inappropriate and contrary to our historic doctrine and understanding of how God's grace is made available in the sacrament (Article XVIII, The Articles of Religion, *BOD*; page 64). If authorized leadership is not available for celebrating the Lord's Supper, other worship services such as love feasts, agape meals, or baptismal reaffirmations are valid alternatives that avoid the misuse of Communion elements.

The consecrated elements of bread and wine are used for distribution to the sick and others who wish to commune but are unable to attend congregational worship. If any bread and wine remain, they should always be disposed of by (1) the pastor and/or others at the pastor's direction consuming them in a reverent manner following the service; (2) returning them to the earth by pouring (2 Samuel 23:16), burying, scattering, or burning.

Hygiene and Table Setting

Principle:

Those who prepare the elements and give them to the people are to demonstrate care that the bread and cup are administered so as to minimize contamination.

Background:

In administering the elements to the people, both perception and reality of hygiene are important. The people have justifiable health concerns that the signs of the body and blood of Christ given to them at the Holy Meal are handled carefully and with concern for hygiene.

This need for care and hygiene should be considered along with scientific studies that make it clear that those who partake in Holy Communion have no higher incidence of illness than those who do not.

Concern and planning are necessary in situations of serious illness and for accommodating at the Table those whose immune systems are compromised. The counsel of Romans 14 and 15 can guide our practice.

Practice:

Those who will prepare and serve the elements should wash their hands. This can be done simply and without creating an additional layer of ceremony in the service.

The piece of bread given should be sizeable enough to be a generous sign and to be able to be dipped in the cup without the fingers of the recipient dipping into the liquid.

Extending the Table
Holy Communion and Evangelism

Principle:

The Lord's Supper forms the church into a community of evangelism that reaches out to preach, teach, baptize, and make new disciples of Christ (Matthew 28:19-20).

Background:

Immediately after his account of the institution of the Lord's Supper in 1 Corinthians 11-12, Paul moves into an extended discussion of the body of Christ composed of many members whose gifts for ministry are diverse. Paul understood the sacrament of Holy Communion to form and shape the church for its mission of redeeming the world. In 2 Corinthians 5:16-6:10, he describes more fully "the ministry of reconciliation" that is the work of the church as "ambassadors for Christ."

United Methodists have inherited a tradition that emphasizes that spiritual benefits are not received for ourselves alone but also to prepare and propel us for the work of evangelism. In our prayer after Communion, we give thanks for what we have received and ask God to "grant that we may go into the world in the strength of your Spirit, to give ourselves for others" (*UMH*; page 11).

The Book of Discipline emphasizes the imperative of evangelism: "The people of God, who are the church made visible in the world, must convince the world of the reality of the gospel or leave it unconvinced. There can be no evasion or delegation of this responsibility; the church is either faithful as a witnessing and serving community, or it loses its vitality and its impact on an unbelieving world" (¶ 128).

Practice:

Through the grace received in continual participation in the Lord's Supper, the community of faith reaches beyond itself to proclaim and exemplify the good news of salvation in Jesus Christ.

In Christian education and congregational life, we teach about the significance and meaning of the sacraments so that the faithful appreciate their own spiritual journey and are empowered to be knowledgeable and hospitable guides to those who seek Christ.

As members of the congregation partake of the Lord's Supper, the bonds of love within are strengthened and the worshiping community is empowered to reach out in dynamic and meaningful ways to evangelize and to work for peace and justice.

Principle:

As followers of Jesus, who ate with sinners and reached out to the marginalized, the church must intentionally concern itself about those who are absent from Christ's Table—those who feel unworthy, the poor, the unconverted, victims of prejudice, and others who are oppressed or neglected.

Background:

One of the themes of the Gospels, most prominent in Luke, is Jesus' ongoing efforts to teach the disciples that God's love and favor are extended to all people, not just those of a certain ethnicity, status, economic or political standing, or gender. The Book of Acts records some of the attempts of the early Christian community to define its limits, and God's continued efforts to broaden its inclusiveness. Peter's vision in Acts 10 is a particularly dramatic example.

Early English Methodists were typically (with some notable exceptions) from the socio-economic groups that we might today speak of as the working poor. Wesley realized that a community of people who lived according to his General Rules (*BOD*; pages 71-74) were inevitably going to rise in status. He preached fervently against the dangers of money and the spiritual weakness that often accompanies prosperity.

In "The Ministry of All Christians," *The Book of Discipline* asserts: "We are called to be faithful to the example of Jesus' ministry to all persons. Inclusiveness means openness, acceptance, and support that enables all persons to participate in the life of the Church, the community, and the world. Thus, inclusiveness denies every semblance of discrimination" (¶ 138).

Practice:

The church is to consciously identify and seek out those who feel unwelcome, even excluded, from its congregations and to invite them to become part of the body of Christ and join in its celebrations of Holy Communion.

Holy Communion and Ethical Christian Discipleship

Principle:

The sacraments are God's gifts to the gathered body of believers to form the church into Christ's body in ministry to the world. Through Holy Communion, the Holy Spirit works to shape our moral and ethical lives. In the ongoing process of conversion, we grow in personal and social holiness and are empowered to work for healing, compassion, reconciliation, justice, and peace.

Background:

The Old Testament prophets denounced the injustice and oppression that they saw around them. They proclaimed a God who acts in favor of the poor and powerless and calls God's people so to act. (Isaiah 1:16-17; 58:6-9; Amos 2:6-8; 5:11-15, 21-24; and Micah 6:6-8 are among a multitude of such passages.) When Jesus began his public ministry, he announced his mission: "The Spirit of the Lord is upon me, because he has anointed me to bring good news to the poor. He has sent me to proclaim release to the captives and recovery of sight to the blind, to let the oppressed go free, to proclaim the year of the Lord's favor" (Luke 4:16-21). He associated with those who were stigmatized and despised. Much of his teaching addressed economic and social inequality. Following his example, the early Christian community tried to care for the needs of all people (Acts 4:32-35; James 1:27; 2:14-17).

The United Methodist Church has a heritage from John Wesley in which ethical discipleship was inextricably related to sacramental worship. From concern by the Holy Club for the imprisoned, through care of the sick by the societies, to Wesley's own lifelong giving away of most of his money, the early Wesleyan movement sought to ease the suffering of the needy. Wesley made the linkage explicit when he wrote, "The Gospel of Christ knows no religion but social, no holiness, but social holiness" (Preface to *Hymns and Sacred Poems*). Collection at the Lord's Supper of alms to be given to the poor is a historic practice that many congregations in our tradition continue.

By the early twentieth century, Methodists had begun to realize that holy living meant even more than acts of charity. Beginning with the Social Creed, American Methodists started to point out injustices caused by economic, social, and political structures and to call for the reform of such structures. The Social Principles in *The Book of Discipline* and the General Conference positions recorded in *The Book of Resolutions* show ongoing response to these concerns.

In carrying out our mission to make disciples of Jesus Christ, *The Book of Discipline* stipulates that the church is to "send persons into the world to live lovingly and justly as servants of Christ by healing the sick, feeding the hungry, caring for the stranger, freeing the oppressed, being and becoming a compassionate, caring presence, and working to develop social structures that are consistent with the gospel" (¶ 122).

Those who partake of Holy Communion are sent from the Table to be in ministry as Christ's presence in the world. God's people are sent to work compassionately for healing, reconciliation, justice, and peace. Such work requires prophetic, subversive actions: "renounc[ing] the spiritual forces of wickedness, reject[ing] the evil powers of this world, . . . accept[ing] the freedom and power God gives . . . to resist evil, injustice, and oppression in whatever forms they present themselves" (vows from the services of the Baptismal Covenant, *BOW*; for example page 88), claiming and making real the victory of the risen Christ over all evil, sin, and death. Such faithful living in the power of the Holy Spirit answers the prayer in the Great Thanksgiving "that we may be for the world the body of Christ" and the petition "your kingdom come, your will be done" in the Lord's Prayer (*UMH*; page 10). Celebrations of Holy Communion are, therefore, a foretaste of the realm of God, when God's future breaks into our present world. Here the church enacts the words of Jesus, "Then people will come from east and west, from north and south, and will eat in the kingdom of God" (Luke 13:29).

Practice:

Holy Communion is to be conducted in ways that make apparent the inherent link between the Table and holy living, both individual and corporate. Participation in the Eucharist bears fruit in the world in attitudes and actions of personal and social holiness.

Communing with others in our congregations is a sign of community and mutual love between Christians throughout the church universal. The church must offer to the world a model of genuine community grounded in God's deep love for every person. As we eat and drink, we are motivated to act compassionately for those whose physical, emotional, and spiritual needs are unmet.

Receiving the bread and wine as products of divine creation reminds us of our duties of stewardship of the natural environment in a time when destruction and pollution imperil the earth and unjust distribution of the planet's resources destroys the hopes and lives of millions.

As we gratefully receive God's abundant grace, we are challenged to accept fully our responsibility and accountability for renewal of the social order, liberation for the oppressed, and the coming of the realm of God.

Holy Communion and the Unity of the Church

Principle:

Holy Communion expresses our oneness in the body of Christ, anticipates Jesus' invitation to feast at the heavenly banquet, and calls us to strive for the visible unity of the church.

Background:

In its Constitution, The United Methodist Church affirms its ecumenical commitment: "As part of the church universal, The United Methodist Church believes that the Lord of the church is calling Christians everywhere to strive toward unity; and therefore it will seek, and work for, unity at all levels of church life" (*BOD*; ¶ 6).

In "Our Doctrinal Heritage" in the *Book of Discipline* (pages 41-43), the church affirms:

"United Methodists share a common heritage with Christians of every age and nation. This heritage is grounded in the apostolic witness to Jesus Christ as Savior and Lord, which is the source and measure of all valid Christian teaching. . . . With Christians of other communions we confess belief in the triune God—Father, Son, and Holy Spirit. This confession embraces the biblical witness to God's activity in creation, encompasses God's gracious self-involvement in the dramas of history, and anticipates the consummation of God's reign."

In the quest for greater visible unity, United Methodism has undertaken numerous concrete actions that express its commitment and promote ecumenical sharing:

1. Since the 1960's, the church has been involved with partners through Churches Uniting in Christ, formerly called the Consultation on Church Union. Throughout most of that history United Methodists have joined the partner churches in Holy Communion using liturgy approved by those churches for celebration together.

2. United Methodists across the world have entered into ecumenical agreements enhancing the unity of the church through recognition and reconciliation of ministries and sacraments.

3. Ecumenical representatives have been invited and encouraged to participate in United Methodist services of Holy Communion.

4. United Methodists have participated in the Eucharist services of other traditions when invited to do so, as an affirmation and reflection of our commitment to the church universal.

Baptism, Eucharist, and Ministry affirms the significance of the sacrament for all Christians:

It is in the eucharist that the community of God's people is fully manifested. Eucharistic celebrations always have to do with the whole Church, and the whole Church is involved in each local eucharistic celebration. In so far as a church claims to be a manifestation of the whole Church, it will take care to order its own life in ways which take seriously the interests and concerns of other churches (page 14).

For churches such as the Orthodox and Roman Catholic, sharing the Eucharist between churches that are not in full agreement with one another is unacceptable because the Eucharist is itself a sign that unity and full agreement have been achieved. For other churches, including The United Methodist Church, the Eucharist can be a means to express the unity in Christ that already exists as a gift from God in spite of our failure to manifest it.

Practice:

United Methodists are encouraged to continue participating in ecumenical services that include Holy Communion. Special care is to be given to the use of commonly approved texts or the development of liturgy that reflects the beliefs and practices of the different traditions. If bishops or superintendents are present, it is appropriate for them to be invited to preside.

Church members can practice hospitality by participating in each others' liturgies with attitudes of respect and openness to learning.

United Methodists are encouraged to receive Communion in other churches when they are invited to do so.

Churches need to address, within official dialogues, the theological barriers to full Eucharistic sharing. Materials already available from the official dialogues shall be part of the study resources of the denomination.

United Methodists need to study and work to answer questions that are critical to ecumenical conversation and sensitive to ecumenical concerns—the presence of Christ ("real presence"), frequency of celebration, who presides at the Table, use of grape juice, and baptism in relation to Eucharist, among others.

Principle:

United Methodists enter into the ecumenical conversation about Eucharist grounded in several historic sources of authority and relate most authentically to other Christian bodies as we remain faithful to these sources.

Background:

Most prominent among United Methodism's sources of authority are the Scriptures of the Old and New Testaments; the hymns and writings of John and Charles Wesley (especially the Standard Sermons, the General Rules, and *Explanatory Notes Upon the New Testament*); the Constitution, Articles of Religion, Confession of Faith, and other doctrinal standards; the writings and traditions emerging from the evangelical experience, through the Wesleyan, Evangelical, and United Brethren movements; and current ecumenical developments and statements that have had United Methodist involvement, especially multilateral and bilateral agreements, some of which have been approved by the World Methodist Council and/or the General Conference.

"Our Doctrinal Heritage" points out some distinctive aspects of the United Methodist tradition:

"Although Wesley shared with many other Christians a belief in grace, justification, assurance, and sanctification, he combined them in a powerful manner to create distinctive emphases for living the full Christian life. The Evangelical United Brethren tradition, particularly as expressed by Phillip William Otterbein from a Reformed background, gave similar distinctive emphases.

"Grace pervades our understanding of Christian faith and life. By grace we mean the undeserved, unmerited, and loving action of God in human existence through the ever-present Holy Spirit. While the grace of God is undivided, it precedes salvation as 'prevenient grace,' continues in 'justifying grace,' and is brought to fruition in 'sanctifying grace'" (*BOD*; pages 45-46).

These distinctive emphases of United Methodists provide the basis for "practical divinity," the experiential realization of the gospel of Jesus Christ in the lives of Christian people. These emphases have been preserved not so much through formal doctrinal declarations as through the vital movement of faith and practice as seen in converted lives and within the disciplined life of the Church.

Devising formal definitions of doctrine has been less pressing for United Methodists than summoning people to faith and nurturing them in the knowledge and love of God. The core of Wesleyan doctrine that informed our past rightly belongs to our common heritage as Christians and remains a prime component within our continuing theological task (*BOD*; pages 49-50).

The General Commission on Christian Unity and Interreligious Concerns spearheads the ecumenical work of the denomination by fulfilling its purpose: "To advocate and work toward the full reception of the gift of Christian unity in every aspect of the Church's life and to foster approaches to ministry and mission that more fully reflect the oneness of Christ's church in the human community" (*BOD*; ¶ 1902.1).

In "Resolution of Intent—With a View to Unity," the 2000 General Conference declared it "our official intent henceforth to interpret all our Articles, Confession, and other 'standards of doctrine' in consonance with our best ecumenical insights and judgment" (*BOR*; page 273).

Practice:

Within all discussions of Holy Communion, United Methodism must remain firmly anchored in its traditional sources of authority. We recognize and respect authorities that other church traditions hold dear. United Methodists remain open to greater Christian unity through the work of the Holy Spirit in response to Jesus' prayer that "they may all be one" (John 17:21).

Committee Members:

L. *Edward Phillips*, Chairperson
Daniel T. Benedict, Jr.
Michael J. Coyner
Jerome King Del Pino
Gayle Carlton Felton
Thelma H. Flores
Barbara Thorington Green
Karen A. Greenwaldt
Susan W. Hassinger
Sally Havens
Dong Hyun (David) Kim
Jon E. McCoy
Sophie Pieh
Arturo L. Razon, Jr.
Bruce W. Robbins
Frank E. Trotter, Jr.
Karen Westerfield Tucker
Hans Växby
Josiah U. Young, III

Notes About This Document

Scripture quotations, unless otherwise indicated, are from the *New Revised Standard Version* of the Bible, copyright © 1989 by the Division of Christian Education of the National Council of the Churches of Christ in the USA. All rights reserved. Used by permission.

BOD, Discipline, and *Book of Discipline* refer to *The Book of Discipline of The United Methodist Church 2004,* copyright © 2004 The United Methodist Publishing House.

UMH refers to *The United Methodist Hymnal,* copyright © 1989 The United Methodist Publishing House.

BOW refers to *The United Methodist Book of Worship,* copyright © 1992 The United Methodist Publishing House.

BOR refers to *The Book of Resolutions of The United Methodist Church 2004,* copyright © 2004 The United Methodist Publishing House.

Quotations from John Wesley are from the Jackson edition of *The Works of John Wesley.*

ADOPTED 2004

354. Seekers on the Internet

WHEREAS, there is a need for a "seeker's link" on the official United Methodist Web site,

Therefore, be it resolved, that a new web page on the General Board of Discipleship website, designed and monitored by the board, provide spiritual guidance for those seeking knowledge of and a relationship with, or belief in Jesus Christ, and that this guidance may include scriptural references, information concerning study guides and prayer resources, and a list of possible contacts in the home area of the seeker (e-mail, phone, etc.), and that this website be linked to The United Methodist Church website.

ADOPTED 2000

355. Church Participation by a Registered Child Sex Offender

The Social Principles of The United Methodist Church declare: "We recognize that family violence and abuse in all its forms—verbal, psychological, physical, sexual—is detrimental to the covenant of the human community. We encourage the Church to provide a safe environment, counsel, and support for the victim. While we deplore the actions of the abuser, we affirm that person to be in need of God's redeeming love."

Increasingly, churches are faced with a dilemma in their attempt to be faithful to both of the last two sentences above. Assuring the safety of children in our care, our facilities and our programs is a sacred duty. We must weigh that duty in the balance with what often seems the conflicting value of participation in the life of the church by a convicted child abuser. Being part of a worshiping community is not the only way for a person to experience God's redeeming love, but it is an important one.

Recent studies suggest a low likelihood that pedophiles can or will change. Without extensive professional treatment, virtually all child sexual offenders will re-offend. Repentance, prayer, and pastoral support, always in combination with lifelong professional treatment, can be crucial in helping to change behavior but, in themselves, offer slim hope of changing the behavior of perpetrators. Welcoming a child sex offender into a congregation must be accompanied by thorough knowledge, careful planning, and long-term monitoring.

A convicted and/or registered sex offender who wishes to be part of a church community should expect to have conditions placed on his or her participation. Indeed, offenders who have been in treatment and are truly committed to living a life free of further abuse will be the first to declare that, in order to accomplish that, they must structure a life that includes on-going treatment, accountability mechanisms, and lack of access to children.

The following steps should be taken in order to be faithful to the Social Principles' commitment both to safety from abuse and to ministry with abusers:

A. Local churches should:

- hold discussions in the church council and in adult education settings about the possibility of facing the situation of a convicted sex offender returning to or joining the church. These discussions should be held and general agreements reached about actions to be taken should the church find itself in this circumstance;
- develop a carefully constructed and openly negotiated covenant between the offender and the church community. The covenant should include agreements in the following areas: participation in a professional counseling program for at least the entire time of church membership or participation; adult "covenant partners" to accompany the offender while on church property or attending church activities; areas of church facilities that are "off limits;" restrictions on leadership in or on behalf of church; no role in church that includes contact with children or youth; any additional conditions for presence or participation; and
- assure that the covenant is maintained by having it written and signed by the offender, the pastor(s), and the chairperson of the church council. While confidentiality of victims should be respected, the covenant should not be secret. Monitoring of the covenant should be taken seriously as a permanent responsibility.

B. Annual conferences should:

- develop similar plans and covenant for situations in which a convicted and/or registered sexual offender is involved or seeks involvement in the conference, its activities or facilities;
- include information about this concern and assistance with implementation of this resolution in its training and resourcing of clergy and local church lay leaders;

C. *The General Board of Discipleship and the General Board of Global Ministries should:*

- cooperatively develop and promote a process and specific guidelines to assist congregations in the education and covenant tasks outlined above.

ADOPTED 2004

356. Service to Reaffirm Ordination Vows

WHEREAS, there is a need for worship resources for the reaffirmation of ordination vows, we therefore suggest that the General Board of Discipleship develop these resources.

ADOPTED 2000

357. Services for the Ordering of Ministry

WHEREAS, the 1996 General Conference adopted changes to the ordering of ministry that required adaptation of the church's official services for ordering ministry published in *The United Methodist Book of Worship* (1992); and

WHEREAS, the General Conference referred the work of revision to the General Board of Discipleship in consultation with the General Board of Higher Education and Ministry, and the Council of Bishops; and

WHEREAS, there continue to be a number of people who began the process toward consecration or ordination under the provisions of the 1992 *Discipline* and there are now many people in the process toward commissioning or ordination under the provisions of the 1996 *Discipline*,

Therefore, the 2000 General Conference adopts *Services for the Ordering of Ministry in The United Methodist Church* (Provisional Texts) as the approved provisional texts for use by the bishops and annual conferences during the 2001-2004 quadrennium and directs the General Board of Discipleship to further revise these services to conform to the 2000 legislation and to present them for adoption by the 2004 General Conference.

ADOPTED 2000

358. Adoption of Services for the Ordering of Ministry

WHEREAS, The United Methodist Church should reflect in the services of ordination the implementation of the ordering of ministry as reflected in *The Book of Discipline;* and

WHEREAS, the 2000 General Conference referred the work of revision of services for the ordering of ministry to the General Board of Discipleship in consultation with the General Board of Higher Education and Ministry and the Council of Bishops; and

WHEREAS, the provisions of the 1992 *Discipline* regarding the consecration of diaconal ministers and the ordination of those in the probationary relationship formally continue until 2008, whereupon further changes in the ritual for ordering ministry will be required;

Therefore, be it resolved, that the 2004 General Conference adopt *Services for the Ordering of Ministry in The United Methodist Church* as the approved texts for use by the bishops and annual conferences during the 2005-2008 quadrennium; and

Be it further resolved, that the 2004 General Conference direct the General Board of Discipleship in consultation with the General Board of Higher Education and Ministry and the Council of Bishops to further revise these services as needed to conform to the 2004 legislation and to present them for adoption by the 2008 General Conference.

ADOPTED 2004

359. Celebration of Full Clergy Rights for Women

WHEREAS, God has given women gifts and graces for ministry to witness faithfully to Jesus Christ; and

WHEREAS, The Church of the United Brethren in Christ gave full clergy rights to women in 1889; and

WHEREAS, in 1947 The Church of the United Brethren in Christ merged with The Evangelical Church to become The Evangelical United Brethren Church and ceased giving full clergy rights to women; and

WHEREAS, in 1956 the General Conference of The Methodist Church granted full clergy rights for women and 2006 will be the 50th anniversary of that event; and

WHEREAS, some women from The Central Jurisdiction of The Methodist Church were dissuaded from seeking full clergy rights; and

WHEREAS, in 1968 The Evangelical United Brethren Church and The Methodist Church, having abolished The Central Jurisdiction, merged to form The United Methodist Church; and

WHEREAS, there are now more than 10,000 clergywomen in The United Methodist Church; and

WHEREAS, the predecessor denominations of The United Methodist Church have a tradition of granting full clergy rights for women reaching back 117 years with 50 continuous years of full clergy rights for women;

Be it resolved, that in 2006 every annual conference of The United Methodist Church celebrate full clergy rights for women including a liturgical act during the conference session; and

Be it further resolved, that all conferences celebrate the anniversary by honoring the names of the conference's clergywomen, past and present; and

Finally, be it resolved, that in 2006 every local congregation observe the celebration of full clergy rights for women.

ADOPTED 2004

360. Celebrating Diversity Within the Global Methodist Family

WHEREAS, modern developments in transportation, communications, and technology have brought peoples and nations closer together; and

WHEREAS, globality tends to be understood in The United Methodist Church basically in terms of the United Methodist presence beyond the boundaries of the United States and almost exclusively in relation to those sections of the Church that are structurally within it; and

WHEREAS, there are a number of churches in the Methodist family that out of a sense of calling by the Holy Spirit, a desire to affirm their own identity, and their need for self-determination have elected to become autonomous;

Therefore, be it resolved, that The United Methodist Church:

1. celebrate the God-given diversity of race, culture, and people at every level of Church life in our worship and other activities;

2. celebrate the global dimension brought to The United Methodist Church by sisters and brothers from all over the globe and the Native American nations, who are a part of U.S. society and The United Methodist Church;

3. celebrate the affiliated autonomous Methodist churches and the Central Conferences of The United Methodist Church as important expressions of the diversity of cultures and peoples called by God to be the church universal;

4. work for a future where The United Methodist Church and the autonomous Methodist churches throughout the world, expressing their faith through their unique, God-given culture, will share resources, personnel, and perspectives as equals in their common task of evangelizing all the world;

5. continue and strengthen its ecumenical commitment; and

6. embody this vision as possible in all United Methodist programs.

ADOPTED 2004

361. Privatization

"The earth is the Lord's and everything in it" (1 Corinthians 10:26). The Lord's people have been given enough—an abundance of all of the things we need for life.

"We believe [that] governments have the responsibility, in the pursuit of justice and order under law, to provide procedures that protect the rights of the whole society as well as those of private ownership" (Social Principles, ¶ 163*A*).

One of our values as Christians is to provide an economy that serves God's vision of abundance to all. (Ecclesiastes 3:22 "So I saw that there is nothing better than that all should enjoy their work for that is their lot," Luke 10:7 and 1 Timothy 5:18 "the laborer deserves to be paid," Matthew 20:8 "Call the laborers and give them their pay.")

Jesus singled out the poor and the sick and imprisoned for special care and the special responsibility of the faithful. Under many privatization schemes, responsibility by the public has been abandoned to private enterprise. Our responsibility to the sick and poor and imprisoned has been left to the devices of private profit. Privatized prisons, nursing homes, hospitals, welfare programs and other social services have sometimes been less dedicated to service and rehabilitation than to cutting service and increasing profits (*Book of Resolutions* #206, Economic Justice for a New Millennium).

(Social Principles ¶ 162) "We support the basic rights of all persons to human services with oversight by the public. "

(Resolution #108) Correcting Injustices in Health Care "private health insurance in all its forms, continues to increase its premium cost while limiting care and /or increasing deductibles and co-payments for care." Just 20 years ago, only about 18 percent of HMOs (Health Maintenance Organizations) were for-profit. By 1995, the market share was 70 percent. HMOs charge up to 25 percent out of every premium dollar for CEO salaries, profits and bureaucracy; Medicare has administrative costs of only 1.2 percent.

(Resolution #9) "We are called to see that all life has a sufficient share of the resources of nature."

Introduction

Corporate interests are rushing to privatize many of the resources of the earth—water, energy, education, natural plants, human and animal genes, cultures and public services such as social security, health care and public safety. Everything from prescription drugs to prisons to welfare programs is considered fair game for corporate profit-making. Wall Street, according to the Economic Policy Institute, is fighting hard for a privatized Social Security system because it would reap an estimated $240 billion in fees for managing these funds during the first 12 years of such a system.

Private Control

Supporters of privatization accuse government of inefficiency and claim that, if allowed to make a profit, these same corporations could control resources more effectively and efficiently, saving public money and delivering services better. The expectation of privatization is that government would continue to collect taxes from the citizens and then provide that tax money to the corporate CEO's who would manage salaries, resources, and functions better. Those who favor privatization argue that they would earn a profit, benefit the economy, and be less encumbered by inefficient bureaucracy and public controls.

The World Bank is actively subsidizing the privatization of public resources worldwide. The World Trade Organization has been quietly re-negotiating and expanding the General Agreement on Trade in Services (GATS). The range of services on the negotiating table is vast, covering such vital areas as water and energy, banking, communications and retail services. Eighty additional countries have been targeted by the European Union for this invasion by foreign corporations. If governments refuse to cooperate, they may be faced with world trade disputes claiming "barriers to free trade."

Public Control

Opponents of privatization point to corporate abuses and criminality in the management of pensions, energy and communications systems.

Those who favor continued public control and regulation of these common resources and services argue that, when private forces take control, there is less accountability to the citizens. They claim that ever-growing profits are the primary interest of the corporations doing the privatizing. They also note that worker salaries and working conditions are usually forfeited in the name of efficiency and in order to increase private profits. Loss of well-paid public sector jobs is a burden to society in many ways, including reduced tax revenues and increasing the need for social welfare programs.

People worldwide are challenging the privatization of commonly held resources such as native seeds and plants under intellectual property rules established under international financial institutions such as the World Trade Organization. Many are calling for public control of resources such as the drugs necessary for stamping out the most devastating diseases of our world and the water that is essential to life on earth.

Discernment

There may be instances where privatization is appropriate. However, the role of Christians requires us to honor the earth's resources and to protect our God-given common heritage. The public must be vigilant to regulate and control any privatization of public resources.

New Laws to Protect Our Common Property

We have rules that protect our private property and our individual property. We also need strong, ethical governments and new laws to protect our common property—the common resources that belong to all of us and the common services that constitute the basis of universal human rights. Responsive governments must be strengthened and supported to provide protection for all, particularly in the most exploited and vulnerable nations and particularly in support of the elements that are necessary to the abundant life provided by God.

There are efforts by the international financial institutions to impose new rules that increase the private invasion of common property. The sovereignty of underdeveloped countries would be undermined by Rule 11 of NAFTA and other free trade agreements such as the proposed Free Trade Area of the Americas. These trade rules strengthen the ability of private interests to force local communities to allow their free trade operations and privatization of common resources without effective regulation. Under Rule 11, if the governments move to regulate the activities of the corporations on behalf of their own workers or their own environment, they face multi-million dollar penalties in private trade courts unattended and unregulated by the public. These rules, called "takings," are increasing the poverty and devastation of communities worldwide.

The Need for Effective Governments

Effective and democratic governments worldwide must be strengthened in order to function on behalf of the interest of their citizens. Our common resources do not belong to government or market, but responsible and effective government is essential for protecting those public properties. Privatization of common property rights should be viewed as a "form of taking" from the people. For decades a body of international rules has been developing led by corporations that would challenge the rights of governments to protect their workers and their natural resources from corporate exploitation.

Call to Action

The United Methodist Church and its predecessors have always had a history of public witness on matters of economic justice. Faced with protecting and securing the common resources and services needed by all humanity, the General Conference calls upon:

1. the General Board of Global Ministries to develop an educational program on the issues posed by privatization worldwide and join in challenging privatization where it endangers public interest;

2. the boards and agencies of The United Methodist Church to create and disseminate materials explaining proposed trade agreements and oppose them when they violate United Methodist ideals supporting a just economy;

3. the General Board of Global Ministries and the General Board of Church and Society to invigorate efforts to acquire national publicly-provided health care for everyone in the United States and that the issue of worldwide health care be put on the agenda for increased support;

4. members of The United Methodist Church to urge our governments to challenge and change the International Monetary Fund (IMF), World Bank and World Trade Organization rules supporting massive privatization;

5. the United Methodist Church to question the IMF investment of billions of public dollars into support for the efforts of private corporations to take over public services and public resources in poor countries;

6. the General Board of Global Ministries and the General Board of Church and Society study ways of supporting world trade rules that would protect our commons resources from the growing trend toward "takings" by private entrepreneurs;

7. the General Board of Global Ministries and the General Board of Church and Society to lead an effort to discern effects to society of privatization of services in the United States and globally and join in opposing detrimental privatization;

8. the General Board of Church and Society to provide studies and actions on the importance of responsible government and ways to enact good governance; and

9. United Methodists to study and act in support of our local governments by insisting that the Federal budget provide for adequate tax money for running public services and regulating private service initiatives for the benefit of all.

ADOPTED 2004

362. Proper Use of Information Communication Technologies

We affirm that the right to communicate and to access information is a basic human right, essential to human dignity and to a just and democratic society.

Our understanding of communication is grounded in Scripture. God is a communicating God.

Christians believe that the creation of the world is rooted in the spoken Word of God.

God made all persons in the divine image. God created the world and all living things for relationship.

The Bible is the inspired Word of God about communication and a God who created the world and all living things for relationship.

The biblical account of the tower of Babel presents a classic example of the integral relationship between communication and being human.

This theme repeats itself in the story of Pentecost, the birthplace of the church. Being filled with the Holy Spirit and in communion with God and one another, the people of God spoke and heard the divine message of God in their own languages. We acknowledge that every right brings with it responsibilities. The whole community—owners, managers and consumers—is responsible for the functioning of communication in society.

Christians have an obligation to advocate that mass media and communication technologies are operated to serve the public good rather than merely commercial interests.

Most peoples of the world have no access to even the most rudimentary communication technologies—telephones, radio—much less the digital, satellite, and other technologies that are rapidly expanding in the developing world.

These technologies allow their owners to manage information and resources at increasingly remote distances from the local cultures and economies affected. The instantaneous nature of global data transmission means that economic powers often have access to information before others do. The global-technological nature of the economy gives tremendous fiscal power to these same developed world and transnational interests.

This system works to advance the cause of the global market and promote commercial values aimed only at profit, often neglecting the aspects of communication and culture that promote the common good. Media companies, as producers and carriers of information, have a far-reaching effect on value formation.

Issues of justice in local and national development cannot be addressed without a consciousness of the role of communication, nor can any people do so without the tools with which to make their views known.

Information Communication Technologies (ICTs) offer enormous benefits. They enable global contact and, when made available for human uses and to address human needs, can significantly enhance life, development, and global consciousness.

Such uses will not become widespread unless concrete enabling steps are taken. Therefore the church's voice is crucial.

The church continues its mission and ministry amid this enormous revolution in communication.

The church quickly embraced the first communication revolution, the invention of the printing press, and used the printed word to disseminate the written word and to teach literacy to millions who were otherwise considered unfit to learn, empowering them to fully engage in the world.

The education of his neighbors was a matter close to John Wesley's heart, and his efforts gave many the education necessary to read and understand the gospel of Jesus Christ and to interpret the events of their world in the light of the gospel.

The Church carries a responsibility for helping its members achieve media literacy, not only to read and understand the gospel but also to discern from the flood of information an understanding of the events of our world today. Citizens cannot get responsible political information without media literacy. The current media revolution challenges all people to resist becoming mere consumers of messages that are created and controlled by a relatively small number of super-powerful transnational media corporations.

Media technologies have great potential to bind the world together, when not beholden entirely to transnational commercial interests.

Therefore, The United Methodist Church commits to:

A. Change of the Church

- Encourage leaders to preach and teach about the impact of media on the quality of life and values of individuals and society and to suggest ways congregations and individuals can both work with the positive forces and resist the negative.
- Use the available ICTs of local churches and other UMC entities to provide training in communication technologies to persons in their communities, particularly children, youth, and the poor, so that they might become active creators of story and culture rather than simply passive consumers.

- Assist members of United Methodist churches, our clergy, seminarians, and those who serve in the Church to become literate and committed to using ICTs for ministry and advocacy. As part of becoming aware of the power of the media, we particularly suggest the study of the Principles of Christian Communication developed by the World Association of Christian Communication.
- Encourage United Methodist institutions of higher education, particularly communication and theology faculties, to address societal communication issues.
- Reevaluate the church's work at every level of the United Methodist connection, including allocation of resources, decisions about programs, ministries, and missions, in light of the vital need to affirm the dignity of all persons by ensuring them equal opportunity to be heard, to have voice in the shaping of the church and of the world, and to communicate their story.

B. Change of Society

- Devote serious attention to the economic, political, and cultural forces that constrain the press and other communication media, challenging the use of communication as a force that supports the powerful, victimizes the powerless, and marginalizes minority opinion.
- Use ICTs for acts of love that liberate.
- We will work to preserve the right to communication for oppressed and persecuted communities, to oppose efforts to deny citizens the right of information, and to develop communication technologies that can be used to protect children from exploitation and psychological harm.
- Advocate for uses of media and communication technologies that promote peace, understanding, cooperation and multiculturalism and oppose those uses of media that encourage violence, factionalism, militarism, and ethnic strife.
- Advocate for technologies that allow consumers to exclude unwanted commercial messages.
- Encourage the production and broadcast of independently owned media, particularly those of developing nations, which encompass artistic and entertainment programming as well as news and information.

C. Change of the World

- Develop methods to educate persons about the importance of communication as a basic right for all persons and advocate for public policies that promote fair and equitable access to ICTs through educational, advocacy, and communications ministries.
- Identify and eliminate the hindrances to communication technologies with a view toward assisting those without those technologies to acquire, access, and use them. In this context the Church supports the development of open source software (General Public License systems). Its availability in the public domain helps overcome some of the digital divide between the developed and developing countries.
- Work through annual conferences and the general boards and agencies with regional, national, and international bodies to provide support for such activities as:
    1. scholarships and training of persons, especially women, in developing countries in communication policy issues and communication management in order that they may be fully prepared to participate in planning for the communications policy, programs, and infrastructure in their respective nations;
    2. participation in communication efforts that offer alternatives to the mass media.
- Integrate sustained work for both domestic and global communications justice into current peace and justice advocacy agendas.
- Work through shareholder groups to persuade companies to respect nations' attempts to protect their cultural sovereignty.

Global communications justice, in the end, is about communication that is just and participatory, equitable and sustainable.

ADOPTED 2004

REQUEST FOR STUDY

363. Organize a Study of Communion in The United Methodist Church

WHEREAS, as United Methodists "we understand ourselves to be part of Christ's universal church when by adoration, proclamation, and service we become conformed to Christ" (¶ 101); and

WHEREAS, "The church . . . is the redeemed and redeeming fellowship in which the Word of God is preached by persons divinely called, and the sacraments are duly administered according to Christ's own appointment" (Preamble to the Constitution); and

WHEREAS, "Through the regular celebration of Holy Communion, we participate in the risen presence of Jesus Christ and are thereby nourished for faithful discipleship" (¶ 101); and

WHEREAS, our heritage emphasizes a " 'practical divinity,' the experiential realization of the gospel of Jesus Christ in the lives of Christian people . . . through the vital movement of faith and practice as seen in converted lives and within the disciplined life of the church" (¶ 101); and

WHEREAS, there should be a strong sense of the importance of Holy Communion in the life of the church, and there is at least an equally strong sense of the absence of any meaningful understanding of Eucharistic theology and practice; and

WHEREAS, there are persistent questions and varied practices including but not limited to frequency, "worthiness," appropriate elements, modes of distribution, authority to administer Communion, length of service, presiding styles, liturgy tone or mood of observance, and understandings of the sacrament of the Lord's Supper; and

WHEREAS, research conducted by the General Board of Discipleship indicates that there is a pervasive, strongly felt need and desire for guidance from the general church on Eucharistic theology, practice, and spirituality; and

WHEREAS, United Methodists expressed enthusiasm for authoritative guidance and interpretation in addition to resources and opportunities for teaching and learning, leading to a fuller understanding and more meaningful practice,

Therefore, be it resolved, that the 2000 General Conference direct the General Board of Discipleship, in collaboration with the Council of Bishops, to organize a committee to develop a comprehensive interpretive document on the theology and practice of Holy Communion in United Methodism and to report their findings and recommendations to the 2004 General Conference;

And be it further resolved, that in order to give the work of the study committee high visibility and priority, at least two bishops named by the Council of Bishops and the general secretaries of the General Board of Discipleship, the General Board of Higher Education and Ministry, and the General Commission on Christian Unity and

Interreligious Concerns be on the study committee as well as laypeople, pastors of local churches, and representatives of central conferences. Membership shall reflect the inclusiveness of our church, with the understanding that the designated agencies (council, boards, and commission) will fund the participation of their staff in the work of the committee and that the General Board of Discipleship will be responsible for costs of the participation of other committee members.

ADOPTED 2000

364. Resources for Study of Evolution and Creation

The 2000 General Conference directs the General Board of Discipleship, working within its own structure, to develop study materials for all levels of the church which will bring all the theories of evolution and creation to the churches in a manner which will compare emerging areas of compatibility and areas yet unresolved in a reconciling approach to the relationship involved.

ADOPTED 2000

365. Task Force to Study Immigration/ Naturalization Issues for Clergy

The general agencies of The United Methodist Church receive numerous inquiries and requests for information on issues related to immigration rules and regulations as they apply to local churches, boards of ordained ministry, districts, and annual conferences.

The Immigration Reform and Control Act of 1986 states, "Employers are to comply with the requirements to confirm that new employees are American citizens or aliens legally authorized to work in the United States."

The 1996 Book of Discipline (¶ 120) states, "United Methodist pastors appointed to local churches are not employees of those churches. It is recognized that for certain limited purposes such as taxation, benefits, and insurance, governments and other entities may classify clergy as employees."

The role of local churches, boards of ordained ministry, bishops, and the annual conference in relation to the appointment of clergy and federal reporting involves a potential conflict between federal laws/regulations and *The Book of Discipline*/United Methodist polity.

Also, situations have arisen in which federal laws/regulations have not been complied with in relation to clergy or other staff which may result in serious penalties, including possible deportation of the individuals.

In the United Methodist polity there is no clear understanding of what entity (local church, district, boards of ordained ministry, conference, or other organization) may be required by law to complete the proper immigration paperwork for newly appointed elders, probationary members, deacons, local pastors, or diaconal ministers.

For all these reasons, it is recommended that General Conference 2000 direct that a task force be appointed to examine the issues of immigration and naturalization with specific regard to complying with federal laws and regulations for United Methodist clergy under appointment; and

It is further recommended that the task force be empowered to study how church organizations can most effectively meet their legal obligations regarding immigration, review who in the church can best fulfill these legal requirements, consider what education and guidance should be given, decide who should disseminate this information and to whom such information and guidance should be given, and as appropriate, forward such recommendations and information to the annual conferences and other church organizations prior to 2004; and

It is further recommended that this task force be instructed and empowered to report its findings, conclusions, and actions to the 2004 General Conference, including, if necessary, proposals for any clarifying legislation to be considered by the 2004 General Conference; and

It is further recommended, that the appointment of the members of this task force include the following:

- one bishop of The United Methodist Church, to be selected by the Council of Bishops;
- one representative of the Division of Ordained Ministry with the General Board of Higher Education and Ministry (GBHEM), selected by GBHEM;
- one representative of the General Board of Global Ministries (GBGM), selected by GBGM; and
- two lay individuals with expertise in the area of immigration and naturalization law.

Costs of travel for task force members named by a United Methodist organization are to be borne by the United Methodist organization that names the individual(s); costs for the last five listed representatives and meeting costs are to be shared jointly by GCFA and GBHEM. There are no new or additional funds being requested from General Conference to fund this task force.

ADOPTED 2000

366. Ethics of Embryonic Stem Cell Research

Preamble

The following statement addresses the ethical implications of using human embryos as a source of stem cells for research. It also examines in-vitro fertilization procedures, as they are the source of most of the embryos that are presently used for research. This statement does not explore in detail other kinds of stem cell research, but finds no moral objections to research involving stem cells derived from adult cells or umbilical cord blood. The United Methodist Church has made a commitment to consider all issues in light of concerns for the welfare of all people and the just distribution of resources. In light of that, we wish to state at the outset our conviction that Christians are called to use their resources to meet the basic health care needs of all people. We reaffirm our theological grounding on these issues as found in Section II of the 2004 *Book of Resolutions*, Resolution #102—"New Developments in Genetic Science."

Description of In Vitro Fertilization

In vitro fertilization (IVF) is a clinical practice in which a woman's ovaries are hyper-stimulated to release several eggs, which are extracted and subsequently fertilized in a laboratory dish. This is for the purpose of creating embryos to be introduced into the uterus in the hope of implantation, gestation, and eventual birth. Current practice usually involves the extraction of up to 15-16 eggs for fertilization. The resulting embryos that are judged most viable are either introduced into the womb in the initial attempt or frozen and stored for possible later use. Some of the embryos are judged to be less viable than others and are discarded. (Those stored embryos that are not later used become the "excess embryos" whose use as a source of embryonic stem cells is currently under discussion.)

Concerns Regarding the Status of Human Embryos

A human embryo, even at its earliest stages, commands our reverence and makes a serious moral claim on us, although not a claim identical to that of a more developed human life. For this reason we should not create embryos with the intention of destroying them, as in the creation of embryos for research purposes. Neither should we, even for reproductive purposes, produce more embryos than we can expect to introduce into the womb in the hope of implantation.

We recommend the following guidelines to minimize the overproduction of embryos:

- We urge clinicians and couples to make the determination of how many eggs to fertilize and implant on a case-by-case basis.
- Only enough embryos should be produced to achieve one pregnancy at a time.
- We insist that rigorous standards of informed consent regarding the procedures, the physical and emotional risks, and the associated ethical issues be applied to all reproductive technologies. This is especially important regarding the disposition of "excess" embryos and should be the norm of practice around the world.

Some Judgments Regarding the Use of Existing Embryos for Stem Cell Research

There has been a great deal of scientific interest recently generated by research on human stem cells. These are the cells that give rise to other cells. There are a number of potential sources for stem cells, including adult tissues, fetal remains, umbilical cord blood, and human embryos. The use of adult stem cells and stem cells derived from umbilical cord blood raise few moral questions. The use of human embryos as a source for stem cells has been the subject of intense moral debate.

Given the reality that most, if not all, of these excess embryos will be discarded—we believe that it is morally tolerable to use existing embryos for stem cell research purposes. This position is a matter of weighing the danger of further eroding the respect due to potential life against the possible, therapeutic benefits that are hoped for from such research. The same judgment of moral tolerability would apply to the use of embryos left from future reproductive efforts if a decision has been made not to introduce them into the womb. We articulate this position with an attitude of caution, not license. We reiterate our opposition to the creation of embryos for the sake of research. (See Book of Resolutions, 2000, p. 254)

The Issue of "Therapeutic Cloning"

In consideration of the potential therapeutic benefits that might eventually arise from research on embryonic stem cells, particular concerns are raised by a proposed practice called "therapeutic cloning." This involves taking a donated human egg, extracting its nucleus, and replacing it with a nucleus taken from another body cell. This newly formed cell would then be electrically stimulated to develop into an embryo. This embryo would be the genetic twin of the person whose body cell was used to obtain the nucleus. The cloned embryo would then be used as a source of stem cells, which would be a genetic match for that donor. This procedure might overcome the problem of immune system rejection of cellular treatments that might be developed for an individual from embryonic stem cells. However, we still believe that human embryos should not be created purely for the sake of research, or created with the advance intention of destroying them, or cloned for harvesting stem cells.-

Resolved, that a task force be formed to complete the charge of the Genetic Science Task force (New Developments in Genetic Science, 90 2000 BOR) (1) to consider the range of issues that are connected with genetic testing, including, but not limited to, pre-implantation genetic diagnosis (PIGD), prenatal testing as a precursor to therapeutic abortion, and predictive testing in children and adults for late onset genetic conditions; (2) to develop resources for pastoral and congregational use. (3) To commission an analysis of the interests which have funded lobbying efforts and public relations efforts regarding funding of embryonic stem cell research and other embryonic research.

Be it further resolved, that the United Methodist 2004 General Conference go on record in support of those persons who wish to enhance medical research by donating their early embryos remaining after in vitro fertilization (IVF) procedures have ended, and

Be it further resolved, that the 2004 General Conference urge that the United States Congress pass legislation that would authorize federal funding for derivation of and medical research on human embryonic stem cells that were generated for IVF and remain after fertilization procedures have been concluded, provided that:

1. these early embryos are no longer required for procreation by those donating them and would simply be discarded;

2. those donating early embryos have given their prior informed consent to their use in stem cell research;

3. the embryos were not deliberately created for research purposes;

4. the embryos were not obtained by sale or purchase; and

Be it further resolved, that the 2004 General Conference of the United Methodist Church urge the United States Secretary of Health and Human Services to establish an interdisciplinary oversight body for all research in both the public and private sectors that involves stem cells from human embryos, parthenotes, sperm cells or egg cells, and have this body in place within six months of passing such legislation; and

Be it further resolved, that the 2004 General Conference of the United Methodist Church direct the General Board of Church and Society to communicate this resolution to appropriate members and committees of the United States Congress and to identify and advocate the legislation called for by this resolution.

ADOPTED 2004

367. Replace "In Defense of Creation" with new Document and Study Guide

WHEREAS, our Abrahamic tradition calls us to seek those things which lead to shalom in our personal lives, our communities, and our world; and

WHEREAS, Jesus Christ calls us to be peacemakers ("blessed are the peacemakers") Matthew 5:9a; and

WHEREAS, our United Methodist Church has a long tradition towards educating and encouraging church members, citizens and governments to seek those things which lead to a just peace; and

WHEREAS, our country is experiencing a new challenge with the escalation of tensions and the rise in worldwide terrorism; and

WHEREAS, the United Methodist Council of Bishops in 1986 at the height of the nuclear arms race published a landmark foundation document and study guide entitled, "In Defense of Creation: The Nuclear

Crisis and a Just Peace," the first draft of this document being adopted at the Council's meeting in Wichita, Kansas November 10-15, 1985;

Therefore, be it resolved, that the Kansas East Conference of The United Methodist Church recommend to General Conference that the Council of Bishops of The United Methodist Church will be charged and funded to publish a new document and study guide similar to "In Defense of Creation," to be published during the next quadrennium.

ADOPTED 2004

368. United Methodist Men Study Committee

WHEREAS, as United Methodists we recognize the critical nature of men's ministries within The United Methodist Church; and

WHEREAS, men's ministry leads to the spiritual growth of men and effective discipleship; and

WHEREAS, each local church or charge shall have an organized unit of United Methodist Men; and

WHEREAS, the purpose of United Methodist Men is to declare the centrality of Christ in every man's life and lead men to spiritual growth and effective discipleship; and

WHEREAS, any organized group of men in a local United Methodist Church constitutes a ministry of men; and

WHEREAS, George Barna's studies indicate that women are 100 percent more likely to be in discipleship than men, 56 percent more likely to be lay leaders, 54 percent more likely to be in a small ministry group, and 39 percent more likely to have personal devotion time; and

WHEREAS, the General Social Survey, shows that 3 out of 10 respondents who attend church weekly also had a father who attended church weekly. Likewise, 3 out of 10 respondents who never attend church also had a father who never attended church at all; and

WHEREAS, research in the area of implied religion shows that men are finding "religion" in groups outside of church—sports, support groups, left wing and right wing radical movements, new religious movements, and new spirituality movements; and

WHEREAS, there is an urgent need to conduct a study of the needs of males in The United Methodist Church in order to develop effective resources, respond to current needs, challenge long-held assumptions, develop effective strategies for reaching men in the 21st century, and effectively understand male spiritual formation issues;

Therefore, be it resolved, that the 2004 General Conference direct the General Commission on United Methodist Men, in cooperation with the Office of Research and Planning, General Council on Ministries (or its equivalent structure for the 2005-2008 quadrennium), to create a study committee for the 2005-2008 quadrennium to undertake a study of men across The United Methodist Church. The study committee will report back to the 2008 General Conference as to its findings.

ADOPTED 2004

INDEX

955